LINUX®
RUTE USER'S TUTORIAL
AND EXPOSITION

ISBN 0-13-033351-4

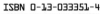

9 790130 333512

90000

LINUX®

RUTE USER'S TUTORIAL AND EXPOSITION

PAUL SHEER

Prentice Hall PTR
Upper Saddle River, New Jersey 07458
www.phptr.com

Library of Congress Cataloging-in-Publication Data

Sheer, Paul.
   Linux: rute user's tutorial and exposition/Paul Sheer.
      p. cm.—(Prentice Hall PTR open source technology series)
   ISBN 0-13-033351-4
   1. Linux. 2. Operating systems (Computers) I. Title. II. Series.

   QA76.76.O63 S5527 2001
   005.4'469—dc21   2001036548

Editorial/production supervision: *Jane Bonnell*
Cover design director: *Jerry Votta*
Cover design: *Anthony Gemmellaro*
Cover illustration: *Tom Post*
Manufacturing buyer: *Maura Zaldivar*
Acquisitions editor: *Mark L. Taub*
Editorial assistant: *Sarah Hand*
Marketing manager: *Bryan Gambrel*

© 2002 by Paul Sheer

Published by Prentice Hall PTR
Prentice-Hall, Inc.
Upper Saddle River, NJ 07458

Prentice Hall books are widely used by corporations and government agencies for training, marketing, and resale.

The publisher offers discounts on this book when ordered in bulk quantities. For more information, contact Corporate Sales Department, Phone: 800-382-3419; FAX: 201-236-7141;
E-mail: corpsales@prenhall.com
Or write: Prentice Hall PTR, Corporate Sales Dept., One Lake Street, Upper Saddle River, NJ 07458

The quotation on p. v from Douglas Adams is reprinted with the kind permission of the Estate of Douglas Adams. © 1979 Completely Unexpected Productions Limited. U.S. edition © 1992 by Random House, Inc.

The quotation on p. v from Alex Garland, *The Beach,* is reproduced by permission of Penguin Books Ltd. and Andrew Nurnberg Associates. Published by Penguin Books 1997, London; copyright © 1996 by Alex Garland. From p. 139.

Linux is a registered trademark of Linus Torvalds. Other product and company names mentioned herein are the trademarks or registered trademarks of their respective owners.

Printed in the United States of America
10 9 8 7 6 5 4 3 2 1

ISBN 0-13-033351-4

Pearson Education LTD.
Pearson Education Australia PTY, Limited
Pearson Education Singapore, Pte. Ltd.
Pearson Education North Asia Ltd.
Pearson Education Canada, Ltd.
Pearson Educación de Mexico, S.A. de C.V.
Pearson Education—Japan
Pearson Education Malaysia, Pte. Ltd.

"The reason we don't sell billions and billions of Guides," continued Harl, after wiping his mouth, "is the expense. What we do is we sell one Guide billions and billions of times. We exploit the multidimensional nature of the Universe to cut down on manufacturing costs. And we don't sell to penniless hitchhikers. What a stupid notion that was! Find the one section of the market that, more or less by definition, doesn't have any money, and try to sell to it. No. We sell to the affluent business traveler and his vacationing wife in a billion, billion different futures. This is the most radical, dynamic and thrusting business venture in the entire multidimensional infinity of space-time-probability ever."

. . .

Ford was completely at a loss for what to do next.

"Look," he said in a stern voice. But he wasn't certain how far saying things like "Look" in a stern voice was necessarily going to get him, and time was not on his side. What the hell, he thought, you're only young once, and threw himself out of the window. That would at least keep the element of surprise on his side.

. . .

In a spirit of scientific inquiry he hurled himself out of the window again.

Douglas Adams
Mostly Harmless

Strangely, the thing that least intrigued me was how they'd managed to get it all done. I suppose I sort of knew. If I'd learned one thing from traveling, it was that the way to get things done was to go ahead and do them. Don't talk about going to Borneo. Book a ticket, get a visa, pack a bag, and it just happens.

Alex Garland
The Beach

Chapter Summary

Contents

Preface

When I began working with GNU/LINUX in 1994, it was straight from the DOS world. Though UNIX was unfamiliar territory, LINUX books assumed that anyone using LINUX was migrating from System V or BSD—systems that I had never heard of. It is a sensible adage to create, for others to share, the recipe that you would most like to have had. Indeed, I am not convinced that a single unifying text exists, even now, without this book. Even so, I give it to you desperately incomplete; but there is only so much one can explain in a single volume.

I hope that readers will now have a single text to guide them through all facets of GNU/LINUX.

Acknowledgments

A special thanks goes to my technical reviewer, Abraham van der Merwe, and my production editor, Jane Bonnell. Thanks to Jonathan Maltz, Jarrod Cinman, and Alan Tredgold for introducing me to GNU/Linux back in 1994 or so. Credits are owed to all the Free software developers that went into LaTeX, TeX, GhostScript, GhostView, Autotrace, XFig, XV, Gimp, the Palatino font, the various LaTeX extension styles, DVIPS, DVIPDFM, ImageMagick, XDVI, XPDF, and LaTeX2HTML without which this document would scarcely be possible. To name a few: John Bradley, David Carlisle, Eric Cooper, John Cristy, Peter Deutsch, Nikos Drakos, Mark Eichin, Brian Fox, Carsten Heinz, Spencer Kimball, Paul King, Donald Knuth, Peter Mattis, Frank Mittelbach, Ross Moore, Derek B. Noonburg, Johannes Plass, Sebastian Rahtz, Chet Ramey, Tomas Rokicki, Bob Scheifler, Rainer Schoepf, Brian Smith, Supoj Sutanthavibul, Herb Swan, Tim Theisen, Paul Vojta, Martin Weber, Mark Wicks, Masatake Yamato, Ken Yap, Herman Zapf.

Thanks to Christopher R. Hertel for contributing his introduction to Samba.

An enormous thanks to the GNU project of the Free Software Foundation, to the countless developers of Free software, and to the many readers that gave valuable feedback on the web site.

Chapter 1

Introduction

Whereas books shelved beside this one will get your feet wet, this one lets you actually paddle for a bit, then thrusts your head underwater while feeding you oxygen.

1.1   What This Book Covers

This book covers GNU/LINUX system administration, for popular distributions like RedHat and Debian, as a tutorial for new users and a reference for advanced administrators. It aims to give concise, thorough explanations and practical examples of each aspect of a UNIX system. Anyone who wants a comprehensive text on (what is commercially called) "LINUX" need look no further—there is little that is not covered here.

1.2   Read This Next...

The ordering of the chapters is carefully designed to allow you to read in sequence without missing anything. You should hence read from beginning to end, in order that later chapters do not reference unseen material. I have also packed in useful examples which you must practice as you read.

1.3   What Do I Need to Get Started?

You will need to install a basic LINUX system. A number of vendors now ship point-and-click-install CDs: you should try get a Debian or "RedHat-like" distribution.

One hint: try and install as much as possible so that when I mention a software package in this text, you are likely to have it installed already and can use it immediately. Most cities with a sizable IT infrastructure will have a LINUX🐧 user group to help you source a cheap CD. These are getting really easy to install, and there is no longer much need to read lengthy installation instructions.

1.4 More About This Book

Chapter 16 contains a fairly comprehensive list of all reference documentation available on your system. This book supplements that material with a tutorial that is both comprehensive and independent of any previous UNIX knowledge.

The book also aims to satisfy the requirements for course notes for a GNU🐂/LINUX🐧 training course. Here in South Africa, I use the initial chapters as part of a 36-hour GNU🐂/LINUX🐧 training course given in 12 lessons. The details of the layout for this course are given in Appendix A.

Note that all "LINUX🐧" systems are really composed mostly of GNU🐂 software, but from now on I will refer to the GNU🐂 system as "LINUX🐧" in the way almost everyone (incorrectly) does.

1.5 I Get Frustrated with UNIX Documentation That I Don't Understand

Any system reference will require you to read it at least three times before you get a reasonable picture of what to do. If you need to read it more than three times, then there is probably some other information that you really should be reading first. If you are reading a document only once, then you are being too impatient with yourself.

It is important to identify the exact terms that you fail to understand in a document. Always try to backtrack to the precise word before you continue.

Its also probably not a good idea to learn new things according to deadlines. Your UNIX knowledge should evolve by grace and fascination, rather than pressure.

1.6 Linux Professionals Institute (LPI) and RedHat Certified Engineer (RHCE) Requirements

The difference between being able to pass an exam and being able to do something useful, of course, is huge.

The LPI and RHCE are two certifications that introduce you to LINUX⌂. This book covers *far* more than both these two certifications in most places, but occasionally leaves out minor items as an exercise. It certainly covers in excess of what you need to know to pass both these certifications.

The LPI and RHCE requirements are given in Appendix B and C.

These two certifications are merely introductions to UNIX. To earn them, users are not expected to write nifty shell scripts to do tricky things, or understand the subtle or advanced features of many standard services, let alone be knowledgeable of the enormous numbers of non-standard and useful applications out there. To be blunt: you can pass these courses and still be considered quite incapable by the standards of companies that do *system integration*. ⬐System integration is my own term. It refers to the act of getting LINUX to do nonbasic functions, like writing complex shell scripts; setting up wide-area dialup networks; creating custom distributions; or interfacing database, web, and email services together.⬏ In fact, these certifications make no reference to computer programming whatsoever.

1.7 Not RedHat: RedHat-*like*

Throughout this book I refer to examples specific to "RedHat" and "Debian☺". What I actually mean by this are systems that use `.rpm` (redHat package manager) packages as opposed to systems that use `.deb` (debian) packages—there are lots of both. This just means that there is no reason to avoid using a distribution like Mandrake, which is `.rpm` based and viewed by many as being better than RedHat.

In short, brand names no longer have any meaning in the Free software community.

(Note that the same applies to the word UNIX which we take to mean the common denominator between all the UNIX variants, including RISC, mainframe, and PC variants of both System V and BSD.)

1.8 Updates and Errata

Corrections to this book will be posted on http://www.icon.co.za/˜psheer/rute-errata.html. Please check this web page before notifying me of errors.

Chapter 2

Computing Sub-basics

This chapter explains some basics that most computer users will already be familiar with. If you are new to UNIX, however, you may want to gloss over the commonly used key bindings for reference.

The best way of thinking about how a computer stores and manages information is to ask yourself how *you* would. Most often the way a computer works is exactly the way you would expect it to if you were inventing it for the first time. The only limitations on this are those imposed by logical feasibility and imagination, but almost anything else is allowed.

2.1   Binary, Octal, Decimal, and Hexadecimal

When you first learned to count, you did so with 10 digits. Ordinary numbers (like telephone numbers) are called "base ten" numbers. Postal codes that include letters *and* digits are called "base 36" numbers because of the addition of 26 letters onto the usual 10 digits. The simplest base possible is "base two" which uses only two digits: 0 and 1. Now, a 7-digit telephone number has $\underbrace{10 \times 10 \times 10 \times 10 \times 10 \times 10 \times 10}_{7\ digits} =$ $10^7 = 10,000,000$ possible combinations. A postal code with four characters has $36^4 = 1,679,616$ possible combinations. However, an 8-digit binary number only has $2^8 = 256$ possible combinations.

Since the internal representation of numbers within a computer is binary and since it is rather tedious to convert between decimal and binary, computer scientists have come up with new bases to represent numbers: these are "base sixteen" and "base eight," known as *hexadecimal* and *octal*, respectively. Hexadecimal numbers use the digits 0 through 9 and the letters A through F, whereas octal numbers use only the digits 0 through 7. Hexadecimal is often abbreviated as *hex*.

Consider a 4-digit binary number. It has $2^4 = 16$ possible combinations and can therefore be easily represented by one of the 16 hex digits. A 3-digit binary number has $2^3 = 8$ possible combinations and can thus be represented by a single octal digit. Hence, a binary number can be represented with hex or octal digits without much calculation, as shown in Table 2.1.

Table 2.1   Binary hexadecimal, and octal representation

Binary	Hexadecimal		Binary	Octal
0000	0		000	0
0001	1		001	1
0010	2		010	2
0011	3		011	3
0100	4		100	4
0101	5		101	5
0110	6		110	6
0111	7		111	7
1000	8			
1001	9			
1010	A			
1011	B			
1100	C			
1101	D			
1110	E			
1111	F			

A binary number 01001011 can be represented in hex as 4B and in octal as 113 by simply separating the binary digits into groups of four or three, respectively.

In UNIX administration, and also in many programming languages, there is often the ambiguity of whether a number is in fact a hex, decimal, or octal number. For instance, a hex number 56 is 01010110, but an octal number 56 is 101110, whereas a decimal number 56 is 111000 (computed through a more tedious calculation). To distinguish between them, hex numbers are often prefixed with the characters "0x", while octal numbers are prefixed with a "0". If the first digit is 1 through 9, then it is a decimal number that is probably being referred to. We would then write 0x56 for hex, and 056 for octal. Another representation is to append the letter H, D, O, or B (or h, d, o, b) to the number to indicate its base.

UNIX makes heavy use of 8-, 16-, and 32-digit binary numbers, often representing them as 2-, 4-, and 8-digit hex numbers. You should get used to seeing numbers like 0xffff (or FFFFh), which in decimal is 65535 and in binary is 1111111111111111.

2.2 Files

Common to every computer system invented is the *file*. A file holds a single contiguous block of data. Any kind of data can be stored in a file, and there is no data that cannot be stored in a file. Furthermore, there is no kind of data that is stored anywhere else except in files. A file holds data of the same type, for instance, a single picture will be stored in one file. During production, this book had each chapter stored in a file. It is uncommon for different types of data (say, text and pictures) to be stored together in the same file because it is inconvenient. A computer will typically contain about 10,000 files that have a great many purposes. Each file will have its own name. The file name on a LINUX⬩ or UNIX machine can be up to 256 characters long.

The file name is usually explanatory—you might call a letter you wrote to your friend something like `Mary_Jones.letter` (from now on, whenever you see the typewriter font ↘A style of print: here is `typewriter font`.↖, it means that those are words that might be read off the screen of the computer). The name you choose has no meaning to the computer and could just as well be any other combination of letters or digits; however, you will refer to that data with that file name whenever you give an instruction to the computer regarding that data, so *you* would like it to be descriptive.   ↘It is important to internalize the fact that computers do not have an interpretation for anything. A computer operates with a set of interdependent logical rules. *Interdependent* means that the rules have no apex, in the sense that computers have no fixed or single way of working. For example, the reason a computer has files at all is because computer *programmers* have decided that this is the most universal and convenient way of storing data, and if you think about it, it really is.↖

The data in each file is merely a long list of numbers. The *size* of the file is just the length of the list of numbers. Each number is called a *byte*. Each byte contains 8 *bits*. Each bit is either a one or a zero and therefore, once again, there are

$$\underbrace{2 \times 2 \times 2 \times 2 \times 2 \times 2 \times 2 \times 2}_{8 \; bits} = \underbrace{256}_{1 \; byte} \text{ possible combinations. Hence a byte can only}$$

hold a number as large as 255. There is no type of data that cannot be represented as a list of bytes. Bytes are sometimes also called *octets*. Your letter to Mary will be *encoded* into bytes for storage on the computer. We all know that a television picture is just a sequence of dots on the screen that scan from left to right. In that way, a picture might be represented in a file: that is, as a sequence of bytes where each byte is interpreted as a level of brightness—0 for black and 255 for white. For your letter, the convention is to store an A as 65, a B as 66, and so on. Each punctuation character also has a numerical equivalent.

A mapping between numbers and characters is called a *character mapping* or a *character set*. The most common character set in use in the world today is the *ASCII* character set which stands for the American Standard Code for Information Interchange. Table 2.2 shows the complete ASCII mappings between characters and their hex, decimal, and octal equivalents.

Table 2.2   ASCII character set

Oct	Dec	Hex	Char	Oct	Dec	Hex	Char	Oct	Dec	Hex	Char	Oct	Dec	Hex	Char
000	0	00	*NUL*	040	32	20	*SPACE*	100	64	40	@	140	96	60	`
001	1	01	*SOH*	041	33	21	!	101	65	41	A	141	97	61	a
002	2	02	*STX*	042	34	22	"	102	66	42	B	142	98	62	b
003	3	03	*ETX*	043	35	23	#	103	67	43	C	143	99	63	c
004	4	04	*EOT*	044	36	24	$	104	68	44	D	144	100	64	d
005	5	05	*ENQ*	045	37	25	%	105	69	45	E	145	101	65	e
006	6	06	*ACK*	046	38	26	&	106	70	46	F	146	102	66	f
007	7	07	*BEL*	047	39	27	'	107	71	47	G	147	103	67	g
010	8	08	*BS*	050	40	28	(	110	72	48	H	150	104	68	h
011	9	09	*HT*	051	41	29	)	111	73	49	I	151	105	69	i
012	10	0A	*LF*	052	42	2A	*	112	74	4A	J	152	106	6A	j
013	11	0B	*VT*	053	43	2B	+	113	75	4B	K	153	107	6B	k
014	12	0C	*FF*	054	44	2C	,	114	76	4C	L	154	108	6C	l
015	13	0D	*CR*	055	45	2D	–	115	77	4D	M	155	109	6D	m
016	14	0E	*SO*	056	46	2E	.	116	78	4E	N	156	110	6E	n
017	15	0F	*SI*	057	47	2F	/	117	79	4F	O	157	111	6F	o
020	16	10	*DLE*	060	48	30	0	120	80	50	P	160	112	70	p
021	17	11	*DC1*	061	49	31	1	121	81	51	Q	161	113	71	q
022	18	12	*DC2*	062	50	32	2	122	82	52	R	162	114	72	r
023	19	13	*DC3*	063	51	33	3	123	83	53	S	163	115	73	s
024	20	14	*DC4*	064	52	34	4	124	84	54	T	164	116	74	t
025	21	15	*NAK*	065	53	35	5	125	85	55	U	165	117	75	u
026	22	16	*SYN*	066	54	36	6	126	86	56	V	166	118	76	v
027	23	17	*ETB*	067	55	37	7	127	87	57	W	167	119	77	w
030	24	18	*CAN*	070	56	38	8	130	88	58	X	170	120	78	x
031	25	19	*EM*	071	57	39	9	131	89	59	Y	171	121	79	y
032	26	1A	*SUB*	072	58	3A	:	132	90	5A	Z	172	122	7A	z
033	27	1B	*ESC*	073	59	3B	;	133	91	5B	[	173	123	7B	{
034	28	1C	*FS*	074	60	3C	<	134	92	5C	\	174	124	7C	|
035	29	1D	*GS*	075	61	3D	=	135	93	5D	]	175	125	7D	}
036	30	1E	*RS*	076	62	3E	>	136	94	5E	^	176	126	7E	~
037	31	1F	*US*	077	63	3F	?	137	95	5F	_	177	127	7F	*DEL*

2.3   Commands

The second thing common to every computer system invented is the *command*. You tell the computer what to do with single words typed into the computer one at a time. Modern computers appear to have done away with the typing of commands by having beautiful graphical displays that work with a mouse, but, fundamentally, all that is happening is that commands are being secretly typed in for you. Using commands is still the only way to have complete power over the computer. You don't really know anything about a computer until you come to grips with the commands it uses. Using a computer will very much involve typing in a word, pressing ⌨Enter↵, and then waiting for the computer screen to spit something back at you. Most commands are typed in to do something useful to a file.

2.4   Login and Password Change

Turn on your LINUX box. After a few minutes of initialization, you will see the *login prompt*. A *prompt* is one or more characters displayed on the screen that you are expected to follow with some typing of your own. Here the prompt may state the name of the computer (each computer has a name—typically consisting of about eight lowercase letters) and then the word `login:`. LINUX machines now come with a graphical desktop by default (most of the time), so you might get a pretty graphical login with the same effect. Now you should type your *login name*—a sequence of about eight lower case letters that would have been assigned to you by your computer administrator—and then press the Enter (or Return) key (that is, Enter↵).

A *password prompt* will appear after which you should type your password. Your password *may* be the same as your *login name*. Note that your password will not be shown on the screen as you type it but will be invisible. After typing your password, press the Enter or Return key again. The screen might show some message and prompt you for a log in again—in this case, you have probably typed something incorrectly and should give it another try. From now on, you will be expected to know that the Enter or Return key should be pressed at the end of every line you type in, analogous to the mechanical typewriter. You will also be expected to know that human error is very common; when you type something incorrectly, the computer will give an error message, and you should try again until you get it right. It is uncommon for a person to understand computer concepts after a first reading or to get commands to work on the first try.

Now that you have logged in you will see a *shell prompt*—a *shell* is the place where you can type commands. The shell is where you will spend most of your time as a system administrator ⟍Computer manager.⟋, but it needn't look as bland as you see now. Your first exercise is to change your password. Type the command `passwd`. You will be asked for a new password and then asked to confirm that password. The password you choose should consist of letters, numbers, and punctuation—you will see later on why this security measure is a good idea. Take good note of your password for the next time you log in. Then the shell will return. The password you have chosen will take effect immediately, replacing the previous password that you used to log in. The password command might also have given some message indicating what effect it actually had. You may not understand the message, but you should try to get an idea of whether the connotation was positive or negative.

When you are using a computer, it is useful to imagine yourself as *being* in different places *within* the computer, rather than just typing commands into it. After you entered the `passwd` command, you were no longer *in* the shell, but moved *into* the password *place*. You could not use the shell until you had moved *out* of the `passwd` command.

9

2.5   Listing Files

Type in the command ls. ls is short for *list*, abbreviated to two letters like most other UNIX commands. ls lists all your current files. You may find that ls does nothing, but just returns you back to the shell. This would be because you have no files as yet. Most UNIX commands do *not* give any kind of message unless something went wrong (the passwd command above was an exception). If there were files, you would see their names listed rather blandly in columns with no indication of what they are for.

2.6   Command-Line Editing Keys

The following keys are useful for editing the *command-line*. Note that UNIX has had a long and twisted evolution from the mainframe, and the Home, End and other keys may not work properly. The following keys bindings are however common throughout many LINUX applications:

Ctrl-a   Move to the beginning of the line (Home).

Ctrl-e   Move to the end of the line (End).

Ctrl-h   Erase backward (←).

Ctrl-d   Erase forward (Delete).

Ctrl-f   Move forward one character (→).

Ctrl-b   Move backward one character (←).

Alt-f   Move forward one word.

Alt-b   Move backward one word.

Alt-Ctrl-f   Erase forward one word.

Alt-Ctrl-b   Erase backward one word.

Ctrl-p   Previous command (up arrow).

Ctrl-n   Next command (down arrow).

Note that the prefixes Alt for Alt, Ctrl for Ctrl, and Shift for ⇧Shift, mean to hold the key down through the pressing and releasing of the letter key. These are known as *key modifiers*. Note also, that the Ctrl key is always case insensitive; hence Ctrl-D (i.e. Ctrl-⇧Shift-D) and Ctrl-d (i.e. Ctrl-D) are identical. The Alt modifier (i.e., Alt-?) is

10

in fact a short way of pressing and releasing Esc before entering the key combination; hence Esc then f is the same as Alt-f—UNIX is different from other operating systems in this use of Esc. The Alt modifier is not case insensitive although some applications will make a special effort to respond insensitively. The Alt key is also sometimes referred to as the Meta key. All of these keys are sometimes referred to by their abbreviations: for example, C-a for Ctrl-a, or M-f for Meta-f and Alt-f. The Ctrl modifier is sometimes also designated with a caret: for example, ^C for Ctrl-C.

Your command-line keeps a history of all the commands you have typed in. Ctrl-p and Ctrl-n will cycle through previous commands entered. New users seem to gain tremendous satisfaction from typing in lengthy commands over and over. *Never* type in anything more than once—use your command history instead.

Ctrl-s is used to suspend the current session, causing the keyboard to stop responding. Ctrl-q reverses this condition.

Ctrl-r activates a search on your command history. Pressing Ctrl-r in the middle of a search finds the next match whereas Ctrl-s reverts to the previous match (although some distributions have this confused with suspend).

The Tab command is tremendously useful for saving key strokes. Typing a partial directory name, file name, or command, and then pressing Tab once or twice in sequence completes the word for you without your having to type it all in full.

You can make Tab and other keys stop beeping in the irritating way that they do by editing the file /etc/inputrc and adding the line

```
set bell-style none
```

and then logging out and logging in again. (More about this later.)

2.7 Console Keys

There are several special keys interpreted directly by the LINUX *console* or text mode interface. The Ctrl-Alt-Del combination initiates a complete shutdown and hardware reboot, which is the preferred method of restarting LINUX.

The Ctrl-PgUp and Ctrl-PgDn keys scroll the console, which is very useful for seeing text that has disappeared off the top of the terminal.

You can use Alt-F2 to switch to a new, independent login session. Here you can log in again and run a separate session. There are six of these *virtual consoles*—Alt-F1 through Alt-F6—to choose from; they are also called *virtual terminals*. If you are in graphical mode, you will have to instead press Ctrl-Alt-F? because the Alt-F? keys are often used by applications. The convention is that the seventh virtual console is graphical, so Alt-F7 will always take you back to graphical mode.

2.8 Creating Files

There are many ways of creating a file. Type `cat > Mary_Jones.letter` and then type out a few lines of text. You will use this file in later examples. The `cat` command is used here to write from the keyboard into a file `Mary_Jones.letter`. At the end of the last line, press `Enter↵` one more time and then press `Ctrl`‖`D`. Now, if you type `ls` again, you will see the file `Mary_Jones.letter` listed with any other files. Type `cat Mary_Jones.letter` *without* the >. You will see that the command `cat` writes the contents of a file to the screen, allowing you to view your letter. It should match exactly what you typed in.

2.9 Allowable Characters for File Names

Although UNIX file names can contain almost any character, standards dictate that only the following characters are preferred in file names:

```
A  B  C  D  E  F  G  H  I  J  K  L  M  N  O  P  Q  R  S  T  U  V  W  X  Y  Z
a  b  c  d  e  f  g  h  i  j  k  l  m  n  o  p  q  r  s  t  u  v  w  x  y  z
0  1  2  3  4  5  6  7  8  9  .  _  -  ~
```

Hence, never use other punctuation characters, brackets, or control characters to name files. Also, never use the space or tab character in a file name, and never begin a file name with a – character.

2.10 Directories

I mentioned that a system may typically contain 10,000 files. Since it would be cumbersome if you were to see all 10,000 of them whenever you typed `ls`, files are placed in different "cabinets" so that files of the same type are placed together and can be easily isolated from other files. For instance, your letter above might go in a separate "cabinet" with other letters. A "cabinet" in computer terms is actually called a directory. This is the third commonality between all computer systems: all files go in one or another directory. To get an idea of how directories work, type the command `mkdir letters`, where `mkdir` stands for *make directory*. Now type `ls`. This will show the file `Mary_Jones.letter` as well as a new file, `letters`. The file `letters` is not really a file at all, but the name of a directory in which a number of other files can be placed. To go *into* the directory `letters`, you can type `cd letters` where `cd` stands for *change directory*. Since the directory is newly created, you would not expect it to contain any files, and typing `ls` will verify such by not listing anything. You can now create a file by using the `cat` command as you did before (try this). To go back to the original directory that you were in, you can use the command `cd ..` where the `..` has the special meaning of taking you out of the current directory. Type `ls` again to verify that you have actually gone *up* a directory.

It is, however, bothersome that we cannot tell the difference between files and directories. The way to differentiate is with the `ls -l` command. `-l` stands for *long* format. If you enter this command, you will see a lot of details about the files that may not yet be comprehensible to you. The three things you can watch for are the file name on the far right, the file size (i.e., the number of bytes that the file contains) in the fifth column from the left, and the file type on the far left. The file type is a string of letters of which you will only be interested in one: the character on the far left is either a – or a d. A – signifies a regular file, and a d signifies a directory. The command `ls -l Mary_Jones.letter` will list only the single file `Mary_Jones.letter` and is useful for finding out the size of a single file.

In fact, there is no limitation on how many directories you can create within each other. In what follows, you will glimpse the layout of all the directories on the computer.

Type the command `cd /`, where the / has the special meaning to go to the topmost directory on the computer called the *root* directory. Now type `ls -l`. The listing may be quite long and may go off the top of the screen; in that case, try `ls -l | less` (then use PgUp and PgDn, and press q when done). You will see that most, if not all, are directories. You can now practice moving around the system with the `cd` command, not forgetting that `cd ..` takes you up and `cd /` takes you to the root directory.

At any time you can type `pwd` *(present working directory) to show the directory you are currently in.*

When you have finished, log out of the computer by using the `logout` command.

Chapter 3

PC Hardware

This chapter explains a little about PC hardware. Readers who have built their own PC or who have configuring myriad devices on Windows can probably skip this section. It is added purely for completeness. This chapter actually comes under the subject of *Microcomputer Organization*, that is, how your machine is electronically structured.

3.1 Motherboard

Inside your machine you will find a single, large circuit board called the *motherboard* (see Figure 3.1). It is powered by a humming power supply and has connector leads to the keyboard and other *peripheral devices*. ↘Anything that is not the motherboard, not the power supply and not purely mechanical.↖

The motherboard contains several large microchips and many small ones. The important ones are listed below.

RAM *Random Access Memory* or just *memory*. The memory is a single linear sequence of bytes that are erased when there is no power. It contains sequences of simple coded *instructions* of one to several bytes in length. Examples are: add this number to that; move this number to this device; go to another part of RAM to get other instructions; copy this part of RAM to this other part. When your machine has "64 megs" (64 megabytes), it has 64 × 1024 × 1024 bytes of RAM. Locations within that space are called *memory addresses*, so that saying "memory address 1000" means the 1000th byte in memory.

ROM A small part of RAM does not reset when the computer switches off. It is called *ROM, Read Only Memory*. It is factory fixed and usually never changes through the life of a PC, hence the name. It overlaps the area of RAM close to the end of

Figure 3.1 Partially assembled motherboard

the first megabyte of memory, so that area of RAM is not physically usable. ROM contains instructions to start up the PC and access certain peripherals.

CPU *Central Processing Unit*. It is the thing that is called 80486, 80586, Pentium, or whatever. On startup, it *jumps* to memory address 1040475 (0xFE05B) and starts reading instructions. The first instructions it gets are actually to fetch more instructions from disk and give a `Boot failure` message to the screen if it finds nothing useful. The CPU requires a timer to drive it. The timer operates at a high speed of hundreds of millions of ticks per second (hertz). That's why the machine is named, for example, a "400 MHz" (400 megahertz) machine. The MHz of the machine is roughly proportional to the number of instructions it can process per second from RAM.

I/O ports Stands for *Input/Output* ports. The ports are a block of RAM that sits in parallel to the normal RAM. There are 65,536 I/O ports, hence I/O is small compared to RAM. I/O ports are used to write to peripherals. When the CPU writes a byte to I/O port 632 (0x278), it is actually sending out a byte through your parallel port. Most I/O ports are not used. There is no specific I/O port chip, though.

There is more stuff on the motherboard:

ISA slots ISA (*eye-sah*) is a shape of socket for plugging in peripheral devices like modem cards and sound cards. Each card expects to be talked to via an I/O port (or several consecutive I/O ports). What I/O port the card uses is sometimes configured by the manufacturer, and other times is selectable on the card through jumpers ⟍Little pin bridges that you can pull off with your fingers.⟍ or switches on the card. Other times still, it can be set by the CPU using a system called *Plug and Pray* ⟍This means that you plug the device in, then beckon your favorite deity for spiritual assistance. Actually, some people complained that this might be taken seriously—no, it's a joke: the real term is Plug 'n Play⟍ or *PnP*. A card also sometimes needs to signal the CPU to indicate that it is ready to send or receive more bytes through an I/O port. They do this through 1 of 16 connectors inside the ISA slot. These are called *Interrupt Request lines* or IRQ lines (or sometimes just *Interrupts*), so numbered 0 through 15. Like I/O ports, the IRQ your card uses is sometimes also jumper selectable, sometimes not. If you unplug an old ISA card, you can often see the actual copper thread that goes from the IRQ jumper to the edge connector. Finally, ISA cards can also access memory directly through one of eight *Direct Memory Access Channels* or *DMA Channels*, which are also possibly selectable by jumpers. Not all cards use DMA, however.

In summary, the peripheral and the CPU need to cooperate on three things: the I/O port, the IRQ, and the DMA. *If any two cards clash by using either the same I/O port, IRQ number, or DMA channel then they won't work (at worst your machine will crash).* ⟍Come to a halt and stop responding.⟍

"8-bit" ISA slots Old motherboards have shorter ISA slots. You will notice yours is a double slot (called "16-bit" ISA) with a gap between them. The larger slot can still take an older 8-bit ISA card: like many modem cards.

PCI slots PCI (*pee-see-eye*) slots are like ISA but are a new standard aimed at high-performance peripherals like networking cards and graphics cards. They also use an IRQ, I/O port and possibly a DMA channel. These, however, are automatically configured by the CPU as a part of the PCI standard, hence there will rarely be jumpers on the card.

AGP slots AGP slots are even higher performance slots for *Accelerated Graphics Processors*, in other words, cards that do 3D graphics for games. They are also auto-configured.

Serial ports A serial port connection may come straight from your motherboard to a socket on your case. There are usually two of these. They may drive an external modem and some kinds of mice and printers. Serial is a simple and cheap way to connect a machine where relatively slow (less that 10 kilobytes per second) data transfer speeds are needed. Serial ports have their own "ISA card" built into the motherboard which uses I/O port 0x3F8–0x3FF and IRQ 4 for the first serial port (also called COM1 under DOS/Windows) and I/O port 0x2F8–0x2FF and IRQ 3 for COM2. A discussion on serial port technology proceeds in Section 3.4 below.

Parallel port Normally, only your printer would plug in here. Parallel ports are, however, extremely fast (being able to transfer 50 kilobytes per second), and hence many types of parallel port devices (like CD-ROM drives that plug into a parallel port) are available. Parallel port cables, however, can only be a few meters in length before you start getting transmission errors. The parallel port uses I/O port 0x378–0x37A and IRQ 7. If you have two parallel ports, then the second one uses I/O port 0x278–0x27A, but does not use an IRQ at all.

USB port The *Universal Serial Bus* aims to allow any type of hardware to plug into one plug. The idea is that one day all serial and parallel ports will be scrapped in favor of a single USB socket from which all external peripherals will daisy chain. I will not go into USB here.

IDE ribbon The IDE ribbon plugs into your hard disk drive or `C:` drive on Windows/DOS and also into your CD-ROM drive (sometimes called an IDE CD-ROM). The IDE cable actually attaches to its own PCI card internal to the motherboard. There are two IDE connectors that use I/O ports 0xF000–0xF007 and 0xF008–0xF00F, and IRQ 14 and 15, respectively. Most IDE CD-ROMs are also ATAPI CD-ROMs. ATAPI is a standard (similar to SCSI, below) that enables many other kinds of devices to plug into an IDE ribbon cable. You get special floppy drives, tape drives, and other devices that plug into the same ribbon. They will be all called ATAPI-(this or that).

SCSI ribbon Another ribbon might be present, coming out of a card (called the SCSI host adaptor or SCSI card) or your motherboard. Home PCs will rarely have SCSI, such being expensive and used mostly for high-end servers. SCSI cables are more densely wired than are IDE cables. They also end in a disk drive, tape drive, CD-ROM, or some other device. SCSI cables are not allowed to just-be-plugged-in: they must be connected end on end with the last device connected in a special way called *SCSI termination*. There are, however, a few SCSI devices that are automatically terminated. More on this on page 477.

3.2 Master/Slave IDE

Two IDE hard drives can be connected to a single IDE ribbon. The ribbon alone has nothing to distinguish which connector is which, so the drive itself has jumper pins on it (see Figure 3.2) that can be set to one of several options. These are one of *Master* (MA), *Slave* (SL), *Cable Select* (CS), or *Master-only/Single-Drive/* and-like. The MA option means that your drive is the "first" drive of two on this IDE ribbon. The SL option means that your drive is the "second" drive of two on this IDE ribbon. The CS option means that your machine is to make its own decision (some boxes only work with this setting), and the Master-only option means that there is no second drive on this ribbon.

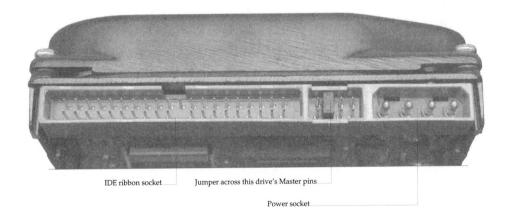

IDE ribbon socket   Jumper across this drive's Master pins

Power socket

Figure 3.2 Connection end of a typical IDE drive

There might also be a second IDE ribbon, giving you a total of four possible drives. The first ribbon is known as *IDE1* (labeled on your motherboard) or the *primary* ribbon, and the second is known as *IDE2* or the *secondary* ribbon. Your four drives are then called *primary master, primary slave, secondary master,* and *secondary slave.* Their labeling under LINUX⚬ is discussed in Section 18.4.

3.3   CMOS

The "CMOS" ↘Stands for *Complementary Metal Oxide Semiconductor,* which has to do with the technology used to store setup information through power-downs.↖ is a small application built into ROM. It is also known as the ROM *BIOS* configuration. You can start it instead of your operating system (OS) by pressing `F2` or `Delete` (or something else) just after you switch your machine on. There will usually be a message `Press <key> to enter setup` to explain this. Doing so will take you inside the CMOS program where you can change your machine's configuration. CMOS programs are different between motherboard manufacturers.

Inside the CMOS, you can enable or disable built-in devices (like your mouses and serial ports); set your machine's "hardware clock" (so that your machine has the correct time and date); and select the boot sequence (whether to load the operating system off the hard drive or CD-ROM—which you will need for installing LINUX⚬ from a bootable CD-ROM). *Boot* means to start up the computer. ↘The term comes from the lack of resources with which to begin: the operating system is on disk, but you might need the operating system to load from the disk—like trying to lift yourself up from your "bootstraps."↖ You can also configure your hard drive. You should always select `Hardrive autodetection` ↘*Autodetection* refers to a system that, though having incomplete information, configures itself. In this case the CMOS program probes the drive to determine its capacity. Very old CMOS programs required you to enter the drive's details manually.↖ whenever installing a new machine or adding/removing disks. Different CMOSs will have different procedures, so browse through all the menus to see what your CMOS can do.

The CMOS is important when it comes to configuring certain devices built into the motherboard. Modern CMOSs allow you to set the I/O ports and IRQ numbers that you would like particular devices to use. For instance, you can make your CMOS switch COM1 with COM2 or use a non-standard I/O port for your parallel port. When it comes to getting such devices to work under LINUX⚬, you will often have to power down your machine to see what the CMOS has to say about that device. More on this in Chapter 42.

3.4   Serial Devices

Serial ports facilitate low speed communications over a short distance using simple 8 core (or less) cable. The standards are old and communication is not particularly fault tolerant. There are so many variations on serial communication that it has become somewhat of a black art to get serial devices to work properly. Here I give a short explanation of the protocols, electronics, and hardware. The Serial-HOWTO and Modem-HOWTO documents contain an exhaustive treatment (see Chapter 16).

Some devices that communicate using serial lines are:

- Ordinary domestic dial-up modems.
- Some permanent modem-like Internet connections.
- Mice and other pointing devices.
- Character text terminals.
- Printers.
- Cash registers.
- Magnetic card readers.
- Uninterruptible power supply (UPS) units.
- Embedded microprocessor devices.

A device is connected to your computer by a cable with a 9-pin or 25-pin, male or female connector at each end. These are known as *DB-9* ( ) or *DB-25* ( ) connectors. Only eight of the pins are ever used, however. See Table 3.1.

Table 3.1 Pin assignments for DB-9 and DB-25 sockets

DB-9 pin number	DB-25 pin number	Acronym	Full-Name	Direction PC device
3	2	TD	Transmit Data	→
2	3	RD	Receive Data	←
7	4	RTS	Request To Send	→
8	5	CTS	Clear To Send	←
6	6	DSR	Data Set Ready	←
4	20	DTR	Data Terminal Ready	→
1	8	CD	Data Carrier Detect	←
9	22	RI	Ring Indicator	←
5	7		Signal Ground	

The way serial devices communicate is very straightforward: A stream of bytes is sent between the computer and the peripheral by dividing each byte into eight bits. The voltage is toggled on a pin called the *TD pin* or *transmit pin* according to whether a bit is 1 or 0. A bit of 1 is indicated by a negative voltage (-15 to -5 volts) and a bit of 0 is indicated by a positive voltage (+5 to +15 volts). The *RD pin* or *receive pin* receives bytes in a similar way. The computer and the serial device need to agree on a *data rate* (also called the *serial port speed*) so that the toggling and reading of voltage levels is properly synchronized. The speed is usually quoted in *bps* (bits per second). Table 3.2 shows a list of possible serial port speeds.

Table 3.2 Serial port speeds in bps

50	200	2,400	57,600	576,000	2,000,000
75	300	4,800	115,200	921,600	2,500,000
110	600	9,600	230,400	1,000,000	3,000,000
134	1,200	19,200	460,800	1,152,000	3,500,000
150	1,800	38,400	500,000	1,500,000	4,000,000

A typical mouse communicates between 1,200 and 9,600 bps. Modems communicate at 19,200, 38,400, 57,600, or 115,200 bps. It is rare to find serial ports or peripherals that support the speeds not blocked in Table 3.2.

To further synchronize the peripheral with the computer, an additional *start bit* proceeds each byte and up to two *stop bits* follow each byte. There may also be a *parity bit* which tells whether there is an even or odd number of 1s in the byte (for error checking). In theory, there may be as many as 12 bits sent for each data byte. These additional bits are optional and device specific. Ordinary modems communicate with an *8N1* protocol—8 data bits, No parity bit, and *1* stop bit. A mouse communicates with 8 bits and no start, stop, or parity bits. Some devices only use 7 data bits and hence are limited to send only ASCII data (since ASCII characters range only up to 127).

Some types of devices use two more pins called the *request to send* (RTS) and *clear to send* (CTS) pins. Either the computer or the peripheral pull the respective pin to +12 volts to indicate that it is ready to receive data. A further two pins call the DTR (data terminal ready) pin and the DSR (data set ready) pin are sometimes used instead—these work the same way, but just use different pin numbers. In particular, domestic modems make full use of the RTS/CTS pins. This mechanism is called *RTS/CTS flow control* or *hardware flow control*. Some simpler devices make no use of flow control at all. *Devices that do not use flow control will loose data which is sent without the receiver's readiness.*

Some other devices also need to communicate whether they are ready to receive data, but do not have RTS/CTS pins (or DSR/DTR pins) available to them. These emit special control characters, sent amid the data stream, to indicate that flow should halt or restart. This is known as *software flow control*. Devices that optionally support either type of flow control should always be configured to use hardware flow control. In particular, a modem used with LINUX*ᴧ* *must* have hardware flow control enabled.

Two other pins are the *ring indicator* (RI) pin and the *carrier detect* (CD) pin. These are only used by modems to indicate an incoming call and the detection of a peer modem, respectively.

The above pin assignments and protocol (including some hard-core electrical specifications which I have omitted) are known as *RS-232*. It is implemented using a standard chip called a 16550 *UART* (Universal Asynchronous Receiver-Transmitter) chip. RS-232 is easily effected by electrical noise, which limits the length and speed at which you can communicate: A half meter cable can carry 115,200 bps without errors, but a 15 meter cable is reliable at no more than 19,200 bps. Other protocols (like RS-423 or RS-422) can go much greater distances and there are converter appliances that give a more advantageous speed/distance tradeoff.

3.5   Modems

Telephone lines, having been designed to carry voice, have peculiar limitations when it comes to transmitting data. It turns out that the best way to send a binary digit over a telephone line is to beep it at the listener using two different pitches: a low pitch for 0 and a high pitch for 1. Figure 3.3 shows this operation schematically.

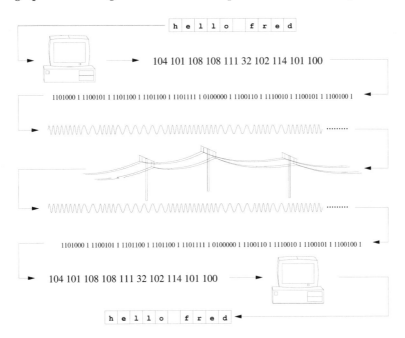

Figure 3.3 Communication between two remote computers by modem

Converting voltages to pitches and back again is known as *modulation-demodulation* and is where the word *modem* comes from. The word *baud* means the number of possible pitch switches per second, which is sometimes used interchangeably with bps. There are many newer modulation techniques used to get the most out of a telephone line, so that 57,600 bps modems are now the standard (as of this writing). Modems also do other things to the data besides modulating it: They may pack the data to reduce redundancies (*bit compression*) and perform error detection and compensation (*error correction*). Such *modem protocols* are given names like *V.90* (57,600 bps), *V.34* (33,600 bps or 28,800 bps), *V.42* (14,400 bps) or *V.32* (14,400 bps and lower). When two modems connect, they need to negotiate a "V" protocol to use. This negotiation is based on their respective capabilities and the current line quality.

A modem can be in one of two states: *command mode* or *connect mode*. A modem is connected if it can hear a peer modem's *carrier signal* over a live telephone call (and is probably transmitting and receiving data in the way explained), otherwise it is in command mode. In command mode the modem does not modulate or transmit data but interprets special text sequences sent to it through the serial line. These text sequences begin with the letters AT and are called AT*tention commands*. AT commands are sent by your computer to configure your modem for the current telephone line conditions, intended function, and serial port capability—for example, there are commands to: enable automatic answering on ring; set the flow control method; dial a number; and hang up. The sequence of commands used to configure the modem is called the *modem initialization string*. How to manually issue these commands is discussed in Section 32.6.3, 34.3, and 41.1 and will become relevant when you want to dial your Internet service provider (ISP).

Because each modem brand supports a slightly different set of modem commands, it is worthwhile familiarizing yourself with your modem manual. Most modern modems now support the *Hayes command set*—a generic set of the most useful modem commands. However, Hayes has a way of enabling hardware flow control that many popular modems do not adhere to. Whenever in this book I give examples of modem initialization, I include a footnote referring to this section. It is usually sufficient to configure your modem to "factory default settings", but often a second command is required to enable hardware flow control. There are no initialization strings that work on all modems. The web sites http://www.spy.net/~dustin/modem/ and http://www.teleport.com/~curt/modems.html are useful resources for finding out modem specifications.

Chapter 4

Basic Commands

> *All of* UNIX *is case sensitive. A command with even a single letter's capitalization altered is considered to be a completely different command. The same goes for files, directories, configuration file formats, and the syntax of all native programming languages.*

4.1 The `ls` Command, Hidden Files, Command-Line Options

In addition to directories and ordinary text files, there are other types of files, although all files contain the same kind of data (i.e., a list of bytes). The *hidden* file is a file that will not ordinarily appear when you type the command `ls` to *list* the contents of a directory. To see a hidden file you must use the command `ls -a`. The `-a` option means to list *all* files as well as hidden files. Another variant is `ls -l`, which lists the contents in *long* format. The `-` is used in this way to indicate variations on a command. These are called *command-line options* or *command-line arguments*, and most UNIX commands can take a number of them. They can be strung together in any way that is convenient ⟍Commands under the GNU🐃 free software license are superior in this way: they have a greater number of options than traditional UNIX commands and are therefore more flexible.⟍, for example, `ls -a -l`, `ls -l -a`, or `ls -al` —any of these will list *all* files in *long* format.

All GNU🐃 commands take the additional arguments `-h` and `--help`. You can type a command with just this on the command-line and get a *usage summary*. This is some brief help that will summarize options that you may have forgotten if you are

25

already familiar with the command—it will never be an exhaustive description of the usage. See the later explanation about `man` pages.

The difference between a *hidden* file and an ordinary file is merely that the file name of a *hidden* file starts with a period. Hiding files in this way is not for security, but for convenience.

The option `ls  -l` is somewhat cryptic for the novice. Its more explanatory version is `ls  --format=long`. Similarly, the *all* option can be given as `ls  --all`, and means the same thing as `ls  -a`.

4.2   Error Messages

Although commands usually do not display a message when they *execute* ↘The computer accepted and processed the command. ↖ successfully, commands do report *errors* in a consistent format. The format varies from one command to another but often appears as follows: *command-name* : *what was attempted* : *error message*. For example, the command `ls  -l qwerty` gives an error `ls: qwerty: No such file or directory`. What actually happened was that the command `ls` attempted to read the file `qwerty`. Since this file does not exist, an error code 2 arose. This error code corresponds to a situation where a file or directory is not being found. The error code is automatically translated into the sentence `No such file or directory`. It is important to understand the distinction between an explanatory message that a command gives (such as the messages reported by the `passwd` command in the previous chapter) and an error code that was just translated into a sentence. The reason is that a lot of different kinds of problems can result in an identical error code (there are only about a hundred different error codes). Experience will teach you that error messages do *not* tell you what to do, only what went wrong, and should not be taken as gospel.

The file `/usr/include/asm/errno.h` contains a complete list of basic error codes. In addition to these, several other header files ↘Files ending in `.h`↖ might define their own error codes. Under UNIX, however, these are 99% of all the errors you are ever likely to get. Most of them will be meaningless to you at the moment but are included in Table 4.1 as a reference.

Table 4.1 LINUX error codes

Number	C define	Message
0		Success
1	EPERM	Operation not permitted
2	ENOENT	No such file or directory
3	ESRCH	No such process
4	EINTR	Interrupted system call
5	EIO	Input/output error
6	ENXIO	Device not configured
7	E2BIG	Argument list too long
8	ENOEXEC	Exec format error
9	EBADF	Bad file descriptor

continues...

Table 4.1 (continued)

Number	C define	Message
10	ECHILD	No child processes
11	EAGAIN	Resource temporarily unavailable
11	EWOULDBLOCK	Resource temporarily unavailable
12	ENOMEM	Cannot allocate memory
13	EACCES	Permission denied
14	EFAULT	Bad address
15	ENOTBLK	Block device required
16	EBUSY	Device or resource busy
17	EEXIST	File exists
18	EXDEV	Invalid cross-device link
19	ENODEV	No such device
20	ENOTDIR	Not a directory
21	EISDIR	Is a directory
22	EINVAL	Invalid argument
23	ENFILE	Too many open files in system
24	EMFILE	Too many open files
25	ENOTTY	Inappropriate ioctl for device
26	ETXTBSY	Text file busy
27	EFBIG	File too large
28	ENOSPC	No space left on device
29	ESPIPE	Illegal seek
30	EROFS	Read-only file system
31	EMLINK	Too many links
32	EPIPE	Broken pipe
33	EDOM	Numerical argument out of domain
34	ERANGE	Numerical result out of range
35	EDEADLK	Resource deadlock avoided
35	EDEADLOCK	Resource deadlock avoided
36	ENAMETOOLONG	File name too long
37	ENOLCK	No locks available
38	ENOSYS	Function not implemented
39	ENOTEMPTY	Directory not empty
40	ELOOP	Too many levels of symbolic links
	EWOULDBLOCK	(*same as* EAGAIN)
42	ENOMSG	No message of desired type
43	EIDRM	Identifier removed
44	ECHRNG	Channel number out of range
45	EL2NSYNC	Level 2 not synchronized
46	EL3HLT	Level 3 halted
47	EL3RST	Level 3 reset
48	ELNRNG	Link number out of range
49	EUNATCH	Protocol driver not attached
50	ENOCSI	No CSI structure available
51	EL2HLT	Level 2 halted
52	EBADE	Invalid exchange
53	EBADR	Invalid request descriptor
54	EXFULL	Exchange full
55	ENOANO	No anode
56	EBADRQC	Invalid request code
57	EBADSLT	Invalid slot
	EDEADLOCK	(*same as* EDEADLK)
59	EBFONT	Bad font file format
60	ENOSTR	Device not a stream
61	ENODATA	No data available
62	ETIME	Timer expired
63	ENOSR	Out of streams resources
64	ENONET	Machine is not on the network
65	ENOPKG	Package not installed
66	EREMOTE	Object is remote
67	ENOLINK	Link has been severed
68	EADV	Advertise error
69	ESRMNT	Srmount error

continues...

Table 4.1 (continued)

Number	C define	Message
70	ECOMM	Communication error on send
71	EPROTO	Protocol error
72	EMULTIHOP	Multihop attempted
73	EDOTDOT	RFS specific error
74	EBADMSG	Bad message
75	EOVERFLOW	Value too large for defined data type
76	ENOTUNIQ	Name not unique on network
77	EBADFD	File descriptor in bad state
78	EREMCHG	Remote address changed
79	ELIBACC	Can not access a needed shared library
80	ELIBBAD	Accessing a corrupted shared library
81	ELIBSCN	.lib section in a.out corrupted
82	ELIBMAX	Attempting to link in too many shared libraries
83	ELIBEXEC	Cannot exec a shared library directly
84	EILSEQ	Invalid or incomplete multibyte or wide character
85	ERESTART	Interrupted system call should be restarted
86	ESTRPIPE	Streams pipe error
87	EUSERS	Too many users
88	ENOTSOCK	Socket operation on non-socket
89	EDESTADDRREQ	Destination address required
90	EMSGSIZE	Message too long
91	EPROTOTYPE	Protocol wrong type for socket
92	ENOPROTOOPT	Protocol not available
93	EPROTONOSUPPORT	Protocol not supported
94	ESOCKTNOSUPPORT	Socket type not supported
95	EOPNOTSUPP	Operation not supported
96	EPFNOSUPPORT	Protocol family not supported
97	EAFNOSUPPORT	Address family not supported by protocol
98	EADDRINUSE	Address already in use
99	EADDRNOTAVAIL	Cannot assign requested address
100	ENETDOWN	Network is down
101	ENETUNREACH	Network is unreachable
102	ENETRESET	Network dropped connection on reset
103	ECONNABORTED	Software caused connection abort
104	ECONNRESET	Connection reset by peer
105	ENOBUFS	No buffer space available
106	EISCONN	Transport endpoint is already connected
107	ENOTCONN	Transport endpoint is not connected
108	ESHUTDOWN	Cannot send after transport endpoint shutdown
109	ETOOMANYREFS	Too many references: cannot splice
110	ETIMEDOUT	Connection timed out
111	ECONNREFUSED	Connection refused
112	EHOSTDOWN	Host is down
113	EHOSTUNREACH	No route to host
114	EALREADY	Operation already in progress
115	EINPROGRESS	Operation now in progress
116	ESTALE	Stale NFS file handle
117	EUCLEAN	Structure needs cleaning
118	ENOTNAM	Not a XENIX named type file
119	ENAVAIL	No XENIX semaphores available
120	EISNAM	Is a named type file
121	EREMOTEIO	Remote I/O error
122	EDQUOT	Disk quota exceeded
123	ENOMEDIUM	No medium found
124	EMEDIUMTYPE	Wrong medium type

4.3   Wildcards, Names, Extensions, and *glob* Expressions

ls can produce a lot of output if there are a large number of files in a directory. Now say that we are only interested in files that ended with the letters tter. To list only these files, you can use ls *tter. The * matches any number of any other characters. So, for example, the files Tina.letter, Mary_Jones.letter and the file splatter, would all be listed if they were present, whereas a file Harlette would not be listed. While the * matches any length of characters, the ? matches only one character. For example, the command ls ?ar* would list the files Mary_Jones.letter and Harlette.

4.3.1   File naming

When naming files, it is a good idea to choose names that group files of the same type together. You do this by adding an *extension* to the file name that describes the type of file it is. We have already demonstrated this by calling a file Mary_Jones.letter instead of just Mary_Jones. If you keep this convention, you will be able to easily list all the files that are letters by entering ls *.letter. The file name Mary_Jones.letter is then said to be composed of two parts: the *name*, Mary_Jones, and the *extension*, letter.

Some common UNIX extensions you may see are:

.a Archive. lib*.a is a static library.

.alias X Window System font alias catalog.

.avi Video format.

.au Audio format (original Sun Microsystems generic sound file).

.awk awk program source file.

.bib bibtex LATEX bibliography source file.

.bmp Microsoft Bitmap file image format.

.bz2 File compressed with the bzip2 compression program.

.cc, .cxx, .C, .cpp C++ program source code.

.cf, .cfg Configuration file or script.

.cgi Executable script that produces web page output.

.conf, .config Configuration file.

.csh `csh` shell script.

.c **C** program source code.

.db Database file.

.dir X Window System font/other database directory.

.deb Debian© package for the Debian distribution.

.diff Output of the `diff` program indicating the difference between files or source trees.

.dvi Device-independent file. Formatted output of `.tex` LATEX file.

.el Lisp program source.

.g3 G3 fax format image file.

.gif, .giff GIF image file.

.gz File compressed with the `gzip` compression program.

.htm, .html, .shtm, .html Hypertext Markup Language. A web page of some sort.

.h **C**/C++ program header file.

.i SWIG source, or **C** preprocessor output.

.in `configure` input file.

.info Info pages read with the `info` command.

.jpg, .jpeg JPEG image file.

.lj LaserJet file. Suitable input to a HP LaserJet printer.

.log Log file of a system service. This file grows with status messages of some system program.

.lsm LINUX Software Map entry.

.lyx LyX word processor document.

.man Man page.

.mf Meta-Font font program source file.

.pbm PBM image file format.

.pcf PCF image file—intermediate representation for fonts. X Window System font.

.pcx PCX image file.

.pfb X Window System font file.

.pdf Formatted document similar to PostScript or dvi.

.php PHP program source code (used for web page design).

.pl Perl program source code.

.ps PostScript file, for printing or viewing.

.py Python program source code.

.rpm RedHat Package Manager `rpm` file.

.sgml Standard Generalized Markup Language. Used to create documents to be converted to many different formats.

.sh `sh` shell script.

.so Shared object file. `lib*.so` is a *Dynamically Linked Library.* Executable program code shared by more than one program to save disk space and memory.

.spd Speedo X Window System font file.

.tar `tar`red directory tree.

.tcl Tcl/Tk source code (programming language).

.texi, .texinfo Texinfo source. Info pages are compiled from these.

.tex T_EX or L_AT_EX document. L_AT_EX is for document processing and typesetting.

.tga TARGA image file.

.tgz Directory tree that has been archived with `tar`, and then compressed with `gzip`. Also a package for the Slackware distribution.

.tiff TIFF image file.

.tfm L_AT_EX font metric file.

.ttf Truetype font.

.txt Plain English text file.

.voc Audio format (Soundblaster's own format).

.wav Audio format (sound files common to Microsoft Windows).

.xpm XPM image file.

.y `yacc` source file.

.Z File compressed with the `compress` compression program.

.zip File compressed with the `pkzip` (or `PKZIP.EXE` for DOS) compression program.

.1, .2 . . . Man page.

In addition, files that have no extension and a capitalized descriptive name are usually plain English text and meant for your reading. They come bundled with packages and are for documentation purposes. You will see them hanging around all over the place.

Some full file names you may see are:

AUTHORS List of people who contributed to or wrote a package.

ChangeLog List of developer changes made to a package.

COPYING Copyright (usually GPL) for a package.

INSTALL Installation instructions.

README Help information to be read first, pertaining to the directory the `README` is in.

TODO List of future desired work to be done to package.

BUGS List of errata.

NEWS Info about new features and changes for the layman about this package.

THANKS List of contributors to a package.

VERSION Version information of the package.

4.3.2 Glob expressions

There is a way to restrict file listings to within the ranges of certain characters. If you only want to list the files that begin with A through M, you can run `ls [A-M]*`. Here the brackets have a special meaning—they match a single character like a `?`, but only those given by the range. You can use this feature in a variety of ways, for example, `[a-dJW-Y]*` matches all files beginning with a, b, c, d, J, W, X or Y; and `*[a-d]id` matches all files ending with `aid`, `bid`, `cid` or `did`; and `*.{cpp,c,cxx}` matches all files ending in `.cpp`, `.c` or `.cxx`. This way of specifying a file name is called a *glob* expression. *Glob* expressions are used in many different contexts, as you will see later.

4.4   Usage Summaries and the Copy Command

The command cp stands for *copy*. It duplicates one or more files. The format is

```
cp <file> <newfile>
cp <file> [<file> ...] <dir>
```

or

```
cp file newfile
cp file [file ...] dir
```

The above lines are called a *usage summary*. The < and > signs mean that you don't actually type out these characters but replace <file> with a file name of your own. These are also sometimes written in italics like, cp *file newfile*. In rare cases they are written in capitals like, cp FILE NEWFILE. <file> and <dir> are called *parameters*. Sometimes they are obviously numeric, like a command that takes <ioport>. ↘Anyone emailing me to ask why typing in literal, <, i, o, p, o, r, t and > characters did not work will get a rude reply.↖ These are common conventions used to specify the usage of a command. The [and] brackets are also not actually typed but mean that the contents between them are optional. The ellipses ... mean that <file> can be given repeatedly, and these also are never actually typed. From now on you will be expected to substitute your own parameters by interpreting the usage summary. You can see that the second of the above lines is actually just saying that one or more file names can be listed with a directory name last.

From the above usage summary it is obvious that there are two ways to use the cp command. If the last name is not a directory, then cp copies that file and renames it to the file name given. If the last name is a directory, then cp copies all the files listed *into* that directory.

The usage summary of the ls command is as follows:

```
ls [-l, --format=long] [-a, --all] <file> <file> ...
ls -al
```

where the comma indicates that either option is valid. Similarly, with the passwd command:

```
passwd [<username>]
```

You should practice using the cp command now by moving some of your files from place to place.

4.5 Directory Manipulation

The `cd` command is used to take you to different directories. Create a directory `new` with `mkdir new`. You *could* create a directory `one` by doing `cd new` and then `mkdir one`, but there is a more direct way of doing this with `mkdir new/one`. You can then change directly to the `one` directory with `cd new/one`. And similarly you can get back to where you were with `cd ../...`. In this way, the `/` is used to represent directories within directories. The directory `one` is called a *subdirectory* of `new`.

The command `pwd` stands for *present working directory* (also called the *current directory*) and tells what directory you are currently in. Entering `pwd` gives some output like `/home/<username>`. Experiment by changing to the root directory (with `cd /`) and then back into the directory `/home/<username>` (with `cd /home/<username>`). The directory `/home/<username>` is called your *home directory*, and is where all your personal files are kept. It can be used at any time with the abbreviation ˜. In other words, entering `cd /home/<username>` is the same as entering `cd ˜`. The process whereby a ˜ is substituted for your home directory is called *tilde expansion*.

To remove (i.e., erase or delete) a file, use the command `rm <filename>`. To remove a directory, use the command `rmdir <dir>`. Practice using these two commands. Note that you cannot remove a directory unless it is empty. To remove a directory as well as any contents it might contain, use the command `rm -R <dir>`. The `-R` option specifies to dive into any subdirectories of `<dir>` and delete their contents. The process whereby a command dives into subdirectories of subdirectories of ... is called recursion. `-R` stands for *recursively*. This is a very dangerous command. Although you may be used to "undeleting" files on other systems, on UNIX a deleted file is, at best, extremely difficult to recover.

The `cp` command also takes the `-R` option, allowing it to copy whole directories. The `mv` command is used to move files and directories. It really just renames a file to a different directory. Note that with `cp` you should use the option `-p` and `-d` with `-R` to preserve all attributes of a file and properly reproduce symlinks (discussed later). Hence, always use `cp -dpR <dir> <newdir>` instead of `cp -R <dir> <newdir>`.

4.6 *Relative* vs. *Absolute* Pathnames

Commands can be given file name arguments in two ways. If you are in the same directory as the file (i.e., the file is in the current directory), then you can just enter the file name on its own (e.g., `cp my_file new_file`). Otherwise, you can enter the *full path name*, like `cp /home/jack/my_file /home/jack/new_file`. Very often administrators use the notation `./my_file` to be clear about the distinction, for instance, `cp ./my_file ./new_file`. The leading `./` makes it clear that both files are relative to the current directory. File names not starting with a / are called *relative* path names, and otherwise, *absolute* path names.

4.7 System Manual Pages

(See Chapter 16 for a complete overview of all documentation on the system, and also how to print manual pages in a properly typeset format.)

The command `man [<section>|-a] <command>` displays help on a particular topic and stands for *manual*. Every command on the entire system is documented in so-named *man pages*. In the past few years a new format of documentation, called *info*, has evolved. This is considered the modern way to document commands, but most system documentation is still available only through `man`. Very few packages are not documented in `man` however.

Man pages are the authoritative reference on how a command works because they are usually written by the very programmer who created the command. Under UNIX, any printed documentation should be considered as being second-hand information. Man pages, however, will often not contain the underlying concepts needed for understanding the context in which a command is used. Hence, it is not possible for a person to learn about UNIX purely from man pages. However, once you have the necessary background for a command, then its man page becomes an indispensable source of information and you can discard other introductory material.

Now, man pages are divided into sections, numbered 1 through 9. Section 1 contains all man pages for system commands like the ones you have been using. Sections 2-7 contain information for programmers and the like, which you will probably not have to refer to just yet. Section 8 contains pages specifically for system administration commands. There are some additional sections labeled with letters; other than these, there are no manual pages besides the sections 1 through 9. The sections are

.../man1	User programs
.../man2	System calls
.../man3	Library calls
.../man4	Special files
.../man5	File formats
.../man6	Games
.../man7	Miscellaneous
.../man8	System administration
.../man9	Kernel documentation

You should now use the `man` command to look up the manual pages for all the commands that you have learned. Type `man cp`, `man mv`, `man rm`, `man mkdir`, `man rmdir`, `man passwd`, `man cd`, `man pwd`, and of course `man man`. Much of the information might be incomprehensible to you at this stage. Skim through the pages to get an idea of how they are structured and what headings they usually contain. Man pages are referenced with notation like cp(1), for the cp command in Section 1, which can be read with man 1 cp. This notation will be used from here on.

4.8 System **info** Pages

info pages contain some excellent reference and tutorial information in hypertext linked format. Type info on its own to go to the top-level menu of the entire info hierarchy. You can also type info <command> for help on many basic commands. Some packages will, however, not have info pages, and other UNIX systems do not support info at all.

info is an interactive program with keys to navigate and search documentation. Inside info, typing H will invoke the help screen from where you can learn more commands.

4.9 Some Basic Commands

You should practice using each of these commands.

bc A calculator program that handles arbitrary precision (very large) numbers. It is useful for doing any kind of calculation on the command-line. Its use is left as an exercise.

cal [[0–12] 1–9999] Prints out a nicely formatted calender of the current month, a specified month, or a specified whole year. Try cal 1 for fun, and cal 9 1752, when the pope had a few days scrapped to compensate for round-off error.

cat <filename> [<filename> ...] Writes the contents of all the files listed to the screen. cat can join a lot of files together with cat <filename> <file-name> ... > <newfile>. The file <newfile> will be an end-on-end *concatenation* of all the files specified.

clear Erases all the text in the current terminal.

date Prints out the current date and time. (The command time, though, does something entirely different.)

df Stands for *disk free* and tells you how much free space is left on your system. The available space usually has the units of kilobytes (1024 bytes) (although on some other UNIX systems this will be 512 bytes or 2048 bytes). The right-most column tells the directory (in combination with any directories below that) under which that much space is available.

dircmp Directory compare. This command compares directories to see if changes have been made between them. You will often want to see where two trees differ (e.g., check for missing files), possibly on different computers. Run `man dircmp` (that is, `dircmp`(1)). (This is a System 5 command and is not present on LINUX⚫. You can, however, compare directories with the Midnight Commander, `mc`).

du <directory> Stands for *disk usage* and prints out the amount of space occupied by a directory. It recurses into any subdirectories and can print only a summary with `du -s <directory>`. Also try `du --max-depth=1 /var` and `du -x /` on a system with `/usr` and `/home` on separate *partitions*. ➘See page 143.➘

dmesg Prints a complete log of all messages printed to the screen during the bootup process. This is useful if you blinked when your machine was initializing. These messages might not yet be meaningful, however.

echo Prints a message to the terminal. Try `echo 'hello there'`, `echo $[10*3+2]`, `echo '$[10*3+2]'`. The command `echo -e` allows interpretation of certain *backslash* sequences, for example `echo -e "\a"`, which prints a *bell*, or in other words, beeps the terminal. `echo -n` does the same without printing the trailing newline. In other words, it does not cause a wrap to the next line after the text is printed. `echo -e -n "\b"`, prints a back-space character only, which will erase the last character printed.

exit Logs you out.

expr <expression> Calculates the numerical expression `expression`. Most arithmetic operations that you are accustomed to will work. Try `expr 5 + 10 '*' 2`. Observe how mathematical precedence is obeyed (i.e., the `*` is worked out before the +).

file <filename> Prints out the type of data contained in a file. `file portrait.jpg` will tell you that `portrait.jpg` is a JPEG image data, JFIF standard. The command `file` detects an enormous amount of file types, across every platform. `file` works by checking whether the first few bytes of a file match certain tell-tale byte sequences. The byte sequences are called *magic numbers*. Their complete list is stored in `/usr/share/magic`. ➘The word "magic" under UNIX normally refers to byte sequences or numbers that have a specific meaning or implication. So-called *magic numbers* are invented for source code, file formats, and file systems.➘

free Prints out available free memory. You will notice two listings: swap space and physical memory. These are contiguous as far as the user is concerned. The swap space is a continuation of your installed memory that exists on disk. It is obviously slow to access but provides the illusion of much more available RAM and avoids the possibility of ever running out of memory (which can be quite fatal).

head [-n <lines>] <filename> Prints the first `<lines>` lines of a file or 10 lines if the `-n` option is not given. (See also `tail` below).

hostname [<new-name>] With no options, `hostname` prints the name of your machine, otherwise it sets the name to `<new-name>`.

kbdrate -r <chars-per-second> -d <repeat-delay> Changes the repeat rate of your keys. Most users will like this rate set to `kbdrate -r 32 -d 250` which unfortunately is the fastest the PC can go.

more Displays a long file by stopping at the end of each page. Run the following: `ls -l /bin > bin-ls`, and then try `more bin-ls`. The first command creates a file with the contents of the output of `ls`. This will be a long file because the directory `/bin` has a great many entries. The second command views the file. Use the space bar to page through the file. When you get bored, just press [Q]. You can also try `ls -l /bin | more` which will do the same thing in one go.

less The GNU🐃 version of `more`, but with extra features. On your system, the two commands may be the same. With `less`, you can use the arrow keys to page up and down through the file. You can do searches by pressing [?], and then typing in a word to search for and then pressing [Enter◄┘]. Found words will be highlighted, and the text will be scrolled to the first found word. The important commands are:

[⇧Shift]┤[G] Go to the end of a file.

[⇧Shift]┤[?]*ssss* Search backward through a file for the text *ssss*.

[?]*ssss* Search forward through a file for the text *ssss*.   ↘Actually *ssss* is a *regular expression*. See Chapter 5 for more info.↖

[⇧Shift]┤[F] Scroll forward and keep trying to read more of the file in case some other program is appending to it—useful for log files.

nnn–[G] Go to line *nnn* of the file.

[Q] Quit. Used by many UNIX text-based applications (sometimes [Q]┤[Enter◄┘]).

(You can make `less` stop beeping in the irritating way that it does by editing the file `/etc/profile` and adding the lines

```
LESS=-Q
export LESS
```

and then logging out and logging in again. But this is an aside that will make more sense later.)

lynx <url> Opens a URL ⟍URL stands for *Uniform Resource Locator*—a web address.⟋ at the
console. Try `lynx http://lwn.net/`.

links <url> Another text-based web browser.

nohup <command> & Runs a command in the background, appending any output
the command may produce to the file `nohup.out` in your home directory. nohup has the useful feature that the command will continue to run even after you
have logged out. Uses for `nohup` will become obvious later.

sleep <seconds> Pauses for `<seconds>` seconds. See also `usleep`.

sort <filename> Prints a file with lines sorted in alphabetical order. Create a file
called `telephone` with each line containing a short telephone book entry. Then
type `sort telephone`, or `sort telephone | less` and see what happens.
`sort` takes many interesting options to sort in reverse (`sort -r`), to eliminate
duplicate entries (`sort -u`), to ignore leading whitespace (`sort -b`), and so on.
See the `sort`(1) for details.

strings [-n <len>] <filename> Writes out a binary file, but strips any unreadable characters. Readable groups of characters are placed on separate lines. If you
have a binary file that you think may contain something interesting but looks
completely garbled when viewed normally, use `strings` to sift out the interesting stuff: try `less /bin/cp` and then try `strings /bin/cp`. By default
`strings` does not print sequences smaller than 4. The `-n` option can alter this
limit.

split ... Splits a file into many separate files. This might have been used when
a file was too big to be copied onto a floppy disk and needed to be split into,
say, 360-KB pieces. Its sister, `csplit`, can split files along specified lines of text
within the file. The commands are seldom used on their own but are very useful
within programs that manipulate text.

tac <filename> [<filename> ...] Writes the contents of all the files listed to
the screen, reversing the order of the lines—that is, printing the last line of the
file first. `tac` is `cat` backwards and behaves similarly.

tail [-f] [-n <lines>] <filename> Prints the last `<lines>` lines of a file or
10 lines if the `-n` option is not given. The `-f` option means to watch the file for
lines being appended to the end of it. (See also `head` above.)

uname Prints the name of the UNIX *operating system* you are currently using. In this
case, LINUX𝕒.

uniq <filename> Prints a file with duplicate lines deleted. The file must first be
sorted.

usleep <microseconds> Pauses for `<microseconds>` microseconds (1/1,000,000 of a second).

wc [-c] [-w] [-l] <filename> Counts the number of bytes (with `-c` for character), or words (with `-w`), or lines (with `-l`) in a file.

whatis <command> Gives the first line of the man page corresponding to <command>, unless no such page exists, in which case it prints `nothing appropriate`.

whoami Prints your login name.

4.10   The mc File Manager

Those who come from the DOS world may remember the famous *Norton Commander* file manager. The GNU project has a Free clone called the *Midnight Commander*, mc. It is essential to at least try out this package—it allows you to move around files and directories extremely rapidly, giving a wide-angle picture of the file system. This will drastically reduce the number of tedious commands you will have to type by hand.

4.11   Multimedia Commands for Fun

You should practice using each of these commands if you have your sound card configured. ⟍I don't want to give the impression that LINUX does not have graphical applications to do all the functions in this section, but you should be aware that for every graphical application, there is a text-mode one that works better and consumes fewer resources.⟋ You may also find that some of these packages are not installed, in which case you can come back to this later.

play [-v <volume>] <filename> Plays linear audio formats out through your sound card. These formats are `.8svx`, `.aiff`, `.au`, `.cdr`, `.cvs`, `.dat`, `.gsm`, `.hcom`, `.maud`, `.sf`, `.smp`, `.txw`, `.vms`, `.voc`, `.wav`, `.wve`, `.raw`, `.ub`, `.sb`, `.uw`, `.sw`, or `.ul` files. In other words, it plays almost every type of "basic" sound file there is: most often this will be a simple Windows `.wav` file. Specify <volume> in percent.

rec <filename> Records from your microphone into a file. (`play` and `rec` are from the same package.)

mpg123 <filename> Plays audio from MPEG files level 1, 2, or 3. Useful options are `-b 1024` (for increasing the buffer size to prevent jumping) and `--2to1` (down-samples by a factor of 2 for reducing CPU load). MPEG files contain sound and/or video, stored very compactly using digital signal processing techniques that the commercial software industry seems to think are very sophisticated.

cdplay Plays a regular music CD⬚. cdp is the interactive version.

aumix Sets your sound card's volume, gain, recording volume, etc. You can use it interactively or just enter aumix -v <volume> to immediately set the volume in percent. Note that this is a dedicated *mixer* program and is considered to be an application separate from any that play music. Preferably do not set the volume from within a sound-playing application, even if it claims this feature—you have much better control with aumix.

mikmod --interpolate -hq --renice Y <filename> Plays *Mod* files. Mod files are a special type of audio format that stores only the duration and pitch of the notes that constitute a song, along with samples of each musical instrument needed to play the song. This makes for high-quality audio with phenomenally small file size. mikmod supports 669, AMF, DSM, FAR, GDM, IMF, IT, MED, MOD, MTM, S3M, STM, STX, ULT, UNI, and XM audio formats—that is, probably every type in existence. Actually, a lot of excellent listening music is available on the Internet in Mod file format. The most common formats are .it, .mod, .s3m, and .xm. ⟍Original .mod files are the product of Commodore-Amiga computers and had only four tracks. Today's 16 (and more) track Mod files are comparable to any recorded music.⟍

4.12 Terminating Commands

You usually use [Ctrl]─[C] to stop an application or command that runs continuously. You must type this at the same prompt where you entered the command. If this doesn't work, the section on *processes* (Section 9.5) will explain about *signalling* a running application to quit.

4.13 Compressed Files

Files typically contain a lot of data that one can imagine might be represented with a smaller number of bytes. Take for example the letter you typed out. The word "the" was probably repeated many times. You were probably also using lowercase letters most of the time. The file was by far not a completely random set of bytes, and it repeatedly used spaces as well as using some letters more than others. ⟍English text in fact contains, on average, only about 1.3 useful bits (there are eight bits in a byte) of data per byte.⟍ Because of this the file can be *compressed* to take up less space. Compression involves representing the same data by using a smaller number of bytes, in such a way that the original data can be reconstructed exactly. Such usually involves finding patterns in the data. The command to compress a file is gzip <filename>, which stands for *GNU zip*. Run gzip on a file in your home directory and then run ls to see what happened. Now, use more to view the compressed file. To uncompress the file use

gzip -d <filename>. Now, use more to view the file again. Many files on the
system are stored in compressed format. For example, man pages are often stored
compressed and are uncompressed automatically when you read them.

You previously used the command cat to view a file. You can use the command zcat to do the same thing with a compressed file. Gzip a file and then type
zcat <filename>. You will see that the contents of the file are written to the screen.
Generally, when commands and files have a z in them they have something to do with
compression—the letter z stands for *zip*. You can use zcat <filename> | less to
view a compressed file proper. You can also use the command zless <filename>,
which does the same as zcat <filename> | less. (Note that your less may ac-
tually have the functionality of zless combined.)

A new addition to the arsenal is bzip2. This is a compression program very
much like gzip, except that it is slower and compresses 20%–30% better. It is useful
for compressing files that will be downloaded from the Internet (to reduce the transfer
volume). Files that are compressed with bzip2 have an extension .bz2. Note that
the improvement in compression depends very much on the type of data being compressed. Sometimes there will be negligible size reduction at the expense of a huge
speed penalty, while occasionally it is well worth it. Files that are frequently compressed and uncompressed should never use bzip2.

4.14   Searching for Files

You can use the command find to search for files. Change to the root directory, and
enter find. It will spew out all the files it can see by *recursively descending* ↘Goes into
each subdirectory and all its subdirectories, and repeats the command find. ↖ into all subdirectories.
In other words, find, when executed from the root directory, prints all the files on the
system. find will work for a long time if you enter it as you have—press [Ctrl]-[C] to
stop it.

Now change back to your home directory and type find again. You will see *all*
your personal files. You can specify a number of options to find to look for specific
files.

find -type d Shows only directories and not the files they contain.

find -type f Shows only files and not the directories that contain them, even
though it will still descend into all directories.

find -name <filename> Finds only files that have the name <filename>. For
instance, find -name '*.c' will find all files that end in a .c extension
(find -name *.c without the quote characters will not work. You will see
why later). find -name Mary_Jones.letter will find the file with the name
Mary_Jones.letter.

find -size [[+|-]]<size> Finds only files that have a size larger (for +) or
smaller (for −) than <size> kilobytes, or the same as <size> kilobytes if the
sign is not specified.

find <directory> [<directory> ...] Starts find in each of the specified directories.

There are many more options for doing just about any type of search for a file. See
find(1) for more details (that is, run man 1 find). Look also at the -exec option
which causes find to execute a command for each file it finds, for example:

```
find /usr -type f -exec ls '-al' '{}' ';'
```

find has the deficiency of actively reading directories to find files. This process
is slow, especially when you start from the root directory. An alternative command is
locate <filename>. This searches through a previously created database of all the
files on the system and hence finds files instantaneously. Its counterpart updatedb
updates the database of files used by locate. On some systems, updatedb runs
automatically every day at 04h00.

Try these (updatedb will take several minutes):

```
updatedb
locate rpm
locate deb
locate passwd
locate HOWTO
locate README
```

4.15   Searching *Within* Files

Very often you will want to search through a number of files to find a particular word
or phrase, for example, when a number of files contain lists of telephone numbers with
people's names and addresses. The command grep does a line-by-line search through
a file and prints only those lines that contain a word that you have specified. grep has
the command summary:

```
grep [options] <pattern> <filename> [<filename> ...]
```

The words *word*, *string*, or *pattern* are used synonymously in this context, basically meaning a short length
of letters and-or numbers that you are trying to find matches for. A *pattern* can also be a string with kinds of
wildcards in it that match different characters, as we shall see later.

Run `grep` for the word "the" to display all lines containing it: `grep 'the' Mary_Jones.letter`. Now try `grep 'the' *.letter`.

grep -n <pattern> <filename> shows the line number in the file where the word was found.

grep -<num> <pattern> <filename> prints out <num> of the lines that came before and after each of the lines in which the word was found.

grep -A <num> <pattern> <filename> prints out <num> of the lines that came After each of the lines in which the word was found.

grep -B <num> <pattern> <filename> prints out <num> of the lines that came Before each of the lines in which the word was found.

grep -v <pattern> <filename> prints out only those lines that do *not* contain the word you are searching for. ↘ You may think that the -v option is no longer doing the same kind of thing that `grep` is advertised to do: i.e., *searching* for strings. In fact, UNIX commands often suffer from this—they have such versatility that their functionality often overlaps with that of other commands. One actually never stops learning new and nifty ways of doing things hidden in the dark corners of man pages.↖

grep -i <pattern> <filename> does the same as an ordinary `grep` but is case insensitive.

4.16 Copying to MS-DOS and Windows Formatted Floppy Disks

A package, called the `mtools` package, enables reading and writing to MS-DOS/Windows floppy disks. These are not standard UNIX commands but are packaged with most LINUX distributions. The commands support Windows "long file name" floppy disks. Put an MS-DOS disk in your `A:` drive. Try

```
mdir A:
touch myfile
mcopy myfile A:
mdir A:
```

Note that there is *no* such thing as an `A:` disk under LINUX. Only the `mtools` package understands `A:` in order to retain familiarity for MS-DOS users. The complete list of commands is

| floppyd | mcopy | mformat | mmount | mshowfat |
| mattrib | mdel | minfo | mmove | mtoolstest |

```
  mbadblocks   mdeltree   mkmanifest   mpartition   mtype
  mcat         mdir       mlabel       mrd          mzip
5 mcd          mdu        mmd          mren         xcopy
```

Entering `info mtools` will give detailed help. In general, any MS-DOS command, put into lower case with an m prefixed to it, gives the corresponding LINUX🐧 command.

4.17   Archives and Backups

> *Never begin any work before you have a fail-safe method of backing it up.*

One of the primary activities of a system administrator is to make backups. It is essential never to underestimate the volatility ⟍Ability to evaporate or become chaotic. ⟍ of information in a computer. *Backups* of data are therefore continually made. A backup is a duplicate of your files that can be used as a replacement should any or all of the computer be destroyed. The idea is that all of the data in a directory ⟍As usual, meaning a directory and all its subdirectories and all the files in those subdirectories, etc. ⟍ are stored in a separate place—often compressed—and can be retrieved in case of an emergency. When we want to store a number of files in this way, it is useful to be able to pack many files into one file so that we can perform operations on that single file only. When many files are packed together into one, this packed file is called an *archive*. Usually archives have the extension .tar, which stands for *tape archive*.

To *create* an archive of a directory, use the tar command:

```
tar -c -f <filename> <directory>
```

Create a directory with a few files in it, and run the tar command to back it up. A file of `<filename>` will be created. Take careful note of any error messages that tar reports. List the file and check that its size is appropriate for the size of the directory you are archiving. You can also use the *verify* option (see the man page) of the tar command to check the integrity of `<filename>`. Now remove the directory, and then restore it with the *extract* option of the tar command:

```
tar -x -f <filename>
```

You should see your directory recreated with all its files intact. A nice option to give to tar is -v. This option lists all the files that are being added to or extracted from the archive as they are processed, and is useful for monitoring the progress of archiving.

It is obvious that you can call your archive anything you like, however; the common practice is to call it <directory>.tar, which makes it clear to all exactly what it is. Another important option is –p which preserves detailed attribute information of files.

Once you have your .tar file, you would probably want to compress it with gzip. This will create a file <directory>.tar.gz, which is sometimes called <directory>.tgz for brevity.

A second kind of archiving utility is cpio. cpio is actually more powerful than tar, but is considered to be more cryptic to use. The principles of cpio are quite similar and its use is left as an exercise.

4.18 The **PATH** Where Commands Are Searched For

When you type a command at the shell prompt, it has to be read off disk out of one or other directory. On UNIX, all such *executable commands* are located in one of about four directories. A file is located in the directory tree according to its type, rather than according to what software package it belongs to. For example, a word processor may have its actual executable stored in a directory with all other executables, while its font files are stored in a directory with other fonts from all other packages.

The shell has a procedure for searching for executables when you type them in. If you type in a command with slashes, like /bin/cp, then the shell tries to run the named program, cp, out of the /bin directory. If you just type cp on its own, then it tries to find the cp command in each of the subdirectories of your PATH. To see what your PATH is, just type

```
echo $PATH
```

You will see a colon separated list of four or more directories. Note that the current directory . is not listed. It is important that the current directory *not* be listed for reasons of security. Hence, to execute a command in the current directory, we hence always ./<command>.

To append, for example, a new directory /opt/gnome/bin to your PATH, do

```
PATH="$PATH:/opt/gnome/bin"
export PATH
```

LINUX⌂ supports the convenience of doing this in one line:

```
export PATH="$PATH:/opt/gnome/bin"
```

There is a further command, `which`, to check whether a command is locatable from the `PATH`. Sometimes there are two commands of the same name in different directories of the `PATH`. ↘This is more often true of Solaris systems than LINUX⚐↖ Typing `which` `<command>` locates the one that your shell would execute. Try:

```
which ls
which cp mv rm
which which
which cranzgots
```

`which` is also useful in shell scripts to tell if there is a command at all, and hence check whether a particular package is installed, for example, `which netscape`.

4.19   The −− Option

If a file name happens to begin with a − then it would be impossible to use that file name as an argument to a command. To overcome this circumstance, most commands take an option −−. This option specifies that no more options follow on the command-line—everything else must be treated as a literal file name. For instance

```
touch -- -stupid_file_name
rm -- -stupid_file_name
```

Chapter 5

Regular Expressions

A regular expression is a sequence of characters that forms a template used to search for *strings* ↘Words, phrases, or just about any sequence of characters. ↖ within text. In other words, it is a search pattern. To get an idea of when you would need to do this, consider the example of having a list of names and telephone numbers. If you want to find a telephone number that contains a 3 in the second place and ends with an 8, regular expressions provide a way of doing that kind of search. Or consider the case where you would like to send an email to fifty people, replacing the word after the "Dear" with their own name to make the letter more personal. Regular expressions allow for this type of searching and replacing.

5.1   Overview

Many utilities use the regular expression to give them greater power when manipulating text. The `grep` command is an example. Previously you used the `grep` command to locate only simple letter sequences in text. Now we will use it to search for regular expressions.

In the previous chapter you learned that the `?` character can be used to signify that any character can take its place. This is said to be a *wildcard* and works with file names. With regular expressions, the wildcard to use is the `.` character. So, you can use the command `grep .3....8 <filename>` to find the seven-character telephone number that you are looking for in the above example.

Regular expressions are used for line-by-line searches. For instance, if the seven characters were spread over two lines (i.e., they had a line break in the middle), then `grep` wouldn't find them. In general, a program that uses regular expressions will consider searches one line at a time.

Here are some regular expression examples that will teach you the regular expression basics. We use the `grep` command to show the use of regular expressions (remember that the `-w` option matches whole words only). Here the expression itself is enclosed in ' quotes for reasons that are explained later.

grep -w 't[a-i]e' Matches the words `tee`, `the`, and `tie`. The brackets have a special significance. They mean to match one character that can be anything from `a` to `i`.

grep -w 't[i-z]e' Matches the words `tie` and `toe`.

grep -w 'cr[a-m]*t' Matches the words `craft`, `credit`, and `cricket`. The `*` means to match any number of the previous character, which in this case is any character from `a` through `m`.

grep -w 'kr.*n' Matches the words `kremlin` and `krypton`, because the `.` matches any character and the `*` means to match the dot any number of times.

egrep -w '(th|sh).*rt' Matches the words `shirt`, `short`, and `thwart`. The `|` means to match either the `th` or the `sh`. `egrep` is just like `grep` but supports *extended regular expressions* that allow for the `|` feature. ↘ The | character often denotes a logical OR, meaning that either the thing on the left or the right of the | is applicable. This is true of many programming languages. ↖ Note how the square brackets mean one-of-several-characters and the round brackets with `|`'s mean one-of-several-words.

grep -w 'thr[aeiou]*t' Matches the words `threat` and `throat`. As you can see, a list of possible characters can be placed inside the square brackets.

grep -w 'thr[^a-f]*t' Matches the words `throughput` and `thrust`. The `^` after the first bracket means to match *any* character *except* the characters listed. For example, the word `thrift` is not matched because it contains an `f`.

The above regular expressions all match whole words (because of the `-w` option). If the `-w` option was not present, they might match parts of words, resulting in a far greater number of matches. Also note that although the `*` means to match any number of characters, it also will match *no* characters as well; for example: `t[a-i]*e` could actually match the letter sequence `te`, that is, a `t` and an `e` with zero characters between them.

Usually, you will use regular expressions to search for *whole lines* that match, and sometimes you would like to match a line that begins or ends with a certain string. The `^` character specifies the beginning of a line, and the `$` character the end of the line. For example, `^The` matches all lines that start with a `The`, and `hack$` matches all lines that end with `hack`, and `'^ *The.*hack *$'` matches all lines that begin with `The` and end with `hack`, even if there is whitespace at the beginning or end of the line.

Because regular expressions use certain characters in a special way (these are **.** \
[ ] * + ?), these characters cannot be used to match characters. This restriction severely
limits you from trying to match, say, file names, which often use the **.** character. To
match a **.** you can use the sequence \. which forces interpretation as an actual **.** and
not as a wildcard. Hence, the regular expression `myfile.txt` might match the letter sequence `myfileqtxt` or `myfile.txt`, but the regular expression `myfile\.txt`
will match only `myfile.txt`.

You can specify most special characters by adding a \ character before them, for
example, use \[for an actual [, a \$ for an actual $, a \\ for and actual \, \+ for an
actual +, and \? for an actual ?. (? and + are explained below.)

5.2   The `fgrep` Command

`fgrep` is an alternative to `grep`. The difference is that while `grep` (the more commonly
used command) matches regular expressions, `fgrep` matches literal strings. In other
words you can use `fgrep` when you would like to search for an ordinary string that is
not a regular expression, instead of preceding special characters with \.

5.3   Regular Expression \{ \} Notation

`x*` matches zero to infinite instances of a character `x`. You can specify other ranges of
numbers of characters to be matched with, for example, `x\{3,5\}`, which will match
at least three but not more than five `x`'s, that is `xxx`, `xxxx`, or `xxxxx`.

`x\{4\}` can then be used to match 4 `x`'s exactly: no more and no less. `x\{7,\}`
will match seven or more `x`'s—the upper limit is omitted to mean that there is no
maximum number of `x`'s.

As in all the examples above, the `x` can be a range of characters (like `[a-k]`) just
as well as a single charcter.

grep -w 'th[a-t]\{2,3\}t' Matches the words `theft`, `thirst`, `threat`,
`thrift`, and `throat`.

grep -w 'th[a-t]\{4,5\}t' Matches the words `theorist`, `thicket`, and
`thinnest`.

5.4   Extended Regular Expression + ? \< \> ( ) | Notation with `egrep`

An enhanced version of regular expressions allows for a few more useful features. Where these conflict with existing notation, they are only available through the `egrep` command.

+ is analogous to \{1,\}. It does the same as * but matches *one* or more characters instead of *zero* or more characters.

? is analogous to "–1"". It matches *zero* or *one* character.

\< \> can surround a string to match only whole words.

( ) can surround several strings, separated by |. This notation will match any of these strings. (`egrep` only.)

\(\) can surround several strings, separated by \|. This notation will match any of these strings. (`grep` only.)

   The following examples should make the last two notations clearer.

grep 'trot' Matches the words `electrotherapist`, `betroth`, and so on, but

grep '\<trot\>' matches only the word `trot`.

egrep -w '(this|that|c[aeiou]*t)' Matches the words `this`, `that`, `cot`, `coat`, `cat`, and `cut`.

5.5   Regular Expression Subexpressions

Subexpressions are covered in Chapter 8.

Chapter 6

Editing Text Files

To edit a text file means to interactively modify its content. The creation and modification of an ordinary text file is known as *text editing*. A word processor is a kind of editor, but more basic than that is the UNIX or DOS text editor.

6.1 `vi`

The important editor to learn how to use is `vi`. After that you can read why, and a little more about other, more user-friendly editors.

Type simply,

```
vi <filename>
```

to edit any file, or the compatible, but more advanced

```
vim <filename>
```

To exit `vi`, press [Esc], then the key sequence `:q!` and then press [Enter↵].

`vi` has a short tutorial which should get you going in 20 minutes. If you get bored in the middle, you can skip it and learn `vi` as you need to edit things. To read the tutorial, enter:

```
vimtutor
```

which edits the file

```
/usr/doc/vim-common-5.7/tutor,
/usr/share/vim/vim56/tutor/tutor, or
/usr/share/doc/vim-common-5.7/tutor/tutor,
```

depending on your distribution. ⟍By this you should be getting an idea of the kinds of differences there are between different LINUX distributions.⟍ You will then see the following at the top of your screen:

```
     ==============================================================================
   = Welcome   to   the   VIM   Tutor   -   Version 1.4   =
     ==============================================================================

 5     Vim is a very powerful editor that has many commands, too many to
       explain in a tutor such as this.  This tutor is designed to describe
       enough of the commands that you will be able to easily use Vim as
       an all-purpose editor.

10     The approximate time required to complete the tutor is 25-30 minutes,
```

You are supposed to edit the `tutor` file itself as practice, following through 6 lessons. Copy it first to your home directory.

Table 6.1 is a quick reference for `vi`. It contains only a few of the many hundreds of available commands but is enough to do all basic editing operations. Take note of the following:

- `vi` has several *modes* of operation. If you press ⎡I⎤, you enter *insert*-mode. You then enter text as you would in a normal DOS text editor, *but you cannot arbitrarily move the cursor and delete characters while in insert mode.* Pressing ⎡Esc⎤ will get you out of insert mode, where you are not able to insert characters, but can now do things like arbitrary deletions and moves.

- Pressing ⎡⇧Shift⎤—⎡;⎤ (i.e., :) gets you into *command-line* mode, where you can do operations like importing files, saving of the current file, searches, and text processing. Typically, you type : then some text, and then hit ⎡Enter←⎤.

- The word *register* is used below. A register is a hidden clipboard.

- A useful tip is to enter `:set ruler` before doing anything. This shows, in the bottom right corner of the screen, what line and column you are on.

Table 6.1 Common vi commands

Key combination	Function
h or ←	Cursor left
l or →	Cursor right.
k or ↑	Cursor up.
j or ↓	Cursor down.
b	Cursor left one word.
w	Cursor right one word.
{	Cursor up one paragraph.
}	Cursor down one paragraph.
^	Cursor to line start.
$	Cursor to line end.
gg	Cursor to first line.
G	Cursor to last line.
Esc	Get out of current mode.
i	Start insert mode.
o	Insert a blank line below the current line and then start insert mode.
O	Insert a blank line above the current line and then start insert mode.
a	Append (start insert mode after the current character).
R	Replace (start insert mode with over-write).
:wq	Save (write) and quit.
:q	Quit.
:q!	Quit forced (without checking whether a save is required).
x	Delete (delete under cursor and copy to register).
X	Backspace (delete left of cursor and copy to register).
dd	Delete line (and copy to register).
:j!	Join line (remove newline at end of current line).
Ctrl-J	Same.
u	Undo.
Ctrl-R	Redo.
de	Delete to word end (and copy to register).

continues...

55

Table 6.1 (continued)

Key combination	Function
db	Delete to word start (and copy to register).
d$	Delete to line end (and copy to register).
d^	Delete to line beginning (and copy to register).
dd	Delete current line (and copy to register).
2dd	Delete two lines (and copy to register).
5dd	Delete five lines (and copy to register).
p	Paste clipboard (insert register).
Ctrl-G	Show cursor position.
5G	Cursor to line five.
16G	Cursor to line sixteen.
G	Cursor to last line.
/*search-string*	Search forwards for *search-string*.
?*search-string*	Search backwards for *search-string*.
:-1,$s/*search-string*/*replace-string*/gc	Search and replace with confirmation starting at current line.
:,$s/*search-string*/*replace-string*/gc	Search and replace with confirmation starting at line below cursor.
:,$s/\<*search-string*\>/*replace-string*/gc	Search and replace whole words.
:8,22s/*search-string*/*replace-string*/g	Search and replace in lines 8 through 22 without confirmation.
:%s/*search-string*/*replace-string*/g	Search and replace whole file without confirmation.
:w *filename*	Save to file *filename*.
:5,20w *filename*	Save lines 5 through 20 to file *filename* (use Ctrl-G to get line numbers if needed).
:5,$w! *filename*	Force save lines 5 through to last line to file *filename*.
:r *filename*	Insert file *filename*.
v	Visual mode (start highlighting).
y	Copy highlighted text to register.
d	Delete highlighted text (and copy to register).
p	Paste clipboard (insert register).
Press v, then move cursor down a few lines, then,	Search and replace within highlighted text.

continues...

Table 6.1 (continued)

Key combination	Function
`:s`/*search-string*/*replace-string*/`g`	
`:help`	Reference manual (open new window with help screen inside—probably the most important command here!).
`:new`	Open new blank window.
`:split` *filename*	Open new window with *filename*.
`:q`	Close current window.
`:qa`	Close all windows.
Ctrl-W j	Move cursor to window below.
Ctrl-W k	Move cursor to window above.
Ctrl-W -	Make window smaller.
Ctrl-W +	Make window larger.

6.2 Syntax Highlighting

Something all UNIX users are used to (and have come to expect) is *syntax highlighting*. This basically means that a `bash` (explained later) script will look like:

```
#!/bin/sh

for file in * ; do
    VAR=`cat $file`
        echo $VAR | tr 'a-z' 'A-Z'
done
```

instead of

```
#!/bin/sh

for file in * ; do
    VAR=`cat $file`
        echo $VAR | tr 'a-z' 'A-Z'
done
```

Syntax highlighting is meant to preempt programming errors by colorizing correct keywords. You can set syntax highlighting in `vim` by using `:syntax on` (but not in `vi`). Enable syntax highlighting whenever possible—all good text editors support it.

6.3 Editors

Although UNIX has had full graphics capability for a long time now, most administration of low-level services still takes place inside text configuration files. Word processing is also best accomplished with typesetting systems that require creation of ordinary text files. ⭢This is in spite of all the hype regarding the WYSIWYG (what you see is what you get) word processor. This document itself was typeset with LATEX and the Cooledit text editor.⭠

Historically, the standard text editor used to be `ed`. `ed` allows the user to see only one line of text of a file at a time (primitive by today's standards). Today, `ed` is mostly used in its streaming version, `sed`. `ed` has long since been superseded by `vi`.

The editor is the place you will probably spend most of your time. Whether you are doing word processing, creating web pages, programming, or administrating. It is your primary interactive application.

6.3.1   Cooledit

(Read this if you "just-want-to-open-a-file-and-start-typing-like-under-Windows.")

`cooledit` The best editor for day-to-day work is Cooledit, ↘As Cooledit's author, I am probably biased in this view.↖ available from *the Cooledit web page* http://cooledit.sourceforge.net/. Cooledit is a graphical (runs under X) editor. It is also a full-featured Integrated Development Environment (IDE) for whatever you may be doing. Those considering buying an IDE for development need look no further than installing Cooledit for free.

People coming from a Windows background will find Cooledit the easiest and most powerful editor to use. It requires no tutelage; just enter `cooledit` under X and start typing. Its counterpart in text mode is `mcedit`, which comes with the GNU🐃 Midnight Commander package `mc`. The text-mode version is inferior to other text mode editors like `emacs` and `jed` but is adequate if you don't spend a lot of time in text mode.

Cooledit has pull-down menus and intuitive keys. It is not necessary to read any documentation before using Cooledit.

6.3.2   `vi` and `vim`

Today `vi` is considered the standard. It is the only editor that *will* be installed by default on *any* UNIX system. `vim` is a "Charityware" version that (as usual) improves upon the original `vi` with a host of features. It is important to learn the basics of `vi` even if your day-to-day editor is not going to be `vi`. The reason is that every administrator is bound to one day have to edit a text file over some really slow network link and `vi` is the best for this.

On the other hand, new users will probably find `vi` unintuitive and tedious and will spend a lot of time learning and remembering how to do all the things they need to. I myself cringe at the thought of `vi` pundits recommending it to new UNIX users.

In defense of `vi`, it should be said that many people use it exclusively, and it is probably the only editor that really can do absolutely *everything*. It is also one of the few editors that has working versions and consistent behavior across all UNIX and non-UNIX systems. `vim` works on AmigaOS, AtariMiNT, BeOS, DOS, MacOS, OS/2, RiscOS, VMS, and Windows (95/98/NT4/NT5/2000) as well as all UNIX variants.

6.3.3   Emacs

Emacs stands for Editor MACroS. It is the monster of all editors and can do almost everything one could imagine that a single software package might. It has become a de facto standard alongside `vi`.

Emacs is more than just a text editor. It is a complete system of using a computer for development, communications, file management, and things you wouldn't even imagine there are programs for. There is even an **X** Window System version available which can browse the web.

6.3.4   Other editors

Other editors to watch out for are `joe`, `jed`, `nedit`, `pico`, `nano`, and many others that try to emulate the look and feel of well-known DOS, Windows, or Apple Mac development environments, or to bring better interfaces by using Gtk/Gnome or Qt/KDE. The list gets longer each time I look. In short, don't think that the text editors that your vendor has chosen to put on your CD are the best or only free ones out there. The same goes for other applications.

Chapter 7

Shell Scripting

This chapter introduces you to the concept of *computer programming*. So far, you have entered commands one at a time. Computer programming is merely the idea of getting a number of commands to be executed, that in combination do some unique powerful function.

7.1 Introduction

To execute a number of commands in sequence, create a file with a `.sh` extension, into which you will enter your commands. The `.sh` extension is not strictly necessary but serves as a reminder that the file contains special text called a *shell script*. From now on, the word *script* will be used to describe any sequence of commands placed in a text file. Now do a

```
chmod 0755 myfile.sh
```

which allows the file to be run in the explained way.

Edit the file using your favorite text editor. The first line should be as follows with no whitespace. ⬊Whitespace are tabs and spaces, and in some contexts, newline (end of line) characters.⬉

```
#!/bin/sh
```

The line dictates that the following program is a *shell* script, meaning that it accepts the same sort of commands that you have normally been typing at the prompt. Now enter a number of commands that you would like to be executed. You can start with

```
echo "Hi there"
```

```
echo "what is your name? (Type your name here and press Enter)"
read NM
echo "Hello $NM"
```

Now, exit from your editor and type `./myfile.sh`. This will *execute* ⬊Cause the computer to read and act on your list of commands, also called *running* the program. ⬉ the file. Note that typing `./myfile.sh` is no different from typing any other command at the shell prompt. Your file `myfile.sh` has in fact become a new UNIX command all of its own.

Note what the `read` command is doing. It creates a pigeonhole called NM, and then inserts text read from the keyboard into that pigeonhole. Thereafter, whenever the shell encounters NM, its contents are written out instead of the letters NM (provided you write a $ in front of it). We say that NM is a *variable* because its contents can vary.

You can use shell scripts like a calculator. Try

```
echo "I will work out X*Y"
echo "Enter X"
read X
echo "Enter Y"
read Y
echo "X*Y = $X*$Y = $[X*Y]"
```

The [and] mean that everything between must be *evaluated* ⬊Substituted, worked out, or reduced to some simplified form. ⬉ as a *numerical expression* ⬊Sequence of numbers with +, −, *, etc. between them. ⬉. You can, in fact, do a calculation at any time by typing at the prompt

```
echo $[3*6+2*8+9]
```

⬊Note that the shell that you are using allows such [ ] notation. On some UNIX systems you will have to use the `expr` command to get the same effect.⬉

7.2 Looping to Repeat Commands: the `while` and `until` Statements

The shell reads each line in succession from top to bottom: this is called *program flow*. Now suppose you would like a command to be executed more than once—you would like to alter the program flow so that the shell reads particular commands repeatedly. The `while` command executes a sequence of commands many times. Here is an example (`-le` stands for *less than or equal*):

```
N=1
while test "$N" -le "10"
do
```

```
          echo "Number $N"
5         N=$[N+1]
   done
```

The `N=1` creates a variable called `N` and places the number 1 into it. The `while` command executes all the commands between the `do` and the `done` repetitively until the `test` condition is no longer true (i.e., until `N` is greater than 10). The `-le` stands for *less than or equal to*. See `test`(1) (that is, run `man 1 test`) to learn about the other types of tests you can do on variables. Also be aware of how `N` is replaced with a new value that becomes 1 greater with each repetition of the `while` loop.

   You should note here that each line is a distinct command—the commands are *newline-separated*. You can also have more than one command on a line by separating them with a semicolon as follows:

```
N=1 ; while test "$N" -le "10"; do echo "Number $N"; N=$[N+1] ; done
```

(Try counting down from 10 with `-ge` (*greater than or equal*).) It is easy to see that shell scripts are extremely powerful, because any kind of command can be executed with conditions and loops.

   The `until` statement is identical to `while` except that the reverse logic is applied. The same functionality can be achieved with `-gt` (*greater than*):

```
N=1 ; until test "$N" -gt "10"; do echo "Number $N"; N=$[N+1] ; done
```

7.3   Looping to Repeat Commands: the `for` Statement

The `for` command also allows execution of commands multiple times. It works like this:

```
for i in cows sheep chickens pigs
do
        echo "$i is a farm animal"
done
5 echo -e "but\nGNUs are not farm animals"
```

   The `for` command takes each string after the `in`, and executes the lines between `do` and `done` with `i` substituted for that string. The strings can be anything (even numbers) but are often file names.

The `if` command executes a number of commands if a condition is met (`-gt` stands for *greater than*, `-lt` stands for *less than*). The `if` command executes all the lines between the `if` and the `fi` ("if" spelled backwards).

```
X=10
Y=5
if test "$X" -gt "$Y" ; then
        echo "$X is greater than $Y"
fi
```

The `if` command in its full form can contain as much as:

```
X=10
Y=5
if test "$X" -gt "$Y" ; then
        echo "$X is greater than $Y"
elif test "$X" -lt "$Y" ; then
        echo "$X is less than $Y"
else
        echo "$X is equal to $Y"
fi
```

Now let us create a script that interprets its arguments. Create a new script called `backup-lots.sh`, containing:

```
#!/bin/sh
for i in 0 1 2 3 4 5 6 7 8 9 ; do
        cp $1 $1.BAK-$i
done
```

Now create a file `important_data` with anything in it and then run `./backup-lots.sh important_data`, which will copy the file 10 times with 10 different extensions. As you can see, the variable `$1` has a special meaning—it is the first argument on the command-line. Now let's get a little bit more sophisticated (`-e` test whether the file *exists*):

```
#!/bin/sh
if test "$1" = "" ; then
        echo "Usage: backup-lots.sh <filename>"
        exit
fi
for i in 0 1 2 3 4 5 6 7 8 9 ; do
        NEW_FILE=$1.BAK-$i
        if test -e $NEW_FILE ; then
                echo "backup-lots.sh: **warning** $NEW_FILE"
                echo "                 already exists - skipping"
        else
                cp $1 $NEW_FILE
```

```
        fi
done
```

7.4 `breaking` Out of Loops and `continueing`

A loop that requires premature termination can include the `break` statement within it:

```
#!/bin/sh
for i in 0 1 2 3 4 5 6 7 8 9 ; do
        NEW_FILE=$1.BAK-$i
        if test -e $NEW_FILE ; then
                echo "backup-lots.sh: **error** $NEW_FILE"
                echo "                already exists - exitting"
                break
        else
                cp $1 $NEW_FILE
        fi
done
```

which causes program execution to continue on the line after the `done`. If two loops are nested within each other, then the command `break` 2 causes program execution to break out of *both* loops; and so on for values above 2.

The `continue` statement is also useful for terminating the current iteration of the loop. This means that if a `continue` statement is encountered, execution will immediately continue from the top of the loop, thus ignoring the remainder of the body of the loop:

```
#!/bin/sh
for i in 0 1 2 3 4 5 6 7 8 9 ; do
        NEW_FILE=$1.BAK-$i
        if test -e $NEW_FILE ; then
                echo "backup-lots.sh: **warning** $NEW_FILE"
                echo "                already exists - skipping"
                continue
        fi
        cp $1 $NEW_FILE
done
```

Note that both `break` and `continue` work inside `for`, `while`, and `until` loops.

7.5   Looping Over Glob Expressions

We know that the shell can expand file names when given *wildcards*. For instance, we can type `ls *.txt` to list all files ending with `.txt`. This applies equally well in any situation, for instance:

```
#!/bin/sh
for i in *.txt ; do
        echo "found a file:" $i
done
```

The `*.txt` is expanded to all matching files. *These files are searched for in the current directory.* If you include an absolute path then the shell will search in that directory:

```
#!/bin/sh
for i in /usr/doc/*/*.txt ; do
        echo "found a file:" $i
done
```

This example demonstrates the shell's ability to search for matching files and expand an absolute path.

7.6   The `case` Statement

The `case` statement can make a potentially complicated program very short. It is best explained with an example.

```
#!/bin/sh
case $1 in
        --test|-t)
                echo "you used the --test option"
                exit 0
        ;;
        --help|-h)
                echo "Usage:"
                echo "        myprog.sh [--test|--help|--version]"
                exit 0
        ;;
        --version|-v)
                echo "myprog.sh version 0.0.1"
                exit 0
        ;;
        -*)
                echo "No such option $1"
                echo "Usage:"
```

```
             echo "          myprog.sh [--test|--help|--version]"
20           exit 1
        ;;
esac

echo "You typed \"$1\" on the command-line"
```

Above you can see that we are trying to process the first argument to a program. It can be one of several options, so using `if` statements will result in a long program. The `case` statement allows us to specify several possible statement blocks depending on the value of a variable. Note how each statement block is separated by `;;`. The strings before the `)` are glob expression matches. The first successful match causes that block to be executed. The `|` symbol enables us to enter several possible glob expressions.

7.7   Using Functions: the `function` Keyword

So far, our programs execute mostly from top to bottom. Often, code needs to be repeated, but it is considered bad programming practice to repeat groups of statements that have the same functionality. Function definitions provide a way to group statement blocks into one. A function groups a list of commands and assigns it a name. For example:

```
#!/bin/sh

function usage ()
{
5       echo "Usage:"
        echo "          myprog.sh [--test|--help|--version]"
}

case $1 in
10      --test|-t)
                echo "you used the --test option"
                exit 0
        ;;
        --help|-h)
15              usage
        ;;
        --version|-v)
                echo "myprog.sh version 0.0.2"
                exit 0
20      ;;
        -*)
```

```
                echo "Error: no such option $1"
                usage
                exit 1
25          ;;
     esac

     echo "You typed \"$1\" on the command-line"
```

Wherever the `usage` keyword appears, it is effectively substituted for the two lines inside the { and }. There are obvious advantages to this approach: if you would like to change the program *usage* description, you only need to change it in one place in the code. Good programs use functions so liberally that they never have more than 50 lines of program code in a row.

7.8 Properly Processing Command-Line Arguments: the `shift` Keyword

Most programs we have seen can take many command-line arguments, sometimes in any order. Here is how we can make our own shell scripts with this functionality. The command-line arguments can be reached with $1, $2, etc. The script,

```
#!/bin/sh

echo "The first argument is: $1, second argument is: $2, third argument is: $3"
```

can be run with

```
myfile.sh dogs cats birds
```

and prints

```
The first argument is: dogs, second argument is: cats, third argument is: birds
```

Now we need to loop through each argument and decide what to do with it. A script like

```
for i in $1 $2 $3 $4 ; do
        <statments>
done
```

doesn't give us much flexibilty. The `shift` keyword is meant to make things easier. It shifts up all the arguments by one place so that $1 gets the value of $2, $2 gets the value of $3, and so on. (!= tests that the "$1" is not equal to "", that is, whether it is empty and is hence past the last argument.) Try

```
while test "$1" != "" ; do
        echo $1
        shift
done
```

and run the program with lots of arguments.

Now we can put any sort of condition statements within the loop to process the arguments in turn:

```
#!/bin/sh

function usage ()
{
        echo "Usage:"
        echo "        myprog.sh [--test|--help|--version] [--echo <text>]"
}

while test "$1" != "" ; do
        case $1 in
                --echo|-e)
                        echo "$2"
                        shift
                ;;
                --test|-t)
                        echo "you used the --test option"
                ;;
                --help|-h)
                        usage
                        exit 0
                ;;
                --version|-v)
                        echo "myprog.sh version 0.0.3"
                        exit 0
                ;;
                -*)
                        echo "Error: no such option $1"
                        usage
                        exit 1
                ;;
        esac
        shift
done
```

`myprog.sh` can now run with multiple arguments on the command-line.

7.9   More on Command-Line Arguments: `$@` and `$0`

Whereas $1, $2, $3, etc. expand to the individual arguments passed to the program, $@ expands to *all* arguments. This behavior is useful for passing all remaining arguments onto a second command. For instance,

```
if test "$1" = "--special" ; then
        shift
        myprog2.sh "$@"
fi
```

$0 means the name of the program itself and not any command-line argument. It is the command used to invoke the current program. In the above cases, it is ./myprog.sh. Note that $0 is immune to shift operations.

7.10   Single Forward Quote Notation

Single forward quotes ′ *protect* the enclosed text from the shell. In other words, you can place any odd characters inside forward quotes, and the shell will treat them literally and reproduce your text exactly. For instance, you may want to echo an actual $ to the screen to produce an output like costs $1000. You can use echo ′costs $1000′ instead of echo "costs $1000".

7.11   Double-Quote Notation

Double quotes   "   have the opposite sense of single quotes. They allow *all* shell interpretations to take place inside them. The reason they are used at all is only to group text containing whitespace into a single word, because the shell will usually break up text along whitespace boundaries. Try,

```
for i in "henry john mary sue" ; do
    echo "$i     is     a      person"
done
```

compared to

```
for i in henry john mary sue ; do
    echo $i     is     a      person
done
```

7.12 Backward-Quote Substitution

Backward quotes ` ` ` have a special meaning to the shell. When a command is inside backward quotes it means that the command should be run and its *output* substituted in place of the backquotes. Take, for example, the `cat` command. Create a small file, `to_be_catted`, with only the text `daisy` inside it. Create a shell script

```
X=`cat to_be_catted`
echo $X
```

The value of `X` is set to the output of the `cat` command, which in this case is the word `daisy`. This is a powerful tool. Consider the `expr` command:

```
X=`expr 100 + 50 '*' 3`
echo $X
```

Hence we can use `expr` and backquotes to do mathematics inside our shell script. Here is a function to calculate factorials. Note how we enclose the `*` in forward quotes. They prevent the shell from expanding the `*` into matching file names:

```
function factorial ()
{
    N=$1
    A=1
    while test $N -gt 0 ; do
        A=`expr $A '*' $N`
        N=`expr $N - 1`
    done
    echo $A
}
```

We can see that the square braces used further above can actually suffice for most of the times where we would like to use `expr`. (However, `$[]` notation is an extension of the GNU shells and is not a standard feature on all varients of UNIX.) We can now run `factorial 20` and see the output. If we want to assign the output to a variable, we can do this with `X=`factorial 20``.

Note that another notation which gives the effect of a backward quote is `$(command)`, which is identical to `` `command` ``. Here, I will always use the older backward quote style.

Chapter 8

Streams and `sed` — The Stream Editor

The ability to use pipes is one of the powers of UNIX. This is one of the principle deficiencies of some non-UNIX systems. Pipes used on the command-line as explained in this chapter are a neat trick, but pipes used inside **C** programs enormously simplify program interaction. Without pipes, huge amounts of complex and buggy code usually needs to be written to perform simple tasks. It is hoped that this chapter will give the reader an idea of why UNIX is such a ubiquitous and enduring standard.

8.1 Introduction

The commands `grep`, `echo`, `df` and so on print some output to the screen. In fact, what is happening on a lower level is that they are printing characters one by one into a theoretical data *stream* (also called a *pipe*) called the *stdout* pipe. The shell itself performs the action of reading those characters one by one and displaying them on the screen. The word *pipe* itself means exactly that: A program places data in the one end of a funnel while another program reads that data from the other end. Pipes allow two separate programs to perform simple communications with each other. In this case, the program is merely communicating with the shell in order to display some output.

The same is true with the `cat` command explained previously. This command, when run with no arguments, reads from the *stdin* pipe. By default, this pipe is the keyboard. One further pipe is the *stderr* pipe to which a program writes error messages. It is not possible to see whether a program message is caused by the program writing to its stderr or stdout pipe because usually both are directed to the screen. Good programs, however, always write to the appropriate pipes to allow output to be specially separated for diagnostic purposes if need be.

8.2 Tutorial

Create a text file with lots of lines that contain the word GNU and one line that contains the word GNU as well as the word Linux. Then run grep GNU my-file.txt. The result is printed to stdout as usual. Now try grep GNU my-file.txt > gnu_lines.txt. What is happening here is that the output of the grep command is being *redirected* into a file. The > gnu_lines.txt tells the shell to create a new file gnu_lines.txt and to fill it with any output from stdout instead of displaying the output as it usually does. If the file already exists, it will be *truncated*. ⟍Shortened to zero length.⟍

Now suppose you want to append further output to this file. Using >> instead of > does *not* truncate the file, but appends output to it. Try

```
echo "morestuff" >> gnu_lines.txt
```

then view the contents of gnu_lines.txt.

8.3 Piping Using | Notation

The real power of pipes is realized when one program can read from the output of another program. Consider the grep command, which reads from stdin when given no arguments; run grep with one argument on the command-line:

```
[root@cericon]# grep GNU
A line without that word in it
Another line without that word in it
A line with the word GNU in it
A line with the word GNU in it
I have the idea now
^C
#
```

grep's default behavior is to read from stdin when no files are given. As you can see, it is doing its usual work of printing lines that have the word GNU in them. Hence, lines containing GNU will be printed twice—as you type them in and again when grep reads them and decides that they contain GNU.

Now try grep GNU myfile.txt | grep Linux. The first grep outputs all lines with the word GNU in them to stdout. The | specifies that all stdout is to be typed as stdin (as we just did above) into the next command, which is also a grep command. The second grep command scans that data for lines with the word Linux in them. grep is often used this way as a *filter* ⟍Something that screens data.⟍ and can be used multiple times, for example,

```
grep L myfile.txt | grep i | grep n | grep u | grep x
```

The < character redirects the contents of a file in place of stdin. In other words, the contents of a file replace what would normally come from a keyboard. Try

```
grep GNU < gnu_lines.txt
```

8.4   A Complex Piping Example

In Chapter 5 we used `grep` on a dictionary to demonstrate regular expressions. This is how a dictionary of words can be created (your dictionary might be under `/var/share/` or under `/usr/lib/aspell` instead):

```
cat /usr/lib/ispell/english.hash | strings | tr 'A-Z' 'a-z' \
| grep '^[a-z]' | sort -u > mydict
```

A backslash \ as the last character on a line indicates that the line is to be continued. You can leave out the \ but then you must leave out the newline as well — this is known as *line continuation.*

The file `english.hash` contains the UNIX dictionary normally used for spell checking. With a bit of filtering, you can create a dictionary that will make solving crossword puzzles a breeze. First, we use the command `strings`, explained previously, to extract readable bits of text. Here we are using its alternate mode of operation where it reads from stdin when no files are specified on its command-line. The command `tr` (abbreviated from *translate*—see `tr(1)`) then converts upper to lower case. The `grep` command then filters out lines that do not start with a letter. Finally, the `sort` command sorts the words in alphabetical order. The `-u` option stands for u*nique*, and specifies that duplicate lines of text should be stripped. Now try `less mydict`.

8.5   Redirecting Streams with `>&`

Try the command `ls nofile.txt > A`. We expect that `ls` will give an error message if the file doesn't exist. The error message is, however, displayed and not written into the file A. The reason is that `ls` has written its error message to stderr while > has only redirected stdout. The way to get both stdout and stderr to both go to the same file is to use a *redirection operator*. As far as the shell is concerned, stdout is called 1 and stderr is called 2, and commands can be appended with a *redirection* like 2>&1 to dictate that stderr is to be mixed into the output of stdout. The actual words stderr and stdout are only used in **C** programming, where the number 1, 2 are known as *file numbers* or *file descriptors*. Try the following:

```
touch existing_file
rm -f non-existing_file
ls existing_file non-existing_file
```

ls will output two lines: a line containing a listing for the file existing_file and a line containing an error message to explain that the file non-existing_file does not exist. The error message would have been written to stderr or file descriptor number 2, and the remaining line would have been written to stdout or file descriptor number 1.

Next we try

```
ls existing_file non-existing_file 2>A
cat A
```

Now A contains the error message, while the remaining output came to the screen. Now try

```
ls existing_file non-existing_file 1>A
cat A
```

The notation 1>A is the same as >A because the shell assumes that you are referring to file descriptor 1 when you don't specify a file descriptor. Now A contains the stdout output, while the error message has been redirected to the screen.

Now try

```
ls existing_file non-existing_file 1>A 2>&1
cat A
```

Now A contains both the error message and the normal output. The >& is called a *redirection operator*. *x>&y tells the shell to write pipe x into pipe y. Redirection is specified from right to left on the command-line.* Hence, the above command means to mix stderr into stdout and *then* to redirect stdout to the file A.

Finally,

```
ls existing_file non-existing_file 2>A 1>&2
cat A
```

We notice that this has the same effect, except that here we are doing the reverse: redirecting stdout into stderr and then redirecting stderr into a file A.

To see what happens if we redirect in reverse order, we can try,

```
ls existing_file non-existing_file 2>&1 1>A
cat A
```

which means to redirect stdout into a file A, and *then* to redirect stderr into stdout. This command will therefore not mix stderr and stdout because the redirection to A came first.

8.6   Using **sed** to Edit Streams

ed used to be the standard text *editor* for UNIX. It is cryptic to use but is compact and programmable. sed stands for *stream editor* and is the only incarnation of ed that is commonly used today. sed allows editing of files non-interactively. In the way that grep can search for words and filter lines of text, sed can do search-replace operations and insert and delete lines into text files. sed is one of those programs with no man page to speak of. Do info sed to see sed's comprehensive info pages with examples.

The most common usage of sed is to replace words in a stream with alternative words. sed reads from stdin and writes to stdout. Like grep, it is line buffered, which means that it reads one line in at a time and then writes that line out again after performing whatever editing operations. Replacements are typically done with

```
cat <file> | sed -e 's/<search-regexp>/<replace-text>/<option>' \
> <resultfile>
```

where <search-regexp> is a regular expression, <replace-text> is the text you would like to replace each occurrence with, and <option> is nothing or g, which means to replace every occurrence in the same line (usually sed just replaces the first occurrence of the regular expression in each line). (There are other <option>; see the sed info page.) For demonstration, type

```
sed -e 's/e/E/g'
```

and type out a few lines of English text.

8.7   Regular Expression Subexpressions

The section explains how to do the apparently complex task of moving text around within lines. Consider, for example, the output of ls: say you want to automatically strip out only the size column—sed can do this sort of editing if you use the special \(\) notation to group parts of the regular expression together. Consider the following example:

```
sed -e 's/\(\<[^ ]*\>\)\([ ]*\)\(\<[^ ]*\>\)/\3\2\1/g'
```

Here sed is searching for the expression \<.*\>[ ]*\<.*\>. From the chapter on regular expressions, we can see that it matches a whole word, an arbitrary amount of whitespace, and then another whole word. The \(\) groups these three so that they can be referred to in <replace-text>. Each part of the regular expression inside \(\) is called a *subexpression* of the regular expression. Each subexpression is numbered—namely, \1, \2, etc. Hence, \1 in <replace-text> is the first \<[^]*\>, \2 is [ ]*, and \3 is the second \<[^]*\>.

Now test to see what happens when you run this:

```
sed -e 's/\(\<[^ ]*\>\)\([ ]*\)\(\<[^ ]*\>\)/\3\2\1/g'
GNU Linux is cool
Linux GNU cool is
```

To return to our ls example (note that this is just an example, to count file sizes you should instead use the du command), think about how we could sum the bytes sizes of all the files in a directory:

```
expr 0 `ls -l | grep '^-' | \
    sed 's/^\([^ ]*[ ]*\)\{4,4\}\([0-9]*\).*$/ + \2/'`
```

We know that ls -l output lines start with - for ordinary files. So we use grep to strip lines not starting with -. If we do an ls -l, we see that the output is divided into four columns of stuff we are not interested in, and then a number indicating the size of the file. A column (or *field*) can be described by the regular expression [^]*[ ]*, that is, a length of text with no whitespace, followed by a length of whitespace. There are four of these, so we bracket it with \(\) and then use the \{ \} notation to specify that we want exactly 4. After that come our number [0-9]*, and then any trailing characters, which we are not interested in, .*$. Notice here that we have neglected to use \< \> notation to indicate whole words. The reason is that sed tries to match the maximum number of characters legally allowed and, in the situation we have here, has exactly the same effect.

If you haven't yet figured it out, we are trying to get that column of byte sizes into a format like

```
+ 438
+ 1525
+ 76
+ 92146
```

so that expr can understand it. Hence, we replace each line with subexpression \2 and a leading + sign. Backquotes give the output of this to expr, which studiously sums them, ignoring any newline characters as though the summation were typed in on a single line. There is one minor problem here: the first line contains a + with nothing before it, which will cause `expr` to complain. To get around this, we can just add a 0 to the expression, so that it becomes 0 + ...

8.8   Inserting and Deleting Lines

`sed` can perform a few operations that make it easy to write scripts that edit configuration files for you. For instance,

```
sed -e '7a\
an extra line.\
another one.\
one more.'
```

appends three lines *after* line 7, whereas

```
sed -e '7i\
an extra line.\
another one.\
one more.'
```

inserts three lines *before* line 7. Then

```
sed -e '3,5D'
```

Deletes lines 3 through 5.

In `sed` terminology, the numbers here are called *addresses*, which can also be regular expressions matches. To demonstrate:

```
sed -e '/Dear Henry/,/Love Jane/D'
```

deletes all the lines starting from a line matching the regular expression `Dear Henry` up to a line matching `Love Jane` (or the end of the file if one does not exist).

This behavior applies just as well to to insertions:

```
sed -e '/Love Jane/i\
Love Carol\
Love Beth'
```

Note that the $ symbol indicates the last line:

```
sed -e '$i\
The new second last line\
```

```
The new last line.'
```

and finally, the negation symbol, `!`, is used to match all lines *not* specified; for instance,

```
sed -e '7,11!D'
```

deletes all lines *except* lines 7 through 11.

Chapter 9

Processes and Environment Variables

From this chapter you will get an idea about what is happening under the hood of your UNIX system, but go have some coffee first.

9.1 Introduction

On UNIX, when you run a program (like any of the shell commands you have been using), the actual computer instructions are read from a file on disk from one of the `bin/` directories and placed in RAM. The program is then executed in memory and becomes a *process*. A *process* is some command/program/shell-script that is being run (or *executed*) in memory. When the process has finished running, it is removed from memory. There are usually about 50 processes running simultaneously at any one time on a system with one person logged in. The CPU hops between each of them to give a share of its *execution time*. ↘Time given to carry out the instructions of a particular program. Note this is in contrast to Windows or DOS where the program itself has to allow the others a share of the CPU: under UNIX, the process has no say in the matter. ↖Each process is given a process number called the *PID* (process ID). Besides the memory actually occupied by the executable, the process itself seizes additional memory for its operations.

In the same way that a file is owned by a particular user and group, a process also has an owner—usually the person who ran the program. Whenever a process tries to access a file, its ownership is compared to that of the file to decide if the access is permissible. Because all devices are files, the only way a process can do *anything* is through a file, and hence file permission restrictions are the only kind of restrictions ever needed on UNIX. ↘There are some exceptions to this.↖ This is how UNIX access control and security works.

81

The center of this operation is called the UNIX *kernel*. The kernel is what actually does the hardware access, execution, allocation of process IDs, sharing of CPU time, and ownership management.

9.2   ps — List Running Processes

Log in on a terminal and type the command ps. You should get some output like:

```
 PID TTY STAT   TIME COMMAND
5995   2 S     0:00 /bin/login -- myname
5999   2 S     0:00 -bash
6030   2 R     0:00 ps
```

ps with no options shows three processes to be running. These are the only three processes visible to you as a user, although there are other system processes not belonging to you. The first process was the program that logged you in by displaying the login prompt and requesting a password. It then ran a second process call bash, the Bourne Again shell ⟍The Bourne shell was the original UNIX shell⟍ where you have been typing commands. Finally, you ran ps, which must have found itself when it checked which processes were running, but then exited immediately afterward.

9.3   Controlling Jobs

The shell has many facilities for controlling and executing processes—this is called job control. Create a small script called proc.sh:

```
#!/bin/sh
echo "proc.sh: is running"
sleep 1000
```

Run the script with chmod 0755 proc.sh and then ./proc.sh. The shell *blocks*, waiting for the process to exit. Now press ^Z. This will cause the process to *stop* (that is, pause but not terminate). Now do a ps again. You will see your script listed. However, it is not presently running because it is in the condition of being stopped. Type bg (for *background*). The script will now be "unstopped" and run in the background. You can now try to run other processes in the meantime. Type fg, and the script returns to the *foreground*. You can then type ^C to interrupt the process.

9.4   Creating Background Processes

Create a program that does something a little more interesting:

```
#!/bin/sh
echo "proc.sh: is running"
while true ; do
        echo -e '\a'
        sleep 2
done
```

Now perform the ^Z, bg, fg, and ^C operations from before. To put a process immediately into the background, you can use:

```
./proc.sh &
```

The **JOB CONTROL** section of the bash man page (bash(1)) looks like this[1]: (the footnotes are mine)

JOB CONTROL

Job control refers to the ability to selectively stop (*suspend*) the execution of processes and continue (*resume*) their execution at a later point. A user typically employs this facility via an interactive interface supplied jointly by the system's terminal driver and **bash**.

The shell associates a *job* with each pipeline. ↘What does this mean? It means that each time you execute something in the background, it gets its own unique number, called the job number.↖ It keeps a table of currently executing jobs, which may be listed with the **jobs** command. When **bash** starts a job asynchronously (in the *background*), it prints a line that looks like:

[1] 25647

indicating that this job is job number 1 and that the process ID of the last process in the pipeline associated with this job is 25647. All of the processes in a single pipeline are members of the same job. **Bash** uses the *job* abstraction as the basis for job control.

To facilitate the implementation of the user interface to job control, the system maintains the notion of a *current terminal process group ID*. Members of this process group (processes whose process group ID is equal to the current terminal process group ID) receive keyboard-generated signals such as **SIGINT**. These processes are said to be in the *foreground*. *Background* processes are those whose process group ID differs from the terminal's; such processes are immune to keyboard-generated

---

[1]Thanks to Brian Fox and Chet Ramey for this material.

signals. Only foreground processes are allowed to read from or write to the terminal. Background processes which attempt to read from (write to) the terminal are sent a **SIGTTIN (SIGTTOU)** signal by the terminal driver, which, unless caught, suspends the process.

If the operating system on which **bash** is running supports job control, **bash** allows you to use it. Typing the *suspend* character (typically ^Z, Control-Z) while a process is running causes that process to be stopped and returns you to **bash**. Typing the *delayed suspend* character (typically ^Y, Control-Y) causes the process to be stopped when it attempts to read input from the terminal, and control to be returned to **bash**. You may then manipulate the state of this job, using the **bg** command to continue it in the background, the **fg** command to continue it in the foreground, or the **kill** command to kill it. A ^Z takes effect immediately, and has the additional side effect of causing pending output and typeahead to be discarded.

There are a number of ways to refer to a job in the shell. The character % introduces a job name. Job number *n* may be referred to as %**n**. A job may also be referred to using a prefix of the name used to start it, or using a substring that appears in its command line. For example, %**ce** refers to a stopped **ce** job. If a prefix matches more than one job, **bash** reports an error. Using %**?ce**, on the other hand, refers to any job containing the string **ce** in its command line. If the substring matches more than one job, **bash** reports an error. The symbols %% and %+ refer to the shell's notion of the *current job*, which is the last job stopped while it was in the foreground. The *previous job* may be referenced using %-. In output pertaining to jobs (e.g., the output of the **jobs** command), the current job is always flagged with a +, and the previous job with a -.

Simply naming a job can be used to bring it into the foreground: %**1** is a synonym for "**fg** %**1**", bringing job 1 from the background into the foreground. Similarly, "%**1** &" resumes job 1 in the background, equivalent to "**bg** %**1**".

The shell learns immediately whenever a job changes state. Normally, **bash** waits until it is about to print a prompt before reporting changes in a job's status so as to not interrupt any other output. If the **-b** option to the **set** builtin command is set, **bash** reports such changes immediately. (See also the description of **notify** variable under **Shell Variables** above.)

If you attempt to exit **bash** while jobs are stopped, the shell prints a message warning you. You may then use the **jobs** command to inspect their status. If you do this, or try to exit again immediately, you are not warned again, and the stopped jobs are terminated.

9.5 killing a Process, Sending Signals

To terminate a process, use the kill command:

```
kill <PID>
```

The `kill` command actually sends a termination *signal* to the process. The sending of a signal simply means that the process is asked to execute one of 30 predefined functions. In some cases, developers would not have bothered to define a function for a particular signal number (called *catching* the signal); in which case the kernel will substitute the default behavior for that signal. The default behavior for a signal is usually to ignore the signal, to stop the process, or to terminate the process. The default behavior for the *termination* signal is to terminate the process.

To send a specific signal to a process, you can name the signal on the command-line or use its numerical equivalent:

```
kill -SIGTERM 12345
```

or

```
kill -15 12345
```

which is the signal that `kill` normally sends when none is specified on the command-line.

To unconditionally terminate a process:

```
kill -SIGKILL 12345
```

or

```
kill -9 12345
```

which should only be used as a last resort. *Processes are prohibited from ever catching the* `SIGKILL` *signal.*

It is cumbersome to have to constantly look up the PID of a process. Hence the GNU utilities have a command, `killall`, that sends a signal to all processes of the same name:

```
killall -<signal> <process_name>
```

This command is useful when you are sure that there is only one of a process running, either because no one else is logged in on the system or because you are not logged in as superuser. *Note that on other* UNIX *systems, the* `killall` *command kills* all *the processes that you are allowed to kill. If you are root, this action would crash the machine.*

9.6   List of Common Signals

The full list of signals can be gotten from `signal(7)`, and in the file `/usr/include/asm/signal.h`.

SIGHUP (1) *Hang up.* If the terminal becomes disconnected from a process, this signal is sent automatically to the process. Sending a process this signal often causes it to reread its configuration files, so it is useful instead of restarting the process. Always check the man page to see if a process has this behavior.

SIGINT (2) *Interrupt* from keyboard. Issued if you press ^C.

SIGQUIT (3) *Quit* from keyboard. Issued if you press ^D.

SIGFPE (8) *Floating point exception.* Issued automatically to a program performing some kind of illegal mathematical operation.

SIGKILL (9) *Kill* signal. This is one of the signals that can never be *caught* by a process. If a process gets this signal it *must* quit immediately and will not perform any clean-up operations (like closing files or removing temporary files). You can send a process a `SIGKILL` signal if there is no other means of destroying it.

SIGUSR1 (10), **SIGUSR2** (12) *User signal.* These signals are available to developers when they need extra functionality. For example, some processes begin logging debug messages when you send them `SIGUSR1`.

SIGSEGV (11) *Segmentation violation.* Issued automatically when a process tries to access memory outside of its allowable address space, equivalent to a **Fatal Exception** or **General Protection Fault** under Windows. Note that programs with bugs or programs in the process of being developed often get these signals. A program receiving a `SIGSEGV`, however, can never cause the rest of the system to be compromised. If the kernel itself were to receive such an error, it would cause the system to come down, but such is extremely rare.

SIGPIPE (13) *Pipe* died. A program was writing to a pipe, the other end of which is no longer available.

SIGTERM (15) *Terminate.* Cause the program to quit gracefully

SIGCHLD (17) *Child terminate.* Sent to a parent process every time one of its spawned processes dies.

9.7   Niceness of Processes, Scheduling Priority

All processes are allocated execution time by the kernel. If all processes were allocated the same amount of time, performance would obviously get worse as the number of processes increased. The kernel uses heuristics ⟍Sets of rules.⟍ to guess how much time each process should be allocated. The kernel tries to be fair—two users competing for CPU usage should both get the same amount.

Most processes spend their time waiting for either a key press, some network input, some device to send data, or some time to elapse. They hence do not consume CPU.

On the other hand, when more than one process runs flat out, it can be difficult for the kernel to decide if it should be given greater *priority* than another process. What if a process is doing some operation more important than another process? How does the kernel tell? The answer is the UNIX feature of *scheduling priority* or *niceness*. Scheduling priority ranges from +20 to −20. You can set a process's niceness with the `renice` command.

```
renice <priority> <pid>
renice <priority> -u <user>
renice <priority> -g <group>
```

A typical example is the *SETI* program. ⟍SETI stands for Search for Extraterrestrial Intelligence. SETI is an initiative funded by various obscure sources to scan the skies for radio signals from other civilizations. The data that SETI gathers has to be intensively processed. SETI distributes part of that data to anyone who wants to run a `seti` program in the background. This puts the idle time of millions of machines to "good" use. There is even a SETI screen-saver that has become quite popular. Unfortunately for the colleague in my office, he runs `seti` at −19 instead of +19 scheduling priority, so nothing on his machine works right. On the other hand, I have inside information that the millions of other civilizations in this galaxy and others are probably not using radio signals to communicate at all :-)⟍ Set its priority to +19 with:

```
renice +19 <pid>
```

to make it disrupt your machine as little as possible.

Note that nice values have the reverse meaning that you would expect: +19 means a process that eats little CPU, while −19 is a process that eats lots. Only superuser can set processes to negative nice values.

Mostly, multimedia applications and some device utilities are the only processes that need negative renicing, and most of these will have their own command-line options to set the nice value. See, for example, cdrecord(1) and mikmod(1) — a negative nice value will prevent skips in your playback. ⟍LINUX will soon have so called *real time* process scheduling. This is a kernel feature that reduces scheduling *latency* (the gaps between CPU execution time of a process, as well as the time it takes for a process to wake). There are already some kernel patches that accomplish this goal.↖

Also useful are the −u and −g options, which set the priority of all the processes that a user or group owns.

Further, we have the `nice` command, which starts a program under a defined niceness relative to the current nice value of the present user. For example,

```
nice +<priority> <pid>
nice -<priority> <pid>
```

Finally, the `snice` command can both display and set the current niceness. This command doesn't seem to work on my machine.

```
snice -v <pid>
```

9.8 Process CPU/Memory Consumption, `top`

The `top` command sorts all processes by their CPU and memory consumption and displays the *top* twenty or so in a table. Use `top` whenever you want to see what's hogging your system. `top -q -d 2` is useful for scheduling the `top` command itself to a high priority, so that it is sure to refresh its listing without lag. `top -n 1 -b > top.txt` lists all processes, and `top -n 1 -b -p <pid>` prints information on one process.

`top` has some useful interactive responses to key presses:

f Shows a list of displayed fields that you can alter interactively. By default the only fields shown are USER PRI NI SIZE RSS SHARE STAT %CPU %MEM TIME COMMAND which is usually what you are most interested in. (The field meanings are given below.)

r Renices a process.

k Kills a process.

The `top` man page describes the field meanings. Some of these are confusing and assume knowledge of the internals of **C** programs. The main question people ask is: *How much memory is a process using?* The answer is given by the RSS field, which stands for *Resident Set Size*. RSS means the amount of RAM that a process consumes alone. The following examples show totals for *all* processes running on my system (which had 65536 kilobytes of RAM at the time). They represent the total of the SIZE, RSS, and SHARE fields, respectively.

```
echo 'echo '0 ' ; top -q -n 1 -b | sed -e '1,/PID *USER *PRI/D' | \
    awk '{print "+" $5}' | sed -e 's/M/\\*1024/' ` | bc
68016

echo 'echo '0 ' ; top -q -n 1 -b | sed -e '1,/PID *USER *PRI/D' | \
    awk '{print "+" $6}' | sed -e 's/M/\\*1024/' ` | bc
58908

echo 'echo '0 ' ; top -q -n 1 -b | sed -e '1,/PID *USER *PRI/D' | \
    awk '{print "+" $7}' | sed -e 's/M/\\*1024/' ` | bc
30184
```

The SIZE represents the total memory usage of a process. RSS is the same, but excludes memory not needing actual RAM (this would be memory swapped to the swap partition). SHARE is the amount shared between processes.

Other fields are described by the top man page (quoted verbatim) as follows:

uptime This line displays the time the system has been up, and the three load averages for the system. The load averages are the average number of processes ready to run during the last 1, 5 and 15 minutes. This line is just like the output of uptime(1). The uptime display may be toggled by the interactive l command.

processes The total number of processes running at the time of the last update. This is also broken down into the number of tasks which are running, sleeping, stopped, or undead. The processes and states display may be toggled by the t interactive command.

CPU states Shows the percentage of CPU time in user mode, system mode, niced tasks, and idle. (Niced tasks are only those whose nice value is negative.) Time spent in niced tasks will also be counted in system and user time, so the total will be more than 100%. The processes and states display may be toggled by the t interactive command.

Mem Statistics on memory usage, including total available memory, free memory, used memory, shared memory, and memory used for buffers. The display of memory information may be toggled by the m interactive command.

Swap Statistics on swap space, including total swap space, available swap space, and used swap space. This and Mem are just like the output of free(1).

PID The process ID of each task.

PPID The parent process ID of each task.

UID The user ID of the task's owner.

USER The user name of the task's owner.

PRI The priority of the task.

NI The nice value of the task. Negative nice values are higher priority.

SIZE The size of the task's code plus data plus stack space, in kilobytes, is shown here.

TSIZE The code size of the task. This gives strange values for kernel processes and is broken for ELF processes.

DSIZE Data + Stack size. This is broken for ELF processes.

TRS Text resident size.

SWAP Size of the swapped out part of the task.

D Size of pages marked dirty.

LIB Size of use library pages. This does not work for ELF processes.

RSS The total amount of physical memory used by the task, in kilobytes, is shown here. For ELF processes used library pages are counted here, for a.out processes not.

SHARE The amount of shared memory used by the task is shown in this column.

STAT The state of the task is shown here. The state is either S for sleeping, D for uninterruptible sleep, R for running, Z for zombies, or T for stopped or traced. These states are modified by a trailing ¡ for a process with negative nice value, N for a process with positive nice value, W for a swapped out process (this does not work correctly for kernel processes).

WCHAN depending on the availability of either /boot/psdatabase or the kernel link map /boot/System.map this shows the address or the name of the kernel function the task currently is sleeping in.

TIME Total CPU time the task has used since it started. If cumulative mode is on, this also includes the CPU time used by the process's children which have died. You can set cumulative mode with the S command line option or toggle it with the interactive command S. The header line will then be changed to CTIME.

%CPU The task's share of the CPU time since the last screen update, expressed as a percentage of total CPU time per processor.

%MEM The task's share of the physical memory.

COMMAND The task's command name, which will be truncated if it is too long to be displayed on one line. Tasks in memory will have a full command line, but swapped-out tasks will only have the name of the program in parentheses (for example, "(getty)").

9.9 Environments of Processes

Each process that runs does so with the knowledge of several *var=value* text pairs. All this means is that a process can look up the value of some variable that it may have inherited from its parent process. The complete list of these text pairs is called the *environment* of the process, and each *var* is called an *environment variable*. Each process has its own environment, which is copied from the parent process's environment.

After you have logged in and have a shell prompt, the process you are using (the shell itself) is just like any other process with an environment with environment variables. To get a complete list of these variables, just type:

```
set
```

This command is useful for finding the value of an environment variable whose name you are unsure of:

```
set | grep <regexp>
```

Try `set | grep PATH` to see the `PATH` environment variable discussed previously.

The purpose of an environment is just to have an alternative way of passing parameters to a program (in addition to command-line arguments). The difference is that an environment is inherited from one process to the next: for example, a shell might have a certain variable set and may run a file manager, which may run a word processor. The word processor inherited its environment from file manager which inherited its environment from the shell. If you had set an environment variable `PRINTER` within the shell, it would have been inherited all the way to the word processor, thus eliminating the need to separately configure which printer the word processor should use.

Try

```
X="Hi there"
echo $X
```

You have set a variable. But now run

```
bash
```

You have now run a new process which is a *child* of the process you were just in. Type

```
echo $X
```

You will see that X is not set. The reason is that the variable was not `exported` as an environment variable and hence was not inherited. Now type

```
exit
```

which breaks to the *parent* process. Then

```
export X
bash
echo $X
```

You will see that the new `bash` now knows about X.

Above we are setting an arbitrary variable for our own use. `bash` (and many other programs) automatically set many of their own environment variables. The `bash` man page lists these (when it talks about unset*ting* a variable, it means using the command `unset <variable>`). You may not understand some of these at the moment, but they are included here as a complete reference for later.

The following is quoted verbatim from the `bash` man page. You will see that some variables are of the type that provide special information and are read but never never set, whereas other variables configure behavioral features of the shell (or other programs) and can be set at any time[2].

Shell Variables
The following variables are set by the shell:

PPID The process ID of the shell's parent.

PWD The current working directory as set by the **cd** command.

OLDPWD The previous working directory as set by the **cd** command.

REPLY Set to the line of input read by the **read** builtin command when no arguments are supplied.

UID Expands to the user ID of the current user, initialized at shell startup.

EUID Expands to the effective user ID of the current user, initialized at shell startup.

BASH Expands to the full pathname used to invoke this instance of **bash**.

BASH_VERSION Expands to the version number of this instance of **bash**.

SHLVL Incremented by one each time an instance of **bash** is started.

RANDOM Each time this parameter is referenced, a random integer is generated. The sequence of random numbers may be initialized by assigning a value to **RANDOM**. If **RANDOM** is unset, it loses its special properties, even if it is subsequently reset.

SECONDS Each time this parameter is referenced, the number of seconds since shell invocation is returned. If a value is assigned to **SECONDS**. the value returned upon subsequent references is the number of seconds since the assignment plus the value assigned. If **SECONDS** is unset, it loses its special properties, even if it is subsequently reset.

LINENO Each time this parameter is referenced, the shell substitutes a decimal number representing the current sequential line number (starting with 1) within a script or function. When not in a script or function, the value substituted is not guaranteed to be meaningful. When in a function, the value is not the number of the source line that the command appears on (that information has been lost by the time the function is executed), but is an approximation of the number of *simple commands* executed in the current function. If **LINENO** is unset, it loses its special properties, even if it is subsequently reset.

HISTCMD The history number, or index in the history list, of the current command. If **HISTCMD** is unset, it loses its special properties, even if it is subsequently reset.

---

[2]Thanks to Brian Fox and Chet Ramey for this material.

OPTARG The value of the last option argument processed by the **getopts** builtin command (see **SHELL BUILTIN COMMANDS** below).

OPTIND The index of the next argument to be processed by the **getopts** builtin command (see **SHELL BUILTIN COMMANDS** below).

HOSTTYPE Automatically set to a string that uniquely describes the type of machine on which **bash** is executing. The default is system-dependent.

OSTYPE Automatically set to a string that describes the operating system on which **bash** is executing. The default is system-dependent.

The following variables are used by the shell. In some cases, **bash** assigns a default value to a variable; these cases are noted below.

IFS The *Internal Field Separator* that is used for word splitting after expansion and to split lines into words with the **read** builtin command. The default value is "<space><tab><newline>".

PATH The search path for commands. It is a colon-separated list of directories in which the shell looks for commands (see **COMMAND EXECUTION** below). The default path is system-dependent, and is set by the administrator who installs **bash**. A common value is "/usr/gnu/bin:/usr/local/bin:/usr/ucb:/bin:/usr/bin:.".

HOME The home directory of the current user; the default argument for the **cd** builtin command.

CDPATH The search path for the **cd** command. This is a colon-separated list of directories in which the shell looks for destination directories specified by the **cd** command. A sample value is ``.:~:/usr''.

ENV If this parameter is set when **bash** is executing a shell script, its value is interpreted as a filename containing commands to initialize the shell, as in *.bashrc*. The value of **ENV** is subjected to parameter expansion, command substitution, and arithmetic expansion before being interpreted as a pathname. **PATH** is not used to search for the resultant pathname.

MAIL If this parameter is set to a filename and the **MAILPATH** variable is not set, **bash** informs the user of the arrival of mail in the specified file.

MAILCHECK Specifies how often (in seconds) **bash** checks for mail. The default is 60 seconds. When it is time to check for mail, the shell does so before prompting. If this variable is unset, the shell disables mail checking.

MAILPATH A colon-separated list of pathnames to be checked for mail. The message to be printed may be specified by separating the pathname from the message with a '?'. $_ stands for the name of the current mailfile. Example: `MAILPATH='/usr/spool/mail/bfox?"You have mail":~/shell-mail?"$_ has mail!"'` **Bash** supplies a default value for this variable, but the location of the user mail files that it uses is system dependent (e.g., /usr/spool/mail/**$USER**).

MAIL_WARNING If set, and a file that **bash** is checking for mail has been accessed since the last time it was checked, the message "The mail in *mailfile* has been read" is printed.

PS1 The value of this parameter is expanded (see **PROMPTING** below) and used as the primary prompt string. The default value is "**bash**"**$** ".

PS2 The value of this parameter is expanded and used as the secondary prompt string. The default is "> ".

PS3 The value of this parameter is used as the prompt for the *select* command (see **SHELL GRAMMAR** above).

PS4 The value of this parameter is expanded and the value is printed before each command **bash** displays during an execution trace. The first character of **PS4** is replicated multiple times, as necessary, to indicate multiple levels of indirection. The default is "+ ".

HISTSIZE The number of commands to remember in the command history (see **HISTORY** below). The default value is 500.

HISTFILE The name of the file in which command history is saved. (See **HISTORY** below.) The default value is ˜/.bash_history. If unset, the command history is not saved when an interactive shell exits.

HISTFILESIZE The maximum number of lines contained in the history file. When this variable is assigned a value, the history file is truncated, if necessary, to contain no more than that number of lines. The default value is 500.

OPTERR If set to the value 1, **bash** displays error messages generated by the **getopts** builtin command (see **SHELL BUILTIN COMMANDS** below). **OPTERR** is initialized to 1 each time the shell is invoked or a shell script is executed.

PROMPT_COMMAND If set, the value is executed as a command prior to issuing each primary prompt.

IGNOREEOF Controls the action of the shell on receipt of an **EOF** character as the sole input. If set, the value is the number of consecutive **EOF** characters typed as the first characters on an input line before **bash** exits. If the variable exists but does not have a numeric value, or has no value, the default value is 10. If it does not exist, **EOF** signifies the end of input to the shell. This is only in effect for interactive shells.

TMOUT If set to a value greater than zero, the value is interpreted as the number of seconds to wait for input after issuing the primary prompt. **Bash** terminates after waiting for that number of seconds if input does not arrive.

FCEDIT The default editor for the **fc** builtin command.

FIGNORE A colon-separated list of suffixes to ignore when performing filename completion (see **READLINE** below). A filename whose suffix matches one of the entries in **FIGNORE** is excluded from the list of matched filenames. A sample value is ".o:˜".

INPUTRC The filename for the readline startup file, overriding the default of ˜/.inputrc (see **READLINE** below).

notify If set, **bash** reports terminated background jobs immediately, rather than waiting until before printing the next primary prompt (see also the **-b** option to the **set** builtin command).

history_control

HISTCONTROL If set to a value of *ignorespace*, lines which begin with a **space** character are not entered on the history list. If set to a value of *ignoredups*, lines matching the last history line are not entered. A value of *ignoreboth* combines the two options. If unset, or if set to any other value than those above, all lines read by the parser are saved on the history list.

command_oriented_history If set, **bash** attempts to save all lines of a multiple-line command in the same history entry. This allows easy re-editing of multi-line commands.

glob_dot_filenames If set, **bash** includes filenames beginning with a '.' in the results of pathname expansion.

allow_null_glob_expansion If set, **bash** allows pathname patterns which match no files (see **Pathname Expansion** below) to expand to a null string, rather than themselves.

histchars The two or three characters which control history expansion and tokenization (see **HISTORY EXPANSION** below). The first character is the *history expansion character*, that is, the character which signals the start of a history expansion, normally '!'. The second character is the *quick substitution* character, which is used as shorthand for re-running the previous command entered, substituting one string for another in the command. The default is '^'. The optional third character is the character which signifies that the remainder of the line is a comment, when found as the first character of a word, normally '#'. The history comment character causes history substitution to be skipped for the remaining words on the line. It does not necessarily cause the shell parser to treat the rest of the line as a comment.

nolinks If set, the shell does not follow symbolic links when executing commands that change the current working directory. It uses the physical directory structure instead. By default, **bash** follows the logical chain of directories when performing commands which change the current directory, such as **cd**. See also the description of the **-P** option to the **set** builtin (**SHELL BUILTIN COMMANDS** below).

hostname_completion_file

HOSTFILE Contains the name of a file in the same format as */etc/hosts* that should be read when the shell needs to complete a hostname. The file may be changed interactively; the next time hostname completion is attempted **bash** adds the contents of the new file to the already existing database.

noclobber If set, **bash** does not overwrite an existing file with the $>$, $>$**&**, and $<>$ redirection operators. This variable may be overridden when creating output files by using the redirection operator $>$— instead of $>$ (see also the **-C** option to the **set** builtin command).

auto_resume This variable controls how the shell interacts with the user and job control. If this variable is set, single word simple commands without redirections are treated as candidates for resumption of an existing stopped job. There is no ambiguity allowed; if there is more than one job beginning with the string typed, the job most recently accessed is selected. The *name* of a stopped job, in this context, is the command line used to start it. If set to the value *exact*, the string supplied must match the name of a stopped job exactly; if set to *substring*, the string supplied needs to match a substring of the name of a stopped job. The *substring* value provides functionality analogous to the %? job id (see **JOB CONTROL** below). If set to any other value, the supplied string must be a prefix of a stopped job's name; this provides functionality analogous to the % job id.

no_exit_on_failed_exec If this variable exists, a non-interactive shell will not exit if it cannot execute the file specified in the **exec** builtin command. An interactive shell does not exit if **exec** fails.

cdable_vars If this is set, an argument to the **cd** builtin command that is not a directory is assumed to be the name of a variable whose value is the directory to change to.

Chapter 10

Mail

Electronic Mail, or *e*mail, is the way most people first come into contact with the Internet. Although you may have used email in a graphical environment, here we show you how mail was first intended to be used on a multiuser system. To a large extent what applies here is really what is going on in the background of any system that supports mail.

A mail message is a block of text sent from one user to another, using some mail command or mailer program. A mail message will usually also be accompanied by a *subject* explaining what the mail is about. The idea of mail is that a message can be sent to someone even though he may not be logged in at the time and the mail will be stored for him until he is around to read it. An email address is probably familiar to you, for example: `bruce@kangeroo.co.au`. This means that `bruce` has a user account on a computer called `kangeroo.co.au`, which often means that he can log in as `bruce` on that machine. The text after the @ is always the name of the machine. Today's Internet does not obey this exactly, but there is always a machine that `bruce` *does* have an account on where mail is eventually sent. ⟍That machine is also usually a UNIX machine.⟍

Sometimes email addresses are written in a more user-friendly form like `Bruce Wallaby <bruce@kangeroo.co.au>` or `bruce@kangeroo.co.au (Bruce Wallaby)`. In this case, the surrounding characters are purely cosmetic; only `bruce@kangeroo.co.au` is ever used.

When mail is received for you (from another user on the system or from a user from another system) it is appended to the file `/var/spool/mail/<username>` called the *mail file* or *mailbox file*; `<username>` is your login name. You then run some program that interprets your mail file, allowing you to browse the file as a sequence of mail messages and read and reply to them.

An actual addition to your mail file might look like this:

```
     From mands@inetafrica.com  Mon Jun  1 21:20:21 1998
     Return-Path: <mands@inetafrica.com>
     Received: from pizza.cranzgot.co.za (root@pizza.cranzgot.co.za [192.168.2.254])
           by onion.cranzgot.co.za (8.8.7/8.8.7) with ESMTP id VAA11942
 5         for <psheer@icon.co.za>; Mon, 1 Jun 1998 21:20:20 +0200
     Received: from mail450.icon.co.za (mail450.icon.co.za [196.26.208.3])
           by pizza.cranzgot.co.za (8.8.5/8.8.5) with ESMTP id VAA19357
           for <psheer@icon.co.za>; Mon, 1 Jun 1998 21:17:06 +0200
     Received: from smtp02.inetafrica.com (smtp02.inetafrica.com [196.7.0.140])
10         by mail450.icon.co.za (8.8.8/8.8.8) with SMTP id VAA02315
           for <psheer@icon.co.za>; Mon, 1 Jun 1998 21:24:21 +0200 (GMT)
     Received: from default [196.31.19.216] (fullmoon)
           by smtp02.inetafrica.com with smtp (Exim 1.73 #1)
           id 0ygTDL-00041u-00; Mon, 1 Jun 1998 13:57:20 +0200
15   Message-ID: <357296DF.60A3@inetafrica.com>
     Date: Mon, 01 Jun 1998 13:56:15 +0200
     From: a person <mands@inetafrica.com>
     Reply-To: mands@inetafrica.com
     Organization: private
20   X-Mailer: Mozilla 3.01 (Win95; I)
     MIME-Version: 1.0
     To: paul sheer <psheer@icon.co.za>
     Subject: hello
     Content-Type: text/plain; charset=us-ascii
25   Content-Transfer-Encoding: 7bit
     Status: RO
     X-Status: A

     hey paul
30   its me
     how r u doing
     i am well
     what u been upot
     hows life
35   hope your well
     amanda
```

Each mail message begins with a `From` at the beginning of a line, followed by a space. Then comes the *mail header*, explaining where the message was routed from to get to your mailbox, who sent the message, where replies should go, the subject of the mail, and various other *mail header fields*. Above, the header is longer than the mail messages. Examine the header carefully.

The header ends with the first blank line. The message itself (or *body*) starts right after. The next header in the file will once again start with a `From`. `From`s on the beginning of a line *never* exist within the body. If they do, the mailbox is considered to be corrupt.

Some mail readers store their messages in a different format. However the above format (called the *mbox* format) is the most common for UNIX. Of interest is a format called *Maildir*, which is one format that does *not* store mail messages in a single contiguous file. Instead, *Maildir* stores each message as a separate file within a directory. The name of the directory is then considered to be the mailbox "file"; by default Maildir uses a directory `Maildir` within the user's home directory.

10.1   Sending and Reading Mail

The simplest way to send mail is to use the `mail` command. Type `mail -s "hello there" <username>`. The `mail` program will then wait for you to type out your message. When you are finished, enter a `.` on its own on a single line. The user name will be another user on your system. If no one else is on your system, then send mail to `root` with `mail -s "Hello there" root` or `mail -s "Hello there" root@localhost` (if the @ is not present, then the local machine, `localhost`, is implied). Sending files over email is discussed in Section 12.6.

You can use `mail` to view your mailbox. This is a primitive utility in comparison with modern graphical mail readers but is probably the only mail reader that can handle arbitrarily sized mailboxes. Sometimes you may get a mailbox that is over a gigabyte in size, and `mail` is the only way to delete messages from it. To view your mailbox, type `mail`, and then `z` to read your next window of messages, and `z-` to view the previous window. Most commands work like *command message_number*, for example, `delete 14` or `reply 7`. The message number is the left column with an `N` next to it (for a New message).

For the state of the art in terminal-based mail readers (also called mail *clients*), try `mutt` and `pine`. ⟍pine's license is not Free.⟋

There are also some graphical mail readers in various stages of development. At the time I am writing this, I have been using `balsa` for a few months, which was the best mail reader I could find.

10.2   The SMTP Protocol — Sending Mail Raw to Port 25

To send mail, you need not use a mail client at all. The mail client just follows *SMTP* (Simple Mail Transfer Protocol), which you can type in from the keyboard.

For example, you can send mail by `telnet`*ing* to *port 25* of a machine that has an *MTA* (Mail Transfer Agent—also called the *mailer daemon* or *mail server*) running. The word *daemon* denotes programs that run silently without user intervention.

This is, in fact, how so-called *anonymous mail* or *spam mail* ⟍Spam is a term used to indicate unsolicited email—that is, junk mail that is posted in bulk to large numbers of arbitrary email addresses. Sending spam is considered unethical Internet practice.⟋ is sent on the Internet. A mailer daemon runs in most small institutions in the world and has the simple task of receiving mail requests and relaying them on to other mail servers. Try this, for example (obviously substituting `mail.cranzgot.co.za` for the name of a mail server that you normally use):

```
[root@cericon]# telnet mail.cranzgot.co.za 25
Trying 192.168.2.1...
```

```
      Connected to 192.168.2.1.
      Escape character is '^]'.
 5    220 onion.cranzgot.co.za ESMTP Sendmail 8.9.3/8.9.3; Wed, 2 Feb 2000 14:54:47 +0200
      HELO cericon.cranzgot.co.za
      250 onion.cranzgot.co.za Hello cericon.ctn.cranzgot.co.za [192.168.3.9], pleased to meet yo
      MAIL FROM:psheer@icon.co.za
      250 psheer@icon.co.za... Sender ok
 10   RCPT TO:mands@inetafrica.com
      250 mands@inetafrica.com... Recipient ok
      DATA
      354 Enter mail, end with "." on a line by itself
      Subject:  just to say hi
 15
      hi there
      heres a short message

      .
 20   250 OAA04620 Message accepted for delivery
      QUIT
      221 onion.cranzgot.co.za closing connection
      Connection closed by foreign host.
      [root@cericon]#
```

The above causes the message "hi there heres a short message" to be delivered to mands@inetafrica.com (the *ReCiPienT*). Of course, I can enter any address that I like as the sender, and it can be difficult to determine who sent the message. In this example, the Subject: is the only header field, although I needn't have supplied a header at all.

Now, you may have tried this and gotten a rude error message. This might be because the MTA is configured *not* to relay mail except from specific trusted machines— say, only those machines within that organization. In this way anonymous email is prevented.

On the other hand, if you are connecting to the user's very own mail server, it has to necessarily receive the mail, regardless of who sent it. Hence, the above is a useful way to supply a bogus FROM address and thereby send mail almost anonymously. By "almost" I mean that the mail server would still have logged the machine from which you connected and the time of connection—there is no perfect anonymity for properly configured mail servers.

The above technique is often the only way to properly test a mail server, and should be practiced for later.

Chapter 11

User Accounts and User Ownerships

UNIX intrinsically supports multiple users. Each user has a personal *home* directory /home/<username> in which the user's files are stored, hidden from other users.

So far you may have been using the machine as the root user, who is the system administrator and has complete access to every file on the system. The root is also called the *superuser*. The home directory of the root user is /root. *Note that there is an ambiguity here: the* root *directory is the topmost directory, known as the* / *directory. The* root *user's home directory is* /root *and is called the* home directory of root.

Other than the superuser, every other user has *limited* access to files and directories. Always use your machine as a normal user. Log in as root only to do system administration. This practice will save you from the destructive power that the root user has. In this chapter we show how to manually and automatically create new users.

Users are also divided into sets, called *groups*. A user can belong to several groups and there can be as many groups on the system as you like. Each group is defined by a list of users that are part of that set. In addition, each user may have a group of the same name (as the user's login name), to which only that user belongs.

11.1   File Ownerships

Each file on a system is *owned* by a particular user and also *owned* by a particular group. When you run ls -al, you can see the user that owns the file in the third column and the group that owns the file in the fourth column (these will often be identical, indicating that the file's group is a group to which only the user belongs). To change the ownership of the file, simply use the chown, *change ownerships*, command as follows.

101

```
chown <user>[:<group>] <filename>
```

11.2 The Password File /etc/passwd

The only place in the whole system where a user name is registered is in this file.
↘Exceptions to this rule are several distributed authentication schemes and the Samba package, but you
needn't worry about these for now.↖ Once a user is added to this file, that user is said to
exist on the system. If you thought that user accounts were stored in some unreachable
dark corner, then this should dispel that idea. This is also known as the *password* file to
administrators. View this file with `less`:

```
    root:x:0:0:Paul Sheer:/root:/bin/bash
    bin:x:1:1:bin:/bin:
    daemon:x:2:2:daemon:/sbin:
    adm:x:3:4:adm:/var/adm:
5   lp:x:4:7:lp:/var/spool/lpd:
    sync:x:5:0:sync:/sbin:/bin/sync
    shutdown:x:6:0:shutdown:/sbin:/sbin/shutdown
    halt:x:7:0:halt:/sbin:/sbin/halt
    mail:x:8:12:mail:/var/spool/mail:
10  news:x:9:13:news:/var/spool/news:
    uucp:x:10:14:uucp:/var/spool/uucp:
    gopher:x:13:30:gopher:/usr/lib/gopher-data:
    ftp:x:14:50:FTP User:/home/ftp:
    nobody:x:99:99:Nobody:/:
15  alias:x:501:501::/var/qmail/alias:/bin/bash
    paul:x:509:510:Paul Sheer:/home/paul:/bin/bash
    jack:x:511:512:Jack Robbins:/home/jack:/bin/bash
    silvia:x:511:512:Silvia Smith:/home/silvia:/bin/bash
```

Above is an extract of my own password file. Each user is stored on a separate
line. Many of these are not human login accounts but are used by other programs.

Each line contains seven *fields* separated by colons. The account for `jack` looks
like this:

jack The user's login name. It should be composed of lowercase letters and numbers.
Other characters are allowed, but are not preferable. In particular, there should
never be two user names that differ only by their capitalization.

x The user's encrypted password. An x in this field indicates that it is stored in a separate file, `/etc/shadow`. This *shadow* password file is a later addition to UNIX
systems. It contains additional information about the user.

511 The user's user identification number, *UID.* ⬊This is used by programs as a short alternative to the user's login name. In fact, internally, the login name is never used, only the UID.⬋

512 The user's group identification number, *GID.* ⬊Similarly applies to the GID. Groups will
be discussed later.⬋

Jack Robbins The user's full name. ⬊Few programs ever make use of this field.⬋

/home/jack The user's home directory. The HOME environment variable will be set
to this when the user logs in.

/bin/bash The shell to start when the user logs in.

11.3   Shadow Password File: `/etc/shadow`

The problem with traditional `passwd` files is that they had to be *world readable* ⬊Ev-
eryone on the system can read the file.⬋ in order for programs to extract information, such as
the user's full name, about the user. This means that everyone can see the encrypted
password in the second field. Anyone can copy any other user's password field and
then try billions of different passwords to see if they match. If you have a hundred
users on the system, there are bound to be several that chose passwords that matched
some word in the dictionary. The so-called *dictionary* attack will simply try all 80,000
common English words until a match is found. If you think you are clever to add a
number in front of an easy-to-guess dictionary word, password cracking algorithms
know about these as well. ⬊And about every other trick you can think of.⬋ To solve this problem the `shadow` password file was invented. The shadow password file is used only
for *authentication* ⬊Verifying that the user is the genuine owner of the account.⬋ and is not world
readable—there is no information in the shadow password file that a common program will ever need—no regular user has permission to see the encrypted password
field. The fields are colon separated just like the `passwd` file.

Here is an example line from a `/etc/shadow` file:

```
jack:Q,Jpl.or6u2e7:10795:0:99999:7:-1:-1:134537220
```

jack The user's login name.

Q,Jpl.or6u2e7 The user's encrypted password known as the *hash* of the password. This is the user's 8-character password with a *one-way hash function* applied to it. It is simply a mathematical algorithm applied to the password that
is known to produce a unique result for each password. To demonstrate: the
(rather poor) password `Loghimin` hashes to `:1Z1F.0VSRRucs:` in the shadow
file. An almost identical password `loghimin` gives a completely different hash

`:CavHIpD1W.cmg:`. Hence, trying to guess the password from the hash can only be done by trying every possible password. Such a *brute force attack* is therefore considered computationally expensive *but not impossible*. To check if an entered password matches, just apply the identical mathematical algorithm to it: if it matches, then the password is correct. This is how the login command works. Sometimes you will see a * in place of a hashed password. This means that the account has been disabled.

10795 Days since January 1, 1970, that the password was last changed.

0 Days before which password may not be changed. Usually zero. This field is not often used.

99999 Days after which password must be changed. This is also rarely used, and will be set to 99999 by default.

7 Days before password is to expire that user is warned of pending password expiration.

-1 Days after password expires that account is considered inactive and disabled. - 1 is used to indicate infinity—that is, to mean we are effectively not using this feature.

-1 Days since January 1, 1970, when account will be disabled.

134537220 Flag reserved for future use.

11.4   The `groups` Command and `/etc/group`

On a UNIX system you may want to give a number of users the same access rights. For instance, you may have five users that should be allowed to access some privileged file and another ten users that are allowed to run a certain program. You can *group* these users into, for example, two groups `previl` and `wproc` and then make the relevant file and directories owned by that group with, say,

```
chown root:previl /home/somefile
chown root:wproc /usr/lib/wproc
```

Permissions ⬝Explained later.⬝ dictate the kind of access, but for the meantime, the file/directory must at least be *owned* by that group.

The `/etc/group` file is also colon separated. A line might look like this:

```
wproc:x:524:jack,mary,henry,arthur,sue,lester,fred,sally
```

wproc The name of the group. There should really also be a user of this name as well.

x The group's password. This field is usually set with an x and is not used.

524 The GID *group ID*. This must be unique in the group's file.

jack,mary,henry,arthur,sue,lester,fred,sally The list of users that belong to the group. This must be comma separated with no spaces.

You can obviously study the `group` file to find out which groups a user belongs to, ↘That is, *not* "which users does a group consist of?" which is easy to see at a glance.↖ but when there are a lot of groups, it can be tedious to scan through the entire file. The `groups` command prints out this information.

11.5 Manually Creating a User Account

The following steps are required to create a user account:

/etc/passwd entry To create an entry in this file, simply edit it and copy an existing line. ↘When editing configuration files, never write out a line from scratch if it has some kind of special format. Always copy an existing entry that has proved itself to be correct, and then edit in the appropriate changes. This will prevent you from making errors.↖ Always add users from the bottom and try to preserve the "pattern" of the file—that is, if you see numbers increasing, make yours fit in; if you are adding a normal user, add it after the existing lines of normal users. Each user must have a unique UID and should usually have a unique GID. So if you are adding a line to the end of the file, make your new UID and GID the same as the last line but incremented by 1.

/etc/shadow entry Create a new shadow password entry. At this stage you do not know what the hash is, so just make it a `*`. You can set the password with the `passwd` command later.

/etc/group entry Create a new group entry for the user's group. Make sure the number in the group entry matches that in the `passwd` file.

/etc/skel This directory contains a template home directory for the user. Copy the entire directory and all its contents into `/home` directory, renaming it to the name of the user. In the case of our `jack` example, you should have a directory `/home/jack`.

Home directory ownerships You need to now change the ownerships of the home directory to match the user. The command `chown -R jack:jack /home/jack` will accomplish this change.

Setting the password Use `passwd <username>` to set the user's password.

11.6   Automatically Creating a User Account: `useradd` and `groupadd`

The above process is tedious. The commands that perform all these updates automatically are `useradd`, `userdel`, and `usermod`. The man pages explain the use of these commands in detail. Note that different flavors of UNIX have different commands to do this. Some may even have graphical programs or web interfaces to assist in creating users.

In addition, the commands `groupadd`, `groupdel`, and `groupmod` do the same with respect to groups.

11.7   User Logins

It is possible to switch from one user to another, as well as view your login status and the status of other users. Logging in also follows a silent procedure which is important to understand.

11.7.1   The `login` command

A user most often gains access to the system through the `login` program. This program looks up the UID and GID from the `passwd` and `group` file and authenticates the user.

The following is quoted from the `login` man page, and explains this procedure in detail:

> **login** is used when signing onto a system. It can also be used to switch from one user to another at any time (most modern shells have support for this feature built into them, however).
>
> If an argument is not given, **login** prompts for the username.
>
> If the user is *not* root, and if */etc/nologin* exists, the contents of this file are printed to the screen, and the login is terminated. This is typically used to prevent logins when the system is being taken down.
>
> If special access restrictions are specified for the user in */etc/usertty*, these must be met, or the login attempt will be denied and a **syslog** ⟍System error log program— `syslog` writes all system messages to the file `/var/log/messages`.⟋ message will be generated. See the section on "Special Access Restrictions."
>
> If the user is `root`, then the login must be occuring on a tty listed in */etc/securetty*. ⟍If this file is not present, then root logins will be allowed from anywhere. It is worth deleting this file if your machine is protected by a firewall and you would like to easily login from

another machine on your LAN. If /etc/securetty is present, then logins are only allowed from the terminals it lists.⟍ Failures will be logged with the **syslog** facility.

After these conditions have been checked, the password will be requested and checked (if a password is required for this username). Ten attempts are allowed before **login** dies, but after the first three, the response starts to get very slow. Login failures are reported via the **syslog** facility. This facility is also used to report any successful root logins.

If the file *.hushlogin* exists, then a "quiet" login is performed (this disables the checking of mail and the printing of the last login time and message of the day). Otherwise, if */var/log/lastlog* exists, the last login time is printed (and the current login is recorded).

Random administrative things, such as setting the UID and GID of the tty are performed. The TERM environment variable is preserved, if it exists (other environment variables are preserved if the **-p** option is used). Then the HOME, PATH, SHELL, TERM, MAIL, and LOGNAME environment variables are set. PATH defaults to */usr/local/bin:/bin:/usr/bin:* . ⟍Note that the **.** —the current directory—is listed in the PATH. This is only the default PATH however.⟍ for normal users, and to */sbin:/bin:/usr/sbin:/usr/bin* for root. Last, if this is not a "quiet" login, the message of the day is printed and the file with the user's name in */usr/spool/mail* will be checked, and a message printed if it has non-zero length.

The user's shell is then started. If no shell is specified for the user in **/etc/passwd**, then **/bin/sh** is used. If there is no directory specified in */etc/passwd*, then / is used (the home directory is checked for the *.hushlogin* file described above).

11.7.2   The *set user*, **su command**

To temporarily become another user, you can use the su program:

```
su jack
```

This command prompts you for a password (unless you are the root user to begin with). It does nothing more than change the current user to have the access rights of jack. Most environment variables will remain the same. The HOME, LOGNAME, and USER environment variables will be set to jack, but all other environment variables will be inherited. su is, therefore, not the same as a normal login.

To get the equivalent of a login with su, run

```
su - jack
```

This will cause all initialization scripts (that are normally run when the user logs in) to be executed. ⟍What actually happens is that the subsequent shell is started with a – in front of the zero'th argument. This makes the shell read the user's personal profile. The login command also does this.⟍ Hence, after running su with the – option, you logged in as if with the login command.

11.7.3 The **who**, **w**, and **users** commands to see who is logged in

who and w print a list of users logged in to the system, as well as their CPU consumption and other statistics. who --help gives:

```
Usage: who [OPTION]... [ FILE | ARG1 ARG2 ]

  -H, --heading      print line of column headings
  -i, -u, --idle     add user idle time as HOURS:MINUTES, . or old
  -m                 only hostname and user associated with stdin
  -q, --count        all login names and number of users logged on
  -s                 (ignored)
  -T, -w, --mesg     add user's message status as +, - or ?
      --message      same as -T
      --writable     same as -T
      --help         display this help and exit
      --version      output version information and exit

If FILE is not specified, use /var/run/utmp.  /var/log/wtmp as FILE is common.
If ARG1 ARG2 given, -m presumed: 'am i' or 'mom likes' are usual.
```

A little more information can be gathered from the info pages for this command. The idle time indicates how long since the user has last pressed a key. Most often, one just types who -Hiw.

w is similar. An extract of the w man page says:

w displays information about the users currently on the machine, and their processes. The header shows, in this order, the current time, how long the system has been running, how many users are currently logged on, and the system load averages for the past 1, 5, and 15 minutes.

The following entries are displayed for each user: login name, the tty name, the remote host, login time, idle time, JCPU, PCPU, and the command line of their current process.

The JCPU time is the time used by all processes attached to the tty. It does not include past background jobs, but does include currently running background jobs.

The PCPU time is the time used by the current process, named in the "what" field.

Finally, from a shell script the users command is useful for just seeing who is logged in. You can use in a shell script, for example:

```
for user in `users` ; do
    <etc>
done
```

11.7.4   The `id` command and *effective* UID

`id` prints your *real* and *effective* UID and GID. A user normally has a UID and a GID but may also have an effective UID and GID as well. The real UID and GID are what a process will generally think you are logged in as. The effective UID and GID are the actual access permissions that you have when trying to read, write, and execute files.

11.7.5   User limits

There is a file `/etc/security/limits.conf` that stipulates the limitations on CPU usage, process consumption, and other resources on a per-user basis. The documentation for this config file is contained in
`/usr/[share/]doc/pam-<version>/txts/README.pam_limits`.

Chapter 12

Using Internet Services

This chapter summarizes remote access and the various methods of transferring files and data over the Internet.

12.1 `ssh`, not `telnet` or `rlogin`

`telnet` is a program for talking to a UNIX network service. It is most often used to do a remote login. Try

```
telnet <remote_machine>
telnet localhost
```

to log in to your remote machine. It needn't matter if there is no physical network; network services always work regardless because the machine always has an internal link to itself.

`rlogin` is like a minimal version of `telnet` that allows login access only. You can type

```
rlogin -l <username> <remote_machine>
rlogin -l jack localhost
```

if the system is configured to support remote logins.

These two services are the domain of old world UNIX; for security reasons, `ssh` is now the preferable service for logging in remotely:

```
ssh [-l <username>] <remote_machine>
```

Though `rlogin` *and* `telnet` *are very convenient, they should* never *be used across a public network because your password can easily be read off the wire as you type it in.*

12.2   rcp and scp

`rcp` stands for *remote copy* and `scp` is the secure version from the `ssh` package. These two commands copy files from one machine to another using a similar notation to `cp`.

```
rcp [-r] [<remote_machine>:]<file> [<remote_machine>:]<file>
scp [-l <username>] [-r] [<remote_machine>:]<file> [<remote_machine>:]<file>
```

Here is an example:

```
   [psheer@cericon]# rcp /var/spool/mail/psheer \
    divinian.cranzgot.co.za:/home/psheer/mail/cericon
   [psheer@cericon]# scp /var/spool/mail/psheer \
    divinian.cranzgot.co.za:/home/psheer/mail/cericon
 5 The authenticity of host 'divinian.cranzgot.co.za' can't be established.
   RSA key fingerprint is 43:14:36:5d:bf:4f:f3:ac:19:08:5d:4b:70:4a:7e:6a.
   Are you sure you want to continue connecting (yes/no)? yes
   Warning: Permanently added 'divinian.cranzgot.co.za' (RSA) to the list of known hosts.
   psheer@divinian's password:
10 psheer              100% |*************************************| 4266 KB    01:18
```

The `-r` option copies recursively and copies can take place in either direction or even between two nonlocal machines.

scp should always be used instead of rcp for security reasons. Notice also the warning given by `scp` for this first-time connection. See the `ssh` documentation for how to make your first connection securely. All commands in the `ssh` package have this same behavior.

12.3   rsh

`rsh` (*remote shell*) is a useful utility for executing a command on a remote machine. Here are some examples:

```
   [psheer@cericon]# rsh divinian.cranzgot.co.za hostname
   divinian.cranzgot.co.za
   [psheer@cericon]# rsh divinian.cranzgot.co.za \
    tar -czf - /home/psheer | dd of=/dev/fd0 bs=1024
 5 tar: Removing leading '/' from member names
   20+0 records in
   20+0 records out
```

```
[psheer@cericon]# cat /var/spool/mail/psheer | rsh divinian.cranzgot.co.za \
 sh -c 'cat >> /home/psheer/mail/cericon'
```

The first command prints the host name of the remote machine. The second command backs up my *remote* home directory to my *local* floppy disk. (More about dd and /dev/fd0 come later.) The last command appends my local mailbox file to a remote mailbox file. Notice how stdin, stdout, and stderr are properly redirected to the local terminal. After reading Chapter 29 see rsh(8) or in.rshd(8) to configure this service.

Once again, for security reasons rsh *should never be available across a public network.*

12.4   FTP

FTP stands for *File Transfer Protocol*. If FTP is set up on your local machine, then other machines can download files. Type

```
ftp metalab.unc.edu
```

or

```
ncftp metalab.unc.edu
```

ftp is the traditional command-line UNIX FTP *client,* ↘*"client" always indicates the user program accessing some remote service.*↖ while *ncftp* is a more powerful client that will not always be installed.

You will now be inside an FTP *session*. You will be asked for a login name and a password. The site metalab.unc.edu is one that allows *anonymous* logins. This means that you can type anonymous as your user name, and then anything you like as a password. You will notice that the session will ask you for an email address as your password. Any sequence of letters with an @ symbol will suffice, but you should put your actual email address out of politeness.

The FTP session is like a reduced shell. You can type cd, ls, and ls -al to view file lists. help brings up a list of commands, and you can also type help <command> to get help on a specific command. You can download a file by using the get <file-name> command, but before you do this, you must set the *transfer type* to *binary*. The *transfer type* indicates whether or not newline characters will be translated to DOS format. Typing ascii turns on this feature, while binary turns it off. You may also want to enter hash which will print a # for every 1024 bytes of download. This is useful for watching the progress of a download. Go to a directory that has a README file in it and enter

```
get README
```

The file will be downloaded into your current directory.

You can also `cd` to the `/incoming` directory and upload files. Try

```
put README
```

to upload the file that you have just downloaded. Most FTP sites have an `/incoming` directory that is flushed periodically.

FTP allows far more than just uploading of files, although the administrator has the option to restrict access to any further features. You can create directories, change ownerships, and do almost anything you can on a local file system.

If you have several machines on a trusted *LAN* (*Local Area Network*—that is, your private office or home network), all should have FTP enabled to allow users to easily copy files between machines. How to install and configure one of the many available FTP servers will become obvious later in this book.

12.5 `finger`

`finger` is a service for remotely listing who is logged in on a remote system. Try `finger @<hostname>` to see who is logged in on `<hostname>`. The *finger* service will often be disabled on machines for security reasons.

12.6 Sending Files by Email

Mail is being used more and more for transferring files between machines. It is bad practice to send mail messages over 64 kilobytes over the Internet because it tends to excessively load mail servers. Any file larger than 64 kilobytes should be uploaded by FTP onto some common FTP server. Most small images are smaller than this size, hence sending a small JPEG ↘A common Internet image file format. These are especially compressed and are usually under 100 kilobytes for a typical screen-sized photograph.↖ image is considered acceptable.

12.6.1 uuencode and uudecode

If you must send files by mail then you can do it by using `uuencode`. This utility packs binary files into a format that mail servers can handle. If you send a mail message containing arbitrary binary data, it will more than likely be corrupted on the way because mail agents are only designed to handle a limited range of characters. `uuencode` represents a binary file with allowable characters, albeit taking up slightly more space.

Here is a neat trick to pack up a directory and send it to someone by mail.

```
tar -czf - <mydir> | uuencode <mydir>.tar.gz \
    | mail -s "Here are some files" <user>@<machine>
```

To unpack a `uuencoded` file, use the `uudecode` command:

```
uudecode <myfile>.uu
```

12.6.2 MIME encapsulation

Most graphical mail readers have the ability to *attach* files to mail messages and read these attachments. The way they do this is not with `uuencode` but in a special format known as *MIME encapsulation*. MIME (*Multipurpose Internet Mail Extensions*) is a way of representing multiple files inside a single mail message. The way binary data is handled is similar to `uuencode`, but in a format known as *base64*.

Each MIME attachment to a mail message has a particular type, known as the *MIME type*. MIME types merely classify the attached file as an image, an audio clip, a formatted document, or some other type of data. The MIME type is a text tag with the format `<major>/<minor>`. The `major` part is called the *major MIME type* and the `minor` part is called the *minor MIME type*. Available major types match all the kinds of files that you would expect to exist. They are usually one of `application`, `audio`, `image`, `message`, `text`, or `video`. The `application` type means a file format specific to a particular utility. The minor MIME types run into the hundreds. A long list of MIME types can be found in `/etc/mime.types`.

If needed, some useful command-line utilities in the same vein as `uuencode` can create and extract MIME messages. These are `mpack`, `munpack`, and `mmencode` (or `mimencode`).

Chapter 13

LINUX Resources

Very often it is not even necessary to connect to the Internet to find the information you need. Chapter 16 contains a description of most of the documentation on a LINUX distribution.

It is, however, essential to get the most up-to-date information where security and hardware driver support are concerned. It is also fun and worthwhile to interact with LINUX users from around the globe. The rapid development of Free software could mean that you may miss out on important new features that could streamline IT services. Hence, reviewing web magazines, reading newsgroups, and subscribing to mailing lists are essential parts of a system administrator's role.

13.1　FTP Sites and the `sunsite` Mirror

The `metalab.unc.edu` FTP site (previously called `sunsite.unc.edu`) is one of the traditional sites for free software. It is mirrored in almost every country that has a significant IT infrastructure. If you point your web browser there, you will find a list of mirrors. For faster access, do pick a mirror in your own country.

It is advisable to browse around this FTP site. In particular you should try to find the locations of:

- The directory where all sources for official GNU packages are stored. This would be a mirror of the Free Software Foundation's FTP archives. These are packages that were commissioned by the FSF and not merely released under the GPL (GNU General Public License). The FSF will distribute them in source form (`.tar.gz`) for inclusion into various distributions. They will, of course, compile and work under any UNIX.

117

- The generic `Linux` download directory. It contains innumerable UNIX packages in source and binary form, categorized in a directory tree. For instance, mail clients have their own directory with many mail packages inside. `metalab` is the place where new developers can host any new software that they have produced. There are instructions on the FTP site to upload software and to request it to be placed into a directory.

- The kernel sources. This is a mirror of the kernel archives where Linus and other maintainers upload new *stable* ↘Meaning that the software is well tested and free of serious bugs.↖ and *beta* ↘Meaning that the software is in its development stages.↖ kernel versions and kernel patches.

- The various distributions. RedHat, Debian◯, and possibly other popular distributions may be present.

This list is by no means exhaustive. Depending on the willingness of the site maintainer, there may be mirrors to far more sites from around the world.

The FTP site is how you will download free software. Often, maintainers will host their software on a web site, but every popular package will almost always have an FTP site where versions are persistently stored. An example is `metalab.unc.edu` in the directory `/pub/Linux/apps/editors/X/cooledit/` where the author's own *Cooledit* package is distributed.

13.2 HTTP — Web Sites

Most users should already be familiar with using a web browser. You should also become familiar with the concept of a *web search*. ↘Do I need to explain this?↖ You search the web when you point your web browser to a popular search engine like http://www.google.com/, http://www.google.com/linux, http://infoseek.go.com/, http://www.altavista.com/, or http://www.yahoo.com/ and search for particular key words. Searching is a bit of a black art with the billions of web pages out there. Always consult the search engine's advanced search options to see how you can do more complex searches than just plain word searches.

The web sites in the FAQ (*Frequently Asked Questions*) (see Appendix D) should all be consulted to get an overview on some of the primary sites of interest to LINUX◊ users.

Especially important is that you keep up with the latest LINUX◊ news. I find the *Linux Weekly News* http://lwn.net/ an excellent source. Also, the famous (and infamous) *SlashDot* http://slashdot.org/ web site gives daily updates about "stuff that matters" (and therefore contains a lot about free software).

Fresh Meat http://freshmeat.net/ is a web site devoted to new software releases. You will find new or updated packages announced every few hours or so.

Linux Planet http://www.linuxplanet.com/ seems to be a new (?) web site that I just found while writing this. It looks like it contains lots of tutorial information on LINUX🐧.

News Forge http://www.newsforge.net/ also contains daily information about software issues.

Lycos http://download.lycos.com/static/advanced_search.asp is an efficient FTP search engine for locating packages. It is one of the few search engines that understand regular expressions.

Realistically, though, a new LINUX🐧 web site is created every week; almost anything prepended or appended to "linux" is probably a web site already.

13.3   SourceForge

A new phenomenon in the free software community is the SourceForge web site, http://www.sourceforge.net/. Developers can use this service at no charge to host their project's web site, FTP archives, and mailing lists. SourceForge has mushroomed so rapidly that it has come to host the better half of all free software projects.

13.4   Mailing Lists

A mailing list is a special address that, when posted to, automatically sends email to a long list of other addresses. You usually subscribe to a mailing list by sending some specially formatted email or by requesting a subscription from the mailing list manager.

Once you have subscribed to a list, any email you post to the list will be sent to every other subscriber, and every other subscriber's posts to the list will be sent to you.

There are mostly three types of mailing lists: the *majordomo* type, the *listserv* type, and the **-request* type.

13.4.1   Majordomo and Listserv

To subscribe to the *majordomo* variety, send a mail message to majordomo@<machine> with no subject and a one-line message:

```
subscribe <mailing-list-name>
```

This command adds your name to the mailing list `<mailing-list-name>@<machine>`, to which messages are posted.

Do the same for *listserv*-type lists, by sending the same message to `listserv@<machine>`.

For instance, if you are an administrator for any machine that is exposed to the Internet, you should get on `bugtraq`. Send email to

```
subscribe bugtraq
```

to `listserv@netspace.org`, and become one of the tens of thousands of users that read and report security problems about LINUX.

To *unsubscribe* to a list is just as simple. Send an email message:

```
unsubscribe <mailing-list-name>
```

Never send `subscribe` *or* `unsubscribe` *messages to the mailing list itself. Send* `subscribe` *or* `unsubscribe` *messages only to to the address* `majordomo@<machine>` *or* `listserv@<machine>`.

13.4.2 *-request

You subscribe to these mailing lists by sending an empty email message to `<mailing-list-name>-request@<machine>` with the word `subscribe` as the subject. The same email with the word `unsubscribe` removes you from the list.

Once again, never send `subscribe` *or* `unsubscribe` *messages to the mailing list itself.*

13.5 Newsgroups

A newsgroup is a notice board that everyone in the world can see. There are tens of thousands of newsgroups and each group is unique in the world.

The client software you use to read a newsgroup is called a *news reader* (or *news client*). `rtin` is a popular text mode reader, while `netscape` is graphical. `pan` is an excellent graphical news reader that I use.

Newsgroups are named like Internet hosts. One you might be interested in is `comp.os.linux.announce`. The `comp` is the broadest subject description for *computers*; `os` stands for *operating systems*; and so on. Many other `linux` newsgroups are devoted to various LINUX issues.

Newsgroups servers are big hungry beasts. They form a tree-like structure on the Internet. When you send mail to a newsgroup it takes about a day or so for the mail you sent to propagate to every other server in the world. Likewise, you can see a list of all the messages posted to each newsgroup by anyone anywhere.

What's the difference between a newsgroup and a mailing list? The advantage of a newsgroup is that you don't have to download the messages you are not interested in. If you are on a mailing list, you get all the mail sent to the list. With a newsgroup you can look at the message list and retrieve only the messages you are interested in.

Why not just put the mailing list on a web page? If you did, then everyone in the world would have to go over international links to get to the web page. It would load the server in proportion to the number of subscribers. This is exactly what SlashDot is. However, your newsgroup server is local, so you retrieve mail over a faster link and save Internet traffic.

13.6 RFCs

An indispensable source of information for serious administrators or developers is the RFCs. RFC stands for *Request For Comments*. RFCs are Internet standards written by authorities to define everything about Internet communication. Very often, documentation will refer to RFCs. ↘There are also a few nonsense RFCs out there. For example there is an RFC to communicate using pigeons, and one to facilitate an infinite number of monkeys trying to write the complete works of Shakespeare. Keep a close eye on *Slashdot* http://slashdot.org/ to catch these.↖

ftp://metalab.unc.edu/pub/docs/rfc/ (and mirrors) has the complete RFCs archived for download. There are about 2,500 of them. The index file `rfc-index.txt` is probably where you should start. It has entries like:

```
2045 Multipurpose Internet Mail Extensions (MIME) Part One: Format of
     Internet Message Bodies. N. Freed & N. Borenstein. November 1996.
     (Format: TXT=72932 bytes) (Obsoletes RFC1521, RFC1522, RFC1590)
     (Updated by RFC2184, RFC2231) (Status: DRAFT STANDARD)

2046 Multipurpose Internet Mail Extensions (MIME) Part Two: Media
     Types. N. Freed & N. Borenstein. November 1996. (Format: TXT=105854
     bytes) (Obsoletes RFC1521, RFC1522, RFC1590) (Status: DRAFT STANDARD)
```

and

```
2068 Hypertext Transfer Protocol -- HTTP/1.1. R. Fielding, J. Gettys,
     J. Mogul, H. Frystyk, T. Berners-Lee. January 1997. (Format:
     TXT=378114 bytes) (Status: PROPOSED STANDARD)
```

Well, you get the idea.

Chapter 14

Permission and Modification Times

Every file and directory on a UNIX system, besides being owned by a user and a group, has access *flags* ↘A switch that can either be on or off.↖ (also called *access bits*) dictating what kind of access that user and group have to the file.

Running `ls -ald /bin/cp /etc/passwd /tmp` gives you a listing like this:

```
-rwxr-xr-x   1 root      root       28628 Mar 24  1999 /bin/cp
-rw-r--r--   1 root      root        1151 Jul 23 22:42 /etc/passwd
drwxrwxrwt   5 root      root        4096 Sep 25 15:23 /tmp
```

In the leftmost column are flags which completely describe the access rights to the file.

So far I have explained that the furthest flag to the left is either – or d, indicating an ordinary file or directory. The remaining nine have a – to indicate an unset value or one of several possible characters. Table 14.1 gives a complete description of file system permissions.

14.1   The chmod Command

You use the chmod command to change the permissions of a file. It's usually used as follows:

```
chmod [-R] [u|g|o|a][+|-][r|w|x|s|t] <file> [<file>] ...
```

Table 14.1 File and directory permissions

	Possible chars, – for unset	Effect for directories	Effect for files
User, u	r	User can read the contents of the directory.	User can read the file.
	w	With x or s, user can create and remove files in the directory.	User can write to the file.
	x s S	User can access the contents of the files in a directory for x or s. S has no effect.	User can execute the file for x or s. s, known as the *setuid* bit, means to set the user owner of the subsequent process to that of the file. S has no effect.
Group, g	r	Group can read the contents of the directory.	Group can read the file.
	w	With x or s, group can create and remove files in the directory.	Group can write to the file.
	x s S	Group can access the contents of the files in a directory for x. For s, force all files in this directory to the same group as the directory. S has no effect.	Group can execute the file for x or s. s, known as the *setgid* bit, means to set the group owner of the subsequent process to that of the file. S has no effect.
Other, o	r	Everyone can read the contents of the directory.	Everyone can read the file.
	w	With x or t, everyone can create and remove files in the directory.	Everyone can write to the file.
	x t T	Everyone can access the contents of the files in a directory for x and t. t, known as the *sticky* bit, prevents users from removing files that they do not own, hence users are free to append to the directory but not to remove other users' files. T has no effect.	Group can execute the file for x or t. For t, save the process text image to the swap device so that future loads will be faster (I don't know if this has an effect on LINUX). T has no effect.

For example,

```
chmod u+x myfile
```

adds execute permissions for the user of `myfile`. And,

```
chmod a-rx myfile
```

removes *read* and *execute* permissions for *all*—that is, user, group, and other.

The -R option, once again means *recursive*, diving into subdirectories as usual.

Permission bits are often represented in their binary form, especially in programs. It is convenient to show the rwxrwxrwx set in octal, ⟍See Section 2.1⟋ where each digit fits conveniently into three bits. Files on the system are usually created with *mode* 0644, meaning rw-r--r--. You can set permissions explicitly with an octal number, for example,

```
chmod 0755 myfile
```

gives myfile the permissions rwxr-xr-x. For a full list of octal values for all kinds of permissions and file types, see /usr/include/linux/stat.h.

In Table 14.1 you can see s, the *setuid* or *setgid* bit. If it is used without execute permissions then it has no meaning and is written as a capitalized S. This bit effectively colorizes an x into an s, so you should read an s as **execute** *with* the setuid or setgid bit set. t is known as the *sticky* bit. It also has no meaning if there are no execute permissions and is written as a capital T.

The leading 0 can in be ignored, but is preferred for explicitness. It *can* take on a value representing the three bits, *setuid* (4), *setgid* (2), and *sticky* (1). Hence a value of 5764 is 101 111 110 100 in binary and gives -rwsrw-r-T.

14.2 The umask Command

umask sets the default permissions for newly created files; it is usually 022. This default value means that the permissions of any new file you create (say, with the touch command) will be *masked* with this number. 022 hence *excludes* write permissions of group and of other. A umask of 006 would exclude read and write permissions of other, but would allow read and write of group. Try

```
umask
touch <file1>
ls -al <file1>
umask 026
touch <file2>
ls -al <file2>
```

026 is probably closer to the kind of mask we like as an ordinary user. Check your /etc/profile file to see what umask your login defaults to, when, and also why.

14.3   Modification Times: `stat`

In addition to permissions, each file has three integers associated with it that represent, in seconds, the last time the file was accessed (read), when it was last modified (written to), and when its permissions were last changed. These are known as the *atime, mtime,* and *ctime* of a file respectively.

To get a complete listing of the file's permissions, use the `stat` command. Here is the result of `stat /etc`:

```
   File: "/etc"
   Size: 4096              Filetype: Directory
   Mode: (0755/drwxr-xr-x)          Uid: (    0/    root)  Gid: (    0/    root)
Device: 3,1    Inode: 14057      Links: 41
Access: Sat Sep 25 04:09:08 1999(00000.15:02:23)
Modify: Fri Sep 24 20:55:14 1999(00000.22:16:17)
Change: Fri Sep 24 20:55:14 1999(00000.22:16:17)
```

The `Size:` quoted here is the actual amount of disk space used to store the directory *listing,* and is the same as reported by `ls`. In this case it is probably four disk blocks of 1024 bytes each. The size of a directory as quoted here does *not* mean the sum of all files contained under it. For a file, however, the `Size:` would be the exact file length in bytes (again, as reported by `ls`).

Chapter 15

Symbolic and Hard Links

Very often, a file is required to be in two different directories at the same time. Think for example of a configuration file that is required by two different software packages that are looking for the file in different directories. The file could simply be copied, but to have to replicate changes in more than one place would create an administrative nightmare. Also consider a document that must be present in many directories, but which would be easier to update at one point. *The way two (or more) files can have the same data is with links.*

15.1 Soft Links

To demonstrate a soft link, try the following:

```
touch myfile
ln -s myfile myfile2
ls -al
cat > myfile
a
few
lines
of
text
^D
cat myfile
cat myfile2
```

Notice that the `ls -al` listing has the letter `l` on the far left next to `myfile2`, and the usual − next to `myfile`. This indicates that the file is a *soft* link (also known as a *symbolic* link or *symlink*) to some other file.

A *symbolic link* contains no data of its own, only a reference to another file. It can even contain a reference to a directory. In either case, programs operating on the link will actually see the file or directory it points to.

Try

```
mkdir mydir
ln -s mydir mydir2
ls -al .
touch ./mydir/file1
touch ./mydir2/file2
ls -al ./mydir
ls -al ./mydir2
```

The directory `mydir2` is a symbolic link to `mydir2` and appears as though it is a replica of the original. Once again the directory `mydir2` does not consume additional disk space—a program that reads from the link is unaware that it is seeing into a different directory.

Symbolic links can also be copied and retain their value:

```
cp mydir2 /
ls -al /
cd /mydir2
```

You have now copied the link to the root directory. However, the link points to a relative path `mydir` in the same directory as the link. Since there is no `mydir` here, an error is raised.

Try

```
rm -f mydir2 /mydir2
ln -s `pwd`/mydir mydir2
ls -al
```

Now you will see `mydir2` has an absolute path. You can try

```
cp mydir2 /
ls -al /
cd /mydir2
```

and notice that it now works.

One of the common uses of symbolic links is to make *mount*ed (see Section 19.4) file systems accessible from a different directory. For instance, you may have a large directory that has to be split over several physical disks. For clarity, you can mount the disks as /disk1, /disk2, etc., and then link the various subdirectories in a way that makes efficient use of the space you have.

Another example is the linking of /dev/cdrom to, say, /dev/hdc so that programs accessing the device file /dev/cdrom (see Chapter 18) actually access the correct IDE drive.

15.2   Hard Links

UNIX allows the data of a file to have more than one name in separate places in the same file system. Such a file with more than one name for the same data is called a *hard-linked* file and is similar to a symbolic link. Try

```
touch mydata
ln mydata mydataB
ls -al
```

The files mydata and mydataB are indistinguishable. They share the same data, and have a 2 in second column of the ls -al listing. This means that they are hard-linked *twice* (that there are two names for this file).

The reason why hard links are sometimes used in preference to symbolic links is that some programs are not fooled by a symbolic link: If you have, say, a script that uses cp to copy a file, it will copy the symbolic link instead of the file it points to. ⟍cp actually has an option to override this behavior.⟍ A hard link, however, will always be seen as a real file.

On the other hand, hard links cannot be made between files on different file systems nor can they be made between directories.

Chapter 16

Pre-installed Documentation

This chapter tells you where to find documentation on a common LINUX⚠ distribution. The paths are derived from a RedHat distribution, but are no less applicable to other distributions, although the exact locations might be different. One difference between distributions is the migration of documentation source from /usr/???? to /usr/share/????—the proper place for them—on account of their being shareable between different machines. See Chapter 35 for the *reason* documentation goes where it does. In many cases, documentation may not be installed or may be in completely different locations. Unfortunately, I cannot keep track of what the 20 major vendors are doing, so it is likely that this chapter will quickly become out of date.

For many proprietary operating systems, the definitive reference for their operating system is printed texts. For LINUX⚠, much of documentation is written by the authors themselves and is included with the source code. A typical LINUX⚠ distribution will package documentation along with the compiled binaries. Common distributions come with *hundreds of megabytes* of printable, hyperlinked, and plain text documentation. There is often no need to go the the World Wide Web unless something is outdated.

If you have not already tried this, run

```
ls -ld /usr/*/doc /usr/*/*/doc /usr/share/*/*/doc \
        /opt/*/doc /opt/*/*/doc
```

This is a somewhat unreliable way to search for potential documentation directories, but it gives at least the following list of directories for an official RedHat 7.0 with a complete set of installed packages:

/usr/X11R6/doc	/usr/share/vim/vim57/doc
/usr/lib/X11/doc	/usr/share/doc
/usr/local/doc	/usr/share/gphoto/doc

```
/usr/share/texmf/doc        /usr/share/lout/doc
```

- *Kernel documentation:* **/usr/src/linux/Documentation/**

This directory contains information on all hardware drivers except graphic cards. The kernel has built-in drivers for networking cards, SCSI controllers, sound cards, and so on. If you need to find out if one of these is supported, this is the first place to look.

- *X Window System graphics hardware support:* **/usr/X11R6/lib/X11/doc/**

(This is the same as /usr/X11R6/doc/.) In this directory you will find documentation on all of the graphics hardware supported by **X**, how to configure **X**, tweak video modes, cope with incompatible graphics cards, and so on. See Section 43.5 for details.

- *TEX and Meta-Font reference:* **/usr/share/texmf/doc/**

This directory has an enormous and comprehensive reference to the TEX typesetting language and the Meta-Font font generation package. It is not, however, an exhaustive reference.

- *LATEX HTML documentation:* **/usr/share/texmf/doc/latex/latex2e-html/**

This directory contains a large reference to the LATEX typesetting language. (This book itself was typeset using LATEX.)

- *HOWTOs:* **/usr/doc/HOWTO** or **/usr/share/doc/HOWTO**

HOWTOs are an excellent source of layman tutorials for setting up almost any kind of service you can imagine. RedHat seems to no longer ship this documentation with their base set of packages. It is worth listing the contents here to emphasize diversity of topics covered. These are mirrored all over the Internet, so you should have no problem finding them from a search engine (in particular, from http://www.linuxdoc.org/):

3Dfx-HOWTO	Finnish-HOWTO	Modem-HOWTO	Security-HOWTO
AX25-HOWTO	Firewall-HOWTO	Multi-Disk-HOWTO	Serial-HOWTO
Access-HOWTO	French-HOWTO	Multicast-HOWTO	Serial-Programming-HOWTO
Alpha-HOWTO	Ftape-HOWTO	NET-3-HOWTO	Shadow-Password-HOWTO
Assembly-HOWTO	GCC-HOWTO	NFS-HOWTO	Slovenian-HOWTO
Bash-Prompt-HOWTO	German-HOWTO	NIS-HOWTO	Software-Release-Practice-HOWTO
Benchmarking-HOWTO	Glibc2-HOWTO	Networking-Overview-HOWTO	Sound-HOWTO
Beowulf-HOWTO	HAM-HOWTO	Optical-Disk-HOWTO	Sound-Playing-HOWTO
BootPrompt-HOWTO	Hardware-HOWTO	Oracle-HOWTO	Spanish-HOWTO
Bootdisk-HOWTO	Hebrew-HOWTO	PCI-HOWTO	TeTeX-HOWTO
Busmouse-HOWTO	INDEX.html	PCMCIA-HOWTO	Text-Terminal-HOWTO

CD-Writing-HOWTO	INFO-SHEET	PPP-HOWTO	Thai-HOWTO
CDROM-HOWTO	IPCHAINS-HOWTO	PalmOS-HOWTO	Tips-HOWTO
COPYRIGHT	IPX-HOWTO	Parallel-Processing-HOWTO	UMSDOS-HOWTO
Chinese-HOWTO	IR-HOWTO	Pilot-HOWTO	UPS-HOWTO
Commercial-HOWTO	ISP-Hookup-HOWTO	Plug-and-Play-HOWTO	UUCP-HOWTO
Config-HOWTO	Installation-HOWTO	Polish-HOWTO	Unix-Internet-Fundamentals-HOWTO
Consultants-HOWTO	Intranet-Server-HOWTO	Portuguese-HOWTO	User-Group-HOWTO
Cyrillic-HOWTO	Italian-HOWTO	PostgreSQL-HOWTO	VAR-HOWTO
DNS-HOWTO	Java-CGI-HOWTO	Printing-HOWTO	VME-HOWTO
DOS-Win-to-Linux-HOWTO	Kernel-HOWTO	Printing-Usage-HOWTO	VMS-to-Linux-HOWTO
DOS-to-Linux-HOWTO	Keyboard-and-Console-HOWTO	Quake-HOWTO	Virtual-Services-HOWTO
DOSEMU-HOWTO	KickStart-HOWTO	README	WWW-HOWTO
Danish-HOWTO	LinuxDoc+Emacs+Ispell-HOWTO	RPM-HOWTO	WWW-mSQL-HOWTO
Distribution-HOWTO	META-FAQ	Reading-List-HOWTO	XFree86-HOWTO
ELF-HOWTO	MGR-HOWTO	Root-RAID-HOWTO	XFree86-Video-Timings-HOWTO
Emacspeak-HOWTO	MILO-HOWTO	SCSI-Programming-HOWTO	XWindow-User-HOWTO
Esperanto-HOWTO	MIPS-HOWTO	SMB-HOWTO	
Ethernet-HOWTO	Mail-HOWTO	SRM-HOWTO	

- *Mini HOWTOs:* **/usr/doc/HOWTO/mini** or **/usr/share/doc/HOWTO/mini**

These are smaller quick-start tutorials in the same vein (also available from http://www.linuxdoc.org/):

3-Button-Mouse	DHCPcd	Leased-Line	PLIP	Software-RAID
ADSL	DPT-Hardware-RAID	Linux+DOS+Win95+OS2	Partition	Soundblaster-AWE
ADSM-Backup	Diald	Linux+FreeBSD	Partition-Rescue	StarOffice
AI-Alife	Diskless	Linux+FreeBSD-mini-HOWTO	Path	Term-Firewall
Advocacy	Ext2fs-Undeletion	Linux+NT-Loader	Pre-Installation-Checklist	TkRat
Alsa-sound	Fax-Server	Linux+Win95	Process-Accounting	Token-Ring
Apache+SSL+PHP+fp	Firewall-Piercing	Loadlin+Win95	Proxy-ARP-Subnet	Ultra-DMA
Automount	GIS-GRASS	Loopback-Root-FS	Public-Web-Browser	Update
Backup-With-MSDOS	GTEK-BBS-550	Mac-Terminal	Qmail+MH	Upgrade
Battery-Powered	Hard-Disk-Upgrade	Mail-Queue	Quota	VAIO+Linux
Boca	INDEX	Mail2News	RCS	VPN
BogoMips	INDEX.html	Man-Page	README	Vesafb
Bridge	IO-Port-Programming	Modules	RPM+Slackware	Visual-Bell
Bridge+Firewall	IP-Alias	Multiboot-with-LILO	RedHat-CD	Windows-Modem-Sharing
Bzip2	IP-Masquerade	NCD-X-Terminal	Remote-Boot	WordPerfect
Cable-Modem	IP-Subnetworking	NFS-Root	Remote-X-Apps	X-Big-Cursor
Cipe+Masq	ISP-Connectivity	NFS-Root-Client	SLIP-PPP-Emulator	XFree86-XInside
Clock	Install-From-ZIP	Netrom-Node	Secure-POP+SSH	Xterm-Title
Coffee	Kerneld	Netscape+Proxy	Sendmail+UUCP	ZIP-Drive
Colour-ls	LBX	Netstation	Sendmail-Address-Rewrite	ZIP-Install
Cyrus-IMAP	LILO	News-Leafsite	Small-Memory	
DHCP	Large-Disk	Offline-Mailing	Software-Building	

- LINUX *documentation project:* **/usr/doc/LDP** or **/usr/share/doc/ldp**

The LDP project's home page is http://www.linuxdoc.org/. The LDP is a consolidation of HOWTOs, FAQs, several books, man pages, and more. The web site will have anything that is not already installed on your system.

- *Web documentation:* **/home/httpd/html** or **/var/www/html**

Some packages may install documentation here so that it goes online automatically if your web server is running. (In older distributions, this directory was /home/httpd/html.)

- *Apache reference:* **/home/httpd/html/manual** or **/var/www/html/manual**

Apache keeps this reference material online, so that it is the default web page shown when you install Apache for the first time. Apache is the most popular web server.

- *Manual pages:* **/usr/man/** or **/usr/share/man/**

Manual pages were discussed in Section 4.7. Other directory superstructures (see page 137) may contain man pages—on some other UNIX systems man pages are littered everywhere.

To convert a man page to PostScript (for printing or viewing), use, for example (for the cp command),

```
groff -Tps -mandoc /usr/man/man1/cp.1 > cp.ps ; gv cp.ps
groff -Tps -mandoc /usr/share/man/man1/cp.1 > cp.ps ; gv cp.ps
```

- *info pages:* **/usr/info/** or **/usr/share/info/**

Info pages were discussed in Section 4.8.

- *Individual package documentation:* **/usr/doc/*** or **/usr/share/doc/***

Finally, all packages installed on the system have their own individual documentation directory. A package foo will most probably have a documentation directory /usr/doc/foo (or /usr/share/doc/foo). This directory most often contains documentation released with the sources of the package, such as release information, feature news, example code, or FAQs. If you have a particular interest in a package, you should always scan its directory in /usr/doc (or /usr/share/doc) or, better still, download its source distribution.

Below are the /usr/doc (or /usr/share/doc) directories that contained more than a trivial amount of documentation for that package. In some cases, the package had complete references. (For example, the complete Python references were contained nowhere else.)

ImageMagick-5.2.2	gcc-c++-2.96	libtool-1.3.5	pmake-2.1.34
LPRng-3.6.24	ghostscript-5.50	libxml-1.8.9	pygtk-0.6.6
XFree86-doc-4.0.1	gimp-1.1.25	lilo-21.4.4	python-docs-1.5.2
bash-2.04	glibc-2.1.92	lsof-4.47	rxvt-2.6.3
bind-8.2.2_P5	gtk+-1.2.8	lynx-2.8.4	sane-1.0.3
cdrecord-1.9	gtk+-devel-1.2.8	ncurses-devel-5.1	sgml-tools-1.0.9
cvs-1.10.8	ipchains-1.3.9	nfs-utils-0.1.9.1	slang-devel-1.4.1
fetchmail-5.5.0	iproute-2.2.4	openjade-1.3	stylesheets-1.54.13rh
freetype-1.3.1	isdn4k-utils-3.1	openssl-0.9.5a	tin-1.4.4
gawk-3.0.6	krb5-devel-1.2.1	pam-0.72	uucp-1.06.1
gcc-2.96	libtiff-devel-3.5.5	pine-4.21	vim-common-5.7

Chapter 17

Overview of the UNIX Directory Layout

Here is an overview of how UNIX directories are structured. This is a simplistic and theoretical overview and not a specification of the LINUX file system. Chapter 35 contains proper details of permitted directories and the kinds of files allowed within them.

17.1 Packages

LINUX systems are divided into hundreds of small *packages*, each performing some logical group of operations. On LINUX, many small, self-contained packages interoperate to give greater functionality than would large, aggregated pieces of software. There is also no clear distinction between what is part of the operating system and what is an application—every function is just a package.

A software package on a RedHat type system is distributed in a single *RedHat Package Manager* (*RPM*) file that has a .rpm extension. On a *Debian* distribution, the equivalent is a .deb package file, and on the *Slackware* distribution there are Slackware .tgz files.

Each package will unpack as many files, which are placed all over the system. Packages generally do not create major directories but unpack files into existing, well-known, major directories.

Note that on a newly installed system there are no files anywhere that do not belong to some package.

17.2   UNIX Directory Superstructure

The root directory on a UNIX system typically looks like this:

```
drwxr-xr-x   2 root      root        2048 Aug 25 14:04 bin
drwxr-xr-x   2 root      root        1024 Sep 16 10:36 boot
drwxr-xr-x   7 root      root       35840 Aug 26 17:08 dev
drwxr-xr-x  41 root      root        4096 Sep 24 20:55 etc
drwxr-xr-x  24 root      root        1024 Sep 27 11:01 home
drwxr-xr-x   4 root      root        3072 May 19 10:05 lib
drwxr-xr-x   2 root      root       12288 Dec 15  1998 lost+found
drwxr-xr-x   7 root      root        1024 Jun  7 11:47 mnt
dr-xr-xr-x  80 root      root           0 Sep 16 10:36 proc
drwxr-xr-x   3 root      root        3072 Sep 23 23:41 sbin
drwxrwxrwt   5 root      root        4096 Sep 28 18:12 tmp
drwxr-xr-x  25 root      root        1024 May 29 10:23 usr
```

The `/usr` directory typically looks like this:

```
drwxr-xr-x   9 root      root        1024 May 15 11:49 X11R6
drwxr-xr-x   6 root      root       27648 Sep 28 17:18 bin
drwxr-xr-x   2 root      root        1024 May 13 16:46 dict
drwxr-xr-x 261 root      root        7168 Sep 26 10:55 doc
drwxr-xr-x   7 root      root        1024 Sep  3 08:07 etc
drwxr-xr-x   2 root      root        2048 May 15 10:02 games
drwxr-xr-x   4 root      root        1024 Mar 21  1999 i386-redhat-linux
drwxr-xr-x  36 root      root        7168 Sep 12 17:06 include
drwxr-xr-x   2 root      root        9216 Sep  7 09:05 info
drwxr-xr-x  79 root      root       12288 Sep 28 17:17 lib
drwxr-xr-x   3 root      root        1024 May 13 16:21 libexec
drwxr-xr-x  15 root      root        1024 May 13 16:35 man
drwxr-xr-x   2 root      root        4096 May 15 10:02 sbin
drwxr-xr-x  39 root      root        1024 Sep 12 17:07 share
drwxr-xr-x   3 root      root        1024 Sep  4 14:38 src
drwxr-xr-x   3 root      root        1024 Dec 16  1998 var
```

The `/usr/local` directory typically looks like this:

```
drwxr-xr-x   3 root      root        4096 Sep 27 13:16 bin
drwxr-xr-x   2 root      root        1024 Feb  6  1996 doc
drwxr-xr-x   4 root      root        1024 Sep  3 08:07 etc
drwxr-xr-x   2 root      root        1024 Feb  6  1996 games
drwxr-xr-x   5 root      root        1024 Aug 21 19:36 include
drwxr-xr-x   2 root      root        1024 Sep  7 09:08 info
drwxr-xr-x   9 root      root        2048 Aug 21 19:44 lib
drwxr-xr-x  12 root      root        1024 Aug  2  1998 man
drwxr-xr-x   2 root      root        1024 Feb  6  1996 sbin
drwxr-xr-x  15 root      root        1024 Sep  7 09:08 share
```

and the `/usr/X11R6` directory also looks similar. What is apparent here is that all these directories contain a similar set of subdirectories. This set of subdirectories is called a *directory superstructure* or *superstructure*. ⟍To my knowledge this is a new term not previously used by UNIX administrators.⟋

The superstructure always contains a `bin` and `lib` subdirectory, but almost all others are optional.

Each package will install under one of these superstructures, meaning that it will unpack many files into various subdirectories of the superstructure. A RedHat package would always install under the `/usr` or `/` superstructure, unless it is a graphical **X** Window System application, which installs under the `/usr/X11R6/` superstructure. Some very large applications may install under a `/opt/<package-name>` superstructure, and homemade packages usually install under the `/usr/local/` superstructure (`local` means *specific to this very machine*). The directory superstructure under which a package installs is often called the *installation prefix*. *Packages almost never install files across different superstructures.* ⟍Exceptions to this are configuration files which are mostly stored in `/etc/`.⟋

Typically, most of the system is under `/usr`. This directory can be read-only, since packages should never need to write to this directory—any writing is done under `/var` or `/tmp` (`/usr/var` and `/usr/tmp` are often just symlinked to `/var` or `/tmp`, respectively). The small amount under `/` that is not part of another superstructure (usually about 40 megabytes) performs essential system administration functions. These are commands needed to bring up or repair the system in the absence of `/usr`.

The list of superstructure subdirectories and their descriptions is as follows:

bin *Binary executables*. Usually all `bin` directories are in the `PATH` environment variable so that the shell will search all these directories for binaries.

sbin *Superuser binary executables*. These are programs for system administration only. Only the `root` will have these executables in their `PATH`.

lib *Libraries*. All other data needed by programs goes in here. Most packages have their own subdirectory under `lib` to store data files into. *Dynamically Linked Libraries* (*DLLs* or `.so` files.) ⟍Executable program code shared by more than one program in the `bin` directory to save disk space and memory.⟋ are stored directly in `lib`.

etc *Et cetera*. Configuration files.

var *Variable data*. Data files that are continually being re-created or updated.

doc *Documentation*. This directory is discussed in Chapter 16.

man *Manual pages*. This directory is discussed in Chapter 16.

info *Info pages*. This directory is discussed in Chapter 16.

share *Shared data*. Architecture-independent files. Files that are independent of the hardware platform go here. This allows them to be shared across different machines, even though those machines may have a different kind of processor altogether.

include C *header files*. These are for development.

src C *source files*. These are sources to the kernel or locally built packages.

tmp *Temporary files*. A convenient place for a running program to create a file for temporary use.

17.3   Linux on a Single 1.44 Megabyte Floppy Disk

You can get Linux to run on a 1.44 megabyte floppy disk if you trim all unneeded files off an old Slackware distribution with a 2.0.3x kernel. You can compile a small 2.0.3x kernel to about 400 kilobytes (compressed) (see Chapter 42). A file system can be reduced to 2–3 megabytes of absolute essentials and when compressed will fit into 1 megabyte. If the total is under 1.44 megabytes, then you have your Linux on one floppy. The file list might be as follows (includes all links):

```
/bin                /etc                  /lib                     /sbin               /var
/bin/sh             /etc/default          /lib/ld.so               /sbin/e2fsck        /var/adm
/bin/cat            /etc/fstab            /lib/libc.so.5           /sbin/fdisk         /var/adm/utmp
/bin/chmod          /etc/group            /lib/ld-linux.so.1       /sbin/fsck          /var/adm/cron
/bin/chown          /etc/host.conf        /lib/libcurses.so.1      /sbin/ifconfig      /var/spool
/bin/cp             /etc/hosts            /lib/libc.so.5.3.12      /sbin/iflink        /var/spool/uucp
/bin/pwd            /etc/inittab          /lib/libtermcap.so.2.0.8 /sbin/ifsetup       /var/spool/uucp/SYSLOG
/bin/dd             /etc/issue            /lib/libtermcap.so.2     /sbin/init          /var/spool/uucp/ERRLOG
/bin/df             /etc/utmp             /lib/libext2fs.so.2.3    /sbin/mke2fs        /var/spool/locks
/bin/du             /etc/networks         /lib/libcom_err.so.2     /sbin/mkfs          /var/tmp
/bin/free           /etc/passwd           /lib/libcom_err.so.2.0   /sbin/mkfs.minix    /var/run
/bin/gunzip         /etc/profile          /lib/libext2fs.so.2      /sbin/mklost+found  /var/run/utmp
/bin/gzip           /etc/protocols        /lib/libm.so.5.0.5       /sbin/mkswap
/bin/hostname       /etc/rc.d             /lib/libm.so.5           /sbin/mount         /home/user
/bin/login          /etc/rc.d/rc.0        /lib/cpp                 /sbin/route
/bin/ls             /etc/rc.d/rc.K                                 /sbin/shutdown      /mnt
/bin/mkdir          /etc/rc.d/rc.M                                 /sbin/swapoff
/bin/mv             /etc/rc.d/rc.S        /usr                     /sbin/swapon        /proc
/bin/ps             /etc/rc.d/rc.inet1    /usr/adm                 /sbin/telinit
/bin/rm             /etc/rc.d/rc.6        /usr/bin                 /sbin/umount        /tmp
/bin/stty           /etc/rc.d/rc.4        /usr/bin/less            /sbin/agetty
/bin/su             /etc/rc.d/rc.inet2    /usr/bin/more            /sbin/update        /dev/<various-devices>
/bin/sync           /etc/resolv.conf      /usr/bin/sleep           /sbin/reboot
/bin/zcat           /etc/services         /usr/bin/reset           /sbin/netcfg
/bin/dircolors      /etc/termcap          /usr/bin/zless           /sbin/killall15
/bin/mount          /etc/motd             /usr/bin/file            /sbin/fsck.minix
/bin/umount         /etc/magic            /usr/bin/fdformat        /sbin/halt
/bin/bash           /etc/DIR_COLORS       /usr/bin/strings         /sbin/badblocks
/bin/domainname     /etc/HOSTNAME         /usr/bin/zgrep           /sbin/kerneld
/bin/head           /etc/mtools           /usr/bin/nc              /sbin/fsck.ext2
/bin/kill           /etc/ld.so.cache      /usr/bin/which
/bin/tar            /etc/psdevtab         /usr/bin/grep
/bin/cut            /etc/mtab             /usr/sbin
/bin/uname          /etc/fastboot         /usr/sbin/showmount
/bin/ping                                 /usr/sbin/chroot
/bin/ln                                   /usr/spool
/bin/ash                                  /usr/tmp
```

Note that the `etc` directory differs from that of a RedHat distribution. The system startup files `/etc/rc.d` are greatly simplified under Slackware.

The /lib/modules directory has been stripped for the creation of this floppy. /lib/modules/2.0.36 would contain dynamically loadable kernel drivers (modules). Instead, all needed drivers are compiled into the kernel for simplicity (explained in Chapter 42).

At some point, try creating a single floppy distribution as an exercise. This task should be most instructive to a serious system administrator. At the very least, you should look through all of the commands in the bin directories and the sbin directories above and browse through the man pages of any that are unfamiliar.

The preceding file system comes from the morecram-1.3 package available from http://rute.sourceforge.net/morecram-1.3.tar.gz. It can be downloaded to provide a useful rescue and setup disk. Note that there are *many* such rescue disks available which are more current than morecram.

Chapter 18

UNIX Devices

UNIX was designed to allow transparent access to hardware devices across all CPU architectures. UNIX also supports the philosophy that all devices be accessible using the same set of command-line utilities.

18.1 Device Files

UNIX has a beautifully consistent method of allowing programs to access hardware. Under UNIX, every piece of hardware is a file. To demonstrate this novelty, try viewing the file /dev/hda (you will have to be `root` to run this command):

```
less -f /dev/hda
```

/dev/hda is not really a file at all. When you read from it, you are actually reading directly from the first physical hard disk of your machine. /dev/hda is known as a device file, and all of them are stored under the /dev directory.

Device files allow access to hardware. If you have a sound card installed and configured, you can try:

```
cat /dev/dsp > my_recording
```

Say something into your microphone and then type:

```
cat my_recording > /dev/dsp
```

The system will play out the sound through your speakers. (Note that this does not always work, since the recording volume or the recording speed may not be set correctly.)

If no programs are currently using your mouse, you can also try:

```
cat /dev/mouse
```

If you now move the mouse, the mouse protocol commands will be written directly to your screen (it will look like garbage). This is an easy way to see if your mouse is working, and is especially useful for testing a serial port. Occasionally this test doesn't work because some command has previously configured the serial port in some odd way. In that case, also try:

```
cu -s 1200 -l /dev/mouse
```

At a lower level, programs that access device files do so in two basic ways:

- They read and write to the device to send and retrieve bulk data (much like `less` and `cat` above).

- They use the **C** `ioctl` (*IO Control*) function to configure the device. (In the case of the sound card, this might set mono versus stereo, recording speed, or other parameters.)

Because every kind of device that one can think of (except for network cards) can be twisted to fit these two modes of operation, UNIX's scheme has endured since its inception and is the universal method of accessing hardware.

18.2   Block and Character Devices

Hardware devices can generally be categorized into random access devices like disk and tape drives, and serial devices like mouse devices, sound cards, and terminals.

Random access devices are usually accessed in large contiguous blocks of data that are stored persistently. They are read from in discrete units (for most disks, 1024 bytes at a time). These are known as *block* devices. Running an `ls -l /dev/hda` shows a `b` on the far left of the listing, which means that your hard disk is a block device:

```
brw-r-----   1 root     disk       3,   64 Apr 27  1995 /dev/hdb
```

Serial devices, on the other hand, are accessed one byte at a time. Data can be read or written only once. For example, after a byte has been read from your mouse, the same byte cannot be read by some other program. Serial devices are called *character* devices and are indicated by a `c` on the far left of the listing. Your `/dev/dsp` (*Digital Signal Processor*—that is, your sound card) device looks like:

142

```
crw-r--r--   1 root      sys        14,   3 Jul 18  1994 /dev/dsp
```

18.3 *Major* and *Minor* Device Numbers

Devices are divided into sets called *major device numbers*. For instance, all SCSI disks are *major number 8*. Further, each individual device has a *minor device number* like /dev/sda, which is *minor device 0*. Major and minor device numbers identify the device to the kernel. The file name of the device is arbitrary and is chosen for convenience and consistency. You can see the major and minor device number (8,   0) in the ls listing for /dev/sda:

```
brw-rw----   1 root      disk        8,   0 May  5  1998 /dev/sda
```

18.4 Common Device Names

A list of common devices and their descriptions follows.   The major numbers are shown in parentheses.   The complete reference for devices is the file /usr/src/linux/Documentation/devices.txt.

/dev/hd?? hd stands for *hard disk*, but refers here only to *IDE* devices—that is, common hard disks. The first letter after the hd dictates the physical disk drive:

/dev/hda (3) First drive, or primary master.

/dev/hdb (3) Second drive, or primary slave.

/dev/hdc (22) Third drive, or secondary master.

/dev/hdd (22) Fourth drive, or secondary slave.

When accessing any of these devices (with, say, less /dev/hda), you would be reading raw from the actual physical disk starting at the first sector of the first track, sequentially, until the last sector of the last track.

Partitions ⬎With all operating systems, disk drives are divided into sections called *partitions*. A typical disk might have 2 to 10 partitions. Each partition acts as a whole disk on its own, giving the effect of having more than one disk. For instance, you might have Windows installed on one partition and LINUX⬦ installed on another. More details come in Chapter 19.⬉ are named /dev/hda1, /dev/hda2, etc., indicating the first, second, etc., partition on physical drive a.

/dev/sd?? **(8)** `sd` stands for *SCSI disk,* the high-end drives mostly used by servers. `sda` is the first physical disk probed, and so on. Probing goes by SCSI ID and has a system completely different from that of IDE devices. `/dev/sda1` is the first partition on the first drive, etc.

/dev/ttyS? **(4)** These are serial devices numbered from 0 up. `/dev/ttyS0` is your first serial port (COM1 under MS-DOS or Windows). If you have a multiport card, these can go to 32, 64, and up.

/dev/psaux **(10)** PS/2 mouse.

/dev/mouse A symlink to `/dev/ttyS0` or `/dev/psaux`. Other mouse devices are also supported.

/dev/modem A symlink to `/dev/ttyS1` or whatever port your modem is on.

/dev/cua? **(4)** Identical to `ttyS?` but now fallen out of use.

/dev/fd? **(2)** *Floppy disk.* `fd0` is equivalent to your `A:` drive and `fd1` your `B:` drive. The `fd0` and `fd1` devices autodetect the format of the floppy disk, but you can explicitly specify a higher density by using a device name like `/dev/fd0H1920`, which gives you access to 1.88 MB, formatted, 3.5-inch floppies. Other floppy devices are shown in Table 18.1.

See Section 19.3.4 on how to format these devices.

/dev/par? **(6)** *Parallel port.* `/dev/par0` is your first parallel port or LPT1 under DOS.

/dev/lp? **(6)** *Line printer.* Identical to `/dev/par?`.

/dev/urandom *Random* number generator. Reading from this device gives pseudo-random numbers.

/dev/st? **(9)** *SCSI tape.* SCSI backup tape drive.

/dev/zero **(1)** Produces zero bytes, and as many of them as you need. This is useful if you need to generate a block of zeros for some reason. Use `dd` (see Section 18.5.2) to read a specific number of zeros.

/dev/null **(1)** *Null device.* Reads nothing. Anything you write to the device is discarded. This is very useful for discarding output.

/dev/pd? *Parallel port IDE disk.*

/dev/pcd? *Parallel port ATAPI CD-ROM.*

/dev/pf? *Parallel port ATAPI disk.*

/dev/sr? *SCSI CD-ROM.*

/dev/scd? *SCSI CD-ROM (Identical, alternate name).*

Table 18.1 Floppy device names

Floppy devices are named /dev/fd*lmnnnn*		
l	0	A: drive
	1	B: drive
m	d	"double density" 360 KB or 5.25 inch
	h	"high density" 1.2 MB or 5.25 inch
	q	"quad density" 5.25 inch
	D	"double density" 720 KB or 3.5 inch
	H	"high density" 1.44 MB or 3.5 inch
	E	Extra density 3.5 inch.
	u	Any 3.5-inch floppy. Note that u now replaces D, H, and E, thus leaving it up to the user to decide if the floppy has enough density for the format.
nnnn	360 410 420 720 800 820 830 880 1040 1120 1200 1440 1476 1494 1600 1680 1722 1743 1760 1840 1920 2880 3200 3520 3840	The size of the format. With D, H, and E, 3.5-inch floppies have devices only for the sizes that are likely to work. For instance, there is no /dev/fd0D1440 because double density disks won't manage 1440 KB. /dev/fd0H1440 and /dev/fd0H1920 are probably the ones you are most interested in.

/dev/sg? *SCSI generic.* This is a general-purpose SCSI command interface for devices like scanners.

/dev/fb? **(29)** *Frame buffer.* This represents the kernel's attempt at a graphics driver.

/dev/cdrom A symlink to /dev/hda, /dev/hdb, or /dev/hdc. It can also be linked to your SCSI CD-ROM.

/dev/ttyI? *ISDN modems.*

/dev/tty? **(4)** *Virtual console.* This is the terminal device for the virtual console itself and is numbered /dev/tty1 through /dev/tty63.

/dev/tty?? **(3) and /dev/pty??** **(2)** Other *TTY* devices used for emulating a terminal. These are called *pseudo-TTYs* and are identified by two lowercase letters and numbers, such as ttyq3. To nondevelopers, these are mostly of theoretical interest.

The file /usr/src/linux/Documentation/devices.txt also has this to say (quoted verbatim):

Recommended links

It is recommended that these links exist on all systems:

/dev/core	/proc/kcore	symbolic	Backward compatibility
/dev/ramdisk	ram0	symbolic	Backward compatibility
/dev/ftape	qft0	symbolic	Backward compatibility
/dev/bttv0	video0	symbolic	Backward compatibility
/dev/radio	radio0	symbolic	Backward compatibility
/dev/i2o*	/dev/i2o/*	symbolic	Backward compatibility
/dev/scd?	sr?	hard	Alternate SCSI CD-ROM name

Locally defined links

The following links may be established locally to conform to the configuration of the system. This is merely a tabulation of existing practice, and does not constitute a recommendation. However, if they exist, they should have the following uses:

/dev/mouse	mouse port	symbolic	Current mouse device
/dev/tape	tape device	symbolic	Current tape device
/dev/cdrom	CD-ROM device	symbolic	Current CD-ROM device
/dev/cdwriter	CD-writer	symbolic	Current CD-writer device
/dev/scanner	scanner	symbolic	Current scanner device
/dev/modem	modem port	symbolic	Current dialout device
/dev/root	root device	symbolic	Current root file system
/dev/swap	swap device	symbolic	Current swap device

/dev/modem should not be used for a modem which supports dial-in as well as dialout, as it tends to cause lock file problems. If it exists, /dev/modem should point to the appropriate primary TTY device (the use of the alternate callout devices is deprecated).

For SCSI devices, /dev/tape and /dev/cdrom should point to the "cooked" devices (/dev/st* and /dev/sr*, respectively), whereas /dev/cdwriter and /dev/scanner should point to the appropriate generic SCSI devices (/dev/sg*).

/dev/mouse may point to a primary serial TTY device, a hardware mouse device, or a socket for a mouse driver program (e.g. /dev/gpmdata).

Sockets and pipes

Non-transient sockets and named pipes may exist in /dev. Common entries are:

/dev/printer	socket	lpd local socket
/dev/log	socket	syslog local socket
/dev/gpmdata	socket	mouse multiplexer

18.5   dd, tar, and Tricks with Block Devices

dd probably originally stood for *disk dump*. It is actually just like cat except it can read and write in discrete blocks. It essentially reads and writes between devices while converting the data in some way. It is generally used in one of these ways:

```
dd if=<in-file> of=<out-file> [bs=<block-size>] \
     [count=<number-of-blocks>] [seek=<output-offset>] \
     [skip=<input-offset>]

dd if=<in-file> [bs=<block-size>] [count=<number-of-blocks>] \
     [skip=<input-offset>] > <outfile>

dd of=<out-file> [bs=<block-size>] [count=<number-of-blocks>] \
     [seek=<output-offset>] < <infile>
```

To use dd, you must specify an input file and an output file with the if= and of= options. If the of= option is omitted, then dd writes to stdout. If the if= option is omitted, then dd reads from stdin. � If you are confused, remember that dd thinks of *in* and *out* with respect to itself.⬆

Note that dd is an unforgiving and destructive command that should be used with caution.

18.5.1   Creating boot disks from boot images

To create a new RedHat boot floppy, find the boot.img file on ftp.redhat.com, and with a new floppy, run:

```
dd if=boot.img of=/dev/fd0
```

This command writes the raw disk image directly to the floppy disk. All distributions will have similar disk images for creating installation floppies (and sometimes rescue floppies).

18.5.2   Erasing disks

If you have ever tried to repartition a LINUX⬆ disk back into a DOS/Windows disk, you will know that DOS/Windows FDISK has bugs in it that prevent it from recreating the partition table. A quick

```
dd if=/dev/zero of=/dev/hda bs=1024 count=10240
```

will write zeros to the first 10 megabytes of your first IDE drive. This will wipe out the partition table as well as any file system information and give you a "brand new" disk.

To zero a floppy disk is just as easy:

```
dd if=/dev/zero of=/dev/fd0 bs=1024 count=1440
```

Even writing zeros to a floppy may not be sufficient. Specialized equipment can probably still read magnetic media after it has been erased several times. If, however, you write random bits to the floppy, it becomes completely impossible to determine what was on it:

```
mknod /dev/urandom c 1 9
for i in 1 2 3 4 ; do
    dd if=/dev/urandom of=/dev/fd0 bs=1024 count=1440
done
```

18.5.3 Identifying data on raw disks

Here is a nice trick to find out something about a hard drive:

```
dd if=/dev/hda1 count=1 bs=512 | file -
```

gives `x86 boot sector.`

To discover what a floppy disk is, try

```
dd if=/dev/fd0 count=1 bs=512 | file -
```

which gives `x86 boot sector, system )k?/bIHC, FAT (12 bit)` for DOS floppies.

18.5.4 Duplicating a disk

If you have two IDE drives that are of identical size, and provided that you are sure they contain no bad sectors and *provided neither are mounted*, you can run

```
dd if=/dev/hdc of=/dev/hdd
```

to copy the entire disk and avoid having to install an operating system from scratch. It doesn't matter what is on the original (Windows, LINUX, or whatever) since each sector is identically duplicated; the new system will work perfectly.

(If they are not the same size, you will have to use `tar` or `mirrordir` to replicate the file system exactly.)

18.5.5   Backing up to floppies

You can use tar to back up to *any* device. Consider periodic backups to an ordinary IDE drive instead of a tape. Here we back up to the secondary slave:

```
tar -cvzf /dev/hdd /bin /boot /dev /etc /home /lib /sbin /usr /var
```

tar can also back up across multiple floppy disks:

```
tar -cvMf /dev/fd0 /home/simon
```

18.5.6   Tape backups

tar traditionally backs up onto tape drives. The commands

```
mt -f /dev/st0 rewind
tar -cvf /dev/st0 /home
```

rewind scsi tape 0 and archive the /home directory onto it. You should not try to use compression with tape drives because they are error prone, and a single error could make the entire archive unrecoverable. The mt command stands for magnetic tape and controls generic SCSI tape devices. See also mt(1).

18.5.7   Hiding program output, creating blocks of zeros

If you don't want to see any program output, just append > /dev/null to the command. For example, we aren't often interested in the output of make. ↘make is discussed later.↖ Here we absorb everything save for error messages.

```
make > /dev/null
```

Then, of course, we can absorb all output *including* error messages with either

```
make >& /dev/null
```

or

```
make > /dev/null 2>&1
```

The device /dev/null finds innumerable uses in shell scripting to suppress the output of a command or to feed a command dummy (empty) input. /dev/null is a *safe* file from a security point of view. It is often used when a file is required for some feature in a configuration script, and you would like the particular feature disabled. For instance, specifying the users shell to /dev/null inside the password file will *certainly* prevent insecure use of a shell, and is an explicit way of saying that that account does *not* allow shell logins.

You can also use /dev/null to create a file containing nothing:

```
cat /dev/null > myfile
```

or alternatively, to create a file containing only zeros. Try

```
dd if=/dev/zero bs=1024 count=<number-of-kilobytes> > myfile
```

18.6   Creating Devices with mknod and /dev/MAKEDEV

Although all devices are listed in the /dev directory, you can create a device anywhere in the file system by using the mknod command:

```
mknod [-m <mode>] <file-name> [b|c] <major-number> <minor-number>
```

The letters b and c are for creating a block or character device, respectively.

To demonstrate, try

```
mknod -m 0600 ~/my-floppy b 2 0
ls -al /dev/fd0 ~/my-floppy
```

my-floppy can be used just like /dev/fd0

Note carefully the *mode* (i.e., the permissions) of /dev/fd0. /dev/fd0 should be readable and writable only to root and to users belonging to the floppy group, since we obviously don't want an arbitrary user to be able to log in (remotely) and overwrite a floppy disk.

In fact, this is the reason for having devices represented as files in the first place. UNIX files naturally support group access control, and therefore so do devices.

To create devices that are missing from your /dev directory (some esoteric devices will not be present by default), simply look up the device's major and minor number in /usr/src/linux/Documentation/devices.txt and use the mknod command. This procedure is, however, somewhat tedious, and the script /dev/MAKEDEV is usually available for convenience. *You must be in the* /dev *directory before you run this script.*

Typical usage of MAKEDEV is

```
cd /dev
./MAKEDEV -v fd0
./MAKEDEV -v fd1
```

to create a complete set of floppy disk devices.

The man page for MAKEDEV contains more details. In particular, it states:

Note that programs giving the error "ENOENT: No such file or directory" normally means that the device file is missing, whereas "ENODEV: No such device" normally means the kernel does not have the driver configured or loaded.

Chapter 19

Partitions, File Systems, Formatting, Mounting

19.1 The Physical Disk Structure

Physical disks are divided into partitions. ↘See **/dev/hd??** under Section 18.4.↖ Information as to how the disk is partitioned up is stored in a *partition table*, which is a small area of the disk separate from the partitions themselves.

19.1.1 Cylinders, heads, and sectors

The physical drive itself usually comprises several actual disks of which both sides are used. The sides are labelled 0, 1, 2, 3, and so on, and are also called *heads* because one magnetic head per side does the actual reading and writing. Each side/head has tracks, and each track is divided into segments called *sectors*. Each sector typically holds 512 bytes. The total amount of space on the drive in bytes is therefore:

512 × (sectors-per-track) × (tracks-per-side) × (number-of-sides)

A single track and all the tracks of the same diameter (on all the sides) are called a *cylinder*. Disks are normally talked about in terms of "cylinders and sectors" instead of "sides, tracks, and sectors." Partitions are (usually) divided along cylinder boundaries. Hence, disks do not have arbitrarily sized partitions; rather, the size of the partition is usually a multiple of the amount of data held in a single cylinder. Partitions therefore have a definite inner and outer diameter. Figure 19.1 illustrates the layout of a hard disk.

153

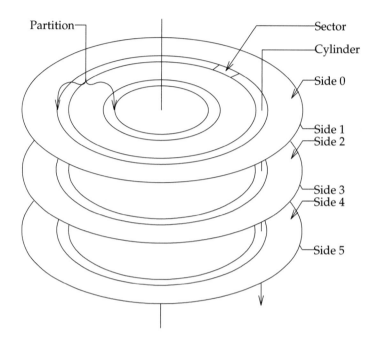

Figure 19.1 Hard drive platters and sector layout

19.1.2   Large Block Addressing

The system above is quite straightforward except for the curious limitation that partition tables have only 10 bits in which to store the partition's cylinder offset. This means that no disk can have more than 1024 cylinders. This limitation was overcome by multiplying up the number of heads in software to reduce the number of cylinders, Called *LBA* (Large Block Addressing) mode. hence portraying a disk of impossible proportions. The user, however, need never be concerned that the physical disk is completely otherwise.

19.1.3   Extended partitions

The partition table has room for only four partitions. For more partitions, one of these four partitions can be divided into many smaller partitions, called *logical* partitions. The original four are then called *primary* partitions. If a primary partition is subdivided in this way, it is known as an *extended primary* or *extended* partition. Typically, the first primary partition will be small (/dev/hda1, say). The second primary partition will fill the rest of the disk as an extended partition (/dev/hda2, say). In this case, the entries in the partition table of /dev/hda3 and /dev/hda4 will be blank. The extended partition can be subdivided repeatedly to give /dev/hda5, /dev/hda6, and so on.

19.2   Partitioning a New Disk

A new disk has no partition information. Typing fdisk will start an interactive partitioning utility. The command

```
fdisk /dev/hda
```

fdisks your primary master.

What follows is an example of the partitioning of a new hard drive. Most distributions these days have a simpler graphical system for creating partitions, so using fdisk will not be necessary at installation time. However, adding a new drive or transferring/copying a LINUX system to new hardware will require partitioning.

On UNIX, each partition has its own *directory. Files under one directory might be stored on a different disk or a different partition to files in another directory.* Typically, the /var directory (and all subdirectories beneath it) is stored on a different partition from the /usr directory (and all subdirectories beneath it).

Table 19.2 offers a general guideline as to how a server machine should be set up (with home computers, you can be far more liberal—most home PCs can do with merely a swap and / partition.). When you install a new server, your distribution should allow you to customize your partitions to match this table.

If another operating system is already installed in the first partition, you can type p and might see:

```
Command (m for help): p

Disk /dev/hda: 255 heads, 63 sectors, 788 cylinders
Units = cylinders of 16065 * 512 bytes

   Device Boot    Start      End    Blocks   Id  System
/dev/hda1             1      312   2506108+   c  Win95 FAT32 (LBA)
```

In such a case, you can just start adding further partitions.

The exact same procedure applies in the case of SCSI drives. The only difference is that /dev/hd? changes to /dev/sd?. (See Chapter 42 for SCSI device driver information.)

Here is a partitioning session with fdisk:

```
[root@cericon /root]# fdisk /dev/hda
Device contains neither a valid DOS partition table, nor Sun or SGI disklabel
```

Table 19.1 Which directories should have their own partitions, and their partitions' sizes

Directory	Size (Megabytes)	Why?
swap	Twice the size of your RAM	This is where memory is drawn from when you run out. The swap partition gives programs the impression that you have more RAM than you actually do, by swapping data in and out of this partition.
		Swap partitions cannot be over 128 MB, but you can have many of them. This limitation has been removed in newer kernels.
		Disk access is obviously slow compared to direct RAM, but when a lot of idle programs are running, swapping to disk allows more real RAM for needy programs.
/boot	5–10	This directory need not be on a different partition to your / partition (below). Whatever you choose, there must be no chance that a file under /boot could span sectors that are over the 1024 cylinder boundary (i.e., outside of the first 500 megabytes of your hard drive). This is why /boot (or /) is often made the first primary partition of the hard drive. If this requirment is not met, you get the famous LI prompt on a nonbooting system. See Section 31.2.4.
/var	100–1000	Here is variable data, like log files, mail spool files, database files, and your web proxy cache (web cache and databases may need to be *much* bigger though). For newer distributions, this directory also contains any local data that this site serves (like FTP files or web pages). If you are going to be using a web cache, either store the stuff in a separate partition/disk or make your /var partition huge. Also, log files can grow to enormous sizes when there are problems. You don't want a full or corrupted /var partition to effect the rest of your disk. This is why it goes in its own partition.
/tmp	50	Here is temporary data. Programs access this frequently and need it to be fast. It goes in a separate partition because programs *really* need to create a temporary file sometimes, and this should not be affected by other partitions becoming full. This partition is also more likely to be corrupted.
/usr	500–1500	Here is your distribution (Debian⊙, RedHat, Mandrake, etc.). It can be mounted read-only. If you have a disk whose write access can physically be disabled (like some SCSI drives), then you can put /usr on a separate drive. Doing so will make for a much more secure system. Since /usr is stock standard, this is the partition you can most afford to lose. Note however that /usr/local/ may be important to you—possibly link this elsewhere.
/home	Remainder of disk	Here are your users' home directories. For older distributions, this directory also contains any local data that this site serves (like FTP files or web pages).
/	50–100	Anything not in any of the other directories is directly under your / directory. These are the /bin (5MB), (possibly) /boot (3MB), /dev (0.1MB), /etc (4MB), /lib (20MB), /mnt (0MB), /proc (0MB), and /sbin (4MB) directories. They are essential for the system to start up and contain minimal utilities for recovering the other partitions in an emergency. As stated above, if the /boot directory is in a separate partition, then / must be below the 1024 cylinder boundary (i.e., within the first 500 megabytes of your hard drive).

```
      Building a new DOS disklabel. Changes will remain in memory only,
      until you decide to write them. After that, of course, the previous
 5    content won't be recoverable.
```

First, we use the p option to print current partitions—

```
      Command (m for help): p

      Disk /dev/hda: 255 heads, 63 sectors, 788 cylinders
      Units = cylinders of 16065 * 512 bytes
 5
         Device Boot    Start      End    Blocks    Id  System
```

—of which there are clearly none. Now n lets us add a new partition:

```
Command (m for help): n
Command action
   e   extended
   p   primary partition (1-4)
p
```

We want to define the first physical partition starting at the first cylinder:

```
Partition number (1-4): 1
First cylinder (1-788, default 1): 1
```

We would like an 80-megabyte partition. fdisk calculates the last cylinder automatically with:

```
Last cylinder or +size or +sizeM or +sizeK (1-788, default 788): +80M
```

Our next new partition will span the rest of the disk and will be an extended partition:

```
Command (m for help): n
Command action
   e   extended
   p   primary partition (1-4)
e
Partition number (1-4): 2
First cylinder (12-788, default 12): 12
Last cylinder or +size or +sizeM or +sizeK (12-788, default 788): 788
```

Our remaining logical partitions fit within the extended partition:

```
Command (m for help): n
Command action
   l   logical (5 or over)
   p   primary partition (1-4)
l
First cylinder (12-788, default 12): 12
Last cylinder or +size or +sizeM or +sizeK (12-788, default 788): +64M

Command (m for help): n
Command action
   l   logical (5 or over)
   p   primary partition (1-4)
l
First cylinder (21-788, default 21): 21
Last cylinder or +size or +sizeM or +sizeK (21-788, default 788): +100M
```

```
   Command (m for help): n
   Command action
      l    logical (5 or over)
20    p    primary partition (1-4)
   l
   First cylinder (34-788, default 34): 34
   Last cylinder or +size or +sizeM or +sizeK (34-788, default 788): +200M

25 Command (m for help): n
   Command action
      l    logical (5 or over)
      p    primary partition (1-4)
   l
30 First cylinder (60-788, default 60): 60
   Last cylinder or +size or +sizeM or +sizeK (60-788, default 788): +1500M

   Command (m for help): n
   Command action
35    l    logical (5 or over)
      p    primary partition (1-4)
   l
   First cylinder (252-788, default 252): 252
   Last cylinder or +size or +sizeM or +sizeK (252-788, default 788): 788
```

The default *partition type* is a single byte that the operating system will look at to determine what kind of file system is stored there. Entering l lists all known types:

```
   Command (m for help): l

      0  Empty           16  Hidden FAT16    61  SpeedStor       a6  OpenBSD
      [...]
5    8  AIX             4d  QNX4.x          82  Linux swap      db  CP/M / CTOS / .
      9  AIX bootable    4e  QNX4.x 2nd part 83  Linux           e1  DOS access
      [...]
     12  Compaq diagnost 56  Golden Bow      a5  BSD/386         ff  BBT
     14  Hidden FAT16 <3 5c  Priam Edisk
```

fdisk will set the type to Linux by default. We only need to explicitly set the type of the swap partition:

```
   Command (m for help): t
   Partition number (1-9): 5
   Hex code (type L to list codes): 82
   Changed system type of partition 5 to 82 (Linux swap)
```

Now we need to set the bootable flag on the first partition, since BIOS's will not boot a disk without at least one bootable partition:

```
   Command (m for help): a
```

```
Partition number (1-10): 1
```

Displaying our results gives:

```
Command (m for help): p

Disk /dev/hda: 255 heads, 63 sectors, 788 cylinders
Units = cylinders of 16065 * 512 bytes

   Device Boot    Start      End    Blocks   Id  System
/dev/hda1   *         1       11     88326   83  Linux
/dev/hda2            12      788  6241252+    5  Extended
/dev/hda5            12       20     72261   82  Linux swap
/dev/hda6            21       33    104391   83  Linux
/dev/hda7            34       59   208813+   83  Linux
/dev/hda8            60      251  1542208+   83  Linux
/dev/hda9           252      788   4313421   83  Linux
```

At this point, nothing has been committed to disk. We write it as follows (**Note:** this step is irreversible):

```
Command (m for help): w
The partition table has been altered!

Calling ioctl() to re-read partition table.
Syncing disks.

WARNING: If you have created or modified any DOS 6.x
partitions, please see the fdisk manual page for additional
information.
```

Even having written the partition, `fdisk` may give a warning that the kernel does not know about the new partitions. This happens if the disk is already in use. In this case, you will need to reboot. For the above partition, the kernel will give the following information at boot time:

```
Partition check:
 hda: hda1 hda2 < hda5 hda6 hda7 hda8 hda9 >
```

The < ... > shows that partition hda2 is extended and is subdivided into five smaller partitions.

19.3   Formatting Devices

19.3.1   File systems

Disk drives are usually read in blocks of 1024 bytes (two sectors). From the point of view of anyone accessing the device, blocks are stored consecutively—there is no need to think about cylinders or heads—so that any program can read the disk as though it were a linear tape. Try

```
less /dev/hda1
less -f /dev/hda1
```

Now a complex directory structure with many files of arbitrary size needs to be stored in this contiguous partition. This poses the problem of what to do with a file that gets deleted and leaves a data "hole" in the partition, or a file that has to be split into parts because there is no single contiguous space big enough to hold it. Files also have to be indexed in such a way that they can be found quickly (consider that there can easily be 10,000 files on a system). UNIX's symbolic/hard links and devices files also have to be stored.

To cope with this complexity, operating systems have a format for storing files called the *file system* (fs). Like MS-DOS with its FAT file system or Windows with its FAT32 file system, LINUX has a file system called the *2nd extended file system*, or ext2.

Whereas ext2 is the traditional native LINUX file system, three other native file systems have recently become available: SGI's XFS file system, the ext3fs file system, and the reiserfs file system. These three support fast and reliable recovery in the event of a power failure, using a feature called *journaling*. A journaling file system prewrites disk alterations to a separate log to facilitate recovery if the file system reaches an incoherent state. (See Section 19.5.)

19.3.2   `mke2fs`

To create a file system on a blank partition, use the command mkfs (or one of its variants). To create a LINUX ext2 file system on the first partition of the primary master run:

```
mkfs -t ext2 -c /dev/hda1
```

or, alternatively

```
mke2fs -c /dev/hda1
```

The -c option means to check for bad blocks by reading through the entire disk first.

This is a *read-only* check and causes unreadable blocks to be flagged as such and not
be used. To do a full *read-write* check, use the `badblocks` command. This command
writes to and verifies every bit in that partition. Although the −c option should always
be used on a new disk, doing a full read-write test is probably pedantic. For the above
partition, this test would be:

```
badblocks -o blocks-list.txt -s -w /dev/hda1 88326
mke2fs -l blocks-list.txt /dev/hda1
```

After running `mke2fs`, we will find that

```
dd if=/dev/hda1 count=8 bs=1024 | file -
```

gives `Linux/i386 ext2 filesystem`.

19.3.3   Formatting floppies and removable drives

New kinds of removable devices are being released all the time. Whatever the device,
the same formatting procedure is used. Most are IDE compatible, which means you
can access them through `/dev/hd?`.

The following examples are a parallel port IDE disk drive, a parallel port ATAPI
CD-ROM drive, a parallel port ATAPI disk drive, and your "A:" floppy drive, respectively:

```
mke2fs -c /dev/pda1
mke2fs -c /dev/pcd0
mke2fs -c /dev/pf0
mke2fs -c /dev/fd0
```

Actually, using an `ext2` file system on a floppy drive wastes a lot of space.
Rather, use an MS-DOS file system, which has less overhead and can be read by anyone
(see Section 19.3.4).

You often will not want to be bothered with partitioning a device that is only
going to have one partition anyway. In this case, you can use the whole disk as one
partition. An example is a removable IDE drive as a primary slave ⬊*LS120* disks and *Jazz*
drives as well as removable IDE brackets are commercial examples.⬉:

```
mke2fs -c /dev/hdb
```

19.3.4   Creating MS-DOS floppies

Accessing files on MS-DOS/Windows floppies is explained in Section 4.16. The command `mformat A:` will format a floppy, but this command merely initializes the file system; it does not check for bad blocks or do the low-level formatting necessary to reformat floppies to odd storage sizes.

A command, called `superformat`, from the `fdutils` package ⟍You may have to find this package on the Internet. See Chapter 24 for how to compile and install source packages.⟍ formats a floppy in any way that you like. A more common (but less thorough) command is `fdformat` from the `util-linux` package. It verifies that each track is working properly and compensates for variations between the mechanics of different floppy drives. To format a 3.5-inch 1440-KB, 1680-KB, or 1920-KB floppy, respectively, run:

```
cd /dev
./MAKEDEV -v fd0
superformat /dev/fd0H1440
superformat /dev/fd0H1690
superformat /dev/fd0H1920
```

Note that these are "long file name" floppies (VFAT), not old 13-character-filename MS-DOS floppies.

Most users would have only ever used a 3.5-inch floppy as a "1.44 MB" floppy. In fact, the disk media and magnetic head can write much more densely than this specification, allowing 24 sectors per track to be stored instead of the usual 18. This is why there is more than one device file for the same drive. Some inferior disks will, however, give errors when trying to format that densely—`superformat` will show errors when this happens.

See Table 18.1 on page 145 for the naming conventions of floppy devices, and their many respective formats.

19.3.5   `mkswap`, `swapon`, and `swapoff`

The `mkswap` command formats a partition to be used as a swap device. For our disk,

```
mkswap -c /dev/hda5
```

`-c` has the same meaning as previously—to check for bad blocks.

Once the partition is formatted, the kernel can be signalled to use that partition as a swap partition with

```
swapon /dev/hda5
```

and to stop usage,

```
swapoff /dev/hda5
```

Swap partitions cannot be larger than 128 MB, although you can have as many of them as you like. You can `swapon` many different partitions simultaneously.

19.4 Device Mounting

The question of how to access files on an arbitrary disk (without `C:`, `D:`, etc., notation, of course) is answered here.

In UNIX, there is only one root file system that spans many disks. Different directories may actually exist on a different physical disk.

> *To bind a directory to a physical device (like a partition or a CD-ROM) so that the device's file system can be read is called* mounting *the device.*

The `mount` command is used as follows:

```
mount [-t <fstype>] [-o <option>] <device> <directory>
umount [-f] [<device>|<directory>]
```

The `-t` option specifies the kind of file system, and can often be omitted since LINUX can autodetect most file systems. `<fstype>` can be one of `adfs`, `affs`, `autofs`, `coda`, `coherent`, `devpts`, `efs`, `ext2`, `hfs`, `hpfs`, `iso9660`, `minix`, `msdos`, `ncpfs`, `nfs`, `ntfs`, `proc`, `qnx4`, `romfs`, `smbfs`, `sysv`, `ufs`, `umsdos`, `vfat`, `xenix`, or `xiafs`. The most common file systems are discussed below. The `-o` option is not usually used. See `mount`(8) for all possible options.

19.4.1 Mounting CD-ROMs

Put your distribution CD-ROM disk into your CD-ROM drive and mount it with

```
ls /mnt/cdrom
mount -t iso9660 -o ro /dev/hdb /mnt/cdrom
```

(Your CD-ROM might be `/dev/hdc` or `/dev/hdd`, however—in this case you should make a soft link `/dev/cdrom` pointing to the correct device. Your distribution may also prefer `/cdrom` over `/mnt/cdrom`.) Now `cd` to your `/mnt/cdrom` directory. You will notice that it is no longer empty, but "contains" the CD-ROM's files. What is happening is that the kernel is redirecting all lookups from the directory /mnt/cdrom to read from the CD-ROM disk. You can browse around these files as though they were already copied onto your hard drive. This is one of the things that makes UNIX cool.

When you are finished with the CD-ROM *unmount* it with

```
umount /dev/hdb
eject /dev/hdb
```

19.4.2   Mounting floppy disks

Instead of using mtools, you could mount the floppy disk with

```
mkdir /mnt/floppy
mount -t vfat /dev/fd0 /mnt/floppy
```

or, for older MS-DOS floppies, use

```
mkdir /mnt/floppy
mount -t msdos /dev/fd0 /mnt/floppy
```

Before you eject the floppy, it is essential to run

```
umount /dev/fd0
```

in order that cached data is committed to the disk. Failing to umount a floppy before ejecting will probably corrupt its file system.

19.4.3   Mounting Windows and NT partitions

Mounting a Windows partition can also be done with the vfat file system, and NT partitions (read-only) with the ntfs file system. VAT32 is also supported (and autodetected). For example,

```
mkdir /windows
mount -t vfat /dev/hda1 /windows
mkdir /nt
mount -t ntfs /dev/hda2 /nt
```

19.5   File System Repair: `fsck`

`fsck` stands for *file system check*. `fsck` scans the file system, reporting and fixing errors. Errors would normally occur only if the kernel halted before the file system was `umount`ed. In this case, it may have been in the middle of a write operation which left the file system in an *incoherent* state. This usually happens because of a power failure. The file system is then said to be *unclean*.

`fsck` is used as follows:

```
fsck [-V] [-a] [-t <fstype>] <device>
```

`-V` means to produce verbose output.   `-a` means to check the file system noninteractively—meaning to not ask the user before trying to make any repairs.

Here is what you would normally do with LINUX if you don't know a whole lot about the `ext2` file system:

```
fsck -a -t ext2 /dev/hda1
```

although you can omit the `-t` option because LINUX autodetects the file system. Note that you should not run `fsck` on a mounted file system. In exceptional circumstances it is permissible to run `fsck` on a file system that has been mounted read-only.

`fsck` actually just runs a program specific to that file system. In the case of `ext2`, the command `e2fsck` (also known as `fsck.ext2`) is run. See `e2fsck`(8) for exhaustive details.

During an interactive check (without the `-a` option, or with the `-r` option—the default), various questions may be asked of you, as regards fixing and saving things. It's best to save stuff if you aren't sure; it will be placed in the `lost+found` directory below the root directory of the particular device. In the example system further below, there would exist the directories `/lost+found`, `/home/lost+found`, `/var/lost+found`, `/usr/lost+found`, etc. After doing a check on, say, `/dev/hda9`, list the `/home/lost+found` directory and delete what you think you don't need. These will usually be temporary files and log files (files that change often). It's rare to lose important files because of an unclean shutdown.

19.6   File System Errors on Boot

Just read Section 19.5 again and run `fsck` on the file system that reported the error.

19.7   Automatic Mounts: `fstab`

Manual mounts are explained above for new and removable disks. It is, of course necessary for file systems to be automatically mounted at boot time. What gets mounted and how is specified in the configuration file `/etc/fstab`.

`/etc/fstab` will usually look something like this for the disk we partitioned above:

```
   /dev/hda1           /                    ext2     defaults          1 1
   /dev/hda6           /tmp                 ext2     defaults          1 2
   /dev/hda7           /var                 ext2     defaults          1 2
   /dev/hda8           /usr                 ext2     defaults          1 2
5  /dev/hda9           /home                ext2     defaults          1 2
   /dev/hda5           swap                 swap     defaults          0 0
   /dev/fd0            /mnt/floppy          auto     noauto,user       0 0
   /dev/cdrom          /mnt/cdrom           iso9660  noauto,ro,user    0 0
   none                /proc                proc     defaults          0 0
10 none                /dev/pts             devpts   mode=0622         0 0
```

For the moment we are interested in the first six lines only. The first three fields (columns) dictate the partition, the directory where it is to be mounted, and the file system type, respectively. The fourth field gives options (the -o option to mount).

The fifth field tells whether the file system contains real files. The field is used by the dump command to decide if it should be backed up. This is not commonly used.

The last field tells the order in which an fsck should be done on the partitions. The / partition should come first with a 1, and all other partitions should come directly after. Placing 2's everywhere else ensures that partitions on different disks can be checked in parallel, which speeds things up slightly at boot time.

The floppy and cdrom entries enable you to use an abbreviated form of the mount command. mount will just look up the corresponding directory and file system type from /etc/fstab. Try

```
mount /dev/cdrom
```

These entries also have the user option, which allows ordinary users to mount these devices. The ro option once again tells to mount the CD-ROM read only, and the noauto command tells mount *not* to mount these file systems at boot time. (More comes further below.)

proc is a kernel information database that looks like a file system. For example /proc/cpuinfo is not any kind of file that actually exists on a disk somewhere. Try cat /proc/cpuinfo.

Many programs use /proc to get dynamic information on the status and configuration of your machine. More on this is discussed in Section 42.4.

The devpts file system is another pseudo file system that generates terminal master/slave pairs for programs. This is mostly of concern to developers.

19.8 Manually Mounting /proc

You can mount the proc file system with the command

```
mount -t proc /proc /proc
```

This is an exception to the normal mount usage. Note that all common LINUX🐧 installations require /proc to be mounted at boot time. The only times you will need this command are for manual startup or when doing a chroot. (See page 178.)

19.9 RAM and Loopback Devices

A *RAM device* is a block device that can be used as a disk but really points to a physical area of RAM.

A *loopback device* is a block device that can be used as a disk but really points to an ordinary file somewhere.

If your imagination isn't already running wild, consider creating a floppy disk with file system, files and all, *without actually having a floppy disk*, and being able to dump this creation to floppy at any time with dd. You can also have a whole other LINUX🐧 system inside a 500 MB file on a Windows partition *and* boot into it—thus obviating having to repartition a Windows machine just to run LINUX🐧. All this can be done with loopback and RAM devices.

19.9.1 Formatting a floppy inside a file

The operations are quite trivial. To create an ext2 floppy inside a 1440 KB *file*, run:

```
dd if=/dev/zero of=~/file-floppy count=1440 bs=1024
losetup /dev/loop0 ~/file-floppy
mke2fs /dev/loop0
mkdir ~/mnt
mount /dev/loop0 ~/mnt
ls -al ~/mnt
```

When you are finished copying the files that you want into ~/mnt, merely run

```
umount ~/mnt
losetup -d /dev/loop0
```

To dump the file system to a floppy, run

```
dd if=~/file-floppy of=/dev/fd0 count=1440 bs=1024
```

A similar procedure for RAM devices is

```
dd if=/dev/zero of=/dev/ram0 count=1440 bs=1024
mke2fs /dev/ram0
mkdir ~/mnt
mount /dev/ram0 ~/mnt
ls -al ~/mnt
```

When you are finished copying the files that you want into ~/mnt, merely run

```
umount ~/mnt
```

To dump the file system to a floppy or file, respectively, run:

```
dd if=/dev/ram0 of=/dev/fd0 count=1440 bs=1024
dd if=/dev/ram0 of=~/file-floppy count=1440 bs=1024
```

19.9.2   CD-ROM files

Another trick is to move your CD-ROM to a file for high-speed access. Here, we use a shortcut instead of the losetup command:

```
dd if=/dev/cdrom of=some_name.iso
mount -t iso9660 -o ro,loop=/dev/loop0 some_name.iso /cdrom
```

19.10   Remounting from Read-Only to Read-Write

A file system that is already mounted as read-only can be remounted as read-write, for example, with

```
mount -o rw,remount /dev/hda1 /
```

This command is useful when you log in in single-user mode with no write access to your root partition.

19.11   Disk sync

The kernel caches write operations in memory for performance reasons. These *flush* (physically commit to the magnetic media) every so often, but you sometimes want to force a flush. This is done simply with

```
sync
```

Chapter 20

Advanced Shell Scripting

This chapter completes our discussion of `sh` shell scripting begun in Chapter 7 and expanded on in Chapter 9. These three chapters represent almost everything you can do with the `bash` shell.

20.1 Lists of Commands

The special operator `&&` and `||` can be used to execute functions in sequence. For instance:

```
grep '^harry:' /etc/passwd || useradd harry
```

The `||` means to only execute the second command if the first command returns an error. In the above case, `grep` will return an exit code of 1 if `harry` is not in the `/etc/passwd` file, causing `useradd` to be executed.

An alternate representation is

```
grep -v '^harry:' /etc/passwd && useradd harry
```

where the `-v` option inverts the sense of matching of `grep`. `&&` has the opposite meaning to `||`, that is, to execute the second command only if the first succeeds.

Adept script writers often string together many commands to create the most succinct representation of an operation:

```
grep -v '^harry:' /etc/passwd && useradd harry || \
    echo "`date`: useradd failed" >> /var/log/my_special_log
```

20.2　Special Parameters: $?, $*,...

An ordinary variable can be expanded with $*VARNAME*. Commonly used variables like PATH and special variables like PWD and RANDOM were covered in Chapter 9. Further special expansions are documented in the following section, quoted verbatim from the bash man page (the footnotes are mine).[1]

Special Parameters

The shell treats several parameters specially. These parameters may only be referenced; assignment to them is not allowed.

$* Expands to the positional parameters (i.e., the command-line arguments passed to the shell script, with **$1** being the first argument, **$2** the second etc.), starting from one. When the expansion occurs within double quotes, it expands to a single word with the value of each parameter separated by the first character of the **IFS** special variable. That is, "**$***" is equivalent to "**$1**$c$**2**$c$**...**", where c is the first character of the value of the **IFS** variable. If **IFS** is unset, the parameters are separated by spaces. If **IFS** is null, the parameters are joined without intervening separators.

$@** Expands to the positional parameters, starting from one. When the expansion occurs within double quotes, each parameter expands to a separate word. That is, "**$@" is equivalent to "**$1**" "**$2**" ... When there are no positional parameters, "**$@**" and **$@** expand to nothing (i.e., they are removed). ↘Hint: this is very useful for writing wrapper shell scripts that just add one argument.↖

$# Expands to the number of positional parameters in decimal (i.e. the number of command-line arguments).

$? Expands to the status of the most recently executed foreground pipeline. ↘I.e., the exit code of the last command.↖

$- Expands to the current option flags as specified upon invocation, by the **set** builtin command, or those set by the shell itself (such as the **-i** option).

$$ Expands to the process ID of the shell. In a () subshell, it expands to the process ID of the current shell, not the subshell.

$! Expands to the process ID of the most recently executed background (asynchronous) command. ↘I.e., after executing a background command with *command* **&**, the variable **$!** will give its process ID.↖

$0 Expands to the name of the shell or shell script. This is set at shell initialization. If **bash** is invoked with a file of commands, **$0** is set to the name of that file. If **bash** is started with the **-c** option, then **$0** is set to the first argument after the string to be executed, if one is present. Otherwise, it is set to the file name used to invoke **bash**, as given by argument zero. ↘Note that **basename $0** is a useful way to get the name of the current command without the leading path.↖

---

[1]Thanks to Brian Fox and Chet Ramey for this material.

$- At shell startup, set to the absolute file name of the shell or shell script being executed as passed in the argument list. Subsequently, expands to the last argument to the previous command, after expansion. Also set to the full file name of each command executed and placed in the environment exported to that command. When checking mail, this parameter holds the name of the mail file currently being checked.

20.3 Expansion

Expansion refers to the way `bash` modifies the command-line before executing it. `bash` performs several textual modifications to the command-line, proceeding in the following order:

Brace expansion We have already shown how you can use, for example, the shorthand `touch file_{one,two,three}.txt` to create multiple files `file_one.txt`, `file_two.txt`, and `file_three.txt`. This is known as brace expansion and occurs before any other kind of modification to the command-line.

Tilde expansion The special character ~ is replaced with the full path contained in the HOME environment variable or the home directory of the users login (if `$HOME` is null). ~+ is replaced with the current working directory and ~- is replaced with the most recent previous working directory. The last two are rarely used.

Parameter expansion This refers to expanding anything that begins with a $. Note that $*VAR* and ${*VAR*} do exactly the same thing, except in the latter case, *VAR* can contain non-"whole word" characters that would normally confuse `bash`.

There are several parameter expansion tricks that you can use to do string manipulation. Most shell programmers never bother with these, probably because they are not well supported by other UNIX systems.

     ${*VAR*:-*default*} This will result in $*VAR* unless *VAR* is unset or null, in which case it will result in *default*.

     ${*VAR*:=*default*} Same as previous except that *default* is also assigned to VAR if it is empty.

     ${*VAR*:-*default*} This will result in an empty string if *VAR* is unset or null; otherwise it will result in *default*. This is the opposite behavior of ${*VAR*:-*default*}.

     ${*VAR*:?*message*} This will result in $*VAR* unless *VAR* is unset or null, in which case an error message containing *message* is displayed.

     ${*VAR*:*offset*} or ${*VAR*:*n*:*l*} This produces the *n*th character of $*VAR* and then the following *l* characters. If *l* is not present, then all characters to the right of the *n*th character are produced. This is useful for splitting up strings. Try:

```
TEXT=scripting_for_phun
echo ${TEXT:10:3}
echo ${TEXT:10}
```

${#VAR} Gives the length of $VAR.

${!PRE*} Gives a list of all variables whose names begin with *PRE*.

${VAR#pattern} $VAR is returned with the glob expression *pattern* removed from the leading part of the string. For instance, `${TEXT#scr}` in the above example will return `ripting_for_phun`.

${VAR##pattern} This is the same as the previous expansion except that if *pattern* contains wild cards, then it will try to match the maximum length of characters.

${VAR%pattern} The same as `${VAR#pattern}` except that characters are removed from the trailing part of the string.

${VAR%%pattern} The same as `${VAR##pattern}` except that characters are removed from the trailing part of the string.

${VAR/search/replace} $VAR is returned with the first occurrence of the string *search* replaced with *replace*.

${VAR/#search/replace} Same as `${VAR/search/replace}` except that the match is attempted from the leading part of $VAR.

${VAR/%search/replace} Same as `${VAR/search/replace}` except that the match is attempted at the trailing part of $VAR.

${VAR//search/replace} Same as `${VAR/search/replace}` except that all instances of *search* are replaced.

Backquote expansion We have already shown backquote expansion in 7.12. Note that the additional notation $ (*command*) is equivalent to `command` except that escapes (i.e., \\) are not required for special characters.

Arithmetic expansion We have already shown arithmetic expansion on page 62. Note that the additional notation $ ((*expression*)) is equivalent to $ [*expression*].

Finally The last modifications to the command-line are the splitting of the command-line into words according to the white space between them. The IFS (*Internal Field Separator*) environment variable determines what characters delimit command-line words (usually whitespace). With the command-line divided into words, path names are expanded according to glob wild cards. Consult bash(1) for a comprehensive description of the pattern matching options that most people don't know about.

20.4   Built-in Commands

Many commands operate some built-in functionality of bash or are especially interpreted. These do not invoke an executable off the file system. Some of these were
described in Chapter 7, and a few more are discussed here. For an exhaustive description, consult bash(1).

: A single colon by itself does nothing. It is useful for a "no operation" line such as:

```
if <command> ; then
    :
else
    echo "<command> was unsuccessful"
fi
```

. *filename args* ... A single dot is the same as the source command. See below.

alias *command=value* Creates a pseudonym for a command. Try:

```
alias necho="echo -n"
necho "hello"
```

Some distributions alias the mv, cp, and rm commands to the same pseudonym
with the -i (interactive) option set. This prevents files from being deleted without prompting, but can be irritating for the administrator. See your ~/.bashrc
file for these settings. See also unalias.

unalias *command* Removes an alias created with alias.

alias -p Prints list of aliases.

eval *arg* ... Executes *arg*s as a line of shell script.

exec *command arg* ... Begins executing *command* under the same process ID as the
current script. This is most often used for shell scripts that are mere "wrapper"
scripts for real programs. The wrapper script sets any environment variables and
then execs the real program binary as its last line. exec should never return.

local *var=value* Assigns a value to a variable. The resulting variable is visible only
within the current function.

pushd *directory* and popd These two commands are useful for jumping around directories. pushd can be used instead of cd, but unlike cd, the directory is saved
onto a list of directories. At any time, entering popd returns you to the previous
directory. This is nice for navigation since it keeps a history of wherever you have
been.

printf *format args ...* This is like the **C** `printf` function. It outputs to the terminal like `echo` but is useful for more complex formatting of output. See `printf`(3) for details and try `printf "%10.3e\n" 12` as an example.

pwd Prints the present working directory.

set Prints the value of all environment variables. See also Section 20.6 on the `set` command.

source *filename args ...* Reads *filename* into the current current shell environment. This is useful for executing a shell script when environment variables set by that script must be preserved.

times Prints the accumulated user and system times for the shell and for processes run from the shell.

type *command* Tells whether *command* is an alias, a built-in or a system executable.

ulimit Prints and sets various user resource limits like memory usage limits and CPU limits. See `bash`(1) for details.

umask See Section 14.2.

unset *VAR* Deletes a variable or environment variable.

unset *-f func* Deletes a function.

wait Pauses until all background jobs have completed.

wait *PID* Pauses until background process with process ID of *PID* has exited, then returns the exit code of the background process.

wait *%job* Same with respect to a job spec.

20.5 Trapping Signals — the `trap` Command

You will often want to make your script perform certain actions in response to a signal. A list of signals can be found on page 86. To trap a signal, create a function and then use the `trap` command to bind the function to the signal.

```
#!/bin/sh

function on_hangup ()
{
    echo 'Hangup (SIGHUP) signal recieved'
}
```

```
     trap on_hangup SIGHUP

10   while true ; do
         sleep 1
     done

     exit 0
```

Run the above script and then send the process ID the −HUP signal to test it. (See Section 9.5.)

An important function of a program is to clean up after itself on exit. The special signal EXIT (not really a signal) executes code on exit of the script:

```
     #!/bin/sh

     function on_exit ()
     {
5        echo 'I should remove temp files now'
     }

     trap on_exit EXIT

10   while true ; do
         sleep 1
     done

     exit 0
```

Breaking the above program will cause it to print its own epitaph.

If − is given instead of a function name, then the signal is unbound (i.e., set to its default value).

20.6   Internal Settings — the **set** Command

The set command can modify certain behavioral settings of the shell. Your current options can be displayed with echo $-. Various set commands are usually entered at the top of a script or given as command-line options to bash. Using set +*option* instead of set −*option* disables the option. Here are a few examples:

set −e Exit immediately if any simple command gives an error.

set −h Cache the location of commands in your PATH. The shell will become confused if binaries are suddenly inserted into the directories of your PATH, perhaps causing a No such file or directory error. In this case, disable this option or restart your shell. This option is enabled by default.

set **-n** Read commands without executing them. This command is useful for syntax checking.

set **-o posix** Comply exactly with the POSIX 1003.2 standard.

set **-u** Report an error when trying to reference a variable that is unset. Usually `bash` just fills in an empty string.

set **-v** Print each line of script as it is executed.

set **-x** Display each command expansion as it is executed.

set **-C** Do not overwrite existing files when using >. You can use >| to force overwriting.

20.7 Useful Scripts and Commands

Here is a collection of useful utility scripts that people are always asking for on the mailing lists. See page 517 for several security check scripts.

20.7.1 chroot

The `chroot` command makes a process think that its root file system is not actually /. For example, on one system I have a complete Debian℗ installation residing under a directory, say, /mnt/debian. I can issue the command

```
chroot /mnt/debian bash -i
```

to run the `bash` shell interactively, under the root file system /mnt/debian. This command will hence run the command /mnt/debian/bin/bash -i. All further commands processed under this shell will have no knowledge of the real root directory, so I can use my Debian℗ installation without having to reboot. All further commands will effectively behave as though they are inside a separate UNIX machine. One caveat: you may have to remount your /proc file system inside your `chroot`'d file system— see page 167.

This useful for improving security. Insecure network services can change to a different root directory—any corruption will not affect the real system.

Most rescue disks have a `chroot` command. After booting the disk, you can manually mount the file systems on your hard drive, and then issue a `chroot` to begin using your machine as usual. Note that the command `chroot <new-root>` without arguments invokes a shell by default.

20.7.2 `if` conditionals

The `if test` ... was used to control program flow in Chapter 7. Bash, however, has a built-in alias for the `test` function: the left square brace, `[`.

Using `[` instead of `test` adds only elegance:

```
if [ 5 -le 3 ] ; then
    echo '5 < 3'
fi
```

It is important at this point to realize that the `if` command understands nothing of arithmetic. It merely executes a command `test` (or in this case `[`) and tests the exit code. If the exit code is zero, then the command is considered to be successful and `if` proceeds with the body of the `if` statement block. The onus is on the `test` command to properly evaluate the expression given to it.

`if` can equally well be used with any command:

```
if echo "$PATH" | grep -qwv /usr/local/bin ; then
    export PATH="$PATH:/usr/local/bin"
fi
```

conditionally adds `/usr/local/bin` if `grep` does not find it in your `PATH`.

20.7.3 `patching` and `diffing`

You may often want to find the differences between two files, for example to see what changes have been made to a file between versions. Or, when a large batch of source code may have been updated, it is silly to download the entire directory tree if there have been only a few small changes. You would want a list of alterations instead.

The `diff` utility dumps the lines that differ between two files. It can be used as follows:

```
diff -u <old-file> <new-file>
```

You can also use `diff` to see difference netween two directory trees. `diff` recursively compares all corresponding files:

```
diff -u --recursive --new-file <old-dir> <new-dir> > <patch-file>.diff
```

The output is known as a *patch file* against a directory tree, that can be used both to see changes, and to bring <old-dir> up to date with <new-dir>.

Patch files may also end in `.patch` and are often `gzip`ped. The patch file can be applied to <old-dir> with

```
cd <old-dir>
patch -p1 -s < <patch-file>.diff
```

which makes <old-dir> identical to <new-dir>. The -p1 option strips the leading directory name from the patch file. The presence of a leading directory name in the patch file often confuses the patch command.

20.7.4   Internet connectivity test

You may want to leave this example until you have covered more networking theory.

The acid test for an Internet connection is a successful DNS query. You can use ping to test whether a server is up, but some networks filter ICMP messages and ping does not check that your DNS is working. dig sends a single UDP packet similar to ping. Unfortunately, it takes rather long to time out, so we fudge in a kill after 2 seconds.

This script blocks until it successfully queries a remote name server. Typically, the next few lines of following script would run fetchmail and a mail server queue flush, or possibly uucico. Do set the name server IP to something appropriate like that of your local ISP; and increase the 2 second time out if your name server typically takes longer to respond.

```
MY_DNS_SERVER=197.22.201.154

while true ; do
    (
        dig @$MY_DNS_SERVER netscape.com IN A &
        DIG_PID=$!
        { sleep 2 ; kill $DIG_PID ; } &
        sleep 1
        wait $DIG_PID
    ) 2>/dev/null | grep -q '^[^;]*netscape.com' && break
done
```

20.7.5   Recursive grep (search)

Recursively searching through a directory tree can be done easily with the find and xargs commands. You should consult both these man pages. The following command pipe searches through the kernel source for anything about the "pcnet" Ethernet card, printing also the line number:

```
find /usr/src/linux -follow -type f | xargs grep -iHn pcnet
```

(You will notice how this command returns rather a lot of data. However, going through it carefully can be quite instructive.)

Limiting a search to a certain file extension is just another common use of this pipe sequence.

```
find /usr/src/linux -follow -type f -name '*.[ch]' | xargs grep -iHn pcnet
```

Note that new versions of grep also have a -r option to recursively search through directories.

20.7.6 Recursive search and replace

Often you will want to perform a search-and-replace throughout all the files in an entire source tree. A typical example is the changing of a function call name throughout lots of **C** source. The following script is a must for any /usr/local/bin/. Notice the way it recursively calls itself.

```
     #!/bin/sh

     N=`basename $0`

5    if [ "$1" = "-v" ] ; then
         VERBOSE="-v"
         shift
     fi

10   if [ "$3" = "" -o "$1" = "-h" -o "$1" = "--help" ] ; then
         echo "$N: Usage"
         echo "            $N [-h|--help] [-v] <regexp-search> \
     <regexp-replace> <glob-file>"
         echo
15       exit 0
     fi

     S="$1" ; shift ; R="$1" ; shift
     T=$$replc

20   if echo "$1" | grep -q / ; then
         for i in "$@" ; do
             SEARCH=`echo "$S" | sed 's,/,\\\\/,g'`
             REPLACE=`echo "$R" | sed 's,/,\\\\/,g'`
25           cat $i | sed "s/$SEARCH/$REPLACE/g" > $T
```

```
            D="$?"
            if [ "$D" = "0" ] ; then
                if diff -q $T $i >/dev/null ; then
                    :
30              else
                    if [ "$VERBOSE" = "-v" ] ; then
                        echo $i
                    fi
                    cat $T > $i
35              fi
                rm -f $T
            fi
        done
    else
40      find . -type f -name "$1" | xargs $0 $VERBOSE "$S" "$R"
    fi
```

20.7.7   cut and `awk` — manipulating text file fields

The cut command is useful for slicing files into fields; try

```
cut -d: -f1 /etc/passwd
cat /etc/passwd | cut -d: -f1
```

The awk program is an interpreter for a complete programming language call AWK. A common use for awk is in field stripping. It is slightly more flexible than cut—

```
cat /etc/passwd | awk -F : '{print $1}'
```

—especially where whitespace gets in the way,

```
ls -al | awk '{print $6 " " $7 " " $8}'
ls -al | awk '{print $5 " bytes"}'
```

which isolates the time and size of the file respectively.

Get your nonlocal IP addresses with:

```
ifconfig | grep 'inet addr:' | fgrep -v '127.0.0.' | \
                    cut -d: -f2 | cut -d' ' -f1
```

Reverse an IP address with:

```
echo 192.168.3.2 | awk -F . '{print $4 "." $3 "." $2 "." $1 }'
```

Print all common user names (i.e., users with UID values greater than 499 on RedHat and greater than 999 on Debian⊘):

```
awk -F: '$3 >= 500 {print $1}' /etc/passwd
( awk -F: '$3 >= 1000 {print $1}' /etc/passwd )
```

20.7.8 Calculations with bc

Scripts can easily use bc to do calculations that expr can't handle. For example, convert to decimal with

```
echo -e 'ibase=16;FFFF' | bc
```

to binary with

```
echo -e 'obase=2;12345' | bc
```

or work out the SIN of 45 degrees with

```
pi=`echo "scale=10; 4*a(1)" | bc -l`
echo "scale=10; s(45*$pi/180)" | bc -l
```

20.7.9 Conversion of graphics formats of many files

The convert program of the *ImageMagick* package is a command many Windows users would love. It can easily be used to convert multiple files from one format to another. Changing a file's extension can be done with echo *filename* | sed - e 's/\.old$/.new/' `. The convert command does the rest:

```
for i in *.pcx ; do
    CMD="convert -quality 625 $i `echo $i | sed -e 's/\.pcx$/.png/' `"
# Show the command-line to the user:
    echo $CMD
# Execute the command-line:
    eval $CMD
done
```

Note that the search-and-replace expansion mechanism could also be used to replace the extensions: ${i/%.pcx/.png} produces the desired result.

Incidentally, the above nicely compresses high-resolution `pcx` files—possibly the output of a scanning operation, or a LaTeX compilation into PostScript rendered with GhostScript (i.e. `gs -sDEVICE=pcx256 -sOutputFile='page%d.pcx'` *file*.ps).

20.7.10   Securely erasing files

Removing a file with `rm` only unlinks the file name from the data. The file blocks may still be on disk, and will only be reclaimed when the file system reuses that data. To erase a file proper, requires writing random bytes into the disk blocks occupied by the file. The following overwrites all the files in the current directory:

```
for i in * ; do
    dd if=/dev/urandom     \
        of="$i"            \
        bs=1024            \
        count=`expr 1 +    \
            \`stat "$i" | grep 'Size:' | awk '{print $2}'\` \
                / 1024`
done
```

You can then remove the files normally with `rm`.

20.7.11   Persistent background processes

Consider trying to run a process, say, the `rxvt` terminal, in the background. This can be done simply with:

```
rxvt &
```

However, `rxvt` still has its output connected to the shell and is a child process of the shell. When a login shell exits, it may take its child processes with it. `rxvt` may also die of its own accord from trying to read or write to a terminal that does not exist without the parent shell. Now try:

```
{ rxvt >/dev/null 2>&1 </dev/null & } &
```

This technique is known as *forking twice*, and *redirecting the terminal to dev null*. The shell can know about its child processes but not about the its "grand child" processes. We have hence create a daemon process proper with the above command.

Now, it is easy to create a daemon process that restarts itself if it happens to die. Although such functionality is best accomplished within **C** (which you will get a taste of in Chapter 22), you can make do with:

```
{ { while true ; do rxvt ; done ; } >/dev/null 2>&1 </dev/null & } &
```

You will notice the effects of all these tricks with:

```
ps awwwxf
```

20.7.12   Processing the process list

The following command uses the custom format option of `ps` to print every conceivable attribute of a process:

```
   ps -awwwxo %cpu,%mem,alarm,args,blocked,bsdstart,bsdtime,c,caught,cmd,comm, \
   command,cputime,drs,dsiz,egid,egroup,eip,esp,etime,euid,euser,f,fgid,fgroup, \
   flag,flags,fname,fsgid,fsgroup,fsuid,fsuser,fuid,fuser,gid,group,ignored, \
   intpri,lim,longtname,lstart,m_drs,m_trs,maj_flt,majflt,min_flt,minflt,ni, \
 5 nice,nwchan,opri,pagein,pcpu,pending,pgid,pgrp,pid,pmem,ppid,pri,rgid,rgroup, \
   rss,rssize,rsz,ruid,ruser,s,sess,session,sgi_p,sgi_rss,sgid,sgroup,sid,sig, \
   sig_block,sig_catch,sig_ignore,sig_pend,sigcatch,sigignore,sigmask,stackp, \
   start,start_stack,start_time,stat,state,stime,suid,suser,svgid,svgroup,svuid, \
   svuser,sz,time,timeout,tmout,tname,tpgid,trs,trss,tsiz,tt,tty,tty4,tty8,ucomm, \
10 uid,uid_hack,uname,user,vsize,vsz,wchan
```

The output is best piped to a file and viewed with a nonwrapping text editor. More interestingly, the `awk` command can print the process ID of a process with

```
ps awwx | grep -w 'htt[p]d' | awk '{print $1}'
```

which prints all the processes having `httpd` in the command name or command-line. This filter is useful for killing `netscape` as follows:

```
kill -9 `ps awx | grep 'netsc[a]pe' | awk '{print $1}'`
```

(Note that the [a] in the regular expression prevents `grep` from finding itself in the process list.)

     Other useful `ps` variations are:

```
  ps awwxf
  ps awwxl
  ps awwxv
  ps awwxu
5 ps awwxs
```

The `f` option is most useful for showing parent-child relationships. It stands for `f`orest, and shows the full process tree. For example, here I am running an **X** desktop with two windows:

```
  PID TTY      STAT    TIME COMMAND
    1 ?        S       0:05 init [5]
    2 ?        SW      0:02 [kflushd]
    3 ?        SW      0:02 [kupdate]
    4 ?        SW      0:00 [kpiod]
    5 ?        SW      0:01 [kswapd]
    6 ?        SW<     0:00 [mdrecoveryd]
  262 ?        S       0:02 syslogd -m 0
  272 ?        S       0:00 klogd
  341 ?        S       0:00 xinetd -reuse -pidfile /var/run/xinetd.pid
  447 ?        S       0:00 crond
  480 ?        S       0:02 xfs -droppriv -daemon
  506 tty1     S       0:00 /sbin/mingetty tty1
  507 tty2     S       0:00 /sbin/mingetty tty2
  508 tty3     S       0:00 /sbin/mingetty tty3
  509 ?        S       0:00 /usr/bin/gdm -nodaemon
  514 ?        S       7:04  \_ /etc/X11/X -auth /var/gdm/:0.Xauth :0
  515 ?        S       0:00  \_ /usr/bin/gdm -nodaemon
  524 ?        S       0:18      \_ /opt/icewm/bin/icewm
  748 ?        S       0:08         \_ rxvt -bg black -cr green -fg whi
  749 pts/0    S       0:00         |  \_ bash
 5643 pts/0    S       0:09         |     \_ mc
 5645 pts/6    S       0:02         |        \_ bash -rcfile .bashrc
25292 pts/6    R       0:00         |           \_ ps awwxf
11780 ?        S       0:16         \_ /usr/lib/netscape/netscape-commu
11814 ?        S       0:00            \_ (dns helper)
15534 pts/6    S       3:12 cooledit -I /root/.cedit/projects/Rute
15535 pts/6    S       6:03  \_ aspell -a -a
```

The u option shows the useful user format, and the others show virtual memory, signal and long format.

20.8   Shell Initialization

Here I will briefly discuss what initialization takes place after logging in and how to modify it.

The interactive shell invoked after login will be the shell specified in the last field of the user's entry in the /etc/passwd file. The login program will invoke the shell after authenticating the user, placing a – in front of the the command name, which indicates to the shell that it is a *login shell,* meaning that it reads and execute several scripts to initialize the environment. In the case of bash, the files it reads are: /etc/profile, ~/.bash_profile, ~/.bash_login and ~/.profile, in that order. In addition, an interactive shell that is not a login shell also reads ~/.bashrc. Note that traditional sh shells only read /etc/profile and ~/.profile.

20.8.1   Customizing the **PATH** and **LD_LIBRARY_PATH**

Administrators can customise things like the environment variables by modifying these startup scripts. Consider the classic case of an installation tree under /opt/. Often, a package like /opt/staroffice/ or /opt/oracle/ will require the PATH and LD_LIBRARY_PATH variables to be adjusted accordingly. In the case of RedHat, a script,

```
for i in /opt/*/bin /usr/local/bin ; do
    test -d $i || continue
    echo $PATH | grep -wq "$i" && continue
    PATH=$PATH:$i
    export PATH
done

if test `id -u` -eq 0 ; then
    for i in /opt/*/sbin /usr/local/sbin ; do
        test -d $i || continue
        echo $PATH | grep -wq "$i" && continue
        PATH=$PATH:$i
        export PATH
    done
fi

for i in /opt/*/lib /usr/local/lib ; do
    test -d $i || continue
    echo $LD_LIBRARY_PATH | grep -wq "$i" && continue
    LD_LIBRARY_PATH=$LD_LIBRARY_PATH:$i
    export LD_LIBRARY_PATH
done
```

can be placed as /etc/profile.d/my_local.sh with execute permissions. This will take care of anything installed under /opt/ or /usr/local/. For Debian©, the script can be inserted directly into /etc/profile.

Page 235 of Section 23.3 contains details of exactly what LD_LIBRARY_PATH is.

(Unrelated, but you should also edit your /etc/man.config to add man page paths that appear under all installation trees under /opt/.)

20.9   File Locking

Often, one would like a process to have *exclusive access* to a file. By this we mean that only one process can access the file at any one time. Consider a mail folder: if two processes were to write to the folder simultaneously, it could become corrupted. We also sometimes want to ensure that a program can never be run twice at the same time; this insurance is another use for "locking."

In the case of a mail folder, if the file is being written to, then *no* other process should try read it or write to it: and we would like to create a *write lock* on the file. However if the file is being read from, *no* other process should try to write to it: and we would like to create a *read lock* on the file. Write locks are sometimes called *exclusive locks*; read locks are sometimes called *shared locks*. Often, *exclusive locks* are preferred for simplicity.

Locking can be implemented by simply creating a temporary file to indicate to other processes to wait before trying some kind of access. UNIX also has some more sophisticated builtin functions.

20.9.1   Locking a mailbox file

There are currently four methods of file locking. ↘The exim sources seem to indicate thorough research in this area, so this is what I am going on.↖

1. "dot lock" file locking. Here, a temporary file is created with the same name as the mail folder and the extension .lock added. So long as this file exists, no program should try to access the folder. This is an exclusive lock only. It is easy to write a shell script to do this kind of file locking.

2. "MBX" file locking. Similar to 1, but a temporary file is created in /tmp. This is also an exclusive lock.

3. fcntl locking. Databases require areas of a file to be locked. fcntl is a system call to be used inside **C** programs.

4. flock file locking. Same as fcntl, but locks whole files.

The following shell function does proper mailbox file locking.

```
function my_lockfile ()
{
        TEMPFILE="$1.$$"
        LOCKFILE="$1.lock"
        echo $$ > $TEMPFILE 2>/dev/null || {
                echo "You don't have permission to access `dirname $TEMPFILE`"
                return 1
        }
        ln $TEMPFILE $LOCKFILE 2>/dev/null && {
                rm -f $TEMPFILE
                return 0
        }
        STALE_PID=`< $LOCKFILE`
```

```
15          test "$STALE_PID" -gt "0" >/dev/null || {
                    return 1
            }
            kill -0 $STALE_PID 2>/dev/null && {
                    rm -f $TEMPFILE
                    return 1
20          }
            rm $LOCKFILE 2>/dev/null && {
                echo "Removed stale lock file of process $STALE_PID"
            }
            ln $TEMPFILE $LOCKFILE 2>/dev/null && {
25                  rm -f $TEMPFILE
                    return 0
            }
            rm -f $TEMPFILE
            return 1
30  }
```

(Note how instead of `cat $LOCKFILE`, we use `< $LOCKFILE`, which is faster.)

You can include the above function in scripts that need to lock any kind file. Use the function as follows:

```
# wait for a lock
until my_lockfile /etc/passwd ; do
        sleep 1
done
5
# The body of the program might go here
# [...]

# Then to remove the lock,
10  rm -f /etc/passwd.lock
```

This script is of academic interest only but has a couple of interesting features. Note how the `ln` function is used to ensure "exclusivity." `ln` is one of the few UNIX functions that is *atomic*, meaning that only one link of the same name can exist, and its creation excludes the possibility that another program would think that it had successfully created the same link. One might naively expect that the program

```
function my_lockfile ()
{
        LOCKFILE="$1.lock"
        test -e $LOCKFILE && return 1
5       touch $LOCKFILE
        return 0
}
```

is sufficient for file locking. However, consider if two programs, running simultaneously, executed line 4 at the same time. *Both* would think that the lock did not exist and proceed to line 5. Then both would successfully create the lock file—not what you wanted.

The `kill` command is then useful for checking whether a process is running. Sending the 0 signal does nothing to the process, but the signal fails if the process does not exist. This technique can be used to remove a lock of a process that died before removing the lock itself: that is, a *stale* lock.

20.9.2   Locking over NFS

The preceding script does *not* work if your file system is mounted over NFS (*network file system*—see Chapter 28). This is obvious because the script relies on the PID of the process, which is not visible across different machines. Not so obvious is that the `ln` function does not work exactly right over NFS—you need to `stat` the file and actually check that the link count has increased to 2.

The commands `lockfile` (from the `procmail` package) and `mutt_dotlock` (from the `mutt` email reader but perhaps not distributed) do similar file locking. These commands, however, but do not store the PID in the lock file. Hence it is not possible to detect a stale lock file. For example, to search your mailbox, you can run:

```
lockfile /var/spool/mail/mary.lock
grep freddy /var/spool/mail/mary
rm -f /var/spool/mail/mary.lock
```

This sequence ensures that you are searching a clean mailbox even if `/var` is a remote NFS share.

20.9.3   Directory versus file locking

File locking is a headache for the developer. The problem with UNIX is that whereas we are intuitively thinking about locking a *file*, what we really mean is locking a *file name* within a directory. *File* locking *per se* should only be used on perpetual files, such as database files. For mailbox and `passwd` files we need *directory locking* ⬊My own term.⬉, meaning the exclusive access of one process to a particular directory entry. In my opinion, lack of such a feature is a serious deficiency in UNIX, but because it will require kernel, NFS, and (possibly) **C** library extensions, will probably not come into being any time soon.

20.9.4   Locking inside C programs

This topic is certainly outside of the scope of this text, except to say that you should consult the source code of reputable packages rather than invent your own locking scheme.

Chapter 21

System Services and `lpd` — the Printer Service

This chapter covers a wide range of concepts about the way UNIX services function.

Every function of UNIX is provided by one or another package. For instance, mail is often handled by the `sendmail` or other package, web by the `apache` package.

Here we examine how to obtain, install, and configure a package, using `lpd` as an example. You can then apply this knowledge to any other package, and later chapters assume that you know these concepts. This discussion will also suffice as an explanation of how to set up and manage printing.

21.1 Using `lpr`

Printing under UNIX on a properly configured machine is as simple as typing `lpr -Plp <filename>` (or `cat <filename> | lpr -Plp`). The "lp" in `-Plp` is the name of the printer *queue* on the local machine you would like to print to. You can omit it if you are printing to the default (i.e., the first listed) queue. A *queue* belongs to a physical printer, so users can predict where paper will come spewing out, by what queue they print to. Queues are conventionally named `lp`, `lp0`, `lp1`, and so on, and any number of them may have been redirected to any other queue on any other machine on the network.

The command `lprm` removes pending jobs from a print queue; `lpq` reports jobs in progress.

The service that facilitates all this is called `lpd`. The `lpr` user program makes a network connection to the `lpd` background process, sending it the print job. `lpd` then queues, filters, and feeds the job until it appears in the print tray.

Printing typifies the *client/server* nature of UNIX services. The `lpd` background process is the *server* and is initiated by the `root` user. The remaining commands are *client* programs, and are run mostly by users.

21.2   Downloading and Installing

The following discussion should relieve the questions of "Where do I get *xxx* service/package?" and "How do I install it?". Full coverage of package management comes in Section 24.2, but here you briefly see how to use package managers with respect to a real system service.

Let us say we know nothing of the service except that it has something to do with a file `/usr/sbin/lpd`. First, we use our package managers to find where the file comes from (Debian◉ commands are shown in parentheses):

```
rpm -qf /usr/sbin/lpd
( dpkg -S /usr/sbin/lpd )
```

Returns `lpr-0.nn-n` (for RedHat 6.2, or `LPRng-n.n.nn-n` on RedHat 7.0, or `lpr` on Debian◉). On RedHat you may have to try this on a different machine because `rpm` does not know about packages that are not installed. Alternatively, if we would like to see whether a package whose name contains the letters `lpr` is installed:

```
rpm -qa | grep -i lpr
( dpkg -l '*lpr*' )
```

If the package is not present, the package file will be on your CD-ROM and is easily installable with (RedHat 7.0 and Debian◉ in braces):

```
rpm -i lpr-0.50-4.i386.rpm
( rpm -i LPRng-3.6.24-2 )
( dpkg -i lpr_0.48-1.deb )
```

(Much more about package management is covered in Chapter 24.)

The list of files which the `lpr` package is comprises (easily obtained with `rpm -ql lpr` or `dpkg -L lpr`) is approximately as follows:

```
/etc/init.d/lpd                 /usr/share/man/man1/lprm.1.gz
/etc/cron.weekly/lpr            /usr/share/man/man5/printcap.5.gz
/usr/sbin/lpf                   /usr/share/man/man8/lpc.8.gz
/usr/sbin/lpc                   /usr/share/man/man8/lpd.8.gz
/usr/sbin/lpd                   /usr/share/man/man8/pac.8.gz
/usr/sbin/pac                   /usr/share/man/man8/lpf.8.gz
/usr/bin/lpq                    /usr/share/doc/lpr/README.Debian
```

```
/usr/bin/lpr                    /usr/share/doc/lpr/copyright
/usr/bin/lprm                   /usr/share/doc/lpr/examples/printcap
/usr/bin/lptest                 /usr/share/doc/lpr/changelog.gz
/usr/share/man/man1/lpr.1.gz    /usr/share/doc/lpr/changelog.Debian.gz
/usr/share/man/man1/lptest.1.gz /var/spool/lpd/lp
/usr/share/man/man1/lpq.1.gz    /var/spool/lpd/remote
```

21.3   LPRng vs. Legacy `lpr-0.`*nn*

(The word *legacy* with regard to software means outdated, superseded, obsolete, or just old.)

RedHat 7.0 has now switched to using LPRng rather than the legacy `lpr` that Debian⊘ and other distributions use. LPRng is a more modern and comprehensive package. It supports the same `/etc/printcap` file and identical binaries as did the legacy `lpr` on RedHat 6.2. The only differences are in the control files created in your spool directories, and a different access control mechanism (discussed below). Note that LPRng has strict permissions requirements on spool directories and is not trivial to install from source.

21.4   Package Elements

A package's many files can be loosely grouped into functional elements. In this sectiom, each element will be explained, drawing on the `lpr` package as an example. Refer to the list of files in Section 21.2.

21.4.1   Documentation files

Documentation should be your first and foremost interest.   Man pages will not always be the only documentation provided.   Above we see that `lpr` does not install very much into the `/usr/share/doc` directory.   However, other packages, like `rpm -ql apache`, reveal a huge user manual (in `/home/httpd/html/manual/` or `/var/www/html/manual/`), and `rpm -ql wu-ftpd` shows lots inside `/usr/doc/wu-ftpd-?.?.?`.

21.4.2   Web pages, mailing lists, and download points

Every package will probably have a team that maintains it as well as a web page. In the case of `lpd`, however, the code is very old, and the various CD vendors do maintenance on it themselves. A better example is the `lprNG` package. Go to *The LPRng Web Page* http://www.astart.com/lprng/LPRng.html with your web browser. There you can see the authors, mailing lists, and points of download. If a particular package is of much interest to you, then you should become familiar with these resources. Good web pages will also have additional documentation like troubleshooting guides and FAQs (Frequently Asked Questions). Some may even have archives of their mailing lists. Note that some web pages are geared more toward CD vendors who are trying to create their own distribution and so will not have packages for download that beginner users can easily install.

21.4.3 User programs

User programs are found in one or another `bin` directory. In this case, we can see `lpq`, `lpr`, `lprm`, and `lptest`, as well as their associated `man` pages.

21.4.4 Daemon and administrator programs

Daemon and administrator command will an `sbin` directory. In this case we can see `lpc`, `lpd`, `lpf`, and `pac`, as well as their associated `man` pages. The only *daemon* (background) program is really the `lpd` program itself, which is the core of the whole package.

21.4.5 Configuration files

The file `/etc/printcap` controls `lpd`. Most system services will have a file in `/etc`. `printcap` is a plain text file that `lpd` reads on startup. Configuring any service primarily involves editing its configuration file. Several graphical configuration tools are available that avoid this inconvenience (`printtool`, which is especially for `lpd`, and `linuxconf`), but these actually just silently produce the same configuration file.

Because printing is so integral to the system, `printcap` is not actually provided by the `lpr` package. Trying `rpm -qf /etc/printcap` gives `setup-2.3.4-1`, and `dpkg -S /etc/printcap` shows it to not be owned (i.e., it is part of the base system).

21.4.6 Service initialization files

The files in `/etc/rc.d/init.d/` (or `/etc/init.d/`) are the startup and shutdown scripts to run `lpd` on boot and shutdown. You can start `lpd` yourself on the command-line with

```
/usr/sbin/lpd
```

but it is preferably to use the given script:

```
/etc/rc.d/init.d/lpd start
/etc/rc.d/init.d/lpd stop
```

(or `/etc/init.d/lpd`). The script has other uses as well:

```
/etc/rc.d/init.d/lpd status
/etc/rc.d/init.d/lpd restart
```

(or `/etc/init.d/lpd`).

To make sure that `lpd` runs on startup, you can check that it has a symlink under the appropriate run level. The symlinks can be explained by running

```
ls -al `find /etc -name '*lpd*'`
find /etc -name '*lpd*' -ls
```

showing,

```
   -rw-r--r--  1 root  root  17335 Sep 25  2000 /etc/lpd.conf
   -rw-r--r--  1 root  root  10620 Sep 25  2000 /etc/lpd.perms
   -rwxr-xr-x  1 root  root   2277 Sep 25  2000 /etc/rc.d/init.d/lpd
   lrwxrwxrwx  1 root  root     13 Mar 21 14:03 /etc/rc.d/rc0.d/K60lpd -> ../init.d/lpd
 5 lrwxrwxrwx  1 root  root     13 Mar 21 14:03 /etc/rc.d/rc1.d/K60lpd -> ../init.d/lpd
   lrwxrwxrwx  1 root  root     13 Mar 21 14:03 /etc/rc.d/rc2.d/S60lpd -> ../init.d/lpd
   lrwxrwxrwx  1 root  root     13 Mar 24 01:13 /etc/rc.d/rc3.d/S60lpd -> ../init.d/lpd
   lrwxrwxrwx  1 root  root     13 Mar 21 14:03 /etc/rc.d/rc4.d/S60lpd -> ../init.d/lpd
   lrwxrwxrwx  1 root  root     13 Mar 28 23:13 /etc/rc.d/rc5.d/S60lpd -> ../init.d/lpd
10 lrwxrwxrwx  1 root  root     13 Mar 21 14:03 /etc/rc.d/rc6.d/K60lpd -> ../init.d/lpd
```

The "3" in `rc3.d` is the what are interested in. Having `S60lpd` symlinked to `lpd` under `rc3.d` means that `lpd` will be started when the system enters *run level* 3, which is the system's state of usual operation.

Note that under RedHat the command `setup` has a menu option `System Services`. The `Services` list will allow you to manage what services come alive on boot, thus creating the symlinks automatically. For Debian⊙, check the man page for the `update-rc.d` command.

More details on bootup are in Chapter 32.

21.4.7 Spool files

Systems services like `lpd`, `innd`, `sendmail`, and `uucp` create intermediate files in the course of processing each request. These are called *spool* files and are stored somewhere under the `/var/spool/` directory, usually to be processed and then deleted in sequence.

`lpd` has a spool directory `/var/spool/lpd`, which may have been created on installation. You can create spool directories for the two printers in the example below, with

```
mkdir -p /var/spool/lpd/lp /var/spool/lpd/lp0
```

21.4.8 Log files

UNIX has a strict policy of not reporting error messages to the user interface whenever there might be no user around to read those messages. Whereas error messages of interactive commands are sent to the terminal screen, error or information messages produced by non-interactive commands are "logged" to files in the directory `/var/log/`.

A log file is a plain text file that continually has one-liner status messages appended to it by a daemon process. The usual directory for log files is `/var/log`. The main log files are `/var/log/messages` and possibly `/var/log/syslog`. It contains kernel messages and messages from a few primary services. When a service would produce large log files (think web access with thousands of hits per hour), the service would use its own log file. `sendmail`, for example, uses `/var/log/maillog`. Actually, `lpd` does not have a log file of its own—one of its failings.

View the system log file with the *follow* option to `tail`:

```
tail -f /var/log/messages
tail -f /var/log/syslog
```

Restarting the `lpd` service gives messages like: ↘Not all distributions log this information.↖

```
Jun 27 16:06:43 cericon lpd: lpd shutdown succeeded
Jun 27 16:06:45 cericon lpd: lpd startup succeeded
```

21.4.9 Log file rotation

Log files are rotated daily or weekly by the `logrotate` package. Its configuration file is `/etc/logrotate.conf`. For each package that happens to produce a log file, there is an additional configuration file under `/etc/logrotate.d/`. It is also easy to write your own—begin by using one of the existing files as an example. *Rotation* means that the log file is renamed with a `.1` extension and then truncated to zero length. The service is notified by the `logrotate` program, sometimes with a SIGHUP. Your `/var/log/` may contain a number of old log files named `.2`, `.3`, etc. The point of log file rotation is to prevent log files from growing indefinitely.

21.4.10   Environment variables

Most user commands of services make use of some environment variables. These can be defined in your shell startup scripts as usual. For `lpr`, if no printer is specified on the command-line, the `PRINTER` environment variable determines the default print queue. For example, `export PRINTER=lp1` will force use of the `lp1` print queue.

21.5   The `printcap` File in Detail

The `printcap` (*printer capabilities*) file is similar to (and based on) the `termcap` (*terminal capabilities*) file. Configuring a printer means adding or removing text in this file. `printcap` contains a list of one-line entries, one for each printer. Lines can be broken by a \ before the newline. Here is an example of a `printcap` file for two printers.

```
lp:\
        :sd=/var/spool/lpd/lp:\
        :mx#0:\
        :sh:\
        :lp=/dev/lp0:\
        :if=/var/spool/lpd/lp/filter:
lp0:\
        :sd=/var/spool/lpd/lp0:\
        :mx#0:\
        :sh:\
        :rm=edison:\
        :rp=lp3:\
        :if=/bin/cat:
```

Printers are named by the first field: in this case `lp` is the first printer and `lp0` the second printer. Each printer usually refers to a different physical device with its own queue. The `lp` printer should always be listed first and is the default print queue used when no other is specified. Here, `lp` refers to a local printer on the device `/dev/lp0` (first parallel port). `lp0` refers to a remote print queue `lp3` on the machine `edison`.

The `printcap` has a comprehensive `man` page. However, the following fields are most of what you will ever need:

sd Spool directory. This directory contains status and spool files.

mx Maximum file size. In the preceding example, unlimited.

sh Suppress headers. The header is a few informational lines printed before or after the print job. This option should always be set to off.

lp Line printer device.

if Input filter. This is an executable script into which printer data is piped. The output of this script is fed directly to the printing device or remote machine. This filter will translate from the application's output into the printer's native code.

rm Remote machine. If the printer queue is not local, this is the machine name.

rp Remote printer queue name. The remote machine will have its own `printcap` file with possibly several printers defined. This specifies which printer to use.

21.6 PostScript and the Print Filter

On UNIX the standard format for all printing is the PostScript file. PostScript `.ps` files are graphics files representing arbitrary scalable text, lines, and images. PostScript is actually a programming language specifically designed to draw things on a page; hence, `.ps` files are really PostScript programs. The last line in any PostScript program is always `showpage`, meaning that all drawing operations are complete and that the page can be displayed. Hence, it is easy to see the number of pages inside a PostScript file by `grepping` for the string `showpage`.

The procedure for printing on UNIX is to convert whatever you would like to print into PostScript. PostScript files can be viewed with a PostScript "emulator," like the `gv` (GhostView) program. A program called `gs` (GhostScript) is the standard utility for converting the PostScript into a format suitable for your printer. The idea behind PostScript is that it is a language that can easily be built into any printer. The so-called "PostScript printer" is one that directly interprets a PostScript file. However, these printers are relatively expensive, and most printers only understand the lesser PCL (printer control language) dialect or some other format.

In short, any of the hundreds of different formats of graphics and text have a utility that will convert a file into PostScript, whereafter `gs` will convert it for any of the hundreds of different kinds of printers. ⟍There are actually many printers not supported by `gs` at the time of this writing. This is mainly because manufacturers refuse to release specifications to their proprietary printer communication protocols⟍. The print filter is the workhorse of this whole operation.

Most applications conveniently output PostScript whenever printing. For example, `netscape`'s <u>Print...</u>   <u>Alt+P</u> menu selection shows

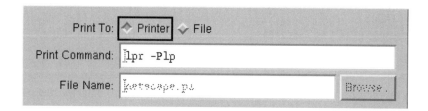

which sends PostScript through the stdin of `lpr`. All applications without their own printer drivers will do the same. This means that we can generally rely on the fact that the print filter will always receive PostScript. `gs`, on the other hand, can convert PostScript for any printer, so all that remains is to determine its command-line options.

If you have chosen "Print To: File," then you can view the resulting output with the `gv` program. Try `gv netscape.ps`, which shows a *print preview*. On UNIX, most desktop applications do *not* have their own preview facility because the PostScript printer itself is emulated by `gv`.

Note that filter programs should not be used with remote filters; remote printer queues can send their PostScript files "as is" with `:if=/bin/cat:` (as in the example `printcap` file above). This way, the machine connected to the device need be the only one especially configured for it.

The filter program we are going to use for the local print queue will be a shell script `/var/spool/lpd/lp/filter`. Create the filter with

```
touch /var/spool/lpd/lp/filter
chmod a+x /var/spool/lpd/lp/filter
```

then edit it so that it looks like

```
#!/bin/bash
cat | gs -sDEVICE=ljet4 -sOutputFile=- -sPAPERSIZE=a4 -r600x600 -q -
exit 0
```

The `-sDEVICE` option describes the printer, in this example a Hewlett Packard LaserJet 1100. Many printers have similar or compatible formats; hence, there are far fewer `DEVICE`'s than different makes of printers. To get a full list of supported devices, use `gs -h` and also consult one of the following files (depending on your distribution):

```
/usr/doc/ghostscript-?.??/devices.txt
/usr/share/doc/ghostscript-?.??/Devices.htm
/usr/share/doc/gs/devices.txt.gz
```

The `-sOutputFile=-` sets to write to stdout (as required for a filter). The `-sPAPERSIZE` can be set to one of `11x17`, `a3`, `a4`, `a5`, `b3`, `b4`, `b5`, `halfletter`, `ledger`, `legal`, `letter`, `note`, and others listed in the `man` page. You can also use `-g<width>x<height>` to set the exact page size in pixels. `-r600x600` sets the resolution, in this case, 600 dpi (dots per inch). `-q` means to set quiet mode, suppressing any informational messages that would otherwise corrupt the PostScript output, and `-` means to read from stdin and not from a file.

Our printer configuration is now complete. What remains is to start `lpd` and test print. You can do that on the command-line with the `enscript` package. `enscript` is a program to convert plain text files into nicely formatted PostScript pages. The `man` page for `enscript` shows an enormous number of options, but we can simply try:

```
echo hello | enscript -p - | lpr
```

21.7 Access Control

You should be very careful about running `lpd` on any machine that is exposed to the Internet. `lpd` has had numerous security alerts ⟍See Chapter 44.⟋ and should really only be used within a trusted LAN.

To prevent any remote machine from using your printer, `lpd` first looks in the file `/etc/hosts.equiv`. This is a simple list of all machines allowed to print to your printers. My own file looks like this:

```
192.168.3.8
192.168.3.9
192.168.3.10
192.168.3.11
```

The file `/etc/hosts.lpd` does the same but doesn't give administrative control by those machines to the print queues. Note that other services, like `sshd` and `rshd` (or `in.rshd`), also check the `hosts.equiv` file and consider any machine listed to be equi*valent*. This means that they are completed trusted and so `rshd` will not request user logins between machines to be authenticated. This behavior is hence a grave security concern.

LPRng on RedHat 7.0 has a different access control facility. It can arbitrarily limit access in a variety of ways, depending on the remote user and the action (such as who is allowed to manipulate queues). The file `/etc/lpd.perms` contains the configuration. The file format is simple, although LPRng's capabilities are rather involved—to make a long story short, the equivalent `hosts.equiv` becomes in `lpd.perms`

```
ACCEPT SERVICE=* REMOTEIP=192.168.3.8
ACCEPT SERVICE=* REMOTEIP=192.168.3.9
ACCEPT SERVICE=* REMOTEIP=192.168.3.10
ACCEPT SERVICE=* REMOTEIP=192.168.3.11
DEFAULT REJECT
```

Large organizations with many untrusted users should look more closely at the LPRng-HOWTO in `/usr/share/doc/LPRng-`*n.n.nn*. It explains how to limit access in more complicated ways.

21.8   Printing Troubleshooting

Here is a convenient order for checking what is not working.

1. Check that your printer is plugged in and working. All printers have a way of printing a test page. Read your printer manual to find out how.

2. Check your printer cable.

3. Check your CMOS settings for your parallel port.

4. Check your printer cable.

5. Try `echo hello > /dev/lp0` to check that the port is operating. The printer should do something to signify that data has at least been received. Chapter 42 explains how to install your parallel port kernel module.

6. Use the `lpc` program to query the `lpd` daemon. Try `help`, then `status lp`, and so on.

7. Check that there is enough space in your `/var` and `/tmp` devices for any intermediate files needed by the print filter. A large print job may require hundreds of megabytes. `lpd` may not give any kind of error for a print filter failure: the print job may just disappear into nowhere. If you are using legacy `lpr`, then complain to your distribution vendor about your print filter not properly logging to a file.

8. For legacy `lpr`, stop `lpd` and remove all of `lpd`'s runtime ⬁At or pertaining to the program being in a running state.⬂ files from `/var/spool/lpd` and from any of its subdirectories. (New LPRng should never require this step.) The unwanted files are `.seq`, `lock`, `status`, `lpd.lock`, and any left over spool files that failed to disappear with `lprm` (these files are recognizable by long file names with a host name and random key embedded in the file name). Then, restart `lpd`.

9. For remote queues, check that you can do forward *and* reverse lookups on both machines of both machine's host names and IP address. If not, you may get `Host name for your address` (*ipaddr*) `unknown` error messages when trying an `lpq`. Test with the command `host <ip-address>` and also `host <machine-name>` on both machines. If any of these do not work, add entries for both machines in `/etc/hosts` from the example on page 278. Note that the `host` command may be ignorant of the file `/etc/hosts` and may still fail. Chapter 40 will explain name lookup configuration.

10. Run your print filter manually to check that it does, in fact, produce the correct output. For example, `echo hello | enscript -p - | /var/spool/lpd/lp/filter > /dev/lp0`.

11. Legacy `lpd` is a bit of a quirky package—meditate.

21.9 Useful Programs

21.9.1 `printtool`

`printtool` is a graphical printer setup program that helps you very quickly set up
`lpd`. It immediately generates a `printcap` file and magic filter, and you need not
know anything about `lpd` configuration.

21.9.2 `apsfilter`

`apsfilter` stands for *any to PostScript filter*. The setup described above requires everything be converted to PostScript before printing, but a filter could foreseeably use
the `file` command to determine the type of data coming in and then invoke a program
to convert it to PostScript before piping it through `gs`. This would enable JPEG, GIF,
plain text, DVI files, or even `gzipped` HTML to be printed directly, since PostScript
converters have been written for each of these. `apsfilter` is one of a few such filters,
which are generally called *magic filters*. ⟍This is because the `file` command uses magic numbers.
See page 37.⟍

I personally find this feature a gimmick rather than a genuine utility, since most
of the time you want to lay out the graphical object on a page before printing, which
requires you to preview it, and hence convert it to PostScript manually. For most situations, the straight PostScript filter above will work adequately, provided users know
to use `enscript` instead of `lpr` when printing plain text.

21.9.3 `mpage`

`mpage` is a useful utility for saving the trees. It resizes PostScript input so that two,
four or eight pages fit on one. Change your print filter to:

```
#!/bin/bash
cat | mpage -4 | gs -sDEVICE=ljet4 -sOutputFile=- -sPAPERSIZE=a4 -r600x600 -q -
exit 0
```

21.9.4 `psutils`

The package `psutils` contains a variety of command-line PostScript manipulation
programs—a must for anyone doing fancy things with filters.

21.10 Printing to Things Besides Printers

The `printcap` allows anything to be specified as the printer device. If we set it to
`/dev/null` and let our filter force the output to an alternative device, then we can use
`lpd` to redirect "print" jobs to any kind of service imaginable.

Here, `my_filter.sh` is a script that might send the print job through an SMB
(Windows NT) print share (using `smbclient`—see Chapter 39), to a printer previewer,
or to a script that emails the job somewhere.

```
lp1:\
        :sd=/var/spool/lpd/lp1:\
        :mx#0:\
        :sh:\
        :lp=/dev/null:\
        :if=/usr/local/bin/my_filter.sh:
```

We see a specific example of redirecting print jobs to a fax machine in Chapter 33.

Chapter 22

Trivial Introduction to C

C was invented for the purpose of writing an operating system that could be recompiled (ported) to different hardware platforms (different CPUs). Because the operating system is written in **C**, this language is the first choice for writing any kind of application that has to communicate efficiently with the operating system.

Many people who don't program very well in **C** think of **C** as an arbitrary language out of many. This point should be made at once: **C** is the fundamental basis of all computing in the world today. UNIX, Microsoft Windows, office suites, web browsers and device drivers are all written in **C**. Ninety-nine percent of your time spent at a computer is probably spent using an application written in **C**. About 70% of all "open source" software is written in **C**, and the remaining 30% written in languages whose compilers or interpreters are written in **C**. ⟍C++ is also quite popular. It is, however, not as fundamental to computing, although it is more suitable in many situations.⟍

Further, there is no replacement for **C**. Since it fulfills its purpose almost flawlessly, there will never be a need to replace it. *Other languages may fulfill other purposes, but* **C** *fulfills its purpose most adequately.* For instance, all future operating systems will probably be written in **C** for a long time to come.

It is for these reasons that your knowledge of UNIX will never be complete until you can program in **C**. On the other hand, just because you can program in **C** does not mean that you *should*. Good **C** programming is a fine art which many veteran **C** programmers never manage to master, even after many years. *It is essential to join a Free software project to properly master an effective style of* **C** *development.*

22.1 C Fundamentals

We start with a simple **C** program and then add fundamental elements to it. Before going too far, you may wish to review `bash` functions in Section 7.7.

22.1.1 The simplest C program

A simple **C** program is:

```
#include <stdlib.h>
#include <stdio.h>

int main (int argc, char *argv[])
{
    printf ("Hello World!\n");
    return 3;
}
```

Save this program in a file `hello.c`. We will now compile the program. ↘*Compiling is the process of turning C code into assembler instructions. Assembler instructions are the program code that your 80?86/SPARC/RS6000 CPU understands directly. The resulting binary executable is fast because it is executed natively by your processor—it is the very chip that you see on your motherboard that does fetch `Hello` byte for byte from memory and executes each instruction. This is what is meant by million instructions per second (MIPS). The megahertz of the machine quoted by hardware vendors is very roughly the number of MIPS. Interpreted languages (like shell scripts) are much slower because the code itself is written in something not understandable to the CPU. The `/bin/bash` program has to interpret the shell program. `/bin/bash` itself is written in **C**, but the overhead of interpretation makes scripting languages many orders of magnitude slower than compiled languages. Shell scripts do not need to be compiled.↖* Run the command

```
gcc -Wall -o hello hello.c
```

The `-o hello` option tells `gcc` ↘GNU **C** Compiler. `cc` on other UNIX systems.↖ to produce the binary file `hello` instead of the default binary file named `a.out`. ↘Called `a.out` for historical reasons.↖ The `-Wall` option means to report `all` warnings during the compilation. This is not strictly necessary but is most helpful for correcting possible errors in your programs. More compiler options are discussed on page 239.

Then, run the program with

```
./hello
```

Previously you should have familiarized yourself with `bash` functions. In **C** *all* code is inside a function. The first function to be called (by the operating system) is the `main` function.

Type `echo $?` to see the return code of the program. You will see it is 3, the return value of the `main` function.

Other things to note are the `"` on either side of the string to be printed. Quotes are required around string literals. Inside a string literal, the `\n` *escape sequence* indicates a newline character. `ascii`(7) shows some other escape sequences. You can also see a proliferation of `;` everywhere in a **C** program. Every statement in **C** is terminated by a `;` unlike statements in shell scripts where a `;` is optional.

Now try:

```
#include <stdlib.h>
#include <stdio.h>

int main (int argc, char *argv[])
{
    printf ("number %d, number %d\n", 1 + 2, 10);
    exit (3);
}
```

`printf` can be thought of as the command to send output to the terminal. It is also what is known as a *standard* **C** *library function*. In other words, it is specified that a **C** implementation should always have the `printf` function and that it should behave in a certain way.

The `%d` specifies that a *decimal* should go in at that point in the text. The number to be substituted will be the first *argument* to the `printf` function after the string literal—that is, the `1 + 2`. The next `%d` is substituted with the second argument—that is, the `10`. The `%d` is known as a *format specifier*. It essentially *converts* an integer number into a decimal representation. See `printf`(3) for more details.

22.1.2 Variables and types

With `bash`, you could use a variable anywhere, anytime, and the variable would just be blank if it had never been assigned a value. In **C**, however, you have to explicitly tell the compiler what variables you are going to need before each block of code. You do this with a variable declaration:

```
#include <stdlib.h>
#include <stdio.h>

int main (int argc, char *argv[])
{
    int x;
    int y;
    x = 10;
    y = 2:
    printf ("number %d, number %d\n", 1 + y, x);
    exit (3);
```

```
  }
```

The int x is a variable declaration. It tells the program to reserve space for one *integer* variable that it will later refer to as x. int is the *type* of the variable. x = 10 assigned a value of 10 to the variable. There are types for each kind of number you would like to work with, and format specifiers to convert them for printing:

```
#include <stdlib.h>
#include <stdio.h>

int main (int argc, char *argv[])
{
    char a;
    short b;
    int c;
    long d;
    float e;
    double f;
    long double g;
    a = 'A';
    b = 10;
    c = 10000000;
    d = 10000000;
    e = 3.14159;
    f = 10e300;
    g = 10e300;
    printf ("%c, %hd, %d, %ld, %f, %f, %Lf\n", a, b, c, d, e, f, g);
    exit (3);
}
```

You will notice that %f is used for both floats *and* doubles. The reason is that a float is always converted to a double before an operation like this. Also try replacing %f with %e to print in exponential notation—that is, less significant digits.

22.1.3 Functions

Functions are implemented as follows:

```
#include <stdlib.h>
#include <stdio.h>

void mutiply_and_print (int x, int y)
{
    printf ("%d * %d = %d\n", x, y, x * y);
}

int main (int argc, char *argv[])
{
    mutiply_and_print (30, 5);
```

```
    mutiply_and_print (12, 3);
    exit (3);
}
```

Here we have a non-main function *called* by the `main` function. The function is first *declared* with

```
void mutiply_and_print (int x, int y)
```

This declaration states the return value of the function (`void` for no return value), the function name (`mutiply_and_print`), and then the *arguments* that are going to be passed to the function. The numbers passed to the function are given their own names, x and y, and are converted to the type of x and y before being passed to the function—in this case, `int` and `int`. The actual **C** code that comprises the function goes between curly braces { and }.

In other words, the above function is equivalent to:

```
void mutiply_and_print ()
{
    int x;
    int y;
    x = <first-number-passed>
    y = <second-number-passed>
    printf ("%d * %d = %d\n", x, y, x * y);
}
```

22.1.4   `for`, `while`, `if`, and `switch` statements

As with shell scripting, we have the `for`, `while`, and `if` statements:

```
#include <stdlib.h>
#include <stdio.h>

int main (int argc, char *argv[])
{
    int x;

    x = 10;

    if (x == 10) {
        printf ("x is exactly 10\n");
        x++;
    } else if (x == 20) {
        printf ("x is equal to 20\n");
    } else {
```

```
            printf ("No, x is not equal to 10 or 20\n");
        }

        if (x > 10) {
20          printf ("Yes, x is more than 10\n");
        }

        while (x > 0) {
            printf ("x is %d\n", x);
25          x = x - 1;
        }

        for (x = 0; x < 10; x++) {
            printf ("x is %d\n", x);
30      }

        switch (x) {
            case 9:
                printf ("x is nine\n");
35              break;
            case 10:
                printf ("x is ten\n");
                break;
            case 11:
40              printf ("x is eleven\n");
                break;
            default:
                printf ("x is huh?\n");
                break;
45      }

        return 0;
    }
```

It is easy to see the format that these statements take, although they are vastly different from shell scripts. **C** code works in *statement blocks* between curly braces, in the same way that shell scripts have do's and done's.

Note that with most programming languages when we want to add 1 to a variable we have to write, say, x = x + 1. In **C**, the abbreviation x++ is used, meaning to *increment* a variable by 1.

The for loop takes three statements between (...): a statement to start things off, a comparison, and a statement to be executed on each completion of the statement block. The statement block after the for is repeatedly executed until the comparison is untrue.

The switch statement is like case in shell scripts. switch considers the argument inside its (...) and decides which case line to jump to. In this example it will obviously be printf ("x is ten\n"); because x was 10 when the previous for loop exited. The break tokens mean that we are through with the switch statement and that execution should continue from Line 46.

Note that in **C** the comparison == is used instead of =. The symbol = means to assign a value to a variable, whereas == is an *equality operator*.

22.1.5 Strings, arrays, and memory allocation

You can define a list of numbers with:

```
int y[10];
```

This list is called an *array*:

```
#include <stdlib.h>
#include <stdio.h>

int main (int argc, char *argv[])
{
    int x;
    int y[10];
    for (x = 0; x < 10; x++) {
        y[x] = x * 2;
    }
    for (x = 0; x < 10; x++) {
        printf ("item %d is %d\n", x, y[x]);
    }
    return 0;
}
```

If an array is of type char*acter*, then it is called a *string*:

```
#include <stdlib.h>
#include <stdio.h>

int main (int argc, char *argv[])
{
    int x;
    char y[11];
    for (x = 0; x < 10; x++) {
        y[x] = 65 + x * 2;
    }
    for (x = 0; x < 10; x++) {
        printf ("item %d is %d\n", x, y[x]);
    }
    y[10] = 0;
    printf ("string is %s\n", y);
    return 0;
}
```

Note that a string has to be *null-terminated*. This means that the last character must be a zero. The code y[10] = 0 sets the 11th item in the array to zero. This also means that strings need to be one char longer than you would think.

213

(Note that the first item in the array is y[0], not y[1], as with some other programming languages.)

In the preceding example, the line char y[11] reserved 11 bytes for the string. But what if you want a string of 100,000 bytes? **C** allows you to request memory from the kernel. This is called *allocate memory*. Any non-trivial program will allocate memory for itself and there is no other way of getting large blocks of memory for your program to use. Try:

```
#include <stdlib.h>
#include <stdio.h>

int main (int argc, char *argv[])
{
    int x;
    char *y;
    y = malloc (11);
    printf ("%ld\n", y);
    for (x = 0; x < 10; x++) {
        y[x] = 65 + x * 2;
    }
    y[10] = 0;
    printf ("string is %s\n", y);
    free (y);
    return 0;
}
```

The declaration char *y means to declare a variable (a number) called y that *points* to a memory location. The * (*asterisk*) in this context means *pointer*. For example, if you have a machine with perhaps 256 megabytes of RAM + swap, then y potentially has a range of this much. The numerical value of y is also printed with printf ("%ld\n", y);, but is of no interest to the programmer.

When you have finished using memory you must give it back to the operating system by using free. Programs that don't free all the memory they allocate are said to *leak* memory.

Allocating memory often requires you to perform a calculation to determine the amount of memory required. In the above case we are allocating the space of 11 chars. Since each char is really a single byte, this presents no problem. But what if we were allocating 11 ints? An int on a PC is 32 bits—four bytes. To determine the size of a type, we use the sizeof keyword:

```
#include <stdlib.h>
#include <stdio.h>

int main (int argc, char *argv[])
{
    int a;
    int b;
```

```
        int c;
        int d;
10      int e;
        int f;
        int g;
        a = sizeof (char);
        b = sizeof (short);
15      c = sizeof (int);
        d = sizeof (long);
        e = sizeof (float);
        f = sizeof (double);
        g = sizeof (long double);
20      printf ("%d, %d, %d, %d, %d, %d, %d\n", a, b, c, d, e, f, g);
        return 0;
}
```

Here you can see the number of bytes required by all of these types. Now we can easily allocate arrays of things other than `char`.

```
#include <stdlib.h>
#include <stdio.h>

int main (int argc, char *argv[])
5  {
        int x;
        int *y;
        y = malloc (10 * sizeof (int));
        printf ("%ld\n", y);
10      for (x = 0; x < 10; x++) {
            y[x] = 65 + x * 2;
        }
        for (x = 0; x < 10; x++) {
            printf ("%d\n", y[x]);
15      }
        free (y);
        return 0;
}
```

On many machines an `int` is four bytes (32 bits), but you should never assume this. *Always use the `sizeof` keyword to allocate memory.*

22.1.6 String operations

C programs probably do more string manipulation than anything else. Here is a program that divides a sentence into words:

```
#include <stdlib.h>
#include <stdio.h>
#include <string.h>

5  int main (int argc, char *argv[])
```

```
   {
       int length_of_word;
       int i;
       int length_of_sentence;
10     char p[256];
       char *q;

       strcpy (p, "hello there, my name is fred.");

15     length_of_sentence = strlen (p);

       length_of_word = 0;

       for (i = 0; i <= length_of_sentence; i++) {
20         if (p[i] == ' ' || i == length_of_sentence) {
               q = malloc (length_of_word + 1);
               if (q == 0) {
                   perror ("malloc failed");
                   abort ();
25             }
               strncpy (q, p + i - length_of_word, length_of_word);
               q[length_of_word] = 0;
               printf ("word: %s\n", q);
               free (q);
30             length_of_word = 0;
           } else {
               length_of_word = length_of_word + 1;
           }
       }
35     return 0;
   }
```

Here we introduce three more *standard* **C** *library functions*. strcpy stands for st*ring*copy. It copies bytes from one place to another sequentially, until it reaches a zero byte (i.e., the end of string). Line 13 of this program copies text *into* the character array p, which is called the *target* of the copy.

strlen stands for st*ring*length. It determines the length of a string, which is just a count of the number of characters up to the null character.

We need to loop over the length of the sentence. The variable i indicates the current position in the sentence.

Line 20 says that if we find a character 32 (denoted by ' '), we know we have reached a word boundary. We also know that the end of the sentence is a word boundary even though there may not be a space there. The token || means **OR**. At this point we can allocate memory for the current word and copy the word into that memory. The strncpy function is useful for this. It copies a string, but only up to a limit of length_of_word characters (the last argument). Like strcpy, the first argument is the target, and the second argument is the place to copy from.

To calculate the position of the start of the last word, we use p + i - length_of_word. This means that we are adding i to the memory location p and then going back `length_of_word` counts thereby pointing `strncpy` to the exact position.

Finally, we null-terminate the string on Line 27. We can then print `q`, `free` the used memory, and begin with the next word.

For a complete list of string operations, see `string`(3).

22.1.7 File operations

Under most programming languages, file operations involve three steps: *opening* a file, *reading* or *writing* to the file, and then *closing* the file. You use the command `fopen` to tell the operating system that you are ready to begin working with a file:

The following program opens a file and spits it out on the terminal:

```
#include <stdlib.h>
#include <stdio.h>
#include <string.h>

int main (int argc, char *argv[])
{
    int c;
    FILE *f;

    f = fopen ("mytest.c", "r");
    if (f == 0) {
        perror ("fopen");
        return 1;
    }
    for (;;) {
        c = fgetc (f);
        if (c == -1)
            break;
        printf ("%c", c);
    }
    fclose (f);
    return 0;
}
```

A new type is presented here: `FILE *`. It is a file operations variable that must be *initialized* with `fopen` before it can be used. The `fopen` function takes two arguments: the first is the name of the file, and the second is a string explaining *how* we want to open the file—in this case `"r"` means *reading* from the start of the file. Other options are `"w"` for *writing* and several more described in `fopen`(3).

If the return value of `fopen` is zero, it means that `fopen` has failed. The `perror` function then prints a textual error message (for example, `No such file or directory`). It is essential to check the return value of all library calls in this way. These checks will constitute about one third of your **C** program.

The command `fgetc` *gets* a character from the file. It retrieves consecutive bytes from the file until it reaches the end of the file, when it returns a −1. The `break` statement says to immediately terminate the `for` loop, whereupon execution will continue from line 21. `break` statements can appear inside `while` loops as well.

You will notice that the `for` statement is empty. This is allowable **C** code and means to loop forever.

Some other file functions are `fread`, `fwrite`, `fputc`, `fprintf`, and `fseek`. See `fwrite`(3), `fputc`(3), `fprintf`(3), and `fseek`(3).

22.1.8 Reading command-line arguments inside C programs

Up until now, you are probably wondering what the (`int argc, char *argv[]`) are for. These are the command-line arguments passed to the program by the shell. `argc` is the total number of command-line arguments, and `argv` is an array of strings of each argument. Printing them out is easy:

```
     #include <stdlib.h>
     #include <stdio.h>
     #include <string.h>

 5   int main (int argc, char *argv[])
     {
         int i;
         for (i = 0; i < argc; i++) {
             printf ("argument %d is %s\n", i, argv[i]);
10       }
         return 0;
     }
```

22.1.9 A more complicated example

Here we put this altogether in a program that reads in lots of files and dumps them as words. Here are some new notations you will encounter: `!=` is the inverse of `==` and tests if *not-equal-to*; `realloc` *reallocates* memory—it resizes an old block of memory so that any bytes of the old block are preserved; `\n`, `\t` mean the newline character, 10, or the tab character, 9, respectively (see `ascii`(7)).

```
     #include <stdlib.h>
     #include <stdio.h>
     #include <string.h>

 5   void word_dump (char *filename)
     {
         int length_of_word;
         int amount_allocated;
```

```
        char *q;
10      FILE *f;
        int c;

        c = 0;

15      f = fopen (filename, "r");
        if (f == 0) {
            perror ("fopen failed");
            exit (1);
        }
20
        length_of_word = 0;

        amount_allocated = 256;
        q = malloc (amount_allocated);
25      if (q == 0) {
            perror ("malloc failed");
            abort ();
        }

30      while (c != -1) {
            if (length_of_word >= amount_allocated) {
                amount_allocated = amount_allocated * 2;
                q = realloc (q, amount_allocated);
                if (q == 0) {
35                  perror ("realloc failed");
                    abort ();
                }
            }

40          c = fgetc (f);
            q[length_of_word] = c;

            if (c == -1 || c == ' ' || c == '\n' || c == '\t') {
                if (length_of_word > 0) {
45                  q[length_of_word] = 0;
                    printf ("%s\n", q);
                }
                amount_allocated = 256;
                q = realloc (q, amount_allocated);
50              if (q == 0) {
                    perror ("realloc failed");
                    abort ();
                }
                length_of_word = 0;
55          } else {
                length_of_word = length_of_word + 1;
            }
        }

60      fclose (f);
    }

    int main (int argc, char *argv[])
    {
65      int i;

        if (argc < 2) {
            printf ("Usage:\n\twordsplit <filename> ...\n");
            exit (1);
70      }

        for (i = 1; i < argc; i++) {
            word_dump (argv[i]);
```

```
75        }

          return 0;
      }
```

This program is more complicated than you might immediately expect. Reading in a file where we are *sure* that a word will never exceed 30 characters is simple. But what if we have a file that contains some words that are 100,000 characters long? GNU🐃 programs are expected to behave correctly under these circumstances.

To cope with normal as well as extreme circumstances, we start off assuming that a word will never be more than 256 characters. If it appears that the word is growing over 256 characters, we `reallocate` the memory space to double its size (lines 32 amd 33). When we start with a new word, we can free up memory again, so we `realloc` back to 256 again (lines 48 and 49). In this way we are using the minimum amount of memory at each point in time.

We have hence created a program that can work efficiently with a 100-gigabyte file just as easily as with a 100-byte file. *This is part of the art of* **C** *programming.*

Experienced **C** programmers may actually scoff at the above listing because it really isn't as "minimalistic" as is absolutely possible. In fact, it is a truly excellent listing for the following reasons:

- The program is easy to understand.

- The program uses an efficient algorithm (albeit not optimal).

- The program contains no arbitrary limits that would cause unexpected behavior in extreme circumstances.

- The program uses no nonstandard **C** functions or notations that would prohibit it compiling successfully on other systems. It is therefore *portable*.

Readability in **C** *is your first priority—it is imperative that what you do is* obvious *to anyone reading the code.*

22.1.10 `#include` statements and prototypes

At the start of each program will be one or more `#include` statements. These tell the compiler to read in another **C** program. Now, "raw" **C** does not have a whole lot in the way of protecting against errors: for example, the `strcpy` function could just as well be used with one, three, or four arguments, and the **C** program would still compile. It would, however, wreak havoc with the internal memory and cause the program to crash. These other `.h` **C** programs are called *header* files. They contain templates for how functions are meant to be called. Every function you might like to use is contained in one or another template file. The templates are called *function prototypes.* ⟍C++ has something called "templates." This is a special C++ term having nothing to do with the discussion here.⟋

A function prototype is written the same as the function itself, but without the code. A function prototype for `word_dump` would simply be:

```
void word_dump (char *filename);
```

The trailing `;` is essential and distinguishes a function prototype from a function.

After a function prototype is defined, any attempt to use the function in a way other than intended—say, passing it to few arguments or arguments of the wrong type—will be met with fierce opposition from `gcc`.

You will notice that the `#include <string.h>` appeared when we started using `string` operations. Recompiling these programs without the `#include <string.h>` line gives the warning message

```
mytest.c:21: warning: implicit declaration of function 'strncpy'
```

which is quite to the point.

The function prototypes give a clear definition of how every function is to be used. Man pages will always first state the function prototype so that you are clear on what arguments are to be passed and what types they should have.

22.1.11   C comments

A **C** comment is denoted with `/* <comment lines> */` and can span multiple lines. Anything between the `/*` and `*/` is ignored. Every function should be commented, and all nonobvious code should be commented. It is a good maxim that a program that *needs* lots of comments to explain it is *badly written*. Also, never comment the obvious, and explain *why* you do things rather that *what* you are doing. It is advisable *not* to make pretty graphics between each function, so rather:

```
/* returns -1 on error, takes a positive integer */
int sqr (int x)
{
    <...>
```

than

```
/************************----SQR----********************************
 *                  x = argument to make the square of            *
 *      return value  =                                           *
 *                              -1 (on error)                     *
 *                              square of x (on success)          *
 ****************************************************************/
```

```
int sqr (int x)
{
    <...>
```

which is liable to cause nausea. In C++, the additional comment `//` is allowed, whereby everything between the `//` and the end of the line is ignored. It is accepted under `gcc`, but should not be used unless you really are programming in C++. In addition, programmers often "comment out" lines by placing a `#if 0 ... #endif` around them, which really does exactly the same thing as a comment (see Section 22.1.12) but allows you to have comments within comments. For example

```
     int x;
     x = 10;
#if 0
     printf ("debug: x is %d\n", x);     /* print debug information */
5 #endif
     y = x + 10;
     <...>
```

comments out Line 4.

22.1.12 `#define` and `#if` — C macros

Anything starting with a # is not actually **C**, but a **C** *preprocessor directive*. A **C** program is first run through a *preprocessor* that removes all spurious junk, like comments, `#include` statements, and anything else beginning with a #. You can make **C** programs much more readable by defining *macros* instead of literal values. For instance,

```
#define START_BUFFER_SIZE 256
```

in our example program, `#defines` the text `START_BUFFER_SIZE` to be the text `256`. Thereafter, wherever in the **C** program we have a `START_BUFFER_SIZE`, the text `256` will be seen by the compiler, and we can use `START_BUFFER_SIZE` instead. This is a much *cleaner* way of programming because, if, say, we would like to change the `256` to some other value, we only need to change it in one place. `START_BUFFER_SIZE` is also more meaningful than a number, making the program more readable.

Whenever you have a *literal constant* like `256`, you should replace it with a macro defined near the top of your program.

You can also check for the existence of macros with the `#ifdef` and `#ifndef` directive. # directives are really a programming language all on their own:

```
/* Set START_BUFFER_SIZE to fine-tune performance before compiling: */
#define START_BUFFER_SIZE 256
/* #define START_BUFFER_SIZE 128 */
/* #define START_BUFFER_SIZE 1024 */
5 /* #define START_BUFFER_SIZE 16384 */
```

```
     #ifndef START_BUFFER_SIZE
     #error This code did not define START_BUFFER_SIZE. Please edit
     #endif
10
     #if START_BUFFER_SIZE <= 0
     #error Wooow! START_BUFFER_SIZE must be greater than zero
     #endif

15   #if START_BUFFER_SIZE < 16
     #warning START_BUFFER_SIZE to small, program may be inefficient
     #elif START_BUFFER_SIZE > 65536
     #warning START_BUFFER_SIZE to large, program may be inefficient
     #else
20   /* START_BUFFER_SIZE is ok, do not report */
     #endif

     void word_dump (char *filename)
     {
25       <...>
         amount_allocated = START_BUFFER_SIZE;
         q = malloc (amount_allocated);
         <...>
```

22.2 Debugging with gdb and strace

Programming errors, or *bugs*, can be found by inspecting program execution. Some developers claim that the need for such inspection implies a sloppy development process. Nonetheless it is instructive to learn **C** by actually watching a program work.

22.2.1 gdb

The GNU🐃 debugger, gdb, is a replacement for the standard UNIX debugger, db. To debug a program means to step through its execution line-by-line, in order to find programming errors as they happen. Use the command gcc -Wall -g -O0 -o word-split wordsplit.c to recompile your program above. The -g option enables debugging support in the resulting executable and the -O0 option disables compiler optimization (which sometimes causes confusing behavior). For the following example, create a test file readme.txt with some plain text inside it. You can then run gdb -q wordsplit. The standard gdb prompt will appear, which indicates the start of a *debugging session*:

```
(gdb)
```

At the prompt, many one letter commands are available to control program execution.

The first of these is *run* which executes the program as though it had been started from a regular shell:

```
(gdb) r
Starting program: /homes/src/wordsplit/wordsplit
Usage:
        wordsplit <filename> ...

Program exited with code 01.
```

Obviously, we will want to set some trial command-line arguments. This is done with the special command, `set args`:

```
(gdb) set args readme.txt readme2.txt
```

The b*reak* command is used like b [[<file>:]<line>|<function>], and sets a *break point* at a function or line number:

```
(gdb) b main
Breakpoint 1 at 0x8048796: file wordsplit.c, line 67.
```

A break point will interrupt execution of the program. In this case the program will stop when it enters the `main` function (i.e., right at the start). Now we can `run` the program again:

```
(gdb) r
Starting program: /home/src/wordsplit/wordsplit readme.txt readme2.txt

Breakpoint 1, main (argc=3, argv=0xbffff804) at wordsplit.c:67
67              if (argc < 2) {
(gdb)
```

As specified, the program stops at the beginning of the `main` function at line 67.

If you are interested in viewing the contents of a variable, you can use the print command:

```
(gdb) p argc
$1 = 3
(gdb) p argv[1]
$2 = 0xbffff988 "readme.txt"
```

which tells us the value of `argc` and `argv[1]`. The *list* command displays the lines about the current line:

```
(gdb) l
63      int main (int argc, char *argv[])
64      {
65          int i;
66
```

```
67              if (argc < 2) {
68                      printf ("Usage:\n\twordsplit <filename> ...\n");
69                      exit (1);
70              }
```

The `list` command can also take an optional file and line number (or even a function name):

```
(gdb) l wordsplit.c:1
1       #include <stdlib.h>
2       #include <stdio.h>
3       #include <string.h>
4
5       void word_dump (char *filename)
6       {
7               int length_of_word;
8               int amount_allocated;
```

Next, we can try setting a break point at an arbitrary line and then using the *continue* command to proceed with program execution:

```
(gdb) b wordsplit.c:48
Breakpoint 2 at 0x804873e: file wordsplit.c, line 48.
(gdb) c
Continuing.
Zaphod

Breakpoint 2, word_dump (filename=0xbffff988 "readme.txt") at wordsplit.c:48
48                      amount_allocated = 256;
```

Execution obediently stops at line 48. At this point it is useful to run a backtrace. This prints out the current *stack* which shows the functions that were called to get to the current line. This output allows you to *trace* the history of execution.

```
(gdb) bt
#0  word_dump (filename=0xbffff988 "readme.txt") at wordsplit.c:48
#1  0x80487e0 in main (argc=3, argv=0xbffff814) at wordsplit.c:73
#2  0x4003db65 in __libc_start_main (main=0x8048790 <main>, argc=3, ubp_av=0xbf
fff814, init=0x8048420 <_init>,
    fini=0x804883c <_fini>, rtld_fini=0x4000df24 <_dl_fini>, stack_end=0xbffff8
0c) at ../sysdeps/generic/libc-start.c:111
```

The `clear` command then deletes the break point at the current line:

```
(gdb) clear
Deleted breakpoint 2
```

The most important commands for debugging are the *next* and *step* commands. The n command simply executes one line of **C** code:

```
(gdb) n
49                      q = realloc (q, amount_allocated);
(gdb) n
50                      if (q == 0) {
(gdb) n
54                      length_of_word = 0;
```

This activity is called *stepping* through your program. The s command is identical to
n except that it dives into functions instead of running them as single line. To see the
difference, step over line 73 first with n, and then with s, as follows:

```
(gdb) set args readme.txt readme2.txt
(gdb) b main
Breakpoint 1 at 0x8048796: file wordsplit.c, line 67.
(gdb) r
Starting program: /home/src/wordsplit/wordsplit readme.txt readme2.txt

Breakpoint 1, main (argc=3, argv=0xbffff814) at wordsplit.c:67
67              if (argc < 2) {
(gdb) n
72              for (i = 1; i < argc; i++) {
(gdb) n
73                      word_dump (argv[i]);
(gdb) n
Zaphod
has
two
heads
72              for (i = 1; i < argc; i++) {
(gdb) s
73                      word_dump (argv[i]);
(gdb) s
word_dump (filename=0xbffff993 "readme2.txt") at wordsplit.c:13
13              c = 0;
(gdb) s
15              f = fopen (filename, "r");
(gdb)
```

An interesting feature of gdb is its ability to attach onto running programs. Try
the following sequence of commands:

```
[root@cericon]# lpd
[root@cericon]# ps awx | grep lpd
28157 ?        S      0:00 lpd Waiting
28160 pts/6    S      0:00 grep lpd
[root@cericon]# gdb -q /usr/sbin/lpd
(no debugging symbols found)...
(gdb) attach 28157
Attaching to program: /usr/sbin/lpd, Pid 28157
0x40178bfe in __select () from /lib/libc.so.6
(gdb)
```

The lpd daemon was not compiled with debugging support, but the point is still made: you can halt and debug *any* running process on the system. Try running a bt for fun. Now release the process with

```
(gdb) detach
Detaching from program: /usr/sbin/lpd, Pid 28157
```

The debugger provides copious amounts of online help. The help command can be run to explain further. The gdb info pages also elaborate on an enormous number of display features and tracing features not covered here.

22.2.2 Examining core files

If your program has a segmentation violation ("segfault") then a core file will be written to the current directory. This is known as a *core dump*. A core dump is caused by a bug in the program—its response to a SIGSEGV signal sent to the program because it tried to access an area of memory outside of its allowed range. These files can be examined using gdb to (usually) reveal where the problem occurred. Simply run gdb <executable> ./core and then type bt (or any gdb command) at the gdb prompt. Typing file ./core will reveal something like

```
/root/core: ELF 32-bit LSB core file of '<executable>' (signal 11), Intel 80386, version 1
```

22.2.3 strace

The strace command prints every *system call* performed by a program. A system call is a function call made *by* a **C** library function to the LINUX⚫ kernel. Try

```
strace ls
strace ./wordsplit
```

If a program has not been compiled with debugging support, the only way to inspect its execution may be with the strace command. In any case, the command can provide valuable information about where a program is failing and is useful for diagnosing errors.

22.3 C Libraries

We made reference to the Standard **C** library. The **C** language on its own does almost nothing; everything useful is an external function. External functions are grouped into libraries. The Standard **C** library is the file `/lib/libc.so.6`. To list all the **C** library functions, run:

```
nm /lib/libc.so.6
nm /lib/libc.so.6 | grep ' T ' | cut -f3 -d' ' | grep -v '^_' | sort -u | less
```

many of these have man pages, but some will have no documentation and require you to read the comments inside the header files (which are often most explanatory). It is better not to use functions unless you are sure that they are *standard* functions in the sense that they are common to other systems.

To create your own library is simple. Let's say we have two files that contain several functions that we would like to compile into a library. The files are `simple_math_sqrt.c`

```
   #include <stdlib.h>
   #include <stdio.h>

   static int abs_error (int a, int b)
5  {
       if (a > b)
           return a - b;
       return b - a;
   }

10
   int simple_math_isqrt (int x)
   {
       int result;
       if (x < 0) {
15         fprintf (stderr,
             "simple_math_sqrt: taking the sqrt of a negative number\n");
           abort ();
       }
       result = 2;
20     while (abs_error (result * result, x) > 1) {
           result = (x / result + result) / 2;
       }
       return result;
   }
```

and `simple_math_pow.c`

```
   #include <stdlib.h>
   #include <stdio.h>

   int simple_math_ipow (int x, int y)
5  {
       int result;
       if (x == 1 || y == 0)
           return 1;
       if (x == 0 && y < 0) {
10         fprintf (stderr,
             "simple_math_pow: raising zero to a negative power\n");
```

228

```
        abort ();
    }
    if (y < 0)
15          return 0;
    result = 1;
    while (y > 0) {
        result = result * x;
        y = y - 1;
20  }
    return result;
}
```

We would like to call the library `simple_math`. It is good practice to name all the functions in the library `simple_math_??????`. The function `abs_error` is not going to be used outside of the file `simple_math_sqrt.c` and so we put the keyword `static` in front of it, meaning that it is a *local* function.

We can compile the code with:

```
gcc -Wall -c simple_math_sqrt.c
gcc -Wall -c simple_math_pow.c
```

The `-c` option means *compile only*. The code is not turned into an executable. The generated files are `simple_math_sqrt.o` and `simple_math_pow.o`. These are called *object* files.

We now need to *archive* these files into a library. We do this with the `ar` command (a predecessor of `tar`):

```
ar libsimple_math.a simple_math_sqrt.o simple_math_pow.o
ranlib libsimple_math.a
```

The `ranlib` command indexes the archive.

The library can now be used. Create a file `mytest.c`:

```
#include <stdlib.h>
#include <stdio.h>

int main (int argc, char *argv[])
5  {
    printf ("%d\n", simple_math_ipow (4, 3));
    printf ("%d\n", simple_math_isqrt (50));
    return 0;
}
```

and run

```
gcc -Wall -c mytest.c
gcc -o mytest mytest.o -L. -lsimple_math
```

The first command compiles the file `mytest.c` into `mytest.o`, and the second function is called *linking* the program, which assimilates `mytest.o` and the libraries into a single executable. The option `L.` means to look in the current directory for any libraries (usually only `/lib` and `/usr/lib` are searched). The option `-lsimple_math` means to assimilate the library `libsimple_math.a` (`lib` and `.a` are added automatically). This operation is called *static* ⟍Nothing to do with the `"static"` keyword.⟍ linking because it happens before the program is run and includes all object files into the executable.

As an aside, note that it is often the case that many static libraries are linked into the same program. Here order is important: the library with the least dependencies should come last, or you will get so-called *symbol referencing errors*.

We can also create a header file `simple_math.h` for using the library.

```
  /* calculates the integer square root, aborts on error */
  int simple_math_isqrt (int x);

  /* calculates the integer power, aborts on error */
5 int simple_math_ipow (int x, int y);
```

Add the line `#include "simple_math.h"` to the top of `mytest.c`:

```
#include <stdlib.h>
#include <stdio.h>
#include "simple_math.h"
```

This addition gets rid of the `implicit declaration of function` warning messages. Usually `#include <simple_math.h>` would be used, but here, this is a header file in the current directory—our *own* header file—and this is where we use `"simple_math.h"` instead of `<simple_math.h>`.

22.4   C Projects — `Makefiles`

What if you make a small change to one of the files (as you are likely to do very often when developing)? You could script the process of compiling and linking, but the script would build everything, and not just the changed file. What we really need is a utility that only recompiles object files whose sources have changed: `make` is such a utility.

`make` is a program that looks inside a `Makefile` in the current directory then does a lot of compiling and linking. `Makefiles` contain lists of rules and *dependencies* describing how to build a program.

Inside a `Makefile` you need to state a list of *what-depends-on-what* dependencies that `make` can work through, as well as the shell commands needed to achieve each goal.

22.4.1 Completing our example **Makefile**

Our first (last?) *dependency* in the process of completing the compilation is that mytest *depends on* both the library, libsimple_math.a, and the object file, mytest.o. In make terms we create a Makefile line that looks like:

```
mytest:    libsimple_math.a mytest.o
```

meaning simply that the files libsimple_math.a mytest.o must exist and be updated before mytest. mytest: is called a make *target*. Beneath this line, we also need to state how to build mytest:

```
        gcc -Wall -o $@ mytest.o -L. -lsimple_math
```

The $@ means the name of the target itself, which is just substituted with mytest. *Note that the space before the* gcc *is a tab character and not 8 space characters.*

The next dependency is that libsimple_math.a depends on simple_math_sqrt.o simple_math_pow.o. Once again we have a dependency, along with a shell script to build the target. The full Makefile *rule* is:

```
libsimple_math.a: simple_math_sqrt.o simple_math_pow.o
        rm -f $@
        ar rc $@ simple_math_sqrt.o simple_math_pow.o
        ranlib $@
```

Note again that the left margin consists of a single tab character and not spaces.

The final dependency is that the files simple_math_sqrt.o and simple_math_pow.o depend on the files simple_math_sqrt.c and simple_math_pow.c. This requires two make target rules, but make has a short way of stating such a rule in the case of many **C** source files,

```
.c.o:
        gcc -Wall -c -o $*.o $<
```

which means that any .o files needed can be built from a .c file of a similar name by means of the command gcc -Wall -c -o $*.o $<, where $*.o means the name of the object file and $< means the name of the file that $*.o depends on, one at a time.

22.4.2 Putting it all together

Makefiles can, in fact, have their rules put in any order, so it's best to state the most obvious rules first for readability.

There is also a rule you should always state at the outset:

```
all:     libsimple_math.a mytest
```

The `all:` target is the rule that `make` tries to satisfy when `make` is run with no command-line arguments. This just means that `libsimple_math.a` and `mytest` are the last two files to be built, that is, they are the top-level dependencies.

Makefiles also have their own form of environment variables, like shell scripts. You can see that we have used the text `simple_math` in three of our rules. It makes sense to define a *macro* for this so that we can easily change to a different library name.

Our final `Makefile` is:

```
      # Comments start with a # (hash) character like shell scripts.
      # Makefile to build libsimple_math.a and mytest program.
      # Paul Sheer <psheer@icon.co.za> Sun Mar 19 15:56:08 2000

  5   OBJS     = simple_math_sqrt.o simple_math_pow.o
      LIBNAME  = simple_math
      CFLAGS   = -Wall

      all:     lib$(LIBNAME).a mytest
 10
      mytest:  lib$(LIBNAME).a mytest.o
               gcc $(CFLAGS) -o $@ mytest.o -L. -l${LIBNAME}

      lib$(LIBNAME).a: $(OBJS)
 15            rm -f $@
               ar rc $@ $(OBJS)
               ranlib $@

      .c.o:
 20            gcc $(CFLAGS) -c -o $*.o $<

      clean:
               rm -f *.o *.a mytest
```

We can now easily type

```
make
```

in the current directory to cause everything to be built.

You can see we have added an additional disconnected target `clean:`. Targets can be run explictly on the command-line like this:

```
make clean
```

which removes all built files.

Makefiles have far more uses than just building **C** programs. Anything that needs to be built from sources can employ a `Makefile` to make things easier.

Chapter 23

Shared Libraries

This chapter follows directly from our construction of *static* .a libraries in Chapter 22. It discusses creation and installation of *Dynamically Linked Libraries* (DLLs). Here I show you both so that you have a good technical overview of how DLLs work on UNIX. You can then promptly forget everything except ldconfig and LD_LIBRARY_PATH discussed below.

The .a library file is good for creating functions that many programs can include. This practice is called *code reuse*. But note how the .a file is *linked into* (included) in the executable mytest in Chapter 22. mytest is enlarged by the size of libsimple_math.a. When hundreds of programs use the same .a file, that code is effectively duplicated all over the file system. Such inefficiency was deemed unacceptable long before LINUX, so library files were invented that only link with the program when it runs—a process known as *dynamic* linking. Instead of .a files, similar .so (*shared object*) files live in /lib/ and /usr/lib/ and are automatically linked to a program when it runs.

23.1 Creating DLL .so Files

Creating a DLL requires several changes to the Makefile on page 232:

```
OBJS        = simple_math_sqrt.o simple_math_pow.o
LIBNAME     = simple_math
SONAME      = libsimple_math.so.1.0.0
SOVERSION   = libsimple_math.so.1.0
CFLAGS      = -Wall

all:    lib$(LIBNAME).so mytest
```

```
     mytest: lib$(LIBNAME).so mytest.o
10           gcc $(CFLAGS) -o $@ mytest.o -L. -l${LIBNAME}

     lib$(LIBNAME).so: $(OBJS)
             gcc -shared $(CFLAGS) $(OBJS) -lc -Wl,-soname -Wl,$(SOVERSION) \
                             -o $(SONAME) && \
15           ln -sf $(SONAME) $(SOVERSION) && \
             ln -sf $(SONAME) lib$(LIBNAME).so

     .c.o:
             gcc -fPIC -DPIC $(CFLAGS) -c -o $*.o $<
20
     clean:
             rm -f *.o *.a *.so mytest
```

The −shared option to gcc builds our shared library. The −W options are linker options that set the version number of the library that linking programs will load at runtime. The −fPIC −DPIC means to generate *position-independent code,* that is, code suitable for dynamic linking.

After running make we have

```
lrwxrwxrwx   1 root     root           23 Sep 17 22:02 libsimple_math.so -> libsimple_math.so.1.0.0
lrwxrwxrwx   1 root     root           23 Sep 17 22:02 libsimple_math.so.1.0 -> libsimple_math.so.1.0.0
-rwxr-xr-x   1 root     root         6046 Sep 17 22:02 libsimple_math.so.1.0.0
-rwxr-xr-x   1 root     root        13677 Sep 17 22:02 mytest
```

23.2   DLL Versioning

You may observe that our three .so files are similar to the many files in /lib/ and /usr/lib/. This complicated system of linking and symlinking is part of the process of *library versioning.* Although generating a DLL is out of the scope of most system admin tasks, library versioning is important to understand.

DLLs have a problem. Consider a DLL that is outdated or buggy: simply overwriting the DLL file with an updated file will affect all the applications that use it. If these applications rely on certain behavior of the DLL code, then they will probably crash with the fresh DLL. UNIX has elegantly solved this problem by allowing multiple versions of DLLs to be present simultaneously. The programs themselves have their required version number built into them. Try

```
ldd mytest
```

which will show the DLL files that mytest is scheduled to link with:

```
libsimple_math.so.1.0 => ./libsimple_math.so.1.0 (0x40018000)
```

```
libc.so.6 => /lib/libc.so.6 (0x40022000)
/lib/ld-linux.so.2 => /lib/ld-linux.so.2 (0x40000000)
```

At the moment, we are interested in `libsimple_math.so.1.0`. Note how it matches the `SOVERSION` variable in the `Makefile`. Note also how we have chosen our symlinks. We are effectively allowing `mytest` to link with any future `libsimple_math.so.1.0.?` (were our `simple_math` library to be upgraded to a new version) purely because of the way we have chosen our symlinks. However, it will not link with any library `libsimple_math.so.1.1.?`, for example. As developers of `libsimple_math`, we are deciding that libraries of a different *minor* ⟍For this example we are considering libraries to be named `libname.so.major.minor.patch`⟍ version number will be incompatible, whereas libraries of a different *patch* level will not be incompatible.

We could also change `SOVERSION` to `libsimple_math.so.1`. This would effectively be saying that future libraries of different minor version numbers are compatible; only a change in the major version number would dictate incompatibility.

23.3   Installing DLL .so Files

If you run `./mytest`, you will be greeted with an `error while loading shared libraries` message. The reason is that the dynamic linker does not search the current directory for `.so` files. To run your program, you will have to install your library:

```
mkdir -p /usr/local/lib
install -m 0755 libsimple_math.so libsimple_math.so.1.0 \
                        libsimple_math.so.1.0.0 /usr/local/lib
```

Then, edit the `/etc/ld.so.conf` file and add a line

```
/usr/local/lib
```

Then, reconfigure your libraries with

```
ldconfig
```

Finally, run your program with

```
export LD_LIBRARY_PATH="$LD_LIBRARY_PATH:/usr/local/lib"
./mytest
```

`ldconfig` configures all libraries on the system. It recreates appropriate symlinks (as we did) and rebuilds a lookup cache. The library directories it considers are `/lib`, `/usr/lib`, and those listed in `/etc/ld.so.config`. The `ldconfig` command should be run automatically when the system boots and manually whenever libraries are installed or upgraded.

The `LD_LIBRARY_PATH` environment variable is relevant to every executable on the system and similar to the `PATH` environment variable. `LD_LIBRARY_PATH` dictates what directories should be searched for library files. Here, we appended `/usr/local/lib` to the search path in case it was missing. Note that even with `LD_LIBRARY_PATH` unset, `/lib` and `/usr/lib` will always be searched.

Chapter 24

Source and Binary Packages

In this chapter you will, first and foremost, learn to build packages from source, building on your knowledge of `Makefile`s in Chapter 22. Most packages, however, also come as `.rpm` (RedHat) or `.deb` (Debian©) files, which are discussed further below.

24.1 Building GNU Source Packages

Almost all packages originally come as **C** sources, `tared` and available from one of the many public FTP sites, like `metalab.unc.edu`. Thoughtful developers would have made their packages *GNU standards compliant*. This means that `untarring` the package will reveal the following files inside the top-level directory:

INSTALL This is a standard document beginning with the line "`These are generic installation instructions.`" Since all GNU packages are installed in the same way, this file should always be the same.

NEWS News of interest to users.

README Any essential information. This is usually an explanation of what the package does, promotional material, and anything special that need be done to install the package.

COPYING The GNU General Public License.

AUTHORS A list of major contributors.

ChangeLog A specially formatted list containing a history of all changes ever done to the package, by whom, and on what date. Used to track work on the package.

Being GNU🐃 standards compliant should also mean that the package can be installed with only the three following commands:

```
./configure
make
make install
```

It also *usually* means that packages will compile on any UNIX system. Hence, this section should be a good guide to getting LINUX🐧 software to work on non-LINUX machines.

An example will illustrate these steps. Begin by downloading `cooledit` from `metalab.unc.edu` in the directory `/pub/Linux/apps/editors/X/cooledit`, using `ftp`. Make a directory `/opt/src` in which to build such custom packages. Now run

```
cd /opt/src
tar -xvzf cooledit-3.17.2.tar.gz
cd cooledit-3.17.2
```

You will notice that most sources have the name *package—major*.*minor*.*patch*.`tar.gz`. The *major* version of the package is changed when the developers make a substantial feature update or when they introduce incompatibilities to previous versions. The minor version is usually updated when small features are added. The patch number (also known as the patch *level*) is updated whenever a new release is made and usually signifies bug fixes.

At this point you can apply any patches you may have. See Section 20.7.3.

You can now `./configure` the package. The `./configure` script is generated by `autoconf`—a package used by developers to create **C** source that will compile on any type of UNIX system. The `autoconf` package also contains the *GNU Coding Standards* to which all software should comply. ↘`autoconf` is the remarkable work of David MacKenzie. I often hear the myth that UNIX systems have so diverged that they are no longer compatible. The fact that sophisticated software like `cooledit` (and countless others) compiles on almost any UNIX machine should dispel this nonsense. There is also hype surrounding developers "porting" commercial software from other UNIX systems to LINUX. If they had written their software in the least bit properly to begin with, there would be no porting to be done. In short, *all* LINUX software runs on *all* UNIXs. The only exceptions are a few packages that use some custom features of the LINUX kernel.↖

```
./configure --prefix=/opt/cooledit
```

Here, `--prefix` indicates the top-level directory under which the package will be installed. (See Section 17.2.). Always also try

```
./configure --help
```

to see package-specific options.

Another trick sets compile options:

```
CFLAGS='-O2 -fomit-frame-pointer -s -pipe' ./configure --prefix=/opt/cooledit
```

-O2 Sets compiler optimizations to be "as fast as possible without making the binary larger." (-O3 almost never provides an advantage.)

-fomit-frame-pointer Permits the compiler to use one extra register that would normally be used for debugging. Use this option only when you are absolutely sure you have no interest in analyzing any running problems with the package.

-s Strips the object code. This reduces the size of the object code by eliminating any debugging data.

-pipe Instructs not to use temporary files. Rather, use pipes to feed the code through the different stages of compilation. This usually speeds compilation.

Compile the package. This can take up to several hours depending on the amount of code and your CPU power. ↘cooledit will compile in under 10 minutes on any entry-level machine at the time of writing.↖

```
make
```

You can also run

```
make CFLAGS='-O0 -g'
```

if you decide that you would rather compile with debug support after all.

Install the package with

```
make install
```

A nice trick to install into a different subdirectory is ↘Not always supported.↖:

```
mkdir /tmp/cooledit
make install prefix=/tmp/cooledit
```

You can use these commands to pack up the completed build for untaring onto a different system. You should, however, never try to run a package from a directory different from the one it was --prefixed to install into, since most packages *compile in* this location and then access installed data from beneath it.

Using a source package is often the best way to install when you want the package to work the way the developers intended. You will also tend to find more documentation, when vendors have neglected to include certain files.

24.2   RedHat and Debian Binary Packages

In this section, we place Debian◯ examples inside parentheses, (...). Since these are examples from actual systems, they do not always correspond.

24.2.1   Package versioning

The package numbering for RedHat and Debian◯ packages is often as follows (although this is far from a rule):

```
<package-name>-<source-version>-<package-version>.<hardware-platform>.rpm
( <package-name>_<source-version>-<package-version>.deb )
```

For example,

```
bash-1.14.7-22.i386.rpm
( bash_2.03-6.deb )
```

is the Bourne Again Shell you are using, major version 1, minor version 14, patch 7, package version 22, compiled for an Intel 386 processor. Sometimes, the Debian◯ package will have the architecture appended to the version number, in the above case, perhaps bash_2.03-6_i386.deb.

    The <source-version> is the version on the original .tar file (as above). The <package-version>, also called the *release*, refers to the .rpm file itself; in this case, bash-1.14.7-22.i386.rpm has been packed together for the 8th time, possibly with minor improvements to the way it installs with each new number. The i386 is called the *architecture* and could also be sparc for a *SPARC* ↘Type of processor used in Sun Microsystems workstations↖ machine, ppc for a *PowerPC* ↘Another non-Intel workstation↖, alpha for a *DEC Alpha* ↘High-end 64 bit server/workstation↖ machine, or several others.

24.2.2   Installing, upgrading, and deleting

To install a package, run the following command on the .rpm or .deb file:

```
rpm -i mirrordir-0.10.48-1.i386.rpm
( dpkg -i mirrordir_0.10.48-2.deb )
```

Upgrading (Debian◯ automatically chooses an upgrade if the package is already present) can be done with the following command,

```
rpm -U mirrordir-0.10.49-1.i386.rpm
( dpkg -i mirrordir_0.10.49-1.deb )
```

and then completely uninstalling with

```
rpm -e mirrordir
( dpkg --purge mirrordir )
```

With Debian☉, a package removal does not remove configuration files, thus allowing you to revert to its current setup if you later decide to reinstall:

```
dpkg -r mirrordir
```

If you need to reinstall a package (perhaps because of a file being corrupted), use

```
rpm -i --force python-1.6-2.i386.rpm
```

Debian☉ reinstalls automatically if the package is present.

24.2.3 Dependencies

Packages often require other packages to already be installed in order to work. The package database keeps track of these *dependencies*. Often you will get an `error: failed dependencies:` (or `dependency problems` for Debian☉) message when you try to install. This means that other packages must be installed first. The same might happen when you try to remove packages. If two packages mutually require each other, you must place them both on the command-line at once when installing. Sometimes a package requires something that is not essential or is already provided by an equivalent package. For example, a program may require `sendmail` to be installed even though `exim` is an adequate substitute. In such cases, the option `--nodeps` skips dependency checking.

```
rpm -i --nodeps <rpm-file>
( dpkg -i --ignore-depends=<required-package> <deb-file> )
```

Note that Debian☉ is far more fastidious about its dependencies; override them only when you are sure what is going on underneath.

24.2.4 Package queries

`.rpm` and `.deb` packages are more than a way of archiving files; otherwise, we could just use `.tar` files. Each package has its file list stored in a database that can be queried. The following are some of the more useful queries that can be done. Note that these are queries on *already* installed packages only:

To get a list of all packages (query all, llist),

```
rpm -qa
```

```
( dpkg -l '*' )
```

To search for a package name,

```
rpm -qa | grep <regular-expression>
( dpkg -l <glob-expression> )
```

Try,

```
rpm -qa | grep util
( dpkg -l '*util*' )
```

To query for the existence of a package, say, `textutils` (query, list),

```
rpm -q textutils
( dpkg -l textutils )
```

gives the name and version

```
textutils-2.0e-7
( ii  textutils    2.0-2    The GNU text file processing utilities. )
```

To get info on a package (query info, status),

```
rpm -qi <package>
( dpkg -s <package> )
```

To list libraries and other packages required by a package,

```
rpm -qR <package>
( dpkg -s <package> | grep Depends )
```

To list what other packages require this one (with Debian we can check by attempting a removal with the `--no-act` option to merely test),

```
rpm -q --whatrequires <package>
( dpkg --purge --no-act <package> )
```

24.2.5   File lists and file queries

To get a file list contained by a package \Once again, *not* for files but packages already installed.\,

```
rpm -ql <package>
( dpkg -L <package> )
```

Package file lists are especially useful for finding what commands and documentation a package provides. Users are often frustrated by a package that they "don't know what to do with." Listing files owned by the package is where to start.

To find out what package a file belongs to,

```
rpm -qf <filename>
( dpkg -S <filename> )
```

For example, rpm -qf /etc/rc.d/init.d/httpd (or rpm -qf /etc/init.d/httpd) gives apache-mod_ssl-1.3.12.2.6.6-1 on my system, and rpm -ql fileutils-4.0w-3 | grep bin gives a list of all other commands from fileutils. A trick to find all the sibling files of a command in your PATH is:

```
rpm -ql `rpm -qf \`which --skip-alias <command> \``
( dpkg -L `dpkg -S \`which <command> \` | cut -f1 -d:` )
```

24.2.6   Package verification

You sometimes might want to query whether a package's files have been modified since installation (possibly by a hacker or an incompetent system administrator). To verify all packages is time consuming but provides some very instructive output:

```
rpm -V `rpm -qa`
( debsums -a )
```

However, there is not yet a way of saying that the package installed is the real package (see Section 44.3.2). To check this, you need to get your actual .deb or .rpm file and verify it with:

```
rpm -Vp openssh-2.1.1p4-1.i386.rpm
( debsums openssh_2.1.1p4-1_i386.deb )
```

Finally, even if you have the package file, how can you be absolutely sure that it is *the* package that the original packager created, and not some Trojan substitution? Use the md5sum command to check:

```
md5sum openssh-2.1.1p4-1.i386.rpm
```

```
( md5sum openssh_2.1.1p4-1_i386.deb )
```

md5sum uses the *MD5* mathematical algorithm to calculate a numeric *hash* value based on the file contents, in this case, 8e8d8e95db7fde99c09e1398e4dd3468. This is identical to password hashing described on page 103. There is no feasible computational method of forging a package to give the same MD5 hash; hence, packagers will often publish their md5sum results on their web page, and you can check these against your own as a security measure.

24.2.7   Special queries

To query a package file that has not been installed, use, for example:

```
rpm -qp --qf '[%{VERSION}\n]' <rpm-file>
( dpkg -f <deb-file> Version )
```

Here, VERSION is a query *tag* applicable to .rpm files. Here is a list of other tags that can be queried:

BUILDHOST	OBSOLETES	RPMTAG_PREUN
BUILDTIME	OS	RPMVERSION
CHANGELOG	PACKAGER	SERIAL
CHANGELOGTEXT	PROVIDES	SIZE
CHANGELOGTIME	RELEASE	SOURCERPM
COPYRIGHT	REQUIREFLAGS	SUMMARY
DESCRIPTION	REQUIRENAME	VENDOR
DISTRIBUTION	REQUIREVERSION	VERIFYSCRIPT
GROUP	RPMTAG_POSTIN	VERSION
LICENSE	RPMTAG_POSTUN	
NAME	RPMTAG_PREIN	

For Debian⊘, Version is a *control field*. Others are

Conffiles	Maintainer	Replaces
Conflicts	Package	Section
Depends	Pre-Depends	Source
Description	Priority	Status
Essential	Provides	Suggests
Installed-Size	Recommends	Version

It is further possible to extract all scripts, config, and control files from a .deb file with:

```
dpkg -e <deb-file> <out-directory>
```

This command creates a directory `<out-directory>` and places the files in it. You can also dump the package as a `tar` file with:

```
dpkg --fsys-tarfile <deb-file>
```

or for an `.rpm` file,

```
rpm2cpio <rpm-file>
```

Finally, package file lists can be queried with

```
rpm -qip <rpm-file>
( dpkg -I <deb-file> )
rpm -qlp <rpm-file>
( dpkg -c <deb-file> )
```

which is analogous to similar queries on already installed packages.

24.2.8 dpkg/apt versus rpm

Only a taste of Debian© package management was provided above. Debian© has two higher-level tools: APT (*Advanced Package Tool*—which comprises the commands `apt-cache`, `apt-cdrom`, `apt-config`, and `apt-get`); and `dselect`, which is an interactive text-based package selector. When you first install Debian©, I suppose the first thing you are supposed to do is run `dselect` (there are other graphical front-ends—search on *Fresh Meat* http://freshmeat.net/), and then install and configure all the things you skipped over during installation. Between these you can do some sophisticated time-saving things like recursively resolving package dependencies through automatic downloads—that is, just mention the package and APT will find it and what it depends on, then download and install everything for you. See `apt`(8), `sources.list`(5), and `apt.conf`(5) for more information.

There are also numerous interactive graphical applications for managing RPM packages. Most are purely cosmetic.

Experience will clearly demonstrate the superiority of Debian© packages over most others. You will also notice that where RedHat-like distributions have chosen a selection of packages that they thought *you* would find useful, Debian© has hundreds of volunteer maintainers selecting what *they* find useful. Almost every free UNIX package on the Internet has been included in Debian©.

24.3   Source Packages — Building RedHat and Debian Packages

Both RedHat and Debian⊙ binary packages begin life as source files from which their binary versions are compiled. Source RedHat packages will end in `.src.rpm`, and Debian⊙ packages will always appear under the source tree in the distribution. The `RPM-HOWTO` details the building of RedHat source packages, and Debian⊙'s `dpkg-dev` and `packaging-manual` packages contain a complete reference to the Debian⊙ package standard and packaging methods (try `dpkg -L dpkg-dev` and `dpkg -L packaging-manual`).

The actual building of RedHat and Debian⊙ source packages is not covered in this edition.

Chapter 25

Introduction to IP

IP stands for *Internet Protocol*. It is the method by which data is transmitted over the Internet.

25.1 Internet Communication

At a hardware level, network cards are capable of transmitting *packets* (also called *datagrams*) of data between one another. A packet contains a small block of, say, 1 kilobyte of data (in contrast to serial lines, which transmit continuously). All Internet communication occurs through transmission of packets, which travel intact, even between machines on opposite sides of the world.

Each packet contains a header of 24 bytes or more which precedes the data. Hence, slightly more than the said 1 kilobyte of data would be found on the wire. When a packet is transmitted, the header would obviously contain the destination machine. Each machine is hence given a unique *IP address*—a 32-bit number. There are no machines on the Internet that do not have an IP address.

The header bytes are shown in Table 25.1.

Table 25.1 IP header bytes

Bytes	Description
0	bits 0–3: Version, bits 4–7: Internet Header Length (IHL)
1	Type of service (TOS)
2–3	Length
4–5	Identification

continues...

Table 25.1 (continued)

6–7	bits 0-3: Flags, bits 4-15: Offset
8	Time to live (TTL)
9	Type
10–11	Checksum
12–15	Source IP address
16–19	Destination IP address
20–IHL*4-1	Options + padding to round up to four bytes
Data begins at IHL*4 and ends at Length-1	

Version for the mean time is 4, although *IP Next Generation* (version 6) is in the (slow) process of deployment. **IHL** is the length of the header divided by 4. **TOS** (*Type of Service*) is a somewhat esoteric field for tuning performance and is not explained here. The **Length** field is the length in bytes of the entire packet including the header. The **Source** and **Destination** are the IP addresses *from* and *to* which the packet is coming/going.

The above description constitutes the view of the Internet that a machine has. However, physically, the Internet consists of many small high-speed networks (like those of a company or a university) called *Local Area Networks*, or *LANs*. These are all connected to each other by lower-speed long distance links. On a LAN, the *raw* medium of transmission is not a packet but an Ethernet *frame*. Frames are analogous to packets (having both a header and a data portion) but are sized to be efficient with particular hardware. IP packets are encapsulated within frames, where the IP packet fits within the **Data** part of the frame. A frame may, however, be too small to hold an entire IP packet, in which case the IP packet is split into several smaller packets. This group of smaller IP packets is then given an identifying number, and each smaller packet will then have the **Identification** field set with that number and the **Offset** field set to indicate its position within the actual packet. On the other side of the connection, the destination machine will reconstruct a packet from all the smaller subpackets that have the same **Identification** field.

The convention for writing an IP address in human readable form is *dotted decimal* notation like `152.2.254.81`, where each number is a byte and is hence in the range of 0 to 255. Hence the entire address *space* is in the range of `0.0.0.0` to `255.255.255.255`. To further organize the assignment of addresses, each 32-bit address is divided into two parts, a *network* and a *host* part of the address, as shown in Figure 25.1.

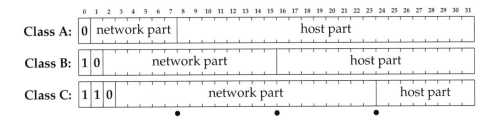

Figure 25.1 IP address classes

The network part of the address designates the LAN, and the host part the particular machine on the LAN. Now, because it was unknown at the time of specification whether there would one day be more LANs or more machines per LAN, three different classes of address were created.

Class A addresses begin with the first bit of the network part set to 0 (hence, a Class A address always has the first dotted decimal number less than 128). The next 7 bits give the identity of the LAN, and the remaining 24 bits give the identity of an actual machine on that LAN. A Class B address begins with a 1 and then a 0 (first decimal number is 128 through 191). The next 14 bits give the LAN, and the remaining 16 bits give the machine. Most universities, like the address above, are Class B addresses. Lastly, Class C addresses start with a 1 1 0 (first decimal number is 192 through 223), and the next 21 bits and then the next 8 bits are the LAN and machine, respectively. Small companies tend use Class C addresses.

In practice, few organizations require Class A addresses. A university or large company might use a Class B address but then would have its own further subdivisions, like using the third dotted decimal as a department (bits 16 through 23) and the last dotted decimal (bits 24 through 31) as the machine within that department. In this way the LAN becomes a micro-Internet in itself. Here, the LAN is called a *network* and the various departments are each called a *subnet*.

25.2   Special IP Addresses

Some special-purposes IP addresses are never used on the open Internet. 192.168.0.0 through 192.168.255.255 are private addresses perhaps used inside a local LAN that does not communicate directly with the Internet. 127.0.0.0 through 127.255.255.255 are used for communication with the *localhost*—that is, the machine itself. Usually, 127.0.0.1 is an IP address pointing to the machine itself. Further, 172.16.0.0 through 172.31.255.255 are additional private addresses for very large internal networks, and 10.0.0.0 through 10.255.255.255 are for even larger ones.

25.3   Network Masks and Addresses

Consider again the example of a university with a Class B address. It might have an IP address range of `137.158.0.0` through `137.158.255.255`. Assume it was decided that the astronomy department should get 512 of its own IP addresses, `137.158.26.0` through `137.158.27.255`. We say that astronomy has a *network address* of `137.158.26.0`. The machines there all have a *network mask* of `255.255.254.0`. A particular machine in astronomy may have an *IP address* of `137.158.27.158`. This terminology is used later. Figure 25.2 illustrates this example.

	Dotted IP	Binary
Netmask	255 . 255 . 254 . 0	1111 1111 1111 1111 1111 1110 0000 0000
Network address	137 . 158 . 26 . 0	1000 1001 1001 1110 0001 1010 0000 0000
IP address	137 . 158 . 27 . 158	1000 1001 1001 1110 0001 1011 1001 1110
Host part	0 . 0 . 1 . 158	0000 0000 0000 0000 0000 0001 1001 1110

Figure 25.2 Dividing an address into network and host portions

25.4   Computers on a LAN

In this section we will use the term LAN to indicate a network of computers that are all more or less connected directly together by Ethernet cables (this is common for small businesses with up to about 50 machines). Each machine has an Ethernet card which is referred to as `eth0` throughout all command-line operations. If there is more than one card on a single machine, then these are named `eth0`, `eth1`, `eth2`, etc., and are each called a *network interface* (or just *interface*, or sometimes *Ethernet port*) of the machine.

LANs work as follows. Network cards transmit a frame to the LAN, and other network cards read that frame from the LAN. If any one network card transmits a frame, then *all* other network cards can see that frame. If a card starts to transmit a frame while another card is in the process of transmitting a frame, then a *clash* is said to have occurred, and the card waits a random amount of time and then tries again. Each network card has a physical address of 48 bits called the *hardware address* (which is inserted at the time of its manufacture and has nothing to do with IP addresses). Each frame has a destination address in its header that tells what network card it is destined for, so that network cards ignore frames that are not addressed to them.

Since frame transmission is governed by the network cards, the destination hardware address must be determined from the destination IP address before a packet is sent to a particular machine. This is done is through the *Address Resolution Protocol*

(ARP). A machine will transmit a special packet that asks "What hardware address is this IP address?" The guilty machine then responds, and the transmitting machine stores the result for future reference. Of course, if you suddenly switch network cards, then other machines on the LAN will have the wrong information, so ARP has time-outs and re-requests built into the protocol. Try typing the command `arp` to get a list of hardware address to IP mappings.

25.5 Configuring Interfaces

Most distributions have a generic way to configure your interfaces. Here, however, we first look at a complete network configuration using only raw networking commands.

We first create a `lo` interface. This is called the *loopback* device (and has nothing to do with loopback block devices: `/dev/loop?` files). The loopback device is an imaginary network card that is used to communicate with the machine itself; for instance, if you are `telnet`ing to the local machine, you are actually connecting via the loopback device. The `ifconfig` (*interface* `config`*ure*) command is used to do anything with interfaces. First, run

```
/sbin/ifconfig lo down
/sbin/ifconfig eth0 down
```

to delete any existing interfaces, then run

```
/sbin/ifconfig lo 127.0.0.1
```

which creates the loopback interface.

Create the Ethernet interface with:

```
/sbin/ifconfig eth0 192.168.3.9 broadcast 192.168.3.255 netmask 255.255.255.0
```

The `broadcast` address is a special address that all machines respond to. It is usually the first or last address of the particular network.

Now run

```
/sbin/ifconfig
```

to view the interfaces. The output will be

```
eth0      Link encap:Ethernet  HWaddr 00:00:E8:3B:2D:A2
          inet addr:192.168.3.9  Bcast:192.168.3.255  Mask:255.255.255.0
          UP BROADCAST RUNNING MULTICAST  MTU:1500  Metric:1
          RX packets:1359 errors:0 dropped:0 overruns:0 frame:0
          TX packets:1356 errors:0 dropped:0 overruns:0 carrier:0
          collisions:0 txqueuelen:100
```

```
                 Interrupt:11 Base address:0xe400

lo               Link encap:Local Loopback
                 inet addr:127.0.0.1  Mask:255.0.0.0
                 UP LOOPBACK RUNNING  MTU:3924  Metric:1
                 RX packets:53175 errors:0 dropped:0 overruns:0 frame:0
                 TX packets:53175 errors:0 dropped:0 overruns:0 carrier:0
                 collisions:0 txqueuelen:0
```

which shows various interesting bits, like the 48-bit hardware address of the network card (hex bytes `00:00:E8:3B:2D:A2`).

25.6 Configuring Routing

The interfaces are now active. However, nothing tells the kernel what packets should go to what interface, even though we might expect such behavior to happen on its own. With UNIX, you must explicitly tell the kernel to send particular packets to particular interfaces.

Any packet arriving through any interface is pooled by the kernel. The kernel then looks at each packet's destination address and decides, based on the destination, where it should be sent. It doesn't matter where the packet came from; once the kernel *has* the packet, it's what its destination address says that matters. It is up to the rest of the network to ensure that packets do not arrive at the wrong interfaces in the first place.

We know that any packet having the network address 127.???.???.??? must go to the loopback device (this is more or less a convention). The command,

```
/sbin/route add -net 127.0.0.0 netmask 255.0.0.0 lo
```

adds a *route* to the network `127.0.0.0`, albeit an imaginary one.

The `eth0` device can be routed as follows:

```
/sbin/route add -net 192.168.3.0 netmask 255.255.255.0 eth0
```

The command to display the current routes is

```
/sbin/route -n
```

(`-n` causes `route` to not print IP addresses as host names) with the following output:

```
Kernel IP routing table
Destination     Gateway         Genmask         Flags Metric Ref    Use Iface
127.0.0.0       0.0.0.0         255.0.0.0       U     0      0        0 lo
192.168.3.0     0.0.0.0         255.255.255.0   U     0      0        0 eth0
```

This output has the meaning, "packets with destination address 127.0.0.0/255.0.0.0 ↘The notation *network/mask* is often used to denote ranges of IP address.↖ must be sent to the `loopback` device," and "packets with destination address 192.168.3.0/255.255.255.0 must be sent to `eth0`." Gateway is zero, hence, is not set (see the following commands).

The routing table now routes `127.` and `192.168.3.` packets. Now we need a route for the remaining possible IP addresses. UNIX can have a route that says to send packets with particular destination IP addresses to another machine on the LAN, from whence they might be forwarded elsewhere. This is sometimes called the *gateway* machine. The command is:

```
/sbin/route add -net <network-address> netmask <netmask> gw \
                                    <gateway-ip-address> <interface>
```

This is the most general form of the command, but it's often easier to just type:

```
/sbin/route add default gw <gateway-ip-address> <interface>
```

when we want to add a route that applies to all remaining packets. This route is called the *default gateway*. `default` signifies all packets; it is the same as

```
/sbin/route add -net 0.0.0.0 netmask 0.0.0.0 gw <gateway-ip-address> \
                                                        <interface>
```

but since routes are ordered according to `netmask`, *more specific routes are used in preference to less specific ones.*

Finally, you can set your host name with:

```
hostname cericon.cranzgot.co.za
```

A summary of the example commands so far is

```
/sbin/ifconfig lo down
/sbin/ifconfig eth0 down
/sbin/ifconfig lo 127.0.0.1
/sbin/ifconfig eth0 192.168.3.9 broadcast 192.168.3.255 netmask 255.255.255.0
/sbin/route add -net 127.0.0.0 netmask 255.0.0.0 lo
/sbin/route add -net 192.168.3.0 netmask 255.255.255.0 eth0
/sbin/route add default gw 192.168.3.254 eth0
hostname cericon.cranzgot.co.za
```

Although these 7 commands will get your network working, you should not do such a manual configuration. The next section explains how to configure your startup scripts.

25.7   Configuring Startup Scripts

Most distributions will have a modular and extensible system of startup scripts that initiate networking.

25.7.1   RedHat networking scripts

RedHat systems contain the directory `/etc/sysconfig/`, which contains configuration files to automatically bring up networking.

The file `/etc/sysconfig/network-scripts/ifcfg-eth0` contains:

```
DEVICE=eth0
IPADDR=192.168.3.9
NETMASK=255.255.255.0
NETWORK=192.168.3.0
BROADCAST=192.168.3.255
ONBOOT=yes
```

The file `/etc/sysconfig/network` contains:

```
NETWORKING=yes
HOSTNAME=cericon.cranzgot.co.za
GATEWAY=192.168.3.254
```

You can see that these two files are equivalent to the example configuration done above. These two files can take an enormous number of options for the various protocols besides IP, but this is the most common configuration.

The file `/etc/sysconfig/network-scripts/ifcfg-lo` for the loopback device will be configured automatically at installation; you should never need to edit it.

To stop and start networking (i.e., to bring up and down the interfaces and routing), type (alternative commands in parentheses):

```
/etc/init.d/network stop
( /etc/rc.d/init.d/network stop )
/etc/init.d/network start
( /etc/rc.d/init.d/network start )
```

which will indirectly read your `/etc/sysconfig/` files.

You can add further files, say, `ifcfg-eth1` (under `/etc/sysconfig/network-scripts/`) for a secondary Ethernet device. For example, `ifcfg-eth1` could contain

```
DEVICE=eth1
IPADDR=192.168.4.1
NETMASK=255.255.255.0
NETWORK=192.168.4.0
BROADCAST=192.168.4.255
ONBOOT=yes
```

and then run `echo "1" > /proc/sys/net/ipv4/ip_forward` to enable packet forwarding between your two interfaces.

25.7.2 Debian networking scripts

Debian☺, on the other hand, has a directory `/etc/network/` containing a file `/etc/network/interfaces`. ↘As usual, Debian☺ has a neat and clean approach.↖ (See also `interfaces`(5).) For the same configuration as above, this file would contain:

```
iface lo inet loopback
iface eth0 inet static
      address 192.168.3.9
      netmask 255.255.255.0
      gateway 192.168.3.254
```

The file `/etc/network/options` contains the same forwarding (and some other) options:

```
ip_forward=no
spoofprotect=yes
syncookies=no
```

To stop and start networking (i.e., bring up and down the interfaces and routing), type

```
/etc/init.d/networking stop
/etc/init.d/networking start
```

which will indirectly read your `/etc/network/interfaces` file.

Actually, the `/etc/init.d/networking` script merely runs the `ifup` and `ifdown` commands. See `ifup`(8). You can alternatively run these commands directly for finer control.

We add further interfaces similar to the RedHat example above by appending to the `/etc/network/interfaces` file. The Debian☺ equivalent is,

255

```
iface lo inet loopback
iface eth0 inet static
    address 192.168.3.9
    netmask 255.255.255.0
    gateway 192.168.3.254
iface eth1 inet static
    address 192.168.4.1
    netmask 255.255.255.0
```

and then set `ip_forward=yes` in your `/etc/network/options` file.

Finally, whereas RedHat sets its host name from the line `HOSTNAME=...` in `/etc/sysconfig/network`, Debian☺ sets it from the contents of the file `/etc/hostname`, which, in the present case, would contain just

```
cericon.cranzgot.co.za
```

25.8 Complex Routing — a Many-Hop Example

Consider two distant LANs that need to communicate. Two dedicated machines, one on each LAN, are linked by some alternative method (in this case, a permanent serial line), as shown in Figure 25.3.

This arrangement can be summarized by five machines **X**, **A**, **B**, **C**, and **D**. Machines **X**, **A**, and **B** form LAN **1** on subnet `192.168.1.0/26`. Machines **C** and **D** form LAN **2** on subnet `192.168.1.128/26`. Note how we use the "`/26`" to indicate that only the first 26 bits are network address bits, while the remaining 6 bits are host address bits. This means that we can have at most $2^6 = 64$ IP addresses on each of LAN **1** and **2**. Our dedicated serial link comes between machines **B** and **C**.

Machine **X** has IP address `192.168.1.1`. This machine is the gateway to the Internet. The Ethernet port of machine **B** is simply configured with an IP address of `192.168.1.2` with a default gateway of `192.168.1.1`. Note that the broadcast address is `192.168.1.63` (the last 6 bits set to 1).

The Ethernet port of machine **C** is configured with an IP address of `192.168.1.129`. No default gateway should be set until serial line is configured.

We will make the network between **B** and **C** subnet `192.168.1.192/26`. It is effectively a LAN on its own, even though only two machines can ever be connected. Machines **B** and **C** will have IP addresses `192.168.1.252` and `192.168.1.253`, respectively, on their facing interfaces.

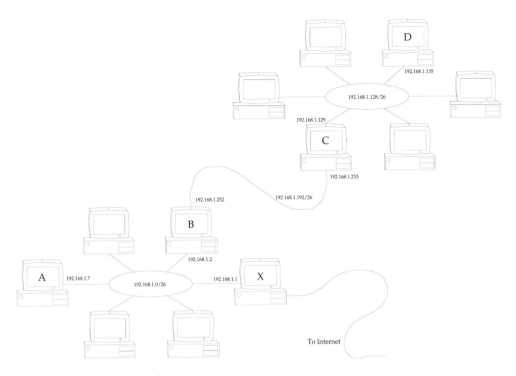

Figure 25.3 Two remotely connected networks

This is a real-life example with an unreliable serial link. To keep the link up requires `pppd` and a shell script to restart the link if it dies. The `pppd` program is covered in Chapter 41. The script for Machine **B** is:

```
#!/bin/sh
while true ; do
    pppd lock local mru 296 mtu 296 nodetach nocrtscts nocdtrcts \
    192.168.1.252:192.168.1.253 /dev/ttyS0 115200 noauth \
    lcp-echo-interval 1 lcp-echo-failure 2 lcp-max-terminate 1 lcp-restart 1
done
```

Note that if the link were an Ethernet link instead (on a second Ethernet card), and/or a genuine LAN between machines **B** and **C** (with subnet `192.168.1.252/26`), then the same script would be just

```
/sbin/ifconfig eth1 192.168.1.252 broadcast 192.168.1.255 netmask \
                                             255.255.255.192
```

in which case all "ppp0" would change to "eth1" in the scripts that follow.

Routing on machine **B** is achieved with the following script, provided the link is up. This script must be executed whenever pppd has negotiated the connection and can therefore be placed in the file /etc/pppd/ip-up, which pppd executes automatically as soon as the ppp0 interface is available:

```
/sbin/route del default
/sbin/route add -net 192.168.1.192 netmask 255.255.255.192 dev ppp0
/sbin/route add -net 192.168.1.128 netmask 255.255.255.192 gw 192.168.1.253
/sbin/route add default gw 192.168.1.1

echo 1 > /proc/sys/net/ipv4/ip_forward
```

Our full routing table and interface list for machine **B** then looks like this ↘RedHat 6 likes to add (redundant) explicit routes to each device. These may not be necessary on your system↖:

```
Kernel IP routing table
Destination     Gateway         Genmask          Flags Metric Ref    Use Iface
192.168.1.2     0.0.0.0         255.255.255.255 UH    0      0        0 eth0
192.168.1.253   0.0.0.0         255.255.255.255 UH    0      0        0 ppp0
192.168.1.0     0.0.0.0         255.255.255.192 U     0      0        0 eth0
192.168.1.192   0.0.0.0         255.255.255.192 U     0      0        0 ppp0
192.168.1.128   192.168.1.253   255.255.255.192 UG    0      0        0 ppp0
127.0.0.0       0.0.0.0         255.0.0.0        U     0      0        0 lo
0.0.0.0         192.168.1.1     0.0.0.0          UG    0      0        0 eth0

eth0      Link encap:Ethernet   HWaddr 00:A0:24:75:3B:69
          inet addr:192.168.1.2  Bcast:192.168.1.63  Mask:255.255.255.192
lo        Link encap:Local Loopback
          inet addr:127.0.0.1  Mask:255.0.0.0
ppp0      Link encap:Point-to-Point Protocol
          inet addr:192.168.1.252  P-t-P:192.168.1.253  Mask:255.255.255.255
```

On machine **C** we can similarly run the script,

```
#!/bin/sh
while true ; do
    pppd lock local mru 296 mtu 296 nodetach nocrtscts nocdtrcts \
    192.168.1.253:192.168.1.252 /dev/ttyS0 115200 noauth \
    lcp-echo-interval 1 lcp-echo-failure 2 lcp-max-terminate 1 lcp-restart 1
done
```

and then create routes with

```
/sbin/route del default
/sbin/route add -net 192.168.1.192 netmask 255.255.255.192 dev ppp0
/sbin/route add default gw 192.168.1.252

echo 1 > /proc/sys/net/ipv4/ip_forward
```

Our full routing table for machine **C** then looks like:

```
Kernel IP routing table
Destination    Gateway          Genmask          Flags Metric Ref    Use Iface
192.168.1.129  0.0.0.0          255.255.255.255 UH    0      0        0 eth0
192.168.1.252  0.0.0.0          255.255.255.255 UH    0      0        0 ppp0
192.168.1.192  0.0.0.0          255.255.255.192 U     0      0        0 ppp0
192.168.1.128  0.0.0.0          255.255.255.192 U     0      0        0 eth0
127.0.0.0      0.0.0.0          255.0.0.0        U     0      0        0 lo
0.0.0.0        192.168.1.252    0.0.0.0          UG    0      0        0 ppp0

eth0      Link encap:Ethernet   HWaddr 00:A0:CC:D5:D8:A7
          inet addr:192.168.1.129  Bcast:192.168.1.191   Mask:255.255.255.192
lo        Link encap:Local Loopback
          inet addr:127.0.0.1  Mask:255.0.0.0
ppp0      Link encap:Point-to-Point Protocol
          inet addr:192.168.1.253  P-t-P:192.168.1.252   Mask:255.255.255.255
```

Machine **D** can be configured like any ordinary machine on a LAN. It just sets its default gateway to 192.168.1.129. Machine **A**, however, has to know to send packets destined for subnet 192.168.1.128/26 *through* machine **B**. Its routing table has an extra entry for the 192.168.1.128/26 LAN. The full routing table for machine **A** is:

```
Kernel IP routing table
Destination    Gateway          Genmask          Flags Metric Ref    Use Iface
192.168.1.0    0.0.0.0          255.255.255.192 U     0      0        0 eth0
192.168.1.128  192.168.1.2      255.255.255.192 UG    0      0        0 eth0
127.0.0.0      0.0.0.0          255.0.0.0        U     0      0        0 lo
0.0.0.0        192.168.1.1      0.0.0.0          UG    0      0        0 eth0
```

To avoid having to add this extra route on machine **A**, you can instead add the same route on machine **X**. This may seem odd, but all that this means is that packets originating from **A** destined for LAN 2 first *try* to go through **X** (since **A** has only one route), and are then redirected *by* **X** to go through **B**.

The preceding configuration allowed machines to properly send packets between machines **A** and **D** and out through the Internet. One caveat: ping sometimes did not work even though telnet did. This may be a peculiarity of the kernel version we were using, **shrug**.

25.9 Interface Aliasing — Many IPs on One Physical Card

(The file /usr/src/linux/Documentation/networking/alias.txt contains the kernel documentation on this.)

If you have one network card which you would like to double as several different IP addresses, you can. Simply name the interface `eth0:`*n* where *n* is from 0 to some large integer. You can use `ifconfig` as before as many times as you like on the same network card—

```
/sbin/ifconfig eth0:0 192.168.4.1 broadcast 192.168.4.255 netmask 255.255.255.0
/sbin/ifconfig eth0:1 192.168.5.1 broadcast 192.168.5.255 netmask 255.255.255.0
/sbin/ifconfig eth0:2 192.168.6.1 broadcast 192.168.6.255 netmask 255.255.255.0
```

—in *addition* to your regular `eth0` device. Here, the same interface can communicate to three LANs having networks `192.168.4.0`, `192.168.5.0`, and `192.168.6.0`. Don't forget to add routes to these networks as above.

25.10 Diagnostic Utilities

It is essential to know how to inspect and test your network to resolve problems. The standard UNIX utilities are explained here.

25.10.1 ping

The `ping` command is the most common network utility. IP packets come in three types on the Internet, represented in the **Type** field of the IP header: *UDP*, *TCP*, and *ICMP*. (The first two, discussed later, represent the two basic methods of communication between two programs running on different machines.) *ICMP* stands for *Internet Control Message Protocol* and is a diagnostic packet that is responded to in a special way. Try:

```
ping metalab.unc.edu
```

or specify some other well-known host. You will get output like:

```
PING metalab.unc.edu (152.19.254.81) from 192.168.3.9 : 56(84) bytes of data.
64 bytes from 152.19.254.81: icmp_seq=0 ttl=238 time=1059.1 ms
64 bytes from 152.19.254.81: icmp_seq=1 ttl=238 time=764.9 ms
64 bytes from 152.19.254.81: icmp_seq=2 ttl=238 time=858.8 ms
64 bytes from 152.19.254.81: icmp_seq=3 ttl=238 time=1179.9 ms
64 bytes from 152.19.254.81: icmp_seq=4 ttl=238 time=986.6 ms
64 bytes from 152.19.254.81: icmp_seq=5 ttl=238 time=1274.3 ms
64 bytes from 152.19.254.81: icmp_seq=6 ttl=238 time=930.7 ms
```

What is happening is that `ping` is sending ICMP packets to `metalab.unc.edu`, which is automatically responding with a return ICMP packet. Being able to `ping` a machine is often the acid test of whether you have a correctly configured and working network interface. Note that some sites explicitly filter out ICMP packets, so, for example, `ping cnn.com` won't work.

`ping` sends a packet every second and measures the time it takes to receive the return packet—like a submarine sonar "ping." Over the Internet, you can get times in excess of 2 seconds if the place is remote enough. On a local LAN this delay will drop to under a millisecond.

If `ping` does not even get to the line `PING metalab.unc.edu...`, it means that `ping` cannot resolve the host name. You should then check that your DNS is set up correctly—see Chapter 27. If `ping` gets to that line but no further, it means that the packets are not getting there or are not getting back. In all other cases, `ping` gives an error message reporting the absence of either routes or interfaces.

25.10.2 `traceroute`

`traceroute` is a rather fascinating utility to identify where a packet has been. It uses UDP packets or, with the `-I` option, ICMP packets to detect the routing path. On my machine,

```
traceroute metalab.unc.edu
```

gives

```
traceroute to metalab.unc.edu (152.19.254.81), 30 hops max, 38 byte packets
 1  192.168.3.254 (192.168.3.254)  1.197 ms  1.085 ms  1.050 ms
 2  192.168.254.5 (192.168.254.5)  45.165 ms  45.314 ms  45.164 ms
 3  cranzgate (192.168.2.254)  48.205 ms  48.170 ms  48.074 ms
 4  cranzposix (160.124.182.254)  46.117 ms  46.064 ms  45.999 ms
 5  cismpjhb.posix.co.za (160.124.255.193)  451.886 ms  71.549 ms  173.321 ms
 6  cisapl.posix.co.za (160.124.112.1)  274.834 ms  147.251 ms  400.654 ms
 7  saix.posix.co.za (160.124.255.6)  187.402 ms  325.030 ms  628.576 ms
 8  ndf-core1.gt.saix.net (196.25.253.1)  252.558 ms  186.256 ms  255.805 ms
 9  ny-core.saix.net (196.25.0.238)  497.273 ms  454.531 ms  639.795 ms
10  bordercore6-serial5-0-0-26.WestOrange.cw.net (166.48.144.105)  595.755 ms  595.174 ms *
11  corerouter1.WestOrange.cw.net (204.70.9.138)  490.845 ms  698.483 ms  1029.369 ms
12  core6.Washington.cw.net (204.70.4.113)  580.971 ms  893.481 ms  730.608 ms
13  204.70.10.182 (204.70.10.182)  644.070 ms  726.363 ms  639.942 ms
14  mae-brdr-01.inet.qwest.net (205.171.4.201)  767.783 ms * *
15  * * *
16  * wdc-core-03.inet.qwest.net (205.171.24.69)  779.546 ms  898.371 ms
17  atl-core-02.inet.qwest.net (205.171.5.243)  894.553 ms  689.472 ms *
18  atl-edge-05.inet.qwest.net (205.171.21.54)  735.810 ms  784.461 ms  789.592 ms
19  * * *
20  * * unc-gw.ncren.net (128.109.190.2)  889.257 ms
21  unc-gw.ncren.net (128.109.190.2)  646.569 ms  780.000 ms *
22  * helios.oit.unc.edu (152.2.22.3)  600.558 ms  839.135 ms
```

You can see that there were twenty machines ↘This is actually a good argument for why "enterprise"-level web servers have no use in non-U.S. markets: there isn't even the network speed to load such servers, thus making any kind of server speed comparisons superfluous.↖ (or *hops*) between mine and `metalab.unc.edu`.

25.10.3 `tcpdump`

`tcpdump` watches a particular interface for *all* the traffic that passes it—that is, all the traffic of all the machines connected to the same hub (also called the *segment* or *network segment*). A network card usually grabs only the frames destined for it, but `tcpdump` puts the card into *promiscuous* mode, meaning that the card is to retrieve all frames regardless of their destination hardware address. Try

```
tcpdump -n -N -f -i eth0
```

tcpdump is also discussed in Section 41.5. Deciphering the output of tcpdump is left for now as an exercise for the reader. More on the *tcp* part of tcpdump in Chapter 26.

Chapter 26

Transmission Control Protocol (TCP) and User Datagram Protocol (UDP)

In the previous chapter we talked about communication between machines in a generic sense. However, when you have two applications on opposite sides of the Atlantic Ocean, being able to send a packet that may or may not reach the other side is not sufficient. What you need is *reliable* communication.

Ideally, a programmer wants to be able to establish a link to a remote machine and then feed bytes in one at a time and be sure that the bytes are being read on the other end, and vice-versa. Such communication is called *reliable stream* communication.

If your only tools are discrete, unreliable packets, implementing a reliable, continuous stream is tricky. You can send single packets and then wait for the remote machine to confirm receipt, but this approach is inefficient (packets can take a long time to get to and from their destination)—you really want to be able to send as many packets as possible at once and then have some means of negotiating with the remote machine when to resend packets that were not received. What *TCP (Transmission Control Protocol)* does is to send data packets one way and then *acknowledgment packets* the other way, saying how much of the stream has been properly received.

We therefore say that *TCP is implemented on top of IP*. This is why Internet communication is sometimes called TCP/IP.

TCP communication has three stages: *negotiation, transfer,* and *detachment.* ⬐This is all my own terminology. This is also somewhat of a schematic representation.⬏

Negotiation The *client* application (say, a web browser) first initiates the connection by using a **C** `connect()` (see `connect`(2)) function. This causes the kernel to send a *SYN* (*SYN*chronization) packet to the remote TCP server (in this case, a web server). The web server responds with a *SYN-ACK* packet (*ACK*nowledge), and finally the client responds with a final SYN packet. This packet negotiation is unbeknown to the programmer.

Transfer: The programmer will use the `send()` (send(2)) and `recv()` (recv(2)) **C** function calls to send and receive an actual stream of bytes. The stream of bytes will be broken into packets, and the packets sent individually to the remote application. In the case of the web server, the first bytes sent would be the line `GET /index.html HTTP/1.0<CR><NL><CR><NL>`. On the remote side, reply packets (also called ACK packets) are sent back as the data arrives, indicating whether parts of the stream went missing and require retransmission. Communication is *full-duplex*—meaning that there are streams in both directions—both data and acknowledge packets are going both ways simultaneously.

Detachment: The programmer will use the **C** function call `shutdown()` and `close()` (see `shutdown()` and `close(2)`) to terminate the connection. A *FIN* packet will be sent and TCP communication will cease.

26.1 The TCP Header

TCP packets are obviously *encapsulated* within IP packets. The TCP packet is inside the **Data begins at...** part of the IP packet. A TCP packet has a header part and a data part. The data part may sometimes be empty (such as in the negotiation stage).

Table 26.1 shows the full TCP/IP header.

Table 26.1 Combined TCP and IP header

Bytes (IP)	Description
0	Bits 0–3: Version, Bits 4–7: Internet Header Length (IHL)
1	Type of service (TOS)
2–3	Length
4–5	Identification
6–7	Bits 0-3: Flags, bits 4-15: Offset
8	Time to live (TTL)
9	Type
10–11	Checksum
12–15	Source IP address
16–19	Destination IP address
20–IHL*4-1	Options + padding to round up to four bytes
Bytes (TCP)	**Description**

continues...

Table 26.1 (continued)

0–1	Source port
2–3	Destination port
4–7	Sequence number
8–11	Acknowledgment number
12	Bits 0–3: number of bytes of additional TCP options / 4
13	Control
14–15	Window
16–17	Checksum
18–19	Urgent pointer
20–(20 + options * 4)	Options + padding to round up to four bytes
TCP data begins at IHL * 4 + 20 + options * 4 and ends at Length - 1	

The minimum combined TCP/IP header is thus 40 bytes.

With Internet machines, several applications often communicate simultaneously. The **Source port** and **Destination port** fields identify and distinguish individual streams. In the case of web communication, the destination port (from the clients point of view) is port 80, and hence all outgoing traffic will have the number 80 filled in this field. The source port (from the client's point of view) is chosen randomly to any unused port number above 1024 before the connection is negotiated; these, too, are filled into outgoing packets. No two streams have the same combinations of source and destination port numbers. The kernel uses the port numbers on incoming packets to determine which application requires those packets, and similarly for the remote machine.

Sequence number is the offset within the stream that this particular packet of data belongs to. The **Acknowledge number** is the point in the stream up to which all data has been received. **Control** is various other flag bits. **Window** is the maximum amount that the receiver is prepared to accept. **Checksum** is used to verify data integrity, and **Urgent pointer** is for interrupting the stream. Data needed by extensions to the protocol are appended after the header as options.

26.2   A Sample TCP Session

It is easy to see TCP working by using `telnet`. You are probably familiar with using `telnet` to log in to remote systems, but `telnet` is actually a generic program to connect to *any* TCP socket as we did in Chapter 10. Here we will try connect to `cnn.com`'s web page.

We first need to get an IP address of `cnn.com`:

```
[root@cericon]# host cnn.com
cnn.com has address 207.25.71.20
```

Now, in one window we run

```
[root@cericon]# tcpdump \
'( src 192.168.3.9 and dst 207.25.71.20 ) or ( src 207.25.71.20 and dst 192.168.3.9 )'
Kernel filter, protocol ALL, datagram packet socket
tcpdump: listening on all devices
```

which says to list all packets having source (src) or destination (dst) addresses of either us or CNN.

Then we use the HTTP protocol to grab the page. Type in the HTTP command GET / HTTP/1.0 and then press ⏎Enter *twice* (as required by the HTTP protocol). The first and last few lines of the sessions are shown below:

```
     [root@cericon root]# telnet 207.25.71.20 80
     Trying 207.25.71.20...
     Connected to 207.25.71.20.
     Escape character is '^]'.
 5   GET / HTTP/1.0

     HTTP/1.0 200 OK
     Server: Netscape-Enterprise/2.01
     Date: Tue, 18 Apr 2000 10:55:14 GMT
10   Set-cookie: CNNid=cf19472c-23286-956055314-2; expires=Wednesday, 30-Dec-2037 16:00:00 GMT;
                                                               path=/; domain=.cnn.com
     Last-modified: Tue, 18 Apr 2000 10:55:14 GMT
     Content-type: text/html

15   <HTML>
     <HEAD>
             <TITLE>CNN.com</TITLE>
             <META http-equiv="REFRESH" content="1800">

20           <!--CSSDATA:956055234-->
             <SCRIPT src="/virtual/2000/code/main.js" language="javascript"></SCRIPT>
             <LINK rel="stylesheet" href="/virtual/2000/style/main.css" type="text/css">
             <SCRIPT language="javascript" type="text/javascript">
                     <!--//
25                   if ((navigator.platform=='MacPPC')&&(navigator.ap

     . . . . . . . . . . . . .
     . . . . . . . . . . . . .

30   </BODY>
     </HTML>
     Connection closed by foreign host.
```

The above commands produce the front page of CNN's web site in raw HTML. This is easy to paste into a file and view off-line.

In the other window, tcpdump is showing us what packets are being exchanged. tcpdump nicely shows us host names instead of IP addresses and the letters www instead of the port number 80. The local "random" port in this case was 4064.

```
[root@cericon]# tcpdump \
'( src 192.168.3.9 and dst 207.25.71.20 ) or ( src 207.25.71.20 and dst 192.168.3.9 )'
Kernel filter, protocol ALL, datagram packet socket
tcpdump: listening on all devices
12:52:35.467121 eth0 > cericon.cranzgot.co.za.4064 > www1.cnn.com.www:
     S 2463192134:2463192134(0) win 32120 <mss 1460,sackOK,timestamp 154031689 0,nop,wscale 0
12:52:35.964703 eth0 < www1.cnn.com.www > cericon.cranzgot.co.za.4064:
     S 4182178234:4182178234(0) ack 2463192135 win 10136 <nop,nop,timestamp 1075172823 154031
12:52:35.964791 eth0 > cericon.cranzgot.co.za.4064 > www1.cnn.com.www:
     . 1:1(0) ack 1 win 32120 <nop,nop,timestamp 154031739 1075172823> (DF)
12:52:46.413043 eth0 > cericon.cranzgot.co.za.4064 > www1.cnn.com.www:
     P 1:17(16) ack 1 win 32120 <nop,nop,timestamp 154032784 1075172823> (DF)
12:52:46.908156 eth0 < www1.cnn.com.www > cericon.cranzgot.co.za.4064:
     . 1:1(0) ack 17 win 10136 <nop,nop,timestamp 1075173916 154032784>
12:52:49.259870 eth0 > cericon.cranzgot.co.za.4064 > www1.cnn.com.www:
     P 17:19(2) ack 1 win 32120 <nop,nop,timestamp 154033068 1075173916> (DF)
12:52:49.886846 eth0 < www1.cnn.com.www > cericon.cranzgot.co.za.4064:
     P 1:278(277) ack 19 win 10136 <nop,nop,timestamp 1075174200 154033068>
12:52:49.887039 eth0 > cericon.cranzgot.co.za.4064 > www1.cnn.com.www:
     . 19:19(0) ack 278 win 31856 <nop,nop,timestamp 154033131 1075174200> (DF)
12:52:50.053628 eth0 < www1.cnn.com.www > cericon.cranzgot.co.za.4064:
     . 278:1176(898) ack 19 win 10136 <nop,nop,timestamp 1075174202 154033068>
12:52:50.160740 eth0 < www1.cnn.com.www > cericon.cranzgot.co.za.4064:
     P 1176:1972(796) ack 19 win 10136 <nop,nop,timestamp 1075174202 154033068>
12:52:50.220067 eth0 > cericon.cranzgot.co.za.4064 > www1.cnn.com.www:
     . 19:19(0) ack 1972 win 31856 <nop,nop,timestamp 154033165 1075174202> (DF)
12:52:50.824143 eth0 < www1.cnn.com.www > cericon.cranzgot.co.za.4064:
     . 1972:3420(1448) ack 19 win 10136 <nop,nop,timestamp 1075174262 154033131>
12:52:51.021465 eth0 < www1.cnn.com.www > cericon.cranzgot.co.za.4064:
     . 3420:4868(1448) ack 19 win 10136 <nop,nop,timestamp 1075174295 154033165>


. . . . . . . . . . . . .
. . . . . . . . . . . . .

12:53:13.856919 eth0 > cericon.cranzgot.co.za.4064 > www1.cnn.com.www:
     . 19:19(0) ack 53204 win 30408 <nop,nop,timestamp 154035528 1075176560> (DF)
12:53:14.722584 eth0 < www1.cnn.com.www > cericon.cranzgot.co.za.4064:
     . 53204:54652(1448) ack 19 win 10136 <nop,nop,timestamp 1075176659 154035528>
12:53:14.722738 eth0 > cericon.cranzgot.co.za.4064 > www1.cnn.com.www:
     . 19:19(0) ack 54652 win 30408 <nop,nop,timestamp 154035615 1075176659> (DF)
12:53:14.912561 eth0 < www1.cnn.com.www > cericon.cranzgot.co.za.4064:
     . 54652:56100(1448) ack 19 win 10136 <nop,nop,timestamp 1075176659 154035528>
12:53:14.912706 eth0 > cericon.cranzgot.co.za.4064 > www1.cnn.com.www:
     . 19:19(0) ack 58500 win 30408 <nop,nop,timestamp 154035634 1075176659> (DF)
12:53:15.706463 eth0 < www1.cnn.com.www > cericon.cranzgot.co.za.4064:
     . 58500:59948(1448) ack 19 win 10136 <nop,nop,timestamp 1075176765 154035634>
12:53:15.896639 eth0 < www1.cnn.com.www > cericon.cranzgot.co.za.4064:
     . 59948:61396(1448) ack 19 win 10136 <nop,nop,timestamp 1075176765 154035634>
12:53:15.896791 eth0 > cericon.cranzgot.co.za.4064 > www1.cnn.com.www:
     . 19:19(0) ack 61396 win 31856 <nop,nop,timestamp 154035732 1075176765> (DF)
12:53:16.678439 eth0 < www1.cnn.com.www > cericon.cranzgot.co.za.4064:
     . 61396:62844(1448) ack 19 win 10136 <nop,nop,timestamp 1075176864 154035732>
12:53:16.867963 eth0 < www1.cnn.com.www > cericon.cranzgot.co.za.4064:
     . 62844:64292(1448) ack 19 win 10136 <nop,nop,timestamp 1075176864 154035732>
12:53:16.868095 eth0 > cericon.cranzgot.co.za.4064 > www1.cnn.com.www:
     . 19:19(0) ack 64292 win 31856 <nop,nop,timestamp 154035829 1075176864> (DF)
12:53:17.521019 eth0 < www1.cnn.com.www > cericon.cranzgot.co.za.4064:
     FP 64292:65200(908) ack 19 win 10136 <nop,nop,timestamp 1075176960 154035829>
12:53:17.521154 eth0 > cericon.cranzgot.co.za.4064 > www1.cnn.com.www:
     . 19:19(0) ack 65201 win 31856 <nop,nop,timestamp 154035895 1075176960> (DF)
12:53:17.523243 eth0 > cericon.cranzgot.co.za.4064 > www1.cnn.com.www:
     F 19:19(0) ack 65201 win 31856 <nop,nop,timestamp 154035895 1075176960> (DF)
12:53:20.410092 eth0 > cericon.cranzgot.co.za.4064 > www1.cnn.com.www:
     F 19:19(0) ack 65201 win 31856 <nop,nop,timestamp 154036184 1075176960> (DF)
12:53:20.940833 eth0 < www1.cnn.com.www > cericon.cranzgot.co.za.4064:
```

```
 . 65201:65201(0) ack 20 win 10136 <nop,nop,timestamp 1075177315 154035895>
103 packets received by filter
```

The preceding output requires some explanation: Line 5, 7, and 9 are the negotiation stage. `tcpdump` uses the format `<Sequence number>:<Sequence number
+ data length>(<data length>)` on each line to show the context of the packet
within the stream. **Sequence number**, however, is chosen randomly at the outset, so
`tcpdump` prints the relative sequence number after the first two packets to make it
clearer what the actual position is within the stream. Line 11 is where I pressed Enter
the first time, and Line 15 was Enter with an empty line. The "`ack 19`"s indicates
the point to which CNN's web server has received incoming data; in this case we only
ever typed in 19 bytes, hence the web server sets this value in every one of its outgoing
packets, while our own outgoing packets are mostly empty of data.

Lines 61 and 63 are the detachment stage.

More information about the `tcpdump` output can be had from `tcpdump`(8) under
the section **TCP Packets**.

26.3   User Datagram Protocol (UDP)

You don't *always* need reliable communication.

Sometimes you want to directly control packets for efficiency, or because you
don't really mind if packets get lost. Two examples are name server communications,
for which single packet transmissions are desired, or voice transmissions for which
reducing lag time is more important than data integrity. Another is NFS (Network File
System), which uses UDP to implement exclusively high bandwidth data transfer.

With UDP the programmer sends and receives individual packets, again encapsulated within IP. Ports are used in the same way as with TCP, but these are merely
identifiers and there is no concept of a stream. The full UDP/IP header is listed in
Table 26.2.

Table 26.2 Combined UDP and IP header

Bytes (IP)	Description
0	bits 0–3: Version, bits 4–7: Internet Header Length (IHL)
1	Type of service (TOS)
2–3	Length
4–5	Identification
6–7	bits 0-3: Flags, bits 4-15: Offset

continues...

Table 26.2 (continued)

8	Time to live (TTL)
9	Type
10–11	Checksum
12–15	Source IP address
16–19	Destination IP address
20–(IHL * 4 - 1)	Options + padding to round up to four bytes
Bytes (UDP)	**Description**
0–1	Source port
2–3	Destination port
4–5	Length
6–7	Checksum
UDP data begins at IHL * 4 + 8 and ends at Length - 1	

26.4 /etc/services File

Various standard port numbers are used exclusively for particular types of services. Port 80 is for web as shown earlier. Port numbers 1 through 1023 are reserved for such standard services and each is given a convenient textual name.

All services are defined for both TCP as well as UDP, even though there is, for example, no such thing as UDP FTP access.

Port numbers below 1024 are used exclusively for root uid programs such as mail, DNS, and web services. Programs of ordinary users are not allowed to *bind* to ports below 1024. ⟍Port binding is where a program reserves a port for listening for an incoming connection, as do all network services. Web servers, for example, *bind* to port 80.⟍ The place where these ports are defined is in the /etc/services file. These mappings are mostly for descriptive purposes—programs can look up port names from numbers and visa versa. *The /etc/services file has nothing to do with the availability of a service.*

Here is an extract of the /etc/services.

```
   tcpmux         1/tcp                        # TCP port service multiplexer
   echo           7/tcp
   echo           7/udp
   discard        9/tcp       sink null
 5 discard        9/udp       sink null
   systat         11/tcp      users
   daytime        13/tcp
   daytime        13/udp
   netstat        15/tcp
10 qotd           17/tcp      quote
   msp            18/tcp                       # message send protocol
   msp            18/udp                       # message send protocol
```

```
     │ ftp-data       20/tcp
     │ ftp            21/tcp
 15  │ fsp            21/udp       fspd
     │ ssh            22/tcp                    # SSH Remote Login Protocol
     │ ssh            22/udp                    # SSH Remote Login Protocol
     │ telnet         23/tcp
     │ smtp           25/tcp       mail
 20  │ time           37/tcp       timserver
     │ time           37/udp       timserver
     │ rlp            39/udp       resource     # resource location
     │ nameserver     42/tcp       name         # IEN 116
     │ whois          43/tcp       nicname
 25  │ domain         53/tcp       nameserver   # name-domain server
     │ domain         53/udp       nameserver
     │ mtp            57/tcp                    # deprecated
     │ bootps         67/tcp                    # BOOTP server
     │ bootps         67/udp
 30  │ bootpc         68/tcp                    # BOOTP client
     │ bootpc         68/udp
     │ tftp           69/udp
     │ gopher         70/tcp                    # Internet Gopher
     │ gopher         70/udp
 35  │ rje            77/tcp       netrjs
     │ finger         79/tcp
     │ www            80/tcp       http         # WorldWideWeb HTTP
     │ www            80/udp                    # HyperText Transfer Protocol
```

26.5 Encrypting and Forwarding TCP

The TCP stream can easily be reconstructed by anyone listening on a wire who happens to see your network traffic, so TCP is known as an inherently insecure service. We would like to encrypt our data so that anything captured between the client and server will appear garbled. Such an encrypted stream should have several properties:

1. It should ensure that the connecting client *really* is connecting to the server in question. In other words it should authenticate the server to ensure that the server is not a Trojan.

2. It should prevent any information being gained by a snooper. This means that any traffic read should appear cryptographically garbled.

3. It should be impossible for a listener to modify the traffic without detection.

The above is relatively easily accomplished with at least two packages. Take the example where we would like to use POP3 to retrieve mail from a remote machine. First, we can verify that POP3 is working by logging in on the POP3 server. Run a `telnet` to port 110 (i.e., the POP3 service) as follows:

```
  telnet localhost 110
  Connected to localhost.localdomain.
  Escape character is '^]'.
  +OK POP3 localhost.localdomain v7.64 server ready
5 QUIT
  +OK Sayonara
  Connection closed by foreign host.
```

For our first example, we use the OpenSSH package. We can initialize and run the sshd Secure Shell daemon if it has not been initialized before. The following commands would be run on the POP3 server:

```
ssh-keygen -b 1024 -f /etc/ssh/ssh_host_key -q -N ''
ssh-keygen -d -f /etc/ssh/ssh_host_dsa_key -q -N ''
sshd
```

To create an encrypted channel shown in Figure 26.1, we use the ssh client login program in a special way. We would like it to listen on a particular TCP port and then encrypt and forward all traffic to the remote TCP port on the server. This is known as *(encrypted) port forwarding*. On the client machine we choose an arbitrary unused port to listen on, in this case 12345:

```
ssh -C -c arcfour -N -n -2 -L 12345:<pop3-server.doma.in>:110 \
                              <pop3-server.doma.in> -l <user> -v
```

where <user> is the name of a shell account on the POP3 server. Finally, also on the client machine, we run:

```
  telnet localhost 12345
  Connected to localhost.localdomain.
  Escape character is '^]'.
  +OK POP3 localhost.localdomain v7.64 server ready
5 QUIT
  +OK Sayonara
  Connection closed by foreign host.
```

Here we get results identical to those above, because, as far as the server is concerned, the POP3 connection comes from a client on the server machine itself, unknowing of the fact that it has originated from sshd, which in turn is forwarding from a remote ssh client. In addition, the -C option compresses all data (useful for low-speed connections). Also note that you should generally never use any encryption besides arcfour and SSH Protocol 2 (option -2).

The second method is the forward program of the mirrordir package. It has a unique encryption protocol that does much of what OpenSSH can, although the pro-

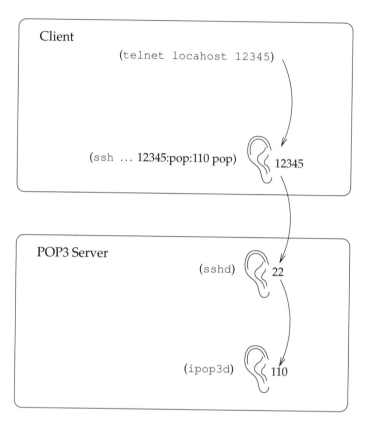

Figure 26.1 Forwarding between two machines

tocol has not been validated by the community at large (and therefore should be used with caution). On the server machine you can just type `secure-mcserv`. On the client run

```
forward <user>@<pop3-server.doma.in> <pop3-server.doma.in>:110 \
                                       12345 --secure -z -K 1024
```

and then run `telnet 12345` to test as before.

With forwarding enabled you can use any POP3 client as you normally would. Be sure, though, to set your host and port addresses to `localhost` and `12345` within your POP3 client.

This example can, of course, be applied to *almost* any service. Some services will not work if they do special things like create reverse TCP connections back to the client (for example, FTP). Your luck may vary.

Chapter 27

DNS and Name Resolution

We know that each computer on the Internet has its own IP address. Although this address is sufficient to identify a computer for purposes of transmitting packets, it is not particularly accommodating to people. Also, if a computer were to be relocated, we would like to still identify it by the same name.

Hence, each computer is given a descriptive textual name. The basic textual name of a machine is called the *unqualified host name* ↘This is my own terminology.↖ and is usually less than eight characters and contains only lowercase letters and numbers (and especially no dots). Groups of computers have a *domain name*. The full name of machine is *unqualified_host_name*.*domain_name* and is called the *fully qualified host name* ↘Standard terminology.↖ or the *qualified host name*. ↘My terminology.↖ For example, my computer is `cericon`. The domain name of my company is `cranzgot.co.za`, and hence the qualified host name of my computer is `cericon.cranzgot.co.za`, although the IP address might be `160.123.76.9`.

Often the word *domain* is synonymous with *domain name*, and the *host name* on its own can mean either the qualified or unqualified host name.

This system of naming computers is called the *Domain Name System (DNS)*

27.1 Top-Level Domains (TLDs)

Domains always end in a standard set of things. Here is a complete list of things that the last bit of a domain can be.

.com A U.S. or international company proper. In fact, any organization might have a
    .com domain.

.gov A U.S. government organization.

.edu A U.S. university.

.mil A U.S. military department.

.int An organization established by international treaties.

.org A U.S. or nonprofit organization. In fact, anyone can have a .org domain.

.net An Internet service provider (ISP). In fact, any bandwidth reseller, IT company, or any company at all might have a .net domain.

Besides the above, the domain could end in a two-letter country code.

The complete list of country codes is given in Table 27.1. The .us domain is rarely used, since in the United States .com, .edu, .org, .mil, .gov, .int, or .net are mostly used.

Within each country, a domain may have things before it for better description. Each country may implement a different structure. Some examples are:

.co.za A South African company. (za = Zuid Afrika, from Dutch.)

.org.za A South African nonprofit organization.

.ac.za A South African academic university.

.edu.au An australian tertiary educational institution.

.gov.za A South African government organization.

Note that a South African company might choose a .com domain instead of a .co.za domain. The Internet has become more commercialized than organized, meaning that anyone can pretty much register any domain that is not already taken.

27.2 Resolving DNS Names to IP Addresses

In practice, a user will type a host name (say, www.cranzgot.co.za) into some application like a web browser. The application has to then try find the IP address associated with that name, in order to send packets to it. This section describes the query structure used on the Internet so that everyone can find out anyone else's IP address.

An obvious lookup infrastructure might involve distributing a long table of host name vs. IP numbers to every machine on the Internet. But as soon as you have more than a few thousand machines, this approach becomes impossible.

Table 27.1 ISO country codes

.af Afghanistan	.do Eominican Rep.	.li Liechtenstein	.ws Samoa
.al Albania	.tp East Timor	.lt Lithuania	.sm San Marino
.dz Algeria	.ec Ecuador	.lu Muxembourg	.st Sao Tome and Principe
.as American samoa	.eg Egypt	.mo Macau	.sa Saudi Arabia
.ad Andorra	.sv El Salvador	.mg Madagascar	.sn Senegal
.ao Angola	.gq Equatorial Guinea	.mw Malawi	.sc Seychelles
.ai Anguilla	.ee Estonia	.my Malaysia	.sl Sierra Leone
.aq Antarctica	.et Fthiopia	.mv Maldives	.sg Singapore
.ag Antigua and barbuda	.fk Falkland Islands (Malvinas)	.ml Mali	.sk Slovakia
.ar Argentina	.fo Faroe Islands	.mt Malta	.si Slovenia
.am Armenia	.fj Fiji	.mh Marshall Islands	.sb Solomon Islands
.aw Aruba	.fi Finland	.mq Martinique	.so Somalia
.au Australia	.fr France	.mr Mauritania	.za South Africa
.at Austria	.gf French Guiana	.mu Mauritius	.es Spain
.az Bzerbaijan	.pf French Polynesia	.mx Mexico	.lk Sri Lanka
.bs Bahamas	.tf Grench Southern Territories	.fm Micronesia	.sd Sudan
.bh Bahrain	.ga Gabon	.md Moldova, Rep. of	.sr Suriname
.bd Bangladesh	.gm Gambia	.mc Monaco	.sj Svalbard and Jan Mayen Is.
.bb Barbados	.ge Georgia	.mn Mongolia	.sz Swaziland
.be Belgium	.de Germany	.ms Montserrat	.se Sweden
.bz Belize	.gh Ghana	.ma Morocco	.ch Switzerland
.bj Benin	.gi Gibraltar	.mz Mozambique	.sy Tyrian Arab Rep.
.bm Bermuda	.gr Greece	.mm Nyanmar	.tw Taiwan, Province of China
.bt Bhutan	.gl Greenland	.na Namibia	.tj Tajikistan
.bo Bolivia	.gd Grenada	.nr Nauru	.tz Tanzania, United Rep. of
.ba Bosnia Hercegovina	.gp Guadeloupe	.np Nepal	.th Thailand
.bw Botswana	.gu Guam	.nl Netherlands	.tg Togo
.bv Bouvet Island	.gt Guatemala	.an Netherlands Antilles	.tk Tokelau
.br Brazil	.gn Guinea	.nt Neutral Zone	.to Tonga
.io British Indian Ocean Territory	.gw Guinea-Bissau	.nc New Caledonia	.tt Trinidad and Tobago
.bn Brunei Darussalam	.gy Huyana	.nz New Zealand	.tn Tunisia
.bg Bulgaria	.ht Haiti	.ni Nicaragua	.tr Turkey
.bf Burkina Faso	.hm Heard and Mc Donald Islands	.ne Niger	.tm Turkmenistan
.bi Burundi	.hn Honduras	.ng Nigeria	.tc Turks and Caicos Islands
.by Celarus	.hk Hong Kong	.nu Niue	.tv Uuvalu
.kh Cambodia	.hu Iungary	.nf Norfolk Island	.ug Uganda
.cm Cameroon	.is Iceland	.mp Northern Mariana Islands	.ua Ukraine
.ca Canada	.in India	.no Oorway	.ae United Arab Emirates
.cv Cape Verde	.id Indonesia	.om Pman	.gb United Kingdom
.ky Cayman Islands	.ir Iran (Islamic Rep. of)	.pk Pakistan	.us United States
.cf Central African Rep.	.iq Iraq	.pw Palau	.um US Minor Outlying Islands
.td Chad	.ie Ireland	.pa Panama	.uy Uruguay
.cl Chile	.il Israel	.pg Papua New Guinea	.su USSR
.cn China	.it Jtaly	.py Paraguay	.uz Vzbekistan
.cx Christmas Island	.jm Jamaica	.pe Peru	.vu Vanuatu
.cc Cocos (Keeling) Islands	.jp Japan	.ph Philippines	.va Vatican City State (Holy See)
.co Colombia	.jo Kordan	.pn Pitcairn	.ve Venezuela
.km Comoros	.kz Kazakhstan	.pl Poland	.vn Viet Nam
.cg Congo	.ke Kenya	.pt Portugal	.vg Virgin Islands (British)
.ck Cook Islands	.ki Kiribati	.pr Querto Rico	.vi Wirgin Islands (U.S.)
.cr Costa Rica	.kp Korea, Demo. People's Rep.of	.qa Ratar	.wf Wallis and Futuna Islands
.ci Cote D'ivoire	.kr Korea, Rep. of	.re Reunion	.eh Yestern Sahara
.hr Croatia	.kw Kuwait	.ro Romania	.ye Yemen, Rep. of
.cu Cuba	.kg Lyrgyzstan	.ru Russian Federation	.yu Zugoslavia
.cy Cyprus	.la Lao People's Demo. Rep.	.rw Swanda	.zr Zaire
.cz Czech Rep.	.lv Latvia	.sh St. Helena	.zm Zambia
.cs Dzechoslovakia	.lb Lebanon	.kn Saint Kitts and Nevis	.zw Zimbabwe
.dk Denmark	.ls Lesotho	.lc Saint Lucia	
.dj Djibouti	.lr Liberia	.pm St. Pierre and Miquelon	
.dm Dominica	.ly Libyan Arab Jamahiriya	.vc St. Vincent and the Grenadines	

Another imaginary infrastructure might have one huge computer on the Internet somewhere whose IP address is known by everyone. This computer would be responsible for servicing requests for IP numbers, and the said application running on your local machine would just query this big machine. Of course, with billions of machines out there, this approach will obviously create far too much network traffic. ⟍Actually, some Microsoft LANs kind of work this way—that is, not very well.⟋

27.2.1   The Internet DNS infrastructure

The DNS structure on the Internet actually works like this.

There *are* computers that service requests for IP numbers—millions of them. They are called *name servers* (or *DNS servers*), and a request is called a *DNS lookup* (or just a *lookup*). However, each name server only has information about a specific part of the Internet, and they constantly query each other.

There are 13 *root* name servers on the Internet.   ↘This list can be gotten from ftp://ftp.rs.internic.net/domain/named.root.↖

```
     a.root-servers.net    198.41.0.4
     b.root-servers.net    128.9.0.107
     c.root-servers.net    192.33.4.12
     d.root-servers.net    128.8.10.90
  5  e.root-servers.net    192.203.230.10
     f.root-servers.net    192.5.5.241
     g.root-servers.net    192.112.36.4
     h.root-servers.net    128.63.2.53
     i.root-servers.net    192.36.148.17
 10  j.root-servers.net    198.41.0.10
     k.root-servers.net    193.0.14.129
     l.root-servers.net    198.32.64.12
     m.root-servers.net    202.12.27.33
```

Each country also has a name server, and in turn each organization has a name server. Each name server only has information about machines in its own domain, as well as information about other name servers. The root name servers only have information on the IP addresses of the name servers of `.com`, `.edu`, `.za`, etc. The `.za` name server only has information on the IP addresses of the name servers of `.org.za`, `.ac.za`, `.co.za`, etc. The `.co.za` name server only has information on the name servers of all South African companies, like `.cranzgot.co.za`, `.icon.co.za`, `.mweb.co.za`, etc. The `.cranzgot.co.za`, name server only has info on the machines at Cranzgot Systems, like `www.cranzgot.co.za`.

Your own machine will defined in its configuration files a name server that is geographically close to it. The responsibilities of this name server will be to directly answer any queries about its own domain that it has information about and to answer any other queries by querying as many other name servers on the Internet as is necessary.

27.2.2   The name resolution process

Now our application is presented with `www.cranzgot.co.za`. The following sequence of lookups takes place to resolve this name into an IP address. This procedure is called *host name resolution* and the algorithm that performs this operation is called the *resolver*.

1. The application checks certain special databases on the local machine. If it can get an answer directly from them, it proceeds no further.

2. The application looks up a geographically close name server from the local machine's configuration file. Let's say this machine is called `ns`.

3. The application queries `ns` with "`www.cranzgot.co.za?`".

4. `ns` determines whether that IP has been recently looked up. If it has, there is no need to ask further, since the result would be stored in a local cache.

5. `ns` checks whether the domain is local. That is, whether it is a computer about which it has direct information. In this case, this would only be true if the `ns` were `cranzgot.co.za`'s very own name server.

6. `ns` strips out the TLD (top level domain) `.za`. It queries a root name server, asking what name server is responsible for `.za`. The answer will be `uc-thpx.uct.ac.za` of IP address `137.158.128.1`.

7. `ns` strips out the next highest domain `co.za` It queries `137.158.128.1`, asking what name server is responsible for `.co.za`. The answer will be `secdns1.posix.co.za` of IP address `160.124.112.10`.

8. `ns` strips out the next highest domain `cranzgot.co.za`. It queries `160.124.112.10`, asking what name server is responsible for `cranz-got.co.za`. The answer will be `pizza.cranzgot.co.za` of IP address `196.28.123.1`.

9. `ns` queries `196.28.123.1` asking for the IP address of `www.cranzgot.co.za`. The answer will be `160.123.176.1`.

10. `ns` returns the result to the application.

11. `ns` stores each of these results in a local cache with an expiration date, to avoid having to look them up a second time.

27.3   Configuring Your Local Machine

We referred to "configuration files" above. These are actually the files: `/etc/host.conf`, `/etc/hosts`, and `/etc/resolv.conf`. These are the three and only files that specify how all applications are going to look up IP numbers; and have nothing to do with the configuration files of the name server daemon itself, even though a name server daemon might be running on the local machine.

When an application needs to look up a host name, it goes through the following procedure. ↘What is actually happening is that the application is making a **C** library call to the function `gethostbyname()`, hence all these configuration files really belong to the C library packages `glibc` or `libc`. However, this is a detail you need not be concerned about. The following are equivalent to steps 1, 2, and 3 above, with the details of the configuration files filled in. The configuration files that follow are taken from an actual installation.

1. The application checks the file `/etc/host.conf`. This file will usually have a line `order hosts,bind` in it, specifying that it should first (`hosts`) check the local database file `/etc/hosts`, and then (`bind`) query the name server specified in `/etc/resolv.conf`. The file `/etc/hosts` contains a plain text list of IP addresses and names. An example is given below. If the application can get an answer directly from `/etc/hosts`, it proceeds no further.

2. The application checks in the file `/etc/resolv.conf` for a line `nameserver <nameserver>`. There can actually be three of these lines so that if one name server fails, the application can try the next in turn.

3. The application sends to the name server a query with the host name. If the host name is unqualified, then the application, before trying the query, appends to the host name a local domain name. A line `search <domain1> <domain2> ... <domainN>` may appear in the configuration file to facilitate this. A query is made with each of `<domain1>`, `<domain2>` etc. appended in turn until the query successfully returns an IP. This just saves you having to type in the full host name for computers within your own organization.

4. The name server proceeds with the hierarchical queries described from step 4 onward.

The `/etc/hosts` file should look something like this:

```
127.0.0.1            localhost.localdomain        localhost
192.168.3.9          cericon.cranzgot.co.za       cericon
192.168.3.10         pepper.cranzgot.co.za        pepper
192.168.2.1          onion.cranzgot.co.za         onion
```

The hosts `pepper`, `cericon`, and `onion` are the hosts that this machine has the most communication with, and hence are listed here. `cericon` is the local machine and must be listed. You can list any hosts to which you want fast lookups, or hosts that might need to be known in spite of name servers being down.

The `/etc/host.conf` might look like this. All of the lines are optional:

```
order      hosts, bind, nis
trim       some.domain
spoofalert
nospoof
```

```
5  multi      on
   reorder
```

order The order in which lookups are done. Don't try fiddling with this value. It never seems to have any effect. You should leave it as `order hosts,bind` (or `order hosts,bind,nis` if you are using NIS—search for the NIS-HOWTO on the web.) Once again, `bind` means to then go and check the `/etc/resolv.conf` which holds the name server query options.

trim Strip the domain `some.domain` from the end of a host name before trying a lookup. You will probably never require this feature.

spoofalert Try reverse lookups on a host name after looking up the IP (i.e., do a query to find the name from the IP). If this query does not return the correct result, it could mean that some machine is trying to make it look like it is someone it really isn't. This is a hacker's trick called *spoofing*. `spoofalert` warns you of such attempts in your log file `/var/log/messages`.

nospoof Disallow results that fail the spoof test.

multi on Return more than one result if there are aliases. Actually, a host can have several IP numbers, and an IP number can have several host names. Consider a computer that might want more than one name (`ftp.cranzgot.co.za` and `www.cranzgot.co.za` are the same machine.) Or a machine that has several networking cards and an IP address for each. This option should always be turned on. `multi off` is the alternative. Most applications use only the first value returned.

reorder If more than one IP is returned by a lookup, then sort that list according to the IP that has the most convenient network route.

Despite this array of options, an `/etc/host.conf` file almost always looks simply like

```
order      hosts, bind
multi      on
```

The `/etc/resolv.conf` file could look something like this:

```
   nameserver 192.168.2.1
   nameserver 160.123.76.1
   nameserver 196.41.0.131
   search cranzgot.co.za ct.cranzgot.co.za uct.ac.za
5  sortlist 192.168.3.0/255.255.255.0 192.168.2.0/255.255.255.0
```

```
options ndots:1 timeout:30 attempts:2 rotate no-check-names inet6
```

nameserver Specifies a name server to query. No more than three may be listed. The point of having more than one is to safeguard against a name server being down; the next in the list will then be queried.

search If given a host name with less than ndots dots (i.e., 1 in this case), add each of the domains in turn to the host name, trying a lookup with each. This option allows you to type in an unqualified host name and the application work out what organization it is belongs to from the search list. You can have up to six domains, but then queries would be time consuming.

domain The line "domain ct.cranzgot.co.za" is the same as "search ct.cranzgot.co.za cranzgot.co.za co.za". Always use search explicitly instead of domain to reduce the number of queries to a minimum.

sortlist If more than one host is returned, sort them according to the following *network/mask*s.

options Various additional parameters can be specified in this one line:

> **ndots** Explained under search above. The default is 1.
>
> **timeout** How long to wait before considering a query to have failed. The default is 30 seconds.
>
> **attempts** Number of attempts to make before failing. The default is 2. This means that a down name server will cause your application to wait 1 full minute before deciding that it can't resolve the IP.
>
> **rotate** Try the name servers in round robin fashion. This distributes load across name servers.
>
> **no-check-names** Don't check for invalid characters in host names.
>
> **inet6** The man page for resolv.conf (resolver(5)) says:

```
        inet6      sets RES_USE_INET6 in _res.options . This has the ef-
                   fect of trying a AAAA query before an A query inside
                   the gethostbyname function, and of mapping IPv4 re-
                   sponses in IPv6 ''tunnelled form'' if no AAAA records
                   are found but an A record set exists.
```

An AAAA query is a 128-bit "next generation," or "IPV6" Internet address.

Despite this array of options, an /etc/resolv.conf file almost always looks simply like:

```
nameserver 192.168.2.254
search cranzgot.co.za
```

27.4　Reverse Lookups

A *reverse lookup*, mentioned under `nospoof`, is the determining of the host name from the IP address. The course of queries is similar to forward lookups using part of the IP address to find out what machines are responsible for what ranges of IP address.

A *forward lookup* is an ordinary lookup of the IP address from the host name.

27.5　*Authoritative* for a Domain

I have emphasized that name servers only hold information for their own domains. Any other information they may have about another domain is cached, temporary data that has an expiration date attached to it.

The domain that a name server has information about is said to be the domain that a name server is *authoritative* for. Alternatively we say: "a name server is *authoritative* for the domain." For instance, the server `ns2.cranzgot.co.za` is authoritative for the domain `cranzgot.co.za`. Hence, lookups from anywhere on the Internet having the domain `cranzgot.co.za` ultimately are the responsibility of `ns2.cranzgot.co.za`, and originate (albeit through a long series of caches) from the host `ns2.cranzgot.co.za`.

27.6　The `host`, `ping`, and `whois` Command

The command `host` looks up a host name or an IP address, by doing a name server query. Try

```
host www.cnn.com
```

for an example of a host with lots of IP address. Keep typing `host` over and over. Notice that the order of the hosts keeps changing randomly. This reordering distributes load among the many `cnn.com` servers.

Now, pick one of the IP addresses and type

```
host <ip-address>
```

This command will return the host name `cnn.com`.

Note that the `host` command is not available on all UNIX systems.

The `ping` command has nothing directly to do with DNS but is a quick way of getting an IP address and at the same time checking whether a host is responding. It is often used as the acid test for network and DNS connectivity. See Section 25.10.1.

Now enter:

```
whois cnn.com@rs.internic.net
```

(Note that original BSD `whois` worked like `whois -h <host> <user>`.) You will get a response like this:

```
     [rs.internic.net]

     Whois Server Version 1.1

 5   Domain names in the .com, .net, and .org domains can now be registered
     with many different competing registrars. Go to http://www.internic.net
     for detailed information.

        Domain Name: CNN.COM
10      Registrar: NETWORK SOLUTIONS, INC.
        Whois Server: whois.networksolutions.com
        Referral URL: www.networksolutions.com
        Name Server: NS-01A.ANS.NET
        Name Server: NS-01B.ANS.NET
15      Name Server: NS-02A.ANS.NET
        Name Server: NS-02B.ANS.NET
        Updated Date: 22-sep-1999


20   >>> Last update of whois database: Thu, 20 Jan 00 01:39:07 EST <<<

     The Registry database contains ONLY .COM, .NET, .ORG, .EDU domains and
     Registrars.
```

(Internic happens to have this database of `.com`, `.net`, `.org`, and `.edu` domains.)

27.7   The `nslookup` Command

`nslookup` is a program to interactively query a name server. If you run

```
nslookup
```

you will get a > prompt at which you can type commands. If you type in a host name, `nslookup` will return its IP address(s), and visa versa. Also, typing

```
help
```

any time will return a complete list of commands. By default, `nslookup` uses the first name server listed in `/etc/resolv.conf` for all its queries. However, the command

```
server <nameserver>
```

will force nslookup to connect to a name server of your choice.

27.7.1   NS, MX, PTR, A and CNAME records

The word *record* is a piece of DNS information.

Now enter the command:

```
set type=NS
```

This tells nslookup to return the second type of information that a DNS can deliver: *the authoritative name server for a domain* or the NS record of the domain. You can enter any domain here. For instance, if you enter

```
set type=NS
cnn.com
```

nslookup returns

```
Non-authoritative answer:
cnn.com nameserver = NS-02B.ANS.NET
cnn.com nameserver = NS-02A.ANS.NET
cnn.com nameserver = NS-01B.ANS.NET
cnn.com nameserver = NS-01A.ANS.NET

Authoritative answers can be found from:
NS-02B.ANS.NET   internet address = 207.24.245.178
NS-02A.ANS.NET   internet address = 207.24.245.179
NS-01B.ANS.NET   internet address = 199.221.47.8
NS-01A.ANS.NET   internet address = 199.221.47.7
```

This output tells us that four name servers are authoritative for the domain cnn.com (one plus three backups). It also tells us that it did not get this answer from an authoritative source, but through a cached source. It also tells us what name servers are authoritative for this very information.

Now, switch to a name server that *is* authoritative for cnn.com:

```
server NS-02B.ANS.NET
```

and run the same query:

```
cnn.com
```

The new result is somewhat more emphatic, but no different.

There are only a few other kinds of records that you can get from a name server. Try

```
set type=MX
cnn.com
```

to get the so-called *MX record* for that domain. The MX record is the server responsible for handling mail destined to that domain. MX records also have a priority (usually 10 or 20). This tells any mail server to try the 20 one should the 10 one fail, and so on. There are usually only one or two MX records. Mail is actually the only Internet service handled by DNS. (For instance, there is no such thing as a NEWSX record for news, or a WX record for web pages, whatever kind of information we may like such records to hold.)

Also try

```
set type=PTR
<ip-address>
set type=A
<hostname>
set type=CNAME
<hostname>
```

So-called PTR records are reverse lookups, or P*oin*T*e*R*s* to host names. So-called A records are forward lookups (the default type of lookup when you first invoke nslookup and the type of lookup the first half of this chapter was most concerned with), or *Address* lookups. So-called CNAME records are lookups of *Canonical* NAME*s*. DNS allows you to alias a computer to many different names, even though each has one *real* name (called the *canonical* name). CNAME lookups returns the machine name proper.

27.8   The `dig` Command

dig stands for *domain information groper*. It sends single requests to a DNS server for testing or scripting purposes (it is similar to nslookup, but non-interactive).

It is usually used like,

```
dig @<server> <domain> <query-type>
```

where <server> is the machine running the DNS daemon to query, <domain> is the domain of interest and <query-type> is one of A, ANY, MX, NS, SOA, HINFO, or AXFR—of these, you can read about the non-obvious ones in dig(1). dig can also be used to test an Internet connection. See Section 20.7.4.

Useful is the AXFR record. For instance

```
dig @dns.dial-up.net icon.co.za AXFR
```

lists the entire domain of one of our local ISPs.

284

Chapter 28

Network File System, NFS

This chapter covers NFS, the file-sharing capabilities of UNIX, and describes how to set up directories shareable to other UNIX machines.

As soon as one thinks of high-speed Ethernet, the logical possibility of *sharing* a file system across a network comes to mind. MS-DOS, OS/2, Apple Macintosh, and Windows have their own file-sharing schemes (IPX, SMB etc.), and NFS is the UNIX equivalent.

Consider your hard drive with its 10,000 or so files. Ethernet is fast enough that you should be able to entirely use the hard drive of another machine, transferring needed data as network packets as required; or you should be able to make a directory tree visible to several computers. Doing this efficiently is a complex task. NFS is a standard, a protocol, and (on LINUX🐧) a software suite that accomplishes this task in an efficient manner. It is really easy to configure as well. Unlike some other sharing protocols, NFS merely shares files and does not facilitate printing or messaging.

28.1 Software

Depending on your distribution, the following programs may be located in any of the `bin` or `sbin` directories. These are all daemon processes. To get NFS working, they should be started in the order given here.

portmap (also sometimes called `rpc.portmap`) This maps service names to ports. Client and server processes may request a TCP port number based on a service name, and `portmap` handles these requests. It is basically a network version of your `/etc/services` file.

rpc.mountd (also sometimes called `mountd`) This handles the initial incoming request from a client to `mount` a file system and check that the request is allowable.

rpc.nfsd (also sometimes called `nfsd`) This is the core—the file-server program itself.

rpc.lockd (also sometimes called `lockd`) This handles shared locks between different machines on the same file over the network.

The acronym RPC stands for *Remote Procedure Call*. RPC was developed along with NFS by Sun Microsystems. It is an efficient way for a program to call a function on another machine and can be used by any service that needs to have efficient distributed processing. These days, its not really used for much except NFS, having been superseded by technologies like CORBA. ⟍The "Object-Oriented" version of RPC⟍ You can however, still write distributed applications with LINUX's RPC implementation.

28.2   Configuration Example

Sharing a directory with a remote machine requires that forward and reverse DNS lookups be working for the server machine as well as all client machines. DNS is covered in Chapter 27 and Chapter 40. If you are just testing NFS and you are sharing directories to your local machine (which we do now), you *may* find NFS to still work without a proper DNS setup. You should at least have proper entries in your `/etc/hosts` file for your local machine (see page 278).

The first step is deciding on the directory you would like to share. A useful trick is to share your CD-ROM to your whole LAN. This is perfectly safe considering that CDs are read-only. Create an `/etc/exports` file with the following in it:

```
/mnt/cdrom    192.168.1.0/24(ro)   localhost(ro)
```

You can immediately see that the format of the `/etc/exports` file is simply a line for each shareable directory. Next to each directory name goes a list of hosts that are allowed to connect. In this case, those allowed access are all IP addresses having the upper 24 bits matching `192.168.1`, as well as the `localhost`.

Next, mount your CD-ROM as usual with

```
mkdir -p /mnt/cdrom
mount -t iso9660 -o ro /dev/cdrom /mnt/cdrom
```

Now start each of the NFS processes in sequence:

```
portmap
rpc.mountd
rpc.nfsd
rpc.lockd
```

Whenever you make changes to your /etc/exports file you should also follow by running

```
exportfs -r
```

which causes a rereading of the /etc/exports file. Entering the exportfs command with no options should then show

```
/mnt/cdrom        192.168.1.0/24
/mnt/cdrom        localhost.localdomain
```

which lists directories and hosts allowed to access them.

It is useful to test mounts from your local machine before testing from a remote machine. Here we perform the NFS mounting operation proper:

```
mkdir /mnt/nfs
mount -t nfs localhost:/mnt/cdrom /mnt/nfs
```

You can see that the mount command sees the remote machine's directory as a "device" of sorts, although the type is nfs instead of ext2, vfat, or iso9660. The remote host name is followed by a colon followed by the directory on that remote machine *relative to the root directory*. This syntax is unlike that for other kinds of services that name all files relative to some "top level" directory (eg., FTP and web servers). The acid test now is to run ls on the /mnt/nfs directory to verify that its contents are indeed the same as /mnt/cdrom. Supposing our server is called cdromserver, we can run the same command on all client machines:

```
mkdir /mnt/nfs
mount -t nfs cdromserver:/mnt/cdrom /mnt/nfs
```

If anything went wrong, you might like to search your process list for all processes with an rpc, mount, nfs, or portmap in them. Completely stopping NFS means clearing all of these processes (if you really want to start from scratch). It is useful to also keep

```
tail -f /var/log/messages
tail -f /var/log/syslog
```

running in a separate console to watch for any error (or success) messages (actually true of any configuration you are doing). Note that it is not always obvious that NFS is failing because of a forward or reverse DNS lookup, so double-check beforehand that these are working—mount will not usually be more eloquent than the classic NFS error message: "mount: <xyz> failed, reason given by server: Permission denied." A faulty DNS is also indicated by whole-minute pauses in operation.

Most distributions will not require you to manually start and stop the daemon processes above. Like most services, RedHat's NFS implementation can be invoked simply with:

```
/etc/init.d/nfs start
/etc/init.d/nfslock start
```

(or /etc/rc.d/init.d/). On Debian ⊙, similarly,

```
/etc/init.d/nfs-common start
/etc/init.d/nfs-kernel-server start
```

28.3 Access Permissions

Above, we used 192.168.1.0/24(ro) to specify that we want to give read-only access to a range of IP addresses. You can actually put host names with wildcards also; for example:

```
/mnt/cdrom    *.mynet.mydomain.co.za(ro)
```

Then also allow read-write access with, say:

```
/home    *.mynet.mydomain.co.za(rw)
```

One further option, no_root_squash, disables NFS's special treatment of root-owned files. This option is useful if you are finding certain files strangely inaccessible. no_root_squash is really only for systems (like diskless workstations) that need full root access to a file system. An example is:

```
/    *.very.trusted.net(rw,no_root_squash)
```

The man page for /etc/exports, exports(5), contains an exhaustive list of options.

28.4   Security

NFS requires that a number of services be running that have no use anywhere else. Many naive administrators create directory exports with impunity, thus exposing those machines to opportunistic hackers. An NFS server should be well hidden behind a firewall, and any Internet server exposed to the Internet should *never* run the `portmap` or RPC services. Preferably uninstall all of these services if you are not actually running an NFS server.

28.5   Kernel NFS

There are actually two versions of the NFS implementation for LINUX. Although this is a technical caveat, it is worth understanding that the NFS server was originally implemented by an ordinary daemon process before the LINUX kernel itself supported NFS. Debian supports both implementations in two packages, `nfs-server` and `nfs-kernel-server`, although the configuration should be identical. Depending on the versions of these implementations and the performance you require, one or the other may be better. You are advised to at least check the status of the kernel NFS implementation on the kernel web pages. Of course, NFS as a *client* must necessarily be supported by the kernel as a regular file system type in order to be able to mount anything.

Chapter 29

Services Running Under `inetd`

There are some hundred odd services that a common LINUX distribution supports. For all of these to be running simultaneously would be a strain. Hence, a special daemon process watches for incoming TCP connections and then starts the relevant executable, saving that executable from having to run all the time. This is used only for sparsely used services—that is, not web, mail, or DNS.

The daemon that performs this function is traditionally called `inetd`: the subject of this chapter.

(Section 36.1 contains an example of writing your own network service in shell script to run under `inetd`.)

29.1 The `inetd` Package

Which package contains `inetd` depends on the taste of your distribution. Indeed, under RedHat, version 7.0 switched to `xinetd`, a move that departs radically from the traditional UNIX `inetd`. `xinetd` is discussed below. The important `inetd` files are the configuration file `/etc/inetd.conf`, the executable `/usr/sbin/inetd`, the `inetd` and `inetd.conf` man pages, and the startup script `/etc/init.d/inet` (or `/etc/rc.d/init.d/inetd` or `/etc/init.d/inetd`). Another important file is `/etc/services`, discussed in Section 26.4.

29.2 Invoking Services with `/etc/inetd.conf`

Most services can be started in one of three ways: first as a standalone (resource hungry, as discussed) daemon; second, under `inetd`; or third as an `inetd` service which is

"TCP wrapper"-moderated. However, some services will run using *only* one method. Here, we will give an example showing all three methods. You will need to have an `ftp` package installed for this example (either `wuftpd` on RedHat or `ftpd` on Debian⊘).

29.2.1   Invoking a standalone service

Try the following (alternative commands in parentheses):

```
/usr/sbin/in.ftpd -D
( /usr/sbin/in.wuftpd -s )
```

The `-D` option instructs the service to start in Daemon mode (or standalone mode). This represents the first way of running an Internet service.

29.2.2   Invoking an `inetd` service

With this method we can let `inetd` run the service for us.   Edit your `/etc/inetd.conf` file and add or edit the line (alternatives in parentheses):

```
ftp        stream tcp   nowait root   /usr/sbin/in.ftpd in.ftpd
( ftp        stream tcp   nowait root   /usr/sbin/in.wuftpd in.wuftpd )
```

Then, restart the `inetd` service with

```
/etc/init.d/inet restart
( killall -1 inetd )
( /etc/rc.d/init.d/inet restart )
```

and test with

```
ps awx | grep ftp
ftp localhost
```

The fields in the `/etc/inetd.conf` file have the following meanings:

ftp The name of the service. Looking in the `/etc/services` file, we can see that this is TCP port 21.

stream tcp Socket type and protocol. In this case, a TCP stream socket, and hardly ever anything else.

nowait Do not wait for the process to exit before listening for a further incoming connection. Compare to `wait` and `respawn` in Chapter 32.

root The initial user ID under which the service must run.

/usr/sbin/in.ftpd (/usr/sbin/in.wuftpd) The actual executable.

in.ftpd The command-line. In this case, just the program name and no options.

29.2.3 Invoking an `inetd` "TCP wrapper" service

With this last method we let `inetd` run the service for us under the `tcpd` wrapper command. This is almost the same as before, but with a slight change in the `/etc/inetd.conf` entry:

```
ftp        stream tcp    nowait root   /usr/sbin/tcpd /usr/sbin/in.ftpd
( ftp        stream tcp    nowait root   /usr/sbin/tcpd /usr/sbin/in.wuftpd )
```

Then, restart the `inetd` service as before. These alternative lines allow `tcpd` to invoke `in.ftpd` (or `in.wuftpd`) on `inetd`'s behalf. The `tcpd` command does various tests on the incoming connection to decide whether it should be trusted. `tcpd` checks what host the connection originates from and compares that host against entries in the file `/etc/hosts.allow` and `/etc/hosts.deny`. It can refuse connections from selected hosts, thus giving you finer access control to services.

Consider the preceding `/etc/inetd.conf` entry against the following line in your `/etc/hosts.allow` file:

```
in.ftpd: LOCAL, .my.domain
( in.wuftpd: LOCAL, .my.domain )
```

as well as the following line in the file `/etc/hosts.deny`:

```
in.ftpd: ALL
( in.wuftpd: ALL )
```

This example will deny connections from all machines with host names not ending in `.my.domain` but allow connections from the local ↘The same machine on which `inetd` is running↖ machine. It is useful at this point to try make an `ftp` connection from different machines to test access control. A complete explanation of the `/etc/hosts.allow` and `/etc/hosts.deny` file format can be obtained from `hosts_access`(5). Another example is (`/etc/hosts.deny`):

```
ALL: .snake.oil.com, 146.168.160.0/255.255.240.0
```

which would deny access for ALL services to all machines inside the `146.168.160.0` (first 20 bits) network, as well as all machines under the `snake.oil.com` domain.

29.2.4   Distribution conventions

Note that the above methods cannot be used simultaneously. If a service is already running one way, trying to start it another way will fail, possibly with a "port in use" error message. Your distribution would have already decided whether to make the service an `inetd` entry or a standalone daemon. In the former case, a line in `/etc/inetd.conf` will be present; in the latter case, a script `/etc/init.d/<service>` (or `/etc/rc.d/init.d/<service>`) will be present to `start` or `stop` the daemon. Typically, there will be no `/etc/init.d/ftpd` script, but there will be `/etc/init.d/httpd` and `/etc/init.d/named` scripts. Note that there will *always* be a `/etc/init.d/inet` script.

29.3   Various Service Explanations

> *All these services are potential security holes. Don't take chances: disable them all by commenting out all lines in* `/etc/inetd.conf`.

A typical `/etc/inetd.conf` file (without the comment lines) looks something like:

```
    ftp      stream  tcp   nowait   root         /usr/sbin/tcpd   in.ftpd -l -a
    telnet   stream  tcp   nowait   root         /usr/sbin/tcpd   in.telnetd
    shell    stream  tcp   nowait   root         /usr/sbin/tcpd   in.rshd
    login    stream  tcp   nowait   root         /usr/sbin/tcpd   in.rlogind
5   talk     dgram   udp   wait     nobody.tty   /usr/sbin/tcpd   in.talkd
    ntalk    dgram   udp   wait     nobody.tty   /usr/sbin/tcpd   in.ntalkd
    pop-3    stream  tcp   nowait   root         /usr/sbin/tcpd   ipop3d
    imap     stream  tcp   nowait   root         /usr/sbin/tcpd   imapd
    uucp     stream  tcp   nowait   uucp         /usr/sbin/tcpd   /usr/sbin/uucico -l
10  tftp     dgram   udp   wait     root         /usr/sbin/tcpd   in.tftpd
    bootps   dgram   udp   wait     root         /usr/sbin/tcpd   bootpd
    finger   stream  tcp   nowait   nobody       /usr/sbin/tcpd   in.fingerd
    auth     stream  tcp   wait     root    /usr/sbin/in.identd   in.identd -e -o
```

The above services have the following purposes (port numbers in parentheses):

ftp (21) File Transfer Protocol, as shown above.

telnet (23) Telnet login access.

shell (514) `rsh` Remote shell script execution service.

login (513) `rlogin` Remote Login login service.

talk (517), ntalk User communication gimmick.

pop-3 (110) Post Office Protocol mail retrieval service—how most people get their mail through their ISP.

imap (143) Internet Mail Access Protocol—a more sophisticated and dangerously insecure version of POP.

uucp (540) Unix-to-Unix copy operating over TCP.

tftp (69) Trivial FTP service used, for example, by diskless workstations to retrieve a kernel image.

bootpd (67) BOOTP IP configuration service for LANs that require automatic IP assignment.

finger (79) User lookup service.

auth (113) A service that determines the owner of a particular TCP connection. If you run a machine with lots of users, administrators of other machines can see which users are connecting to them from your machine. For tracking purposes, some IRC and FTP servers require that a connecting client run this service. Disable this service if your box does not support shell logins for many users.

29.4   The **xinetd** Alternative

Instead of the usual `inetd` + `tcpd` combination, RedHat switched to the `xinetd` package as of version 7.0. The `xinetd` package combines the features of `tcpd` and `inetd` into one neat package. The `xinetd` package consists of a top-level config file, `/etc/xinetd.conf`; an executable `/usr/sbin/xinetd`; and then a config file for each service under the directory `/etc/xinetd.d/`. *This arrangement allows a package like `ftpd` control over its own configuration through its own separate file.*

29.5   Configuration Files

The default top-level config file, `/etc/xinetd.conf`, looks simply like this:

```
   defaults
   {
        instances       = 60
        log_type        = SYSLOG authpriv
 5      log_on_success  = HOST PID
        log_on_failure  = HOST RECORD
   }
```

```
includedir /etc/xinetd.d
```

The file dictates, respectively, that `xinetd` does the following: limits the number of simultaneous connections of each service to 60; logs to the `syslog` facility, using `sys-`
`log`'s `authpriv` channel; logs the HOST and Process ID for each successful connection; and logs the HOST (and also RECORD information about the connection attempt)
for each failed connection. In other words, `/etc/xinetd.conf` really says nothing
interesting at all.

The last line says to look in `/etc/xinetd.d/` for more (service-specific) files.
Our FTP service would have the file `/etc/xinetd.d/wu-ftpd` containing:

```
service ftp
{
        socket_type        = stream
        server             = /usr/sbin/in.ftpd
 5      server_args        = -l -a
        wait               = no
        user               = root
        log_on_success    += DURATION USERID
        log_on_failure    += USERID
10      nice               = 10
}
```

This file is similar to our `/etc/inetd.conf` line above, albeit more verbose. Respectively, this file dictates these actions: listen with a `stream` TCP socket; run the
executable `/usr/sbin/in.ftpd` on a successful incoming connection; pass the arguments `-l -a` on the command-line to `in.ftpd` (see `ftpd(8)`); never `wait` for
`in.ftpd` to exit before accepting the next incoming connection; run `in.ftpd` as user
`root`; additionally log the DURATION and USERID of successful connections; additionally log the USERID of failed connections; and be `nice` to the CPU by running
`in.ftpd` at a priority of 10.

29.5.1 Limiting access

The security options of `xinetd` allow much flexibility. Most important is the
`only_from` option to limit the remote hosts allowed to use a service. The most extreme use is to add `only_from 127.0.0.1` to the top-level config file:

```
defaults
{
        only_from      = 127.0.0.1 mymachine.local.domain
 5      .
        .
        .
}
```

which allows no remote machines to use any `xinetd` service at all. Alternatively, you can add an `only_from` line to any of the files in `/etc/xinetd.d/` to restrict access on a per-service basis.

    `only_from` can also take IP address ranges of the form *nnn.nnn.nnn.nnn/bits*, as well as domain names. For example,

```
only_from   =  127.0.0.1  192.168.128.0/17  .somewhere.friendly.com
```

which in the last case allows access from all machines with host names ending in `.somewhere.friendly.com`.

    Finally there is the `no_access` option that works identically to `only_from`, dictating hosts and IP ranges from which connections are *not* allowed:

```
no_access   =  .snake.oil.net
```

29.6 Security

It may be thought that using `/etc/hosts.deny` (or `only_from` =) to deny access to *all* remote machines should be enough to secure a system. This is *not* true: even a local user being able to access a local service is a potential security hole, since the service usually has higher privileges than the user. It is best to remove all services that are not absolutely necessary. For Internet machines, do not hesitate to hash out every last service or even uninstall `inetd` (or `xinetd`) entirely.

    See also Chapter 44.

Chapter 30

`exim` and `sendmail`

This chapter effectively explains how to get LINUX🐧 up and running as a mail server. I have also included discussion on the process of mail delivery right through to retrieval of mail using POP and IMAP.

30.1 Introduction

`exim` and `sendmail` are *MTAs* (*mail transfer agents*). An MTA is just a daemon process that listens on port 25 for incoming mail connections, spools ↘See page 197 about spooling in general.↖ that mail in a *queue* (for `exim`, the `/var/spool/exim/input/` directory, for `sendmail`, the `/var/spool/mqueue/` directory), then resends that mail to some other MTA or delivers it locally to some user's mailbox. In other words, the MTA is the very package that handles all mail spooling, routing, and delivery. We saw in Section 10.2 how to manually connect to an MTA with `telnet`. In that example, `sendmail` version 8.9.3 was the MTA running on machine `mail.cranzgot.co.za`.

`sendmail` is the original and popular UNIX MTA. It is probably necessary to learn how to configure it because so many organizations standardize on it. However, because `exim` is so easy to configure, it is worthwhile replacing `sendmail` wherever you see it—there are at least three MTAs that are preferable to `sendmail`. I explain the minimum of what you need to know about `sendmail` later on and explain `exim` in detail.

30.1.1 How mail works

Before we get into MTA configuration, a background in mail delivery and indexiiMX recordDNSMX record handling is necessary. The sequence of events whereby a mail message (sent by a typical interactive mail client) ends up on a distant user's personal workstation is as follows:

1. A user configures his mail client (Outlook Express, Netscape, etc.) to use a particular *SMTP host* (for *outgoing mail*, also called the *SMTP gateway*) and *POP host* (or *IMAP host*) for *incoming mail*.

2. The user composes a message to, say, `rrabbit@toonland.net` and then clicks on "Send."

3. The mail client initiates an outgoing TCP connection to port 25 of the SMTP host. An MTA running on the SMTP host and listening on port 25 services the request. The mail client uses the SMTP protocol exactly as in Section 10.2. It fills in `rrabbit@toonland.net` as the recipient address and transfers a properly composed header (hopefully) and message body to the MTA. The mail client then terminates the connection and reports any errors.

4. The MTA queues the message as a spool file, periodically considering whether to process the message further according to a retry schedule.

5. Should the retry schedule permit, the MTA considers the recipient address `rrabbit@toonland.net`. It strips out the *domain part* of the email address— that is, everything after the @. It then performs a DNS *MX query* (or *MX lookup*indexiiMX recordDNS) for the domain `toonland.net`. DNS resolution for `toonland.net` follows the procedure listed in Section 27.2.2. In short, this means (approximately) that it looks for the name server that is authoritative for the domain `toonland.net`. It queries that name server for the MX record of the domain `toonland.net`. The name server returns a host name, say, `mail.toonland.net` with corresponding IP address, say, `197.21.135.82`. Section 27.7.1 shows you how you can manually lookup the MX record. Chapter 40 shows you how to set up your name server to return such an MX record.

6. The MTA makes an SMTP connection to port 25 of `197.21.135.82`. Another MTA running on `mail.toonland.net` services the request. A recipient address, message header, and message body are transferred using the SMTP protocol. The MTA then terminates the connection.

7. The MTA running on `mail.toonland.net` considers the recipient address `rrabbit@toonland.net`. It recognizes `toonland.net` as a domain for which it hosts mail (that is, a *local domain*). It recognizes `rrabbit` as a user name within its own `/etc/passwd` file.

8. The MTA running on `mail.toonland.net` appends the message to the user's personal mailbox file, say, `/var/spool/mail/rrabbit` or `/home/rrabbit/Maildir/`. *The delivery is now complete. How the email gets from the mailbox on* `mail.toonland.net` *to Mr Rabbit's personal workstation is* not *the responsibility of the MTA and does* not *happen through SMTP.*

9. Mr Rabbit would have configured his mail client (running on his personal work-station) to use a POP/IMAP host `mail.toonland.net` for incoming mail. `mail.toonland.net` runs a POP or IMAP service on port 110 or 143, respectively.

10. Mr Rabbit's mail client makes a TCP connection to port 110 (or 143) and communicates using the POP or IMAP protocol. The POP or IMAP service is responsible for feeding the message to the mail client and deleting it from the mailbox file.

11. Mr Rabbit's mail client stores the message on his workstation using its own methods and displays the message as a "new" message.

30.1.2   Configuring a POP/IMAP server

POP and IMAP are invoked by `inetd` or `xinetd`—see Chapter 29. Except for limiting the range of clients that are allowed to connect (for security reasons), no configuration is required. Client connections authenticate themselves using the normal UNIX login name and password. There are specialized POP and IMAP packages for supporting different mailbox types (like Maildir).

30.1.3   Why `exim`?

The `exim` *home page* http://www.exim.org/ gives you a full rundown. Here I will just say that `exim` is the simplest MTA to configure. Moreover, its configuration file works the same way you imagine mail to work. It's really easy to customize the `exim` configuration to do some really weird things. The whole package fits together cleanly, logically, and intuitively. This is in contrast to `sendmail`'s `sendmail.cf` file, which is widely considered to be extremely cryptic and impractical. `exim` also seems to have been written with proper security considerations, although many people argue that `postfix` and `qmail` are the last word in secure mail.

30.2   `exim` Package Contents

You can get `exim` as a `.rpm` or `.deb` file. After installation, the file `/usr/share/doc/exim-?.??/doc/spec.txt` ↘or `/usr/doc/`↖ contains the complete `exim` documentation; there is also an HTML version on the `exim` web page, whereas the man page contains only command-line information. `exim` is a drop-in replacement for `sendmail`, meaning that for every critical `sendmail` command, there is an `exim` command of the same name that takes the same options, so that needy scripts won't know the difference. These are:

```
  /etc/aliases
  /usr/bin/mailq
  /usr/bin/newaliases
  /usr/bin/rmail
5 /usr/lib/sendmail
  /usr/sbin/sendmail
```

Finally, there is the `exim` binary itself, `/usr/sbin/exim`, and configuration file `/etc/exim/config`, `/etc/exim.conf`, or `/etc/exim/exim.conf`, depending on your LINUX distribution. Then there are the usual start/stop scripts, `/etc/init.d/exim`. or `/etc/rc.d/init.d/exim`

30.3   **exim** Configuration File

As a preliminary example, here we create a simple spooling mail server for a personal workstation, `cericon.cranzgot.co.za`.

Client applications (especially non-UNIX ones) are usually configured to connect to an MTA running on a remote machine, however, using a remote SMTP host can be irritating if the host or network go down. Running `exim` on the local workstation enables all applications to use `localhost` as their SMTP gateway: that is, `exim` takes care of queuing and periodic retries.

Here is the configuration. The difference between this and a full-blown mail server is actually very slight.

```
   ##################### MAIN CONFIGURATION SETTINGS #####################
   log_subject
   errors_address = postmaster
   freeze_tell_mailmaster = yes
5  queue_list_requires_admin = false
   prod_requires_admin = false
   trusted_users = psheer
   local_domains = localhost : ${primary_hostname}
   never_users = root
10 # relay_domains = my.equivalent.domains : more.equivalent.domains
   host_accept_relay = localhost : *.cranzgot.co.za : 192.168.0.0/16
   exim_user = mail
   exim_group = mail
   end
15
   ##################### TRANSPORTS CONFIGURATION #####################
   remote_smtp:
       driver = smtp
       hosts = 192.168.2.1
20     hosts_override
   local_delivery:
       driver = appendfile
```

```
         file = /var/spool/mail/${local_part}
         delivery_date_add
25       envelope_to_add
         return_path_add
         group = mail
         mode_fail_narrower =
         mode = 0660
30  end

    #################### DIRECTORS CONFIGURATION ####################
    localuser:
         driver = localuser
35       transport = local_delivery
    end

    #################### ROUTERS CONFIGURATION ####################
    lookuphost:
40       driver = lookuphost
         transport = remote_smtp
    literal:
         driver = ipliteral
         transport = remote_smtp
45  end

    #################### RETRY CONFIGURATION ####################
    *                        *            F,2h,15m; G,16h,1h,1.5; F,4d,8h
    end
50
    #################### REWRITE CONFIGURATION ####################
    *@cericon.cranzgot.co.za   psheer@icon.co.za
```

30.3.1 Global settings

The `exim` config file is divided into six logical sections separated by the `end` keyword.
The top or `MAIN` section contains global settings. The global settings have the following
meanings:

log_subject Tells `exim` to log the subject in the mail log file. For example, `T="I`
  `LOVE YOU"` will be added to the log file.

errors_address The mail address where errors are to be sent. It doesn't matter what
  you put here, because all mail will get rewritten to `psheer@icon.co.za`, as we
  see later.

freeze_tell_mailmaster Tells `errors_address` about *frozen* messages. *frozen*
  messages are messages that could not be delivered for some reason (like a permissions problem, or a failed message whose return address is invalid) and are
  flagged to sit idly in the mail queue, and not be processed any further. Note that

frozen messages sometimes mean that something is wrong with your system or mail configuration.

local_domains Each mail message received is processed in one of two ways: by either a local or remote delivery. A local delivery is one to a user on the local machine, and a remote delivery is one to somewhere else on the Internet. `local_domains` distinguishes between these two. For example, according to the config line above, a message destined to `psheer@localhost` or `psheer@cericon.cranzgot.co.za` is local, whereas a message to `psheer@elsewhere.co.za` is remote. Note that the list is colon delimited.

never_users Never become this user. Just for security.

exim_user Specifies the user that `exim` should run as.

exim_group Specifies the group that `exim` should run as.

> It is important to understand the `host_accept_relay` and `relay_domains` options for security.

host_accept_relay This option specifies machines that are allowed to use `cericon.cranzgot.co.za` as a *relay*. A relay is a host that sends mail on another machine's behalf: that is, we are acting as a relay when we process a mail message that neither originated from our machine nor is destined for a user on our machine.

We *never* want to relay from an untrusted host. Why? Because it may, for example, allow someone to send 100,000 messages to 100,000 different addresses, each with *us* in the message header.

`host_accept_relay` specifies a list of trusted hosts that are allowed to send such arbitrary messages through us. Note again that the list is colon delimited. In this example, we don't even need to put in addresses of other machines on our LAN, except if we are feeling friendly.

relay_domains `relay_domains` gives an additional condition for which an arbitrary host is allowed to use us as a relay. Consider that we are a backup mail server for a particular domain; mail to the domain does not originate from us nor is destined for us yet must be allowed *only if the destination address matches the domains for which we are a backup*. We put such domains under `relay_domains`.

30.3.2 Transports

The transport section comes immediately after the main configuration options. It defines various *methods* of delivering mail. We are going to refer to these methods later in the configuration file. Our manual `telnet`ing to port 25 was *transport*ing a mail message by SMTP. Appending a mail message to the end of a mail folder is also a transport method. These are represented by the `remote_smtp:` and `local_delivery:` labels, respectively.

`remote_smtp:` This transport has the following suboptions:

> **`driver`** The actual method of delivery. `driver` = always specifies the kind of transport, director, or router.
>
> **`hosts_override` and `hosts`** Using these two options together overrides any list of hosts that may have been looked up by DNS MX queries. By "list of hosts" we mean machines established from the recipients email address to which we might like to make an SMTP delivery, but which we are not going to use. Instead we send all mail to `192.168.2.1`, which is this company's internal mail server.

`local_delivery:` This transport has the following suboptions:

> **`driver`** The actual method of delivery. `driver` = always specifies the kind of transport, director, or router.
>
> **`file`** The file to append the mail message to. `${local_part}` is replaced with everything before the @ character of the recipient's address.
>
> **`delivery_date_add`, `envelope_to_add`, and `return_path_add`** Various things to add to the header.
>
> **`group`, `mode_fail_narrower` and `mode`** Various permission settings.

(It should be obvious at this stage what these two transports are going to be used for. As far as MTAs are concerned, the only two things that ever happen to an email message are that it either (a) gets sent through SMTP to another host or (b) gets appended to a file.)

30.3.3 Directors

If a message arrives and it is listed in `local_domains`, `exim` will attempt a local delivery. This means `exim` works through the list of *directors* until it finds one that does not fail. The only director listed here is the one labeled `localuser:` with `local_delivery` as its transport. So quite simply, email messages having recipient addresses that are listed under `local_domains` are appended to a user's mailbox file—not very complicated.

A director *directs* mail to a mailbox.

30.3.4 Routers

If a message arrives and it is not listed in `local_domains`, `exim` attempts a remote delivery. Similarly, this means `exim` works through the list of *routers* until it finds one that does not fail.

Two routers are listed here. The first is for common email addresses. It uses the `lookuphost` driver, which does a DNS MX query on the domain part of the email address (i.e., everything after the @). The MX records found are then passed to the `remote_smtp` transport (and in our case, then ignored). The `lookuphost` driver will fail if the domain part of the email address is a bracketed literal IP address.

The second router uses the `ipliteral` driver. It sends mail directly to an IP address in the case of bracketed, literal email addresses. For example, `root@[111.1.1.1]`.

A router *routes* mail to another host.

30.4 Full-blown Mail server

An actual mail server config file contains very little extra. This one is the example config file that comes by default with `exim-3.16`:

```
#################### MAIN CONFIGURATION SETTINGS ####################
# primary_hostname =
# qualify_domain =
# qualify_recipient =
# local_domains =
never_users = root
# host_accept_relay = localhost
# host_accept_relay = my.friends.host : 131.111.0.0/16
# relay_domains = my.equivalent.domains : more.equivalent.domains
host_lookup = 0.0.0.0/0
# receiver_unqualified_hosts =
# sender_unqualified_hosts =
rbl_domains = rbl.maps.vix.com
no_rbl_reject_recipients
sender_reject = "*@*.sex*.net:*@sex*.net"
host_reject = "open-relay.spamming-site.com"
rbl_warn_header
# rbl_domains = rbl.maps.vix.com:dul.maps.vix.com:relays.orbs.org
# percent_hack_domains = *
end
#################### TRANSPORTS CONFIGURATION ####################
remote_smtp:
  driver = smtp
# procmail transport goes here <---
local_delivery:
  driver = appendfile
```

```
       file = /var/spool/mail/${local_part}
       delivery_date_add
       envelope_to_add
30     return_path_add
       group = mail
       mode = 0660
     address_pipe:
       driver = pipe
35     return_output
     address_file:
       driver = appendfile
       delivery_date_add
       envelope_to_add
40     return_path_add
     address_reply:
       driver = autoreply
     end
     ##################### DIRECTORS CONFIGURATION #####################
45   # routers because of a "self=local" setting (not used in this configuration).
     system_aliases:
       driver = aliasfile
       file = /etc/aliases
       search_type = lsearch
50     user = mail
       group = mail
       file_transport = address_file
       pipe_transport = address_pipe
     userforward:
55     driver = forwardfile
       file = .forward
       no_verify
       no_expn
       check_ancestor
60   # filter
       file_transport = address_file
       pipe_transport = address_pipe
       reply_transport = address_reply
     # procmail director goes here <---
65   localuser:
       driver = localuser
       transport = local_delivery
     end
     ##################### ROUTERS CONFIGURATION #####################
70   # widen_domains = "sales.mycompany.com:mycompany.com"
     lookuphost:
       driver = lookuphost
       transport = remote_smtp
     # widen_domains =
75   literal:
       driver = ipliteral
       transport = remote_smtp
     end
     ##################### RETRY CONFIGURATION #####################
80   *                      *            F,2h,15m; G,16h,1h,1.5; F,4d,8h
     end
```

```
###################################################################
```

For `procmail` support (see `procmail(1)`, `procmailrc(6)`, and `proc-mailex(5)`), simply add

```
procmail:
    driver = pipe
    command = "/usr/bin/procmail -Y -d ${local_part}"
```

after your `remote_smtp` transport, and then also,

```
procmail:
  driver = localuser
  transport = procmail
  require_files = /usr/bin/procmail
```

after your `user_forward` director.

30.5 Shell Commands for **exim** Administration

As with other daemons, you can stop `exim`, start `exim`, and cause `exim` to reread its configuration file with:

```
/etc/init.d/exim stop
/etc/init.d/exim start
/etc/init.d/exim reload
```

You should always do a `reload` to cause config file changes to take effect. The `startup` script actually just runs `exim -bd -q30m`, which tells `exim` to start as a standalone daemon, listening for connections on port 25, and then execute a `runq` (explained below) every 30 minutes.

To cause `exim` ↘and many other MTAs for that matter↖ to loop through the queue of pending messages and consider each one for deliver, run

```
runq
```

which is the same as `exim -q`.

To list mail that is queued for delivery, use

```
mailq
```

which is the same as `exim -bp`.

To forcibly attempt delivery on any mail in the queue, use

```
exim -qf
```

and then to forcibly retry even frozen messages in the queue, use

```
exim -qff
```

To delete a message from the queue, use

```
exim -Mrm <message-id>
```

The man page exim(8) contains exhaustive treatment of command-line options. Those above are most of what you will use, however.

30.6 The Queue

It is often useful to check the queue directory /var/spool/exim/input/ for mail messages, just to get an inside look at what's going on. The simple session—

```
[root@cericon]# mailq
  0m   320 14Epss-0008DY-00 <psheer@icon.co.za>
          freddy@elmstreet.org

  0m   304 14Ept8-0008Dg-00 <psheer@icon.co.za>
          igor@ghostbusters.com

[root@cericon]# ls -l /var/spool/exim/input/
total 16
-rw-------   1 root      root           25 Jan  6 11:43 14Epss-0008DY-00-D
-rw-------   1 root      root          550 Jan  6 11:43 14Epss-0008DY-00-H
-rw-------   1 root      root           25 Jan  6 11:43 14Ept8-0008Dg-00-D
-rw-------   1 root      root          530 Jan  6 11:43 14Ept8-0008Dg-00-H
```

—clearly shows that two messages are queued for delivery. The files ending in -H are *envelope headers*, and those ending in -D are message bodies. The spec.txt document will show you how to interpret the contents of the header files.

Don't be afraid to manually rm files from this directory, but always delete them in pairs (i.e., remove the both the header *and* the body file), and make sure exim is not running at the time. In the above example, the commands,

```
[root@cericon]# exim -Mrm 14Epss-0008DY-00 14Ept8-0008Dg-00
Message 14Epss-0008DY-00 has been removed
Message 14Ept8-0008Dg-00 has been removed
[root@cericon]# mailq
```

```
5  [root@cericon]#
```

work even better.

30.7 `/etc/aliases` for Equivalent Addresses

Often, we would like certain local addresses to *actually* deliver to other addresses. For instance, we would like all mail destined to user `MAILER-DAEMON` to actually go to user `postmaster`; or perhaps some user has two accounts but would like to read mail from only one of them.

The `/etc/aliases` file performs this mapping. This file has become somewhat of an institution; however you can see that in the case of `exim`, aliasing is completely arbitrary: you can specify a lookup on *any* file under the `system_aliases:` director provided that file is colon delimited.

A default `/etc/aliases` file could contain as much as the following; you should check that the `postmaster` account does exist on your system, and test whether you can read, send, and receive mail as user `postmaster`.

```
    # This is a combination of what I found in the Debian
    # and RedHat distributions.

    MAILER-DAEMON:            postmaster
 5  abuse:                    postmaster
    anonymous:                postmaster
    backup:                   postmaster
    backup-reports:           postmaster
    bin:                      postmaster
10  daemon:                   postmaster
    decode:                   postmaster
    dns:                      postmaster
    dns-admin:                postmaster
    dumper:                   postmaster
15  fetchmail-daemon:         postmaster
    games:                    postmaster
    gnats:                    postmaster
    ingres:                   postmaster
    info:                     postmaster
20  irc:                      postmaster
    list:                     postmaster
    listmaster:               postmaster
    lp:                       postmaster
    mail:                     postmaster
25  mailer-daemon:            postmaster
    majordom:                 postmaster
    man:                      postmaster
    manager:                  postmaster
    msql:                     postmaster
30  news:                     postmaster
```

```
     nobody:                   postmaster
     operator:                 postmaster
     postgres:                 postmaster
     proxy:                    postmaster
35   root:                     postmaster
     sync:                     postmaster
     support:                  postmaster
     sys:                      postmaster
     system:                   postmaster
40   toor:                     postmaster
     uucp:                     postmaster
     warnings:                 postmaster
     web-master:               postmaster
     www-data:                 postmaster
45
     # some users who want their mail redirected
     arny:                     mail@swartzneger.co.us
     larry:                    lking@cnn.com
```

You can remove a lot of these aliases, since they assume services to be running that might not be installed—games, ingres, for example. Aliases can do two things: firstly, anticipate what mail people are likely to use if they need to contact the administrator; and secondly, catch any mail sent by system daemons: for example the, email address of the DNS administrator is dictated by the DNS config files, as explained on page 445.

Note that an alias in the /etc/aliases file does not have to have an account on the system—larry and arny need not have entries in the /etc/passwd file.

30.8 Real-Time Blocking List — Combating Spam

30.8.1 What is *spam*?

Spam refers to unsolicited ⟍Not looked for or requested; unsought⟍ bulk mail sent to users usually for promotional purposes. That is, mail is sent automatically to many people with whom the sender has no relationship, and where the recipient did nothing to prompt the mail: all on the *chance* that the recipient might be interested in the subject matter.

Alternatively, spam can be thought of as any mail sent to email addresses, where those addresses were obtained without their owners consent. More practically, anyone who has had an email account for very long will have gotten messages like Subject: Fast way to earn big $$$!, which clutters my mailbox. The longer you have an email address, the more of these messages you will get, and the more irritated you will get.

To send spam is easy. Work your way around the Internet till you find a mail server that allows relaying. Then send it 10,000 email addresses and a message about where to get pictures of naked underage girls. Now you are a genuine worthy-of-being-arrested spammer. Unfortunately for the unsuspecting administrator of that machine and provided you have even a little clue what you're doing, he will probably never be able to track you down. Several other tricks are employed to get the most out of your $100-for-1,000,000-genuine-email-addresses.

Note that spam is not merely email you are not interested in. People often confuse mail with other types of communication. . . like telephone calls: if you get a telephone call, you *have* to pick up the phone then and there—the call is an an invasion of your privacy. The beauty of email is that you never need to have your privacy invaded. You can simply delete the mail. If you never want to get email from a particular person again, you can simply add a filter that blocks mail from that person's address (see procmailex(5)).   ⟍If you are irritated by the presumption of the sender, then that's *your* problem. Replying to that person with "Please don't email me..." not only shows that you are insecure, but also that you are clueless, don't get much mail, and are therefore also unpopular.⟍

The point at which email becomes intrusive is purely a question of volume, much like airwave advertisements. *Because it comes from a different place each time, you cannot protect yourself against it with a simple mail filter.*

Typical spam mail will begin with a spammer subject like Create Wealth From Home Now!! and then the spammer will audaciously append the footer:

> This is not a SPAM. You are receiving this because you are on a list of email addresses that I have bought. And you have opted to receive information about business opportunities. If you did not opt in to receive information on business opportunities then please accept our apology. To be REMOVED from this list simply reply with REMOVE as the subject. And you will NEVER receive another email from me.

Need I say that you should be wary of replying with REMOVE, since it clearly tells the sender that your email is a valid address.

30.8.2 Basic spam prevention

You can start by at least adding the following lines to your MAIN configuration section:

```
headers_check_syntax
headers_sender_verify
sender_verify
receiver_verify
```

The option headers_check_syntax causes exim to check all headers of incoming mail messages for correct syntax, failing them otherwise. The next three options check that one of the `Sender:`, `Reply-To:` or `From:` headers, as well as both the addresses in the SMTP `MAIL` and `RCPT` commands, are genuine email addresses.

The reasoning here is that spammers will often use malformed headers to trick the MTA into sending things it ordinarily wouldn't, I am not sure exactly how this applies in `exim`'s case, but these are for the good measure of rejecting email messages at the point where the SMTP exchange is being initiated.

30.8.3   Real-time blocking list

To find out a lot more about spamming, banning hosts, reporting spam and email usage in general, see *MAPS (Mail Abuse Prevention System LLC)* http://www.mail-abuse.org/, as well as *Open Relay Behavior-modification System* http://www.orbs.org/. ⟍If this site is not working, there is also http://www.orbl.org/ and http://www.ordb.org/.⟍ *Real-time Blocking Lists* or RBL's are a not-so-new idea that has been incorporated into `exim` as a feature. It works as follows. The spammer has to use a host that allows relays. The IP of that relay host will be clear to the MTA at the time of connection. The MTA can then check that against a database of publicly available *banned IP addresses* of relay hosts. For `exim`, this means the list under `rbl_domains`. If the `rbl_domains` friendly has this IP blacklisted, then `exim` denies it also. You can enable this capability with ⟍This example comes from `exim`'s front web page.⟍

```
  # reject messages whose sending host is in MAPS/RBL
  # add warning to messages whose sending host is in ORBS
  rbl_domains = blackholes.mail-abuse.org/reject : \
          dialups.mail-abuse.org/reject : \
5         relays.mail-abuse.org/reject : \
          relays.orbs.org/warn
  # check all hosts other than those on internal network
  rbl_hosts = !192.168.0.0/16:0.0.0.0/0
  # but allow mail to postmaster@my.dom.ain even from rejected host
10 recipients_reject_except = postmaster@my.dom.ain
  # change some logging actions (collect more data)
  rbl_log_headers          # log headers of accepted RBLed messages
  rbl_log_rcpt_count       # log recipient info of accepted RBLed messages
```

in your `MAIN` configuration section.   Also remember to remove the line `no_rbl_reject_recipients`; otherwise, `exim` will only log a warning message and not actually refuse email.

30.8.4   Mail administrator and user responsibilities

Mail administrator and email users are expected to be aware of the following:

- Spam is evil.

- Spam is caused by poorly configured mail servers.

- It is the responsibility of the mail administrator to ensure that proper measures have been taken to prevent spam.

- Even as a user, you should follow up spam by checking where it came from and complaining to those administrators.

- Many mail administrators are not aware there is an issue. Remind them.

30.9 Sendmail

sendmail's configuration file is /etc/sendmail.cf. This file format was inherited from the first UNIX servers and references simpler files under the directory /etc/mail/. You can do most ordinary things by editing one or another file under /etc/mail/ without having to deal with the complexities of /etc/sendmail.cf.

Like most stock MTAs shipped with LINUX distributions, the sendmail package will work by default as a mailer without any configuration. However, as always, you will have to add a list of relay hosts. This is done in the file /etc/mail/access for sendmail-8.10 and above. To relay from yourself and, say, the hosts on network 192.168.0.0/16, as well as, say, the domain *hosts*.trusted.com, you must have at least:

```
localhost.localdomain        RELAY
localhost                    RELAY
127.0.0.1                    RELAY
192.168                      RELAY
trusted.com                  RELAY
```

which is exactly what the host_accept_relay option does in the case of exim.

The domains for which you are acting as a backup mail server must be listed in the file /etc/mail/relay-domains, each on a single line. This is analogous to the relay_domains option of exim.

Then, of course, the domains for which sendmail is going to receive mail must also be specified. This is analogous to the local_domains option of exim. These are listed in the file /etc/mail/local-host-names, each on a single line.

The same /etc/aliases file is used by exim and sendmail.

Having configured anything under /etc/mail/, you should now run make in this directory to rebuild lookup tables for these files. You also have to run the command `newaliases` whenever you modify the `/etc/aliases` file. In both cases, you must restart `sendmail`.

`sendmail` has received a large number of security alerts in its time. It is imperative that you install the latest version. Note that older versions of `sendmail` have configurations that allowed relaying by default—another reason to upgrade.

A useful resource to for finding out more tricks with `sendmail` is *The Sendmail FAQ* http://www.sendmail.org/faq/.

Chapter 31

lilo, initrd, and Booting

lilo stands for *linux loader*. LILO: is the prompt you first see after boot up, from which you can usually choose the OS you would like to boot and give certain boot options to the kernel. This chapter explains how to configure lilo and kernel boot options, and to get otherwise non-booting systems to boot.

The lilo package itself contains the files

```
/boot/boot.b        /boot/message       /sbin/lilo
/boot/chain.b       /boot/os2_d.b       /usr/bin/keytab-lilo
/usr/share/doc/lilo-<version>
```

which is not that interesting, except to know that the technical and user documentation is there if hard-core details are needed.

31.1 Usage

When you first start your LINUX system, the LILO: prompt, at which you can enter boot options, is displayed. Pressing [Tab] displays a list of things to type. The purpose is to allow the booting of different LINUX installations on the same machine, or different operating systems stored in different partitions on the same disk. Later, you can actually view the file /proc/cmdline to see what boot options (including default boot options) were used.

317

31.2 Theory

31.2.1 Kernel boot sequence

A UNIX kernel, to be booted, must be loaded into memory from disk and be executed. The execution of the kernel causes it to uncompress itself and then run. ⬭The word *boot* itself comes from the concept that a computer cannot begin executing without program code, and program code cannot get into memory without other program code—like trying to lift yourself up by your bootstraps, and hence the name.⬭ The first thing the kernel does after it runs is initialize various hardware devices. It then mounts the root file system on a specified partition. Once the root file system is mounted, the kernel executes /sbin/init to begin the UNIX operating system. This is how all UNIX systems begin life.

31.2.2 Master boot record

PCs begin life with a small program in the ROM BIOS that loads the very first sector of the disk into memory, called the *boot sector* of the *master boot record* or *MBR*. This piece of code is up to 512 bytes long and is expected to start the operating system. In the case of LINUX🐧, the boot sector loads the file /boot/map, which contains a list of the precise location of the disk sectors that the LINUX🐧 *kernel image* (usually the file /boot/vmlinuz) spans. It loads each of these sectors, thus reconstructing the kernel image in memory. Then it jumps to the kernel to execute it.

You may ask how it is possible to load a file from a file system when the file system is not mounted. Further, the boot partition is a small and simple program and certainly does not support the many types of file systems and devices that the kernel image may reside in. Actually, lilo doesn't have to support a file system to access a file, as long as it has a list of the sectors that the file spans and is prepared to use the BIOS *interrupts* ⬭Nothing to do with "interrupting" or hardware interrupts, but refers to BIOS functions that are available for use by the operating system. Hardware devices may insert custom BIOS functions to provided rudimentary support needed for themselves at startup. This support is distinct from that provided by the hardware device drivers of the booted kernel.⬭ to read those sectors. If the file is never modified, that sector list will never change; this is how the /boot/map and /boot/vmlinuz files are loaded.

31.2.3 Booting partitions

In addition to the MBR, each primary partition has a boot sector that can boot the operating system in that partition. MS-DOS (Windows) partitions have this, and hence lilo can optionally load and execute these *partition boot sectors* to start a Windows installation in another partition.

31.2.4   Limitations

BIOSs have inherited several limitations because of lack of foresight of their designers.

First, some BIOSs do not support more than one IDE. ⬊At least according to the lilo documentation.⬋ I myself have not come across this as a problem.

The second limitation is most important to note. As explained, lilo uses BIOS functions to access the IDE drive, *but the BIOS of a PC is often limited to accessing the first 1024 cylinders of the disk.* Hence, whatever LILO reads *must* reside within the first 1024 cylinders (the first 500 megabytes of disk space). Here is the list of things whose sectors are required to be within this space:

1. /boot/vmlinuz

2. Various lilo files /boot/*.b

3. Any non-LINUX partition boot sector you would like to boot

However a LINUX⬟ root partition can reside anywhere because the boot sector program never reads this partition except for the abovementioned files. A scenario where the /boot/ directory is a small partition below the 500 megabyte boundary and the / partition is above the 500 megabyte boundary, is quite common. See page 155.

Note that newer "LBA" BIOS's support more than the first 512 megabytes—even up to 8 Gigabytes. I personally do not count on this.

31.3   `lilo.conf` and the `lilo` Command

To "do a lilo" means running the lilo command as root, with a correct /etc/lilo.conf file. The lilo.conf file will doubtless have been set up by your distribution (check yours). A typical lilo.conf file that allows booting of a Windows partition and two LINUX⬟ partitions is as follows:

```
   boot=/dev/hda
   prompt
   timeout = 50
   compact
 5 vga = extended
   lock
   password = jAN]")Wo
   restricted
   append = "ether=9,0x300,0xd0000,0xd4000,eth0 hisax=1,3,5,0xd8000,0xd80,HiSax"
10 image = /boot/vmlinuz-2.2.17
           label = linux
           root = /dev/hda5
           read-only
```

```
     image = /boot/vmlinuz-2.0.38
15           label = linux-old
             root = /dev/hda6
             read-only
     other = /dev/hda2
             label = win
20           table = /dev/hda
```

Running `lilo` will install into the MBR a boot loader that understands where to get the `/boot/map` file, which in turn understands where to get the `/boot/vmlinuz-2.2.12-20` file. It gives output like:

```
[root@cericon]# lilo
Added linux *
Added linux-old
Added win
```

It also backs up your existing MBR, if this has not previously been done, into a file `/boot/boot.0300` (where `0300` refers to the device's major and minor number).

Let's go through the options:

boot Device to boot. It will most always be `/dev/hda` or `/dev/sda`.

prompt Display a prompt where the user can enter the OS to boot.

timeout How many tenths of a seconds to display the prompt (after which the first image is booted).

compact String together adjacent sector reads. This makes the kernel load *much* faster.

vga We would like 80×50 text mode. Your startup scripts may reset this to 80×25— search `/etc/rc.d` recursively for any file containing "`textmode`".

lock Always default to boot the last OS booted ⬊A very useful feature which is seldom used.⬈.

password Require a password to boot.

restricted Require a password only if someone attempts to enter special options at the `LILO:` prompt.

append A *kernel boot option*. Kernel boot options are central to `lilo` and kernel modules and are discussed in Chapter 42.5. They are mostly not needed in simple installations.

image A LINUX🐧 kernel to boot.

label The text to type at the boot prompt to cause this kernel/partition to boot.

root The root file system that the kernel must mount.

read-only Flag to specify that the root file system must initially be mounted read-only.

other Some other operating system to boot: in this case, a Windows partition.

table Partition table info to be passed to the partition boot sector.

Further other = partitions can follow, and many image = kernel images are allowed.

The preceding lilo.conf file assumed a partition scheme as follows:

/dev/hda1 10-megabyte ext2 partition to be mounted on /boot.

/dev/hda2 Windows 98 partition over 500 megabytes in size.

/dev/hda3 Extended partition.

/dev/hda4 Unused primary partition.

/dev/hda5 ext2 root file system.

/dev/hda6 Second ext2 root file system containing an older distribution.

/dev/hda? LINUX swap, /home, and other partitions.

31.4   Creating Boot Floppy Disks

If LILO is broken or absent, we require an alternative boot method. A floppy disk capable of booting our system must contain a kernel image, the means to load the image into memory, and the means to mount /dev/hda5 as the root file system. To create such a floppy, insert a *new* floppy disk into a running LINUX system, and overwrite it with the following commands:

```
dd if=/boot/vmlinuz-2.2.17 of=/dev/fd0
rdev /dev/fd0 /dev/hda5
```

Then simply boot the floppy. This procedure requires a second LINUX installation at least. If you only have an MS-DOS or Windows system at your disposal then you will have to download the RAWRITE.EXE utility as well as a raw boot disk image. Many of these are available and will enable you to create a boot floppy from a DOS prompt. I will not go into detail about this here.

31.5   SCSI Installation Complications and `initrd`

Some of the following descriptions may be difficult to understand without knowledge of kernel modules explained in Chapter 42. You may want to come back to it later.

Consider a system with zero IDE disks and one SCSI disk containing a LINUX🐧 installation. There are BIOS interrupts to read the SCSI disk, just as there were for the IDE, so LILO can happily access a kernel image somewhere inside the SCSI partition. However, the kernel is going to be lost without a *kernel module* ↘See Chapter 42. The kernel doesn't support every possible kind of hardware out there all by itself. It is actually divided into a main part (the kernel image discussed in this chapter) and hundreds of modules (loadable parts that reside in `/lib/modules/`) that support the many type of SCSI, network, sound etc., peripheral devices.↖ that understands the particular SCSI driver. So although the kernel can load and execute, it won't be able to mount its root file system without loading a SCSI module first. But the module itself resides in the root file system in `/lib/modules/`. This is a tricky situation to solve and is done in one of two ways: either (a) using a kernel with preenabled SCSI support or (b) using what is known as an `initrd` *preliminary root file system image.*

The first method is what I recommend. It's a straightforward (though time-consuming) procedure to create a kernel with SCSI support for your SCSI card built-in (and not in a separate module). Built-in SCSI and network drivers will also autodetect cards most of the time, allowing immediate access to the device—they will work without being given any options ↘Discussed in Chapter 42.↖ and, most importantly, without your having to read up on how to configure them. This setup is known as *compiled-in* support for a hardware driver (as opposed to *module* support for the driver). The resulting kernel image will be larger by an amount equal to the size of module. Chapter 42 discusses such kernel compiles.

The second method is faster but trickier. LINUX🐧 supports what is known as an `initrd` image (initial rAM disk image). This is a small, ±1.5 megabyte file system that is loaded by LILO and mounted by the kernel instead of the real file system. The kernel mounts this file system as a RAM disk, executes the file `/linuxrc`, and then only mounts the real file system.

31.6   Creating an `initrd` Image

Start by creating a small file system. Make a directory `~/initrd` and copy the following files into it.

```
drwxr-xr-x   7 root     root        1024 Sep 14 20:12 initrd/
drwxr-xr-x   2 root     root        1024 Sep 14 20:12 initrd/bin/
-rwxr-xr-x   1 root     root      436328 Sep 14 20:12 initrd/bin/insmod
-rwxr-xr-x   1 root     root      424680 Sep 14 20:12 initrd/bin/sash
```

```
  5   drwxr-xr-x    2 root      root         1024 Sep 14 20:12 initrd/dev/
      crw-r--r--    1 root      root       5,   1 Sep 14 20:12 initrd/dev/console
      crw-r--r--    1 root      root       1,   3 Sep 14 20:12 initrd/dev/null
      brw-r--r--    1 root      root       1,   1 Sep 14 20:12 initrd/dev/ram
      crw-r--r--    1 root      root       4,   0 Sep 14 20:12 initrd/dev/systty
 10   crw-r--r--    1 root      root       4,   1 Sep 14 20:12 initrd/dev/tty1
      crw-r--r--    1 root      root       4,   1 Sep 14 20:12 initrd/dev/tty2
      crw-r--r--    1 root      root       4,   1 Sep 14 20:12 initrd/dev/tty3
      crw-r--r--    1 root      root       4,   1 Sep 14 20:12 initrd/dev/tty4
      drwxr-xr-x    2 root      root         1024 Sep 14 20:12 initrd/etc/
 15   drwxr-xr-x    2 root      root         1024 Sep 14 20:12 initrd/lib/
      -rwxr-xr-x    1 root      root           76 Sep 14 20:12 initrd/linuxrc
      drwxr-xr-x    2 root      root         1024 Sep 14 20:12 initrd/loopfs/
```

On my system, the file initrd/bin/insmod is the *statically linked* ⟍meaning it does not require shared libraries.⟋ version copied from /sbin/insmod.static—a member of the modutils-2.3.13 package. initrd/bin/sash is a statically linked shell from the sash-3.4 package. You can recompile insmod from source if you don't have a statically linked version. Alternatively, copy the needed DLLs from /lib/ to initrd/lib/. (You can get the list of required DLLs by running ldd /sbin/insmod. Don't forget to also copy symlinks and run strip -s <lib> to reduce the size of the DLLs.)

Now copy into the initrd/lib/ directory the SCSI modules you require. For example, if we have an Adaptec AIC-7850 SCSI adapter, we would require the aic7xxx.o module from /lib/modules/<version>/scsi/aic7xxx.o. Then, place it in the initrd/lib/ directory.

```
-rw-r--r--    1 root      root       129448 Sep 27  1999 initrd/lib/aic7xxx.o
```

The file initrd/linuxrc should contain a script to load all the modules needed for the kernel to access the SCSI partition. In this case, just the aic7xxx module ⟍insmod can take options such as the IRQ and IO-port for the device. See Chapter 42.⟋:

```
#!/bin/sash

aliasall

echo "Loading aic7xxx module"
insmod /lib/aic7xxx.o
```

Now double-check all your permissions and then chroot to the file system for testing.

```
chroot ~/initrd /bin/sash
```

```
/linuxrc
```

Now, create a file system image similar to that in Section 19.9:

```
  dd if=/dev/zero of=~/file-inird count=2500 bs=1024
  losetup /dev/loop0 ~/file-inird
  mke2fs /dev/loop0
  mkdir ~/mnt
5 mount /dev/loop0 ~/mnt
  cp -a initrd/* ~/mnt/
  umount ~/mnt
  losetup -d /dev/loop0
```

Finally, `gzip` the file system to an appropriately named file:

```
gzip -c ~/file-inird > initrd-<kernel-version>
```

31.7 Modifying `lilo.conf` for `initrd`

Your `lilo.conf` file can be changed slightly to force use of an `initrd` file system.
Simply add the `initrd` option. For example:

```
   boot=/dev/sda
   prompt
   timeout = 50
   compact
5  vga = extended
   linear
   image = /boot/vmlinuz-2.2.17
           initrd = /boot/initrd-2.2.17
           label = linux
10         root = /dev/sda1
           read-only
```

Notice the use of the `linear` option. This is a BIOS trick that you can read about
in `lilo`(5). It is often necessary but can make SCSI disks nonportable to different
BIOSs (meaning that you will have to rerun `lilo` if you move the disk to a different
computer).

31.8 Using `mkinitrd`

Now that you have learned the manual method of creating an `initrd` image, you
can read the `mkinitrd` man page. It creates an image in a single command. This is
command is peculiar to RedHat.

Chapter 32

init, ?getty, and UNIX Run Levels

This chapter explains how LINUX⟨ (and a UNIX system in general) initializes itself. It follows on from the kernel boot explained in Section 31.2. We also go into some advanced uses for mgetty, like receiving of faxes.

32.1 init — the First Process

After the kernel has been unpacked into memory, it begins to execute, initializing hardware. The last thing it does is mount the root file system, which necessarily contains a program /sbin/init, which the kernel executes. init is one of the only programs the kernel ever executes explicitly; the onus is then on init to bring the UNIX system up. init always has the process ID 1.

For the purposes of init, the (rather arbitrary) concept of a UNIX *run level* was invented. The run level is the current operation of the machine, numbered run level 0 through run level 9. When the UNIX system is *at* a particular run level, it means that a certain selection of services is running. In this way, the machine could be a mail server or an X Window workstation depending on what run level it is in.

The traditionally defined run levels are:

0	Halt.
1	Single-user mode.
2	Multiuser, without network file system (NFS).
3	Full multiuser mode.
4	Unused.

5 | **X** Window System Workstation (usually identical to run level 3).
6 | Reboot.
7 | Undefined.
8 | Undefined.
9 | Undefined.

The idea here is that `init` begins at a particular run level that can then be manually changed to any other by the superuser. `init` uses a list of scripts for each run level to start or stop each of the many services pertaining to that run level. These scripts are `/etc/rc?.d/KNNservice` or `/etc/rc?.d/SNNservice` ⟍On some systems `/etc/rc.d/rc?.d/...` ⟍, where *NN*, K, or S is a prefix to force the order of execution (since the files are executed in alphabetical order).

These scripts all take the options `start` and `stop` on the command-line, to begin or terminate the service.

For example, when `init` enters, say, run level 5 from run level 3, it executes the particular scripts from `/etc/rc3.d/` and `/etc/rc5.d/` to bring up or down the appropriate services. This may involve, say, executing

```
/etc/rc3.d/S20exim stop
```

and similar commands.

32.2 /etc/inittab

`init` has one config file: `/etc/inittab` which is scanned once on bootup.

32.2.1 Minimal configuration

A minimal `inittab` file might consist of the following.

```
id:3:initdefault:

si::sysinit:/etc/rc.d/rc.sysinit

l0:0:wait:/etc/rc.d/rc 0
l1:1:wait:/etc/rc.d/rc 1
l2:2:wait:/etc/rc.d/rc 2
l3:3:wait:/etc/rc.d/rc 3
l4:4:wait:/etc/rc.d/rc 4
l5:5:wait:/etc/rc.d/rc 5
l6:6:wait:/etc/rc.d/rc 6
```

```
     ud::once:/sbin/update

15   1:2345:respawn:/sbin/getty 38400 tty1
     2:2345:respawn:/sbin/getty 38400 tty2
     3:2345:respawn:/sbin/getty 38400 tty3
     4:2345:respawn:/sbin/getty 38400 tty4

20   S0:2345:respawn:/sbin/mgetty -n 3 -s 115200 ttyS0 57600

     S4:2345:respawn:/sbin/mgetty -r -s 19200 ttyS4 DT19200

     x:5:respawn:/usr/bin/X11/xdm -nodaemon
```

The lines are colon-separated fields and have the following meaning (lots more can be gotten from `inittab(5)`):

id:3:initdefault: This dictates that the default run level is 3. It is the run level that the system will boot up into. This field usually has a 3 or a 5, which are most often the only two run levels that the system ever sits in.

si::sysinit:/etc/rc.d/rc.sysinit This says to run a script on bootup to initialize the system. If you view the file /etc/rc.d/rc.sysinit, you will see a fairly long script that does the following: mounts the proc file system; initializes the keyboard maps, console font, NIS domain, host name, and swap partition; runs `isapnp` and `depmod -a`; cleans the `utmp` file; as well as other things. *This script is only run once on bootup.* On Debian℗ this is a script, /etc/init.d/rcS, that runs everything under /etc/rcS.d/. ↘As usual, Debian℗ gravitated to the most clean, elegant and extensible solution.↖

13:3:wait:/etc/rc.d/rc 3 The first field is a descriptive tag and could be anything. The second is a list of run levels under which the particular script (last field) is to be invoked: in this case, /etc/rc.d/rc 3 is to be run when entering run level 3. The `wait` means to pause until /etc/rc.d/rc has finished execution. If you view the file /etc/rc.d/rc, you will see it merely executes scripts under /etc/rc?.d/ as appropriate for a run level change.

ud::once:/sbin/update This flushes the disk cache on each run level change.

1:2345:respawn:/sbin/getty 38400 tty1 This says to run the command /sbin/getty 38400 tty1 when in run level 2 through 5. `respawn` means to restart the process if it dies.

x:5:respawn:/usr/bin/X11/xdm -nodaemon This says to run the command /usr/bin/X11/xdm -nodaemon when in run level 5. This is the **X** Window System graphical login program.

32.2.2 Rereading `inittab`

If you modify the `inittab` file, `init` will probably not notice until you issue it a
`SIGHUP`. This is the same as typing

```
telinit q
```

which causes `init` to reread `/etc/inittab`.

32.2.3 The `respawning too fast` error

You get a `respawning too fast` error when an `inittab` line makes no sense
↘These errors are common and very irritating when you are doing console work, hence an explicit section on it.↖: like a `getty` running on a non-functioning serial port. Simply comment
out or delete the appropriate line and then run

```
telinit q
```

32.3 Useful Run Levels

Switching run levels manually is something that is rarely done. The most common
way of shutting down the machine is to use:

```
shutdown -h now
```

which effectively goes to run level 0, and

```
shutdown -r now
```

which effectively goes to run level 6.

You can also specify the run level at the `LILO:` prompt. Type

```
linux 1
```

or

```
linux single
```

to enter single-user mode when booting your machine. You change to single-user
mode on a running system with:

```
telinit S
```

You can forcefully enter any run level with

```
telinit <N>
```

32.4 `getty` Invocation

The `getty` man page begins with:

> **getty** opens a tty port, prompts for a login name and invokes the /bin/login command. It is normally invoked by *init(8)*.

Note that `getty`, `agetty`, `fgetty` and `mingetty` are just different implementations of `getty`.

The most noticeable effect of `init` running at all is that it spawns a login to each of the LINUX⠪ virtual consoles. It is the `getty` (or sometimes `mingetty`) command as specified in the `inittab` line above that displays this login. Once the login name is entered, `getty` invokes the `/bin/login` program, which then prompts the user for a password.

The `login` program (discussed in Section 11.7) then executes a shell. When the shell dies (as a result of the user `exit`ing the session) `getty` is just `respawned`.

32.5 Bootup Summary

Together with Chapter 31 you should now have a complete picture of the entire bootup process:

1. First sector loaded into RAM and executed—`LILO:` prompt appears.
2. Kernel loaded from sector list.
3. Kernel executed; unpacks.
4. Kernel initializes hardware.
5. Kernel mounts root file system, say `/dev/hda1`.
6. Kernel executes `/sbin/init` as PID 1.
7. `init` executes all scripts for default run level.
8. `init` spawns `getty` programs on each terminal.

9. `getty` prompts for login.
10. `getty` executes `/bin/login` to authentic user.
11. `login` starts shell.

32.6   Incoming Faxes and Modem Logins

32.6.1   mgetty with character terminals

The original purpose of `getty` was to manage character terminals on mainframe computers. `mgetty` is a more comprehensive `getty` that deals with proper serial devices. A typical `inittab` entry is

```
S4:2345:respawn:/sbin/mgetty -r -s 19200 ttyS4 DT19200
```

which would open a login on a terminal connected to a serial line on `/dev/ttyS4`. See page 479 for information on configuring multiport serial cards.

(The LINUX☺ devices `/dev/tty1` through `/dev/tty12` as used by `getty` emulate classic terminals in this way.)

32.6.2   mgetty log files

`mgetty` will log to `/var/log/mgetty.log.ttyS?`. This log file contains everything you need for troubleshooting. It is worthwhile running `tail -f` on these files while watching a login take place.

32.6.3   mgetty with modems

Running `mgetty` (see `mgetty(8)`) is a common and trivial way to get a dial login to a LINUX machine. Your `inittab` entry is just

```
S0:2345:respawn:/sbin/mgetty -n 3 -s 115200 ttyS0 57600
```

where `-n 3` says to answer the phone after the 3rd ring. Nothing more is needed than to plug your modem into a telephone. You can then use `dip -t`, as done in Section 41.1.1, to dial this machine from another LINUX machine. Here is an example session:
This example assumes that an initialization string of AT&F1 is sufficient. See Section 3.5.

```
[root@cericon]# dip -t
DIP: Dialup IP Protocol Driver version 3.3.7o-uri (8 Feb 96)
Written by Fred N. van Kempen, MicroWalt Corporation.
```

```
 5  DIP> port ttyS0
    DIP> speed 57600
    DIP> term
    [ Entering TERMINAL mode.  Use CTRL-] to get back ]
    AT&F1
10  OK
    ATDT5952521
    CONNECT 19200/ARQ/V34/LAPM/V42BIS

    Red Hat Linux release 6.1 (Cartman)
15  Kernel 2.2.12-20 on an i686

    remote.dialup.private login:
```

Note that this is purely a login session having nothing to do with PPP dialup.

32.6.4 **mgetty receiving faxes**

mgetty receives faxes by default, provided your modem supports faxing ⟍If your modem says it supports faxing, and this still does not work, you will have to spend a lot of time reading through your modem's AT command set manual, as well as the mgetty info documentation.⟍ and provided it has not been explicitly disabled with the −D option. An appropriate inittab line is,

```
S0:2345:respawn:/sbin/mgetty -x 4 -n 3 -s 57600 -I '27 21 7654321' ttyS0 57600
```

The options mean, respectively, to set the debug level to 4, answer after 3 rings, set the port speed to 57600, and set the fax ID number to 27 21 7654321. Alternatively, you can use the line

```
S0:2345:respawn:/sbin/mgetty ttyS0 57600
```

and instead put your configuration options in the file mgetty.config under /etc/mgetty+sendfax/:

```
debug 4
rings 3
speed 57600
fax-id 27 21 7654321
```

Faxes end up in /var/spool/fax/incoming/ as useless .g3 format files, but note how the command

```
strings /sbin/mgetty | grep new_fax
```

gives

331

```
/etc/mgetty+sendfax/new_fax
```

which is a script that `mgetty` secretly runs when new faxes arrive. It can be
used to convert faxes into something (like `.gif` graphics files ⟍I recommend `.png` over
`.gif` any day, however.⟍) readable by typical office programs. The following example
`/etc/mgetty+sendfax/new_fax` script puts incoming faxes into `/home/fax/` as
`.gif` files that all users can access. ⟍Modified from the `mgetty` contribs.⟍ Note how it uses
the CPU-intensive `convert` program from the `ImageMagic` package.

```
     #!/bin/sh

     # you must have pbm tools and they must be in your PATH
     PATH=/usr/bin:/bin:/usr/X11R6/bin:/usr/local/bin
 5
     HUP="$1"
     SENDER="$2"
     PAGES="$3"

10   shift 3
     P=1

     while [ $P -le $PAGES ] ; do
         FAX=$1
15       BASENAME=`basename $FAX`
         RES=`echo $BASENAME | sed 's/.\(.\).*/\1/'`
         if [ "$RES" = "n" ] ; then
             STRETCH="-s"
         else
20           STRETCH=""
         fi
         nice g32pbm $STRETCH $FAX > /tmp/$BASENAME.pbm \
             && rm -f $FAX \
             && nice convert -colorspace gray -colors 16 -geom \
25               '50%x50%' /tmp/$BASENAME.pbm /home/fax/$BASENAME.gif \
             && rm -f /tmp/$BASENAME.pbm \
             && chmod 0666 /home/fax/$BASENAME.gif
         shift
         P=`expr $P + 1`
30   done

     exit 0
```

Chapter 33

Sending Faxes

This chapter discusses the `sendfax` program, with reference to the specific example of setting up an artificial printer that will automatically use a modem to send its print jobs to remote fax machines.

33.1   Fax Through Printing

Continuing from Section 21.10...

You should go now and read the `sendfax` section of the `info` page for `mgetty`. The `sendfax` command is just one program that sends faxes through the modem. Like `mgetty`, it reads a config file in `/etc/mgetty+sendfax/`. This config file is just `sendfax.config` and can contain as little as

```
verbose y
debug 5
fax-devices ttyS0
fax-id 27 21 7654321
max-tries 3
max-tries-continue y
```

Below, `fax_filter.sh` is a script that sends the print job through the fax machine after requesting the telephone number through `gdialog`. ⟍`gdialog` is part of the `gnome-utils` package.⟍ An appropriate `/etc/printcap` entry is:

```
fax:\
        :sd=/var/spool/lpd/fax:\
        :mx#0:\
```

```
      :sh:\
5     :lp=/dev/null:\
      :if=/var/spool/lpd/fax/fax_filter.sh:
```

The file `fax_filter.sh` itself could contain a script like this ⟍Remember to rotate
the `/var/log/fax` log file, see page 198.⟍ for a modem on `/dev/ttyS0`:

```
#!/bin/sh

exec 1>>/var/log/fax
exec 2>>/var/log/fax
5
echo
echo
echo $@

10 echo "Starting fax `date`: I am `id`"

export DISPLAY=localhost:0.0
export HOME=/home/lp

15 function error()
{
    gdialog --title "Send Fax" --msgbox "$1" 10 75 || \
        echo 'Huh? no gdialog on this machine'
    cd /
20  rm -Rf /tmp/$$fax || \
        gdialog \
            --title "Send Fax" \
            --msgbox "rm -Rf /tmp/$$fax failed" \
            10 75
25  exit 1
}

mkdir /tmp/$$fax || error "mkdir /tmp/$$fax failed"
cd /tmp/$$fax || error "cd /tmp/$$fax failed"
30
cat > fax.ps

if /usr/bin/gdialog \
            --title "Send Fax" \
35          --inputbox "Enter the phone number to fax:" \
            10 75 "" 2>TEL ; then
    :
else
    echo "gdialog failed `< TEL`"
40  rm -Rf /tmp/$$fax
    exit 0
fi

TEL=`< TEL`
45 test -z "$TEL" && error 'no telephone number given'
```

```
cat fax.ps | gs -r204x98 -sOutputFile=- -sDEVICE=faxg3 -dBATCH -q - \
    1>fax.ps.g3 || error 'gs failed'

50  ls -al /var/lock/
    /usr/sbin/sendfax -x 5 -n -l ttyS0 $TEL fax.ps.g3 || \
        error "sendfax failed"

    rm -Rf /tmp/$$fax

55
    exit 0
```

33.2 Setgid Wrapper Binary

The above script is not enough however. Above, sendfax requires access to the
/dev/ttyS0 device as well as the /var/lock/ directory (to create a modem lock
file—see Section 34.4). It cannot do that as the lp user (under which the above filter
runs). On RedHat, the command ls -ald /var/lock /dev/ttyS0 reveals that
only uucp is allowed to access modems. We can get around this restriction by creating
a setgid (see Chapter 14) binary that runs as the uucp user. Do this by compiling the **C**
program,

```
    #include <stdlib.h>
    #include <string.h>
    #include <stdio.h>
    #include <unistd.h>
5
    int main (int argc, char **argv)
    {
        char **a;
        int i;
10
    /* set the real group ID to that of the effective group ID */
        if (setgid (getegid ())) {
            perror ("sendfax_wrapper: setgid failed");
            exit (1);
15
        }

    /* copy all arguments */
        a = (char **) malloc ((argc + 1) * sizeof (char *));
        for (i = 1; i < argc; i++)
20          a[i] = (char *) strdup (argv[i]);
        a[argc] = NULL;

    /* execute sendfax */
        a[0] = "/usr/sbin/sendfax";
25      execvp (a[0], a);

    /* exit on failure */
        perror ("sendfax_wrapper: failed to exececute /usr/sbin/sendfax");
        exit (1);
30  }
```

using the commands,

```
gcc sendfax_wrapper.c -o /usr/sbin/sendfax_wrapper -Wall
chown lp:uucp /usr/sbin/sendfax_wrapper
chmod g+s,o-rwx /usr/sbin/sendfax_wrapper
```

Then, replace `sendfax` with `sendfax_wrapper` in the filter script. You can see that `sendfax_wrapper` just executes `sendfax` after changing the group ID to the *effective group ID* (GID) as obtained from the `getegid` function on line 12. The effective group ID is `uucp` because of the setgid group bit (i.e., `g+s`) in the `chmod` command, and hence `sendfax` runs under the `uucp` group with full access to the modem device.

On your own system it may be cleaner to try implement this without a wrapper. Debian©, for example, has a `dialout` group for the purposes of accessing modems. Also be aware that some distributions may not use the `uucp` user in the way RedHat does and you may have to create an alternative user especially for this task.

Chapter 34

uucp and uux

uucp is a command to copy a file from one UNIX system to another. uux executes a command on another UNIX system, even if that command is receiving data through stdin on the local system. uux is extremely useful for automating many kinds of distributed functions, like mail and news.

The uucp and uux commands both come as part of the uucp (*Unix-to-Unix Copy*) package. uucp may sound ridiculous considering the availability of modern commands like rcp, rsh, or even FTP transfers (which accomplish the same thing), but uucp has features that these do not, making it an essential, albeit antiquated, utility. For instance, uucp never executes jobs immediately. It will, for example, queue a file copy for later processing and then dial the remote machine during the night to complete the operation.

uucp predates the Internet: It was originally used to implement a mail system, using only modems and telephone lines. It hence has sophisticated protocols for ensuring that your file/command *really does get there*, with the maximum possible fault tolerance and the minimum of retransmission. This is why it should always be used for automated tasks wherever there are unreliable (i.e., modem) connections. The uucp version that comes with most LINUX distributions is called Taylor UUCP after its author.

Especially important is that when a uucp operation is interrupted by a line break, the connection time is not wasted: uucp will not have discarded any partially transmitted data. This means that no matter how slow or error prone the connection, progress is always made. Compare this to an SMTP or POP3/IMAP connection: Any line break halfway through a large mail message will necessitate that the entire operation to be restarted from scratch.

34.1 Command-Line Operation

To copy a file from one machine to another, simply enter

```
uucp <filename> <machine>!<path>
```

You can also run commands on the remote system, like

```
echo -n 'Hi, this is a short message\n\n-paul' | \
                              uux - 'cericon!rmail' 'john'
```

which runs `rmail` on the remote system `cericon`, feeding some text to the `rmail` program. Note how you should quote the `!` character to prevent it from being interpreted by the shell. (These commands will almost always fail with `permission denied by remote`. The error will come in a mail message to the user that ran the command.)

34.2 Configuration

`uucp` comes with comprehensive documentation in HTML format (`/usr/doc/uucp-`*version*`/uucp.html` or `/usr/share/...`) on RedHat, and `info` format on Debian and RedHat. Here, I sketch a basic and typical configuration.

The `uucp` package has a long history of revisions, beginning with the first modem-based mail networks. The latest GNU editions that come with LINUX distributions have a configuration file format that will probably differ from that which old `uucp` hands are used to.

Dialup networks today typically use `uucp` in combination with normal PPP dialup, probably not using `uucp`'s dial-in facilities at all. For example, if you are deploying a number of remote hosts that are using modems, these hosts should always use `uucp` to upload and retrieve mail, rather than POP3/IMAP or straight SMTP, because of the retransmission problem discussed above. In other words, `uucp` is really working as an ordinary TCP service, albeit with far more fault tolerance.

To make `uucp` into a TCP server, place it into `/etc/inetd.conf` as follows

```
uucp   stream tcp   nowait uucp  /usr/sbin/tcpd /usr/lib/uucp/uucico -l
```

being also *very* careful to limit the hosts that can connect by using the techniques discussed in Chapter 29. Similarly for `xinetd`, create a file `/etc/xinetd.d/uucp` containing,

```
service uucp
{
    only_from      = 127.0.0.1 192.168.0.0/16
    socket_type    = stream
    wait           = no
    user           = uucp
    server         = /usr/lib/uucp/uucico
    server_args    = -1
    disable        = no
}
```

uucp configuration files are stored under /etc/uucp/. Now we configure a client machine, machine1.cranzgot.co.za, to send mail through
server1.cranzgot.co.za, where server1.cranzgot.co.za is running the
uucico service above.

uucp has an antiquated authentication mechanism that uses its own list of users
and passwords completely distinct from those of ordinary UNIX accounts. We must
first add a common "user" and password to both machines for authentication purposes. For machine1.cranzgot.co.za, we can add to the file /etc/uucp/call
the line

```
server1    machine1login    pAsSwOrD123
```

which tells uucp to use the login machine1login whenever trying to
speak to server1. On server1.cranzgot.co.za we can add to the file
/etc/uucp/passwd the line,

```
machine1login    pAsSwOrD123
```

Note that the uucp name server1 was chosen for the machine
server1.cranzgot.co.za for convenience. uucp names, however, have nothing to do with domain names.

Next, we need to tell uucp about the intentions of machine1. Any machine that
you might connect to or from must be listed in the /etc/uucp/sys file. Our entry
looks like

```
system machine1
call-login *
call-password *
commands rmail
protocol t
```

and can have as many entries as we like. The only things server1 has to know about
machine1 are the user and password and the preferred protocol. The *'s mean to look

up the user and password in the `/etc/uucp/passwd` file, and `protocol t` means to use a simple non-error, correcting protocol (as appropriate for use over TCP). The `commands` option takes a space-separated list of permitted commands—for security reasons, commands not in this list cannot be executed. (This is why I stated above that commands will almost always fail with `permission denied by remote`—they are usually not listed under `commands`.)

The `/etc/uucp/sys` file on `machine1` will contain:

```
  system server1
  call-login *
  call-password *
  time any
5 port TCP
  address 192.168.3.2
  protocol t
```

Here `time any` specifies which times of the day `uucp` may make calls to `server1`. The default is `time Never`. ⟍See the uucp documentation under **Time Strings** for more info.⟍ The option `port TCP` means that we are using a *modem* named `TCP` to execute the dialout. All modems are defined in the file `/etc/uucp/port`. We can add our modem entry to `/etc/uucp/port` as follows,

```
port TCP
type tcp
```

which clearly is not really a modem at all.

Finally, we can queue a mail transfer job with

```
echo -e 'Hi Jack\n\nHow are you?\n\n-jill" | \
                        uux - --nouucico 'server1!rmail' 'jack@beanstalk.com'
```

and copy a file with

```
uucp --nouucico README 'cericon!/var/spool/uucppublic'
```

Note that `/var/spool/uucppublic/` is the only directory you are allowed access to by default. You should probably keep it this way for security.

uucico

Although we have queued a job for processing, nothing will transfer until the program `uucico` (which stands for *Unix-to-Unix copy in copy out*) is run. The idea is that both `server1` and `machine1` may have queued a number of jobs; then when `uucico` is running on both machines and talking to each other, all jobs on both machines are processed in turn, regardless of which machine initiated the connection.

Usually `uucico` is run from a `crond` script every hour. (Even having run `uucico`, nothing will transfer if the time of day does not come within the ranges specified under `time ....`) Here we can run `tail -f /var/log/uucp/Log` while running `uucico` manually as follows:

```
uucico --debug 3 --force --system server1
```

The higher the debug level, the more verbose output you will see in the `Log` file. This will `--forceably` dial the `--system server1` regardless of when it last dialed (usually there are constraints on calling soon after a failed call: `--force` overrides this).

If your mail server on `server1` is configured correctly, it should now have queued the message on the remote side.

34.3 Modem Dial

If you are really going to use `uucp` the old-fashioned way, you can use `mgetty` to answer `uucp` calls on `server1` by adding the following to your `/etc/inittab` file:

```
S0:2345:respawn:/sbin/mgetty -s 57600 ttyS0
```

And then add the line

```
machine1login  uucp  machine1login  /usr/sbin/uucico -l -u machine1login
```

to the file `/etc/mgetty+sendfax/login.config` (`/etc/mgetty/login.config` for Debian©). You will then also have to add a UNIX account `machine1login` with password `pAsSwOrD123`. This approach works is because `mgetty` and `uucico` have the same login prompt and password prompt, but `mgetty` uses `/etc/passwd` instead of `/etc/uucp/passwd` to authenticate. Also, for a modem connection, `protocol t` is error prone: change it to `protocol g`, which has small packet sizes and error correction.

Note that the above configuration also supports faxes, logins, voice, and PPP (see Section 41.4) on the same modem, because `mgetty` only starts `uucico` if the user name is `machine1login`.

To dial out from `machine1`, you first need to add a modem device (besides TCP) to your `/etc/uucp/port` file:

```
port ACU
type modem
device /dev/ttyS0
dialer mymodem
speed 57600
```

ACU is antiquated terminology and stands for *Automatic Calling Unit* (i.e., a modem). We have to specify the usual types of things for serial ports, like the device (`/dev/ttyS0` for a modem on COM1) and speed of the serial line. We also must specify a means to initialize the modem: the `dialer mymodem` option. A file `/etc/uucp/dial` should then contain an entry for our type of modem matching "mymodem" as follows: ↘This example assumes that an initialization string of `AT&F1` is sufficient. See Section 3.5.↖

```
   dialer mymodem
   chat "" AT&F1\r\d\c OK\r ATDT\D CONNECT
   chat-fail RING
   chat-fail NO\sCARRIER
 5 chat-fail ERROR
   chat-fail NO\sDIALTONE
   chat-fail BUSY
   chat-fail NO\sANSWER
   chat-fail VOICE
10 complete \d\d+++\d\dATH\r\c
   abort \d\d+++\d\dATH\r\c
```

More about modems and dialing is covered with pppd in Chapter 41.

With the modem properly specified, we can change our entry in the `sys` file to

```
   system server1
   call-login *
   call-password *
   time any
 5 port ACU
   phone 555-6789
   protocol g
```

The same uux commands should now work over dialup.

34.4   tty/UUCP Lock Files

I hinted about lock files in Section 33.2. A more detailed explanation follows.

You will have noticed by now that several services use serial devices, and many of them can use the same device at different times. This creates a possible conflict should two services wish to use the same device at the same time. For instance, what if someone wants to send a fax, while another person is dialing in?

The solution is the *UUCP lock file*. This is a file created by a process in `/var/lock/` of the form `LCK..`*device* that indicates the serial port is being used by that process. For instance, when running `sendfax` through a modem connected on

/dev/ttyS0, a file /var/lock/LCK..ttyS0 suddenly appears. This is because
sendfax, along with all other mgetty programs, obeys the UUCP lock file convention. The contents of this file actually contain the process ID of the program using the
serial device, so it is easy to check whether the lock file is bogus. A lock file of such a
dead process is called a *stale lock file* and can be removed manually.

34.5   Debugging uucp

uucp implementations rarely run smoothly the first time. Fortunately, you have
available a variety of verbose debugging options. uucico takes the --debug
option to specify the level of debug output. You should examine the files
/var/log/uucp/Log, /var/log/uucp/Debug, and /var/log/uucp/Stats to
get an idea about what is going on in the background. Also important is the
spool directory /var/spool/uucp/. You can specify the debugging level with -
-debug *level* where *level* is in the range of 0 through 11. You can also use --
debug chat to only see modem communication details. A full description of other
options follows ⬰Credits to the uucp documentation.⬰:

--debug abnormal Output debugging messages for abnormal situations, such as
    recoverable errors.
--debug chat Output debugging messages for chat scripts.
--debug handshake Output debugging messages for the initial handshake.
--debug uucp protocol Output debugging messages for the UUCP session protocol.
--debug proto Output debugging messages for the individual link protocols.
--debug port Output debugging messages for actions on the communication port.
--debug config Output debugging messages while reading the configuration files.
--debug spooldir Output debugging messages for actions in the spool directory.
--debug execute Output debugging messages whenever another program is exe-
    cuted.
--debug incoming List all incoming data in the debugging file.
--debug outgoing List all outgoing data in the debugging file.
--debug all All of the above.

34.6   Using uux with exim

On machine1 we would like exim to spool all mail through uucp. Using uucp requires a pipe transport (exim transports are discussed in Section 30.3.2). exim merely
sends mail through stdin of the uux command and then forgets about it. uux is then
responsible for executing rmail on server1. The complete exim.conf file is simply
as follows.

```
#################### MAIN CONFIGURATION SETTINGS ####################
log_subject
errors_address = admin
local_domains = localhost : ${primary_hostname} : machine1 : \
                                    machine1.cranzgot.co.za
host_accept_relay = 127.0.0.1 : localhost : ${primary_hostname} : \
                                 machine1 : machine1.cranzgot.co.za
never_users = root
exim_user = mail
exim_group = mail
end
##################### TRANSPORTS CONFIGURATION #####################
uucp:
  driver = pipe
  user = nobody
  command = "/usr/bin/uux - --nouucico ${host}!rmail \
                                ${local_part}@${domain}"
  return_fail_output = true
local_delivery:
  driver = appendfile
  file = /var/spool/mail/${local_part}
  delivery_date_add
  envelope_to_add
  return_path_add
  group = mail
  mode_fail_narrower =
  mode = 0660
end
##################### DIRECTORS CONFIGURATION #####################
localuser:
  driver = localuser
  transport = local_delivery
end
#################### ROUTERS CONFIGURATION ####################
touucp:
  driver = domainlist
  route_list = "* server1"
  transport = uucp
end
#################### RETRY CONFIGURATION ####################
*                     *              F,2m,1m
end
```

On machine server1, exim must however be running as a full-blown mail
server to properly route the mail elsewhere. Of course, on server1, rmail is the
sender; hence, it appears to exim that the mail is coming from the local machine. This
means that no extra configuration is required to support mail coming *from* a uux command.

Note that you can add further domains to your route_list so that your dialouts
occur directly to the recipient's machine. For instance:

```
route_list = "machine2.cranzgot.co.za machine2 ; \
              machine2                 machine2 ; \
              machine3.cranzgot.co.za machine3 ; \
              machine3                 machine3 ; \
              *                        server1"
```

You can then add further entries to your /etc/uucp/sys file as follows:

```
system machine2
call-login *
call-password *
time any
port ACU
phone 555-6789
protocol g

system machine3
call-login *
call-password *
time any
port ACU
phone 554-3210
protocol g
```

The exim.conf file on server1 must also have a router to get mail back to machine1. The router will look like this:

```
##################### ROUTERS CONFIGURATION #######################
touucp:
  driver = domainlist
  route_list = "machine2.cranzgot.co.za machine2 ; \
                machine2                 machine2 ; \
                machine3.cranzgot.co.za machine3 ; \
                machine3                 machine3"
  transport = uucp
lookuphost:
  driver = lookuphost
  transport = remote_smtp
end
```

This router sends all mail matching our dial-in hosts through the uucp transport while all other mail (destined for the Internet) falls through to the lookuphost router.

34.7 Scheduling Dialouts

Above, we used `uucico` only manually. `uucico` does not operate as a daemon process on its own and must be invoked by `crond`. All systems that use `uucp` have a `/etc/crontab` entry or a script under `/etc/cron.hourly`.

A typical `/etc/crontab` for `machine1` might contain:

```
45 *         * * * uucp /usr/lib/uucp/uucico --master
40 8,13,18 * * * root /usr/bin/uux -r server1!
```

The option `--master` tells `uucico` to loop through all pending jobs and call any machines for which jobs are queued. It does this every hour. The second line queues a null command three times daily for the machine `server1`. This will force `uucico` to dial out to `server1` at least three times a day on the appearance of real work to be done. The point of this to pick up any jobs coming the other way. This process is known as creating a *poll file*.

Clearly, you can use `uucp` over a TCP link initiated by `pppd`. If a dial link is running in demand mode, a `uucp` call will trigger a dialout and make a straight TCP connection through to the remote host. A common situation occurs when a number of satellite systems are dialing an ISP that has no `uucp` facility. To service the satellite machines, a separate `uucp` server is deployed that has no modems of its own. The server will have a permanent Internet connection and listen on TCP for `uucp` transfers.

Chapter 35

The LINUX File System Standard

This chapter reproduces the *Filesystem Hierarchy Standard*, translated into LATEX with some minor formatting changes and the addition of this book's chapter number to all the section headers. An original can be obtained from *the FHS home page* http://www.pathname.com/fhs/.

If you have ever asked the questions "Where in my file system does file *xxx* go?" or "What is directory *yyy* for?", then consult this document. It can be considered to provide the final word on such matters. Although this is mostly a reference for people creating new LINUX distributions, all administrators can benefit from an understanding of the rulings and explanations provided here.

Filesystem Hierarchy Standard — Version 2.2 final

Filesystem Hierarchy Standard Group

edited by Rusty Russell and Daniel Quinlan

ABSTRACT

This standard consists of a set of requirements and guidelines for file and directory placement under UNIX-like operating systems. The guidelines are intended to support interoperability of applications, system administration tools, development tools, and scripts as well as greater uniformity of documentation for these systems.

May 23, 2001

All trademarks and copyrights are owned by their owners, unless specifically noted otherwise. Use of a term in this document should not be regarded as affecting the validity of any trademark or service mark.

35.1 Introduction

35.1.1 Purpose

This standard enables

- Software to predict the location of installed files and directories, and
- Users to predict the location of installed files and directories.

We do this by

- Specifying guiding principles for each area of the filesystem,
- Specifying the minimum files and directories required,
- Enumerating exceptions to the principles, and
- Enumerating specific cases where there has been historical conflict.

The FHS document is used by

- Independent software suppliers to create applications which are FHS compliant, and work with distributions which are FHS complaint,
- OS creators to provide systems which are FHS compliant, and
- Users to understand and maintain the FHS compliance of a system.

35.1.2 Conventions

A constant-width font is used for displaying the names of files and directories.

Components of filenames that vary are represented by a description of the contents enclosed in "<" and ">" characters, `<thus>`. Electronic mail addresses are also enclosed in "<" and ">" but are shown in the usual typeface.

Optional components of filenames are enclosed in "[" and "]" characters and may be combined with the "<" and ">" convention. For example, if a filename is allowed to occur either with or without an extension, it might be represented by `<filename>[.<extension>]`.

Variable substrings of directory names and filenames are indicated by "*".

35.2 The Filesystem

This standard assumes that the operating system underlying an FHS-compliant file system supports the same basic security features found in most UNIX filesystems.

It is possible to define two independent categories of files: shareable vs. unshareable and variable vs. static. There should be a simple and easily understandable mapping from directories to the type of data they contain: directories may be mount points for other filesystems with different characteristics from the filesystem on which they are mounted.

Shareable data is that which can be shared between several different hosts; unshareable is that which must be specific to a particular host. For example, user home directories are shareable data, but device lock files are not.

Static data includes binaries, libraries, documentation, and anything that does not change without system administrator intervention; variable data is anything else that does change without system administrator intervention.

BEGIN RATIONALE

The distinction between shareable and unshareable data is needed for several reasons:

- In a networked environment (i.e., more than one host at a site), there is a good deal of data that can be shared between different hosts to save space and ease the task of maintenance.

- In a networked environment, certain files contain information specific to a single host. Therefore these filesystems cannot be shared (without taking special measures).

- Historical implementations of UNIX-like filesystems interspersed shareable and unshareable data in the same hierarchy, making it difficult to share large portions of the filesystem.

The "shareable" distinction can be used to support, for example:

- A /usr partition (or components of /usr) mounted (read-only) through the network (using NFS).

- A /usr partition (or components of /usr) mounted from read-only media. A CD-ROM is one copy of many identical ones distributed to other users by the postal mail system and other methods. It can thus be regarded as a read-only filesystem shared with other FHS-compliant systems by some kind of "network".

The "static" versus "variable" distinction affects the filesystem in two major ways:

- Since / contains both variable and static data, it needs to be mounted read-write.

- Since the traditional /usr contains both variable and static data, and since we may want to mount it read-only (see above), it is necessary to provide a method to have /usr mounted read-only. This is done through the creation of a /var hierarchy that is mounted read-write (or is a part of another read-write partition, such as /), taking over much of the /usr partition's traditional functionality.

Here is a summarizing chart. This chart is only an example for a common FHS-compliant system, other chart layouts are possible within FHS-compliance.

	shareable	unshareable
static	/usr	/etc
	/opt	/boot
variable	/var/mail	/var/run
	/var/spool/news	/var/lock

END RATIONALE

35.3 The Root Filesystem

35.3.1 Purpose

The contents of the root filesystem must be adequate to boot, restore, recover, and/or repair the system.

- To boot a system, enough must be present on the root partition to mount other filesystems. This includes utilities, configuration, boot loader information, and other essential start-up data. `/usr`, `/opt`, and `/var` are designed such that they may be located on other partitions or filesystems.

- To enable recovery and/or repair of a system, those utilities needed by an experienced maintainer to diagnose and reconstruct a damaged system must be present on the root filesystem.

- To restore a system, those utilities needed to restore from system backups (on floppy, tape, etc.) must be present on the root filesystem.

BEGIN RATIONALE

The primary concern used to balance these considerations, which favor placing many things on the root filesystem, is the goal of keeping root as small as reasonably possible. For several reasons, it is desirable to keep the root filesystem small:

- It is occasionally mounted from very small media.

- The root filesystem contains many system-specific configuration files. Possible examples include a kernel that is specific to the system, a specific hostname, etc. This means that the root filesystem isn't always shareable between networked systems. Keeping it small on servers in networked systems minimizes the amount of lost space for areas of unshareable files. It also allows workstations with smaller local hard drives.

- While you may have the root filesystem on a large partition, and may be able to fill it to your heart's content, there will be people with smaller partitions. If you have more files installed, you may find incompatibilities with other systems using root filesystems on smaller partitions. If you are a developer then you may be turning your assumption into a problem for a large number of users.

- Disk errors that corrupt data on the root filesystem are a greater problem than errors on any other partition. A small root filesystem is less prone to corruption as the result of a system crash.

Software must never create or require special files or subdirectories in the root directory. Other locations in the FHS hierarchy provide more than enough flexibility for any package.

There are several reasons why introducing a new subdirectory of the root filesystem is prohibited:

- It demands space on a root partition which the system administrator may want kept small and simple for either performance or security reasons.

- It evades whatever discipline the system administrator may have set up for distributing standard file hierarchies across mountable volumes.

END RATIONALE

35.3.2 Requirements

The following directories, or symbolic links to directories, are required in /.

```
/ ———— the root directory
  └ bin     Essential command binaries
  └ boot    Static files of the boot loader
  └ dev     Device files
  └ etc     Host-specific system configuration
  └ lib     Essential shared libraries and kernel modules
  └ mnt     Mount point for mounting a filesystem temporarily
  └ opt     Add-on application software packages
  └ sbin    Essential system binaries
  └ tmp     Temporary files
  └ usr     Secondary hierarchy
  └ var     Variable data
```

Each directory listed above is specified in detail in separate subsections below. /usr and /var each have a complete section in this document due to the complexity of those directories.

35.3.3 Specific Options

The following directories, or symbolic links to directories, must be in /, if the corresponding subsystem is installed:

```
/ ———— the root directory
  └ home          User home directories (optional)
  └ lib<qual>     Alternate format essential shared libraries (optional)
  └ root          Home directory for the root user (optional)
```

Each directory listed above is specified in detail in separate subsections below.

35.3.4 /bin : Essential user command binaries (for use by all users)

35.3.4.1 Purpose

/bin contains commands that may be used by both the system administrator and by users, but which are required when no other filesystems are mounted (e.g. in single user mode). It may also contain commands which are used indirectly by scripts.[1]

35.3.4.2 Requirements

There must be no subdirectories in /bin.

The following commands, or symbolic links to commands, are required in /bin.

cat	Utility to concatenate files to standard output
chgrp	Utility to change file group ownership
chmod	Utility to change file access permissions
chown	Utility to change file owner and group
cp	Utility to copy files and directories
date	Utility to print or set the system data and time
dd	Utility to convert and copy a file
df	Utility to report filesystem disk space usage
dmesg	Utility to print or control the kernel message buffer
echo	Utility to display a line of text
false	Utility to do nothing, unsuccessfully
hostname	Utility to show or set the system's host name
kill	Utility to send signals to processes
ln	Utility to make links between files
login	Utility to begin a session on the system
ls	Utility to list directory contents
mkdir	Utility to make directories
mknod	Utility to make block or character special files
more	Utility to page through text
mount	Utility to mount a filesystem
mv	Utility to move/rename files
ps	Utility to report process status
pwd	Utility to print name of current working directory
rm	Utility to remove files or directories
rmdir	Utility to remove empty directories
sed	The 'sed' stream editor
sh	The Bourne command shell
stty	Utility to change and print terminal line settings
su	Utility to change user ID
sync	Utility to flush filesystem buffers

---

[1]Command binaries that are not essential enough to place into /bin must be placed in /usr/bin, instead. Items that are required only by non-root users (the X Window System, chsh, etc.) are generally not essential enough to be placed into the root partition.

`true`	Utility to do nothing, successfully
`umount`	Utility to unmount file systems
`uname`	Utility to print system information

If `/bin/sh` is not a true Bourne shell, it must be a hard or symbolic link to the real shell command.

The `[` and `test` commands must be placed together in either `/bin` or `/usr/bin`.

BEGIN RATIONALE

For example bash behaves differently when called as `sh` or `bash`. The use of a symbolic link also allows users to easily see that `/bin/sh` is not a true Bourne shell.

The requirement for the `[` and `test` commands to be included as binaries (even if implemented internally by the shell) is shared with the POSIX.2 standard.

END RATIONALE

35.3.4.3   Specific Options

The following programs, or symbolic links to programs, must be in `/bin` if the corresponding subsystem is installed:

`csh`	The C shell (optional)
`ed`	The 'ed' editor (optional)
`tar`	The tar archiving utility (optional)
`cpio`	The cpio archiving utility (optional)
`gzip`	The GNU compression utility (optional)
`gunzip`	The GNU uncompression utility (optional)
`zcat`	The GNU uncompression utility (optional)
`netstat`	The network statistics utility (optional)
`ping`	The ICMP network test utility (optional)

If the gunzip and zcat programs exist, they must be symbolic or hard links to gzip. `/bin/csh` may be a symbolic link to `/bin/tcsh` or `/usr/bin/tcsh`.

BEGIN RATIONALE

The tar, gzip and cpio commands have been added to make restoration of a system possible (provided that `/` is intact).

Conversely, if no restoration from the root partition is ever expected, then these binaries might be omitted (e.g., a ROM chip root, mounting `/usr` through NFS). If restoration of a system is planned through the network, then `ftp` or `tftp` (along with everything necessary to get an ftp connection) must be available on the root partition.

END RATIONALE

35.3.5   /boot : Static files of the boot loader

35.3.5.1   Purpose

This directory contains everything required for the boot process except configuration files and the map installer. Thus `/boot` stores data that is used before the kernel begins executing user-mode programs. This may include saved master boot sectors, sector map files, and other data that is not directly edited by hand.[2]

35.3.5.2 Specific Options

The operating system kernel must be located in either `/` or `/boot`.[3]

35.3.6 /dev : Device files

35.3.6.1 Purpose

The `/dev` directory is the location of special or device files.

35.3.6.2 Specific Options

If it is possible that devices in `/dev` will need to be manually created, `/dev` must contain a command named `MAKEDEV`, which can create devices as needed. It may also contain a `MAKEDEV.local` for any local devices.

If required, `MAKEDEV` must have provisions for creating any device that may be found on the system, not just those that a particular implementation installs.

35.3.7 /etc : Host-specific system configuration

35.3.7.1 Purpose

`/etc` contains configuration files and directories that are specific to the current system.[4]

35.3.7.2 Requirements

No binaries may be located under `/etc`.

The following directories, or symbolic links to directories are required in `/etc`:

```
/etc  ────── Host-specific system configuration
   └ opt    Configuration for /opt
```

---

[2]Programs necessary to arrange for the boot loader to be able to boot a file must be placed in `/sbin`. Configuration files for boot loaders must be placed in `/etc`.

[3]On some i386 machines, it may be necessary for `/boot` to be located on a separate partition located completely below cylinder 1024 of the boot device due to hardware constraints.

Certain MIPS systems require a `/boot` partition that is a mounted MS-DOS filesystem or whatever other filesystem type is accessible for the firmware. This may result in restrictions with respect to usable filenames within `/boot` (only for affected systems).

[4]The setup of command scripts invoked at boot time may resemble System V, BSD or other models. Further specification in this area may be added to a future version of this standard.

35.3.7.3 Specific Options

The following directories, or symbolic links to directories must be in /etc, if the corresponding subsystem is installed:

```
/etc        ——— Host-specific system configuration
    └ X11      Configuration for the X Window System (optional)
    └ sgml     Configuration for SGML and XML (optional)
```

The following files, or symbolic links to files, must be in /etc if the corresponding subsystem is installed:[5]

csh.login	Systemwide initialization file for C shell logins (optional)
exports	NFS filesystem access control list (optional)
fstab	Static information about filesystems (optional)
ftpusers	FTP daemon user access control list (optional)
gateways	File which lists gateways for routed (optional)
gettydefs	Speed and terminal settings used by getty (optional)
group	User group file (optional)
host.conf	Resolver configuration file (optional)
hosts	Static information about host names (optional)
hosts.allow	Host access file for TCP wrappers (optional)
hosts.deny	Host access file for TCP wrappers (optional)
hosts.equiv	List of trusted hosts for rlogin, rsh, rcp (optional)
hosts.lpd	List of trusted hosts for lpd (optional)
inetd.conf	Configuration file for inetd (optional)
inittab	Configuration file for init (optional)
issue	Pre-login message and identification file (optional)
ld.so.conf	List of extra directories to search for shared libraries (optional)
motd	Post-login message of the day file (optional)
mtab	Dynamic information about filesystems (optional)
mtools.conf	Configuration file for mtools (optional)
networks	Static information about network names (optional)
passwd	The password file (optional)
printcap	The lpd printer capability database (optional)
profile	Systemwide initialization file for sh shell logins (optional)
protocols	IP protocol listing (optional)
resolv.conf	Resolver configuration file (optional)
rpc	RPC protocol listing (optional)
securetty	TTY access control for root login (optional)
services	Port names for network services (optional)
shells	Pathnames of valid login shells (optional)
syslog.conf	Configuration file for syslogd (optional)

---

[5]Systems that use the shadow password suite will have additional configuration files in /etc (/etc/shadow and others) and programs in /usr/sbin (useradd, usermod, and others).

mtab does not fit the static nature of /etc: it is excepted for historical reasons.[6]

35.3.7.4   /etc/opt : Configuration files for /opt

35.3.7.4.1   Purpose

Host-specific configuration files for add-on application software packages must be installed within the directory /etc/opt/<package>, where <package> is the name of the subtree in /opt where the static data from that package is stored.

35.3.7.4.2   Requirements

No structure is imposed on the internal arrangement of /etc/opt/<package>.

If a configuration file must reside in a different location in order for the package or system to function properly, it may be placed in a location other than /etc/opt/<package>.

> BEGIN RATIONALE
> Refer to the rationale for /opt.
> END RATIONALE

35.3.7.5   /etc/X11 : Configuration for the X Window System (optional)

35.3.7.5.1   Purpose

/etc/X11 is the location for all X11 host-specific configuration. This directory is necessary to allow local control if /usr is mounted read only.

35.3.7.5.2   Specific Options

The following files, or symbolic links to files, must be in /etc/X11 if the corresponding subsystem is installed:

Xconfig	The configuration file for early versions of XFree86 (optional)
XF86Config	The configuration file for XFree86 versions 3 and 4 (optional)
Xmodmap	Global X11 keyboard modification file (optional)

Subdirectories of /etc/X11 may include those for xdm and for any other programs (some window managers, for example) that need them.[7] We recommend that window managers with only one configuration file which is a default .*wmrc file must name it system.*wmrc (unless there is a widely-accepted alternative name) and not use a subdirectory. Any window manager subdirectories must be identically named to the actual window manager binary.

---

[6]On some Linux systems, this may be a symbolic link to /proc/mounts, in which case this exception is not required.

[7]/etc/X11/xdm holds the configuration files for xdm. These are most of the files previously found in /usr/lib/X11/xdm. Some local variable data for xdm is stored in /var/lib/xdm.

35.3.7.6 /etc/sgml : Configuration files for SGML and XML (optional)

35.3.7.6.1 Purpose

Generic configuration files defining high-level parameters of the SGML or XML systems are installed here. Files with names `*.conf` indicate generic configuration files. File with names `*.cat` are the DTD-specific centralized catalogs, containing references to all other catalogs needed to use the given DTD. The super catalog file `catalog` references all the centralized catalogs.

35.3.8 /home : User home directories (optional)

35.3.8.1 Purpose

`/home` is a fairly standard concept, but it is clearly a site-specific filesystem.[8] The setup will differ from host to host. Therefore, no program should rely on this location.[9]

35.3.9 /lib : Essential shared libraries and kernel modules

35.3.9.1 Purpose

The `/lib` directory contains those shared library images needed to boot the system and run the commands in the root filesystem, ie. by binaries in `/bin` and `/sbin`.[10]

35.3.9.2 Requirements

At least one of each of the following filename patterns are required (they may be files, or symbolic links):

`libc.so.*`	The dynamically-linked C library (optional)
`ld*`	The execution time linker/loader (optional)

---

[8]Different people prefer to place user accounts in a variety of places. This section describes only a suggested placement for user home directories; nevertheless we recommend that all FHS-compliant distributions use this as the default location for home directories.

On small systems, each user's directory is typically one of the many subdirectories of `/home` such as `/home/smith`, `/home/torvalds`, `/home/operator`, etc. On large systems (especially when the `/home` directories are shared amongst many hosts using NFS) it is useful to subdivide user home directories. Subdivision may be accomplished by using subdirectories such as `/home/staff`, `/home/guests`, `/home/students`, etc.

[9]If you want to find out a user's home directory, you should use the `getpwent(3)` library function rather than relying on `/etc/passwd` because user information may be stored remotely using systems such as NIS.

[10]Shared libraries that are only necessary for binaries in `/usr` (such as any X Window binaries) must not be in `/lib`. Only the shared libraries required to run binaries in `/bin` and `/sbin` may be here. In particular, the library `libm.so.*` may also be placed in `/usr/lib` if it is not required by anything in `/bin` or `/sbin`.

If a C preprocessor is installed, `/lib/cpp` must be a reference to it, for historical reasons.[11]

35.3.9.3 Specific Options

The following directories, or symbolic links to directories, must be in `/lib`, if the corresponding subsystem is installed:

```
/lib       ——— essential shared libraries and kernel modules
    └ modules    Loadable kernel modules (optional)
```

35.3.10 /lib<qual> : Alternate format essential shared libraries (optional)

35.3.10.1 Purpose

There may be one or more variants of the `/lib` directory on systems which support more than one binary format requiring separate libraries.[12]

35.3.10.2 Requirements

If one or more of these directories exist, the requirements for their contents are the same as the normal `/lib` directory, except that `/lib<qual>/cpp` is not required.[13]

35.3.11 /mnt : Mount point for a temporarily mounted filesystem

35.3.11.1 Purpose

This directory is provided so that the system administrator may temporarily mount a filesystem as needed. The content of this directory is a local issue and should not affect the manner in which any program is run.

This directory must not be used by installation programs: a suitable temporary directory not in use by the system must be used instead.

---

[11]The usual placement of this binary is `/usr/lib/gcc-lib/<target>/<version>/cpp`. `/lib/cpp` can either point at this binary, or at any other reference to this binary which exists in the filesystem. (For example, `/usr/bin/cpp` is also often used.)

[12]This is commonly used for 64-bit or 32-bit support on systems which support multiple binary formats, but require libraries of the same name. In this case, `/lib32` and `/lib64` might be the library directories, and `/lib` a symlink to one of them.

[13]`/lib<qual>/cpp` is still permitted: this allows the case where `/lib` and `/lib<qual>` are the same (one is a symbolic link to the other).

35.3.12   /opt : Add-on application software packages

35.3.12.1   Purpose

/opt is reserved for the installation of add-on application software packages.

A package to be installed in /opt must locate its static files in a separate /opt/<package> directory tree, where <package> is a name that describes the software package.

35.3.12.2   Requirements

```
/opt      ———— Add-on application software packages
   └── <package>    Static package objects
```

The directories /opt/bin, /opt/doc, /opt/include, /opt/info, /opt/lib, and /opt/man are reserved for local system administrator use. Packages may provide "front-end" files intended to be placed in (by linking or copying) these reserved directories by the local system administrator, but must function normally in the absence of these reserved directories.

Programs to be invoked by users must be located in the directory /opt/<package>/bin. If the package includes UNIX manual pages, they must be located in /opt/<package>/man and the same substructure as /usr/share/man must be used.

Package files that are variable (change in normal operation) must be installed in /var/opt. See the section on /var/opt for more information.

Host-specific configuration files must be installed in /etc/opt. See the section on /etc for more information.

No other package files may exist outside the /opt, /var/opt, and /etc/opt hierarchies except for those package files that must reside in specific locations within the filesystem tree in order to function properly. For example, device lock files must be placed in /var/lock and devices must be located in /dev.

Distributions may install software in /opt, but must not modify or delete software installed by the local system administrator without the assent of the local system administrator.

BEGIN RATIONALE

The use of /opt for add-on software is a well-established practice in the UNIX community. The System V Application Binary Interface [AT&T 1990], based on the System V Interface Definition (Third Edition), provides for an /opt structure very similar to the one defined here.

The Intel Binary Compatibility Standard v. 2 (iBCS2) also provides a similar structure for /opt.

Generally, all data required to support a package on a system must be present within /opt/<package>, including files intended to be copied into /etc/opt/<package> and /var/opt/<package> as well as reserved directories in /opt.

The minor restrictions on distributions using /opt are necessary because conflicts are possible between distribution-installed and locally-installed software, especially in the case of fixed pathnames found in some binary software.

END RATIONALE

35.3.13 /root : Home directory for the root user (optional)

35.3.13.1 Purpose

The root account's home directory may be determined by developer or local preference, but this is the recommended default location.[14]

35.3.14 /sbin : System binaries

35.3.14.1 Purpose

Utilities used for system administration (and other root-only commands) are stored in /sbin, /usr/sbin, and /usr/local/sbin. /sbin contains binaries essential for booting, restoring, recovering, and/or repairing the system in addition to the binaries in /bin.[15] Programs executed after /usr is known to be mounted (when there are no problems) are generally placed into /usr/sbin. Locally-installed system administration programs should be placed into /usr/local/sbin.[16]

35.3.14.2 Requirements

The following commands, or symbolic links to commands, are required in /sbin.

shutdown   Command to bring the system down.

35.3.14.3 Specific Options

The following files, or symbolic links to files, must be in /sbin if the corresponding subsystem is installed:

---

[14]If the home directory of the root account is not stored on the root partition it will be necessary to make certain it will default to / if it can not be located.

We recommend against using the root account for tasks that can be performed as an unprivileged user, and that it be used solely for system administration. For this reason, we recommend that subdirectories for mail and other applications not appear in the root account's home directory, and that mail for administration roles such as root, postmaster, and webmaster be forwarded to an appropriate user.

[15]Originally, /sbin binaries were kept in /etc.

[16]Deciding what things go into "sbin" directories is simple: if a normal (not a system administrator) user will ever run it directly, then it must be placed in one of the "bin" directories. Ordinary users should not have to place any of the sbin directories in their path.

For example, files such as chfn which users only occasionally use must still be placed in /usr/bin. ping, although it is absolutely necessary for root (network recovery and diagnosis) is often used by users and must live in /bin for that reason.

We recommend that users have read and execute permission for everything in /sbin except, perhaps, certain setuid and setgid programs. The division between /bin and /sbin was not created for security reasons or to prevent users from seeing the operating system, but to provide a good partition between binaries that everyone uses and ones that are primarily used for administration tasks. There is no inherent security advantage in making /sbin off-limits for users.

`fastboot`	Reboot the system without checking the disks (optional)
`fasthalt`	Stop the system without checking the disks (optional)
`fdisk`	Partition table manipulator (optional)
`fsck`	File system check and repair utility (optional)
`fsck.*`	File system check and repair utility for a specific filesystem (optional)
`getty`	The getty program (optional)
`halt`	Command to stop the system (optional)
`ifconfig`	Configure a network interface (optional)
`init`	Initial process (optional)
`mkfs`	Command to build a filesystem (optional)
`mkfs.*`	Command to build a specific filesystem (optional)
`mkswap`	Command to set up a swap area (optional)
`reboot`	Command to reboot the system (optional)
`route`	IP routing table utility (optional)
`swapon`	Enable paging and swapping (optional)
`swapoff`	Disable paging and swapping (optional)
`update`	Daemon to periodically flush filesystem buffers (optional)

35.3.15   /tmp : Temporary files

35.3.15.1   Purpose

The /tmp directory must be made available for programs that require temporary files.

Programs must not assume that any files or directories in /tmp are preserved between invocations of the program.

> **BEGIN RATIONALE**
>
> IEEE standard P1003.2 (POSIX, part 2) makes requirements that are similar to the above section.
>
> Although data stored in /tmp may be deleted in a site-specific manner, it is recommended that files and directories located in /tmp be deleted whenever the system is booted.
>
> FHS added this recommendation on the basis of historical precedent and common practice, but did not make it a requirement because system administration is not within the scope of this standard.
>
> **END RATIONALE**

35.4   The /usr Hierarchy

35.4.1   Purpose

/usr is the second major section of the filesystem. /usr is shareable, read-only data. That means that /usr should be shareable between various FHS-compliant hosts and must not be written to. Any information that is host-specific or varies with time is stored elsewhere.

Large software packages must not use a direct subdirectory under the /usr hierarchy.

35.4.2 Requirements

The following directories, or symbolic links to directories, are required in /usr.

```
/usr    ──────Secondary Hierarchy
   └ bin         Most user commands
   └ include     Header files included by C programs
   └ lib         Libraries
   └ local       Local hierarchy (empty after main installation)
   └ sbin        Non-vital system binaries
   └ share       Architecture-independent data
```

35.4.3 Specific Options

```
/usr    ──────Secondary Hierarchy
   └ X11R6       X Window System, version 11 release 6 (optional)
   └ games       Games and educational binaries (optional)
   └ lib<qual>   Alternate Format Libraries (optional)
   └ src         Source code (optional)
```

An exception is made for the X Window System because of considerable precedent and widely-accepted practice.

The following symbolic links to directories may be present. This possibility is based on the need to preserve compatibility with older systems until all implementations can be assumed to use the /var hierarchy.

```
/usr/spool -> /var/spool
/usr/tmp -> /var/tmp
/usr/spool/locks -> /var/lock
```

Once a system no longer requires any one of the above symbolic links, the link may be removed, if desired.

35.4.4 /usr/X11R6 : X Window System, Version 11 Release 6 (optional)

35.4.4.1 Purpose

This hierarchy is reserved for the X Window System, version 11 release 6, and related files.

To simplify matters and make XFree86 more compatible with the X Window System on other systems, the following symbolic links must be present if /usr/X11R6 exists:

```
/usr/bin/X11 -> /usr/X11R6/bin
/usr/lib/X11 -> /usr/X11R6/lib/X11
/usr/include/X11 -> /usr/X11R6/include/X11
```

In general, software must not be installed or managed via the above symbolic links. They are intended for utilization by users only. The difficulty is related to the release version of the X Window System — in transitional periods, it is impossible to know what release of X11 is in use.

35.4.4.2 Specific Options

Host-specific data in `/usr/X11R6/lib/X11` should be interpreted as a demonstration file. Applications requiring information about the current host must reference a configuration file in `/etc/X11`, which may be linked to a file in `/usr/X11R6/lib`.[17]

35.4.5 /usr/bin : Most user commands

35.4.5.1 Purpose

This is the primary directory of executable commands on the system.

35.4.5.2 Specific Options

The following directories, or symbolic links to directories, must be in `/usr/bin`, if the corresponding subsystem is installed:

`/usr/bin` ——— Binaries that are not needed in single-user mode
     └ mh   Commands for the MH mail handling system (optional)

`/usr/bin/X11` must be a symlink to `/usr/X11R6/bin` if the latter exists.

The following files, or symbolic links to files, must be in `/usr/bin`, if the corresponding subsystem is installed:

`perl`	The Practical Extraction and Report Language (optional)
`python`	The Python interpreted language (optional)
`tclsh`	Simple shell containing Tcl interpreter (optional)
`wish`	Simple Tcl/Tk windowing shell (optional)
`expect`	Program for interactive dialog (optional)

BEGIN RATIONALE

Because shell script interpreters (invoked with `#!`<path> on the first line of a shell script) cannot rely on a path, it is advantageous to standardize their locations. The Bourne shell and C-shell interpreters are already fixed in `/bin`, but Perl, Python, and Tcl are often found

---

[17]Examples of such configuration files include `Xconfig`, `XF86Config`, or `system.twmrc`)

in many different places. They may be symlinks to the physical location of the shell interpreters.

END RATIONALE

35.4.6   /usr/include : Directory for standard include files.

35.4.6.1   Purpose

This is where all of the system's general-use include files for the C programming language should be placed.

35.4.6.2   Specific Options

The following directories, or symbolic links to directories, must be in /usr/include, if the corresponding subsystem is installed:

```
/usr/include    ———— Include files
            └─ bsd    BSD compatibility include files (optional)
```

The symbolic link /usr/include/X11 must link to /usr/X11R6/include/X11 if the latter exists.

35.4.7   /usr/lib : Libraries for programming and packages

35.4.7.1   Purpose

/usr/lib includes object files, libraries, and internal binaries that are not intended to be executed directly by users or shell scripts.[18]

Applications may use a single subdirectory under /usr/lib. If an application uses a subdirectory, all architecture-dependent data exclusively used by the application must be placed within that subdirectory.[19]

35.4.7.2   Specific Options

For historical reasons, /usr/lib/sendmail must be a symbolic link to /usr/sbin/sendmail if the latter exists.[20]

---

[18]Miscellaneous architecture-independent application-specific static files and subdirectories must be placed in /usr/share.

[19]For example, the perl5 subdirectory for Perl 5 modules and libraries.

[20]Some executable commands such as makewhatis and sendmail have also been traditionally placed in /usr/lib. makewhatis is an internal binary and must be placed in a binary directory; users access only catman. Newer sendmail binaries are now placed by default in /usr/sbin. Additionally, systems using a sendmail-compatible mail transfer agent must provide /usr/sbin/sendmail as a symbolic link to the appropriate executable.

If `/lib/X11` exists, `/usr/lib/X11` must be a symbolic link to `/lib/X11`, or to whatever `/lib/X11` is a symbolic link to.[21]

35.4.8 /usr/lib<qual> : Alternate format libraries (optional)

35.4.8.1 Purpose

`/usr/lib<qual>` performs the same role as `/usr/lib` for an alternate binary format, except that the symbolic links `/usr/lib<qual>/sendmail` and `/usr/lib<qual>/X11` are not required.[22]

35.4.9 /usr/local : Local hierarchy

35.4.9.1 Purpose

The `/usr/local` hierarchy is for use by the system administrator when installing software locally. It needs to be safe from being overwritten when the system software is updated. It may be used for programs and data that are shareable amongst a group of hosts, but not found in `/usr`.

Locally installed software must be placed within `/usr/local` rather than `/usr` unless it is being installed to replace or upgrade software in `/usr`.[23]

35.4.9.2 Requirements

The following directories, or symbolic links to directories, must be in `/usr/local`

```
/usr/local   ────── Local hierarchy
          └ bin        Local binaries
          └ games      Local game binaries
          └ include    Local C header files
          └ lib        Local libraries
          └ man        Local online manuals
          └ sbin       Local system binaries
          └ share      Local architecture-independent hierarchy
```

---

[21]Host-specific data for the X Window System must not be stored in `/usr/lib/X11`. Host-specific configuration files such as `Xconfig` or `XF86Config` must be stored in `/etc/X11`. This includes configuration data such as `system.twmrc` even if it is only made a symbolic link to a more global configuration file (probably in `/usr/X11R6/lib/X11`).

[22]The case where `/usr/lib` and `/usr/lib<qual>` are the same (one is a symbolic link to the other) these files and the per-application subdirectories will exist.

[23]Software placed in `/` or `/usr` may be overwritten by system upgrades (though we recommend that distributions do not overwrite data in `/etc` under these circumstances). For this reason, local software must not be placed outside of `/usr/local` without good reason.

        └─ `src`   Local source code

No other directories, except those listed below, may be in `/usr/local` after first installing a FHS-compliant system.

35.4.9.3   Specific Options

If directories `/lib<qual>` or `/usr/lib<qual>` exist, the equivalent directories must also exist in `/usr/local`.

35.4.10   /usr/sbin : Non-essential standard system binaries

35.4.10.1   Purpose

This directory contains any non-essential binaries used exclusively by the system administrator. System administration programs that are required for system repair, system recovery, mounting `/usr`, or other essential functions must be placed in `/sbin` instead.[24]

35.4.11   /usr/share : Architecture-independent data

35.4.11.1   Purpose

The `/usr/share` hierarchy is for all read-only architecture independent data files.[25]

This hierarchy is intended to be shareable among all architecture platforms of a given OS; thus, for example, a site with i386, Alpha, and PPC platforms might maintain a single `/usr/share` directory that is centrally-mounted. Note, however, that `/usr/share` is generally not intended to be shared by different OSes or by different releases of the same OS.

Any program or package which contains or requires data that doesn't need to be modified should store that data in `/usr/share` (or `/usr/local/share`, if installed locally). It is recommended that a subdirectory be used in `/usr/share` for this purpose.

Game data stored in `/usr/share/games` must be purely static data. Any modifiable files, such as score files, game play logs, and so forth, should be placed in `/var/games`.

35.4.11.2   Requirements

The following directories, or symbolic links to directories, must be in `/usr/share`

`/usr/share` ──────── Architecture-independent data
        └─ `man`   Online manuals
        └─ `misc`   Miscellaneous architecture-independent data

---

[24]Locally installed system administration programs should be placed in `/usr/local/sbin`.
[25]Much of this data originally lived in `/usr` (man, doc) or `/usr/lib` (dict, terminfo, zoneinfo).

35.4.11.3   Specific Options

The following directories, or symbolic links to directories, must be in `/usr/share`, if the corresponding subsystem is installed:

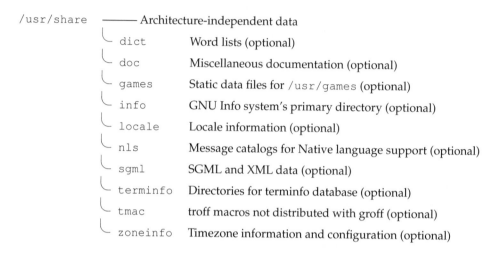

`/usr/share`	—— Architecture-independent data
`dict`	Word lists (optional)
`doc`	Miscellaneous documentation (optional)
`games`	Static data files for `/usr/games` (optional)
`info`	GNU Info system's primary directory (optional)
`locale`	Locale information (optional)
`nls`	Message catalogs for Native language support (optional)
`sgml`	SGML and XML data (optional)
`terminfo`	Directories for terminfo database (optional)
`tmac`	troff macros not distributed with groff (optional)
`zoneinfo`	Timezone information and configuration (optional)

It is recommended that application-specific, architecture-independent directories be placed here. Such directories include `groff`, `perl`, `ghostscript`, `texmf`, and `kbd` (Linux) or `syscons` (BSD). They may, however, be placed in `/usr/lib` for backwards compatibility, at the distributor's discretion. Similarly, a `/usr/lib/games` hierarchy may be used in addition to the `/usr/share/games` hierarchy if the distributor wishes to place some game data there.

35.4.11.4   /usr/share/dict : Word lists (optional)

35.4.11.4.1   Purpose

This directory is the home for word lists on the system; Traditionally this directory contains only the English `words` file, which is used by `look(1)` and various spelling programs. `words` may use either American or British spelling.

> **BEGIN RATIONALE**
>
> The reason that only word lists are located here is that they are the only files common to all spell checkers.
>
> **END RATIONALE**

35.4.11.4.2   Specific Options

The following files, or symbolic links to files, must be in `/usr/share/dict`, if the corresponding subsystem is installed:

`words`	List of English words (optional)

Sites that require both American and British spelling may link words to /usr/share/dict/american-english or /usr/share/dict/british-english.

Word lists for other languages may be added using the English name for that language, e.g., /usr/share/dict/french, /usr/share/dict/danish, etc. These should, if possible, use an ISO 8859 character set which is appropriate for the language in question; if possible the Latin1 (ISO 8859-1) character set should be used (this is often not possible).

Other word lists must be included here, if present.

35.4.11.5 /usr/share/man : Manual pages

35.4.11.5.1 Purpose

This section details the organization for manual pages throughout the system, including /usr/share/man. Also refer to the section on /var/cache/man.

The primary <mandir> of the system is /usr/share/man. /usr/share/man contains manual information for commands and data under the / and /usr filesystems.[26]

Manual pages are stored in <mandir>/<locale>/man<section>/<arch>. An explanation of <mandir>, <locale>, <section>, and <arch> is given below.

A description of each section follows:

- man1: User programs
  Manual pages that describe publicly accessible commands are contained in this chapter. Most program documentation that a user will need to use is located here.

- man2: System calls
  This section describes all of the system calls (requests for the kernel to perform operations).

- man3: Library functions and subroutines
  Section 3 describes program library routines that are not direct calls to kernel services. This and chapter 2 are only really of interest to programmers.

- man4: Special files
  Section 4 describes the special files, related driver functions, and networking support available in the system. Typically, this includes the device files found in /dev and the kernel interface to networking protocol support.

- man5: File formats
  The formats for many data files are documented in the section 5. This includes various include files, program output files, and system files.

- man6: Games
  This chapter documents games, demos, and generally trivial programs. Different people have various notions about how essential this is.

- man7: Miscellaneous
  Manual pages that are difficult to classify are designated as being section 7. The troff and other text processing macro packages are found here.

---

[26]Obviously, there are no manual pages in / because they are not required at boot time nor are they required in emergencies.[27]

[27]Really.

- `man8`: System administration
  Programs used by system administrators for system operation and maintenance are documented here. Some of these programs are also occasionally useful for normal users.

35.4.11.5.2 Specific Options

The following directories, or symbolic links to directories, must be in `/usr/share/<mandir>/<locale>`, unless they are empty:[28]

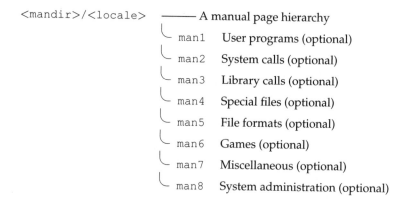

`<mandir>/<locale>`	——— A manual page hierarchy
`man1`	User programs (optional)
`man2`	System calls (optional)
`man3`	Library calls (optional)
`man4`	Special files (optional)
`man5`	File formats (optional)
`man6`	Games (optional)
`man7`	Miscellaneous (optional)
`man8`	System administration (optional)

The component `<section>` describes the manual section.

Provisions must be made in the structure of `/usr/share/man` to support manual pages which are written in different (or multiple) languages. These provisions must take into account the storage and reference of these manual pages. Relevant factors include language (including geographical-based differences), and character code set.

This naming of language subdirectories of `/usr/share/man` is based on Appendix E of the POSIX 1003.1 standard which describes the locale identification string — the most well-accepted method to describe a cultural environment. The `<locale>` string is:

```
<language>[_<territory>][.<character-set>][,<version>]
```

The `<language>` field must be taken from ISO 639 (a code for the representation of names of languages). It must be two characters wide and specified with lowercase letters only.

The `<territory>` field must be the two-letter code of ISO 3166 (a specification of representations of countries), if possible. (Most people are familiar with the two-letter codes used for the country codes in email addresses.[29]) It must be two characters wide and specified with uppercase letters only.

The `<character-set>` field must represent the standard describing the character set. If the `<character-set>` field is just a numeric specification, the number represents the number of

---

[28]For example, if `/usr/local/man` has no manual pages in section 4 (Devices), then `/usr/local/man/man4` may be omitted.

[29]A major exception to this rule is the United Kingdom, which is 'GB' in the ISO 3166, but 'UK' for most email addresses.

the international standard describing the character set. It is recommended that this be a numeric representation if possible (ISO standards, especially), not include additional punctuation
symbols, and that any letters be in lowercase.

A parameter specifying a `<version>` of the profile may be placed after the
`<character-set>` field, delimited by a comma. This may be used to discriminate between different cultural needs; for instance, dictionary order versus a more systems-oriented
collating order. This standard recommends not using the `<version>` field, unless it is
necessary.

Systems which use a unique language and code set for all manual pages may omit the
`<locale>` substring and store all manual pages in `<mandir>`. For example, systems
which only have English manual pages coded with ASCII, may store manual pages (the
man`<section>` directories) directly in `/usr/share/man`. (That is the traditional circumstance and arrangement, in fact.)

Countries for which there is a well-accepted standard character code set may omit the
`<character-set>` field, but it is strongly recommended that it be included, especially for
countries with several competing standards.

Various examples:

Language	Territory	Character Set	Directory
English	—	ASCII	`/usr/share/man/en`
English	United Kingdom	ASCII	`/usr/share/man/en_GB`
English	United States	ASCII	`/usr/share/man/en_US`
French	Canada	ISO 8859-1	`/usr/share/man/fr_CA`
French	France	ISO 8859-1	`/usr/share/man/fr_FR`
German	Germany	ISO 646	`/usr/share/man/de_DE.646`
German	Germany	ISO 6937	`/usr/share/man/de_DE.6937`
German	Germany	ISO 8859-1	`/usr/share/man/de_DE.88591`
German	Switzerland	ISO 646	`/usr/share/man/de_CH.646`
Japanese	Japan	JIS	`/usr/share/man/ja_JP.jis`
Japanese	Japan	SJIS	`/usr/share/man/ja_JP.sjis`
Japanese	Japan ·	UJIS (or EUC-J)	`/usr/share/man/ja_JP.ujis`

Similarly, provision must be made for manual pages which are architecture-dependent,
such as documentation on device-drivers or low-level system administration commands.
These must be placed under an `<arch>` directory in the appropriate man`<section>` directory; for example, a man page for the i386 ctrlaltdel(8) command might be placed in
`/usr/share/man/<locale>/man8/i386/ctrlaltdel.8`.

Manual pages for commands and data under `/usr/local` are stored in `/usr/local/man`.
Manual pages for X11R6 are stored in `/usr/X11R6/man`. It follows that all manual page hierarchies in the system must have the same structure as `/usr/share/man`.

The cat page sections (`cat<section>`) containing formatted manual page entries are also
found within subdirectories of `<mandir>/<locale>`, but are not required nor may they be
distributed in lieu of nroff source manual pages.

The numbered sections "1" through "8" are traditionally defined. In general, the file name for
manual pages located within a particular section end with `.<section>`.

In addition, some large sets of application-specific manual pages have an additional suffix appended to the manual page filename. For example, the MH mail handling system manual pages must have mh appended to all MH manuals. All X Window System manual pages must have an x appended to the filename.

The practice of placing various language manual pages in appropriate subdirectories of /usr/share/man also applies to the other manual page hierarchies, such as /usr/local/man and /usr/X11R6/man. (This portion of the standard also applies later in the section on the optional /var/cache/man structure.)

35.4.11.6 /usr/share/misc : Miscellaneous architecture-independent data

This directory contains miscellaneous architecture-independent files which don't require a separate subdirectory under /usr/share.

35.4.11.6.1 Specific Options

The following files, or symbolic links to files, must be in /usr/share/misc, if the corresponding subsystem is installed:

ascii	ASCII character set table (optional)
magic	Default list of magic numbers for the file command (optional)
termcap	Terminal capability database (optional)
termcap.db	Terminal capability database (optional)

Other (application-specific) files may appear here,[30] but a distributor may place them in /usr/lib at their discretion.

35.4.11.7 /usr/share/sgml : SGML and XML data (optional)

35.4.11.7.1 Purpose

/usr/share/sgml contains architecture-independent files used by SGML or XML applications, such as ordinary catalogs (not the centralized ones, see /etc/sgml), DTDs, entities, or style sheets.

35.4.11.7.2 Specific Options

The following directories, or symbolic links to directories, must be in /usr/share/sgml, if the corresponding subsystem is installed:

---

[30]Some such files include:

```
{ airport, birthtoken, eqnchar, getopt, gprof.callg, gprof.flat, inter.phone,
  ipfw.samp.filters, ipfw.samp.scripts, keycap.pcvt, mail.help, mail.tildehelp,
  man.template, map3270, mdoc.template, more.help, na.phone, nslookup.help, oper-
  ator, scsi_modes, sendmail.hf, style, units.lib, vgrindefs, vgrindefs.db, zipcodes
  }
```

```
/usr/share/sgml ————SGML and XML data
              └ docbook    docbook DTD (optional)
              └ tei        tei DTD (optional)
              └ html       html DTD (optional)
              └ mathml     mathml DTD (optional)
```

Other files that are not specific to a given DTD may reside in their own subdirectory.

35.4.12 /usr/src : Source code (optional)

35.4.12.1 Purpose

Any non-local source code should be placed in this subdirectory.

35.5 The /var Hierarchy

35.5.1 Purpose

/var contains variable data files. This includes spool directories and files, administrative and logging data, and transient and temporary files.

Some portions of /var are not shareable between different systems. For instance, /var/log, /var/lock, and /var/run. Other portions may be shared, notably /var/mail, /var/cache/man, /var/cache/fonts, and /var/spool/news.

/var is specified here in order to make it possible to mount /usr read-only. Everything that once went into /usr that is written to during system operation (as opposed to installation and software maintenance) must be in /var.

If /var cannot be made a separate partition, it is often preferable to move /var out of the root partition and into the /usr partition. (This is sometimes done to reduce the size of the root partition or when space runs low in the root partition.) However, /var must not be linked to /usr because this makes separation of /usr and /var more difficult and is likely to create a naming conflict. Instead, link /var to /usr/var.

Applications must generally not add directories to the top level of /var. Such directories should only be added if they have some system-wide implication, and in consultation with the FHS mailing list.

35.5.2 Requirements

The following directories, or symbolic links to directories, are required in /var.

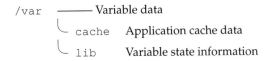

```
/var ————Variable data
      └ cache    Application cache data
      └ lib      Variable state information
```

```
└ local    Variable data for /usr/local
└ lock     Lock files
└ log      Log files and directories
└ opt      Variable data for /opt
└ run      Data relevant to running processes
└ spool    Application spool data
└ tmp      Temporary files preserved between system reboots
```

Several directories are 'reserved' in the sense that they must not be used arbitrarily by some new application, since they would conflict with historical and/or local practice. They are:

```
/var/backups
/var/cron
/var/msgs
/var/preserve
```

35.5.3 Specific Options

The following directories, or symbolic links to directories, must be in /var, if the corresponding subsystem is installed:

```
/var    ——— Variable data
└ account    Process accounting logs (optional)
└ crash      System crash dumps (optional)
└ games      Variable game data (optional)
└ mail       User mailbox files (optional)
└ yp         Network Information Service (NIS) database files (optional)
```

35.5.4 /var/account : Process accounting logs (optional)

35.5.4.1 Purpose

This directory holds the current active process accounting log and the composite process usage data (as used in some UNIX-like systems by lastcomm and sa).

35.5.5 /var/cache : Application cache data

35.5.5.1 Purpose

/var/cache is intended for cached data from applications. Such data is locally generated as a result of time-consuming I/O or calculation. The application must be able to regenerate or restore the data. Unlike /var/spool, the cached files can be deleted without data loss. The data must remain valid between invocations of the application and rebooting the system.

Files located under /var/cache may be expired in an application specific manner, by the system administrator, or both. The application must always be able to recover from manual deletion of these files (generally because of a disk space shortage). No other requirements are made on the data format of the cache directories.

BEGIN RATIONALE

The existence of a separate directory for cached data allows system administrators to set different disk and backup policies from other directories in /var.

END RATIONALE

35.5.5.2 Specific Options

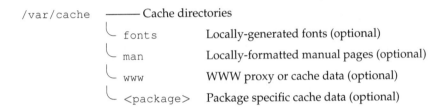

/var/cache	—— Cache directories
	└ fonts	Locally-generated fonts (optional)
	└ man	Locally-formatted manual pages (optional)
	└ www	WWW proxy or cache data (optional)
	└ \<package>	Package specific cache data (optional)

35.5.5.3 /var/cache/fonts : Locally-generated fonts (optional)

35.5.5.3.1 Purpose

The directory /var/cache/fonts should be used to store any dynamically-created fonts. In particular, all of the fonts which are automatically generated by mktexpk must be located in appropriately-named subdirectories of /var/cache/fonts.[31]

35.5.5.3.2 Specific Options

Other dynamically created fonts may also be placed in this tree, under appropriately-named subdirectories of /var/cache/fonts.

35.5.5.4 /var/cache/man : Locally-formatted manual pages (optional)

35.5.5.4.1 Purpose

This directory provides a standard location for sites that provide a read-only /usr partition, but wish to allow caching of locally-formatted man pages. Sites that mount /usr as writable (e.g., single-user installations) may choose not to use /var/cache/man and may write formatted man pages into the cat\<section> directories in /usr/share/man directly. We recommend that most sites use one of the following options instead:

- Preformat all manual pages alongside the unformatted versions.

---

[31]This standard does not currently incorporate the TEX Directory Structure (a document that describes the layout TEX files and directories), but it may be useful reading. It is located at ftp://ctan.tug.org/tex/.

- Allow no caching of formatted man pages, and require formatting to be done each time a man page is brought up.

- Allow local caching of formatted man pages in /var/cache/man.

The structure of /var/cache/man needs to reflect both the fact of multiple man page hierarchies and the possibility of multiple language support.

Given an unformatted manual page that normally appears in <path>/man/<locale>/man<section>, the directory to place formatted man pages in is /var/cache/man/<catpath>/<locale>/cat<section>, where <catpath> is derived from <path> by removing any leading usr and/or trailing share pathname components.[32] (Note that the <locale> component may be missing.)

Man pages written to /var/cache/man may eventually be transferred to the appropriate preformatted directories in the source man hierarchy or expired; likewise formatted man pages in the source man hierarchy may be expired if they are not accessed for a period of time.

If preformatted manual pages come with a system on read-only media (a CD-ROM, for instance), they must be installed in the source man hierarchy (e.g. /usr/share/man/cat<section>). /var/cache/man is reserved as a writable cache for formatted manual pages.

BEGIN RATIONALE

Release 1.2 of the standard specified /var/catman for this hierarchy. The path has been moved under /var/cache to better reflect the dynamic nature of the formatted man pages. The directory name has been changed to man to allow for enhancing the hierarchy to include post-processed formats other than "cat", such as PostScript, HTML, or DVI.

END RATIONALE

35.5.6 /var/crash : System crash dumps (optional)

35.5.6.1 Purpose

This directory holds system crash dumps. As of the date of this release of the standard, system crash dumps were not supported under Linux.

35.5.7 /var/games : Variable game data (optional)

35.5.7.1 Purpose

Any variable data relating to games in /usr should be placed here. /var/games should hold the variable data previously found in /usr; static data, such as help text, level descriptions, and so on, must remain elsewhere, such as /usr/share/games.

BEGIN RATIONALE

---

[32]For example, /usr/share/man/man1/ls.1 is formatted into /var/cache/man/cat1/ls.1, and /usr/X11R6/man/<locale>/man3/XtClass.3x into /var/cache/man/X11R6/<locale>/-cat3/XtClass.3x.

/var/games has been given a hierarchy of its own, rather than leaving it merged in with the old /var/lib as in release 1.2. The separation allows local control of backup strategies, permissions, and disk usage, as well as allowing inter-host sharing and reducing clutter in /var/lib. Additionally, /var/games is the path traditionally used by BSD.

END RATIONALE

35.5.8   /var/lib : Variable state information

35.5.8.1   Purpose

This hierarchy holds state information pertaining to an application or the system. State information is data that programs modify while they run, and that pertains to one specific host. Users must never need to modify files in /var/lib to configure a package's operation.

State information is generally used to preserve the condition of an application (or a group of inter-related applications) between invocations and between different instances of the same application. State information should generally remain valid after a reboot, should not be logging output, and should not be spooled data.

An application (or a group of inter-related applications) must use a subdirectory of /var/lib for its data.[33] There is one required subdirectory, /var/lib/misc, which is intended for state files that don't need a subdirectory; the other subdirectories should only be present if the application in question is included in the distribution.

/var/lib/<name> is the location that must be used for all distribution packaging support. Different distributions may use different names, of course.

35.5.8.2   Requirements

The following directories, or symbolic links to directories, are required in /var/lib:

```
/var/lib    ──────── Variable state information
        └─ misc     Miscellaneous state data
```

35.5.8.3   Specific Options

The following directories, or symbolic links to directories, must be in /var/lib, if the corresponding subsystem is installed:

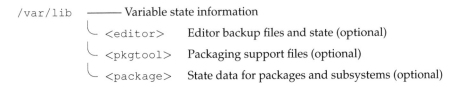

```
/var/lib    ──────── Variable state information
        └─ <editor>     Editor backup files and state (optional)
        └─ <pkgtool>    Packaging support files (optional)
        └─ <package>    State data for packages and subsystems (optional)
```

---

[33] An important difference between this version of this standard and previous ones is that applications are now required to use a subdirectory of /var/lib.

    └─ hwclock   State directory for hwclock (optional)

    └─ xdm   X display manager variable data (optional)

35.5.8.4 /var/lib/<editor> : Editor backup files and state (optional)

35.5.8.4.1 Purpose

These directories contain saved files generated by any unexpected termination of an editor (e.g., elvis, jove, nvi).

Other editors may not require a directory for crash-recovery files, but may require a well-defined place to store other information while the editor is running. This information should be stored in a subdirectory under /var/lib (for example, GNU Emacs would place lock files in /var/lib/emacs/lock).

Future editors may require additional state information beyond crash-recovery files and lock files — this information should also be placed under /var/lib/<editor>.

> **BEGIN RATIONALE**
>
> Previous Linux releases, as well as all commercial vendors, use /var/preserve for vi or its clones. However, each editor uses its own format for these crash-recovery files, so a separate directory is needed for each editor.
>
> Editor-specific lock files are usually quite different from the device or resource lock files that are stored in /var/lock and, hence, are stored under /var/lib.
>
> **END RATIONALE**

35.5.8.5 /var/lib/hwclock : State directory for hwclock (optional)

35.5.8.5.1 Purpose

This directory contains the file /var/lib/hwclock/adjtime.

> **BEGIN RATIONALE**
>
> In FHS 2.1, this file was /etc/adjtime, but as hwclock updates it, that was obviously incorrect.
>
> **END RATIONALE**

35.5.8.6 /var/lib/misc : Miscellaneous variable data

35.5.8.6.1 Purpose

This directory contains variable data not placed in a subdirectory in /var/lib. An attempt should be made to use relatively unique names in this directory to avoid namespace conflicts.[34]

---

[34]This hierarchy should contain files stored in /var/db in current BSD releases. These include locate.database and mountdtab, and the kernel symbol database(s).

35.5.9   /var/lock : Lock files

35.5.9.1   Purpose

Lock files should be stored within the /var/lock directory structure.

Lock files for devices and other resources shared by multiple applications, such as the serial device lock files that were originally found in either /usr/spool/locks or /usr/spool/uucp, must now be stored in /var/lock. The naming convention which must be used is LCK.. followed by the base name of the device file. For example, to lock /dev/ttyS0 the file LCK..ttyS0 would be created.
[35]

The format used for the contents of such lock files must be the HDB UUCP lock file format. The HDB format is to store the process identifier (PID) as a ten byte ASCII decimal number, with a trailing newline. For example, if process 1230 holds a lock file, it would contain the eleven characters: space, space, space, space, space, space, one, two, three, zero, and newline.

35.5.10   /var/log : Log files and directories

35.5.10.1   Purpose

This directory contains miscellaneous log files. Most logs must be written to this directory or an appropriate subdirectory.

35.5.10.2   Specific Options

The following files, or symbolic links to files, must be in /var/log, if the corresponding subsystem is installed:

lastlog	record of last login of each user
messages	system messages from syslogd
wtmp	record of all logins and logouts

35.5.11   /var/mail : User mailbox files (optional)

35.5.11.1   Purpose

The mail spool must be accessible through /var/mail and the mail spool files must take the form <username>.[36]

User mailbox files in this location must be stored in the standard UNIX mailbox format.

BEGIN RATIONALE

---

[35]Then, anything wishing to use /dev/ttyS0 can read the lock file and act accordingly (all locks in /var/lock should be world-readable).

[36]Note that /var/mail may be a symbolic link to another directory.

The logical location for this directory was changed from /var/spool/mail in order to bring FHS in-line with nearly every Unix implementation. This change is important for inter-operability since a single /var/mail is often shared between multiple hosts and multiple Unix implementations (despite NFS locking issues).

It is important to note that there is no requirement to physically move the mail spool to this location. However, programs and header files must be changed to use /var/mail.
END RATIONALE

35.5.12 /var/opt : Variable data for /opt

35.5.12.1 Purpose

Variable data of the packages in /opt must be installed in /var/opt/<package>, where <package> is the name of the subtree in /opt where the static data from an add-on software package is stored, except where superseded by another file in /etc. No structure is imposed on the internal arrangement of /var/opt/<package>.

BEGIN RATIONALE
Refer to the rationale for /opt.
END RATIONALE

35.5.13 /var/run : Run-time variable data

35.5.13.1 Purpose

This directory contains system information data describing the system since it was booted. Files under this directory must be cleared (removed or truncated as appropriate) at the beginning of the boot process. Programs may have a subdirectory of /var/run; this is encouraged for programs that use more than one run-time file.[37] Process identifier (PID) files, which were originally placed in /etc, must be placed in /var/run. The naming convention for PID files is <program-name>.pid. For example, the crond PID file is named /var/run/crond.pid.

35.5.13.2 Requirements

The internal format of PID files remains unchanged. The file must consist of the process identifier in ASCII-encoded decimal, followed by a newline character. For example, if crond was process number 25, /var/run/crond.pid would contain three characters: two, five, and newline.

Programs that read PID files should be somewhat flexible in what they accept; i.e., they should ignore extra whitespace, leading zeroes, absence of the trailing newline, or additional lines in the PID file. Programs that create PID files should use the simple specification located in the above paragraph.

The utmp file, which stores information about who is currently using the system, is located in this directory.

Programs that maintain transient Unix-domain sockets must place them in this directory.

---

[37]/var/run should be unwritable for unprivileged users (root or users running daemons); it is a major security problem if any user can write in this directory.

35.5.14   /var/spool : Application spool data

35.5.14.1   Purpose

`/var/spool` contains data which is awaiting some kind of later processing.   Data in `/var/spool` represents work to be done in the future (by a program, user, or administrator); often data is deleted after it has been processed.[38]

35.5.14.2   Specific Options

The following directories, or symbolic links to directories, must be in `/var/spool`, if the corresponding subsystem is installed:

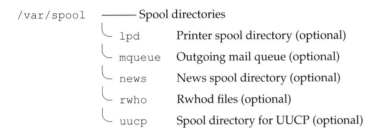

```
/var/spool      ――――― Spool directories
      └─ lpd          Printer spool directory (optional)
      └─ mqueue       Outgoing mail queue (optional)
      └─ news         News spool directory (optional)
      └─ rwho         Rwhod files (optional)
      └─ uucp         Spool directory for UUCP (optional)
```

35.5.14.3   /var/spool/lpd : Line-printer daemon print queues (optional)

35.5.14.3.1   Purpose

The lock file for `lpd`, `lpd.lock`, must be placed in `/var/spool/lpd`. It is suggested that the lock file for each printer be placed in the spool directory for that specific printer and named `lock`.

35.5.14.3.2   Specific Options

```
/var/spool/lpd    ――――― Printer spool directory
       └─ <printer>    Spools for a specific printer (optional)
```

35.5.14.4   /var/spool/rwho : Rwhod files (optional)

35.5.14.4.1   Purpose

This directory holds the `rwhod` information for other systems on the local net.

   BEGIN RATIONALE

---

[38]UUCP lock files must be placed in `/var/lock`. See the above section on `/var/lock`.

Some BSD releases use `/var/rwho` for this data; given its historical location in `/var/spool` on other systems and its approximate fit to the definition of 'spooled' data, this location was deemed more appropriate.
END RATIONALE

35.5.15   /var/tmp : Temporary files preserved between system reboots

35.5.15.1   Purpose

The `/var/tmp` directory is made available for programs that require temporary files or directories that are preserved between system reboots. Therefore, data stored in `/var/tmp` is more persistent than data in `/tmp`.

Files and directories located in `/var/tmp` must not be deleted when the system is booted. Although data stored in `/var/tmp` is typically deleted in a site-specific manner, it is recommended that deletions occur at a less frequent interval than `/tmp`.

35.5.16   /var/yp : Network Information Service (NIS) database files (optional)

35.5.16.1   Purpose

Variable data for the Network Information Service (NIS), formerly known as the Sun Yellow Pages (YP), must be placed in this directory.

> **BEGIN RATIONALE**
> `/var/yp` is the standard directory for NIS (YP) data and is almost exclusively used in NIS documentation and systems.[39]
> **END RATIONALE**

35.6   Operating System Specific Annex

This section is for additional requirements and recommendations that only apply to a specific operating system. The material in this section should never conflict with the base standard.

35.6.1   Linux

This is the annex for the Linux operating system.

35.6.1.1   / : Root directory

On Linux systems, if the kernel is located in `/`, we recommend using the names `vmlinux` or `vmlinuz`, which have been used in recent Linux kernel source packages.

---

[39]NIS should not be confused with Sun NIS+, which uses a different directory, `/var/nis`.

35.6.1.2 /bin : Essential user command binaries (for use by all users)

Linux systems which require them place these additional files into /bin.

```
{ setserial }
```

35.6.1.3 /dev : Devices and special files

All devices and special files in /dev should adhere to the *Linux Allocated Devices* document, which is available with the Linux kernel source. It is maintained by H. Peter Anvin <hpa@zytor.com>.

Symbolic links in /dev should not be distributed with Linux systems except as provided in the *Linux Allocated Devices* document.

> **BEGIN RATIONALE**
>
> The requirement not to make symlinks promiscuously is made because local setups will often differ from that on the distributor's development machine. Also, if a distribution install script configures the symbolic links at install time, these symlinks will often not get updated if local changes are made in hardware. When used responsibly at a local level, however, they can be put to good use.
>
> **END RATIONALE**

35.6.1.4 /etc : Host-specific system configuration

Linux systems which require them place these additional files into /etc.

```
{ lilo.conf }
```

35.6.1.5 /proc : Kernel and process information virtual filesystem

The proc filesystem is the de-facto standard Linux method for handling process and system information, rather than /dev/kmem and other similar methods. We strongly encourage this for the storage and retrieval of process information as well as other kernel and memory information.

35.6.1.6 /sbin : Essential system binaries

Linux systems place these additional files into /sbin.

- Second extended filesystem commands (optional):

```
{ badblocks, dumpe2fs, e2fsck, mke2fs, mklost+found, tune2fs }
```

- Boot-loader map installer (optional):

```
{ lilo }
```

Optional files for /sbin:

- Static binaries:

{ ldconfig, sln, ssync }

Static `ln` (`sln`) and static `sync` (`ssync`) are useful when things go wrong. The primary use of `sln` (to repair incorrect symlinks in `/lib` after a poorly orchestrated upgrade) is no longer a major concern now that the `ldconfig` program (usually located in `/usr/sbin`) exists and can act as a guiding hand in upgrading the dynamic libraries. Static `sync` is useful in some emergency situations. Note that these need not be statically linked versions of the standard `ln` and `sync`, but may be.

The `ldconfig` binary is optional for `/sbin` since a site may choose to run `ldconfig` at boot time, rather than only when upgrading the shared libraries. (It's not clear whether or not it is advantageous to run `ldconfig` on each boot.) Even so, some people like `ldconfig` around for the following (all too common) situation:

1. I've just removed `/lib/<file>`.
2. I can't find out the name of the library because `ls` is dynamically linked, I'm using a shell that doesn't have `ls` built-in, and I don't know about using "echo *" as a replacement.
3. I have a static `sln`, but I don't know what to call the link.

- Miscellaneous:

{ ctrlaltdel, kbdrate }

So as to cope with the fact that some keyboards come up with such a high repeat rate as to be unusable, `kbdrate` may be installed in `/sbin` on some systems.

Since the default action in the kernel for the Ctrl-Alt-Del key combination is an instant hard reboot, it is generally advisable to disable the behavior before mounting the root filesystem in read-write mode. Some `init` suites are able to disable Ctrl-Alt-Del, but others may require the `ctrlaltdel` program, which may be installed in `/sbin` on those systems.

35.6.1.7   /usr/include : Header files included by C programs

These symbolic links are required if a C or C++ compiler is installed and only for systems not based on glibc.

```
/usr/include/asm -> /usr/src/linux/include/asm-<arch>
/usr/include/linux -> /usr/src/linux/include/linux
```

35.6.1.8   /usr/src : Source code

For systems based on glibc, there are no specific guidelines for this directory. For systems based on Linux libc revisions prior to glibc, the following guidelines and rationale apply:

The only source code that should be placed in a specific location is the Linux kernel source code. It is located in `/usr/src/linux`.

If a C or C++ compiler is installed, but the complete Linux kernel source code is not installed, then the include files from the kernel source code must be located in these directories:

```
/usr/src/linux/include/asm-<arch>
/usr/src/linux/include/linux
```

`<arch>` is the name of the system architecture.

Note: `/usr/src/linux` *may be a symbolic link to a kernel source code tree.*

BEGIN RATIONALE

It is important that the kernel include files be located in `/usr/src/linux` and not in `/usr/include` so there are no problems when system administrators upgrade their kernel version for the first time.

END RATIONALE

35.6.1.9   /var/spool/cron : cron and at jobs

This directory contains the variable data for the `cron` and `at` programs.

35.7 Appendix

35.7.1 The FHS mailing list

The FHS mailing list is located at <fhs-discuss@ucsd.edu>. To subscribe to the list send mail to <listserv@ucsd.edu> with body "`ADD fhs-discuss`".

Thanks to Network Operations at the University of California at San Diego who allowed us to use their excellent mailing list server.

As noted in the introduction, please do not send mail to the mailing list without first contacting the FHS editor or a listed contributor.

35.7.2 Background of the FHS

The process of developing a standard filesystem hierarchy began in August 1993 with an effort to restructure the file and directory structure of Linux. The FSSTND, a filesystem hierarchy standard specific to the Linux operating system, was released on February 14, 1994. Subsequent revisions were released on October 9, 1994 and March 28, 1995.

In early 1995, the goal of developing a more comprehensive version of FSSTND to address not only Linux, but other UNIX-like systems was adopted with the help of members of the BSD development community. As a result, a concerted effort was made to focus on issues that were general to UNIX-like systems. In recognition of this widening of scope, the name of the standard was changed to Filesystem Hierarchy Standard or FHS for short.

Volunteers who have contributed extensively to this standard are listed at the end of this document. This standard represents a consensus view of those and other contributors.

35.7.3 General Guidelines

Here are some of the guidelines that have been used in the development of this standard:

- Solve technical problems while limiting transitional difficulties.
- Make the specification reasonably stable.
- Gain the approval of distributors, developers, and other decision-makers in relevant development groups and encourage their participation.
- Provide a standard that is attractive to the implementors of different UNIX-like systems.

35.7.4 Scope

This document specifies a standard filesystem hierarchy for FHS filesystems by specifying the location of files and directories, and the contents of some system files.

This standard has been designed to be used by system integrators, package developers, and system administrators in the construction and maintenance of FHS compliant filesystems. It is primarily intended to be a reference and is not a tutorial on how to manage a conforming filesystem hierarchy.

The FHS grew out of earlier work on FSSTND, a filesystem organization standard for the Linux operating system. It builds on FSSTND to address interoperability issues not just in the Linux community but in a wider arena including 4.4BSD-based operating systems. It incorporates lessons learned in the BSD world and elsewhere about multi-architecture support and the demands of heterogeneous networking.

Although this standard is more comprehensive than previous attempts at filesystem hierarchy standardization, periodic updates may become necessary as requirements change in relation to emerging technology. It is also possible that better solutions to the problems addressed here will be discovered so that our solutions will no longer be the best possible solutions. Supplementary drafts may be released in addition to periodic updates to this document. However, a specific goal is backwards compatibility from one release of this document to the next.

Comments related to this standard are welcome. Any comments or suggestions for changes may be directed to the FHS editor (Daniel Quinlan <quinlan@pathname.com>) or the FHS mailing list. Typographical or grammatical comments should be directed to the FHS editor.

Before sending mail to the mailing list it is requested that you first contact the FHS editor in order to avoid excessive re-discussion of old topics.

Questions about how to interpret items in this document may occasionally arise. If you have need for a clarification, please contact the FHS editor. Since this standard represents a consensus of many participants, it is important to make certain that any interpretation also represents their collective opinion. For this reason it may not be possible to provide an immediate response unless the inquiry has been the subject of previous discussion.

35.7.5   Acknowledgments

The developers of the FHS wish to thank the developers, system administrators, and users whose input was essential to this standard. We wish to thank each of the contributors who helped to write, compile, and compose this standard.

The FHS Group also wishes to thank those Linux developers who supported the FSSTND, the predecessor to this standard. If they hadn't demonstrated that the FSSTND was beneficial, the FHS could never have evolved.

35.7.6   Contributors

Brandon S. Allbery	<bsa@kf8nh.wariat.org>
Keith Bostic	<bostic@cs.berkeley.edu>
Drew Eckhardt	<drew@colorado.edu>
Rik Faith	<faith@cs.unc.edu>
Stephen Harris	<sweh@spuddy.mew.co.uk>
Ian Jackson	<ijackson@cus.cam.ac.uk>
John A. Martin	<jmartin@acm.org>
Ian McCloghrie	<ian@ucsd.edu>
Chris Metcalf	<metcalf@lcs.mit.edu>
Ian Murdock	<imurdock@debian.org>
David C. Niemi	<niemidc@clark.net>
Daniel Quinlan	<quinlan@pathname.com>

Eric S. Raymond	`<esr@thyrsus.com>`
Rusty Russell	`<rusty@rustcorp.com.au>`
Mike Sangrey	`<mike@sojurn.lns.pa.us>`
David H. Silber	`<dhs@glowworm.firefly.com>`
Thomas Sippel-Dau	`<t.sippel-dau@ic.ac.uk>`
Theodore Ts'o	`<tytso@athena.mit.edu>`
Stephen Tweedie	`<sct@dcs.ed.ac.uk>`
Fred N. van Kempen	`<waltje@infomagic.com>`
Bernd Warken	`<bwarken@mayn.de>`

Chapter 36

`httpd` — Apache Web Server

In this chapter, we will show how to set up a web server running virtual domains and dynamic CGI web pages. HTML is not covered, and you are expected to have some understanding of what HTML is, or at least where to find documentation about it.

36.1 Web Server Basics

In Section 26.2 we showed a simple HTTP session with the `telnet` command. A *web server* is really nothing more than a program that reads a file from the hard disk whenever a `GET /<filename>.html HTTP/1.0` request comes in on port 80. Here, we will show a simple web server written in shell script. ⟍Not by me. The author did not put his name in the source, so if you are out there, please drop me an email.⟋ You will need to add the line

```
www  stream  tcp  nowait  nobody  /usr/local/sbin/sh-httpd
```

to your `/etc/inetd.conf` file. If you are running `xinetd`, then you will need to add a file containing

```
service www
{
        socket_type             = stream
        wait                    = no
        user                    = nobody
        server                  = /usr/local/sbin/sh-httpd
}
```

to your `/etc/xinetd.d/` directory. Then, you must stop any already running web servers and restart `inetd` (or `xinetd`).

389

You will also have to create a log file (`/usr/local/var/log/sh-httpd.log`) and at least one web page (`/usr/local/var/sh-www/index.html`) for your server to serve. It can contain, say:

```
    <HTML>
     <HEAD>
      <TITLE>My First Document</TITLE>
     </HEAD>
5    <BODY bgcolor=#CCCCCC text="#000000">
    This is my first document<P>
    Please visit
      <A HREF="http://rute.sourceforge.net/">
       The Rute Home Page
10    </A>
    for more info.</P>
     </BODY>
    </HTML>
```

Note that the server runs as `nobody`, so the log file must be writable by the nobody user, and the `index.html` file must be readable. Also note the use of the `get-peername` command, which can be changed to `PEER=""` if you do not have the `net-pipes` package installed. ↘I am not completely sure if other commands used here are unavailable on other UNIX systems.↖.

```
    #!/bin/sh
    VERSION=0.1
    NAME="ShellHTTPD"
    DEFCONTENT="text/html"
5    DOCROOT=/usr/local/var/sh-www
    DEFINDEX=index.html
    LOGFILE=/usr/local/var/log/sh-httpd.log

    log() {
10       local REMOTE_HOST=$1
         local REFERRER=$2
         local CODE=$3
         local SIZE=$4

15       echo "$REMOTE_HOST $REFERRER - [$REQ_DATE] \
    \"${REQUEST}\" ${CODE} ${SIZE}" >> ${LOGFILE}
    }

    print_header() {
20       echo -e "HTTP/1.0 200 OK\r"
         echo -e "Server: ${NAME}/${VERSION}\r"
         echo -e "Date: `date`\r"
    }

25  print_error() {
         echo -e "HTTP/1.0 $1 $2\r"
```

```
          echo -e "Content-type: $DEFCONTENT\r"
          echo -e "Connection: close\r"
          echo -e "Date: `date`\r"
30        echo -e "\r"
          echo -e "$2\r"
          exit 1
      }

35    guess_content_type() {
          local FILE=$1
          local CONTENT

          case ${FILE##*.} in
40            html) CONTENT=$DEFCONTENT ;;
              gz) CONTENT=application/x-gzip ;;
              *) CONTENT=application/octet-stream ;;
          esac

45        echo -e "Content-type: $CONTENT"
      }

      do_get() {
          local DIR
50        local NURL
          local LEN

          if [ ! -d $DOCROOT ]; then
              log ${PEER} - 404 0
55            print_error 404 "No such file or directory"
          fi

          if [ -z "${URL##*/}" ]; then
              URL=${URL}${DEFINDEX}
60        fi

          DIR="`dirname $URL`"
          if [ ! -d ${DOCROOT}/${DIR} ]; then
              log ${PEER} - 404 0
65            print_error 404 "Directory not found"
          else
              cd ${DOCROOT}/${DIR}
              NURL="`pwd`/`basename ${URL}`"
              URL=${NURL}
70        fi

          if [ ! -f ${URL} ]; then
              log ${PEER} - 404 0
              print_error 404 "Document not found"
75        fi

          print_header
          guess_content_type ${URL}
          LEN="`ls -l ${URL} | tr -s ' ' | cut -d ' ' -f 5`"
80        echo -e "Content-length: $LEN\r\n\r"
          log ${PEER} - 200 ${LEN}
```

```
        cat ${URL}
        sleep 3
   }
85
   read_request() {
        local DIRT
        local COMMAND

90      read REQUEST
        read DIRT

        REQ_DATE="`date +"%d/%b/%Y:%H:%M:%S %z"`"
        REQUEST="`echo ${REQUEST} | tr -s [:blank:]`"
95      COMMAND="`echo ${REQUEST} | cut -d ' ' -f 1`"
        URL="`echo ${REQUEST} | cut -d ' ' -f 2`"
        PROTOCOL="`echo ${REQUEST} | cut -d ' ' -f 3`"

        case $COMMAND in
100         HEAD)
                print_error 501 "Not implemented (yet)"
                ;;
            GET)
                do_get
105             ;;
            *)
                print_error 501 "Not Implemented"
                ;;
        esac
110 }

   #
   # It was supposed to be clean - without any non-standard utilities
   # but I want some logging where the connections come from, so
115 # I use just this one utility to get the peer address
   #
   # This is from the netpipes package
   PEER="`getpeername | cut -d ' ' -f 1`"

120 read_request

   exit 0
```

Now run `telnet localhost 80`, as in Section 26.2. If that works and your log files are being properly appended (use `tail -f ...`), you can try to connect to http://localhost/ with a web browser like Netscape.

Notice also that the command `getsockname` (which tells you which of your own IP addresses the remote client connected to) could allow the script to serve pages from a different directory for each IP address. This is *virtual domains* in a nutshell. ⟍Groovy, baby, I'm in a giant nutshell.... how do I get out?⟋

392

36.2   Installing and Configuring Apache

Because all distributions package Apache in a different way, here I assume Apache to have been installed from its source tree, rather than from a .deb or .rpm package. You can refer to Section 24.1 on how to install Apache from its source .tar.gz file like any other GNU😊 package. (You can even install it under Windows, Windows NT, or OS/2.) The source tree is, of course, available from *The Apache Home Page* http://www.apache.org. Here I assume you have installed it in --prefix=/opt/apache/. In the process, Apache will have dumped a huge reference manual into /opt/apache/htdocs/manual/.

36.2.1   Sample `httpd.conf`

Apache has several legacy configuration files: access.conf and srm.conf are two of them. These files are now deprecated and should be left empty. A single configuration file /opt/apache/conf/httpd.conf may contain at minimum:

```
    ServerType standalone
    ServerRoot "/opt/apache"
    PidFile /opt/apache/logs/httpd.pid
    ScoreBoardFile /opt/apache/logs/httpd.scoreboard
 5  Port 80
    User nobody
    Group nobody
    HostnameLookups Off
    ServerAdmin webmaster@cranzgot.co.za
10  UseCanonicalName On
    ServerSignature On
    DefaultType text/plain
    ErrorLog /opt/apache/logs/error_log
    LogLevel warn
15  LogFormat "%h %l %u %t \"%r\" %>s %b" common
    CustomLog /opt/apache/logs/access_log common
    DocumentRoot "/opt/apache/htdocs"
    DirectoryIndex index.html
    AccessFileName .htaccess
20  <Directory />
        Options FollowSymLinks
        AllowOverride None
        Order Deny,Allow
        Deny from All
25  </Directory>
    <Files ~ "^\.ht">
        Order allow,deny
        Deny from all
    </Files>
30  <Directory "/opt/apache/htdocs">
        Options Indexes FollowSymLinks MultiViews
        AllowOverride All
```

```
         Order allow,deny
         Allow from all
35   </Directory>
     <Directory "/opt/apache/htdocs/home/*/www">
         Options Indexes MultiViews
         AllowOverride None
         Order allow,deny
40       Allow from all
     </Directory>
     UserDir /opt/apache/htdocs/home/*/www
```

With the config file ready, you can move the index.html file above to /opt/apache/htdocs/. You will notice the complete Apache manual and a demo page already installed there; you can move them to another directory for the time being. Now run

```
/opt/apache/bin/httpd -X
```

and then point your web browser to http://localhost/ as before.

36.2.2   Common directives

Here is a description of the options.   Each option is called a *directive* in Apache terminology.   A complete list of basic directives is in the file /opt/apache/htdocs/manual/mod/core.html.

ServerType As discussed in Section 29.2, some services can run standalone or from inetd (or xinetd). This directive can be exactly standalone or inetd. If you choose inetd, you will need to add an appropriate line into your inetd configuration, although a web server should almost certainly choose standalone mode.

ServerRoot This is the directory superstructure ⬎See page 137.⬏ under which Apache is installed. It will always be the same as the value passed to --prefix=.

PidFile Many system services store the process ID in a file for shutdown and monitoring purposes. On most distributions, the file is /var/run/httpd.pid.

ScoreBoardFile This option is used for communication between Apache parent and child processes on some non-UNIX systems.

Port This is the TCP port for standalone servers to listen on.

User, Group This option is important for security. It forces httpd to user nobody privileges. If the web server is ever hacked, the attack will not be able to gain more than the privileges of the nobody user.

HostnameLookups To force a reverse DNS lookup on every connecting host, set this directive to `on`. To force a forward lookup on every reverse lookup, set this to `double`. This option is for logging purposes since access control does a reverse and forward reverse lookup anyway if required. It should certainly be `off` if you want to reduce latency.

ServerAdmin Error messages include this email address.

UseCanonicalName If Apache has to return a URL for any reason, it will normally return the full name of the server. Setting to `off` uses the very host name sent by the client.

ServerSignature Add the server name to HTML error messages.

DefaultType All files returned to the client have a type field specifying how the file should be displayed. If Apache cannot deduce the type, it assumes the MIME Type to be `text/plain`. See Section 12.6.2 for a discussion of MIME types.

ErrorLog Where errors get logged, usually `/var/log/httpd/error_log`

LogLevel How much info to log.

LogFormat Define a new log format. Here we defined a log format and call it common. Multiple lines are allowed. Lots of interesting information can actually be logged: See `/opt/apache/htdocs/manual/mod/mod_log_config.html` for a full description.

CustomLog The log file name and its (previously defined) format.

DocumentRoot This directive specifies the top-level directory that client connections will see. The string `/opt/apache/htdocs/` is prepended to any file lookup, and hence a URL http://localhost/manual/index.html.en will return the file `/opt/apache/htdocs/manual/index.html.en`.

DirectoryIndex This directive gives the default file to try serve for URLs that contain only a directory name. If a file `index.html` does not exist under that directory, an index of the directory is sent to the client. Other common configurations use `index.htm` or `default.html`.

AccessFileName Before serving a file to a client, Apache reads additional directives from a file `.htaccess` in the same directory as the requested file. If a parent directory contains a `.htaccess` instead, this one will take priority. The `.htaccess` file contains directives that limit access to the directory, as discussed below.

The above is merely the general configuration of Apache. To actually serve pages, you need to define directories, each with a particular purpose, containing particular HTML or graphic files. The Apache configuration file is very much like an HTML document. Sections are started with *<section parameter>* and ended with *</section>*.

The most common directive of this sort is <Directory /*directory*> which does such directory definition. Before defining any directories, we need to limit access to the root directory. This control is critical for security.

```
<Directory />
    Options FollowSymLinks
    Deny from All
    Order Deny,Allow
    AllowOverride None
</Directory>
```

This configuration tells Apache about the root directory, giving clients very restrictive access to it. The directives are ⟍Some of these are extracted from the Apache manual.⟋:

Options The Options directive controls which server features are available in a particular directory. There is also the syntax +*option* or −*option* to include the options of the parent directory, for example, Options +FollowSymLinks −Indexes.

FollowSymLinks The server will follow any symbolic links beneath the directory. Be careful about what symbolic links you have beneath directories with FollowSymLinks. You can, for example, give everyone access to the root directory by having a link ../../../ under htdocs—not what you want.

ExecCGI Execution of CGI scripts is permitted.

Includes Server-side includes are permitted (more on this later).

IncludesNOEXEC Server-side includes are permitted, but the #exec command and #include of CGI scripts are disabled.

Indexes If a client asks for a directory by name and no index.html file (or whatever DirectoryIndex file you specified) is present, then a pretty listing of the contents of that directory is created and returned. For security you may want to turn this option off.

MultiViews Content-negotiated MultiViews are allowed (more on this later).

SymLinksIfOwnerMatch The server will only follow symbolic links for which the target file or directory is owned by the same user ID as the link (more on this later).

All All options except for MultiViews. This is the default setting.

Deny Hosts that are not allowed to connect. You can specify a host name or IP address, for example, as:

```
Deny from 10.1.2.3
Deny from 192.168.5.0/24
Deny from cranzgot.co.za
```

which will deny access to 10.1.2.3, all hosts beginning with 192.168.5., and all hosts ending in .cranzgot.co.za, including the host cranzgot.co.za.

Allow Hosts that are allowed to connect. This directive uses the same syntax as Deny.

Order If order is Deny,Allow, then the Deny directives are checked first and any client that does not match a Deny directive or does match an Allow directive will be *allowed* access to the server.

If order is Allow,Deny, then the Allow directives are checked first and any client that does not match an Allow directive or does match a Deny directive will be *denied* access to the server.

AllowOverride In addition to the directives specified here, additional directives will be read from the file specified by AccessFileName, usually called .htaccess. This file would usually exist alongside your .html files or otherwise in a parent directory. If the file exists, its contents are read into the current <Directory ...> directive. AllowOverride says what directives the .htaccess file is allowed to squash. The complete list can be found in /opt/apache/htdocs/manual/mod/core.html.

You can see that we give very restrictive Options to the root directory, as well as very restrictive access. The only server feature we allow is FollowSymLinks, then we Deny any access, and then we remove the possibility that a .htaccess file could override our restrictions.

The <Files ...> directive sets restrictions on all files matching a particular regular expression. As a security measure, we use it to prevent access to all .htaccess files as follows:

```
<Files ~ "^\.ht">
    Order allow,deny
    Deny from all
</Files>
```

We are now finally ready to add actual web page directories. These take a less restrictive set of access controls:

```
<Directory "/opt/apache/htdocs">
    Options Indexes FollowSymLinks MultiViews
    AllowOverride All
    Order allow,deny
    Allow from all
</Directory>
```

36.2.3   User HTML directories

Our users may require that Apache know about their private web page directories `~/www/`. This is easy to support with the special `UserDir` directive:

```
<Directory "/opt/apache/htdocs/home/*/www">
    Options Indexes MultiViews
    AllowOverride None
    Order allow,deny
    Allow from all
</Directory>
UserDir /opt/apache/htdocs/home/*/www
```

For this feature to work, you must symlink `/opt/apache/htdocs/home` to `/home`, and create a directory `www/` under each user's home directory. Hitting the URL http://localhost/~jack/index.html will then retrieve the file `/opt/apache/htdocs/home/jack/www/index.html`. You will find that Apache gives a `Forbidden` error message when you try to do this. This is probably because `jack`'s home directory's permissions are too restrictive. Your choices vary between now making `jack`'s home directory less restricted or increasing the privileges of Apache. Running Apache under the `www` group by using `Group www`, and then running

```
groupadd -g 65 www
chown jack:www /home/jack /home/jack/www
chmod 0750 /home/jack /home/jack/www
```

is a reasonable compromise.

36.2.4   Aliasing

Sometimes, HTML documents will want to refer to a file or graphic by using a simple prefix, rather than a long directory name. Other times, you want two different references to source the same file. The `Alias` directive creates virtual links between directories. For example, adding the following line, means that a URL `/icons/bomb.gif` will serve the file `/opt/apache/icons/bomb.gif`:

```
Alias /icons/ "/opt/apache/icons/"
```

We do, of course, need to tell Apache about this directory:

```
<Directory "/opt/apache/icons">
    Options None
    AllowOverride None
    Order allow,deny
```

```
5    Allow from all
</Directory>
```

36.2.5   Fancy indexes

You will find the directory lists generated by the preceding configuration rather bland. The directive

```
IndexOptions FancyIndexing
```

causes nice descriptive icons to be printed to the left of the file name. What icons match what file types is a trick issue. You can start with:

```
AddIconByEncoding (CMP,/icons/compressed.gif) x-compress x-gzip
AddIconByType (TXT,/icons/text.gif) text/*
AddIconByType (IMG,/icons/image2.gif) image/*
AddIconByType (SND,/icons/sound2.gif) audio/*
AddIconByType (VID,/icons/movie.gif) video/*
AddIcon /icons/compressed.gif .Z .z .tgz .gz .zip
AddIcon /icons/a.gif .ps .eps
AddIcon /icons/layout.gif .html .shtml .htm
```

This requires the `Alias` directive above to be present. The default Apache configuration contains a far more extensive map of file types.

36.2.6   Encoding and language negotiation

You can get Apache to serve `gzip`ped files with this:

```
AddEncoding x-compress Z
AddEncoding x-gzip gz
```

Now if a client requests a file `index.html`, but only a file `index.html.gz` exists, Apache decompresses it on-the-fly. Note that you must have the `MultiViews` options enabled.

The next options cause Apache to serve `index.html.`*language-code* when `index.html` is requested, filling in the preferred language code sent by the web browser. Adding these directives causes your Apache manual to display correctly and will properly show documents that have non-English translations. Here also, the `MultiViews` must be present.

```
AddLanguage en .en
```

```
     AddLanguage da .dk
     AddLanguage nl .nl
     AddLanguage et .ee
5    AddLanguage fr .fr
     AddLanguage de .de
     AddLanguage el .el
     AddLanguage ja .ja
     AddLanguage ru .ru
10   LanguagePriority en da nl et fr de el ja ru
```

The LanguagePriority directive indicates the preferred language if the browser did not specify any.

Some files might contain a .koi8-r extension, indicating a Russian character set encoding for this file. Many languages have such custom character sets. Russian files are named *webpage*.html.ru.koi8-r. Apache must tell the web browser about the encoding type, based on the extension. Here are directives for Japanese, Russian, and UTF-8 ⟍UTF-8 is a Unicode character set encoding useful for any language.⟍, as follows:

```
AddCharset ISO-2022-JP   .jis
AddCharset KOI8-R        .koi8-r
AddCharset UTF-8         .utf8
```

Once again, the default Apache configuration contains a far more extensive map of languages and character sets.

36.2.7   Server-side includes — SSI

Apache actually has a built-in programming language that interprets .shtml files as scripts. The output of such a script is returned to the client. Most of a typical .shtml file will be ordinary HTML, which will be served unmodified. However, lines like

```
<!--#echo var="DATE_LOCAL" -->
```

will be interpreted, and their output *included* into the HTML—hence the name *server-side includes*. Server-side includes are ideal for HTML pages that contain mostly static HTML with small bits of dynamic content. To demonstrate, add the following to your httpd.conf:

```
     AddType text/html .shtml
     AddHandler server-parsed .shtml
     <Directory "/opt/apache/htdocs/ssi">
         Options Includes
5        AllowOverride None
         Order allow,deny
```

```
      Allow from all
</Directory>
```

Create a directory `/opt/apache/htdocs/ssi` with the index file `index.shtml`:

```
<HTML>
The date today is <!--#echo var="DATE_LOCAL" -->.<P>
Here is a directory listing:<br>
 <PRE>
  <!--#exec cmd="ls -al" -->
 </PRE>
<!--#include virtual="footer.html" -->
</HTML>
```

and then a file `footer.html` containing anything you like. It is obvious how useful this procedure is for creating many documents with the same banner by means of a `#include` statement. If you are wondering what other variables you can print besides DATE_LOCAL, try the following:

```
<HTML>
 <PRE>
  <!--#printenv -->
 </PRE>
</HTML>
```

You can also goto http://localhost/manual/howto/ssi.html to see some other examples.

36.2.8   CGI — Common Gateway Interface

(I have actually never managed to figure out why CGI is called CGI.) CGI is where a URL points to a script. What comes up in your browser is the output of the script (were it to be executed) instead of the contents of the script itself. To try this, create a file `/opt/apache/htdocs/test.cgi`:

```
#!/bin/sh

echo 'Content-type: text/html'
echo
echo '<HTML>'
echo ' <HEAD>'
echo '  <TITLE>My First CGI</TITLE>'
echo ' </HEAD>'
echo ' <BODY bgcolor=#CCCCCC text="#000000">'
echo 'This is my first CGI<P>'
echo 'Please visit'
```

```
      echo '   <A HREF="http://rute.sourceforge.net/">'
      echo '     The Rute Home Page'
      echo '   </A>'
15    echo 'for more info.</P>'
      echo '  </BODY>'
      echo '</HTML>'
```

Make this script executable with `chmod a+x test.cgi` and test the output by running it on the command-line. Add the line

```
AddHandler cgi-script .cgi
```

to your `httpd.conf` file. Next, modify your `Options` for the directory `/opt/apache/htdocs` to include `ExecCGI`, like this:

```
<Directory "/opt/apache/htdocs">
    Options Indexes FollowSymLinks MultiViews ExecCGI
    AllowOverride All
    Order allow,deny
5    Allow from all
</Directory>
```

After restarting Apache you should be able to visit the URL http://localhost/test.cgi. If you run into problems, don't forget to run `tail /opt/apache/logs/error_log` to get a full report.

To get a full list of environment variables available to your CGI program, try the following script:

```
#!/bin/sh

echo 'Content-type: text/html'
echo
5    echo '<HTML>'
echo '<PRE>'
set
echo '</PRE>'
echo '</HTML>'
```

The script will show ordinary `bash` environment variables as well as more interesting variables like QUERY_STRING: Change your script to

```
#!/bin/sh

echo 'Content-type: text/html'
echo
```

```
5  echo '<HTML>'
   echo '<PRE>'
   echo $QUERY_STRING
   echo '</PRE>'
   echo '</HTML>'
```

and then go to the URL http://localhost/test/test.cgi?xxx=2&yyy=3. It is easy to see how variables can be passed to the shell script.

The preceding example is not very interesting. However, it gets useful when scripts have complex logic or can access information that Apache can't access on its own. In Chapter 38 we see how to deploy an SQL database. When you have covered SQL, you can come back here and replace your CGI script with,

```
   #!/bin/sh

   echo 'Content-type: text/html'
   echo
5
   psql -d template1 -H -c "SELECT * FROM pg_tables;"
```

This script will dump the table list of the `template1` database if it exists. Apache will have to run as a user that can access this database, which means changing `User` nobody to `User postgres`. ⟍Note that for security you should *really* limit who can connect to the `postgres` database. See Section 38.4.⟍

36.2.9 Forms and CGI

To create a functional form, use the HTTP `<FORM>` tag as follows. A file `/opt/apache/htdocs/test/form.html` could contain:

```
   <HTML>
     <FORM name="myform" action="test.cgi" method="get">
       <TABLE>
         <TR>
5          <TD colspan="2" align="center">
             Please enter your personal details:
           </TD>
         </TR>
         <TR>
10           <TD>Name:</TD><TD><INPUT type="text" name="name"></TD>
         </TR>
         <TR>
           <TD>Email:</TD><TD><INPUT type="text" name="email"></TD>
         </TR>
15         <TR>
```

```
       <TD>Tel:</TD><TD><INPUT type="text" name="tel"></TD>
     </TR>
     <TR>
       <TD colspan="2" align="center">
20        <INPUT type="submit" value="Submit">
       </TD>
     </TR>
    </TABLE>
   </FORM>
25 </HTML>
```

which looks like:

Note how this form calls our existing `test.cgi` script. Here is a script that adds the entered data to a `postgres` SQL table:

```
#!/bin/sh

echo 'Content-type: text/html'
echo

5
opts=`echo "$QUERY_STRING" | \
    sed -e 's/[^A-Za-z0-9 %&+,.\/:=@_~-]//g' -e 's/&/ /g' -e q`

for opt in $opts ; do
10    case $opt in
        name=*)
            name=${opt/name=/}
            ;;
        email=*)
15            email=${opt/email=/}
            ;;
        tel=*)
            tel=${opt/tel=/}
            ;;
20    esac
```

```
     done

     if psql -d template1 -H -c "\
     INSERT INTO people (name, email, tel) \
25   VALUES ('$name', '$email', '$tel')" 2>&1 | grep -q '^INSERT ' ; then
         echo "<HTML>Your details \"$name\", \"$email\" and \"$tel\"<BR>"
         echo "have been succesfully recorded.</HTML>"
     else
         echo "<HTML>Database error, please contact our webmaster.</HTML>"
30   fi

     exit 0
```

Note how the first lines of script remove all unwanted characters from QUERY_STRING. Such processing is imperative for security because shell scripts can easily execute commands should characters like $ and ` be present in a string.

To use the alternative "POST" method, change your FORM tag to

```
<FORM name="myform" action="test.cgi" method="post">
```

The POST method sends the query text through stdin of the CGI script. Hence, you need to also change your `opts=` line to

```
opts=`cat | \
      sed -e 's/[^A-Za-z0-9 %&+,.\/:=@_~-]//g' -e 's/&/ /g' -e q`
```

36.2.10   Setuid CGIs

Running Apache as a privileged user has security implications. Another way to get this script to execute as user `postgres` is to create a setuid binary. To do this, create a file `test.cgi` by compiling the following **C** program similar to that in Section 33.2.

```
#include <unistd.h>

int main (int argc, char *argv[])
{
     setreuid (geteuid (), geteuid ());
5    execl ("/opt/apache/htdocs/test/test.sh", "test.sh", 0);
     return 0;
}
```

Then run `chown postgres:www test.cgi` and `chmod a-w,o-rx,u+s test.cgi` (or `chmod 4550 test.cgi`). Recreate your shell script as `test.sh` and go to the URL again. Apache runs `test.cgi`, which becomes user `postgres`, and then executes the script as the `postgres` user. Even with Apache as `User nobody` your script will still work. Note how your setuid program is insecure: it takes no arguments and performs only a single function, but it takes environment variables (or input from stdin) that could influence its functionality. If a login user could execute the script, that user could send data via these variables that could cause the script to behave in an unforeseen way. An alternative is:

```
#include <unistd.h>

int main (int argc, char *argv[])
{
    char *envir[] = {0};
    setreuid (geteuid (), geteuid ());
    execle ("/opt/apache/htdocs/test/test.sh", "test.sh", 0, envir);
    return 0;
}
```

This script nullifies the environment before starting the CGI, thus forcing you to use the POST method only. Because the only information that can be passed to the script is a single line of text (through the `-e q` option to `sed`) and because that line of text is carefully stripped of unwanted characters, we can be much more certain of security.

36.2.11   Apache modules and PHP

CGI execution is extremely slow if Apache has to invoke a shell script for each hit. Apache has a number of facilities for built-in interpreters that will parse script files with high efficiency. A well-known programming language developed specifically for the Web is PHP. PHP can be downloaded as source from *The PHP Home Page* http://www.php.net and contains the usual GNU installation instructions.

Apache has the facility for adding functionality at runtime using what it calls DSO (*Dynamic Shared Object*) files. This feature is for distribution vendors who want to ship split installs of Apache that enable users to install only the parts of Apache they like. This is conceptually the same as what we saw in Section 23.1: To give your program some extra feature provided by some library, you can *either* statically link the library to your program *or* compile the library as a shared `.so` file to be linked at run time. The difference here is that the library files are (usually) called mod_*name* and are stored in `/opt/apache/libexec/`. They are also only loaded if a `Load-Module` *name*_module appears in `httpd.conf`. To enable DSO support, rebuild and reinstall Apache starting with:

```
./configure --prefix=/opt/apache --enable-module=so
```

Any source package that creates an Apache module can now use the Apache utility `/opt/apache/bin/apxs` to tell it about the current Apache installation, so you should make sure this executable is in your `PATH`.

You can now follow the instructions for installing PHP, possibly beginning with `./configure --prefix=/opt/php --with-apxs=/opt/apache/bin/apxs --with-pgsql=/usr`. (This assumes that you want to enable support for the `postgres` SQL database and have `postgres` previously installed as a package under `/usr`.) Finally, check that a file `libphp4.so` eventually ends up in `/opt/apache/libexec/`.

Your `httpd.conf` then needs to know about PHP scripts. Add the following lines

```
LoadModule php4_module /opt/apache/libexec/libphp4.so
AddModule mod_php4.c
AddType application/x-httpd-php .php
```

and then create a file `/opt/apache/htdocs/hello.php` containing

```
<html>
<head>
<title>Example</title>
</head>
<body>
<?php echo "Hi, I'm a PHP script!"; ?>
</body>
</html>
```

and test by visiting the URL http://localhost/hello.php.

Programming in the PHP language is beyond the scope of this book.

36.2.12   Virtual hosts

Virtual hosting is the use of a single web server to serve the web pages of multiple domains. Although the web browser seems to be connecting to a web site that is an isolated entity, that web site may in fact be hosted alongside many others on the same machine.

Virtual hosting is rather trivial to configure. Let us say that we have three domains: `www.domain1.com`, `www.domain2.com`, and `www.domain3.com`. We want domains `www.domain1.com` and `www.domain2.com` to share IP address `196.123.45.1`, while `www.domain3.com` has its own IP address of `196.123.45.2`. The sharing of a single IP address is called *name-based virtual hosting*, and the use of a different IP address for each domain is called *IP-based virtual hosting*.

If our machine has one IP address, 196.123.45.1, we may need to configure a separate IP address on the same network card as follows (see Section 25.9):

```
ifconfig eth0:1 196.123.45.2 netmask 255.255.255.0 up
```

For each domain /opt/apache/htdocs/www.domain?.com/, we now create a top-level directory. We need to tell Apache that we intend to use the IP address 196.123.45.1 for several hosts. We do that with the NameVirtualHost directive. Then for each host, we must specify a top-level directory as follows:

```
NameVirtualHost 196.123.45.1

<VirtualHost 196.123.45.1>
    ServerName www.domain1.com
    DocumentRoot /opt/apache/htdocs/www.domain1.com/
</VirtualHost>

<VirtualHost 196.123.45.1>
    ServerName www.domain2.com
    DocumentRoot /opt/apache/htdocs/www.domain2.com/
</VirtualHost>

<VirtualHost 196.123.45.2>
    ServerName www.domain3.com
    DocumentRoot /opt/apache/htdocs/www.domain3.com/
</VirtualHost>
```

All that remains is to configure a correct DNS zone for each domain so that lookups of www.domain1.com and www.domain2.com return 196.123.45.1 while lookups of www.domain3.com return 196.123.45.2.

You can then add index.html files to each directory.

Chapter 37

crond and atd

crond and atd are two very simple and important services that everyone should be familiar with. crond does the job of running commands periodically (daily, weekly), and atd's main feature is to run a command once at some future time.

These two services are so basic that we are not going to detail their package contents and invocation.

37.1 /etc/crontab Configuration File

The /etc/crontab file dictates a list of periodic jobs to be run—like updating the locate (see page 43) and whatis (see page 40) databases, rotating logs (see Section 21.4.9), and possibly performing backup tasks. If anything needs to be done periodically, you can schedule that job in this file. /etc/crontab is read by crond on startup. crond will already be running on all but the most broken of UNIX systems.

After modifying /etc/crontab, you should restart crond with /etc/rc.d/init.d/crond restart (or /etc/init.d/crond restart, or /etc/init.d/cron restart).

/etc/crontab consists of single line definitions for the time of the day/week/month at which a particular command should be run. Each line has the form,

```
<time> <user> <executable>
```

where <time> is a time pattern that the current time must match for the command to be executed, <user> tells under what user the command is to be executed, and <executable> is the command to be run.

The time pattern gives the minute, hour, day of the month, month, and weekday that the current time is compared. The comparison is done at the start of *every single minute.* If crond gets a match, it will execute the command. A simple time pattern is as follows.

```
50 13 2 9 6 root /usr/bin/play /etc/theetone.wav
```

which will play en WAV Sat Sep 2 13:50:00 every year, and

```
50 13 2 * * root /usr/bin/play /etc/theetone.wav
```

will play it at 13:50:00 on the 2nd of every month, and

```
50 13 * * 6 root /usr/bin/play /etc/theetone.wav
```

will do the same on every Saturday. Further,

```
50 13,14 * * 5,6,7 root /usr/bin/play /etc/theetone.wav
```

will play at 13:50:00 *and* at 14:50:00 on Friday, Saturday, and Sunday, while

```
*/10 * * * 6 root /usr/bin/play /etc/theetone.wav
```

will play every 10 minutes the whole of Saturday. The / is a special notation meaning "in steps of".

Note that in the above examples, the play command is executed as root.

The following is an actual /etc/crontab file:

```
   # Environment variables first
   SHELL=/bin/bash
   PATH=/sbin:/bin:/usr/sbin:/usr/bin
   MAILTO=root
5  HOME=/

   # Time specs
   30 20 * * *   root   /etc/cron-alarm.sh
   35 19 * * *   root   /etc/cron-alarm.sh
10 58 18 * * *   root   /etc/cron-alarm.sh
   01 *  * * *   root   run-parts /etc/cron.hourly
   02 4  * * *   root   run-parts /etc/cron.daily
   22 4  * * 0   root   run-parts /etc/cron.weekly
   42 4  1 * *   root   run-parts /etc/cron.monthly
```

Note that the # character is used for comments as usual. crond also allows you to specify environment variables under which commands are to be run.

Your time additions should come like mine have, to remind me of the last three Metro trains of the day.

The last four entries are vendor supplied. The `run-parts` command is a simple script to run *all* the commands listed under `/etc/cron.hourly`, `/etc/cron.daily`, etc. Hence, if you have a script that needs to be run every day but not at a specific time, you needn't edit your `crontab` file: rather just place the script with the others in `/etc/cron.<interval>`.

My own `/etc/cron.daily/` directory contains:

```
     total 14
     drwxr-xr-x    2 root       root            1024 Sep  2 13:22 .
     drwxr-xr-x   59 root       root            6144 Aug 31 13:11 ..
     -rwxr-xr-x    1 root       root             140 Aug 13 16:16 backup
   5 -rwxr-xr-x    1 root       root              51 Jun 16  1999 logrotate
     -rwxr-xr-x    1 root       root             390 Sep 14  1999 makewhatis.cron
     -rwxr-xr-x    1 root       root             459 Mar 25  1999 radiusd.cron.daily
     -rwxr-xr-x    1 root       root              99 Jul 23 23:48 slocate.cron
     -rwxr-xr-x    1 root       root             103 Sep 25  1999 tetex.cron
  10 -rwxr-xr-x    1 root       root             104 Aug 30  1999 tmpwatch
```

It is advisable to go through each of these now to see what your system is doing to itself behind your back.

37.2   The at Command

`at` will execute a command at some future time, and only once. I suppose it is essential to know, although I never used it myself until writing this chapter. `at` is the front end to the `atd` daemon which, like `crond` will almost definitely be running.

Try our wave file example, remembering to press ⌨ Ctrl - D to get the <EOT> (End Of Text):

```
     [root@cericon /etc]# at 14:19
     at> /usr/bin/play /etc/theetone.wav
     at> <EOT>
     warning: commands will be executed using /bin/sh
   5 job 3 at 2000-09-02 14:19
```

You can type `atq` to get a list of current jobs:

```
     3           2000-09-02 14:19 a
```

a means is the queue name, 3 is the job number, and `2000-09-02 14:19` is the scheduled time of execution. While `play` is executing, `atq` will display:

411

```
3          2000-09-02 14:19 =
```

The at and atd man pages contain additional information.

Note that atd should generally be disabled for security.

37.3 Other cron Packages

There are many crond implementations. Some have more flexible config files, and others have functionality cope with job schedules that run when the machine is typically switched off (like home PCs). Your distribution may have chosen one of these packages instead.

Chapter 38

postgres SQL Server

This chapter will show you how to set up an SQL server for free.

38.1 Structured Query Language

Structured Query Language (SQL) is a programming language developed specifically to access data arranged in tables of rows and columns—as in a database—as well as do searching, sorting and cross-referencing of that data.

Typically, the database tables will sit in files managed by an *SQL server* daemon process. The SQL server will listen on a TCP socket for incoming requests from client machines and will service those requests.

SQL has become a de facto industry standard. However, the protocols (over TCP/IP) by which those SQL requests are sent are different from implementation to implementation.

SQL requests can usually be typed in manually from a command-line interface. This is difficult for most users, so a GUI interface will usually hide this process from the user.

SQL servers and SQL support software is major institution. Management of database tables is actually a complicated affair. A good SQL server will properly streamline multiple simultaneous requests that may access and modify rows in the same table. Doing this efficiently, along with the many types of complex searches and cross-referencing, while also ensuring data integrity, is a complex task.

413

38.2 postgres

postgres (*PostGreSQL*) is a free SQL server written under the BSD license. postgres supports an extended subset of SQL92. ↘The definitive SQL standard.↖ It does a *lot* of very nifty things that no other database can (it seems). About the only commercial equivalent worth buying over postgres is a certain very expensive industry leader. postgres runs on every flavor of UNIX and also on Windows NT.

The postgres documentation proudly states:

> The Object-Relational Database Management System now known as PostgreSQL (and briefly called Postgres95) is derived from the Postgres package written at Berkeley. With over a decade of development behind it, PostgreSQL is the most advanced open-source database available anywhere, offering multi-version concurrency control, supporting almost all SQL constructs (including subselects, transactions, and user-defined types and functions), and having a wide range of language bindings available (including C, C++, Java, Perl, Tcl, and Python).

postgres is also fairly dry. Most people ask why it doesn't have a graphical frontend. Considering that it runs on so many different platforms, it makes sense for it to be purely a back-end engine. A graphical interface is a different kind of software project that would probably support more than one type of database server at the back and possibly run under only one kind of graphical interface.

The postgres package consists of the files described in the next two sections:

38.3 postgres Package Content

The postgres packages consists of the user programs

```
createdb        dropdb          pg_dump         psql
createlang      droplang        pg_dumpall      vacuumdb
createuser      dropuser        pg_id
```

and the server programs

```
initdb          pg_ctl          pg_upgrade      postgresql-dump
initlocation    pg_encoding     pg_version      postmaster
ipcclean        pg_passwd       postgres
```

Each of these programs has a man page which you should get an inkling of.

Further man pages provide references to actual SQL commands. Try man 1 se-lect (explained further on):

```
SELECT(1)                                          SELECT(1)


NAME
       SELECT - Retrieve rows from a table or view.

SYNOPSIS
       SELECT [ ALL | DISTINCT [ ON ( expression [, ...] ) ] ]
           expression [ AS name ] [, ...]
           [ INTO [ TEMPORARY | TEMP ] [ TABLE ] new_table ]
           [ FROM table [ alias ] [, ...] ]
           [ WHERE condition ]
           [ GROUP BY column [, ...] ]
           [ HAVING condition [, ...] ]
           [ { UNION [ ALL ] | INTERSECT | EXCEPT } select ]
           [ ORDER BY column [ ASC | DESC | USING operator ] [, ...] ]
           [ FOR UPDATE [ OF class_name [, ...] ] ]
           LIMIT { count | ALL } [ { OFFSET | , } start ]
```

Most important is the enormous amount of HTML documentation that comes with `postgres`. Point your web browser to `/usr/doc/postgresql-?.?.?` (or `/usr/share/doc/...`), then dive into the `admin`, `user`, `programmer`, `tutorial`, and `postgres` directories.

Finally, there are the start and stop scripts in `/etc/rc.d/init.d/` (or `/etc/init.d/`) and the directory in which the database tables themselves are stored: `/var/lib/pgsql/`.

38.4   Installing and Initializing **postgres**

`postgres` can be gotten prepackaged for your favorite distribution. Simply install the package using `rpm` or `dpkg` and then follow the instructions given below.

Stop the `postgres` server if it is running; the `init.d` script may be called `postgres` or `postgresql` (Debian⊙ commands in parentheses):

```
/etc/rc.d/init.d/postgres stop
( /etc/init.d/postgresql stop )
```

Edit the `init.d` script to support TCP requests. There will be a line like the following to which you can add the `-i` option. Mine looks like:

```
su -l postgres -c "/usr/bin/pg_ctl -D $PGDATA \
```

```
        -p /usr/bin/postmaster -o '-i -o -e' start >/dev/null 2>&1"
```

which also (with the −o −e option) forces European date formats (28/4/1984 instead of 4/28/1984). Note that hosts will not be able to connect unless you edit your `/var/lib/pgsql/data/pg_hba.conf` (`/etc/postgresql/pg_hba.conf` on Debian(⊘) file, and add lines like

```
host     mydatabase    192.168.4.7    255.255.255.255     trust
```

In either case, you should check this file to ensure that only trusted hosts can connect to your database, or remove the −i option altogether if you are only connecting from the local machine. To a limited extent, you can also limit what users can connect within this file.

It would be nice if the UNIX domain socket that `postgres` listens on (i.e., `/tmp/.s.PGSQL.5432`) had permissions 0770 instead of 0777. That way, you could limit connections to only those users belonging to the `postgres` group. You can add this feature by searching for the **C** chmod command within `src/backend/libpq/pqcomm.c` inside the `postgres-7.0` sources. Later versions may have added a feature to set the permissions on this socket.

To run `postgres`, you need a user of that name. If you do not already have one then enter

```
/usr/sbin/useradd postgres
```

and restart the server with

```
/etc/rc.d/init.d/postgresql restart
```

The `postgres init.d` script initializes a template database on first run, so you may have to start it twice.

Now you can create your own database. The following example creates a database `finance` as well as a `postgres` user `finance`. It does these creations while being user `postgres` (this is what the −U option is for). You should run these commands as user `root` or as user `postgres` without the −U postgres.

```
[root@cericon]# /usr/sbin/useradd finance
[root@cericon]# createuser -U postgres --adduser --createdb finance
CREATE USER
[root@cericon]# createdb -U finance finance
CREATE DATABASE
[root@cericon]#
```

38.5 Database Queries with `psql`

Now that the database exists, you can begin running SQL queries.

```
[root@cericon]# psql -U finance
Welcome to psql, the PostgreSQL interactive terminal.

Type:  \copyright for distribution terms
       \h for help with SQL commands
       \? for help on internal slash commands
       \g or terminate with semicolon to execute query
       \q to quit

finance=# select * from pg_tables;
     tablename    | tableowner | hasindexes | hasrules | hastriggers
 -----------------+------------+------------+----------+-------------
  pg_type         | postgres   | t          | f        | f
  pg_attribute    | postgres   | t          | f        | f
  pg_proc         | postgres   | t          | f        | f
  pg_class        | postgres   | t          | f        | f
  pg_group        | postgres   | t          | f        | f
  pg_database     | postgres   | f          | f        | f
  pg_variable     | postgres   | f          | f        | f
  pg_log          | postgres   | f          | f        | f
  pg_xactlock     | postgres   | f          | f        | f
  pg_attrdef      | postgres   | t          | f        | f
  pg_relcheck     | postgres   | t          | f        | f
  pg_trigger      | postgres   | t          | f        | f
  pg_inherits     | postgres   | t          | f        | f
  pg_index        | postgres   | t          | f        | f
  pg_statistic    | postgres   | t          | f        | f
  pg_operator     | postgres   | t          | f        | f
  pg_opclass      | postgres   | t          | f        | f
  pg_am           | postgres   | t          | f        | f
  pg_amop         | postgres   | t          | f        | f
  pg_amproc       | postgres   | f          | f        | f
  pg_language     | postgres   | t          | f        | f
  pg_aggregate    | postgres   | t          | f        | f
  pg_ipl          | postgres   | f          | f        | f
  pg_inheritproc  | postgres   | f          | f        | f
  pg_rewrite      | postgres   | t          | f        | f
  pg_listener     | postgres   | t          | f        | f
  pg_description  | postgres   | t          | f        | f
  pg_shadow       | postgres   | f          | f        | t
 (28 rows)
```

The preceeding rows are `postgres`'s internal tables. Some are actual tables, and some are *views* of tables. ↘A selective representation of an actual table.↖

To get a list of databases, try:

```
finance=# select * from pg_database;
```

417

```
    datname  | datdba | encoding |  datpath
   ----------+--------+----------+-----------
    template1 |    24 |        0 | template1
5   finance   |    26 |        0 | finance
   (2 rows)
```

38.6　Introduction to SQL

The following are 99% of the commands you are ever going to use. (Note that all SQL commands require a semicolon at the end—you won't be the first person to ask why nothing happens when you press ⏎ without the semicolon.)

38.6.1　Creating tables

To create a table called `people`, with three columns:

```
CREATE TABLE people ( name text, gender bool, address text );
```

The created table will title the columns, `name`, `gender`, and `address`. Columns are *typed*. This means that only the kind of data that was specified at the time of creation can go in that column. In the case of `gender`, it can only be *true* or *false* for the `boolean` type, which we will associate to the male and female genders. There is probably no reason to use the boolean value here: using an integer or text field can often be far more descriptive and flexible. In the case of `name` and `address`, these can hold anything, since they are of the `text` type, which is the most encompassing type of all.

　　Note that in the `postgres` documentation, a "column" is called an "attribute" for historical reasons.

　　You should try to choose types according to the kind of *searches* you are going to do and *not* according to the data it holds. Table 38.1 lists the most of the useful types as well as their SQL92 equivalents. The types in bold are to be used in preference to other similar types for greater range or precision:

Table 38.1　Common `postgres` types

Postgres Type	SQL92 or SQL3 Type	Description
bool	boolean	logical boolean (true/false)
box		rectangular box in 2D plane
char(n)	character(n)	fixed-length character string
cidr		IP version 4 network or host address

continues...

418

Table 38.1 (continued)

Postgres Type	SQL92 or SQL3 Type	Description
circle		circle in 2D plane
date	date	calendar date without time of day
decimal	decimal(p,s)	exact numeric for p ¡= 9, s = 0
float4	float(p), p ¡ 7	floating-point number with precision p
float8	float(p), 7 ¡= p ¡ 16	floating-point number with precision p
inet		IP version 4 network or host address
int2	smallint	signed 2-byte integer
int4	int, integer	signed 4-byte integer
int8		signed 8-byte integer
interval	interval	general-use time span
line		infinite line in 2D plane
lseg		line segment in 2D plane
money	decimal(9,2)	U.S.-style currency
numeric	numeric(p,s)	exact numeric for p == 9, s = 0
path		open and closed geometric path in 2D plane
point		geometric point in 2D plane
polygon		closed geometric path in 2D plane
serial		unique ID for indexing and cross-reference
time	time	time of day
text		arbitrary length text (up to 8k for postgres 7)
timetz	time with time zone	time of day, including time zone
timestamp	timestamp with time zone	accurate high range, high precision date/time with zone
varchar(n)	character varying(n)	variable-length character string

38.6.2 Listing a table

The SELECT statement is the most widely used statement in SQL. It returns data from tables and can do searches:

```
finance=# SELECT * FROM PEOPLE;
 name | gender | address
------+--------+---------
(0 rows)
```

38.6.3 Adding a column

The `ALTER` statement changes something:

```
finance=# ALTER TABLE people ADD COLUMN phone text;
ALTER
finance=# SELECT * FROM people;
 name | gender | address | phone
------+--------+---------+-------
(0 rows)
```

38.6.4 Deleting (dropping) a column

You cannot drop columns in `postgres`; you must create a new table from the old table without the column. How to do this will become obvious further on.

38.6.5 Deleting (dropping) a table

Use the `DROP` command to delete most things:

```
DROP TABLE people;
```

38.6.6 Inserting rows, "object relational"

Insert a row with (you can continue typing over multiple lines):

```
finance=# INSERT INTO people (name, gender, address, phone)
finance-# VALUES ('Paul Sheer', true, 'Earth', '7617224');
INSERT 20280 1
```

The return value is the `oid` (*Object ID*) of the row. `postgres` is an *Object Relational* database. This term gets thrown around a lot, but it really means that every table has a hidden column called the `oid` column that stores a unique identity number for each row. The identity number is unique across the entire database. Because it uniquely identifies rows across all tables, you could call the rows "objects." The `oid` feature is most useful to programmers.

38.6.7 Locating rows

The `oid` of the above row is `20280`. To find it:

```
finance=# SELECT * FROM people WHERE oid = 20280;
    name     | gender | address |  phone
------------+--------+---------+---------
 Paul Sheer | true   | Earth   | 7617224
(1 row)
```

38.6.8 Listing selected columns, and the `oid` column

To list selected columns, try:

```
SELECT name, address FROM people;
SELECT oid, name FROM people;
SELECT oid, * FROM people;
```

It should be obvious what these do.

38.6.9 Creating tables from other tables

Here we create a new table and fill two of its columns from columns in our original table:

```
finance=# CREATE TABLE sitings (person text, place text, siting text);
CREATE
finance=# INSERT INTO sitings (person, place) SELECT name, address FROM people;
INSERT 20324 1
```

38.6.10 Deleting rows

Delete selected rows, like

```
finance=# DELETE FROM people WHERE name = 'Paul Sheer';
DELETE 1
```

38.6.11 Searches

About the simplest search you can do with `postgres` is

```
SELECT * FROM people WHERE name LIKE '%Paul%';
```

Or alternatively, case insensitively and across the `address` field:

```
SELECT * FROM people WHERE lower(name) LIKE '%paul%' OR lower(address) LIKE '%paul%';
```

The first `%` is a wildcard that matches any length of text before the `Paul`, and the final `%` matches any text after. It is the usual way of searching with a field, instead of trying to get an exact match.

The possibilities are endless:

```
SELECT * FROM people WHERE gender = true AND phone = '8765432';
```

38.6.12 Migrating from another database; dumping and restoring tables as plain text

Migrating from another database;
dumping and restoring tables as plain text

The command

```
COPY people TO '/tmp/people.txt';
```

dumps the `people` table to `/tmp/people.txt`, as tab delimeter, newline terminated rows.

The command,

```
COPY people WITH OIDS TO '/tmp/people.txt' DELIMITERS ',' WITH NULL AS '(null)';
```

dumps the `people` table to `/tmp/people.txt`, as comma-delimited, newline-terminated rows, with (`null`) whereever there is supposed to be a zero byte.

Similarly, the command

```
COPY people FROM '/tmp/people.txt';
```

inserts into the table `people` the rows from `/tmp/people.txt`. It assumes one line per row and the tab character between each cell.

Note that unprintable characters are escaped with a backslash \ in both output and the interpretation of input.

Hence, it is simple to get data from another database. You just have to work out how to dump it as text.

38.6.13   Dumping an entire database

The command `pg_dump <database-name>` dumps your entire database as plain text. If you try this on your database, you will notice that the output contains straightforward SQL commands. Your database can be reconstructed from scratch by piping this output through stdin of the `psql` command. In other words, `pg_dump` merely produces the exact sequence of SQL commands necessary to reproduce your database.

Sometimes a new version of `postgres` will switch to a database file format that is incompatible with your previous files. In this case it is prudent to do a `pg_dumpall` (and carefully save the output) before upgrading. The output of `pg_dumpall` can once again be fed through stdin of the `psql` command and contains all the commands necessary to reconstruct all your databases as well as all the data they contain.

38.6.14   More advanced searches

When you have some very complicated set of tables in front of you, you are likely to want to merge, select, search, and cross-reference them in innumerable ways to get the information you want out of them.

Being able to efficiently query the database in this way is the true power of SQL, but this is about as far as I am going to go here. The `postgres` documentation cited above contains details on everything you can do.

38.7   Real Database Projects

University Computer Science majors learn about subjects like *Entity Modeling, Relational Algebra,* and *Database Normalization*. These are formal academic methods according to which good databases are designed. You should not venture into constructing any complex database without these methods.

Most university book shops will have academic books that teach formal database theory.

Chapter 39

smbd — Samba NT Server

The following introduction is quoted from the Samba online documentation.

39.1   Samba: An Introduction by Christopher R. Hertel

A lot of emphasis has been placed on peaceful coexistence between UNIX and Windows. Unfortunately, the two systems come from very different cultures and they have difficulty getting along without mediation. ... and that, of course, is Samba's job. *Samba* http://samba.org/ runs on UNIX platforms, but speaks to Windows clients like a native. It allows a UNIX system to move into a Windows "Network Neighborhood" without causing a stir. Windows users can happily access file and print services without knowing or caring that those services are being offered by a UNIX host.

All of this is managed through a protocol suite which is currently known as the "Common Internet File System," or *CIFS* http://www.cifs.com. This name was introduced by Microsoft, and provides some insight into their hopes for the future. At the heart of CIFS is the latest incarnation of the Server Message Block (SMB) protocol, which has a long and tedious history. Samba is an open source CIFS implementation, and is available for free from the http://samba.org/ mirror sites.

Samba and Windows are not the only ones to provide CIFS networking. OS/2 supports SMB file and print sharing, and there are commercial CIFS products for Macintosh and other platforms (including several others for UNIX). Samba has been ported to a variety of non-UNIX operating systems, including VMS, AmigaOS, and NetWare. CIFS is also supported on dedicated file server platforms from a variety of vendors. In other words, this stuff is all over the place.

History — the (hopefully) Untedious Version

It started a long time ago, in the early days of the PC, when IBM and Sytec co-developed a simple networking system designed for building small LANs. The system included something called

NetBIOS, or *Network Basic Input Output System.* NetBIOS was a chunk of software that was loaded into memory to provide an interface between programs and the network hardware. It included an addressing scheme that used 16-byte names to identify workstations and network-enabled applications. Next, Microsoft added features to DOS that allowed disk I/O to be *redirected* to the NetBIOS interface, which made disk space sharable over the LAN. The file-sharing protocol that they used eventually became known as SMB, and now CIFS.

Lots of other software was also written to use the NetBIOS API (*Application Programmer's Interface*), which meant that it would never, ever, ever go away. Instead, the workings beneath the API were cleverly gutted and replaced. NetBEUI (*NetBIOS Enhanced User Interface*), introduced by IBM, provided a mechanism for passing NetBIOS packets over Token Ring and Ethernet. Others developed NetBIOS LAN emulation over higher-level protocols including DECnet, IPX/SPX and, of course, TCP/IP.

NetBIOS and TCP/IP made an interesting team. The latter could be routed between interconnected networks (internetworks), but NetBIOS was designed for isolated LANs. The trick was to map the 16-byte NetBIOS names to IP addresses so that messages could actually find their way through a routed IP network. A mechanism for doing just that was described in the Internet RFC1001 and RFC1002 documents. As Windows evolved, Microsoft added two additional pieces to the SMB package. These were service announcement, which is called "browsing," and a central authentication and authorization service known as Windows NT Domain Control.

Meanwhile, on the Other Side of the Planet...

Andrew Tridgell, who is both tall and Australian, had a bit of a problem. He needed to mount disk space from a UNIX server on his DOS PC. Actually, this wasn't the problem at all because he had an NFS (*Network File System*) client for DOS and it worked just fine. Unfortunately, he also had an application that required the NetBIOS interface. Anyone who has ever tried to run multiple protocols under DOS knows that it can be...er...quirky.

So Andrew chose the obvious solution. He wrote a packet sniffer, reverse engineered the SMB protocol, and implemented it on the UNIX box. Thus, he made the UNIX system appear to be a PC file server, which allowed him to mount shared filesystems from the UNIX server while concurrently running NetBIOS applications. Andrew published his code in early 1992. There was a quick, but short succession of bug-fix releases, and then he put the project aside. Occasionally he would get email about it, but he otherwise ignored it. Then one day, almost two years later, he decided to link his wife's Windows PC with his own Linux system. Lacking any better options, he used his own server code. He was actually surprised when it worked.

Through his email contacts, Andrew discovered that NetBIOS and SMB were actually (though nominally) documented. With this new information at his fingertips he set to work again, but soon ran into another problem. He was contacted by a company claiming trademark on the name that he had chosen for his server software. Rather than cause a fuss, Andrew did a quick scan against a spell-checker dictionary, looking for words containing the letters "smb". "Samba" was in the list. Curiously, that same word is not in the dictionary file that he uses today. (Perhaps they know it's been taken.)

The Samba project has grown mightily since then. Andrew now has a whole team of programmers, scattered around the world, to help with Samba development. When a new release is announced, thousands of copies are downloaded within days. Commercial systems vendors, including Silicon Graphics, bundle Samba with their products. There are even Samba T-shirts available. Perhaps one of the best measures of the success of Samba is that it was listed in the "Halloween Documents", a pair of internal Microsoft memos that were leaked to the Open Source community. These memos list Open Source products which Microsoft considers to be competitive threats. The absolutely best measure of success, though, is that Andrew can still share the printer with his wife.

What Samba Does

Samba consists of two key programs, plus a bunch of other stuff that we'll get to later. The two key programs are smbd and nmbd. Their job is to implement the four basic modern-day CIFS services, which are:

- File and print services
- Authentication and Authorization
- Name resolution
- Service announcement (browsing)

File and print services are, of course, the cornerstone of the CIFS suite. These are provided by smbd, the SMB daemon. Smbd also handles "share mode" and "user mode" authentication and authorization. That is, you can protect shared file and print services by requiring passwords. In share mode, the simplest and least recommended scheme, a password can be assigned to a shared directory or printer (simply called a "share"). This single password is then given to everyone who is allowed to use the share. With user mode authentication, each user has their own username and password and the System Administrator can grant or deny access on an individual basis.

The Windows NT Domain system provides a further level of authentication refinement for CIFS. The basic idea is that a user should only have to log in once to have access to all of the authorized services on the network. The NT Domain system handles this with an authentication server, called a Domain Controller. An NT Domain (which should *not* be confused with a *Domain Name System* (DNS) Domain) is basically a group of machines which share the same Domain Controller.

The NT Domain system deserves special mention because, until the release of Samba version 2, only Microsoft owned code to implement the NT Domain authentication protocols. With version 2, Samba introduced the first non-Microsoft-derived NT Domain authentication code. The eventual goal, of course, it to completely mimic a Windows NT Domain Controller.

The other two CIFS pieces, name resolution and browsing, are handled by nmbd. These two services basically involve the management and distribution of lists of NetBIOS names.

Name resolution takes two forms: broadcast and point-to-point. A machine may use either or both of these methods, depending upon its configuration. Broadcast resolution is the closest to the original NetBIOS mechanism. Basically, a client looking for a service named Trillian will call out ``Yo! Trillian! Where are you?'', and wait for the machine with that name to answer with an IP address. This can generate a bit of broadcast traffic (a lot of shouting in the streets), but it is restricted to the local LAN so it doesn't cause too much trouble.

The other type of name resolution involves the use of an NBNS (*NetBIOS Name Service*) server. (Microsoft called their NBNS implementation WINS, for Windows Internet Name Service, and that acronym is more commonly used today.) The NBNS works something like the wall of an old-fashioned telephone booth. (Remember those?) Machines can leave their name and number (IP address) for others to see.

```
Hi, I'm node Voomba.  Call me for a good time!  192.168.100.101
```

It works like this: The clients send their NetBIOS names and IP addresses to the NBNS server, which keeps the information in a simple database. When a client wants to talk to another client, it sends the other client's name to the NBNS server. If the name is on the list, the NBNS hands back an IP address. You've got the name, look up the number.

Clients on different subnets can all share the same NBNS server so, unlike broadcast, the point-to-point mechanism is not limited to the local LAN. In many ways the NBNS is similar to the DNS, but the NBNS name list is almost completely dynamic and there are few controls to ensure that only authorized clients can register names. Conflicts can, and do, occur fairly easily.

Finally, there's browsing. This is a whole 'nother kettle of worms, but Samba's nmbd handles it anyway. This is not the web browsing we know and love, but a browsable list of services (file and print shares) offered by the computers on a network.

On a LAN, the participating computers hold an election to decide which of them will become the Local Master Browser (LMB). The "winner" then identifies itself by claiming a special NetBIOS name (in addition to any other names it may have). The LMB's job is to keep a list of available services, and it is this list that appears when you click on the Windows "Network Neighborhood" icon.

In addition to LMBs, there are *Domain* Master Browsers (DMBs). DMBs coordinate browse lists across NT Domains, even on routed networks. Using the NBNS, an LMB will locate its DMB to exchange and combine browse lists. Thus, the browse list is propagated to all hosts in the NT Domain. Unfortunately, the synchronization times are spread apart a bit. It can take more than an hour for a change on a remote subnet to appear in the Network Neighborhood.

Other Stuff

Samba comes with a variety of utilities. The most commonly used are:

smbclient A simple SMB client, with an interface similar to that of the FTP utility. It can be used from a UNIX system to connect to a remote SMB share, transfer files, and send files to remote print shares (printers).

nmblookup A NetBIOS name service client. Nmblookup can be used to find NetBIOS names on a network, look up their IP addresses, and query a remote machine for the list of names the machine believes it owns.

swat The *Samba Web Administration Tool*. Swat allows you to configure Samba remotely, using a web browser.

There are more, of course, but describing them would require explaining even more bits and pieces of CIFS, SMB, and Samba. That's where things really get tedious, so we'll leave it alone for now.

SMB Filesystems for Linux

One of the cool things that you can do with a Windows box is use an SMB file share as if it were a hard disk on your own machine. The `N:` drive can look, smell, feel, and act like your own disk space, but it's really disk space on some other computer somewhere else on the network.

Linux systems can do this too, using the `smbfs` filesystem. Built from Samba code, `smbfs` (which stands for *SMB Filesystem*) allows Linux to map a remote SMB share into its directory structure. So, for example, the `/mnt/zarquon` directory might actually be an SMB share, yet you can read, write, edit, delete, and copy the files in that directory just as you would local files.

The `smbfs` is nifty, but it only works with Linux. In fact, it's not even part of the Samba suite. It is distributed with Samba as a courtesy and convenience. A more general solution is the new `smbsh` (*SMB shell*, which is still under development at the time of this writing). This is a cool gadget. It is run like a UNIX shell, but it does some funky fiddling with calls to UNIX libraries. By intercepting these calls, `smbsh` can make it look as though SMB shares are mounted. All of the read, write, etc. operations are available to the `smbsh` user. Another feature of `smbsh` is that it works on a per user, per shell basis, while mounting a filesystem is a system-wide operation. This allows for much finer-grained access controls.

Setup and Management

Samba is configured using the `smb.conf` file. This is a simple text file designed to look a lot like those *.ini files used in Windows. The goal, of course, is to give network administrators familiar with Windows something comfortable to play with. Over time, though, the number of things that can be configured in Samba has grown, and the percentage of Network Admins willing to edit a Windows *.ini file has shrunk. For some people, that makes managing the `smb.conf` file a bit daunting.

Still, learning the ins and outs of `smb.conf` is a worthwhile penance. Each of the `smb.conf` variables has a purpose, and a lot of fine-tuning can be accomplished. The file structure contents are fully documented, so as to give administrators a running head start, and `smb.conf` can be manipulated using `swat`, which at least makes it nicer to look at.

The Present

Samba 2.0 was released in January 1999. One of the most significant and cool features of the 2.0 release was improved speed. Ziff-Davis Publishing used their Netbench software to benchmark Samba 2.0 on Linux against Windows NT4. They ran all of their tests on the same PC hardware, and their results showed Samba's throughput under load to be at least twice that of NT. Samba is shipped with all major Linux distributions, and Ziff-Davis tested three of those.

Another milestone was reached when Silicon Graphics (SGI) became the first commercial UNIX vendor to support Samba. In their December 1998 press release, they claimed that their Origin series servers running Samba 2.0 were the most powerful line of file servers for Windows clients available. SGI now offers commercial support for Samba as do several other providers, many of which are listed on the Samba web site (see http://samba.org/). Traditional

Internet support is, of course, still available via the `comp.protocols.smb` newsgroup and the `samba@samba.org` mailing list.

The Samba Team continues to work on new goodies. Current interests include NT ACLs (*Access Control Lists*), support for LDAP (the Lightweight Directory Access Protocol), NT Domain Control, and Microsoft's DFS (*Distributed File System*).

The Future

Windows 2000 looms on the horizon like a lazy animal peeking its head over the edge of its burrow while trying to decide whether or not to come out. No one is exactly sure about the kind of animal it will be when it does appear, but folks are fairly certain that it will have teeth.

Because of their dominance on the desktop, Microsoft gets to decide how CIFS will grow. Windows 2000, like previous major operating system releases, will give us a whole new critter to study. Based on the beta copies and the things that Microsoft has said, here are some things to watch for:

CIFS Without NetBIOS Microsoft will attempt to decouple CIFS and NetBIOS. NetBIOS won't go away, mind you, but it won't be *required* for CIFS networking either. Instead, the SMB protocol will be carried natively over TCP/IP. Name lookups will occur via the DNS.

Dynamic DNS Microsoft will implement Dynamic DNS, a still-evolving system designed by the IETF (*Internet Engineering Task Force*). Dynamic DNS allows names to be added to a DNS server on-the-fly.

Kerberos V Microsoft has plans to use Kerberos V. The Microsoft K5 tickets are supposed to contain a Privilege Attribute Certificate *(PAC)* http://www.usenix.org/publications/login/1997-11/embraces.html, which will include user and group ID information from the Active Directory. Servers will be looking for this PAC when they grant access to the services that they provide. Thus, Kerberos may be used for both authentication and authorization.

Active Directory The Active Directory appears to be at the heart of Windows 2000 networking. It is likely that legacy NetBIOS services will register their names in the Active Directory.

Hierarchical NT Domains Instead of isolated Domain Controllers, the NT Domain system will become hierarchical. The naming system will change to one that is remarkably similar to that of the DNS.

One certainty is that W2K (as it is often called) is, and will be, under close scrutiny. Windows has already attracted the attention of some of the Internet Wonderland's more curious inhabitants, including security analysts, standards groups, crackers dens, and general all-purpose geeks. The business world, which has finally gotten a taste of the freedom of Open Source Software, may be reluctant to return to the world of proprietary, single-vendor solutions. Having the code in your hands is both reassuring and empowering.

Whatever the next Windows animal looks like, it will be Samba's job to help it get along with its peers in the diverse world of the Internet. The Samba Team, a microcosm of the Internet community, are among those watching W2K to see how it develops. Watching does not go hand-in-hand with waiting, though, and Samba is an on-going and open effort. Visit the Samba web site, join the mailing lists, and see what's going on.

Participate in the future.

39.2 Configuring Samba

That said, configuring `smbd` is really easy. A typical LAN will require a UNIX machine that can share `/home/*` directories to Windows clients, where each user can log in as the name of their home directory. It must also act as a print share that redirects print jobs through `lpr`; and then in PostScript, the way we like it. Consider a Windows machine `divinian.cranzgot.co.za` on a local LAN `192.168.3.0/24`. The user of that machine would have a UNIX login `psheer` on the server `cericon.cranzgot.co.za`.

The usual place for Samba's configuration file is `/etc/samba/smb.conf` on most distributions. A minimalist configuration file to perform the above functions might be:

```
     [global]
        workgroup = MYGROUP
        server string = Samba Server
        hosts allow = 192.168. 127.
  5     printcap name = /etc/printcap
        load printers = yes
        printing = bsd
        log file = /var/log/samba/%m.log
        max log size = 0
 10     security = user
        socket options = TCP_NODELAY SO_RCVBUF=8192 SO_SNDBUF=8192
        encrypt passwords = yes
        smb passwd file = /etc/samba/smbpasswd
     [homes]
 15     comment = Home Directories
        browseable = no
        writable = yes
     [printers]
        comment = All Printers
 20     path = /var/spool/samba
        browseable = no
        guest ok = no
        printable = yes
```

The SMB protocol stores passwords differently from UNIX. It therefore needs its own password file, usually `/etc/samba/smbpasswd`. There is also a mapping between UNIX logins and Samba logins in `/etc/samba/smbusers`, but for simplicity we will use the same UNIX name as the Samba login name. We can add a new UNIX user and Samba user and set both their passwords with

```
smbadduser psheer:psheer
useradd psheer
smbpasswd psheer
passwd psheer
```

Note that with SMB there are all sorts of issues with case interpretation—an incorrectly typed password could still work with Samba but obviously won't with UNIX.

To start Samba, run the familiar

```
/etc/init.d/smbd start
( /etc/rc.d/init.d/smbd start )
( /etc/init.d/samba start )
```

For good measure, there should also be a proper DNS configuration with forward and reverse lookups for all client machines.

At this point you can test your Samba server from the UNIX side. LINUX has native support for SMB shares with the `smbfs` file system. Try mounting a share served by the local machine:

```
mkdir -p /mnt/smb
mount -t smbfs -o username=psheer,password=12345 //cericon/psheer /mnt/smb
```

You can now run `tail -f /var/log/samba/cericon.log`. It should contain messages like:

```
cericon (192.168.3.2) connect to service psheer as user psheer (uid=500, gid=500) (pid 942)
```

where a "service" means either a directory share or a print share.

The useful utility `smbclient` is a generic tool for running SMB requests, but is mostly useful for printing. Make sure your printer daemon is running (and working) and then try

```
echo hello | smbclient //cericon/lp 12345 -U psheer -c 'print -'
```

which will create a small entry in the `lp` print queue. Your log file will be appended with:

```
cericon (192.168.3.2) connect to service lp as user psheer (uid=500, gid=500) (pid 1014)
```

39.3   Configuring Windows

Configuration from Windows begins with a working TCP/IP configuration:

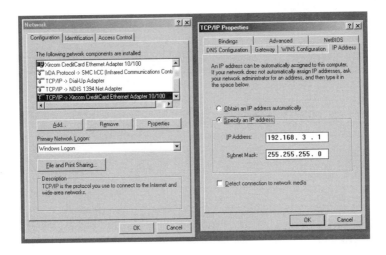

Next, you need to **Log Off** from the **Start** menu and log back in as your Samba user.

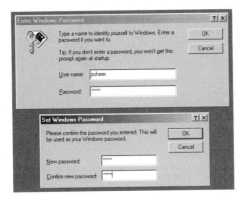

Finally, go to **Run...** in the **Start** menu and enter \\cericon\psheer. You will be prompted for a password, which you should enter as for the smbpasswd program above.

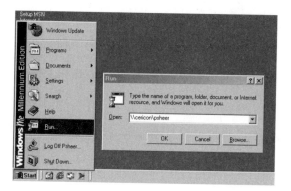

This should bring up your home directory like you have probably never seen it before.

39.4　Configuring a Windows Printer

Under **Settings** in your **Start** menu, you can add new printers. Your UNIX lp print queue is visible as the \\cericon\lp network printer and should be entered as such in the configuration wizard. For a printer driver, you should choose "Apple Color Laserwriter," since this driver just produces regular PostScript output. In the printer driver options you should also select to optimize for "portability."

39.5　Configuring swat

swat is a service, run from inetd, that listens for HTTP connections on port 901. It allows complete remote management of Samba from a web browser. To configure, add the service swat　901/tcp to your /etc/services file, and the following to your /etc/inetd.conf file.

```
swat stream tcp nowait root /usr/sbin/tcpd /usr/sbin/swat
```

being *very careful who you allow connections from*. If you are running xinetd, create a file /etc/xinetd.d/swat:

```
   service swat
   {
       port            = 901
       socket_type     = stream
 5     wait            = no
       only_from       = localhost 192.168.0.0/16
       user            = root
       server          = /usr/sbin/swat
       server_args     = -s /etc/samba/smb.conf
10     log_on_failure  += USERID
```

```
    disable = no
}
```

After restarting `inetd` (or `xinetd`), you can point your web browser to http://cericon:901/. Netscape will request a user and password. You should login as `root` (`swat` does not use `smbpasswd` to authenticate this login). The web page interface is extremely easy to use—

Welcome to SWAT!

—and, being written by the Samba developers themselves, can be trusted to produce working configurations. The web page also gives a convenient interface to all the documentation. Do note that it will completely overwrite your existing configuration file.

39.6   Windows NT Caveats

Windows SMB servers compete to be the name server of their domain by version number and uptime. By this we again mean the Windows name service and not the DNS service. How exactly this works I will not cover here, ⤵Probably because I have no idea what I am talking about.⤴ but do be aware that configuring a Samba server on a network of many NT machines and getting it to work can be a nightmare. A solution once attempted was to shut down all machines on the LAN, then pick one as the domain server, then bring it up first after waiting an hour for all possible timeouts to have elapsed. After verifying that it was working properly, the rest of the machines were booted.

Then of course, don't forget your `nmblookup` command.

Chapter 40

named — Domain Name Server

In Chapter 27 we dealt with the "client" side of DNS. In this chapter we configure the name server that services such requests.

There seems to be a lot of hype that elevates the name server to something mystical and illusive. In fact, setting up a name server is a standard and trivial exercise. A name server daemon is also no heavyweight service: The `named` executable is 500 KB and consumes little CPU.

The package that the name server comes in is called `bind`. This chapter assumes a `bind` of approximately `bind-8.2` or later. `bind` stands for *Berkeley Internet Name Domain*.

The difficulty with setting up a name server is that the configuration files are impossible to construct from the specification without some kind of typing error being made. The solution is quite simple: *Never* create a name server config file from scratch. *Always* copy one from an existing working name server. Here we give more example configuration files than explanation. You can copy these examples to create your own name server.

Please note before running `bind` that it has security vulnerabilities. Hence, it may be possible for someone to hack your machine if you are running an old version. Many people are also skeptical about even the latest versions of `bind` (9.1 at the time of writing) even though no security holes had been announced for this version. An alternative is `djbdns`, which is purported to be the ultimate DNS server.

Before you even start working on name server configuration, you should start a new terminal window with the command (Debian alternative in parentheses):

```
tail -f /var/log/messages
( tail -f /var/log/syslog )
```

Keep this window throughout the entire setup and testing procedure. From now on, when I refer to *messages*, I am referring to a message in this window.

40.1   Documentation

The man pages for `named` are `hostname`(7), `named-xfer`(8), `named`(8), and `ndc`(8). These pages reference a document called the "Name Server Operations Guide for BIND." What they actually mean is the PostScript file `/usr/[share/]doc/bind-<version>/bog/file.psf` (or `/usr/share/doc/bind/bog.ps`).

The problem with some of this documentation is that it is still based on the old (now deprecated) `named.boot` configuration file. There is a script `/usr/doc/bind-<version>/named-bootconf/named-bootconf` (or `/usr/sbin/named-bootconf`) that reads a `named.boot` file from stdin and writes a `named.conf` file to stdout. I found it useful to `echo "old config line" | named-bootconf` to see what a new style equivalent would be.

The directory `/usr/[share/]doc/bind[-<version>]/html/` contains the most important general information. It is a complete reference to `bind` configuration. Parallel directories also contain FAQ documents and various theses on security. A file `style.txt` contains the recommended layout of the configuration files for consistent spacing and readability. Finally an `rfc/` directory contains the relevant RFCs (see Section 13.6).

40.2   Configuring `bind`

There is only one main configuration file for `named`: `/etc/named.conf` (or `/etc/bind/named.conf` on Debian⊘—here we assume a `/etc/named.conf` file for simplicity). The `named` service once used a file `/etc/named.boot`, but this has been scrapped. If there is a `named.boot` file in your `/etc` directory, then it is not being used, except possibly by a very old version of `bind`.

Here we will show example configurations necessary for typical scenarios of a name server.

40.2.1   Example configuration

The `named.conf` file will have in it the line `directory "/var/named";` (or `directory "/etc/named";` or `directory "/var/cache/bind";`). This directory holds various files containing textual lists of the name to IP address mappings that `bind` will serve. The following example is a name server for a company that has been given a range of IP addresses 196.28.144.16/29 (i.e., 196.28.144.16–23), as well as one single IP address (160.123.181.44). This example also must support a range of internal IP addresses (192.168.2.0–255) The trick is not to think about how everything works. If you just copy and edit things in a consistent fashion, carefully reading the comments, bind will work fine. I will now list all necessary files.

• *Local client configuration:* **/etc/resolv.conf**

```
domain localdomain
nameserver 127.0.0.1
```

• *Top-level config file:* **/etc/named.conf**

```
/*
 * The ''directory'' line tells named that any further file name's
 * given are under the /var/named/ directory.
 */
5  options {
        directory "/var/named";
        /*
         * If there is a firewall between you and nameservers you want
         * to talk to, you might need to uncomment the query-source
10       * directive below.  Previous versions of BIND always asked
         * questions using port 53, but BIND 8.1 uses an unprivileged
         * port by default.
         */
        // query-source address * port 53;
15 };

   /* The list of root servers: */
   zone "." {
        type hint;
20      file "named.ca";
   };

   /* Forward lookups of the localhost: */
   zone "localdomain" {
25      type master;
        file "named.localdomain";
   };

   /* Reverse lookups of the localhost: */
30 zone "1.0.0.127.in-addr.arpa" {
        type master;
        file "named.127.0.0.1";
   };

35 /* Forward lookups of hosts in my domain: */
   zone "cranzgot.co.za" {
        type master;
        file "named.cranzgot.co.za";
   };

40 /* Reverse lookups of local IP numbers: */
   zone "2.168.192.in-addr.arpa" {
```

```
           type master;
           file "named.192.168.2";
45    };

     /* Reverse lookups of 196.28.144.* Internet IP numbers: */
     zone "144.28.196.in-addr.arpa" {
           type master;
50         file "named.196.28.144";
     };

     /* Reverse lookup of 160.123.181.44 only: */
     zone "44.181.123.160.in-addr.arpa" {
55         type master;
           file "named.160.123.181.44";
     };
```

• *Root name server list:* **/var/named/named.ca**

```
    ; Get the original of this file from ftp://ftp.rs.internic.net/domain/named.root
    ;
    ; formerly ns.internic.net
    .                         3600000   IN  NS    a.root-servers.net.
5   a.root-servers.net.       3600000       A     198.41.0.4
    .                         3600000       NS    b.root-servers.net.
    b.root-servers.net.       3600000       A     128.9.0.107
    .                         3600000       NS    c.root-servers.net.
    c.root-servers.net.       3600000       A     192.33.4.12
10  .                         3600000       NS    d.root-servers.net.
    d.root-servers.net.       3600000       A     128.8.10.90
    .                         3600000       NS    e.root-servers.net.
    e.root-servers.net.       3600000       A     192.203.230.10
    .                         3600000       NS    f.root-servers.net.
15  f.root-servers.net.       3600000       A     192.5.5.241
    .                         3600000       NS    g.root-servers.net.
    g.root-servers.net.       3600000       A     192.112.36.4
    .                         3600000       NS    h.root-servers.net.
    h.root-servers.net.       3600000       A     128.63.2.53
20  .                         3600000       NS    i.root-servers.net.
    i.root-servers.net.       3600000       A     192.36.148.17
    .                         3600000       NS    j.root-servers.net.
    j.root-servers.net.       3600000       A     198.41.0.10
    .                         3600000       NS    k.root-servers.net.
25  k.root-servers.net.       3600000       A     193.0.14.129
    .                         3600000       NS    l.root-servers.net.
    l.root-servers.net.       3600000       A     198.32.64.12
    .                         3600000       NS    m.root-servers.net.
    m.root-servers.net.       3600000       A     202.12.27.33
```

• *Local forward lookups:* **/var/named/named.localdomain**

```
    $TTL 259200
    @              IN      SOA    localhost.localdomain. dns-admin.localhost.localdomain. (
                   2000012101     ; Serial number
                   10800          ; Refresh every 3 hours
5                  3600           ; Retry every hour
```

```
            3600000         ; Expire after 42 days
            259200 )        ; Minimum Time to Live (TTL) of 3 days

            IN      NS      localhost.localdomain.
localhost   IN      A       127.0.0.1
```

- *Local reverse lookups:* `/var/named/named.127.0.0.1`

```
$TTL 259200
@           IN      SOA     localhost. dns-admin.localhost. (
            2000012101      ; Serial number
            10800           ; Refresh every 3 hours
            3600            ; Retry every hour
            3600000         ; Expire after 42 days
            259200 )        ; Minimum Time to Live (TTL) of 3 days

            IN      NS      localhost.

            IN      PTR     localhost.
```

- *Authoritative domain file:* `/var/named/named.cranzgot.co.za`

```
$TTL 259200
@           IN      SOA     ns1.cranzgot.co.za. dns-admin.ns1.cranzgot.co.za. (
            2000012101      ; Serial number
            10800           ; Refresh every 3 hours
            3600            ; Retry every hour
            3600000         ; Expire after 42 days
            259200 )        ; Minimum Time to Live (TTL) of 3 days

            IN      NS      ns1.cranzgot.co.za.
            IN      NS      ns2.cranzgot.co.za.

            IN      A       160.123.181.44
            IN      MX      10 mail1.cranzgot.co.za.
            IN      MX      20 mail2.cranzgot.co.za.
; We will use the first IP address for the name server itself:
ns1         IN      A       196.28.144.16

; our backup name server is faaar away:
ns2         IN      A       146.143.21.88

; FTP server:
ftp         IN      A       196.28.144.17

; Aliases:
www         IN      CNAME   cranzgot.co.za.
mail1       IN      CNAME   ns1.cranzgot.co.za.
mail2       IN      CNAME   ns2.cranzgot.co.za.
gopher      IN      CNAME   ftp.cranzgot.co.za.
pop         IN      CNAME   mail1.cranzgot.co.za.
proxy       IN      CNAME   ftp.cranzgot.co.za.
```

```
      ; Reserved for future web servers:
      unused18        IN      A       196.28.144.18
35    unused19        IN      A       196.28.144.19
      unused20        IN      A       196.28.144.20
      unused21        IN      A       196.28.144.21
      unused22        IN      A       196.28.144.22
      unused23        IN      A       196.28.144.23
40
      ; local LAN:
      pc1             IN      A       192.168.2.1
      pc2             IN      A       192.168.2.2
      pc3             IN      A       192.168.2.3
45    pc4             IN      A       192.168.2.4
      ; and so on... to 192.168.2.255
```

- **LAN** *reverse lookups:* **/var/named/named.192.168.2**

```
      $TTL 259200
      @               IN      SOA     ns1.cranzgot.co.za. dns-admin.ns1.cranzgot.co.za. (
                      2000012101      ; Serial number
                      10800           ; Refresh every 3 hours
5                     3600            ; Retry every hour
                      3600000         ; Expire after 42 days
                      259200 )        ; Minimum Time to Live (TTL) of 3 days

                      IN      NS      ns1.cranzgot.co.za.
10
      1               IN      PTR     pc1.cranzgot.co.za.
      2               IN      PTR     pc2.cranzgot.co.za.
      3               IN      PTR     pc3.cranzgot.co.za.
      4               IN      PTR     pc4.cranzgot.co.za.
15    ; and so on... to 255
```

- *Authoritative reverse lookups (1):* **/var/named/named.196.28.144**

```
      $TTL 259200
      @               IN      SOA     ns1.cranzgot.co.za. dns-admin.ns1.cranzgot.co.za. (
                      2000012101      ; Serial number
                      10800           ; Refresh every 3 hours
5                     3600            ; Retry every hour
                      3600000         ; Expire after 42 days
                      259200 )        ; Minimum Time to Live (TTL) of 3 days

                      IN      NS      dns.big-isp.net.
10
      0               IN      NS      dns.big-isp.net.
      1               IN      NS      dns.big-isp.net.
      2               IN      NS      dns.big-isp.net.
      3               IN      NS      dns.big-isp.net.
15    4               IN      NS      dns.big-isp.net.
      5               IN      NS      dns.big-isp.net.
      6               IN      NS      dns.big-isp.net.
      7               IN      NS      dns.big-isp.net.
```

442

```
     8              IN      NS      dns.big-isp.net.
20   9              IN      NS      dns.big-isp.net.
     10             IN      NS      dns.big-isp.net.
     11             IN      NS      dns.big-isp.net.
     12             IN      NS      dns.big-isp.net.
     13             IN      NS      dns.big-isp.net.
25   14             IN      NS      dns.big-isp.net.
     15             IN      NS      dns.big-isp.net.

     16             IN      PTR     ns1.cranzgot.co.za.
     17             IN      PTR     ftp.cranzgot.co.za.
30   18             IN      PTR     unused18.cranzgot.co.za.
     19             IN      PTR     unused19.cranzgot.co.za.
     20             IN      PTR     unused20.cranzgot.co.za.
     21             IN      PTR     unused21.cranzgot.co.za.
     22             IN      PTR     unused22.cranzgot.co.za.
35   23             IN      PTR     unused23.cranzgot.co.za.

     24             IN      NS      dns.big-isp.net.
     25             IN      NS      dns.big-isp.net.
     26             IN      NS      dns.big-isp.net.
40   ; and so on... up to 255
```

- *Authoritative reverse lookups (2):* **/var/named/named.160.123.181.44**

```
    $TTL 259200
    @              IN      SOA     ns1.cranzgot.co.za. dns-admin.ns1.cranzgot.co.za. (
                   2000012101      ; Serial number
                   10800           ; Refresh every 3 hours
5                  3600            ; Retry every hour
                   3600000         ; Expire after 42 days
                   259200 )        ; Minimum Time to Live (TTL) of 3 days

                   IN      NS      ns1.cranzgot.co.za.
10                 IN      NS      ns2.cranzgot.co.za.

                   IN      PTR     cranzgot.co.za.
```

40.2.2   Starting the name server

If you have created a configuration similar to that above, you can then run the bind
package initialization commands. The actions available are (alternative commands in
parentheses):

```
   /etc/rc.d/init.d/named start
   ( /etc/init.d/named start )
   ( /etc/init.d/bind start )
   /etc/rc.d/init.d/named stop
5  /etc/rc.d/init.d/named restart
   /etc/rc.d/init.d/named status
```

443

You should get messages like:

```
Jul  8 15:45:23 ns1 named[17656]: starting.  named 8.2.2-P5 Sat Aug  5 13:21:24 EDT 2000 ^I
Jul  8 15:45:23 ns1 named[17656]: hint zone "" (IN) loaded (serial 0)
Jul  8 15:45:23 ns1 named[17656]: master zone "localhost" (IN) loaded (serial 2000012101)
Jul  8 15:45:23 ns1 named[17656]: master zone "1.0.0.127.in-addr.arpa" (IN) loaded (serial
Jul  8 15:45:23 ns1 named[17656]: master zone "cranzgot.co.za" (IN) loaded (serial 20000121
Jul  8 15:45:23 ns1 named[17656]: master zone "myisp.co.za" (IN) loaded (serial 2000012101)
Jul  8 15:45:23 ns1 named[17656]: master zone "2.168.192.in-addr.arpa" (IN) loaded (serial
Jul  8 15:45:23 ns1 named[17656]: master zone "144.28.196.in-addr.arpa" (IN) loaded (serial
Jul  8 15:45:23 ns1 named[17656]: master zone "44.181.123.160.in-addr.arpa" (IN) loaded (se
Jul  8 15:45:23 ns1 named[17656]: listening on [127.0.0.1].53 (lo)
Jul  8 15:45:23 ns1 named[17656]: listening on [196.28.144.16].53 (eth0)
Jul  8 15:45:23 ns1 named[17656]: Forwarding source address is [0.0.0.0].1041
Jul  8 15:45:23 ns1 named: named startup succeeded
Jul  8 15:45:23 ns1 named[17657]: group = 25
Jul  8 15:45:23 ns1 named[17657]: user = named
Jul  8 15:45:23 ns1 named[17657]: Ready to answer queries.
```

If you have made typing errors, or named files incorrectly, you will get appropriate error messages. *Novice administrators are wont to edit* named *configuration files and restart* named *without checking* /var/log/messages *(or* /var/log/syslog*) for errors.* NEVER *do this.*

40.2.3   Configuration in detail

If there are no apparent errors in your config files, you can now more closely examine the contents of the files.

40.2.3.1   Top-level **named.conf**

The top-level configuration file /etc/named.conf has an obvious **C** style format. Comments are designated by /* */ or //.

The options section in our case specifies only one parameter: the directory for locating any files. The file options.html under the bind documentation directories has a complete list of options. Some of these are esoteric, but a few have common uses.

The lines zone "." {...   will be present in all name server configurations. They tell named that the whole Internet is governed by the file named.ca. named.ca in turn contains the list of root name servers.

The lines zone "localdomain" {...   are common.   They specify that forward lookups for *host*.localdomain are contained in the file /var/named/named.localdomain. This file gives a correct result for any lookup for localhost. Many applications query the name server for this name and a fastidious configuration ought to return it correctly. Note that such a lookup works together with `resolv.conf`—it has a line `search localdomain` so that a query for `local-host` gives the same result as a query for `localhost.localdomain`.

The lines `zone "1.0.0.127.in-addr.arpa" {...` resolve reverse lookups for the IP address `127.0.0.1` (stored in the file `named.127.0.0.1`). Note that `1.0.0.127` is `127.0.0.1` written backwards. In fact, reverse lookups are just forward lookups under the domain `.in-addr.arpa`. Many applications reverse lookup any received connection to check its authenticity, even from `localhost`, so you may want to have these lines present to prevent such applications failing or blocking.

The rest of the file is the configuration specific to our domain.

The lines `zone "cranzgot.co.za" {...` say that information for forward lookups is located in the file `named.cranzgot.co.za`.

The lines `zone "1.168.192.in-addr.arpa" {...` say that information for reverse lookups on the IP address range `192.168.1.0`–`255` is located in the file `named.192.168.1`.

The lines `zone "44.182.124.160.in-addr.arpa" {...` says that information for reverse lookups on the IP address `160.124.182.44` is located in the file `named.160.124.182.44`.

40.2.3.2   Domain SOA records

Each of the other `named.` files has a similar format. They begin with `$TTL` line and then an `@ IN SOA`. TTL stands for *Time To Live*, the default expiration time for all subsequent entries. This line not only prevents a `No default TTL set...` warning message, but really tells the rest of the Internet how long to cache an entry. If you plan on moving your site soon or often, set this to a smaller value. SOA stands for *Start of Authority*. The host name on the second line specifies the authority for that domain, and the adjacent `<user>.<hostname>` specifies the email address of the responsible person.

The next few lines contain timeout specifications for cached data and data propagation across the net. These are reasonable defaults, but if you would like to tune these values, consult the relevant documentation listed on page 438. The values are all in seconds.

The *serial number* for the file (i.e., `2000012101`) is used to tell when a change has been made and hence that new data should be propagated to other servers. When updating the file in any way, you must increment this serial number. The format is conventionally *YYYYMMDDxx*—exactly ten digits. *xx* begins with, say, `01` and is incremented with each change made during a day.

It is absolutely essential that the serial number be updated whenever a file is edited. If not, the changes will not be reflected through the rest of the Internet.

40.2.3.3   Dotted and non-dotted host names

If a host name ends in a **.** then the dot signifies a fully qualified host name. If it does
not end in a **.** then the absence of a dot signifies that the domain should be appended
to the host name. This feature is purely to make files more elegant.

For instance, the line

```
ftp                     IN      A       196.28.144.17
```

could just as well be written

```
ftp.cranzgot.co.za.   IN      A       196.28.144.17
```

Always be careful to properly end qualified host names with a dot, since failing to do so causes
named to append a further domain.

40.2.3.4   Empty host names

If a host name is omitted from the start of the line, then the domain is substituted. The
purpose of this notation is also for elegance. For example,

```
                        IN      NS      ns1.cranzgot.co.za.
```

is the same as

```
cranzgot.co.za.       IN      NS      ns1.cranzgot.co.za.
```

40.2.3.5   NS, MX, PTR, A, and CNAME records

Each DNS record appears on a single line, associating some host name / domain or IP
address with some other host name or IP address. Hence, it is easy to construct a file
that makes the Internet think anything you want it to about your organization.

The most basic types of record are the A and PTR records. They simply associate
a host name with an IP number, or an IP number with a host name, respectively. You
should not have more than one host associated to a particular IP number.

The CNAME record says that a host is just an alias to another host. So have

```
ns1             IN      A       196.28.144.1
mail1           IN      CNAME   ns1.cranzgot.co.za.
```

rather than

```
ns1             IN      A       196.28.144.1
mail1           IN      A       196.28.144.1
```

Finally, NS and MX records

```
<domain>        IN      NS      <nameserver>
<domain>        IN      MX      <mailserver>
```

just state that domain <domain> has a name server or mail server <nameserver> or <mailserver>, respectively. MTAs can now locate your mail server as being responsible for email addresses of the form *user*@cranzgot.co.za.

40.2.3.6   Reverse lookups configuration

The file /var/named/named.196.28.144 contains reverse lookup data on all 255 IP addresses under 196.28.144.. It is, however, our ISP (called big-isp.net) that is responsible for this address range, possibly having bought all 65536 addresses under 196.28.. The Internet is going to query big-isp.net when trying to do a reverse lookup for 196.28.144.?. The problem here is that there are many companies comprising the 196.28.144.? range, each with their own name server, so no single name server can be authoritative for the whole domain 144.28.196.in-addr.arpa. This is the reason for lines in /var/named/named.196.28.144 like

```
5               IN      NS      dns.big-isp.net.
```

IP address 196.28.144.5 is not our responsibility, and hence we refer any such query to a more authoritative name server. On the ISP side, the name server dns.big-isp.net must have a file /var/named/named.196.28.144 that contains something like:

```
$TTL 259200
@               IN      SOA     dns.dns.big-isp.net. dns-admin.dns.big-isp.net. (
                2000012101      ; Serial number
                10800           ; Refresh every 3 hours
                3600            ; Retry every hour
                3600000         ; Expire after 42 days
                259200 )        ; Minimum Time to Live (TTL) of 3 days

                IN      NS      dns.big-isp.net.

0               IN      NS      ns1.dali.co.za.
1               IN      NS      ns1.dali.co.za.
2               IN      NS      ns1.dali.co.za.
3               IN      NS      ns1.dali.co.za.
4               IN      NS      ns1.dali.co.za.
5               IN      NS      ns1.dali.co.za.
6               IN      NS      ns1.dali.co.za.
7               IN      NS      ns1.dali.co.za.
```

```
20   8                 IN      NS      ns1.picasso.co.za.
     9                 IN      NS      ns1.picasso.co.za.
     10                IN      NS      ns1.picasso.co.za.
     11                IN      NS      ns1.picasso.co.za.
     12                IN      NS      ns1.picasso.co.za.
25   13                IN      NS      ns1.picasso.co.za.
     14                IN      NS      ns1.picasso.co.za.
     15                IN      NS      ns1.picasso.co.za.

     16                IN      NS      ns1.cranzgot.co.za.
30   17                IN      NS      ns1.cranzgot.co.za.
     18                IN      NS      ns1.cranzgot.co.za.
     19                IN      NS      ns1.cranzgot.co.za.
     20                IN      NS      ns1.cranzgot.co.za.
     21                IN      NS      ns1.cranzgot.co.za.
35   22                IN      NS      ns1.cranzgot.co.za.
     23                IN      NS      ns1.cranzgot.co.za.

     24                IN      NS      ns1.matisse.co.za.
     25                IN      NS      ns1.matisse.co.za.
40   26                IN      NS      ns1.matisse.co.za.
     27                IN      NS      ns1.matisse.co.za.
     28                IN      NS      ns1.matisse.co.za.
     29                IN      NS      ns1.matisse.co.za.
     30                IN      NS      ns1.matisse.co.za.
45   31                IN      NS      ns1.matisse.co.za.
     ; and so on... up to 255
```

Here, Matisse, Dali, and Picasso are other companies that have bought small IP address blocks from big-isp. Each of these lines will redirect queries to the appropriate name server.

40.3   Round-Robin Load-Sharing

If you have more than one A record for a particular machine, then named will return multiple IP addresses upon a lookup. Load sharing between several web servers is now possible—the record ordering is randomized with each new lookup and your web browser will only choose the first listed IP address. For instance, host cnn.com returns several IP addresses. Their zone file configuration might look like

```
     cnn.com.    IN    A    207.25.71.5
     cnn.com.    IN    A    207.25.71.6
     .
     .
5    .
     cnn.com.    IN    A    207.25.71.29
     cnn.com.    IN    A    207.25.71.30
```

40.4   Configuring named for Dialup Use

If you have a dialup connection, the name server should be configured as what is called a *caching-only* name server. Of course, there is no such thing as a caching-*only* name server—the term just means that the name. files have only a few essential records in them. The point of a caching server is to prevent spurious DNS lookups that may eat modem bandwidth or cause a dial-on-demand server to initiate a dialout. It also prevents applications blocking, waiting for a DNS lookup. (Typical examples are send-mail, which blocks for a couple of minutes when a machine is turned on without the network plugged in; and netscape 4, which tries to look up the IP address of news.<localdomain>.)

40.4.1   Example caching name server

For a caching name server, the /etc/name.conf file should look as follows. Replace <nameserver> with the IP address of the name server your ISP has given you. Your local machine name is assumed to be cericon.priv.ate. (The following listings are minus superfluous comments and newlines for brevity):

```
options {
        forwarders {
                <nameserver>;
        };
        directory "/var/named";
};

zone "." { type hint; file "named.ca"; };
zone "localdomain" { type master; file "named.localdomain"; };
zone "1.0.0.127.in-addr.arpa" { type master; file "named.127.0.0.1";};
zone "priv.ate" { type master; file "named.priv.ate"; };
zone "168.192.in-addr.arpa" { type master; file "named.192.168"; };
```

The /var/named/named.priv.ate file should look like:

```
$TTL 259200
@         IN      SOA     cericon.priv.ate. root.cericon.priv.ate.
          ( 2000012101 10800 3600 3600000 259200 )
          IN      NS      cericon.priv.ate.
cericon   IN      A       192.168.1.1
news      IN      A       192.168.1.2
```

The /var/named/named.192.168 file should look like:

```
$TTL 259200
@          IN      SOA     localhost. root.localhost.
           ( 2000012101 10800 3600 3600000 259200 )
           IN      NS      localhost.
1.1        IN      PTR     cericon.priv.ate.
```

The remaining files are the same as before. In addition to the above, your host name has to be configured as in Chapter 27.

40.4.2 Dynamic IP addresses

The one contingency of dialup machines is that IP addresses are often dynamically assigned, so your `192.168.` addresses aren't going to apply. Probably one way to get around this is to dial in a few times to get a feel for what IP addresses you are likely to get. Assuming you know that your ISP always gives you `196.26.`*x*.*x*, you can have a reverse lookup file `named.196.26` with nothing in it. This will just cause reverse lookups to fail instead of blocking.

Such a "hack" is probably unnecessary. It is best to identify the particular application that is causing a spurious dialout or causing a block, and then apply your creativity to the particular case.

40.5 Secondary or Slave DNS Servers

`named` can operate as a backup server to another server, also called a *slave* or *secondary* server.

Like the caching-*only* server there, is no such thing as a *secondary* server. It's just the same `named` running with reduced capacity.

Let's say we would like `ns2.cranzgot.co.za` to be a secondary to `ns1.cranzgot.co.za`. The `named.conf` file would look as follows:

```
options {
        directory "/var/named";
};

zone "." {
        type hint;
        file "named.ca";
};

zone "localdomain" {
```

```
               type master;
               file "named.localdomain";
      };

15    zone "1.0.0.127.in-addr.arpa" {
               type master;
               file "named.127.0.0.1";
      };

20    zone "cranzgot.co.za" {
               type slave;
               file "named.cranzgot.co.za";
               masters {
                       196.28.144.16;
25             };
      };

      zone "2.168.192.in-addr.arpa" {
               type slave;
30             file "named.192.168.2";
               masters {
                       196.28.144.16;
               };
      };
35
      zone "144.28.196.in-addr.arpa" {
               type slave;
               file "named.196.28.144";
               masters {
40                     196.28.144.16;
               };
      };

      zone "44.181.123.160.in-addr.arpa" {
45             type slave;
               file "named.160.123.181.44";
               masters {
                       196.28.144.16;
               };
50    };
```

When an entry has a "master" in it, you must supply the appropriate file. When an entry has a "slave" in it, named will automatically download the file from 196.28.144.16 (i.e., ns1.cranzgot.co.za) the first time a lookup is required from that domain.

And that's DNS!

Chapter 41

Point-to-Point Protocol — Dialup Networking

Dialup networking is unreliable and difficult to configure. The reason is simply that telephones were not designed for data. However, considering that the telephone network is by far the largest electronic network on the globe, it makes sense to make use of it. This is why modems were created. On the other hand, the advent of ISDN is slightly more expensive and a better choice for all but home dialup. See Section 41.6 for more information.

41.1 Basic Dialup

For home use, dialup networking is not all that difficult to configure. The PPP HOWTO contains lots on this (see Section 16). For my machine this boils down to creating the files `/etc/ppp/chap-secrets` and `/etc/ppp/pap-secrets`, both containing the following line of text:

```
<username>   *   <password>   *
```

although only one of the files will be used, then running the following command at a shell prompt: ⬊This example assumes that an initialization string of AT&F1 is sufficient. See Section 3.5.⬉

```
pppd connect \
         "chat -S -s -v \
         '' 'AT&F1' \
         OK ATDT<tel-number> CONNECT '' \
         name: <username> assword: '\q<password>' \
```

453

```
        con: ppp" \
/dev/<modem> 57600 debug crtscts modem lock nodetach \
hide-password defaultroute \
user <username> \
noauth
```
10

This is a minimalist's dial-in command and it's specific to *my* ISP only. Don't use the exact command unless you have an account with the Internet Solution ISP in South Africa, before January 2000.

The command-line options are explained as follows:

connect <script> Specifies the script that pppd must use to start things up. When you use a modem manually (as is shown further below), you need to go through the steps of initializing the modem, causing a dial, connecting, logging in, and finally telling the remote computer that you would like to set the connection to "data communication" mode, called the *point-to-point protocol*, or *PPP*. The <script> is the automation of this manual procedure.

chat -S -s -v <expect> <send> <expect> <send> ... The <script> proper. chat has a man page and uses other than modem communication. -S means to log messages to the terminal and not to syslog; -s means to log to stderr; -v means verbose output. After the options comes a list of things the modem is likely to say, alternated with appropriate responses. This is called an *expect–send* sequence. The sequence AT&F1 is the modem initialization string. ↘This example assumes that an initialization string of AT&F1 is sufficient. See Section 3.5.↖ \q means to *not* print the password amid the debug output—very important.

/dev/tty?? Specifies the device you are going to use. This will usually be /dev/ttyS0, /dev/ttyS1, /dev/ttyS2, or /dev/ttyS3.

57600 The speed the modem is to be set to. This is only the speed between the PC and the modem and has nothing to do with the actual data throughput. It should be set as high as possible except in the case of very old machines whose serial ports may possibly only handle 38400. It's best to choose 115200 unless this doesn't work.

debug Output debug information. This option is useful for diagnosing problems.

crtscts Use hardware flow control.

modem Use modem control lines. This is actually the default.

lock Create a UUCP lock file in /var/lock/. As explained in Section 34.4, this is a file of the form /var/lock/LCK..tty?? that tells other applications that the serial device is in use. For this reason, you *must not* call the device /dev/modem or /dev/cua?.

nodetach Remain always a foreground process. This allows you to watch pppd run
   and stop it with ^C.

defaultroute Create an IP route after PPP comes alive. Henceforth, packets will go
   to the right place.

hide-password Hide the password from the logs. This is important for security.

user <username> Specifies the line from the /etc/ppp/chap-secrets and
   /etc/ppp/pap-secrets file to use. For a home PC there is usually only one
   line.

41.1.1   Determining your chat script

To determine the list of expect–send sequences, you need to do a manual dial-in. The
command

```
dip -t
```

stands for *dial-IP* and talks directly to your modem.

   The following session demonstrates a manual dial for user psheer. Using dip
manually like this is a game of trying to get the garbage lines you see below: this is
PPP starting to talk. When you get this junk, you have won and can press ^C. Then,
copy and paste your session for future reference.

```
[root@cericon]# dip -t
DIP: Dialup IP Protocol Driver version 3.3.7o-uri (8 Feb 96)
Written by Fred N. van Kempen, MicroWalt Corporation.

DIP> port ttyS0
DIP> speed 57600
DIP> term
[ Entering TERMINAL mode.  Use CTRL-] to get back ]
AT&F1
OK
ATDT4068500
CONNECT 26400/ARQ/V34/LAPM/V42BIS
Checking authorization, please wait...
name:psheer
password:

c2-ctn-icon:ppp
Entering PPP mode.
Async interface address is unnumbered (FastEthernet0)
Your IP address is 196.34.157.148. MTU is 1500 bytes

~y}#A!}!e} }3}"}&} }*} } }~}&4}2Iq}'}"}(}"N$~~y}#A!}!r} }4}"}&} }
[ Back to LOCAL mode. ]
DIP> quit
```

```
25   [root@cericon]#
```

Now you can modify the above `chat` script as you need. The kinds of things that will differ are trivial: like having `login:` instead of `name:`. Some systems also require you to type something instead of `ppp`, and some require nothing to be typed after your password. Some further require nothing to be typed at all, thus immediately entering PPP mode.

Note that `dip` also creates UUCP lock files as explained in Section 34.4.

41.1.2 CHAP and PAP

You may ask why there are `/etc/ppp/chap-secrets` and `/etc/ppp/pap-secrets` files if a user name and password are already specified inside the the `chat` script. *CHAP* (Challenge Handshake Authentication Protocol) and *PAP* (Password Authentication Protocol) are authentication mechanisms used *after* logging in—in other words, somewhere amid the

˜y}#A!}!e} }3}"}&} }*} } }˜}&4}2Iq}'}"}(}"N$˜˜y}#A!}!r} }4}"}&} }.

41.1.3 Running pppd

If you run the `pppd` command above, you will get output something like this:

```
     send (AT&F1^M)
     expect (OK)
     AT&F1^M^M
     OK
 5    -- got it

     send (ATDT4068500^M)
     expect (CONNECT)
     ^M
10   ATDT4068500^M^M
     CONNECT
      -- got it

     send (^M)
15   expect (name:)
      45333/ARQ/V90/LAPM/V42BIS^M
     Checking authorization, Please wait...^M
     username:
      -- got it
20
     send (psheer^M)
     expect (assword:)
     psheer^M
     password:
25    -- got it

     send (??????)
     expect (con:)
```

456

```
     ^M
30   ^M
     c2-ctn-icon:
     -- got it

     send (ppp^M)
35   Serial connection established.
     Using interface ppp0
     Connect: ppp0 <--> /dev/ttyS0
     sent [LCP ConfReq id=0x1 <asyncmap 0x0> <magic 0x88c5a54f> <pcomp> <accomp>]
     rcvd [LCP ConfReq id=0x3d <asyncmap 0xa0000> <magic 0x3435476c> <pcomp> <accomp>]
40   sent [LCP ConfAck id=0x3d <asyncmap 0xa0000> <magic 0x3435476c> <pcomp> <accomp>]
     rcvd [LCP ConfAck id=0x1 <asyncmap 0x0> <magic 0x88c5a54f> <pcomp> <accomp>]
     sent [IPCP ConfReq id=0x1 <addr 192.168.3.9> <compress VJ 0f 01>]
     sent [CCP ConfReq id=0x1 <deflate 15> <deflate(old#) 15> <bsd v1 15>]
     rcvd [IPCP ConfReq id=0x45 <addr 168.209.2.67>]
45   sent [IPCP ConfAck id=0x45 <addr 168.209.2.67>]
     rcvd [IPCP ConfRej id=0x1 <compress VJ 0f 01>]
     sent [IPCP ConfReq id=0x2 <addr 192.168.3.9>]
     rcvd [LCP ProtRej id=0x3e 80 fd 01 01 00 0f 1a 04 78 00 18 04 78 00 15 03 2f]
     rcvd [IPCP ConfNak id=0x2 <addr 196.34.157.131>]
50   sent [IPCP ConfReq id=0x3 <addr 196.34.157.131>]
     rcvd [IPCP ConfAck id=0x3 <addr 196.34.157.131>]
     local  IP address 196.34.25.95
     remote IP address 168.209.2.67
     Script /etc/ppp/ip-up started (pid 671)
55   Script /etc/ppp/ip-up finished (pid 671), status = 0x0
      Terminating on signal 2.
     Script /etc/ppp/ip-down started (pid 701)
     sent [LCP TermReq id=0x2 "User request"]
     rcvd [LCP TermAck id=0x2]
```

You can see the expect–send sequences working, so it's easy to correct them if you made a mistake somewhere.

At this point you might want to type `route -n` and `ifconfig` in another terminal:

```
     [root@cericon]# route -n
     Kernel IP routing table
     Destination     Gateway         Genmask         Flags Metric Ref    Use Iface
     168.209.2.67    0.0.0.0         255.255.255.255 UH    0      0        0 ppp0
5    127.0.0.0       0.0.0.0         255.0.0.0       U     0      0        0 lo
     0.0.0.0         168.209.2.69    0.0.0.0         UG    0      0        0 ppp0
     [root@cericon]# ifconfig
     lo        Link encap:Local Loopback
               inet addr:127.0.0.1  Mask:255.0.0.0
10             UP LOOPBACK RUNNING  MTU:3924  Metric:1
               RX packets:2547933 errors:0 dropped:0 overruns:0 frame:0
               TX packets:2547933 errors:0 dropped:0 overruns:0 carrier:0
               collisions:0 txqueuelen:0

15   ppp0      Link encap:Point-to-Point Protocol
               inet addr:196.34.25.95  P-t-P:168.209.2.67  Mask:255.255.255.255
               UP POINTOPOINT RUNNING NOARP MULTICAST  MTU:1500  Metric:1
               RX packets:7 errors:0 dropped:0 overruns:0 frame:0
               TX packets:7 errors:0 dropped:0 overruns:0 carrier:0
20             collisions:0 txqueuelen:10
```

This clearly shows what `pppd` has done: created a network device and a route to it.

If your name server is configured, you should now be able to `ping meta-lab.unc.edu` or some well-known host.

41.2   Demand-Dial, Masquerading

Dial-on-demand really just involves adding the `demand` option to the `pppd` command-line above. The other way of doing dial-on-demand is to use the `diald` package, but here we discuss the `pppd` implementation. The `diald` package is, however, a far more thorough solution.

With the `demand` option, you will notice that spurious dialouts take place. You need to add some filtering rules to ensure that only the services you are interested in cause a dialout. These services should only make outgoing connections when absolutely necessary.

A firewall script might look as follows. This example uses the old `ipfwadm` command, possibly called `/sbin/ipfwadm-wrapper` on your machine. ⟍The newer `ipchains` command is now superseded by a completed different packet filtering system in kernel 2.4.⟋ See the `Firewall-HOWTO` for more information on building a firewall.

```
    # Enable ip forwarding and dynamic address changing:
    echo 1 > /proc/sys/net/ipv4/ip_forward
    echo 1 > /proc/sys/net/ipv4/ip_dynaddr

 5  # Clear all firewall rules:
    /sbin/ipfwadm -O -f
    /sbin/ipfwadm -I -f
    /sbin/ipfwadm -F -f

10  /sbin/ipfwadm -O -p deny
    /sbin/ipfwadm -I -p deny

    # Allow all local communications:
    /sbin/ipfwadm -O -a accept -D 192.168.0.0/16 -S 0.0.0.0/0
15  /sbin/ipfwadm -O -a accept -D 127.0.0.0/24   -S 127.0.0.0/24
    /sbin/ipfwadm -O -a accept -S 192.168.0.0/16 -D 127.0.0.0/24
    /sbin/ipfwadm -O -a accept -S 192.168.0.0/16 -D 192.168.0.0/16
    /sbin/ipfwadm -I -a accept -S 192.168.0.0/16 -D 0.0.0.0/0
    /sbin/ipfwadm -I -a accept -S 127.0.0.0/24   -D 127.0.0.0/24
20  /sbin/ipfwadm -I -a accept -D 192.168.0.0/16 -S 127.0.0.0/24
    /sbin/ipfwadm -I -a accept -D 192.168.0.0/16 -S 192.168.0.0/16

    # Allow ports outgoing:
    /sbin/ipfwadm -O -a accept -P tcp -S 0.0.0.0/0 \
25                             -D 0.0.0.0/0 20 21 22 25 53 80 110 119 143
```

```
/sbin/ipfwadm -O -a accept -P udp -S 0.0.0.0/0 -D 0.0.0.0/0 53

# # Add this line to allow FTP from masqueraded machines:
# /sbin/ipfwadm -O -a accept -P tcp -S 0.0.0.0/0 -D 0.0.0.0/0 1024:65535

# Allow ports incoming:
/sbin/ipfwadm -I -a accept -P tcp -S 0.0.0.0/0 -D 0.0.0.0/0 20 113
/sbin/ipfwadm -I -a accept -P tcp -S 0.0.0.0/0 -D 0.0.0.0/0 1024:65535
/sbin/ipfwadm -I -a accept -P udp -S 0.0.0.0/0 -D 0.0.0.0/0 1024:65535
```

The ports we are using are

20	ftp-data
21	ftp
22	ssh
25	smtp
53	domain
80	www
110	pop3
113	auth
119	nntp
143	imap2

The `auth` service is not needed but should be kept open so that connecting services get a failure instead of waiting for a timeout. You can comment out the `auth` line in `/etc/inetd.conf` for security.

If you have a LAN of machines that needs to share the same dialup link, then you can give them all `192.168.` addresses and *masquerade* the LAN through the PPP interface. IP masquerading or NAT (*network address translation*) can be done with:

```
# Masquerading for ftp requires special handling on older kernels:
/sbin/modprobe ip_masq_ftp

# Masquerade the domain 192.168.2.0/255.255.128.0
/sbin/ipfwadm -F -f
/sbin/ipfwadm -F -p deny
/sbin/ipfwadm -F -a m -S 192.168.0.0/17 -D 0.0.0.0/0
```

The `pppd` script becomes (note that you need `pppd-2.3.11` or later for this to work as I have it here):

```
pppd connect \
        "chat -S -s -v \
        '' 'AT&F1' \
        OK ATDT<tel-number> CONNECT '' \
        name: <username> assword: '\q<password>' \
        con: ppp" \
```

```
     /dev/ttyS0 57600 debug crtscts modem lock nodetach \
     hide-password defaultroute \
     user <username> \
10   demand \
     :10.112.112.112 \
     idle 180 \
     holdoff 30
```

41.3   Dialup DNS

Your DNS service, to be used on a dialup server, requires some customization. Replace your `options` section from the DNS configurations in Chapter 40 with the following:

```
options {
        forwarders { 196.7.173.2; /* example only */ };
        listen-on { 192.168.2.254; };
        directory "/var/cache/bind";
5       dialup yes; notify no; forward only;
};
```

The options `dialup yes; notify no; forward only;` tell `bind` to use the link as little as possible; not send notify messages (there are no slave servers on our LAN to notify) and to forward requests to `192.168.2.254` rather than trying to answer them itself; respectively. The option `listen-on` causes the name server to bind to the network interface `192.168.2.254` only. In this example, the interface `192.168.2.254` is our Ethernet card which routes packets from the local LAN. This is important for security, because it prevents any possible connection from the outside.

There is also a DNS package written specifically for use by dialup servers. It is called `dnrd` and is much easier to configure than `bind`.

41.4   Dial-in Servers

`pppd` is really just a way to initiate a network device over a serial port, regardless of whether you initiate or listen for a connection. As long as there is a serial connection between two machines, `pppd` will negotiate a link.

To *listen* for a `pppd` dial-*in*, you need just add the following line to your `/etc/inittab` file:

```
S0:2345:respawn:/sbin/mgetty -s 115200 ttyS0
```

and then the line

```
/AutoPPP/ - a_ppp   /usr/sbin/pppd
```

to the file /etc/mgetty+sendfax/login.config (/etc/mgetty/login.config
for Debian). For security, you would probably want to run chmod a-
s /usr/sbin/pppd, since mgetty runs pppd as root anyway. Your
/etc/ppp/options file could contain

```
proxyarp mtu 552 mru 552 require-chap <hostname>:
```

Note that we dispense with the serial line options (i.e., speed and flow control) because
mgetty would have already initialized the serial line. <hostname> is just the name
of the local machine. The proxyarp setting adds the remote client to the ARP tables.
This enables your client to connect through to the Internet on the other side of the line
without extra routes. The file /etc/ppp/chap-secrets can be filled with lines like,

```
dialup * <passwd> 192.168.254.123
```

to specify the IP address and password of each user.

Next, add a user dialup and perhaps set its password to that in the chap-
secrets file. You can then test your configuration from a remote machine with dip -
t as above. If that works (i.e., mgetty answers, and you get your garbage lines as
on page 456), then a proper pppd dial-in should also work. The /etc/ppp/chap-
secrets file can contain:

```
dialup * <passwd> *
```

and you can dial out using a typical pppd command, like this:

```
pppd \
    connect "chat -S -s -v '' 'AT&F1' OK ATDT<telephone> CONNECT '' "
    /dev/<modem> 57600 debug crtscts modem lock nodetach
    hide-password defaultroute \
    user dialup \
    noauth
```

You should be carefully to have a proper DNS configuration for forward and
reverse lookups of your pppd IP addresses. This is so that no services block with
long timeouts and also so that other Internet machines will be friendly to your user's
connections.

Note that the above also supports faxes, logins, voice, and uucp (see Section
34.3) on the same modem because mgetty only starts pppd if it sees an LCP request (part of the PPP protocol). If you just want PPP, read the config files in
/etc/mgetty+sendfax/ (Debian /etc/mgetty/) to disable the other services.

41.5   Using `tcpdump`

If a dialout does occur unexpectedly, you can run `tcpdump` to dump packets going to your `ppp0` device. This output will probably highlight the error. You can then look at the TCP port of the service and try to figure out what process the packet might have come from. The command is:

```
tcpdump -n -N -f -i ppp0
```

`tcpdump` is also discussed in Section 25.10.3.

41.6   ISDN Instead of Modems

For those who are not familiar with ISDN, this paragraph gives you a quick summary. ISDN stands for *Integrated Services Digital Network*. ISDN lines are like regular telephone lines, except that an ISDN line comes with two analog and two digital channels. The analog channels are regular telephone lines in every respect—just plug your phone in and start making calls. The digital lines each support 64 kilobits/second data transfer; only ISDN communication equipment is meant to plug in to these and the charge rate is the same as that of a telephone call. To communicate over the digital line, you need to dial an ISP just as with a regular telephone. PPP runs over ISDN in the same way as a modem connection. It used to be that only very expensive ISDN routers could work with ISDN, but ISDN modems and ISDN ISA/PCI cards have become cheap enough to allow anyone to use ISDN, and most telephone companies will install an ISDN line as readily as a regular telephone line. So you may ask what's with the "Integrated Services." I suppose it was thought that this service, in allowing both data and regular telephone, would be the ubiquitous communications service. It remains to be seen, however, if video conferencing over 64-Kb lines becomes mainstream.

ISDN is not covered in detail here, although ample HOWTOs exists on the subject. Be wary when setting up ISDN. ISDN dials *really* fast. It can dial out a thousand times in a few minutes, which is expensive.

Chapter 42

The LINUX Kernel Source, Modules, and Hardware Support

This chapter explains how to configure, patch, and build a kernel from source. The configuration of device drivers and modules is also discussed in detail.

42.1 Kernel Constitution

A kernel installation consists of the kernel boot image, the kernel modules, the `System.map` file, the kernel headers (needed only for development), and various support daemons (already provided by your distribution). These constitute everything that is called "Linux" under LINUX, and are built from about 50 megabytes of **C** code of around 1.5 million lines.

- The LINUX kernel image is a 400 to 600-KB file that sits in `/boot/` (see Chapter 31). If you look in this directory, you might see several kernels. The choice of which to boot is probably available to you at boot time, through `lilo`.

    The kernel in `/boot/` is compressed. That is, it is `gzip` compressed and is actually about twice the size when unpacked into memory on boot.

- The kernel also has detached parts called *modules*. These all sit in `/lib/modules/<version>/`. They are categorized into the subdirectories below this directory. In kernel `2.2` there were about 400, modules totaling about 9 megabytes.

    Modules are actually just shared object files, like the `.o` files we created in Section 23.1. They are not quite the same as Windows device drivers, in that it is

463

not generally possibly to use a module on a kernel other than the one it was compiled for—hence the name "module" is used instead of "driver." Modules are separated out of the kernel image purely to save RAM. Modules are sometimes *compiled into* the kernel in the same way that our `test` program was statically linked on page 230. In this case, they would be absent from `/lib/modules/<version>/` and should not really be called modules. In this chapter I show how to create compiled-in or compiled-out versions of modules when rebuilding the kernel.

- Next is the `System.map` file, also in `/boot`. It is used by `klogd` to resolve kernel address references to symbols, so as to write logs about them, and then also by `depmod` to work out *module dependencies* (what modules need what other modules to be loaded first).

- Finally, the kernel headers `/usr/src/linux/include` are used when certain packages are built.

- The "various support daemons" should be running already. Since `2.2`, these have been reduced to `klogd` only. The other kernel daemons that appear to be running are generated by the kernel itself.

42.2 Kernel Version Numbers

The kernel is versioned like other packages: `linux-`*major*`.`*minor*`.`*patch*. Development kernels are given odd minor version numbers; stable kernels are given even minor version numbers. At the time of writing, the stable kernel was `2.2.17`, and `2.4.0` was soon to be released. By the time you read this, `2.4.0` will be available. This chapter should be entirely applicable to future stable releases of `2.4`.

42.3 Modules, `insmod` Command, and Siblings

A module is usually a device driver pertaining to some device node generated with the `mknod` command or already existing in the `/dev/` directory. For instance, the SCSI driver automatically locks onto device major = 8, minor = 0, 1,..., when it loads; and the Sound module onto device major = 14, minor = 3 (`/dev/dsp`), and others. The modules people most often play with are SCSI, Ethernet, and Sound modules. There are also many modules that support extra features instead of hardware.

Modules are loaded with the `insmod` command, and removed with the `rmmod` command. This is somewhat like the operation of linking shown in the `Makefile` on page 233. To list currently loaded modules, use `lsmod`. Try (kernel `2.4` paths are different and are given in braces)

```
insmod /lib/modules/<version>/fs/fat.o
( insmod /lib/modules/<version>/kernel/fs/fat/fat.o )
lsmod
rmmod fat
lsmod
```

`rmmod -a` further removes all unused modules.

Modules sometimes need other modules to be present in order to load. If you try to load a module and it gives `<module-name>: unresolved symbol <symbol-name>` error messages, then it requires something else to be loaded first. The `modprobe` command loads a module along with other modules that it depends on. Try

```
insmod /lib/modules/2.2.12-20/fs/vfat.o
( insmod /lib/modules/<version>/kernel/fs/vfat/vfat.o )
modprobe vfat
```

`modprobe`, however, requires a table of *module dependencies*. This table is the file `/lib/modules/<version>/modules.dep` and is generated automatically by your startup scripts with the command

```
/sbin/depmod -a
```

although you can run it manually at any time. The `lsmod` listing also shows module dependencies in brackets.

```
Module            Size   Used by
de4x5            41396   1    (autoclean)
parport_probe     3204   0    (autoclean)
parport_pc        5832   1    (autoclean)
lp                4648   0    (autoclean)
parport           7320   1    (autoclean) [parport_probe parport_pc lp]
slip              7932   2    (autoclean)
slhc              4504   1    (autoclean) [slip]
sb               33812   0
uart401           6224   0    [sb]
sound            57464   0    [sb uart401]
soundlow           420   0    [sound]
soundcore         2596   6    [sb sound]
loop              7872   2    (autoclean)
nls_iso8859-1     2272   1    (autoclean)
nls_cp437         3748   1    (autoclean)
vfat              9372   1    (autoclean)
fat              30656   1    (autoclean) [vfat]
```

42.4   Interrupts, I/O Ports, and DMA Channels

A loaded module that drives hardware will often consume I/O ports, IRQs, and possibly a DMA channel, as explained in Chapter 3. You can get a full list of occupied resources from the /proc/ directory:

```
[root@cericon]# cat /proc/ioports

0000-001f : dma1
0020-003f : pic1
0040-005f : timer
0060-006f : keyboard
0070-007f : rtc
0080-008f : dma page reg
00a0-00bf : pic2
00c0-00df : dma2
00f0-00ff : fpu
0170-0177 : ide1
01f0-01f7 : ide0
0220-022f : soundblaster
02f8-02ff : serial(auto)
0330-0333 : MPU-401 UART
0376-0376 : ide1
0378-037a : parport0
0388-038b : OPL3/OPL2
03c0-03df : vga+
03f0-03f5 : floppy
03f6-03f6 : ide0
03f7-03f7 : floppy DIR
03f8-03ff : serial(auto)
e400-e47f : DC21140 (eth0)
f000-f007 : ide0
f008-f00f : ide1

[root@cericon]# cat /proc/interrupts

          CPU0
   0:    8409034          XT-PIC   timer
   1:     157231          XT-PIC   keyboard
   2:          0          XT-PIC   cascade
   3:     104347          XT-PIC   serial
   5:          2          XT-PIC   soundblaster
   6:         82          XT-PIC   floppy
   7:          2          XT-PIC   parport0
   8:          1          XT-PIC   rtc
  11:          8          XT-PIC   DC21140 (eth0)
  13:          1          XT-PIC   fpu
```

```
  14:       237337             XT-PIC   ide0
  15:        16919             XT-PIC   ide1
NMI:            0

[root@cericon]# cat /proc/dma

  1: SoundBlaster8
  2: floppy
  4: cascade
  5: SoundBlaster16
```

The above configuration is typical. Note that the second column of the IRQ listing shows the number of interrupts signals received from the device. Moving my mouse a little and listing the IRQs again gives me

```
   3:       104851             XT-PIC   serial
```

showing that several hundred interrupts were since received. Another useful entry is /proc/devices, which shows what major devices numbers were allocated and are being used. This file is extremely useful for seeing what peripherals are "alive" on your system.

42.5 Module Options and Device Configuration

Device modules often need information about their hardware configuration. For instance, ISA device drivers need to know the IRQ and I/O port that the ISA card is physically configured to access. This information is passed to the module as *module options* that the module uses to initialize itself. Note that most devices will *not* need options at all. PCI cards mostly autodetect; it is mostly ISA cards that require these options.

42.5.1 Five ways to pass options to a module

1. If a module is compiled into the kernel, then the module will be initialized at boot time. lilo passes module options to the kernel from the command-line at the LILO: prompt. For instance, at the LILO: prompt, you can type ⟍See Section 4.4⟍:

```
linux aha1542=<portbase>[,<buson>,<busoff>[,<dmaspeed>]]
```

467

to initialize the Adaptec 1542 SCSI driver. What these options are and exactly what goes in them can be learned from the file `/usr/src/linux-<version>/drivers/scsi/aha1542.c`. Near the top of the file are comments explaining the meaning of these options.

2. If you are using `LOADLIN.EXE` or some other DOS or Windows kernel loader, then it, too, can take similar options. I will not go into these.

3. `/etc/lilo.conf` can take the `append =` option, as discussed on page 320. This options passes options to the kernel as though you had typed them at the `LILO:` prompt. The equivalent `lilo.conf` line is

```
append = aha1542=<portbase>[,<buson>,<busoff>[,<dmaspeed>]]
```

This is the most common way of giving kernel boot options.

4. The `insmod` and `modprobe` commands can take options that are passed to the module. These are vastly different from the way you pass options with `append =`. For instance, you can give options to a compiled-in Ethernet module with the commands

```
append = ether=9,0x300,0xd0000,0xd4000,eth0
append = ether=0,0,eth1
```

from within `/etc/lilo.conf`. But then, using `modprobe` on the same "compiled-out" modules, these options have to be specified like this:

```
modprobe wd irq=9 io=0x300 mem=0xd0000 mem_end=0xd4000
modprobe de4x5
```

Note that the `0xd0000,0xd4000` are only applicable to a few Ethernet modules and are usually omitted. Also, the 0's in `ether=0,0,eth1` mean to try autodetect. To find out what options a module will take, you can use the `modinfo` command which shows that the `wd` driver is one of the few Ethernet drivers where you can set their RAM usage. ⟍This has not been discussed, but cards can sometimes use areas of memory directly.⟍

```
[root@cericon]# modinfo -p /lib/modules/<version>/net/wd.o
( [root@cericon]# modinfo -p /lib/modules/<version>/kernel/drivers/net/wd.o )
io int array (min = 1, max = 4)
irq int array (min = 1, max = 4)
mem int array (min = 1, max = 4)
mem_end int array (min = 1, max = 4)
```

5. The file `/etc/modules.conf` ⟍Also sometimes called `/etc/conf.modules`, but now deprecated.⟍ contains default options for `modprobe`, instead of our giving them on the `modprobe` command-line. This is the preferred and most common way of giving module options. Our Ethernet example becomes:

```
alias eth0 wd
alias eth1 de4x5
options wd irq=9 io=0x300 mem=0xd0000 mem_end=0xd4000
```

Having set up an `/etc/modules.conf` file allows module *dynamic loading* to take place. This means that the kernel automatically loads the necessary module whenever the device is required (as when `ifconfig` is first used for Ethernet devices). The kernel merely tries an `/sbin/modprobe eth0`, and the `alias` line hints to `modprobe` to actually run `/sbin/modprobe wd`. Further, the `options` line means to run `/sbin/modprobe wd irq=9 io=0x300 mem=0xd0000 mem_end=0xd4000`. In this way, `/etc/modules.conf` maps devices to drivers.

42.5.2 Module documentation sources

You might like to see a complete summary of all module options with examples of each of the five ways of passing options. No such summary exists at this point, simply because there is no overall consistency and because people are mostly interested in getting one particular device to work, which will doubtless have peculiarities best discussed in a specialized document. Further, some specialized modules are mostly used in compiled-out form, whereas others are mostly used in compiled-in form.

To get an old or esoteric device working, it is best to read the appropriate HOWTO documents: `BootPrompt-HOWTO`, `Ethernet-HOWTO`, and `Sound-HOWTO`. The device could also be documented in `/usr/linux-<version>/Documentation/` or under one of its subdirectories like `sound/` and `networking/`. This is documentation written by the driver authors themselves. Of particular interest is the file `/usr/src/linux/Documentation/networking/-net-modules.txt`, which, although outdated, has a fairly comprehensive list of networking modules and the module options they take. Another source of documentation is the driver **C** code itself, as in the `aha1542.c` example above. It may explain the `/etc/lilo.conf` or `/etc/modules.conf` options to use but will often be quite cryptic. A driver is often written with only one of compiled-in or compiled-out support in mind (even though it really supports both). Choose whether to compile-in or compiled-out based on what is implied in the documentation or **C** source.

42.6   Configuring Various Devices

Further examples on getting common devices to work now follow but only a few devices are discussed. See the documentation sources above for more info. We concentrate here on what is *normally* done.

42.6.1   Sound and `pnpdump`

Plug-and-Play (PnP) ISA sound cards (like SoundBlaster cards) are possibly the more popular of any cards that people have gotten to work under LINUX🐧. Here, we use the sound card example to show how to get a PnP ISA card working in a few minutes. *This is, of course, applicable to cards other than sound.*

A utility called `isapnp` takes one argument, the file `/etc/isapnp.conf`, and configures all ISA Plug-and-Play devices to the IRQs and I/O ports specified therein. `/etc/isapnp.conf` is a complicated file but can be generated with the `pnpdump` utility. `pnpdump` outputs an example `isapnp.conf` file to stdout, which contains IRQ and I/O port values allowed by your devices. You must edit these to unused values. Alternatively, you can use `pnpdump --config` to get a `/etc/isapnp.conf` file with the correct IRQ, I/O port, and DMA channels automatically guessed from an examination of the `/proc/` entries. This comes down to

```
[root@cericon]# pnpdump --config | grep -v '^\(#.*\|\)$' > /etc/isapnp.conf
[root@cericon]# isapnp /etc/isapnp.conf

Board 1 has Identity c9 00 00 ab fa 29 00 8c 0e:  CTL0029 Serial No 44026 [checksum c9]
CTL0029/44026[0]{Audio      }: Ports 0x220 0x330 0x388; IRQ5 DMA1 DMA5 --- Enabled OK
CTL0029/44026[1]{IDE        }: Ports 0x168 0x36E; IRQ10 --- Enabled OK
CTL0029/44026[2]{Game       }: Port 0x200; --- Enabled OK
```

which gets any ISA PnP card configured with just two commands. Note that the `/etc/isapnp.gone` file can be used to make `pnpdump` avoid using certain IRQ and I/O ports. Mine contains

```
IO 0x378,2
IRQ 7
```

to avoid conflicting with my parallel port. `isapnp /etc/isapnp.conf` must be run each time at boot and is probably already in your startup scripts.

Now that your ISA card is enabled, you can install the necessary modules. You can read the `/etc/isapnp.conf` file and also `isapnp`'s output above to reference the I/O ports to the correct module options:

```
alias sound-slot-0 sb
alias sound-service-0-0 sb
alias sound-service-0-1 sb
```

```
   alias sound-service-0-2 sb
 5 alias sound-service-0-3 sb
   alias sound-service-0-4 sb
   alias synth0 sb
   post-install sb /sbin/modprobe "-k" "adlib_card"
   options sb io=0x220 irq=5 dma=1 dma16=5 mpu_io=0x330
10 options adlib_card io=0x388      # FM synthesizer
```

Now run `tail -f /var/log/messages /var/log/syslog`, and then at another terminal type:

```
depmod -a
modprobe sb
```

If you get no kernel or other errors, then the devices are working.

Now we want to set up dynamic loading of the module. Remove all the sound and other modules with `rmmod -a` (or manually), and then try:

```
aumix
```

You should get a kernel log like this:

```
Sep 24 00:45:19 cericon kernel: Soundblaster audio driver
 Copyright (C) by Hannu Savolainen 1993-1996
Sep 24 00:45:19 cericon kernel: SB 4.13 detected OK (240)
```

Then try:

```
playmidi <somefile>.mid
```

You should get a kernel log like this one:

```
Sep 24 00:51:34 cericon kernel: Soundblaster audio driver
 Copyright (C) by Hannu Savolainen 1993-1996
Sep 24 00:51:34 cericon kernel: SB 4.13 detected OK (240)
Sep 24 00:51:35 cericon kernel: YM3812 and OPL-3 driver
 5 Copyright (C) by Hannu Savolainen, Rob Hooft 1993-1996
```

If you had to comment out the `alias` lines, then a kernel message like `modprobe: Can't locate module sound-slot-0` would result. This indicates that the kernel is attempting a `/sbin/modprobe sound-slot-0`: a cue to insert an `alias` line. Actually, `sound-service-0-0,1,2,3,4` are the `/dev/mixer,sequencer,midi,dsp,audio` devices, respectively. `sound-slot-0` means a card that should supply all of these. The `post-install` option means to run an additional command after installing the `sb` module; this takes care of the Adlib sequencer driver. ⟍I was tempted to try removing the `post-install` line and adding a `alias sound-service-0-1 adlib_card`. This works, but not if you run `aumix` before `playmidi`, ⁎⁎*shrug*⁎⁎.⟍

42.6.2 Parallel port

The parallel port module is much less trouble:

```
alias parport_lowlevel parport_pc
options parport_lowlevel io=0x378 irq=7
```

Merely make sure that your IRQ and I/O port match those in your CMOS (see Section 3.3), and that they do not conflict with any other devices.

42.6.3 NIC — Ethernet, PCI, and old ISA

Here I demonstrate non-PnP ISA cards and PCI cards, using Ethernet devices as an example. (NIC stands for Network Interface Card, that is, an Ethernet 10 or 100 Mb card.)

For old ISA cards with jumpers, you will need to check your `/proc/` files for unused IRQ and I/O ports and then physically set the jumpers. Now you can do a `modprobe` as usual, for example:

```
modinfo -p ne
modprobe ne io=0x300 irq=9
```

Of course, for dynamic loading, your `/etc/modules.conf` file must have the lines:

```
alias eth0 ne
options ne io=0x300 irq=9
```

On some occasions you will come across a card that has software configurable jumpers, like PnP, but that can only be configured with a DOS utility. In this case compiling the module into the kernel will cause it to be autoprobed on startup *without needing any other configuration.*

A worst case scenario is *a card whose make is unknown, as well its IRQ and I/O ports.* The chip number on the card can sometimes give you a hint (`grep` the kernel sources for this number), but not always. To get this card working, compile in support for several modules, one of which the card is likely to be. Experience will help you make better guesses. If one of your guesses is correct, your card will almost certainly be discovered on reboot. You can find its IRQ and I/O port values in /proc/ or you can run dmesg to see the autoprobe message line; the message will begin with eth0: ... and contain some information about the driver. This information can be used if you decide later to use modules instead of your custom kernel.

As explained, PCI devices almost never require IRQ or I/O ports to be given as options. As long as you have the correct module, a simple

```
modprobe <module>
```

will always work. Finding the correct module can still be a problem, however, because suppliers will call a card all sorts of marketable things besides the actual chipset it is compatible with. The utility scanpci (which is actually part of **X**) checks your PCI slots for PCI devices. Running scanpci might output something like:

```
     .
     .
     .
   pci bus 0x0 cardnum 0x09 function 0x0000: vendor 0x1011 device 0x0009
5    Digital DC21140 10/100 Mb/s Ethernet

   pci bus 0x0 cardnum 0x0b function 0x0000: vendor 0x8086 device 0x1229
    Intel 82557/8/9 10/100MBit network controller

10  pci bus 0x0 cardnum 0x0c function 0x0000: vendor 0x1274 device 0x1371
    Ensoniq es1371
```

Another utility is lspci from the pciutils package, which gives comprehensive information where scanpci sometimes gives none. Then a simple script (kernel 2.4 paths in parentheses again),

```
   for i in /lib/modules/<version>/net/* ; do strings $i \
                                  | grep -q -i 21140 && echo $i ; done
   ( for i in /lib/modules/<version>/kernel/drivers/net/* \
                          ; do strings $i | grep -q -i 21140 && echo $i ; done )
5  for i in /lib/modules/<version>/net/* ; do strings $i \
                                  | grep -q -i 8255 && echo $i ; done
   ( for i in /lib/modules/<version>/kernel/drivers/net/* \
                          ; do strings $i | grep -q -i 8255 && echo $i ; done )
```

faithfully outputs three modules de4x5.o, eepro100.o, and tulip.o, of which two are correct. On another system lspci gave

```
     .
     .
     .
   00:08.0 Ethernet controller: Macronix, Inc. [MXIC] MX987x5 (rev 20)
5  00:0a.0 Ethernet controller: Accton Technology Corporation SMC2-1211TX (rev 10)
```

and the same `for...grep...Accton` gave `rtl8139.o` and `tulip.o` (the former of which was correct), and `for...grep...Macronix` (or even `987`) gave `tulip.o`, which hung the machine. I have yet to get that card working, although Eddie across the room claims he got a similar card working fine. Cards are cheap—there are enough working brands so that you don't have to waist your time on difficult ones.

42.6.4   PCI vendor ID and device ID

PCI supports the useful concept that every vendor and device have unique hex IDs. For instance, Intel has chosen to represent themselves by the completely random number 0x8086 as their vendor ID. PCI cards will provide their IDs on request. You will see numerical values listed in the output of `lspci`, `scanpci`, and `cat /proc/pci`, especially if the respective utility cannot look up the vendor name from the ID number. The file `/usr/share/pci.ids` (`/usr/share/misc/pci.ids` on Debian ⊙) from the `pciutils` package contains a complete table of all IDs and their corresponding names. The `kudzu` package also has a table `/usr/share/kudzu/pcitable` containing the information we are *really* looking for: ID to kernel module mappings. This enables you to use the intended scientific method for locating the correct PCI module from the kernel's `/proc/pci` data. The file format is easy to understand, and as an exercise you should try writing a shell script to do the lookup automatically.

42.6.5   PCI and sound

The `scanpci` output just above also shows the popular Ensoniq sound card, sometimes built into motherboards. Simply adding the line

```
alias sound es1371
```

to your `modules.conf` file will get this card working. It is relatively easy to find the type of card from the card itself—Ensoniq cards actually have es1371 printed on one of the chips.

42.6.6   Commercial sound drivers

If your card is not listed in `/usr/src/<version>/Documentation/sound/`, then you might be able to get a driver from *Open Sound* http://www.opensound.com. If you still can't find a driver, complain to the manufacturer by email.

There are a lot of sound (and other) cards whose manufacturers refuse to supply the Free software community with specs. Disclosure of programming information would enable LINUX △ *users to buy their cards; Free software developers would produce a driver at no cost. Actually, manufacturers' reasons are often just pig-headedness.*

42.6.7   The ALSA sound project

The ALSA (*Advanced Linux Sound Architecture* http://www.alsa-project.org/) project aims to provide better kernel sound support. If your card is not supported by the standard kernel or you are not getting the most out of the standard kernel drivers, then do check this web site.

42.6.8   Multiple Ethernet cards

If you have more than one Ethernet card, you can easily specify both in your `modules.conf` file, as shown in Section 42.5 above. Modules compiled into the kernel only probe a single card (`eth0`) by default. Adding the line

```
append = "ether=0,0,eth1 ether=0,0,eth2 ether=0,0,eth3"
```

will cause `eth1`, `eth2`, and `eth3` to be probed as well. Further, replacing the 0's with actual values can force certain interfaces to certain physical cards. If all your cards are PCI, however, you will have to get the order of assignment by experimentation.

    If you have two of the same card, your kernel may complain when you try to load the same module twice. The `-o` option to `insmod` specifies a different internal name for the driver to trick the kernel into thinking that the driver is not really loaded:

```
alias eth0 3c509
alias eth1 3c509
options eth0 -o 3c509-0 io=0x280 irq=5
options eth1 -o 3c509-1 io=0x300 irq=7
```

However, with the following two PCI cards that deception was not necessary:

```
alias eth0 rtl8139
alias eth1 rtl8139
```

42.6.9   SCSI disks

SCSI (pronounced *scuzzy*) stands for *Small Computer System Interface*. SCSI is a ribbon, a specification, and an electronic protocol for communication between devices and computers. Like your IDE ribbons, SCSI ribbons can connect to their own SCSI hard disks. SCSI ribbons have gone through some versions to make SCSI faster, the latest "Ultra-Wide" SCSI ribbons are thin, with a dense array of pins. Unlike your IDE, SCSI can also connect tape drives, scanners, and many other types of peripherals. SCSI theoretically allows multiple computers to share the same device, although I have not seen this implemented in practice. Because many UNIX hardware platforms only support SCSI, it has become an integral part of UNIX operating systems.

SCSIs also introduce the concept of *LUNs* (which stands for *Logical Unit Number*), *Buses,* and *ID.* These are just numbers given to each device in order of the SCSI cards you are using (if more than one), the SCSI cables on those cards, and the SCSI devices on those cables—the SCSI standard was designed to support a great many of these. The kernel assigns each SCSI drive in sequence as it finds them: /dev/sda, /dev/sdb, and so on, so these details are usually irrelevant.

An enormous amount should be said on SCSI, but the bare bones is that for 90% of situations, insmod <pci-scsi-driver> is all you are going to need. You can then immediately begin accessing the device through /dev/sd? for disks, /dev/st? for tapes, /dev/scd? for CD-ROMs, or /dev/sg? for scanners. ↘Scanner user programs will have docs on what devices they access.↖ SCSIs often also come with their own BIOS that you can enter on startup (like your CMOS). This will enable you to set certain things. In some cases, where your distribution compiles-out certain modules, you may have to load one of sd_mod.o, st.o, sr_mod.o, or sg.o, respectively. The core scsi_mod.o module may also need loading, and /dev/ devices may need to be created. A safe bet is to run

```
cd /dev
./MAKEDEV -v sd
./MAKEDEV -v st0 st1 st2 st3
./MAKEDEV -v scd0 scd1 scd2 scd3
./MAKEDEV -v sg
```

to ensure that all necessary device files exist in the first place.

It is recommended that you compile into your kernel support for your SCSI card (also called the *SCSI Host Adapter*) that you have, as well as support for tapes, CD-ROMs, etc. When your system next boots, everything will just autoprobe. An example system with a SCSI disk and tape gives the following at bootup:

```
(scsi0) <Adaptec AIC-7895 Ultra SCSI host adapter> found at PCI 0/12/0
(scsi0) Wide Channel A, SCSI ID=7, 32/255 SCBs
(scsi0) Cables present (Int-50 YES, Int-68 YES, Ext-68 YES)
(scsi0) Illegal cable configuration!!  Only two
(scsi0) connectors on the SCSI controller may be in use at a time!
(scsi0) Downloading sequencer code... 384 instructions downloaded
(scsi1) <Adaptec AIC-7895 Ultra SCSI host adapter> found at PCI 0/12/1
(scsi1) Wide Channel B, SCSI ID=7, 32/255 SCBs
(scsi1) Downloading sequencer code... 384 instructions downloaded
scsi0 : Adaptec AHA274x/284x/294x (EISA/VLB/PCI-Fast SCSI) 5.1.28/3.2.4
        <Adaptec AIC-7895 Ultra SCSI host adapter>
scsi1 : Adaptec AHA274x/284x/294x (EISA/VLB/PCI-Fast SCSI) 5.1.28/3.2.4
        <Adaptec AIC-7895 Ultra SCSI host adapter>
scsi : 2 hosts.
(scsi0:0:0:0) Synchronous at 40.0 Mbyte/sec, offset 8.
  Vendor: FUJITSU   Model: MAE3091LP        Rev: 0112
```

```
     Type:   Direct-Access                    ANSI SCSI revision: 02
    Detected scsi disk sda at scsi0, channel 0, id 0, lun 0
    (scsi0:0:3:0) Synchronous at 10.0 Mbyte/sec, offset 15.
20   Vendor: HP        Model: C1533A          Rev: A708
     Type:   Sequential-Access                ANSI SCSI revision: 02
    Detected scsi tape st0 at scsi0, channel 0, id 3, lun 0
    scsi : detected 1 SCSI tape 1 SCSI disk total.
    SCSI device sda: hdwr sector= 512 bytes. Sectors= 17826240 [8704 MB] [8.7 GB]
25   .
     .
     .
    Partition check:
     sda: sda1
30   hda: hda1 hda2 hda3 hda4
     hdb: hdb1
```

You should also check Section 31.5 to find out how to boot SCSI disks when the needed module... is on a file system... inside a SCSI disk... that needs the module.

For actually using a tape drive, see page 149.

42.6.10   SCSI termination and cooling

This is the most important section to read regarding SCSI. You may be used to IDE ribbons that just plug in and work. SCSI ribbons are not of this variety; they need to be impedance matched and terminated. These are electrical technicians' terms. Basically, it means that you must use high-quality SCSI ribbons and *terminate* your SCSI device. SCSI ribbons allow many SCSI disks and tapes to be connected to one ribbon. *Terminating* means setting certain jumpers or switches on the last devices on the ribbon. It may also mean plugging the last cable connector into something else. Your adapter documentation and disk documentation should explain what to do. If you terminate incorrectly, everything may work fine, but you may get disk errors later in the life of the machine. Also note that some newer SCSI devices have automatic termination.

Cooling is another important consideration. When the documentation for a disk drive recommends **forced air cooling** for that drive, *it usually means it*. SCSI drives get extremely hot and can burn out in time. Forced air cooling can mean as little as buying a cheap circuit box fan and tying it in a strategic position. You should also use very large cases with several inches of space between drives. Anyone who has opened up an expensive high end server will see the attention paid to air cooling.

42.6.11   CD writers

A system with an ATAPI (IDE CD-Writer *and* ordinary CD-ROM will display a message at bootup like,

```
hda: FUJITSU MPE3084AE, ATA DISK drive
hdb: CD-ROM 50X L, ATAPI CDROM drive
hdd: Hewlett-Packard CD-Writer Plus 9300, ATAPI CDROM drive
```

Note that these devices should give BIOS messages before `LILO:` *starts to indicate that they are correctly installed.*

The `/etc/modules.conf` lines to get the CD-writer working are:

```
alias    scd0 sr_mod            # load sr_mod upon access of /dev/scd0
alias    scsi_hostadapter ide-scsi   # SCSI hostadaptor emulation
options ide-cd ignore="hda hdc hdd"  # Our normal IDE CD is on /dev/hdb
```

The `alias scd0` line must be omitted if `sr_mod` is compiled into the kernel—search your `/lib/modules/<version>/` directory. Note that the kernel does not support ATAPI CD-Writers directly. The `ide-scsi` module *emulates* a SCSI adapter on behalf of the ATAPI CD-ROM. CD-Writer software expects to speak to `/dev/scd?`, and the `ide-scsi` module makes this device appear like a real SCSI CD writer. ↘Real SCSI CD writers are much more expensive.↖ There is one caveat: your ordinary IDE CD-ROM driver, `ide-cd`, will also want to probe your CD writer as if it were a normal CD-ROM. The `ignore` option makes the `ide-cd` module overlook any drives that should not be probed—on this system, these would be the hard disk, CD writer, and non-existent secondary master. *However*, there is no way of giving an `ignore` option to a compiled-in `ide-cd` module (which is how many distributions ship), so read on.

An alternative is to compile in support for `ide-scsi` and completely leave out support for `ide-cd`. Your normal CD-ROM will work perfectly as a read-only CD-ROM under SCSI emulation. ↘Even with music CDs.↖ This means setting the relevant sections of your kernel configuration menu:

```
<*> Enhanced IDE/MFM/RLL disk/cdrom/tape/floppy support
< >     Include IDE/ATAPI CDROM support
<*>     SCSI emulation support

<*> SCSI support
<*> SCSI CD-ROM support
[*]     Enable vendor-specific extensions (for SCSI CDROM)
<*> SCSI generic support
```

No further configuration is needed, and on bootup, you will find messages like:

```
scsi0 : SCSI host adapter emulation for IDE ATAPI devices
scsi : 1 host.
  Vendor: E-IDE      Model: CD-ROM 50X L     Rev: 12
  Type:   CD-ROM                             ANSI SCSI revision: 02
Detected scsi CD-ROM sr0 at scsi0, channel 0, id 0, lun 0
  Vendor: HP         Model: CD-Writer+ 9300  Rev: 1.0b
```

```
    Type:   CD-ROM                        ANSI SCSI revision: 02
Detected scsi CD-ROM sr1 at scsi0, channel 0, id 1, lun 0
scsi : detected 2 SCSI generics 2 SCSI cdroms total.
sr0: scsi3-mmc drive: 4x/50x cd/rw xa/form2 cdda tray
Uniform CD-ROM driver Revision: 3.10
sr1: scsi3-mmc drive: 32x/32x writer cd/rw xa/form2 cdda tray
```

If you do have a real SCSI writer, compiling in support for your SCSI card will detect it in a similar fashion. Then, for this example, the device on which to mount your CD-ROM is /dev/scd0 and your CD-Writer, /dev/scd1.

For actually recording a CD disc, the cdrecord command-line program is simple and robust, although there are also many pretty graphical front ends. To locate your CD disc ID, run

```
cdrecord -scanbus
```

which will give a comma-separated numeric sequence. You can then use this sequence as the argument to cdrecord's dev= option. On my machine I type

```
mkisofs -a -A 'Paul Sheer' -J -L -r -P PaulSheer \
        -p www.icon.co.za/~psheer/ -o my_iso /my/directory
cdrecord dev=0,1,0 -v speed=10 -isosize -eject my_iso
```

to create an ISO9660 CD-ROM out of everything below a directory /my/directory. This is most useful for backups. (The -a option should be omitted in newer versions of this command.) Beware not to exceed the speed limit of your CD writer.

42.6.12 Serial devices

You don't need to load any modules to get your mouse and modem to work. Regular serial devices (COM1 through COM4 under DOS/Windows) will autoprobe on boot and are available as /dev/ttyS0 through /dev/ttyS3. A message on boot, like

```
Serial driver version 4.27 with MANY_PORTS MULTIPORT SHARE_IRQ enabled
ttyS00 at 0x03f8 (irq = 4) is a 16550A
ttyS01 at 0x02f8 (irq = 3) is a 16550A
```

will testify to their correct detection.

On the other hand, multiport serial cards can be difficult to configure. These devices are in a category all of their own. Most use a chip called the *16550A UART* (Universal Asynchronous Receiver Transmitter), which is similar to that of your built-in serial port. The kernel's generic serial code supports them, and you will not need a separate driver. The UART really *is* the serial port and comes in the flavors 8250, 16450, 16550, 16550A, 16650, 16650V2, and 16750.

To get these cards working requires the use of the `setserial` command. It is used to configure the kernel's built-in serial driver. A typical example is an 8-port non-PnP ISA card with jumpers set to unused IRQ 5 and ports `0x180–0x1BF`. Note that unlike most devices, many serial devices can share the same IRQ. ↘The reason is that serial devices set an I/O port to tell which device is sending the interrupt. The CPU just checks every serial device whenever an interrupt comes in.↖ The card is configured with this script:

```
     cd /dev/
     ./MAKEDEV -v ttyS4
     ./MAKEDEV -v ttyS5
     ./MAKEDEV -v ttyS6
5    ./MAKEDEV -v ttyS7
     ./MAKEDEV -v ttyS8
     ./MAKEDEV -v ttyS9
     ./MAKEDEV -v ttyS10
     ./MAKEDEV -v ttyS11
10   /bin/setserial -v /dev/ttyS4 irq 5 port 0x180 uart 16550A skip_test
     /bin/setserial -v /dev/ttyS5 irq 5 port 0x188 uart 16550A skip_test
     /bin/setserial -v /dev/ttyS6 irq 5 port 0x190 uart 16550A skip_test
     /bin/setserial -v /dev/ttyS7 irq 5 port 0x198 uart 16550A skip_test
     /bin/setserial -v /dev/ttyS8 irq 5 port 0x1A0 uart 16550A skip_test
15   /bin/setserial -v /dev/ttyS9 irq 5 port 0x1A8 uart 16550A skip_test
     /bin/setserial -v /dev/ttyS10 irq 5 port 0x1B0 uart 16550A skip_test
     /bin/setserial -v /dev/ttyS11 irq 5 port 0x1B8 uart 16550A skip_test
```

You should immediately be able to use these devices as regular ports. Note that you would expect to see the interrupt in use under `/proc/interrupts`. For serial devices this is only true after data actually starts to flow. However, you can check `/proc/tty/driver/serial` to get more status information. The `setserial` man page contains more about different UARTs and their compatibility problems. It also explains autoprobing of the UART, IRQ, and I/O ports (although it is better to be sure of your card and never use autoprobing).

Serial devices give innumerable problems. There is a very long `Serial-HOWTO` that will help you solve most of them; It goes into more technical detail. It will also explain special kernel support for many "nonstandard" cards.

42.7 Modem Cards

Elsewhere in this book I refer only to ordinary external modems that connect to your machine's auxiliary serial port. However, internal ISA modem cards are cheaper and include their own internal serial port. This card can be treated as above, like an ISA multiport serial card with only one port: just set the I/O port and IRQ jumpers and then run `setserial /dev/ttyS3`... .

Beware that a new variety of modem has been invented called the "win-modem." These cards are actually just sound cards. Your operating system has to generate the signals needed to talk the same protocol as a regular modem. Because the CPU has to be very fast to do this, such modems were probably not viable before 1997 or so. http://linmodems.technion.ac.il/, http://www.idir.net/˜gromitkc/winmodem.html, and http://www.-linmodems.org/ are three resources that cover these modems.

42.8 More on `LILO`: Options

The `BootPrompt-HOWTO` contains an exhaustive list of things that can be typed at the boot prompt to do interesting things like NFS root mounts. This document is important to read if only to get an idea of the features that LINUX⌂ supports.

42.9 Building the Kernel

Summary:

```
cd /usr/src/linux/
make mrproper
make menuconfig
make dep
make clean
make bzImage
make modules
make modules_install
cp /usr/src/linux/arch/i386/boot/bzImage /boot/vmlinuz-<version>
cp /usr/src/linux/System.map /boot/System.map-<version>
```

Finally, edit `/etc/lilo.conf` and run `lilo`. Details on each of these steps follow.

42.9.1 Unpacking and patching

The LINUX⌂ kernel is available from various places as `linux-?.?.?.tar.gz`, but primarily from *the* LINUX⌂ *kernel's home* ftp://ftp.kernel.org/pub/linux/kernel/.

The kernel can easily be unpacked with

```
cd /usr/src
mv linux linux-OLD
tar -xzf linux-2.4.0-test6.tar.gz
mv linux linux-2.4.0-test6
ln -s linux-2.4.0-test6 linux
cd linux
```

and possibly patched with (see Section 20.7.3):

```
  bzip2 -cd ../patch-2.4.0-test7.bz2 | patch -s -p1
  cd ..
  mv linux-2.4.0-test6 linux-2.4.0-test7
  ln -sf linux-2.4.0-test7 linux
5 cd linux
  make mrproper
```

Your 2.4.0-test6 kernel source tree is now a 2.4.0-test7 kernel source tree. You will often want to patch the kernel with features that Linus did not include, like security patches or commercial hardware drivers.

Important is that the following include directories point to the correct directories in the kernel source tree:

```
[root@cericon]# ls -al /usr/include/{linux,asm} /usr/src/linux/include/asm
lrwxrwxrwx  1 root   root    24 Sep  4 13:45 /usr/include/asm -> ../src/linux/include/asm
lrwxrwxrwx  1 root   root    26 Sep  4 13:44 /usr/include/linux -> ../src/linux/include/linux
lrwxrwxrwx  1 root   root     8 Sep  4 13:45 /usr/src/linux/include/asm -> asm-i386
```

Before continuing, you should read the Changes file (under /usr/src/linux/Documentation/) to find out what is required to build the kernel. If you have a kernel source tree supplied by your distribution, everything will already be up-to-date.

42.9.2 Configuring

(A kernel tree that has suffered from previous builds may need you to run

```
make mrproper
```

before anything else. This completely cleans the tree, as though you had just unpacked it.)

There are three kernel configuration interfaces. The old line-for-line y/n interface is painful to use. For a better text mode interface, you can type

```
make menuconfig
```

otherwise, under **X** enter

```
make xconfig
```

to get the graphical configurator. For this discussion, I assume that you are using the text-mode interface.

The configure program enables you to specify an enormous number of features. It is advisable to skim through all the sections to get a feel for the different things you can do. Most options are about specifying whether you want a feature **[*]** compiled into the kernel image, **[M]** compiled as a module, or **[ ]** not compiled at all. You can also turn off module support altogether from **Loadable module support --->**. The kernel configuration is one LINUX⚓ program that offers lots of help—select **< Help >** on any feature. The raw help file is `/usr/src/linux/Documentation/Configure.help` (nearly 700 kilobytes) and is worth reading.

When you are satisfied with your selection of options, select **< Exit >** and select **save your new kernel configuration**.

The kernel configuration is saved in a file `/usr/src/linux/.config`. Next time you run `make menuconfig`, your configuration will default to these settings. The file `/usr/src/linux/arch/i386/defconfig` contains defaults to use in the absence of a `.config` file. Note that the command `make mrproper` removes the `.config` file.

42.10   Using Packaged Kernel Source

Your distribution will probably have a kernel source package ready to build. This package is better to use than downloading the source yourself because all the default build options will be present; for instance, RedHat 7.0 comes with the file `/usr/src/linux-2.2.16/configs/kernel-2.2.16-i586-smp.config`, which can be copied over the `/usr/src/linux-2.2.16/.config` to build a kernel optimized for SMP (*Symmetric Multiprocessor Support*) with all of Red-Hat's defaults enabled. It also comes with a custom `defconfig` file to build kernels identical to those of RedHat. Finally, RedHat would have applied many patches to add features that may be time consuming to do yourself. The same goes for Debianⓒ.

You should try to enable or "compile-in" features rather than disable anything, since the default RedHat kernel supports almost every kernel feature, and later it may be more convenient to have left it that way. On the other hand, a minimal kernel will compile much faster.

42.11   Building, Installing

Run the following commands to build the kernel; this process may take anything from a few minutes to several hours, depending on what you have enabled. After each command completes, check the last few messages for errors (or check the return code, `$?`), rather than blindly typing the next commands.

```
  make dep && \
  make clean && \
  make bzImage && \
  make modules && \
5 make modules_install
```

The command `make modules_install` would have installed all modules into
`/lib/modules/<version>`. ↘You may like to clear out this directory at some point and rerun
`make modules_install`, since stale modules cause problems with `depmod -a`.↖

The kernel image itself, `/usr/src/linux/arch/i386/boot/bzImage`, and
`/usr/src/linux/System.map` are two other files produced by the build. These
must be copied to `/boot/`, possibly creating neat symlinks:

```
cp /usr/src/linux/arch/i386/boot/bzImage /boot/vmlinuz-<version>
cp /usr/src/linux/System.map /boot/System.map-<version>
ln -sf System.map-<version> /boot/System.map
ln -sf /boot/vmlinuz-<version> vmlinuz
```

Finally, your `lilo.conf` may be edited as described in Chapter 31. Most people
now forget to run `lilo` and find their system unbootable. Do run `lilo`, making sure
that you have left your old kernel in as an option, in case you need to return to it. Also
make a boot floppy from your kernel, as shown in Section 31.4.

Chapter 43

The X Window System

Before *The X Window System* (from now on called **X**), UNIX was terminal based and had no proper graphical environment, sometimes called a *GUI*. ↘Graphical User Interface.↖ **X** was designed to fulfill that need and to incorporate into graphics all the power of a networked computer.

X was developed in 1985 at the Massachusetts Institute of Technology by the X Consortium and is now owned by the Open Software Foundation (OSF). It comprises over 2 million lines of **C** code that run on every variant of UNIX.

You might imagine that allowing an application to put graphics on a screen involves nothing more than creating a user library that can perform various graphical functions like line drawing, font drawing, and so on. To understand why **X** is more than merely this, consider the example of character terminal applications: these are programs that run on a *remote* machine while displaying to a character terminal and receiving feedback (keystrokes) from that character terminal. There are two distinct entities at work—the application and the user's character terminal display; these two are connected by some kind of serial or network link. Now what if the character terminal could display windows and other graphics (in addition to text), while giving feedback to the application with a mouse (as well as a keyboard)? This is what **X** achieves.

43.1 The X Protocol

X is a protocol of commands that are sent and received between an application and a special graphical terminal called an *X Server* (from now on called the *server*). ↘The word "server" is confusing, because there are lots of X servers for each client machine, and the user sits on the server side. This is in the opposite sense to what we usually mean by a server.↖ How the server actually draws graphics on the hardware is irrelevant to the developer; all the application

485

needs to know is that if it sends a particular sequence of bytes down the TCP/IP link, the server will interpret them to mean that a line, circle, font, box, or other graphics entity should be drawn on its screen. In the other direction, the application needs to know that particular sequences of bytes mean that a keyboard key was pressed or that a mouse has moved. This TCP communication is called the *X protocol*.

When you are using **X**, you will probably not be aware that this interaction is happening. The server and the application might very well be on the same machine. The real power of **X** is evident when they are *not* on the same machine. Consider, for example, that 20 users can be logged in to a single machine and be running different programs that are displayed on 20 different remote **X** servers. It is as though a single machine was given multiple screens and keyboards. It is for this reason that **X** is called a *network transparent windowing system*.

The developer of a graphical application can then dispense with having to know anything about the graphics hardware itself (consider DOS applications where each had to build in support for many different graphics cards), and that developer can also dispense with having to know what machine the graphics will be displayed on.

The precise program that performs this miracle is `/usr/X11/bin/X`. A typical sequence of events to get a graphical program to run is as follows. (This is an illustration. In practice, numerous utilities perform these functions in a more generalized and user-friendly way.)

1. The program `/usr/X11R6/bin/X` is started and run in the background. **X** will detect through configuration files (`/etc/XF86Config` or `/etc/X11/XF86Config` on LINUX⚙), and possibly through hardware autodetection, what graphics hardware (like a graphics add-on card) is available. It then initializes that hardware into graphics mode.

2. It then opens a socket connection to listen for incoming requests on a specific port (usually TCP port 6000), being ready to interpret any connection as a stream of graphics commands.

3. An application is started on the local machine or on a remote machine. *All* **X** programs have a configuration option by which you can specify (with an IP address or host name) where you would like the program to connect, that is, on which server you would like the resulting output to display.

4. The application opens a socket connection to the specified server over the network. This is the most frequent source of errors. Applications fail to connect to a server because the server is not running, because the server was specified incorrectly, or because the server refuses a connection from an untrusted host.

5. The application begins sending **X** protocol requests, waiting for them to be processed, and then receiving and processing the resulting **X** protocol responses. From the user's point of view, the application now appears to be "running" on the server's display.

Communication between the application and the server is somewhat more complex than the mere drawing of lines and rectangles and reporting of mouse and key events. The server must be able to handle multiple applications connecting from multiple machines, and these applications may interact with each other (think of *cut* and *paste* operations between applications that are actually running on different machines.) Some examples of the fundamental *X Protocol* requests that an application can make to a server are the following:

"Create Window" A window is a logical rectangle on the screen, owned by particular application, into which graphics can be drawn.

"List Fonts" To list fonts available to the application.

"Allocate Color" Will define a color of the specified name or RGB value for later use.

"Create Graphics Context" A Graphics Context is a definition of how graphics are to be drawn within a window—for example, the default background color, line style, clipping, and font.

"Get Selection Owner" Find which window (possibly belonging to another application) owns the selection (i.e., a "cut" of text).

In return, the server replies by sending *events* back to the application. The application is required to constantly poll the server for these events. Besides events detailing the user's mouse and keyboard input, there are other events, for example, that indicate that a window has been *exposed* (a window on top of another window was moved, thus exposing the window beneath it. The application should then send the appropriate commands needed to redraw the graphics within the window now on top). Another example is a notification to request a *paste* from another application. The file `/usr/include/X11/Xproto.h` contains the full list of **X** protocol requests and events.

The programmer of an **X** application need not be directly concerned with these requests. A high-level library handles the details of the server interaction. This library is called the *X Library*, `/usr/X11R6/lib/libX11.so.6`.

One of the limitations of such a protocol is that developers are restricted to the set of commands that have been defined. **X** overcame this problem by making the protocol *extensible* ↘Being able to add extensions and enhancements without complicating or breaking compatibility.↖ from the start. These days there are extensions to **X** to allow, for example, the display of 3D graphics on the server, the interpretation of PostScript commands, and many other capabilities that improve aesthetic appeal and performance. Each extension comes with a new group of **X** protocol requests and events, as well as a programmers' library interface.

An example of a real **X** program follows. This is about the simplest an **X** program is ever going to get. The program displays a small XPM image file in a window and waits for a key press or mouse click before exiting. You can compile it with `gcc -o splash splash.c -lX11 -L/usr/X11R6/lib`. (You can see right away why there are few applications written directly in **X**.) Notice that all **X** library functions are prefixed by an X.

```c
/* splash.c - display an image */

#include <stdlib.h>
#include <stdio.h>
#include <string.h>

#include <X11/Xlib.h>

/* XPM */
static char *graham_splash[] = {
/* columns rows colors chars-per-pixel */
"28 32 16 1",
"  c #34262e", ". c #4c3236", "X c #673a39", "o c #543b44",
"O c #724e4e", "+ c #6a5459", "@ c #6c463c", "# c #92706c",
"$ c #92685f", "% c #987e84", "& c #aa857b", "n c #b2938f",
"= c #bca39b", "- c #a89391", "; c #c4a49e", ": c #c4a8a4",
/* pixels */
"--%#%%nnnn#-nnnnnn=====;;=;:", "--------n-nnnnnn=n==;==;=:;:",
"----n--n-n-n-n-nn===:::::::", "-----&------nn-n=n====:::::::",
"----------------n===;=:::::::", "----%&-%--%##%---n===::::::::",
"------%#%+++o+++----=:::::::", "--#-%%#+++oo. oo+#--=::::::::",
"-%%%%++++o..  .++&-==:::::::", "---%#+#+++o.    oo+&n=::::::",
"--%###+$+++Oo.    o+#-:=::", "-&%#########++Oo    @$-==::",
"####$$$+####$++OX   .O+&==", "&##$O+OXo+++$#+Oo.  ..O&&-",
"&##+OX..... .oOO@@... o@+&&", "&####$Oo.o++    ..oX@oo@O$&-",
"n###$$$$O$o ...X.. .XXX@$$$&", "nnn##$$#$OO. .XX+@ .XXX@$$#&",
"nnn&&%####$OX.X$$@.  XX$$$$&", "nnnnn&&###$$$OX$$X..XXX@O$&n",
"nnnnnn&&%###$$$$@XXXXX@O$&&n", ";n=;nnnn&&#$$$$$@@@@@O$&n;",
";n;=nn;nnnn#&$$$@X@O$@@$$&n;", "=n=;;;n;;nn&&$$$OO$$$$&;;",
"n;=n;;=nn&n&&&&$$$$$##&&n;", "n;=;;;;;;;&&n&&&&&&&#&n=;",
";n;n;;=n;&;&;&n&&&&&&&nn;;;", "n;=;;;;;;;n;&&n&&n&nnnn;;;",
"n=;;;;;=;;nn;&n;&n&nnnnnnn=;", "nn;;;;;;;;;;;;;n&nnnnnnn===;",
"=nn;;;;n;;;;&&&n&&nnnnnn;=;", "n====;;;;&&&&&&nnnnnnnnnn;;"
};

int main (int argc, char **argv)
{
    int i, j, x, y, width, height, n_colors;
    XSetWindowAttributes xswa;
    XGCValues gcv;
    Display *display;
    char *display_name = 0;
    int depth = 0;
    Visual *visual;
    Window window;
    Pixmap pixmap;
    XImage *image;
    Colormap colormap;
    GC gc;
    int bytes_per_pixel;
    unsigned long colors[256];
    unsigned char **p, *q;
    for (i = 1; i < argc - 1; i++)
        if (argv[i])
            if (!strcmp (argv[i], "-display"))
                display_name = argv[i + 1];
    display = XOpenDisplay (display_name);
    if (!display) {
        printf ("splash: cannot open display\n");
```

```
60          exit (1);
        }
        depth = DefaultDepth (display, DefaultScreen (display));
        visual = DefaultVisual (display, DefaultScreen (display));
        p = (unsigned char **) graham_splash;
65      q = p[0];
        width = atoi ((const char *) q);
        q = (unsigned char *) strchr (q, ' ');
        height = atoi ((const char *) ++q);
        q = (unsigned char *) strchr (q, ' ');
70      n_colors = atoi ((const char *) ++q);

        colormap = DefaultColormap (display, DefaultScreen (display));
        pixmap =
            XCreatePixmap (display, DefaultRootWindow (display), width, height,
75                         depth);
        gc = XCreateGC (display, pixmap, 0, &gcv);

        image =
            XCreateImage (display, visual, depth, ZPixmap, 0, 0, width, height,
80                        8, 0);
        image->data = (char *) malloc (image->bytes_per_line * height + 16);

/* create color palette */
        for (p = p + 1, i = 0; i < n_colors; p++, i++) {
85          XColor c, c1;
            unsigned char *x;
            x = *p + 4;
            if (*x == '#') {
                unsigned char *h = (unsigned char *) "0123456789abcdef";
90              x++;
                c.red =
                    ((unsigned long) strchr (h, *x++) -
                    (unsigned long) h) << 12;
                c.red |=
95                  ((unsigned long) strchr (h, *x++) -
                    (unsigned long) h) << 8;
                c.green =
                    ((unsigned long) strchr (h, *x++) -
                    (unsigned long) h) << 12;
100             c.green |=
                    ((unsigned long) strchr (h, *x++) -
                    (unsigned long) h) << 8;
                c.blue =
                    ((unsigned long) strchr (h, *x++) -
105                 (unsigned long) h) << 12;
                c.blue |=
                    ((unsigned long) strchr (h, *x++) -
                    (unsigned long) h) << 8;
                if (!XAllocColor (display, colormap, &c))
110                 printf ("splash: could not allocate color cell\n");
            } else {
                if (!XAllocNamedColor (display, colormap, (char *) x, &c, &c1))
                    printf ("splash: could not allocate color cell\n");
            }
115         colors[(*p)[0]] = c.pixel;
        }

        bytes_per_pixel = image->bytes_per_line / width;

120 /* cope with servers having different byte ordering and depths */
        for (j = 0; j < height; j++, p++) {
            unsigned char *r;
            unsigned long c;
            q = image->data + image->bytes_per_line * j;
```

```
125        r = *p;
           if (image->byte_order == MSBFirst) {
               switch (bytes_per_pixel) {
               case 4:
                   for (i = 0; i < width; i++) {
130                    c = colors[*r++];
                       *q++ = c >> 24;
                       *q++ = c >> 16;
                       *q++ = c >> 8;
                       *q++ = c;
135                }
                   break;
               case 3:
                   for (i = 0; i < width; i++) {
                       c = colors[*r++];
140                    *q++ = c >> 16;
                       *q++ = c >> 8;
                       *q++ = c;
                   }
                   break;
145            case 2:
                   for (i = 0; i < width; i++) {
                       c = colors[*r++];
                       *q++ = c >> 8;
                       *q++ = c;
150                }
                   break;
               case 1:
                   for (i = 0; i < width; i++)
                       *q++ = colors[*r++];
155                break;
               }
           } else {
               switch (bytes_per_pixel) {
               case 4:
160                for (i = 0; i < width; i++) {
                       c = colors[*r++];
                       *q++ = c;
                       *q++ = c >> 8;
                       *q++ = c >> 16;
165                    *q++ = c >> 24;
                   }
                   break;
               case 3:
                   for (i = 0; i < width; i++) {
170                    c = colors[*r++];
                       *q++ = c;
                       *q++ = c >> 8;
                       *q++ = c >> 16;
                   }
175                break;
               case 2:
                   for (i = 0; i < width; i++) {
                       c = colors[*r++];
                       *q++ = c;
180                    *q++ = c >> 8;
                   }
                   break;
               case 1:
                   for (i = 0; i < width; i++)
185                    *q++ = colors[*r++];
                   break;
               }
           }
       }
```

```
190    XPutImage (display, pixmap, gc, image, 0, 0, 0, 0, width, height);

       x = (DisplayWidth (display, DefaultScreen (display)) - width) / 2;
       y = (DisplayHeight (display, DefaultScreen (display)) - height) / 2;
195
       xswa.colormap = colormap;
       xswa.background_pixmap = pixmap;

       window =
200        XCreateWindow (display, DefaultRootWindow (display), x, y, width,
                          height, 0, depth, InputOutput, visual,
                          CWColormap | CWBackPixmap, &xswa);
       XSelectInput (display, window, KeyPressMask | ButtonPressMask);

205    XMapRaised (display, window);

       while (1) {
           XEvent event;
           XNextEvent (display, &event);
210        if (event.xany.type == KeyPress || event.xany.type == ButtonPressMask)
               break;
       }
       XUnmapWindow (display, window);
       XCloseDisplay (display);
215    return 0;
   }
```

You can learn to program **X** from the documentation in the **X** Window System sources—see below. The preceding program is said to be "written directly in X-lib" because it links only with the lowest-level **X** library, `libX11.so`. The advantage of developing this way is that your program will work across every variant of UNIX without any modifications. Notice also that the program deals with any type of display device regardless of its *resolution* (width × height or pixels-per-inch), color capacity, or hardware design.

43.2   Widget Libraries and Desktops

To program in **X** is tedious. Therefore, most developers will use a higher-level *widget library*. Most users of GUIs will be familiar with *widgets*: buttons, menus, text input boxes, and so on. **X** programmers have to implement these manually. The reason widgets were not built into the **X** protocol is to allow different user interfaces to be built on top of **X**. This flexibility makes **X** the enduring technology that it is.

43.2.1   Background

The *X Toolkit* (`libXt.so`) is a widget library that has always come free with **X**. It is crude-looking by today's standards. It doesn't feature 3D (shadowed) widgets, although it is comes free with **X**. ↘The excellent `xfig` application, an X Toolkit application, was in fact used to do the diagrams in this book.↖ *Motif* (`libM.so`) is a modern, full-featured widget library that had become an industry standard. Motif is, however, bloated, slow, and dependent on the **X** toolkit. It has always been an expensive proprietary library. *Tk* (tee-kay, `libtk.so`) is a library that is primarily used with the *Tcl* scripting language. It was probably the first platform-independent library (running on Windows, all UNIX variants, and the Apple Mac). It is, however, slow and has limited features (this is progressively changing). Both Tcl and Motif are not very elegant-looking.

Around 1996, we saw a lot of widget libraries popping up with different licenses. *V*, *xforms*, and *graphix* come to mind. (This was when I started to write *coolwidgets*—my own widget library.) There was no efficient, multipurpose, Free, and elegant-looking widget library for UNIX. This was a situation that sucked and was retarding Free software development.

43.2.2   Qt

At about that time, a new GUI library was released. It was called *Qt* and was developed by *Troll Tech*. It was not free, but it was an outstanding technical accomplishment in that it worked efficiently and cleanly on many different platforms. It was shunned by some factions of the Free software community because it was written in C++, ↘Which is not considered to be the standard development language by the Free Software Foundation because it is not completely portable and possibly for other reasons.↖ and was only free for noncommercial applications to link with.

Nevertheless, advocates of Qt went ahead and began producing the outstanding KDE desktop project—a set of higher-level development libraries, a window manager, and many core applications that together make up the KDE Desktop. The licensing issues with Qt have relaxed somewhat, and it is now available under both the GPL and a proprietary license.

43.2.3   Gtk

At one point, before KDE was substantially complete, Qt antagonists reasoned that since there were more lines of Qt code than of KDE code, it would be better to develop a widget library from scratch—but that is an aside. The Gtk widget library was written especially for `gimp` (*GNU Image Manipulation Program*), is GPL'd and written entirely in **C** in low-level **X** calls (i.e., without the X Toolkit), object oriented, fast, clean, extensible and having a staggering array of features. It comprises *Glib*, a library meant to extend standard **C**, providing higher-level functions usually akin only to scripting languages, like hash tables and lists; *Gdk*, a wrapper around raw **X** Library to give GNU🐾 naming conventions to **X**, and to give a slightly higher level interface to **X**; and the *Gtk* library itself.

Using Gtk, the *Gnome* project began, analogous to KDE, but written entirely in **C**.

43.2.4   GNUStep

OpenStep (based on NeXTStep) was a GUI specification published in 1994 by Sun Microsystems and NeXT Computers, meant for building applications. It uses the *Objective-C* language, which is an object-oriented extension to **C**, that is arguably more suited to this kind of development than is C++.

OpenStep requires a *PostScript display engine* that is analogous to the **X** protocol, but it is considered superior to **X** because all graphics are independent of the pixel resolution of the screen. In other words, high-resolution screens would improve the picture quality without making the graphics smaller.

The GNUStep project has a working PostScript display engine and is meant as a Free replacement to OpenStep.

43.3   XFree86

X was developed by the X Consortium as a standard as well as a reference implementation of that standard. There are ports to every platform that supports graphics. The current version of the standard is 11 release 6 (hence the directory /usr/X11R6/). There will probably never be another version.

XFree86 http://www.xfree86.org/ is a free port of **X** that includes LINUX Intel machines among its supported hardware. **X** has some peculiarities that are worth noting if you are a Windows user, and XFree86 has some over those. XFree86 has its own versioning system beneath the "11R6" as explained below.

43.3.1   Running X and key conventions

(See Section 43.6 for configuring **X**).

At a terminal prompt, you can type:

```
X
```

to start **X** (provided **X** is not already running). If you have configured **X** properly (including putting /usr/X11R6/bin in your PATH), then this command will initiate the graphics hardware and a black-and-white stippled background will appear with a single **X** as the mouse cursor. Contrary to intuition, this means that **X** is actually working properly.

- *To kill the* **X** *server*, use the key combination [Ctrl]—[Alt]—[←].

- *To switch to the text console*, use [Ctrl]—[Alt]—[F1] ... [Ctrl]—[Alt]—[F6].

493

- *To switch to the* **X** *console, use* . The seven common virtual consoles of LINUX are 1–6 as text terminals, and 7 as an **X** terminal (as explained in Section 2.7).

- *To zoom in or out of your* **X** *session, use* ` Ctrl `—` Alt `—` + ` *and* ` Ctrl `—` Alt `—` _ `.

43.3.2   Running X utilities

`/usr/X11R6/bin/` contains a large number of **X** utilities that most other operating systems have based theirs on. Most of these begin with an `x`. The basic XFree86 programs are:

SuperProbe	iceauth	rstartd	xcmsdb	xhost	xmessage
X	ico	scanpci	xconsole	xieperf	xmodmap
XFree86	lbxproxy	sessreg	xcutsel	xinit	xon
Xmark	listres	setxkbmap	xditview	xkbbell	xprop
Xprt	lndir	showfont	xdm	xkbcomp	xrdb
Xwrapper	makepsres	showrgb	xdpyinfo	xkbevd	xrefresh
appres	makestrs	smproxy	xedit	xkbprint	xset
atobm	mergelib	startx	xev	xkbvleds	xsetmode
bdftopcf	mkcfm	twm	xeyes	xkbwatch	xsetpointer
beforelight	mkdirhier	viewres	xf86config	xkill	xsetroot
bitmap	mkfontdir	x11perf	xfd	xload	xsm
bmtoa	oclock	x11perfcomp	xfindproxy	xlogo	xstdcmap
dga	pcitweak	xauth	xfontsel	xlsatoms	xterm
editres	proxymngr	xbiff	xfs	xlsclients	xvidtune
fsinfo	resize	xcalc	xfwp	xlsfonts	xwd
fslsfonts	revpath	xclipboard	xgamma	xmag	xwininfo
fstobdf	rstart	xclock	xgc	xman	xwud

To run an **X** program, you need to tell the program what remote server to connect to. Most programs take the option `-display` to specify the **X** server. With **X** running in your seventh virtual console, type into your first virtual console:

```
xterm -display localhost:0.0
```

`localhost` refers to the machine on which the **X** server is running—in this case, our own. The first 0 means the screen we want to display on (**X** supports multiple physical screens in its specification). The second 0 refers to the *root window* we want to display on. Consider a *multiheaded* ⟍For example, two adjacent monitors that behave as one continuous screen.⟍ display: we would like to specify which monitor the application pops up on.

While `xterm` is running, switching to your **X** session will reveal a character terminal where you can type commands.

A better way to specify the display is to use the `DISPLAY` environment variable:

```
DISPLAY=localhost:0.0
export DISPLAY
```

causes all subsequent **X** applications to display to `localhost:0.0`, although a `-display` on the command-line takes first priority.

The **X** utilities listed above are pretty ugly and unintuitive. Try, for example, `xclock`, `xcalc`, and `xedit`. For fun, try `xbill`. Also run

```
rpm -qa | grep '^x'
```

43.3.3 Running two X sessions

You can start up a second **X** server on your machine. The command

```
/usr/X11R6/bin/X :1
```

starts up a second **X** session in the virtual console 8. You can switch to it by using `Ctrl`-`Alt`-`F8` or `Alt`-`F8`.

You can also start up a second **X** server *within* your current **X** display:

```
/usr/X11R6/bin/Xnest :1 &
```

A smaller **X** server that uses a subwindow as a display device will be started. You can easily create a third **X** server within that, *ad infinitum*.

To get an application to display to this second server, use, as before,

```
DISPLAY=localhost:1.0
export DISPLAY
xterm
```

or

```
xterm -display localhost:1.0
```

43.3.4 Running a window manager

Manually starting **X** and then running an application is *not* the way to use **X**. We want a window manager to run applications properly. The best window manager available (sic) is `icewm`, available from *icewm.cjb.net* http://icewm.cjb.net/. Window managers enclose each application inside a resizable bounding box and give you the ▬, ⊡, and

<kbd>X</kbd> buttons, as well as possibly a task bar and a Start button that you may be familiar with. A window manager is just another **X** application that has the additional task of managing the positions of basic **X** applications on your desktop. Window managers executables are usually suffixed by a `wm`. If you don't have `icewm`, the minimalist's `twm` window manager will almost always be installed.

- *Clicking on the background* is common convention of **X** user interfaces. Different mouse buttons may bring up a menu or a list of actions. It is often analogous to a Start button.

An enormous amount of religious attention is given to window managers. There are about 20 useful choices to date. Remember that any beautiful graphics are going to irritate you after you sit in front of the computer for a few hundred hours. You also don't want a window manager that eats too much memory or uses too much space on the screen.

43.3.5   X access control and remote display

The way we described an **X** server may leave you wondering if anyone on the Internet can start an application on your display. By default, **X** prohibits access from all machines except your own. The `xhost` command enables access from particular machines. For instance, you can run `xhost +192.168.5.7` to allow that host to display to your machine. The command `xhost +` completely disables access control. A typical procedure is the running of an application on a remote machine to a local machine. A sample session follows:

```
[psheer@divinian]# xhost +192.168.3.2
192.168.3.2 being added to access control list
[psheer@divinian]# ifconfig | grep inet
        inet addr:192.168.3.1  Bcast:192.168.3.255  Mask:255.255.255.0
        inet addr:127.0.0.1  Mask:255.0.0.0
[psheer@divinian]# telnet 192.168.3.2
Trying 192.168.3.2...
Connected to 192.168.3.2.
Escape character is '^]'.
Debian GNU/Linux 2.2 cericon
cericon login: psheer
Password:
Last login: Fri Jul 13 18:46:43 2001 from divinian on pts/1
[psheer@cericon]# export DISPLAY=192.168.3.1:0.0
[psheer@cericon]# nohup rxvt &
[1] 32573
nohup: appending output to 'nohup.out'
[psheer@cericon]# exit
Connection closed by foreign host.
```

43.3.6 X selections, cutting, and pasting

Start an `xterm` to demonstrate the following mouse operations.

X predates the cut-and-paste conventions of Windows and the Mac. **X** requires a three-button mouse, although pushing the two outer buttons simultaneously is equivalent to pushing the middle button. ↘That is, provided **X** has been configured for this—see the `Emulate3Buttons` option in the configuration file example below.↖ Practice the following:

- *Dragging the left mouse button* is the common way to *select* text. This automatically places the highlighted text into a *cut buffer*, also sometimes called the *clipboard*.

- *Dragging the right mouse button* extends the selection, that is, enlarges or reduces the selection.

- *Clicking the middle mouse button* pastes the selection. Note that **X** becomes virtually unusable without the capability of pasting in this way.

Modern Gtk and Qt applications have tried to retain compatibility with these mouse conventions.

43.4 The X Distribution

The official **X** distribution comes as an enormous source package available in `tgz` format at http://www.xfree86.org/. It is traditionally packed as three `tgz` files to be unpacked over each other—the total of the three is about 50 megabytes compressed. This package has nothing really to do with the version number `X11R6`—it is a subset of `X11R6`.

Downloading and installing the distribution is a major undertaking, but you should do it if you are interested in **X** development.

All UNIX distributions come with a compiled and (mostly) configured **X** installation; hence, the official **X** distribution should never be needed except by developers.

43.5 X Documentation

The **X** Window System comes with tens of megabytes of documentation.

43.5.1 Programming

All the books describing all of the programming APIs are included inside the **X** distribution. Most of these are of specialized interest and will not be including in your distribution by default—download the complete distribution if you want them. You can then look inside `xc/doc/specs` (especially `xc/doc/specs/X11`) to begin learning how to program under **X**.

Debian Ⓞ also comes with the `xbooks` package, and RedHat with the `XFree86-doc` packages.

43.5.2 Configuration documentation

Important to configuring **X** is the directory `/usr/X11R6/lib/X11/doc/` or `/usr/share/doc/xserver-common/`. It may contain, for example,

AccelCards.gz	README.Mach64.gz	README.ark.gz	README.neo.gz
Devices.gz	README.NVIDIA.gz	README.ati.gz	README.r128.gz
Monitors.gz	README.Oak.gz	README.chips.gz	README.rendition.gz
QuickStart.doc.gz	README.P9000.gz	README.cirrus.gz	README.trident.gz
README.3DLabs.gz	README.S3.gz	README.clkprog.gz	README.tseng.gz
README.Config.gz	README.S3V.gz	README.cyrix.gz	RELNOTES.gz
README.DGA.gz	README.SiS.gz	README.epson.gz	changelog.Debian.gz
README.Debian	README.Video7.gz	README.fbdev.gz	copyright
README.I128.gz	README.W32.gz	README.gz	examples
README.Linux.gz	README.WstDig.gz	README.i740.gz	xinput.gz
README.MGA.gz	README.agx.gz	README.i810.gz	
README.Mach32.gz	README.apm.gz	README.mouse.gz	

As you can see, there is documentation for each type of graphics card. Learning how to configure **X** is a simple matter of reading the `QuickStart` guide and then checking the specifics for your card.

43.5.3 XFree86 web site

Any missing documentation can be found on the *XFree86* http://www.xfree86.org/ web site.

New graphics cards are coming out all the time. *XFree86* http://www.xfree86.org/ contains FAQs about cards and the latest binaries, should you not be able to get your card working from the information below. Please always search the XFree86 web site for information on your card and for newer **X** releases before reporting a problem.

43.6   X Configuration

Configuring **X** involves editing XFree86's configuration file `/etc/X11/XF86Config`. Such a file may have been produced at installation time but will not always be correct. You will hence frequently find yourself having to make manual changes to get **X** running in full resolution.

Note that XFree86 has a slightly different configuration file format for the new version 4. Differences are explained below.

43.6.1   Simple 16-color **X** server

The documentation discussed above is a lot to read. The simplest possible way to get **X** working is to determine what mouse you have, and then create a file, `/etc/X11/XF86Config` (back up your original) containing the following. Adjust the `"Pointer"` section for your correct `Device` and `Protocol`. If you are running **X** version 3.3, you should also comment out the `Driver "vga"` line. You may also have to switch the line containing `25.175` to `28.32` for some laptop displays.

```
   Section "Files"
        RgbPath    "/usr/X11R6/lib/X11/rgb"
        FontPath   "/usr/X11R6/lib/X11/fonts/misc/"
   EndSection
 5 Section "ServerFlags"
   EndSection
   Section "Keyboard"
        Protocol   "Standard"
        AutoRepeat 500 5
10      XkbDisable
        XkbKeymap  "xfree86(us)"
   EndSection
   Section "Pointer"
   #    Protocol   "Busmouse"
15 #    Protocol   "IntelliMouse"
   #    Protocol   "Logitech"
        Protocol   "Microsoft"
   #    Protocol   "MMHitTab"
   #    Protocol   "MMSeries"
20 #    Protocol   "MouseMan"
   #    Protocol   "MouseSystems"
   #    Protocol   "PS/2"
        Device     "/dev/ttyS0"
   #    Device     "/dev/psaux"
25      Emulate3Buttons
        Emulate3Timeout 150
   EndSection
   Section "Monitor"
        Identifier "My Monitor"
30      VendorName "Unknown"
        ModelName  "Unknown"
```

```
      HorizSync  31.5 - 57.0
      VertRefresh 50-90
#     Modeline "640x480"      28.32  640  664  760  800   480  491  493  525
      Modeline "640x480"      25.175 640  664  760  800   480  491  493  525
EndSection
Section "Device"
      Identifier "Generic VGA"
      VendorName "Unknown"
      BoardName  "Unknown"
      Chipset    "generic"
#     Driver     "vga"
      Driver     "vga"
EndSection
Section "Screen"
      Driver     "vga16"
      Device     "Generic VGA"
      Monitor    "My Monitor"
      Subsection "Display"
          Depth    4
          Modes    "640x480"
          Virtual  640 480
      EndSubsection
EndSection
```

You can then start **X**. For XFree86 version 3.3, run

```
/usr/X11R6/bin/XF86_VGA16 -cc 0
```

or for XFree86 version 4, run

```
/usr/X11R6/bin/XFree86 -cc 0
```

Both of these will print out a status line containing `clocks: ...` confirming whether your choice of `25.175` was correct. ↘This is the speed, in Megahertz, that pixels can come from your card and is the only variable to configuring a 16-color display.↖

You should now have a working gray-level display that is actually almost usable. It has the advantage that it *always* works.

43.6.2   Plug-and-Play operation

XFree86 version 4 has "Plug-and-Play" support. Simply run

```
/usr/X11R6/bin/XFree86 -configure
```

to produce a working `XF86Config` file. You can copy this file to `/etc/X11/XF86Config` and immediately start running **X**. However, the file you get may be less than optimal. Read on for detailed configuration.

43.6.3   Proper X configuration

A simple and reliable way to get **X** working is given by the following steps (if this fails, then you will have to read some of the documentation described above). There is also a tool called `Xconfigurator` which provides a user-friendly graphical front-end.

1. Back up your `/etc/X11/XF86Config` to `/etc/X11/XF86Config.ORIG`.

2. Run `SuperProbe` at the character console. It will blank your screen and then spit out what graphics card you have. Leave that information on your screen and switch to a different virtual terminal. If `SuperProbe` fails to recognize your card, it usually means that XFree86 will also fail.

3. Run `xf86config`. This is the official **X** configuration script. Run through all the options, being very sure not to guess. You can set your monitor to `31.5`, `35.15`, `35.5; Super VGA...` if you have no other information to go on. Vertical sync can be set to 50–90. Select your card from the card database (check the `SuperProbe` output), and check which **X** server the program recommends— this will be one of `XF86_SVGA`, `XF86_S3`, `XF86_S3V`, etc. Whether you "set the symbolic link" or not, or "modify the /etc/X11/Xserver file" is irrelevant. Note that you do not need a "RAM DAC" setting with most modern PCI graphics cards. The same goes for the "Clockchip setting."

4. Do *not* run **X** at this point.

5. The `xf86config` command should have given you an *example* `/etc/X11/XF86Config` file to work with. You need not run it again. You will notice that the file is divided into sections, like

```
  Section "<section-name>"
      <config-line>
      <config-line>
      <config-line>
5 EndSection
```

Search for the `"Monitor"` section. A little further down you will see lots of lines like:

```
  # 640x480 @ 60 Hz, 31.5 kHz hsync
  Modeline "640x480"      25.175 640  664  760  800    480  491  493  525
  # 800x600 @ 56 Hz, 35.15 kHz hsync
  ModeLine "800x600"        36    800  824  896 1024    600  601  603  625
5 # 1024x768 @ 87 Hz interlaced, 35.5 kHz hsync
  Modeline "1024x768"      44.9  1024 1048 1208 1264    768  776  784  817 Interlace
```

These are timing settings for different monitors and screen resolutions. Choosing one that is too fast could blow an old monitor but will usually give you a lot of garbled fuzz on your screen. We are going to eliminate all but the three above; we do that by commenting them out with # or deleting the lines entirely. (You may want to back up the file first.) You could leave it up to **X** to choose the correct `Modeline` to match the capabilities of the monitor, but this doesn't always work. I always like to explicitly choose a selection of `Modeline`s.

If you don't find modelines in your `XF86Config` you can use this as your monitor section:

```
Section "Monitor"
     Identifier   "My Monitor"
     VendorName   "Unknown"
     ModelName    "Unknown"
     HorizSync    30-40
     VertRefresh  50-90
     Modeline     "320x200"    12.588 320   336  384  400    200  204  205  225 Doublescan
     ModeLine     "400x300"    18     400   416  448  512    300  301  302  312 Doublescan
     Modeline     "512x384"    20.160 512   528  592  640    384  385  388  404 -HSync -VSync
     Modeline     "640x480"    25.175 640   664  760  800    480  491  493  525
     ModeLine     "800x600"    36     800   824  896  1024   600  601  603  625
     Modeline     "1024x768"   44.9   1024 1048 1208 1264    768  776  784  817 Interlace
EndSection
```

6. Edit your `"Device"` section. You can make it as follows for XFree86 version 3.3, and there should be only one `"Device"` section.

```
Section "Device"
     Identifier   "My Video Card"
     VendorName   "Unknown"
     BoardName    "Unknown"
     VideoRam     4096
EndSection
```

For XFree86 version 4, you must add the device driver module. On my laptop, this is `ati`:

```
Section "Device"
     Identifier   "My Video Card"
     Driver       "ati"
     VendorName   "Unknown"
     BoardName    "Unknown"
     VideoRam     4096
EndSection
```

Several options that can also be added to the `"Device"` section to tune your card. Three possible lines are

```
     Option       "no_accel"
     Option       "sw_cursor"
     Option       "no_pixmap_cache"
```

which disable graphics hardware acceleration, hardware cursor support, and video memory pixmap caching, respectively. The last refers to the use of the card's unused memory for intermediate operations. You should try these options if there are glitches or artifacts in your display.

7. Your "Screen" section should properly order the modes specified in the "Monitor" section. It should use your single "Device" section and single "Monitor" section, "My Video Card" and "My Monitor", respectively. Note that XFree86 version 3.3 does not take a DefaultDepth option.

```
Section "Screen"
    Identifier   "My Screen"
    Device       "My Video Card"
    Monitor      "My Monitor"
5
    DefaultDepth 16

    Subsection "Display"
        ViewPort    0 0
10      Virtual 1024 768
        Depth   16
        Modes   "1024x768" "800x600" "640x480" "512x384" "400x300" "320x240"
    EndSubsection
    Subsection "Display"
15      ViewPort    0 0
        Virtual 1024 768
        Depth   24
        Modes   "1024x768" "800x600" "640x480" "512x384" "400x300" "320x240"
    EndSubsection
20  Subsection "Display"
        ViewPort    0 0
        Virtual 1024 768
        Depth   8
        Modes   "1024x768" "800x600" "640x480" "512x384" "400x300" "320x240"
25  EndSubsection
EndSection
```

8. At this point you need to run the **X** program itself. For XFree86 version 3.3, there will be a separate package for each video card, as well as a separate binary with the appropriate driver code statically compiled into it. These binaries are of the form /usr/X11R6/bin/XF86_cardname. The relevant packages can be found with the command dpkg -l 'xserver-*' for Debian⊙, and rpm -qa | grep XFree86 for RedHat 6 (or RedHat/RPMS/XFree86-* on your CD-ROM). You can then run

```
/usr/X11R6/bin/XFree86-<card> -bpp 16
```

which also sets the display *depth* to 16, that is, the number of bits per pixel, which translates to the number of colors.

For XFree86 version 4, card support is compiled as separate modules named
`/usr/X11R6/lib/modules/drivers/`*cardname*`_drv.o`. A single binary executable `/usr/X11R6/bin/XFree86` loads the appropriate module based on
the `Driver` "*cardname*" line in the "`Device`" section. Having added this, you
can run

```
/usr/X11R6/bin/XFree86
```

where the depth is set from the `DefaultDepth 16` line in the "`Screen`" section. You can find what driver to use by `grep`ing the modules with the name of
your graphics card. This is similar to what we did with kernel modules on page
473.

9. A good idea is to now create a script, `/etc/X11/X.sh`, containing your `-bpp`
   option with the server you would like to run. For example,

```
#!/bin/sh
exec /usr/X11R6/bin/<server> -bpp 16
```

10. You can then symlink `/usr/X11R6/bin/X` to this script. It is also worth sym-
    linking `/etc/X11/X` to this script since some configurations look for it there.
    There should now be no chance that **X** could be started except in the way you
    want. Double-check by running `X` on the command-line by itself.

43.7   Visuals

X introduces the concept of a *visual*. A visual is the hardware method used to represent
colors on your screen. There are two common and four specialized types:

TrueColor(4) The most obvious way of representing a color is to use a byte for each of
the red, green, and blue values that a pixel is composed of. Your video buffer will
hence have 3 bytes per pixel, or 24 bits. You will need $800 \times 600 \times 3 = 1440000$
bytes to represent a typical 800 by 600 display.

Another way is to use two bytes, with 5 bits for red, 6 for green, and then 5 for
blue. This gives you 32 shades of red and blue, and 64 shades of green (green
should have more levels because it has the most influence over the pixel's overall
brightness).

Displays that use 4 bytes usually discard the last byte, and are essentially 24-bit
displays. Note also that most displays using a full 8 bits per color discard the
trailing bits, so there is often no appreciable difference between a 16-bit display
and a 32-bit display. If you have limited memory, 16 bits is preferable; it is also
faster.

PseudoColor(3) If you want to display each pixel with only one byte and still get a wide range of colors, the best way is to make that pixel index a dynamic table of 24-bit palette values: 256 of them exactly. 8-bit depths work this way. You will have just as many possible colors, but applications will have to pick what colors they want to display at once and compete for entries in the color palette.

StaticGray(0) These are gray-level displays usually with 1 byte or 4 bits per pixel, or monochrome displays with 1 byte per pixel, like the legacy Hercules Graphics Card (HGC, or MDA—monochrome graphics adapter). Legacy VGA cards can be set to 640 × 480 in 16-color "black and white." **X** is almost usable in this mode and has the advantage that it *always* works, regardless of what hardware you have.

StaticColor(2) This usually refers to 4-bit displays like the old (and obsolete) CGA and EGA displays having a small fixed number of colors.

DirectColor(5) This is rarely used and refers to displays that have a separate palette for each of red, green, and blue.

GrayScale(1) These are like StaticGray, but the gray levels are programmable like PseudoColor. This is also rarely used.

You can check the visuals that your display supports with the `xdpyinfo` command. You will notice more than one visual listed, since **X** can effectively support a simple StaticColor visual with PseudoColor, or a DirectColor visual with TrueColor. The default visual is listed first and can be set with the `-cc` option as we did above for the 16-color server. The argument to the `-cc` option is the number code above in parentheses.

Note that good **X** applications check the list of available visuals and choose an appropriate one. There are also those that require a particular visual, and some that take a `-visual` option on the command-line.

43.8   The `startx` and `xinit` Commands

The action of starting an **X** server, then a window manager should obviously be automated. The classic way to start **X** is to run the `xinit` command on its own. On LINUX🐧 this has been superseded by

```
startx
```

which is a script that runs `xinit` after setting some environment variables. These commands indirectly call a number of configuration scripts in `/etc/X11/xinit/` and your home directory, where you can specify your window manager and startup applications. See `xinit`(1) and `startx`(1) for more information.

43.9 Login Screen

init runs mgetty, which displays a login: prompt on every attached character terminal. init can also run xdm, which displays a graphical login box on every **X** server. Usually, there will only be one **X** server: the one on your own machine.

The interesting lines inside your inittab file are

```
id:5:initdefault:
```

and

```
x:5:respawn:/usr/X11R6/bin/xdm -nodaemon
```

which state that the default run level is 5 and that xdm should be started at run level 5. This should only be attempted if you are sure that **X** works (by running X on the command-line by itself). If it doesn't, then xdm will keep trying to start **X**, effectively disabling the console. On systems besides RedHat and Debian☺, these may be run levels 2 versus 3, where run level 5 is reserved for something else. In any event, there should be comments in your /etc/inittab file to explain your distribution's convention.

43.10 X Font Naming Conventions

Most **X** applications take a -fn or -font option to specify the font. In this section, I give a partial guide to **X** font naming.

A font name is a list of words and numbers separated by hyphens. A typical font name is -adobe-courier-medium-r-normal--12-120-75-75-m-60-iso8859-1. Use the xlsfonts command to obtain a complete list of fonts.

The font name fields have the following meanings:

adobe The name of the font's maker. Others are

abisource	b&h	daewoo	gnu	macromedia	monotype	software	urw
adobe	bitstream	dec	isas	microsoft	mutt	sony	xfree86
arabic	cronyx	dtp	jis	misc	schumacher	sun	

courier The font family. This is the real name of the font. Some others are

arial	dingbats	lucidux serif	starbats
arial black	fangsong ti	marlett	starmath
arioso	fixed	mincho	symbol
avantgarde	goth	new century schoolbook	tahoma
bitstream charter	gothic	newspaper	tera special
bookman	helmet	nil	terminal

506

century schoolbook	helmetcondensed	nimbus mono	times
charter	helvetic	nimbus roman	times new roman
chevara	helvetica	nimbus sans	timmons
chevaraoutline	impact	nimbus sans condensed	unifont
clean	lucida	open look cursor	utopia
comic sans ms	lucida console	open look glyph	verdana
conga	lucidabright	palatino	webdings
courier	lucidatypewriter	palladio	wingdings
courier new	lucidux mono	song ti	zapf chancery
cursor	lucidux sans	standard symbols	zapf dingbats

medium The font weight: it can also be `bold`, `demibold`, or `regular`.

r Indicate that the font is `roman`; `i` is for italic and `o` is for oblique.

normal Character width and intercharacter spacing. It can also be `condensed`, `semicondensed`, `narrow`, or `double`.

12 The pixel size. A zero means a scalable font that can be selected at any pixel size. The largest fixed sized font is about 40 points.

120 The size in tenths of a printers point. This is usually 10 times the pixel size.

75-75 Horizontal and vertical pixel resolution for which the font was designed. Most monitors today are 75 pixels per inch. The only other possible values are `72-72` or `100-100`.

m The font spacing. Other values are `monospaced`, `proportional`, or `condensed`.

60 The average width of all characters in the font in tenths of a pixel.

iso8859-1 The ISO character set. In this case, the 1 indicates **ISO Latin 1**, a superset of the ASCII character set. This last bit is the locale setting, which you would normally omit to allow **X** to determine it according to your locale settings.

As an example, start `cooledit` with

```
cooledit -font '-*-times-medium-r-*--20-*-*-*-p-*-iso8859-1'
cooledit -font '-*-times-medium-r-*--20-*-*-*-p-*'
cooledit -font '-*-helvetica-bold-r-*--14-*-*-*-p-*-iso8859-1'
cooledit -font '-*-helvetica-bold-r-*--14-*-*-*-p-*'
```

These invoke a newspaper font and an easy-reading font respectively. A `*` means that the **X** server can place default values into those fields. That way, you do not have to specify a font exactly.

The `xfontsel` command is the traditional **X** utility for displaying fonts and the `showfont` command dumps fonts as ASCII text.

43.11 Font Configuration

Fonts used by **X** are conventionally stored in `/usr/X11R6/lib/X11/fonts/`. Each directory contains a `fonts.alias` file that maps full font names to simpler names, and a `fonts.alias` file which lists the fonts contained in that directory. To create these files, you must `cd` to each directory and run `mkfontdir` as follows:

```
mkfontdir -e /usr/X11R6/lib/X11/fonts/encodings -e /usr/X11R6/lib/X11/fonts/encodings/large
```

You can rerun this command at any time for good measure.

To tell **X** to use these directories add the following lines to your `"Files"` section. A typical configuration will contain

```
Section "Files"
    RgbPath  "/usr/X11R6/lib/X11/rgb"
    FontPath "/usr/X11R6/lib/X11/fonts/misc/:unscaled"
    FontPath "/usr/X11R6/lib/X11/fonts/75dpi/:unscaled"
    FontPath "/usr/X11R6/lib/X11/fonts/Speedo/"
    FontPath "/usr/X11R6/lib/X11/fonts/Type1/"
    FontPath "/usr/X11R6/lib/X11/fonts/misc/"
    FontPath "/usr/X11R6/lib/X11/fonts/75dpi/"
EndSection
```

Often you will add a directory without wanting to restart **X**. The command to add a directory to the **X** *font path* is:

```
xset +fp /usr/X11R6/lib/X11/fonts/<new-directory>
```

and to remove a directory, use

```
xset -fp /usr/X11R6/lib/X11/fonts/<new-directory>
```

To set the font path, use

```
xset fp= /usr/X11R6/lib/X11/fonts/misc,/usr/X11R6/lib/X11/fonts/75dpi
```

and reset it with

```
xset fp default
```

If you change anything in your font directories, you should run

```
xset fp rehash
```

to cause **X** to reread the font directories.

The command `chkfontpath` prints out your current font path setting.

Note that XFree86 version 4 has a TrueType engine. TrueType (`.ttf`) fonts are common to Windows. They are high-quality, scalable fonts designed for graphical displays. You can add your TrueType directory alongside your other directories above, and run

```
ttmkfdir > fonts.scale
mkfontdir -e /usr/X11R6/lib/X11/fonts/encodings -e /usr/X11R6/lib/X11/fonts/encodings/large
```

inside each one. Note that the `ttmkfdir` is needed to catalog TrueType fonts as scalable fonts.

43.12 The Font Server

Having all fonts stored on all machines is expensive. Ideally, you would like a large font database installed on one machine and fonts to be read off this machine, over the network and on demand. You may also have an **X** that does not support a particular font type; if it can read the font from the network, built-in support will not be necessary. The daemon `xfs` (**X** *font server*) facilitates all of this.

`xfs` reads its own simple configuration file from `/etc/X11/fs/config` or `/etc/X11/xfs/config`. It might contain a similar list of directories:

```
     client-limit = 10
     clone-self = on
     catalogue = /usr/X11R6/lib/X11/fonts/misc:unscaled,
             /usr/X11R6/lib/X11/fonts/75dpi:unscaled,
5            /usr/X11R6/lib/X11/fonts/ttf,
             /usr/X11R6/lib/X11/fonts/Speedo,
             /usr/X11R6/lib/X11/fonts/Type1,
             /usr/X11R6/lib/X11/fonts/misc,
             /usr/X11R6/lib/X11/fonts/75dpi
10   default-point-size = 120
     default-resolutions = 75,75,100,100
     deferglyphs = 16
     use-syslog = on
     no-listen = tcp
```

You can start the font server by using:

```
/etc/init.d/xfs start
( /etc/rc.d/init.d/xfs start )
```

and change your font paths in `/etc/X11/XF86Config` to include only a minimal set of fonts:

```
    Section "Files"
        RgbPath  "/usr/X11R6/lib/X11/rgb"
        FontPath "/usr/X11R6/lib/X11/fonts/misc/:unscaled"
        FontPath "unix/:7100"
 5  EndSection
```

Or otherwise use `xset`:

```
xset +fp unix/:7100
```

Note that no other machines can use your own font server because of the `no-listen = tcp` option. Deleting this line (and restarting `xfs`) allows you to instead use

```
    FontPath "inet/127.0.0.1:7100"
```

which implies an open TCP connection to your font server, along with all its security implications. Remote machines can use the same setting after changing `127.0.0.1` to your IP address.

Finally, note that for XFree86 version 3.3, which does not have TrueType support, the font server name `xfstt` is available on *Fresh Meat* http://freshmeat.net/.

Chapter 44

UNIX Security

This is probably the most important chapter of this book.[1]

LINUX🐧 has been touted as both the most secure and insecure of all operating systems. The truth is both. Take no heed of advice from the LINUX🐧 community, and your server *will* be hacked eventually. Follow a few simple precautions, and it will be safe for years without much maintenance.

The attitude of most novice administrators is "Since the UNIX system is so large and complex and since there are so many millions of them on the Internet, it is unlikely that *my* machine will get hacked." Of course, it won't necessarily be a person *targeting* your organization that is the problem. It could be a person who has written an automatic scanner that tries to hack every computer in your city. It could also be a person who is not an expert in hacking at all, but who has merely downloaded a small utility to do it for him. Many seasoned experts write such utilities for public distribution, while so-called *script kiddies* (because the means to execute a script is all the expertise needed) use these to do real damage. ⬦The word *hack* means gaining unauthorized access to a computer. However, programmers sometimes use the term to refer to enthusiastic work of any kind. Here we refer to the malicious definition.⬦

In this chapter you will get an idea of the kinds of ways a UNIX system gets hacked. Then you will know what to be wary of, and how you can minimize risk.

44.1 Common Attacks

I personally divide attacks into two types: attacks that can be attempted by a user on the system, and network attacks that come from outside of a system. If a server

---

[1]Thanks to Ryan Rubin for reviewing this chapter.

511

is, say, only used for mail and web, shell logins may not be allowed *at all*; hence, the former type of security breach is of less concern. Here are some of the ways security is compromised, just to give an idea of what UNIX security is about. In some cases, I indicate when it is of more concern to multiuser systems.

Note also that attacks from users become an issue when a remote attack succeeds and a hacker gains user privileges to your system (even as a `nobody` user). This is an issue even if you do not host logins.

44.1.1 Buffer overflow attacks

Consider the following **C** program. If you don't understand **C** that well, it doesn't matter—it's the concept that is important. (Before trying this example, you should unplug your computer from the network.)

```
#include <stdio.h>

void do_echo (void)
{
    char buf[256];
    gets (buf);
    printf ("%s", buf);
    fflush (stdout);
}


int main (int argc, char **argv)
{
    for (;;) {
        do_echo ();
    }
}
```

You can compile this program with `gcc -o /usr/local/sbin/myechod myechod.c`. Then, make a system service out of it as follows: For `xinetd`, create file `/etc/xinetd.d/myechod` containing:

```
service myechod
{
        flags           = REUSE
        socket_type     = stream
        wait            = no
        user            = root
        server          = /usr/local/sbin/myechod
        log_on_failure  += USERID
}
```

while for `inetd` add the following line to your `/etc/inetd.conf` file:

```
myechod stream  tcp      nowait  root     /usr/local/sbin/myechod
```

Of course, the service `myechod` does not exist. Add the following line to your `/etc/services` file:

```
myechod         400/tcp          # Temporary demo service
```

and then restart `xinetd` (or `inetd`) as usual.

You can now run `netstat -na`. You should see a line like this somewhere in the output:

```
tcp     0       0 0.0.0.0:400          0.0.0.0:*           LISTEN
```

You can now run `telnet localhost 400` and type away happily. As you can see, the `myechod` service simply prints lines back to you.

Someone reading the code will realize that typing more than 256 characters will write into uncharted memory of the program. How can they use this effect to *cause the program to behave outside of its design*? The answer is simple. Should they be able to write processor instructions into an area of memory that may get executed later, they can cause the program to do anything at all. The process runs with `root` privileges, so a few instructions sent to the kernel could, for example, cause the `passwd` file to be truncated, or the file system superblock to be erased. A particular technique that works on a particular program is known as an *exploit* for a vulnerability. In general, an attack of this type is known as a *buffer overflow attack*.

To prevent against such attacks is easy when you are writing new programs. Simply make sure that any incoming data is treated as being dangerous. In the above case, the `fgets` function should preferably be used, since it limits the number of characters that could be written to the buffer. There are, however, many functions that behave in such a dangerous way: even the `strcpy` function writes up to a null character that may not be present; `sprintf` writes a format string that could be longer than the buffer. `getwd` is another function that also does no bound checking.

However, when programs grow long and complicated, it becomes difficult to analyze where there may be loopholes that could be exploited indirectly. A program is a legal contract with an impartial jury.

44.1.2   Setuid programs

A program like `su` must be *setuid* (see Chapter 14). Such a program has to run with `root` privileges in order to switch UIDs to another user. The onus is, however, on `su` to refuse privileges to anyone who isn't trusted. Hence, `su` requests a password and checks it against the `passwd` file before doing anything.

Once again, the logic of the program has to hold up to ensure security, as well as to provide insurance against buffer overflow attacks. Should `su` have a flaw in the authentication logic, it would enable someone to change to a UID that they were not privileged to hold.

Setuid programs should hence be considered with the utmost suspicion. Most setuid programs try be small and simple, to make it easy to verify the security of their logic. A vulnerability is more likely to be found in any setuid program that is large and complex.

(Of slightly more concern in systems hosting many untrusted user logins.)

44.1.3   Network client programs

Consider when your FTP client connects to a remote untrusted site. If the site server returns a response that the FTP client cannot handle (say, a response that is too long— a buffer overflow), it could allow malicious code to be executed by the FTP client on behalf of the server.

Hence, it is quite possible to exploit a security hole in a client program by just waiting for that program to connect to your site.

(Mostly a concern in systems that host user logins.)

44.1.4   `/tmp` file vulnerability

If a program creates a temporary file in your `/tmp/` directory and it is possible to predict the name of the file it is going to create, then it may be possible to create that file in advance or quickly modify it without the program's knowledge. Programs that create temporary files in a predictable fashion or those that do not set correct permissions (with exclusive access) to temporary files are liable to be exploited. For instance, if a program running as superuser truncates a file `/tmp/9260517.TMP` and it was possible to predict that file name in advance, then a hacker could create a symlink to `/etc/passwd` of the same name, resulting in the superuser program actually truncating the `passwd` file.

(Of slightly more concern in systems that host many untrusted user logins.)

44.1.5   Permission problems

It is easy to see that a directory with permissions `660` and ownerships `root:admin` cannot be accessed by user `jsmith` if he is outside of the `admin` group. Not so easy to see is when you have thousands of directories and hundreds of users and groups. Who can access what, when, and why becomes complicated and often requires scripts to be written to do permission tests and sets. Even a badly set `/dev/tty*` device can cause a user's terminal connection to become vulnerable.

(Of slightly more a concern in systems that host many untrusted user logins.)

44.1.6   Environment variables

There are lots of ways of creating and reading environment variables to either exploit a vulnerability or obtain some information that will compromise security. Environment variables should never hold secret information like passwords.

On the other hand, when handling environment variables, programs should consider the data they contain to be potentially malicious and do proper bounds checking and verification of their contents.

(Of more concern in systems that host many untrusted user logins.)

44.1.7   Password sniffing

When `telnet`, `ftp`, `rlogin`, or in fact any program at all that authenticates over the network without encryption is used, the password is transmitted over the network in *plain text*, that is, human-readable form. These programs are all common network utilities that old UNIX hands were accustomed to using. The sad fact is that what is being transmitted can easily be read off the wire with the most elementary tools (see `tcpdump` on page 266). None of these services should be exposed to the Internet. Use within a local LAN is safe, provided the LAN is firewalled, and your local users are trusted.

44.1.8   Password cracking

This concept is discussed in Section 11.3.

44.1.9   Denial of service attacks

A denial of service (DoS) attack is one which does not compromise the system but prevents other users from using a service legitimately. It can involve repetitively loading a service to the point that no one else can use it. In each particular case, logs or TCP traffic dumps might reveal the point of origin. You might then be able to deny access with a firewall rule. There are many types of DoS attacks that can be difficult or impossible to protect against.

44.2   Other Types of Attack

The preceding lists are far from exhaustive. It never ceases to amaze me how new loopholes are discovered in program logic. Not all of these exploits can be classified; indeed, it is precisely because new and innovative ways of hacking systems are always being found, that security needs constant attention.

44.3   Counter Measures

Security first involves removing known risks, then removing potential risks, then (possibly) making life difficult for a hacker, then using custom UNIX security paradigms, and finally being proactively cunning in thwarting hack attempts.

44.3.1   Removing known risks: outdated packages

It is especially sad to see naive administrators install packages that are *well known* to be vulnerable and for which "script kiddy" exploits are readily available on the Internet.

If a security hole is discovered, the package will usually be updated by the distribution vendor or the author. The `bugtraq` http://www.securityfocus.com/forums/bugtraq/-intro.html mailing list announces the latest exploits and has many thousands of subscribers worldwide. You should get on this mailing list to be aware of new discoveries. *The Linux Weekly News* http://lwn.net/ is a possible source for security announcements if you only want to read once a week. You can then download and install the binary or source distribution provided for that package. Watching security announcements is critical. ⭲I often ask "administrators" if they have upgraded the *xxx* service and get the response, that either they are not sure if they need it, do not believe it is vulnerable, do not know if it is running, where to get a current package, or even how to perform the upgrade; as if their ignorance absolves them of their responsibility. If the janitor were to duct-tape your safe keys to a window pane, would you fire him?⭱

This goes equally for new systems that you install: never install outdated packages. Some vendors ship updates to their older distributions. This means that you can install from an old distribution and then upgrade all your packages from an "update" package list. Your packages would be then as secure as the packages of the distribution that has the highest version number. For instance, you can install RedHat 6.2 from a 6-month-old CD, then download a list of RedHat 6.2 "update" packages. Alternatively, you can install the latest RedHat version 7.? which has a completely different set of packages. On the other hand, some other vendors may "no longer support" an older distribution, meaning that those packages will never be updated. In this case, you should be sure to install or upgrade with the vendor's most current distribution or manually recompile vulnerable packages by yourself.

Over and above this, remember that vendors are sometimes slow to respond to security alerts. Hence, trust the free software community's alerts over anything vendors may fail to tell you.

Alternatively, if you discover that a service is insecure, you may just want to disable it (or better still, uninstall it) if it's not really needed.

44.3.2 Removing known risks: compromised packages

Packages that are modified by a hacker can allow him a back door into your system: so called *Trojans*. Use the package verification commands discussed in Section 24.2.6 to check package integrity.

44.3.3 Removing known risks: permissions

It is easy to locate world-writable files. There should be only a few in the /dev and /tmp directories:

```
find / -perm -2 ! -type l -ls
```

Files without any owner are an indication of mismanagement or compromise of your system. Use the find command with

```
find / -nouser -o -nogroup -ls
```

44.3.4 Password management

It is obvious that variety in user passwords is more secure. It is a good idea to rather not let novice users choose their own passwords. Create a randomizing program to generate completely arbitrary 8 character passwords for them. You should also use the pwconv utility from the shadow-utils package to create the shadow password files (explained in Section 11.3). See pwconv(8) for information.

44.3.5 Disabling inherently insecure services

Services that are inherently insecure are those that allow the password to be sniffed over the Internet or provide no proper authentication to begin with. Any service that does not encrypt traffic should not be used for authentication over the Internet. These are `ftp`, `telnet`, `rlogin`, `uucp`, `imap`, `pop3`, and any service that does not use encryption and yet authenticates with a password.

Instead, you should use `ssh` and `scp`. There are secure versions of POP and IMAP (SPOP3 and SIMAP), but you may not be able to find good client programs. If you really *have* to use a service, you should limit the networks that are allowed to connect to it, as described on page 293 and 296.

Old UNIX hands are notorious for exporting NFS shares (`/etc/exports`) that are readable (and writable) from the Internet. The group of functions to do Sun Microsystems' port mapping and NFS—the `nfs-utils` (`rpc....`) and `portmap` packages—don't give me a warm, fuzzy feeling. Don't use these on machines exposed to the Internet.

44.3.6 Removing potential risks: network

Install `libsafe`. This is a library that wraps all those vulnerable **C** functions discussed above, thus testing for a buffer overflow attempt with each call. It is trivial to install, and sends email to the administrator upon hack attempts. Go to http://www.avayalabs.com/project/libsafe/index.html for more information, or send email to `libsafe@research.avayalabs.com`. The `libsafe` library effectively solves 90% of the buffer overflow problem. There is a *very* slight performance penalty, however.

Disable all services that you are not using. Then, try to evaluate whether the remaining services are really needed. For instance, do you *really* need IMAP or would POP3 suffice? IMAP has had a lot more security alerts than POP3 because it is a much more complex service. Is the risk worth it?

`xinetd` (or `inetd`) runs numerous services, of which only a few are needed. You should trim your `/etc/xinetd.d` directory (or `/etc/inetd.conf` file) to a minimum. For `xinetd`, you can add the line `disable = yes` to the relevant file. Only one or two files should be enabled. Alternatively, your `/etc/inetd.conf` should have only a few lines in it. A real-life example is:

```
ftp       stream  tcp     nowait  root    /usr/sbin/tcpd  in.ftpd -l -a
pop-3     stream  tcp     nowait  root    /usr/sbin/tcpd  ipop3d
imap      stream  tcp     nowait  root    /usr/sbin/tcpd  imapd
```

This advice should be taken quite literally. The rule of thumb is that if you don't know what a service does, you should disable it. See also Section 29.6.

In the above real-life case, the services were additionally limited to permit only certain networks to connect (see page 293 and 296).

`xinetd` (or `inetd`) is not the only problem. There are many other problematic services. Entering `netstat -nlp` gives initial output, like

```
 (Not all processes could be identified, non-owned process info
  will not be shown, you would have to be root to see it all.)
 Active Internet connections (only servers)
 Proto Recv-Q Send-Q Local Address      Foreign Address    State    PID/Program name
 tcp        0      0 0.0.0.0:25          0.0.0.0:*          LISTEN   2043/exim
 tcp        0      0 0.0.0.0:400         0.0.0.0:*          LISTEN   32582/xinetd
 tcp        0      0 0.0.0.0:21          0.0.0.0:*          LISTEN   32582/xinetd
 tcp        0      0 172.23.80.52:53     0.0.0.0:*          LISTEN   30604/named
 tcp        0      0 127.0.0.1:53        0.0.0.0:*          LISTEN   30604/named
 tcp        0      0 0.0.0.0:6000        0.0.0.0:*          LISTEN   583/X
 tcp        0      0 0.0.0.0:515         0.0.0.0:*          LISTEN   446/
 tcp        0      0 0.0.0.0:22          0.0.0.0:*          LISTEN   424/sshd
 udp        0      0 0.0.0.0:1045        0.0.0.0:*                   30604/named
 udp        0      0 172.23.80.52:53     0.0.0.0:*                   30604/named
 udp        0      0 127.0.0.1:53        0.0.0.0:*                   30604/named
 raw        0      0 0.0.0.0:1           0.0.0.0:*          7        -
 raw        0      0 0.0.0.0:6           0.0.0.0:*          7        -
```

but doesn't show that PID `446` is actually `lpd`. For that information just type `ls -al /proc/446/`.

You can see that ten services are actually open: `1`, `6`, `21`, `22`, `25`, `53`, `400`, `515`, `1045`, and `6000`. `1` and `6` are kernel ports, and `21` and `400` are FTP and our echo daemon, respectively. Such a large number of open ports provides ample opportunity for attack.

At this point, you should go through each of these services and **(1)**, decide whether you really need them. Then **(2)**, make sure you have the latest version; finally **(3)**, consult the packages documentation so that you can limit the networks that are allowed to connect to those services.

It is interesting that people are wont to make assumptions about packages to the tune of "This service is so popular it can't possibly be vulnerable." The exact opposite is, in fact, true: The more obscure and esoteric a service is, the less likely that someone has taken the trouble to find a vulnerability. In the case of `named` (i.e., `bind`), a number of most serious vulnerabilities were made public as regards every Bind release prior to 9. Hence, upgrading to the latest version (9.1 at the time of writing) from source was prudent for all the machines I administered (a most-time consuming process).

44.3.7   Removing potential risks: setuid programs

It is easy to find all the setuid programs on your system:

```
find / -type f -perm +6000 -ls
```

Disabling them is just as easy:

```
chmod -s /bin/ping
```

There is nothing wrong with the decision that ordinary users are *not* allowed to use even the `ping` command. If you do allow any shell logins on your system, then you should remove setuid permissions from all shell commands.

44.3.8 Making life difficult

There is much that you can do that is not "security" *per se* but that will make life considerably more difficult for a hacker, and certainly impossible for a stock standard attack, even if your system is vulnerable. A hack attempt often relies on a system being configured a certain way. Making your system different from the standard can go a long way.

Read-only partitions: It is allowable to mount your /usr partition (and critical top-level directories like /bin) read-only since these are, by definition, static data. Of course, anyone with root access can remount it as writable, but a generic attack script may not know this. Some SCSI disks can be configured as read-only by using dip switches (or so I hear). The /usr partition can be made from an ISO 9660 partition (CD-ROM file system) which is read-only by design. You can also mount your CD-ROM as a /usr partition: access will be slow, but completely unmodifiable. Finally, you can manually modify your kernel code to fail write-mount attempts on /usr.

Read-only attributes: LINUX🐧 has additional file attributes to make a file unmodifiable over and above the usual permissions. These attributes are controlled by the commands `chattr` and `lsattr`. You can make a log file append-only with `chatter +a /var/log/messages /var/log/syslog` or make files immutable with, `chatter +i /bin/login`: both actions are a good idea. The command

```
chattr -R +i /bin /boot /lib /sbin /usr
```

is a better idea still. Of course, anyone with superuser privileges can switch them back.

Periodic system monitoring: It is useful to write your own `crond` scripts to check whether files have changed. the scripts can check for new setuid programs, permissions, or changes to binary files; or you can reset permissions to what you think is secure. Just remember that `cron` programs can be modified by anyone who hacks into the system. A simple command

```
find / -mtime 2 -o -ctime 2
```

searches for all files that have been modified in the last two days.

Nonstandard packages: If you notice many security alerts for a package, switch to a different one. There are alternatives to `bind`, `wu-ftpd`, `sendmail` (as covered in Chapter 30), and almost every service you can think of. You can also try installing an uncommon or security-specialized distribution. Switching entirely to FreeBSD is also one way of reducing your risk considerably. ⬐This is not a joke.⬏

Nonstandard messages: Many services provide banners and informational messages which give away the version of your software. For example, mail servers have default `HELO` responses to advertise themselves; and login and FTP banners often display the operating system you are running. These messages should be customized to provide less information on which to base an attack. You can begin by editing `/etc/motd`.

Minimal kernels: Its easy to compile your kernel without module support, with an absolutely minimal set of features. Loading of Trojan modules has been a source of insecurity in the past. Such a kernel can only make you safer.

Non-Intel architecture: Hackers need to learn assembly language to exploit many vulnerabilities. The most common assembly language is that of Intel 80?86 processors. Using a non-Intel platform adds that extra bit of obscurity.

Removing fingerprints: Your system identifies itself to

OpenWall project: This has a kernel patch that makes the stack of a process non-executable (which will thwart most kinds of buffer overflow attempts) and does some other cute things with the `/tmp` directory and process I/O.

44.3.9 Custom security paradigms

Hackers have limited resources. Take oneupmanship away and security is about the cost of hacking a system versus the reward of success. If you feel the machine you administer is bordering on this category then you need to start billing far more for your hours and doing things like those described below. It *is* possible to go to lengths that will make a LINUX system secure against a large government's defense budget.

Capabilities: This is a system of security that gives limited kinds of superuser access to programs that would normally need to be full-blown setuid `root` executables. Think: Most processes that run with `root` (setuid) privileges do so because of the need to access only a single privileged function. For instance, the `ping` program does not need *complete* superuser privileges (run `ls -l /bin/ping` and note the setuid bit). Capabilities are a fine-grained set of privileges that say that a process can do particular things that an ordinary user can't, *without* ever having full `root` access. In the case of `ping`, its capability would be certain networking access that only `root` is normally allowed to do.

Access control lists: These lists extend the simple "user/group/other" permissions of UNIX files to allow arbitrary lists of users to access particular files. This really does nothing for network security but is useful if you have many users on the system and you would like to restrict them in odd ways. (ACL is a little out of place in this list.)

DTE: *Domain and Type Enforcement* works like this: When a program is executed, it is categorized and only allowed to do certain things even if it is running as root. These limitations are extended to child processes that it may execute. This is *real* security; there are kernel patches to do this. The National Security Agency (of the U.S.) (NSA) actually has a LINUX distribution built around DTE.

medusa: This is a security system that causes the kernel to query a user daemon before letting any process on the system do anything. It is the most ubiquitous security system out because it is entirely configurable—you can make the user daemon restrict anything however you like.

VXE: *Virtual eXecuting Environment* dictates that a program executes in its own protected space while VXE executes a Lisp program to check whether a system call is allowed. This is effectively a lot like `medusa`.

MAC: *Mandatory Access Controls*. This is also about virtual environments for processes. MAC is a POSIX standard.

RSBAC and RBAC: *Rule-Set-Based Access Controls* and *Role-Based Access Controls*. These look like a combination of some of the above.

LIDS: *Linux Intrusion Detection System* does some meager preventive measures to restrict module loading, file modifications, and process information.

Kernel patches exist to do all of the above. Many of these projects are well out of the test phase but are not in the mainstream kernel, possibly because developers are not sure of the most enduring approach to UNIX security. They all have one thing in common: double-checking what a privileged process does, which can only be a good thing.

44.3.10 Proactive cunning

Proactive cunning means attack monitoring and reaction, and intrusion monitoring and reaction. Utilities that do this come under a general class called *network intrusion detection* software. The idea that one might detect and react to a hacker has an emotional appeal, but it automatically implies that your system is insecure to begin with—which is probably true, considering the rate at which new vulnerabilities are being reported. I am weary of so-called intrusion detection systems that administrators implement even before the most elementary of security measures. Really, one must implement all of the above security measures before thinking about intrusion monitoring.

To picture the most basic form of monitoring, consider this: To hack a system, one usually needs to test for open services. To do this, one tries to connect to every port on the system to see which are open. This is known as a *port scan*. There are simple tools to detect a port scan, which will then start a firewall rule that will deny further access from the offending host although this can work against you if the hacker has spoofed your own IP address. More importantly, the tools will report the IP address from which the attack arose. A reverse lookup will give the domain name, and then a `whois` query on the appropriate authoritative DNS registration site will reveal the physical address and telephone number of the domain owner.

Port scan monitoring is the most elementary form of monitoring and reaction. From there up, you can find innumerable bizarre tools to try and read into all sorts of network and process activity. I leave this to your own research, although you might want to start with the *Snort traffic scanner* http://www.snort.org/, the *Tripwire intrusion detection system* http://www.tripwiresecurity.com/, and *IDSA* http://jade.cs.uct.ac.za/idsa/.

A point to such monitoring is also as a deterrent to hackers. A network should be able to find the origins of an attack and thereby trace the attacker. The threat of discovery makes hacking a far less attractive pastime, and you should look into the legal recourse you may have against people who try to compromise your system.

44.4   Important Reading

The preceding is a practical guide. It gets much more interesting than this. A place to start is the `comp.os.linux.security` FAQ. This FAQ gives the most important UNIX security references available on the net. You can download it from http://www.memeticcandiru.com/colsfaq.html, http://www.linuxsecurity.com/docs/-colsfaq.html or http://www.geocities.com/swan_daniel/colsfaq.html. The *Linux Security* http://www.linuxsecurity.com/ web page also has a security quick reference card that summarizes most everything you need to know in two pages.

44.5   Security Quick-Quiz

- *How many security reports have you read?*
- *How many packages have you upgraded because of vulnerabilities?*
- *How many services have you disabled because you were unsure of their security?*
- *How many access limit rules do you have in your* `hosts.*`/`xinetd` *services?*

If your answer to any of these questions is fewer than 5, you are not being conscientious about security.

44.6 Security Auditing

This chapter is mostly concerned with securing your own LINUX server. However, if you have a large network, *security auditing* is a more extensive evaluation of your systems' vulnerabilities. Security auditing becomes an involved procedure when multiple administrators maintain many different platforms across a network. There are companies that specialize in this work: Any network that does not dedicate an enlightened staff member should budget generously for their services.

Auditing your network might involve the following:

- Doing penetration testing of firewalls.
- Port scanning.
- Installing intrusion detection software.
- Analyzing and reporting on Internet attack paths.
- Evaluating service access within your local LAN.
- Tracking your administrators' maintenance activities.
- Trying password cracking on all authentication services.
- Monitoring the activity of legitimate user accounts.

> *Network attacks cost companies billions of dollars each year in service downtime and repair. Failing to pay attention to security is a false economy.*

Appendix A

Lecture Schedule

The following sections describe a 36-hour lecture schedule in 12 lessons, 2 per week, of 3 hours each. The lectures are interactive, following the text closely, but sometimes giving straightforward chapters as homework.

A.1 Hardware Requirements

The course requires that students have a LINUX system to use for their homework assignments. For past courses, most people were willing to repartition their home machines, buy a new hard drive, or use a machine of their employer.

The classroom itself should have 4 to 10 places. It is imperative that students have their own machine, since the course is *highly* interactive. The lecturer need not have a machine. I myself prefer to write everything on a whiteboard. The machines should be networked with Ethernet and configured so that machines can telnet to each other's IPs. A *full* LINUX installation is preferred—everything covered by the lectures must be installed. This would include all services, several desktops, and **C** and kernel development packages.

LINUX CDs should also be available for those who need to set up their home computers.

Most notably, each student should have his own copy of this text.

A.2 Student Selection

This lecture layout is designed for seasoned administrators of MS-DOS or Windows systems, those who at least have some kind of programming background, or those who, at the very least, are experienced in assembling hardware and installing operating systems. At the other end of the scale, "end users" with no knowledge of command-line interfaces, programming, hardware assembly, or networking, would require a far less intensive lecture schedule and would certainly not cope with the abstraction of a shell interface.

Of course, people of high intelligence can cover this material quite quickly, regardless of their IT experience, and it is smoothest when the class is at the same level. The most controversial method would be to simply place a tape measure around the cranium (since the latest data puts the correlation between IQ and brain size at about 0.4).

A less intensive lecture schedule would probably cover about half of the material, with more personalized tuition, and having more in-class assignments.

A.3   Lecture Style

Lessons are three hours each. In my own course, these were in the evenings from 6 to 9, with two 10 minute breaks on the hour. It is important that there are a few days between each lecture for students to internalize the concepts and practice them by themselves.

The course is completely interactive, following a "type this now class..." genre. The text is replete with examples, so these should be followed in sequence. In some cases, repetitive examples are skipped. Examples are written on the whiteboard, perhaps with slight changes for variety. Long examples are not written out: "Now class, type in the example on page...".

The motto of the lecture style is: *keep 'em typing*.

Occasional diversions from the lecturer's own experiences are always fun when the class gets weary.

The lecturer will also be aware that students get stuck occasionally. I check their screens from time to time, typing in the odd command for them, to speed the class along.

Lesson 1

A background to UNIX and LINUX history is explained, crediting the various responsible persons and organizations. The various copyrights are explained, with emphasis on the GPL.

Chapter 4 then occupies the remainder of the first three hours.

Homework: Appendix D and E to be read. Students to install their own LINUX
distributions. Chapter 6 should be covered to learn basic operations with `vi`.

Lesson 2

Chapter 5 (Regular Expressions) occupies the first hour, then Chapter 7 (Shell Scripting) the remaining time. Lecturers should doubly emphasize to the class the importance of properly understanding regular expressions, as well as their wide use in UNIX.

Homework: Research different desktop configurations and end-user applications. Students should become familiar with the different desktops and major applications that
they offer.

Lesson 3

First hour covers Chapter 8. Second hour covers Chapters 9 and 10. Third hour covers
Chapter 11.

Homework: Research LINUX on the Internet. All resources mentioned in Chapters
16 and 13 should be accessed.

Lesson 4

First two hours cover Chapters 12, 13, 14, 15. Third hour covers Chapters 16 and 17.

Homework: Chapters 18 through 21 to be covered. Students will not be able to modify the house's partitions, and printers will not be available, so these experiments are
given for homework. Chapter 20 is not considered essential. Students are to attempt
to configure their own printers and report back with any problems.

Lesson 5

First hour covers Chapter 22, second hour covers Chapter 24. For the third hour, student read Chapter 25 and Chapter 26, asking questions about any unclear points.

Homework: Optionally, Chapters 23, then rereading of Chapter 25 and 26.

Lesson 6

Lectured coverage of Chapter 25 and Chapter 26. Also demonstrate an attempt to sniff the password of a `telnet` session with `tcpdump`. Then the same attempt with `ssh`.

Homework: Read Chapter 27 through Chapter 29 in preparation for next lesson.

Lesson 7

Chapters 27 through 29 covered in first and second hour. A DNS server should be up for students to use. Last hour explains how Internet mail works, in theory only, as well as the structure of the `exim` configuration file.

Homework: Read through Chapter 30 in preparation for next lesson.

Lesson 8

First and second hours cover Chapter 30. Students to configure their own mail server. A DNS server should be present to test MX records for their domain. Last hour covers Chapters 31 and 32, excluding anything about modems.

Homework: Experiment with Chapter 33. Chapter 34 not covered. Chapter 35 to be studied in detail. Students to set up a web server from Chapter 36 and report back with problems. Apache itself is not covered in lectures.

Lesson 9

First hour covers Chapter 37. Second and third hours cover Chapter 40. Students to configure their own name servers with forward and reverse lookups. Note that Samba is not covered if there are no Windows machines or printers to properly demonstrate it. An alternative would be to set up printing and file-sharing using `smbmount`.

Homework: Chapter 41 for homework—students to configure dialup network for themselves. Read through Chapter 42 in preparation for next lesson.

Lesson 10

First and second hours cover Chapter 42. Students to at least configure their own network card if no other hardware devices are available. Build a kernel with some customizations. Third hour covers the **X** Window System in theory and use of the `DISPLAY` environment variable to display applications to each other's **X** servers.

Homework: Study Chapter 28.

Lesson 11

First hour covers configuring of NFS, noting the need for a name server with forward and reverse lookups. Second and third hours cover Chapter 38.

Homework: Download and read the Python tutorial. View the weeks security reports online. Study Chapter 44.

Lesson 12

First and second hours cover the security chapter and an introduction to the Python programming language. Last hour comprises the course evaluation. The final lesson could possibly hold an examination if a certification is offered for this particular course.

Appendix B

LINUX Professionals Institute Certification Cross-Reference

These requirements are quoted verbatim from the LPI web page http://www.lpi.org/. *For each objective, the relevant chapter or section from this book is referenced in parentheses: these are my additions to the text. In some cases, outside references are given. Note that the LPI level 2 exams have not been finalized as of this writing. However, the preliminary draft of the level 2 curricula is mostly covered by this book.*

Each objective is assigned a weighting value. The weights range roughly from 1 to 8, and indicate the relative importance of each objective. Objectives with higher weights will be covered by more exam questions.

B.1   Exam Details for 101

General LINUX, part I

This is a required exam for certification level I. It covers fundamental system administration activities that are common across all flavors of LINUX.

Topic 1.3: GNU and UNIX Commands

Obj 1: Work Effectively on the UNIX command line
Weight of objective: 4

Interact with shells and commands using the command line (Chapter 4). Includes typing valid commands and command sequences (Chapter 4), defining, referencing and exporting environment variables (Chapter 9), using command history and editing facilities (Section 2.6), invoking commands in the path and outside the path (Section 4.6), using command substitution, and applying commands recursively through a directory tree (Section 20.7.5).

Obj 2: Process text streams using text processing filters
Weight of objective: 7

Send text files and output streams through text utility filters to modify the output in a useful way (Chapter 8). Includes the use of standard UNIX commands found in the GNU textutils package such as sed, sort, cut, expand, fmt, head, join, nl, od, paste, pr, split, tac, tail, tr, and wc (see the man pages for each of these commands in conjunction with Chapter 8).

Obj 3: Perform basic file management
Weight of objective: 2

Use the basic UNIX commands to copy and move files and directories (Chapter 4). Perform advanced file management operations such as copying multiple files recursively and moving files that meet a wildcard pattern (Chapter 4). Use simple and advanced wildcard specifications to refer to files (Chapter 4.3).

Obj 4: Use UNIX streams, pipes, and redirects
Weight of objective: 3

Connect files to commands and commands to other commands to efficiently process textual data. Includes redirecting standard input, standard output, and standard error; and piping one command's output into another command as input or as arguments (using xargs); sending output to stdout and a file (using tee) (Chapter 8).

Obj 5: Create, monitor, and kill processes
Weight of objective: 5

Includes running jobs in the foreground and background (Chapter 9), bringing a job from the background to the foreground and vise versa, monitoring active processes, sending signals to processes, and killing processes. Includes using commands ps, top, kill, bg, fg, and jobs (Chapter 9).

Obj 6: Modify process execution priorities
Weight of objective: 2

Run a program with higher or lower priority, determine the priority of a process, change the priority of a running process (Section 9.7). Includes the command nice and its relatives (Section 9.7).

Obj 7: Perform searches of text files making use of regular expressions
Weight of objective: 3

Includes creating simple regular expressions and using related tools such as grep and sed to perform searches (Chapters 5 and 8).

Topic 2.4: Devices, LINUX File Systems, Filesystem Hierarchy Standard

Obj 1: Create partitions and filesystems
Weight of objective: 3

Create disk partitions using fdisk, create hard drive and other media filesystems using mkfs (Chapter 19).

Obj 2: Maintain the integrity of filesystems
Weight of objective: 5

Verify the integrity of filesystems, monitor free space and inodes, fix simple filesystem problems. Includes commands fsck, du, df (Chapter 19).

Obj 3: Control filesystem mounting and unmounting
Weight of objective: 3

Mount and unmount filesystems manually, configure filesystem mounting on bootup, configure user-mountable removable file systems. Includes managing file /etc/fstab (Chapter 19).

Obj 4: Set and view disk quota
Weight of objective: 1

Setup disk quota for a filesystem, edit user quota, check user quota, generate reports of user quota. Includes quota, edquota, repquota, quotaon commands. (Quotas are not covered but are easily learned form the Quota mini-HOWTO.)

Obj 5: Use file permissions to control access to files
Weight of objective: 3

Set permissions on files, directories, and special files, use special permission modes such as suid and sticky bit, use the group field to grant file access to workgroups, change default file creation mode. Includes chmod and umask commands. Requires understanding symbolic and numeric permissions (Chapter 14).

Obj 6: Manage file ownership
Weight of objective: 2

Change the owner or group for a file, control what group is assigned to new files created in a directory. Includes chown and chgrp commands (Chapter 11).

Obj 7: Create and change hard and symbolic links
Weight of objective: 2

Create hard and symbolic links, identify the hard links to a file, copy files by following or not following symbolic links, use hard and symbolic links for efficient system administration (Chapter 15).

Obj 8: Find system files and place files in the correct location
Weight of objective: 2

Understand the filesystem hierarchy standard, know standard file locations, know the purpose of various system directories, find commands and files. Involves using the commands: find, locate, which, updatedb . Involves editing the file: /etc/updatedb.conf (Section 4.14 and Chapters 17 and 35).

Topic 2.6: Boot, Initialization, Shutdown, Run Levels

Obj 1: Boot the system
Weight of objective: 3

Guide the system through the booting process, including giving options to the kernel at boot time, and check the events in the log files. Involves using the commands: dmesg (lilo). Involves reviewing the files: /var/log/messages, /etc/lilo.conf, /etc/conf.modules — /etc/modules.conf (Sections 21.4.8 and 42.5.1 and Chapters 31 and 32).

Obj 2: Change runlevels and shutdown or reboot system
Weight of objective: 3

Securely change the runlevel of the system, specifically to single user mode, halt (shutdown) or reboot. Make sure to alert users beforehand, and properly terminate processes. Involves using the commands: shutdown, init (Chapter 32).

Topic 1.8: Documentation

Obj 1: Use and Manage Local System Documentation
Weight of objective: 5

Use and administer the man facility and the material in /usr/doc/. Includes finding relevant man pages, searching man page sections, finding commands and manpages related to one, configuring access to man sources and the man system, using system documentation stored in /usr/doc/ and related places, determining what documentation to keep in /usr/doc/ (Section 4.7 and Chapter 16; you should also study the man page of the man command itself).

Obj 2: Find Linux documentation on the Internet
Weight of objective: 2

Find and use Linux documentation at sources such as the Linux Documentation Project, vendor and third-party websites, newsgroups, newsgroup archives, mailing lists (Chapter 13).

Obj 3: Write System Documentation
Weight of objective: 1

Write documentation and maintain logs for local conventions, procedures, configuration and configuration changes, file locations, applications, and shell scripts. (You should learn how to write a man page yourself. There are many man pages to copy as examples. It is difficult to say what the LPI had in mind for this objective.)

Obj 4: Provide User Support
Weight of objective: 1

Provide technical assistance to users via telephone, email, and personal contact. (This is not covered. Providing user support can be practiced by answering questions on the newsgroups or mailing lists.)

Topic 2.11: Administrative Tasks

Obj 1: Manage users and group accounts and related system files
Weight of objective: 7

Add, remove, suspend user accounts, add and remove groups, change user/group info in passwd/group databases, create special purpose and limited accounts. Includes commands useradd, userdel, groupadd, gpasswd, passwd, and file passwd, group, shadow, and gshadow. (Chapter 11. You should also study the `useradd` and `groupadd` man pages in detail.)

Obj 2: Tune the user environment and system environment variables
Weight of objective: 4

Modify global and user profiles to set environment variable, maintain skel directories for new user accounts, place proper commands in path. Involves editing /etc/profile and /etc/skel/ (Chapter 11 and Section 20.8).

Obj 3: Configure and use system log files to meet administrative and security needs
Weight of objective: 3

Configure the type and level of information logged, manually scan log files for notable activity, arrange for automatic rotation and archiving of logs, track down problems noted in logs. Involves editing /etc/syslog.conf (Sections 21.4.8 and 21.4.9).

Obj 4: Automate system administration tasks by scheduling jobs to run in the future
Weight of objective: 4

Use cron to run jobs at regular intervals, use at to run jobs at a specific time, manage cron and at jobs, configure user access to cron and at services (Chapter 37).

Obj 5: Maintain an effective data backup strategy
Weight of objective: 3

Plan a backup strategy, backup filesystems automatically to various media, perform partial and manual backups, verify the integrity of backup files, partially or fully restore backups (Section 4.17 and Chapter 18).

B.2 Exam Details for 102

General LINUX, part II

Topic 1.1: Hardware and Architecture

Obj 1: Configure fundamental system hardware
Weight of objective: 3

Demonstrate a proper understanding of important BIOS settings, set the date and time, ensure IRQs and I/O addresses are correct for all ports including serial and parallel, make a note of IRQs and I/Os, be aware of the issues associated with drives larger than 1024 cylinders (Chapters 3 and 42).

Obj 2: Setup SCSI and NIC devices
Weight of objective: 4

Manipulate the SCSI BIOS to detect used and available SCSI IDs, set the SCSI ID to the correct ID number for the boot device and any other devices required, format the SCSI drive—low level with manufacturer's installation tools—and properly partition and system format with LINUX fdisk and mke2fs, set up NIC using manufacturer's setup tools setting the I/O and the IRQ as well as the DMA if required. (Sections 42.6.3 and 42.6.9. Each hardware vendor has their own specific tools. There are few such NICs still left to practice on.)

Obj 3: Configure modem, sound cards
Weight of objective: 3

Ensure devices meet compatibility requirements (particularly that the modem is NOT a win-modem), verify that both the modem and sound card are using unique and correct IRQs, I/O, and DMA addresses, if the sound card is PnP install and run sndconfig and isapnp, configure modem for outbound dialup, configure modem for outbound PPP — SLIP — CSLIP connection, set serial port for 115.2 Kbps (Sections 42.6.1, 42.6.12, and 42.7 and Chapters 34 and 41).

Topic 2.2: LINUX Installation and Package Management

Obj 1: Design hard-disk layout
Weight of objective: 2

Design a partitioning scheme for a LINUX system, depending on the hardware and system use (number of disks, partition sizes, mount points, kernel location on disk, swap space). (Chapter 19.)

Obj 2: Install a boot manager
Weight of objective: 3

Select, install and configure a boot loader at an appropriate disk location. Provide alternative and backup boot options (like a boot floppy disk). Involves using the command: lilo . Involves editing the file: /etc/lilo.conf (Chapter 31).

Obj 3: Make and install programs from source
Weight of objective: 5

Manage (compressed) archives of files (unpack "tarballs"), specifically GNU source packages. Install and configure these on your systems. Do simple manual customization of the Makefile if necessary (like paths, extra include dirs) and make and install the executable. Involves using the commands: gunzip, tar, ./configure, make, make install . Involves editing the files: ./Makefile (Chapter 24).

Obj 4: Manage shared libraries
Weight of objective: 3

Determine the dependencies of executable programs on shared libraries, and install these when necessary. Involves using the commands: ldd, ldconfig . Involves editing the files: /etc/ld.so.conf (Chapter 23).

Obj 5: Use Debian package management
Weight of objective: 5

Use the Debian package management system, from the command line (dpkg) and with interactive tools (dselect). Be able to find a package containing specific files or software; select and retrieve them from archives; install, upgrade or uninstall them; obtain status information like version, content, dependencies, integrity, installation status; and determine which packages are installed and from which package a specific file has been installed. Be able to install a non-Debian package on a Debian system (Chapter 24).

Involves using the commands and programs: dpkg, dselect, apt, apt-get, alien . Involves reviewing or editing the files and directories: /var/lib/dpkg/* .

Obj 6:Use Red Hat Package Manager (rpm)
Weight of objective: 6

Use rpm from the command line. Familiarize yourself with these tasks: Install a package, uninstall a package, determine the version of the package and the version of the software it contains, list the files in a package, list documentation files in a package, list configuration files or installation or uninstallation scripts in a package, find out for a certain file from which package it was installed, find out which packages have been installed on the system (all packages, or from a subset of packages), find out in which package a certain program or file can be found, verify the integrity of a package, verify the PGP or GPG signature of a package, upgrade a package. Involves using the commands and programs: rpm, grep (Chapter 24).

Topic 1.5: Kernel

Obj 1: Manage kernel modules at runtime
Weight of objective: 3

Learn which functionality is available through loadable kernel modules, and manually load and unload the modules as appropriate. Involves using the commands: lsmod, insmod, rmmod, modinfo, modprobe. Involves reviewing the files: /etc/modules.conf — /etc/conf.modules (* depends on distribution *), /lib/modules/{kernel-version}/modules.dep (Chapter 42).

Obj 2: Reconfigure, build, and install a custom kernel and modules
Weight of objective: 4

Obtain and install approved kernel sources and headers (from a repository at your site, CD, kernel.org, or your vendor); customize the kernel configuration (i.e., reconfigure the kernel from the existing .config file when needed, using oldconfig, menuconfig or xconfig); Make a new LINUX kernel and modules; Install the new kernel and modules at the proper place; Reconfigure and run lilo. N.B.: This does not require to upgrade the kernel to a new version (full source nor patch). Requires the commands: make (dep, clean, menuconfig, bzImage, modules, modules_install), depmod, lilo. Requires reviewing or editing the files: /usr/src/linux/.config , /usr/src/linux/Makefile, /lib/modules/{kernelversion}/modules.dep, /etc/conf.modules — /etc/modules.conf, /etc/lilo.conf (Chapter 42).

Topic 1.7: Text Editing, Processing, Printing

Obj 1: Perform basic file editing operations using vi
Weight of objective: 2

Edit text files using vi. Includes vi navigation, basic modes, inserting, editing and deleting text, finding text, and copying text (Chapter 6).

Obj 2: Manage printers and print queues
Weight of objective: 2

Monitor and manage print queues and user print jobs, troubleshoot general printing problems. Includes the commands: lpc, lpq, lprm and lpr . Includes reviewing the file: /etc/printcap (Chapter 21).

Obj 3: Print files
Weight of objective: 1

Submit jobs to print queues, convert text files to postscript for printing. Includes lpr command (Section 21.6).

Obj 4: Install and configure local and remote printers
Weight of objective: 3

Install a printer daemon, install and configure a print filter (e.g.: apsfilter, magicfilter). Make local and remote printers accessible for a LINUX system, including postscript, non-postscript, and Samba printers. Involves the daemon: lpd . Involves editing or reviewing the files and directories: /etc/printcap , /etc/apsfilterrc , /usr/lib/apsfilter/filter/*/ , /etc/magicfilter/*/ , /var/spool/lpd/*/ (why *not* to use apsfilter is discussed in Section 21.9.2).

Topic 1.9: Shells, Scripting, Programming, Compiling

Obj 1: Customize and use the shell environment
Weight of objective: 4

Customize your shell environment: set environment variables (e.g. PATH) at login or when spawning a new shell; write bash functions for frequently used sequences of commands. Involves editing these files in your home directory: .bash_profile — .bash_login — .profile ; .bashrc ; .bash_logout ; .inputrc (Chapter 20).

Obj 2: Customize or write simple scripts
Weight of objective: 5

Customize existing scripts (like paths in scripts of any language), or write simple new (ba)sh scripts. Besides use of standard sh syntax (loops, tests), be able to do things like: command substitution and testing of command return values, test of file status, and conditional mailing to the superuser. Make sure the correct interpreter is called on the first (#!) line, and consider location, ownership, and execution- and suid-rights of the script (Chapter 20; setuid is covered in Sections 33.2 and 36.2.10 from a slightly more utilitarian angle).

Topic 2.10: X

Obj 1: Install and configure XFree86
Weight of objective: 4

Verify that the video card and monitor are supported by an X server, install the correct X server, configure the X server, install an X font server, install required fonts for X (may require a manual edit of /etc/X11/XF86Config in the "Files" section), customize and tune X for videocard and monitor. Commands: XF86Setup, xf86config. Files: /etc/X11/XF86Config, .xresources (Chapter 43).

Obj 2: Setup XDM
Weight of objective: 1

Turn xdm on and off, change the xdm greeting, change default bitplanes for xdm, set-up xdm for use by X-stations (see the xdm man page for comprehensive information).

Obj 3: Identify and terminate runaway X applications
Weight of objective: 1

Identify and kill X applications that won't die after user ends an X-session. Example: netscape, tkrat, etc.

Obj 4: Install and customize a Window Manager Environment
Weight of objective: 4

Select and customize a system-wide default window manager and/or desktop environment, demonstrate an understanding of customization procedures for window manager menus, configure menus for the window manager, select and configure the desired x-terminal (xterm, rxvt, aterm etc.), verify and resolve library dependency issues for X applications, export an X-display to a client workstation. Commands: Files: .xinitrc, .Xdefaults, various .rc files. (The `xinit`, `startx`, and `xdm` man pages provide this information.)

Topic 1.12: Networking Fundamentals

Obj 1: Fundamentals of TCP/IP
Weight of objective: 4

Demonstrate an understanding of network masks and what they mean (i.e. determine a network address for a host based on its subnet mask), understand basic TCP/IP protocols (TCP, UDP, ICMP) and also PPP, demonstrate an understanding of the purpose and use of the more common ports found in /etc/services (20, 21, 23, 25, 53, 80, 110, 119, 139, 143, 161), demonstrate an correct understanding of the function and application of a default route. Execute basic TCP/IP tasks: FTP, anonymous FTP, telnet, host, ping, dig, traceroute, whois (Chapters 25 and 26).

Obj 2: (superseded)
Obj 3: TCP/IP troubleshooting and configuration
Weight of objective: 10

Demonstrate an understanding of the techniques required to list, configure and verify the operational status of network interfaces, change, view or configure the routing table, check the existing route table, correct an improperly set default route, manually add/start/stop/restart/delete/reconfigure network interfaces, and configure LINUX as a DHCP client and a TCP/IP host and debug associated problems. May involve reviewing or configuring the following files or directories: /etc/HOSTNAME — /etc/hostname, /etc/hosts, /etc/networks, /etc/host.conf, /etc/resolv.conf, and other network configuration files for your distribution. May involve the use of the following commands and programs: dhcpd, host, hostname (domainname, dnsdomainname), ifconfig, netstat, ping, route, traceroute, the network scripts run during system initialization (Chapters 25 and 27).

Obj 4: Configure and use PPP
Weight of objective: 4

Define the chat sequence to connect (given a login example), setup commands to be run automatically when a PPP connection is made, initiate or terminate a PPP connection, initiate or terminate an ISDN connection, set PPP to automatically reconnect if disconnected (Chapter 41).

Topic 1.13: Networking Services

Obj 1: Configure and manage inetd and related services
Weight of objective: 5

Configure which services are available through inetd, use tcpwrappers to allow or deny services on a host-by-host basis, manually start, stop, and restart Internet services, configure basic network services including telnet and ftp. Includes managing inetd.conf, hosts.allow, and hosts.deny (Chapter 29).

Obj 2: Operate and perform basic configuration of sendmail
Weight of objective: 5

Modify simple parameters in sendmail config files (modify the DS value for the "Smart Host" if necessary), create mail aliases, manage the mail queue, start and stop sendmail, configure mail forwarding (.forward), perform basic troubleshooting of sendmail. Does not include advanced custom configuration of sendmail. Includes commands mailq, sendmail, and newaliases. Includes aliases and mail/ config files (Chapter 30).

Obj 3: Operate and perform basic configuration of apache
Weight of objective: 3

Modify simple parameters in apache config files, start, stop, and restart httpd, arrange for automatic restarting of httpd upon boot. Does not include advanced custom configuration of apache. Includes managing httpd conf files (Chapter 36).

Obj 4: Properly manage the NFS, smb, and nmb daemons
Weight of objective: 4

Mount remote filesystems using NFS, configure NFS for exporting local filesystems, start, stop, and restart the NFS server. Install and configure Samba using the included GUI tools or direct edit of the /etc/smb.conf file (Note: this deliberately excludes advanced NT domain issues but includes simple sharing of home directories and printers, as well as correctly setting the nmbd as a WINS client). (Chapters 28 and 39.)

Obj 5: Setup and configure basic DNS services
Weight of objective: 3

Configure hostname lookups by maintaining the /etc/hosts, /etc/resolv.conf, /etc/host.conf, and /etc/nsswitch.conf files, troubleshoot problems with local caching-only name server. Requires an understanding of the domain registration and DNS translation process. Requires understanding key differences in config files for bind 4 and bind 8. Includes commands nslookup, host. Files: named.boot (v.4) or named.conf (v.8) (Chapters 27 and 40).

Topic 1.14: Security

Obj 1: Perform security admin tasks
Weight of objective: 4

Configure and use TCP wrappers to lock down the system, list all files with SUID bit set, determine if any package (.rpm or .deb) has been corrupted, verify new packages prior to install, use setgid on dirs to keep group ownership consistent, change a user's password, set expiration dates on user's passwords, obtain, install and configure ssh (Chapter 44).

Obj 2: Setup host security
Weight of objective: 4

Implement shadowed passwords, turn off unnecessary network services in inetd, set the proper mailing alias for root and setup syslogd, monitor CERT and BUGTRAQ, update binaries immediately when security problems are found (Chapter 44).

Obj 3: Setup user level security
Weight of objective: 2

Set limits on user logins, processes, and memory usage (Section 11.7.5).

Appendix C

RedHat Certified Engineer Certification Cross-Reference

RedHat has encouraged a larger number of overlapping courses, some of which contain lighter and more accessible material. They concentrate somewhat on RedHat specific issues that are not always applicable to other distributions. In some areas they expect more knowledge than the LPI, so it is worth at least reviewing RedHat's requirements for purposes of self-evaluation. The information contained in this appendix was gathered from discussions with people who had attended the RedHat courses. This is intended purely for cross-referencing purposes and is possibly outdated. By no means should it be taken as definitive. Visit http://redhat.com/training/rhce/courses/ for the official guide.

For each objective, the relevant chapter or section from this book is referenced in parentheses.

C.1 RH020, RH030, RH033, RH120, RH130, and RH133

These courses are *beneath* the scope of this book: They cover LINUX from a user and desktop perspective. Although they include administrative tasks, they keep away from technicalities. They often prefer graphical configuration programs to do administrative tasks. One objective of one of these courses is configuring Gnome panel applets; another is learning the `pico` text editor.

C.2 RH300

This certification seems to be for administrators of non-LINUX systems who want to extend their knowledge. The requirements below lean toward understanding available LINUX∆ alternatives and features, rather than expecting the user to actually configure anything complicated. Note that I abbreviate the RedHat Installation Guide(s) as RHIG. This refers to the install help in the installation program itself or, for RedHat 6.2 systems, the HTML installation guide on the CD. It also refers to the more comprehensive online documentation at http://www.redhat.com/support/-manuals/.

Unit 1: Hardware selection and RedHat installation

- Finding Web docs. Using HOWTOs to locate supported hardware (Chapter 16).
- Knowledge of supported architectures and SMP support (Chapter 42).
- Use of `kudzu` (I do not cover `kudzu` and recommend that you uninstall it).
- Hardware concepts—IRQ, PCI, EISA, AGP, and I/O ports (Chapters 3 and 42).
- `isapnp`, `pciscan` (Chapter 42).
- Concepts of LINUX∆ support for PCMCIA, PS/2, tapes, scanners, USB (Chapter 42).
- Concepts of serial, parallel, SCSI, IDE, CD-ROM and floppy devices, and their `/dev/` listings (Chapter 18).
- `hdparm` (`hdparm`(8)).
- Concepts of IDE geometry, BIOS limitations (Chapter 19).
- Disk sector and partition structure. Use of `fdisk`, `cfdisk`, and diskdruid (Chapter 19).
- Creation of a partitioning structure (Chapter 19).
- Management of swap, native, and foreign partitions during installation (RHIG).
- Concept of distribution of directories over different partitions (Chapter 19).
- Configuring `lilo` on installation (Chapter 31 refers to general use of `lilo`).
- BIOS configuration (Chapter 3).
- Conceptual understanding of different disk images. Creating and booting disk images from their `boot.img`, `bootnet.img`, or `pcmcia.img` (RHIG).
- Use of the installer to create RAID devices (RHIG).
- Package selection (RHIG).
- X video configuration (Chapter 43 and RHIG).

Unit 2: Configuring and administration

- Using `setup`, `mouseconfig`, `Xconfigurator`, `kbdconfig`, `timeconfig`, `netconfig`, `authconfig`, `sndconfig`. (These are higher level interactive utilities than the ones I cover in Chapter 42 and elsewhere. Run each of these commands for a demo.)
- Understanding `/etc/sysconfig/network-scripts/ifcfg-*` (Chapter 25).
- Using `netcfg` or `ifconfig` (Chapter 25).
- Using `ifup`, `ifdown`, `rp3`, `usernet`, and `usernetctl` (Chapter 25).

- Using `pnpdump`, `isapnp` and editing `/etc/isapnp.conf` (Chapter 42).
- Conceptual understanding of `/etc/conf.modules`, `esd`, and `kaudioserver` (Chapter 42; man pages for same).
- Using `mount`, editing `/etc/fstab` (Chapter 19).
- Using `lpr`, `lpc`, `lpq`, `lprm`, `printtool` and understanding concepts of `/etc/printcap` (Chapter 21).
- Virtual consoles concepts: changing in `/etc/inittab` (Chapter 32).
- Using `useradd`, `userdel`, `usermod`, and `passwd` (Chapter 11).
- Creating accounts manually and with `userconf` and with `linuxconf`. (The use of graphical tools is discouraged by this book.)
- Understanding concepts of the `/etc/passwd` and `/etc/group` files and `/etc/skel` and contents (Chapter 11).
- Editing `bashrc`, `.bashrc`, `/etc/profile`, `/etc/profile.d` (Chapter 20).
- General use of `linuxconf`. (The use of graphical tools is discouraged by this book.)
- Using `cron`, `anacron`, editing `/var/spool/cron/<username>` and `/etc/crontab`. `tmpwatch`, `logrotate`, and locate cron jobs.
- Using `syslogd`, `klogd`, `/etc/syslog.conf`, `swatch`, `logcheck`.
- Understanding and using `rpm`. Checksums, file listing, forcing, dependencies, querying, verifying querying tags, provides, and requires. FTP and HTTP installs, `rpmfind`, `gnorpm`, and `kpackage` (Chapter 24).
- Building `.src.rpm` files. Customizing and rebuilding packages. (See the RPM-HOWTO.)
- `/usr/sbin/up2date`. (The use of package is discouraged by this book.)
- Finding documentation (Chapter 16).

Unit 3: Alternative installation methods

- Laptops, PCMCIA, `cardmanager`, and `apm`. (See the RHIG, PCMCIA-HOWTO and Laptop-HOWTO.)
- Multiboot systems, boot options, and alternative boot image configuration (Chapter 31).
- Network installations using `netboot.img` (RHIG).
- Serial console installation (RHIG?).
- Kickstart concepts.

Unit 4: Kernel

- `/proc` file system concepts and purpose of various subdirectories (see Section 42.4 and the index entries for `/proc/`). Tuning parameters with `/etc/sysctl.conf` (see `sysctl.conf(5)`).
- Disk quotas. `quota`, `quotaon`, `quotaoff`, `edquota`, `repquota`, `quotawarn`, `quotastats`. (Quotas are not covered but are easily learned form the Quota mini-HOWTO.)

- System startup scripts' initialization sequences. `inittab`, switching run levels. Conceptual understanding of various `/etc/rc.d/` files. SysV scripts, `chkconfig`, `ntsysv`, `tksysv`, `ksysv` (Chapter 32).
- Configuring software RAID. Using `raidtools` to activate and test RAID devices (see the RAID-HOWTO).
- Modules Management. `modprobe`, `depmod`, `lsmod`, `insmod`, `rmmod` commands. `kernelcfg`. Editing of `/etc/conf.modules`, aliasing and `optioning` modules (Chapter 42).
- Concepts of kernel source, `.rpm` versions, kernel versioning system. Configuring, compiling and installing kernels (Chapter 42).

Unit 5: Basic network services

- TCP/IP concepts. `inetd`. Port concepts and service-port mappings (Chapters 25 and 26).
- `apache`, config files, virtual hosts (Chapter 36).
- `sendmail`, config files, `mailconf`, m4 macro concepts (Chapter 30).
- POP and IMAP concepts (Chapters 29 and 30).
- `named` configuration (Chapter 40).
- FTP configuration. (I did not cover FTP because of the huge number of FTP services available. It is recommended that you try the `vsftpd` package.)
- configuration, `/etc/rc.d/init.d/netfs` (Chapter 28).
- smbd, file-sharing and print-sharing concepts. Security concepts config file overview. Use of `testparam`, `smbclient`, `nmblookup`, `smbmount`, Windows authentication concepts (Chapter 39).
- dhcpd and BOOTP, config files and concepts. Configuration with `netcfg`, `netconfig` or `linuxconf`. using `pump` (see the DHCP mini-HOWTO).
- Understanding `squid` caching and forwarding concepts. (The squid configuration file `/etc/squid/squid.conf` provides ample documentation for actually *setting up* squid.)
- Overview of `lpd`, `mars-nwe`, time services, and news services (Chapter 21).

Unit 6: X Window System

- X client server architecture (Section 43.1).
- Use of `Xconfigurator`, `xf86config`, `XF86Setup`, and concepts of `/etc/X11/XF86Config` (Section 43.6.3).
- Knowledge of various window managers, editing `/etc/sysconfig/desktop`. Understanding of concepts of different user interfaces: Gnome, KDE. Use of `switchdesk` (Section 43.3.4).
- `init` run level 5 concepts, `xdm`, `kdm`, `gdm`, `prefdm` alternatives (Section 43.9).
- `xinit`, `xinitrc` concepts. User config files `.xsession` and `.Xclients` (see `xinit`(1), `xdm`(1), `startx`(1), and read the scripts under `/etc/X11/xinit/` and `/etc/X11/xdm`).

- Use of `xhost` (Section 43.3.5). Security issues. `DISPLAY` environment variable. Remote displays (Section 43.3.2).
- `xfs` concepts (Section 43.12).

Unit 7: Security

- Use of `tcp_wrappers` (Chapter 29). User and host based access restrictions. PAM access. Port restriction with `ipchains` (see the Firewall-HOWTO).
- PAM concepts. Editing of `/etc/pam.d`, `/etc/security` config files. PAM documentation (see `/usr/share/doc/pam-0.72/txts/pam.txt`).
- NIS concepts and config files. `ypbind, yppasswd ypserv, yppasswdd, makedbm, yppush` (see the NIS-HOWTO).
- LDAP concepts. OpenLDAP package, `slapd, ldapd, slurpd`, and config files. PAM integration.
- `inetd` concepts. Editing of `/etc/inetd.conf`, interface to `tcp_wrappers`. Editing of `/etc/hosts.allow` and `/etc/hosts.deny`. `portmap, tcpdchk, tcpdmatch, twist` (see the LDAP-HOWTO).
- `ssh` client server and security concepts (Chapters 12 and 44).

Unit 8: Firewalling, routing and clustering, troubleshooting

- Static and dynamic routing with concepts. `/etc/sysconfig/static-routes`. Use of `linuxconf` and `netcfg` to edit routes. (Use of graphical tools is discouraged by this book.)
- Forwarding concepts. Concepts of forwarding other protocols: X.25, frame-relay, ISDN, and PPP. (By "concepts of" I take it to mean that mere knowledge of these features is sufficient. See also Chapter 41.)
- `ipchains` and ruleset concepts. Adding, deleting, listing, flushing rules. Forwarding, masquerading. Protocol-specific kernel modules (see the Firewall-HOWTO).
- High availability concepts. Concepts of `lvs, pulse, nanny`, config files, and web-based configuration. Piranha, failover concepts. (A conceptual understanding again.)
- High performance clustering concepts. Parallel virtual machine for computational research (conceptual understanding only).
- Troublshooting: Networking (Chapter 25), X (Chapter 43), booting (Chapter 31), DNS (Chapters 27 and 40), authentication (Chapter 11), file system corruption (Section 19.5).
- `mkbootdisk` and rescue floppy concepts. Use of the rescue disk environment and available commands (see `mkbootdisk`(8)).

C.3   RH220 (RH253 Part 1)

RH220 is the networking module. It covers services sparsely, possibly intending that the student learn only the bare bones of what is necessary to configure a service.

Unit 1: DNS

A treatment of `bind`, analogous to **Topic 1.13, Obj 5** of LPI (page 541). Expects exhaustive understanding of the Domain Name System, an understanding of `SOA`, `NS`, `A`, `CNAME`, `PTR`, `MX` and `HINFO` records, ability to create master domain servers from scratch, caching-only servers, and round-robin load sharing configuration (Chapter 40).

Unit 2: Samba

Overview of SMB services and concepts. Configuring Samba for file and print sharing. Using Samba client tools. Using `linuxconf` and `swat`. Editing `/etc/smb.conf`. Understanding types of shares. Support Wins. Setting authentication method. Using client utilities (Chapter 39).

Unit 3: NIS

Conceptual understanding of NIS. NIS master and slave configure. Use of client utilities. LDAP concepts. OpenLDAP package, `slapd`, `ldapd`, `slurpd`, and config files (see the NIS-HOWTO).

Unit 4: Sendmail and procmail

Understanding of mail spooling and transfer. Understanding the purpose of all `sendmail` config files. Editing config file for simple client (i.e., forwarding) configuration. Editing `/etc/sendmail.mc`, `/etc/mail/virtusertable`, `/etc/mail/access`. Restricting relays. Viewing log files. Creating simple `.procmail` folder and email redirectors. (Chapter 30. Also see *The Sendmail FAQ* http://www.sendmail.org/faq/ as well as `procmail`(1), `procmailrc`(6), and `procmailex`(5).)

Unit 5: Apache

Configuring virtual hosts. Adding MIME types. Manipulating directory access and directory aliasing. Allowing restricting of CGI access. Setting up user and password databases. Understanding important modules (Chapter 36).

Unit 6: pppd and DHCP

Setting up a basic `pppd` server. Adding dial-in user accounts. Restricting users. Understanding `dhcpd` and BOOTP config files and concepts. Configuring with `netcfg`, `netconfig`, or `linuxconf`. Using `pump`. Editing `/etc/dhcpd.conf`. (Chapter 41. See also the DHCP-HOWTO.)

C.4 RH250 (RH253 Part 2)

RH250 is the security module. It goes through basic administration from a security perspective.

Unit 1: Introduction

Understanding security requirements. Basic terminology: *hacker, cracker, denial of service, virus, trojan horse, worm*. Physical security and security policies (Chapter 44).

Unit 2: Local user security

Understanding user accounts concepts, restricting access based on groups. Editing pam config files. /etc/nologin; editing /etc/security/ files. Using console group, cug; configuring and using clobberd and sudo. Checking logins in log files. Using last (Chapters 11 and 44).

Unit 3: Files and file system security

Exhaustive treatment of groups and permissions. chattr and lsattr commands. Use of find to locate permission problems. Use of tmpwatch. Installation of tripwire. Managment of NFS exports for access control (Chapters 14, 28, and 44).

Unit 4: Password security and encryption

Encryption terms: *Public/Private Key, GPG, one-way hash, MD5*. xhost, xauth. ssh concepts and features. Password-cracking concepts (Section 11.3 and Chapter 12).

Unit 5: Process security and monitoring

Use PAM to set resource limits (Section 11.7.5). Monitor process memory usage and CPU consumption; top, gtop, kpm, xosview, xload, xsysinfo. last, ac, accton, lastcomm (Chapter 9). Monitor logs with swatch (see swatch(5) and swatch(8)).

Unit 6: Building firewalls

ipchains and ruleset concepts. Adding, deleting, listing, flushing rules. Forwarding, many-to-one and one-to-one masquerading. Kernels options for firewall support. Static and dynamic routing with concepts (see the Firewall-HOWTO). /etc/sysconfig/static-routes. Use of linuxconf and netcfg to edit routes. tcp_wrappers (Chapter 29).

Unit 7: Security tools

Concepts of `nessus`, SAINT, SARA, SATAN. Concepts of `identd`. Use of `sniffit`, `tcpdump`, `traceroute`, `ping -f`, `ethereal`, `iptraf`, `mk-ftp-stats`, `lurkftp`, `mrtg`, `netwatch`, `webalizer`, `trafshow`. (These tools may be researched on the web.)

Appendix D

LINUX Advocacy Frequently-Asked-Questions

The capabilities of LINUX *are constantly expanding. Please consult the various Internet resources listed for up-to-date information.*

D.1 LINUX Overview

This section covers questions that pertain to LINUX as a whole.

What is LINUX?

LINUX is the core of a free UNIX operating system for the PC and other hardware platforms. Developement of this operating system started in 1984; it was called the GNU project of the Free Software Foundation (FSF). The LINUX core (or kernel), named after its author, Linus Torvalds, began development in 1991—the first usable releases where made in 1993. LINUX is often called GNU/LINUX because much of the OS (operating system) results from the efforts of the GNU project.

UNIX systems have been around since the 1960s and are a proven standard in industry. LINUX is said to be POSIX compliant, meaning that it confirms to a certain definite computing standard laid down by academia and industry. This means that LINUX is largely compatible with other UNIX systems (the same program can be easily ported to run on another UNIX system with few (sometimes no) modifications) and will network seamlessly with other UNIX systems.

Some commercial UNIX systems are IRIX (for Silicon Graphics); Solaris or SunOS for Sun Microsystem SPARC workstations; HP UNIX for Hewlett Packard servers; SCO for the PC; OSF

551

for the DEC Alpha machine and AIX for the PowerPC/RS6000. Because the UNIX name is a registered trademark, most systems are not called UNIX.

Some freely available UNIX systems are NetBSD, FreeBSD, and OpenBSD and also enjoy widespread popularity.

UNIX systems are multitasking and multiuser systems, meaning that multiple concurrent users running multiple concurrent programs can connect to and use the same machine.

What are UNIX systems used for? What can LINUX do?

UNIX systems are the backbone of the Internet. Heavy industry, mission-critical applications, and universities have always used UNIX systems. High-end servers and multiuser mainframes are traditionally UNIX based. Today, UNIX systems are used by large ISPs through to small businesses as a matter of course. A UNIX system is the standard choice when a hardware vendor comes out with a new computer platform because UNIX is most amenable to being ported. UNIX systems are used as database, file, and Internet servers. UNIX is used for visualization and graphics rendering (as for some Hollywood productions). Industry and universities use UNIX systems for scientific simulations and UNIX clusters for number crunching. The embedded market (small computers without operators that exist inside appliances) has recently turned toward LINUX systems, which are being produced in the millions.

LINUX itself can operate as a web, file, SMB (WinNT), Novell, printer, FTP, mail, SQL, masquerading, firewall, and POP server to name but a few. It can do anything that any other network server can do, more efficiently and reliably.

LINUX's up-and-coming graphical user interfaces (GUI) are the most functional and aesthetically pleasing ever to have graced the computer screen. LINUX has now moved into the world of the desktop.

What other platforms does LINUX run on including the PC?

LINUX runs on

- 386/486/Pentium processors.
- DEC 64-bit Alpha processors.
- Motorola 680x0 processors, including Commodore Amiga, Atari-ST/TT/Falcon and HP Apollo 68K.
- Sun Microsystems SPARC workstations, including sun4c, sun4m, sun4d, and sun4u architectures. Multiprocessor machines are supported as is full 64-bit support on the Ultra-SPARC.
- Advanced Risc Machine (ARM) processors.
- MIPS R3000/R4000 processors, including Silicon Graphics machines.
- PowerPC machines.
- Intel Architecture 64-bit processors.

- IBM 390 mainframe.
- ETRAX-100 processor.

Other projects are in various stages of completion. For example, you may get LINUX up and running on many other hardware platforms, but it would take some time and expertise to install, and you might not have graphics capabilities. Every month or so support is announced for some new esoteric hardware platform. Watch the *Linux Weekly News* http://lwn.net/ to catch these.

What is meant by GNU/LINUX as opposed to LINUX?

(See also "What is GNU?" and "What is LINUX?".)

In 1984 the Free Software Foundation (FSF) set out to create a free UNIX-like system. It is only because of their efforts that the many critical packages that go into a UNIX distribution are available. It is also because of them that a freely available, comprehensive, legally definitive, free-software license is available. Because many of the critical components of a typical LINUX distribution are really just GNU tools developed long before LINUX, it is unfair to merely call a distribution "LINUX". The term GNU/LINUX is more accurate and gives credit to the larger part of LINUX.

What web pages should I look at?

Hundreds of web pages are devoted to LINUX. Thousands of web pages are devoted to different free software packages. A net search will reveal the enormous amount of information available.

- Three places for general LINUX information are:
    - *Alan Cox's Linux web page* http://www.linux.org.uk/
    - *Linux Online* http://www.linux.org/
    - *Linux International* http://www.li.org/
- For kernel information, see
    - *Linux Headquarters* http://www.linuxhq.com/
- A very important site is
    - *FSF Home Pages* http://www.gnu.org/

    which is the home page of the Free Software Foundation and explains their purpose and the philosophy of software that can be freely modified and redistributed.
- Some large indexes of reviewed free and proprietary LINUX software are:
    - *Fresh Meat* http://freshmeat.net/
    - *Source Forge* http://www.sourceforge.net/
    - *Tu Cows* http://linux.tucows.com/

- – *Scientific Applications for Linux (SAL)* http://SAL.KachinaTech.COM/index.shtml

- Announcements for new software are mostly made on

  - – *Fresh Meat* http://freshmeat.net/

- The Linux Weekly News brings up-to-date info covering a wide range of Linux issues:

  - – *Linux Weekly News* http://lwn.net/

- Three major Linux desktop projects are:

  - – *Gnome Desktop* http://www.gnome.org/

  - – *KDE Desktop* http://www.kde.org/

  - – *GNUstep* http://gnustep.org/

But don't stop there—there are hundreds more.

What are Debian, RedHat, Caldera, SuSE? Explain the different Linux distributions.

All applications, network server programs, and utilities that go into a full Linux machine are free software programs recompiled to run under the Linux kernel. Most can (and do) actually work on any other of the Unix systems mentioned above.

Hence, many efforts have been made to package all of the utilities needed for a Unix system into a single collection, usually on a single easily installable CD.

Each of these efforts combines hundreds of *packages* (e.g., the Apache web server is one package, the Netscape web browser is another) into a Linux *distribution*.

Some of the popular Linux distributions are:

- *Caldera OpenLinux* http://www.calderasystems.com/
- *Debian GNU/*Linux http://www.debian.org/
- *Mandrake* http://www.linux-mandrake.com/
- *RedHat* http://www.redhat.com/
- *Slackware* http://www.slackware.com/
- *SuSE* http://www.suse.com/
- *TurboLinux* http://www.turbolinux.com/

There are now about 200 distributions of Linux. Some of these are single floppy routers or rescue disks, and others are modifications of popular existing distributions. Still others have a specialized purpose, like real time work or high security.

Who developed LINUX?

LINUX was largely developed by the *Free Software Foundation* http://www.gnu.org/.

The *Orbiten Free Software Survey* http://www.orbiten.org/ came up with the following break-down of contributors after surveying a wide array of open source packages. The following lists the top 20 contributors by amount of code written:

Serial	Author	Bytes	Percentage	Projects
1	Free Software Foundation, Inc.	125565525	(11.246%)	546
2	Sun Microsystems, Inc.	20663713	(1.85%)	66
3	The Regents of the University of California	15192791	(1.36%)	156
4	Gordon Matzigkeit	13599203	(1.218%)	267
5	Paul Houle	11647591	(1.043%)	1
6	Thomas G. Lane	8746848	(0.783%)	17
7	The Massachusetts Institute of Technology	8513597	(0.762%)	38
8	Ulrich Drepper	6253344	(0.56%)	142
9	Lyle Johnson	5906249	(0.528%)	1
10	Peter Miller	5871392	(0.525%)	3
11	Eric Young	5607745	(0.502%)	48
12	login-belabas	5429114	(0.486%)	2
13	Lucent Technologies, Inc.	4991582	(0.447%)	5
14	Linus Torvalds	4898977	(0.438%)	10
15	(uncredited-gdb)	4806436	(0.43%)	1
16	Aladdin Enterprises	4580332	(0.41%)	27
17	Tim Hudson	4454381	(0.398%)	26
18	Carnegie Mellon University	4272613	(0.382%)	23
19	James E. Wilson, Robert A. Koeneke	4272412	(0.382%)	2
20	ID Software, Inc.	4038969	(0.361%)	1

This listing contains the top 20 contributors by number of projects contributed to:

Serial	Author	Bytes	Percentage	Projects
1	Free Software Foundation, Inc.	125565525	(11.246%)	546
2	Gordon Matzigkeit	13599203	(1.218%)	267
3	The Regents of the University of California	15192791	(1.36%)	156
4	Ulrich Drepper	6253344	(0.56%)	142
5	Roland Mcgrath	2644911	(0.236%)	99
6	Sun Microsystems, Inc.	20663713	(1.85%)	66
7	RSA Data Security, Inc.	898817	(0.08%)	59
8	Martijn Pieterse	452661	(0.04%)	50
9	Eric Young	5607745	(0.502%)	48
10	login-vern	3499616	(0.313%)	47
11	jot@cray	691862	(0.061%)	47
12	Alfredo K. Kojima	280990	(0.025%)	40
13	The Massachusetts Institute of Technology	8513597	(0.762%)	38
14	Digital Equipment Corporation	2182333	(0.195%)	37

15	David J. Mackenzie	337388	(0.03%)	37
16	Rich Salz	365595	(0.032%)	35
17	Jean-Loup Gailly	2256335	(0.202%)	31
18	eggert@twinsun	387923	(0.034%)	30
19	Josh Macdonald	1994755	(0.178%)	28
20	Peter Mattis, Spencer Kimball	1981094	(0.177%)	28

The preceding tables are rough approximations. They do, however, give an idea of the spread of contributions.

Why should I not use LINUX?

If you are a private individual with no UNIX expertise available to help you when you run into problems and you are not interested in learning about the underlying workings of a UNIX system, then you shouldn't install LINUX.

D.2 LINUX, GNU, and Licensing

This section answers questions about the nature of free software and the concepts of GNU.

What is LINUX's license?

The LINUX kernel is distributed under the GNU General Public License (GPL) which is reproduced in Appendix E and is available from the *FSF Home Page* http://www.gnu.org/.

Most of all other software in a typical LINUX distribution is also under the GPL or the LGPL (see below).

There are many other types of free software licenses. Each of these is based on particular commercial or moral outlooks. Their acronyms are as follows (as defined by the LINUX Software Map database) in no particular order:

PD: Placed in public domain.

Shareware: Copyrighted, no restrictions, contributions solicited.

MIT: MIT X Consortium license (like that of BSDs but with no advertising requirement).

BSD: Berkeley Regents copyright (used on BSD code).

Artistic License: Same terms as Perl Artistic License.

FRS: Copyrighted, freely redistributable, might have some restrictions on redistribution of modified sources.

GPL: GNU General Public License.

GPL+LGPL: GNU GPL and Library GPL.

restricted: Less free than any of the above.

More information on these licenses can be had from the *Metalab license List* ftp://metalab.unc.-edu/pub/Linux/LICENSES

What is GNU?

GNU (pronounced with a hard G) is an acronym for GNUs Not UNIX. A gnu is a large beast and is the motif of the Free Software Foundation (FSF). GNU is a *recursive acronym*.

Richard Stallman is the founder of the FSF and the creator of the GNU General Public License. One of the purposes of the FSF is to promote and develop free alternatives to proprietary software. The GNU project is an effort to create a free UNIX-like operating system from scratch; the project was started in 1984.

GNU represents this software licensed under the GNU General Public License—it is called Free software. GNU software is software designed to meet a higher set of standards than its proprietary counterparts.

GNU has also become a movement in the computing world. When the word GNU is mentioned, it usually evokes feelings of extreme left-wing geniuses who in their spare time produce free software that is far superior to anything even large corporations can come up with through years of dedicated development. It also means distributed and open development, encouraging peer review, consistency, and portability. GNU means doing things once in the best way possible, providing solutions instead of quick fixes and looking exhaustively at possibilities instead of going for the most brightly colored or expedient approach.

GNU also means a healthy disrespect for the concept of a deadline and a release schedule.

Why is GNU software better than proprietary software?

Proprietary software is often looked down upon in the free software world for many reasons:

- The development process is closed to external scrutiny.
- Users are unable to add features to the software.
- Users are unable to correct errors (bugs) in the software.
- Users are not allowed to share the software.

The result of these limitations is that proprietary software

- Does not conform to good standards for information technology.
- Is incompatible with other proprietary software.
- Is buggy.
- Cannot be fixed.
- Costs far more than it is worth.
- Can do anything behind your back without your knowing.
- Is insecure.
- Tries to be better than other proprietary software without meeting real technical and practical needs.
- Wastes a lot of time duplicating the effort of other proprietary software.

- Fails to build on existing software because of licensing issues.

GNU software, on the other hand, is open for anyone to scrutinize. Users can (and do) freely fix and enhance software for their own needs, and then allow others the benefit of their extensions. Many developers of different areas of expertise collaborate to find the best way of doing things. Open industry and academic standards are adhered to, to make software consistent and compatible. Collaborated effort between different developers means that code is shared and effort is not replicated. Users have close and direct contact with developers, ensuring that bugs are fixed quickly and that user needs are met. Because source code can be viewed by anyone, developers write code more carefully and are more inspired and more meticulous.

Possibly the most important reason for the superiority of Free software is peer review. Sometimes this means that development takes longer as more people quibble over the best way of doing things. However, most of the time peer review results in a more reliable product.

Another partial reason for this superiority is that GNU software is often written by people from academic institutions who are in the center of IT research and are most qualified to dictate software solutions. In other cases, authors write software for their own use out of their own dissatisfaction for existing proprietary software—a powerful motivation.

Explain the restrictions of LINUX's "free"GNU General Public License.

The following is quoted from the GPL itself.

> When we speak of free software, we are referring to freedom, not price. Our General Public Licenses are designed to make sure that you have the freedom to distribute copies of free software (and charge for this service if you wish), that you receive source code or can get it if you want it, that you can change the software or use pieces of it in new free programs; and that you know you can do these things.

> To protect your rights, we need to make restrictions that forbid anyone to deny you these rights or to ask you to surrender the rights. These restrictions translate to certain responsibilities for you if you distribute copies of the software, or if you modify it.

> For example, if you distribute copies of such a program, whether gratis or for a fee, you must give the recipients all the rights that you have. You must make sure that they, too, receive or can get the source code. And you must show them these terms so they know their rights.

If LINUX is free, where do companies have the right to make money from selling CDs?

See "Where do I get LINUX?" on page 562.

What if Linus Torvalds decided to change the copyright on the kernel? Could he sell out to a company?

This situation is not possible. Because of the legal terms of the GPL, for LINUX to be distributed under a different copyright would require the consent of all 200+ persons that have ever contributed to the LINUX source code. These people come from such a variety of places, that such a task is logistically infeasible. Even if it did happen, new developers would probably rally in defiance and continue to work on the kernel as it is. This free kernel would amass more followers and would quickly become the standard, with or without Linus.

What if Linus Torvalds stopped supporting LINUX? What if kernel development split?

There are many kernel developers who have sufficient knowledge to do the job of Linus. Most probably, a team of core developers would take over the task if Linus no longer worked on the kernel. LINUX might even split into different development teams if a disagreement did break out about some programming issue, and it might rejoin later on. This is a process that many GNU software packages are continually going through, to no ill effect. It doesn't really matter much from the end user's perspective, since GNU software by its nature always tends to gravitate towards consistency and improvement, one way or another. It is also doesn't matter to the end user because the end user has selected a popular LINUX distribution packaged by someone who has already dealt with these issues.

What is Open Source vs. Free vs. Shareware?

Open Source is a new catch phrase that is ambiguous in meaning but is often used synonymously with Free. It sometimes refers to any proprietary vendor releasing source code to their package, even though that source code is not free in the sense of users being able to modify it and redistribute it. Sometimes it means "public domain" software that anyone can modify but which can be incorporated into commercial packages where later versions will be unavailable in source form.

Open Source advocates vie for the superiority of the Open Source development model.

GNU supporters don't like to use the term Open Source. Free software, in the sense of *freedom* to modify and redistribute is the preferred term and necessitates a copyright license along the same vein as the GPL. Unfortunately, it's not a marketable term because it requires this very explanation, which tends to bore people who don't really care about licensing issues.

Free software advocates vie for the ethical responsibility of making source code available and encouraging others to do the same.

Shareware refers to completely nonfree software that is encouraged to be redistributed at no charge, but which requests a small fee if it happens to land on your computer. It is not Free software at all.

D.3 LINUX Distributions

This section covers questions that about how LINUX software is packaged and distributed and how to obtain LINUX.

If everyone is constantly modifying the source, isn't this bad for the consumer? How is the user protected from bogus software?

You as the user are not going to download arbitrary untested software any more than you would if you were using Windows.

When you get LINUX, it will be inside a standard distribution, probably on a CD. Each of these packages is selected by the distribution vendors to be a genuine and stable release of that package. This is the responsibility taken on by those who create LINUX distributions.

Note that no corporate body oversees LINUX. Everyone is on their own mission. But a package will not find its way into a distribution unless someone feels that it is a useful one. For people to feel it is useful means that they have to have used it over a period of time; in this way only good, thoroughly reviewed software gets included.

Maintainers of packages ensure that official releases are downloadable from their home pages and will upload original versions onto well-established FTP servers.

It is not the case that any person is free to modify original distributions of packages and thereby hurt the names of the maintainers of that package.

For those who are paranoid that the software they have downloaded is not the genuine article distributed by the maintainer of that software, digital signatures can verify the packager of that software. Cases where vandals have managed to substitute a bogus package for a real one are extremely rare and entirely preventable.

There are so many different LINUX versions — is this not confusion and incompatibility?

(See also next question.)

The LINUX kernel is now on release version 2.4.3 as of this writing. The only other stable release of the kernel was the previous 2.2 series which was the standard for more than a year.

The LINUX kernel version does not affect the LINUX user. LINUX programs will work regardless of the kernel version. Kernel versions speak of features, not compatibility.

Each LINUX distribution has its own versioning system. RedHat has just released version 7.0 of its distribution, Caldera, 2.2, Debian, 2.1, and so forth. Each new incarnation of a distribution will have newer versions of packages contained therein and better installation software. There may also have been subtle changes in the file system layout.

The LINUX UNIX **C** library implementation is called `glibc`. When RedHat brought out version 5.0 of its distribution, it changed to `glibc` from the older `libc5` library. Because all packages require this library, this was said to introduce incompatibility. It is true, however, that multiple versions of libraries can coexist on the same system, and hence no serious compatibility problem was ever introduced in this transition. Other vendors have since followed suit in making the transition to `glibc` (also known as `libc6`).

The LINUX community has also produced a document called the LINUX Filesystem Standard. Most vendors try to `comply` with this standard, and hence LINUX systems will look very similar from one distribution to another.

There are hence no prohibitive compatibility problems between LINUX distributions.

Will a program from one LINUX Distribution run on another? How compatible are the different distributions?

The different distributions are very similar and share binary compatibility (provided that they are for the same type of processor of course)—that is, LINUX binaries compiled on one system will work on another. This is in contrast to the differences between, say, two UNIX operating systems (compare Sun vs. IRIX). Utilities also exist to convert packages meant for one distribution to be installed on a different distribution. Some distributions are, however, created for specific hardware, and thus their packages will only run on that hardware. However, all software specifically written for LINUX will recompile without any modifications on another LINUX platform in addition to compiling with *few* modifications on other UNIX systems.

The rule is basically this: If you have three packages that you would need to get working on a different distribution, then it is trivial to make the adjustments to do this. If you have a hundred packages that you need to get working, then you have a problem.

What is the best distribution to use?

If you are an absolute beginner and don't really feel like thinking about what distribution to get, one of the most popular and easiest to install is Mandrake. RedHat is also supported quite well in industry.

The attributes of some distributions are:

Mandrake: Mandrake is RedHat with some packages added and updated. It has recently become the most popular and may be worth using in preference to RedHat.

Debian: This is probably the most technically advanced. It is completely free and very well structured as well as standards conformant. It is slightly less elegant to install. Debian package management is vastly superior to any other. The distribution has legendary technical excellence and stability.

RedHat: This is possibly the most popular.

Slackware: This was the first LINUX distribution and is supposed to be the most current (software is always the latest). It's a pain to install and manage, although school kids who don't know any better love it.

What's nice about RPM based distributions (RedHat, Mandrake, and others) is that almost all developers provide RedHat `.rpm` files (the file that a RedHat package comes in). Debian `.deb` package files are usually provided, but not as often as `.rpm`. On the other hand, Debian packages are mostly created by people on the Debian development team, who have rigorous standards to adhere to.

TurboLinux, SuSE, and some others are also very popular. You can find reviews on the Internet.

Many other popular distributions are worth installation. Especially worthwhile are distributions developed in your own country that specialize in the support of your local language.

Where do I get LINUX?

Once you have decided on a distribution (see previous question), you need to download that distribution or buy or borrow it on CD. Commercial distributions may contain proprietary software that you may not be allowed to install multiple times. However, Mandrake, RedHat, Debian, and Slackware are all committed to freedom and hence will not have any software that is not redistributable. Hence, if you get one of these on CD, feel free to install it as many times as you like.

Note that the GPL does not say that GNU software is without cost. You are allowed to charge for the service of distributing, installing, and maintaining software. It is the nonprohibition to redistribute and modify GNU software that is meant by the word free.

An international mirror for LINUX distributions is *Metalab distributions mirror* ftp://metalab.unc.edu/pub/Linux/distributions/. Also consult the resources in Chapter 13, "What web pages should I look at?" on page 553, and the **Web sites** entry in the index.

Downloading from an FTP site is going to take a long time unless you have a really fast link. Hence, rather ask around who locally sells LINUX on CD. Also make sure you have the latest version of whatever it is you're buying or downloading. Under no circumstance install from a distribution that has been superseded by a newer version.

How do I install LINUX?

It helps to think more laterally when trying to get information about LINUX:

> Would-be LINUX users everywhere need to know how to install LINUX. Surely the Free software community has long since generated documentation to help them? Where is that documentation?

Most distributions have very comprehensive installation guides, which is the reason I do not cover installation in this book. Browse around your CD to find it or consult your vendor's web site.

Also try see what happens when you do a net search with "linux installation guide." You need to read through the install guide in detail. It will explain everything you need to know about setting up partitions, dual boots, and other installation goodies.

The installation procedure will be completely different for each distribution.

D.4   LINUX Support

This section explains where to get free and commercial help with LINUX.

Where does a person get LINUX support? My purchased software is supported; how does LINUX compete?

LINUX is supported by the community that uses LINUX. With commercial systems, users are too stingy to share their knowledge because they feel that they owe nothing for having spent money on software.

LINUX users, on the other hand, are very supportive of other LINUX users. People can get far better support from the Internet community than they would from their commercial software vendors. Most packages have email lists where the very developers are available for questions. Most cities have mailing lists where responses to email questions are answered within hours. New LINUX users discover that help abounds and that they never lack friendly discussions about any computing problem they may have. Remember that LINUX is *your* operating system.

Newsgroups provide assistance where LINUX issues are discussed and help is given to new users; there are many such newsgroups. Using a newsgroup has the benefit of the widest possible audience.

The web is also an excellent place for support. Because users constantly interact and discuss LINUX issues, 99% of the problems a user is likely to have would have already been documented or covered in mailing list archives, often obviating the need to ask anyone at all.

Finally, many professional companies provide assistance at comparable hourly rates.

D.5   LINUX Compared to Other Systems

This section discusses the relative merits of different UNIX systems and NT.

What is the most popular UNIX in the world?

LINUX has several times the installed base of any UNIX system.

How many LINUX systems are there out there?

This is an answer nobody really knows. Various estimates have been put forward based on statistical considerations. As of early 2001 the figure was about 10–20 million. As LINUX begins to dominate the embedded market, that number will soon surpass the number of all other operating systems combined.

What is clear is that the number of LINUX users is doubling consistently every year. This is evident from user interest and industry involvement in LINUX; journal subscriptions, web hits, media attention, support requirements, software ports, and other criteria.

Because it is easy to survey online machines, it is well-established that over 25% of all web servers run LINUX.

What is the total cost of installing and running LINUX compared to a proprietary non-UNIX system?

Although LINUX is free, a good knowledge of UNIX is required to install and configure a reliable server. This tends to cost you in time or support charges.

On the other hand, your Windows or OS/2 server, for example, has to be licensed.

Many arguments put forward regarding server costs fail to take into account the complete lifetime of the server. This has resulted in contrasting reports that either claim that LINUX costs nothing or claim that it is impossible to use because of the expense of the expertise required. Neither of these extreme views is true.

The total cost of a server includes the following:

- Cost of the OS license.
- Cost of dedicated software that provides functions not inherently supported by the operating system.
- Cost of hardware.
- Availability of used hardware and the OS's capacity to support it.
- Cost of installation.
- Cost of support.
- Implicit costs of server downtime because of software bugs.
- Implicit costs of server downtime because of security breaches.
- Cost of maintenance.
- Cost of repair.
- Cost of essential upgrades.
- Negative cost of multiple servers: LINUX can run many services (mail, file, Web) from the same server rather than requiring dedicated servers, and this can be a tremendous saving.

When all these factors are considered, any company should probably make a truly enormous saving by choosing a LINUX server over a commercial operating system.

What is the total cost of installing and running a LINUX system compared to a proprietary UNIX system?

(See previous question.)

Proprietary UNIX systems are not as user friendly as LINUX. LINUX is also considered far easier to maintain than any commercial UNIX system because of its widespread use and hence easy access to LINUX expertise. LINUX has a far more dedicated and "beginner friendly" documentation project than any commercial UNIX, and many more user-friendly interfaces and commands.

The upshot of this is that although your proprietary UNIX system will perform as reliably as LINUX, it will be more time consuming to maintain.

UNIX systems that run on specialized hardware are almost never worth what you paid for them in terms of a cost/performance ratio. That is doubly if you are also paying for an operating system.

How does LINUX compare to other operating systems in performance?

LINUX typically performs 50% to 100% better than other operating systems on the same hardware. There are no commercial exceptions to this rule for a basic PC.

There have been a great many misguided attempts to show that LINUX performs better or worse than other platforms. I have never read a completely conclusive study. Usually these studies are done with one or other competing system having better expertise at its disposal and are, hence, grossly biased. In some supposedly independent tests, LINUX tended to outperform NT as a web server, file server, and database server by an appreciable margin.

In general, the performance improvement of a LINUX machine is quite visible to users and administrators. It is especially noticeable how fast the file system access is and how it scales smoothly when multiple services are being used simultaneously. LINUX also performs well when loaded by many services simultaneously.

There is also criticism of LINUX's SMP (multiprocessor) support, and lack of a journalling file system. These two issues are discussed in the next question.

In our experience (from both discussions and development), LINUX's critical operations are always pedantically optimized—far more than would normally be encouraged in a commercial organization. Hence, if your hardware is not performing the absolute best it can, it's by a very small margin.

It's also probably not worthwhile debating these kinds of speed issues when there are so many other good reasons to prefer LINUX.

What about SMP and a journalling file system? Is LINUX enterprise-ready?

LINUX is supposed to lack proper SMP support and therefore not be as scalable as other OSs. This is somewhat true and has been the case until kernel 2.4 was released in January 2001.

LINUX has a proper journalling file system called ReiserFS. This means that in the event of a power failure, there is very little chance that the file system would ever be corrupted, or that manual intervention would be required to fix the file system.

Does LINUX only support 2 Gigs of memory and 128 Meg of swap?

LINUX supports a full 64 gigabytes of memory, with 1 gigabyte of unshared memory per process.

If you really need this much memory, you should be using a 64-bit system, like a DEC Alpha, or Sun UltraSPARC machine.

On 64-bit systems, LINUX supports more memory than most first-world governments can afford to buy.

LINUX supports as much swap space as you like. For technical reasons, however, the swap space formerly required division into separate partitions of 128 megabytes each.

Isn't UNIX antiquated? Isn't its security model outdated?

The principles underlying OS development have not changed since the concept of an OS was invented some 40+ years ago. It is really academia that develops the theoretical models for computer science—industry only implements these.

There are a great many theoretical paradigms of operating system that vary in complexity and practicality. Of the popular server operating systems, UNIX certainly has the most versatile, flexible, and applicable security model and file system structure.

How does FreeBSD compare to LINUX?

FreeBSD is like a LINUX distribution in that it also relies on a large number of GNU packages. Most of the packages available in LINUX distributions are also available for FreeBSD.

FreeBSD is not merely a kernel but also a distribution, a development model, an operating system standard, and a community infrastructure. FreeBSD should rather be compared to Debian than LINUX.

The arguments comparing the FreeBSD kernel to the LINUX kernel center around the differences between how various kernel functions are implemented. Depending on the area you look at, either LINUX or FreeBSD will have a better implementation. On the whole, FreeBSD is thought to have a better architecture, although LINUX has had the benefit of having been ported to many platforms, has a great many more features, and supports far more hardware. It is questionable whether the performance penalties we are talking about are of real concern in most practical situations.

Another important consideration is that the FreeBSD maintainers go to far more effort securing FreeBSD than does any LINUX vendor. This makes FreeBSD a more trustworthy alternative.

GPL advocates take issue with FreeBSD because its licensing allows a commercial organization to use FreeBSD without disclosing additions to the source code.

None of these arguments offset the fact that either of these systems is preferable to a proprietary one.

D.6   Migrating to LINUX

What are the principal issues when migrating to LINUX from a non-UNIX system?

Most companies tend to underestimate how entrenched they are in Windows skills. An office tends to operate organically with individuals learning tricks from each other over long periods of time. For many people, the concept of a computer is synonymous with the Save As and My Documents buttons. LINUX departs completely from every habit they might have learned about their computer. The average secretary will take many frustrating weeks gaining confidence with a different platform, while the system administrator will battle for much longer.

Whereas Windows does not offer a wide range of options with regards to desktops and office suites, the look-and-feel of a LINUX machine can be as different between the desktops of two users as is Windows 98 different from an Apple Macintosh. Companies will have to make careful decisions about standardizing what people use, and creating customizations peculiar to their needs.

Note that Word and Excel documents can be read by various LINUX office applications *but complex formatting will not convert cleanly.* For instance, document font sizes, page breaking, and spacing will not be preserved exactly.

LINUX can interoperate seamlessly with Windows shared file systems, so this is one area where you will have few migration problems.

GUI applications written specifically for Windows are difficult to port to a UNIX system. The Wine project now allows pure **C** Windows applications to be recompiled under UNIX, and Borland has developed Kylix (a LINUX version of Delphi). There are more examples of LINUX versions of Windows languages, however, any application that interfaces with many proprietary tools and is written in a proprietary language is extremely difficult to port. The developer who does the porting will need to be an expert in UNIX development *and* an expert in Windows development. Such people are rare and expensive to hire.

What are the principal issues when migrating to LINUX from another UNIX system?

The following is based on my personal experience during the migration of three large companies to LINUX.

Commercial UNIX third party software that has been ported to LINUX will pose very little problem at all. You can generally rely on performance improvements and reduced costs. You should have no hesitation to install these on LINUX.

Managers will typically request that "LINUX" skills be taught to their employees through a training course. What is often missed, is that their staff have little basic UNIX experience to begin with. For instance, it is entirely feasible to run Apache (a web server package) on a SCO, IRIX, or Sun systems, yet managers will request, for example, that their staff be taught how to configure a LINUX "web server" in order to avoid web server licensing fees.

It is important to gauge whether your staff have a real understanding of the TCP/IP networks and UNIX systems that you are depending on, rather then merely using a trial-and-error approach to configuring your machines. Fundamentally, LINUX is just a UNIX system, and a very user-friendly one at that, so any difficulties with LINUX ought not to be greater than those with your proprietary UNIX system.

Should their basic UNIX knowledge be incomplete, a book like this one will provide a good reference.

Many companies also develop in-house applications specific to their corporation's services. Being an in-house application, the primary concern of the developers was to "get it working", and that might have been accomplished only by a very small margin. Suddenly running the code on a different platform will unleash havoc, especially if it was badly written. In this case, it will be essential to hire an experienced developer who is familiar with the GNU compiler tools.

Well written UNIX applications (even GUI applications) will, however, port very easily to LINUX and of course to other UNIX systems.

How should a supervisor proceed after making the decision to migrate to LINUX?

Before installing any LINUX machines, you should identify what each person in your organization does with their computer. This undertaking is difficult but very instructive. If you have any custom applications, you need to identify what they do and create a detailed specification of their capabilities.

The next step is to encourage practices that lean toward interoperability. You may not be able to migrate to LINUX immediately, but you can save yourself enormous effort by taking steps in anticipation of that possibility. For instance, make a policy that all documents must be saved in a portable format that is not bound to a particular wordprocessor package.

Wean people off tools and network services that do not have UNIX equivalents. SMTP and POP/IMAP servers are an Internet standard and can be replaced with LINUX servers. SMB file servers can be replaced by LINUX Samba servers. There are web mail and web groupware services that run on LINUX servers that can be used from Internet Explorer. There are some word processors that have both UNIX and Windows versions whose operation is identical on both OSs.

Force your developers to test their Web pages on Netscape/Mozilla as well as Internet Explorer. Do not develop using tools that are tied very closely to the operating system and are therefore unlikely to ever have UNIX versions; there are Free cross platform development tools that are more effective than popular commercial IDEs: Use these languages instead. If you are developing using a compiler language, your developers should ensure that code compiles cleanly with independent brands of compiler. This will not only improve code quality but will make the code more portable.

Be aware that people will make any excuse to avoid having to learn something new. Make the necessary books available to them. Identify common problems and create procedures for solving them. Learn about the capabilities of LINUX by watching Internet publications: A manager who is not prepared to do this much should not expect their staff to do better.

D.7   Technical

This section covers various specific and technical questions.

Are LINUX CDs readable from Windows?

Yes. You can browse the installation documentation on the CD (if it has any) using Internet Explorer. LINUX software tends to prefer Windows floppy disk formats, and ISO9660 CD formats, even though almost everything else uses a different format.

Can I run LINUX and Windows on the same machine?

Yes, LINUX will occupy two or more partitions, while Windows will sit in one of the primary partitions. At boot time, a boot prompt will ask you to select which operating system you would like to boot into.

How much space do I need to install LINUX?

A useful distribution of packages that includes the **X** Window System (UNIX's graphical environment) will occupy less than 1 gigabyte. A network server that does not have to run X can get away with about 100-300 megabytes. LINUX can run on as little as a single stiffy disk—that's 1.4 megabytes—and still perform various network services.

What are the hardware requirements?

LINUX runs on many different hardware platforms, as explained above. Typical users should purchase an entry-level PC with at least 16 megabytes of RAM if they are going to run the X Window System (UNIX's graphical environment) smoothly.

A good LINUX machine is a PII 300 (or AMD, K6, Cyrix, etc.) with 64 megabytes of RAM and a 2-megabyte graphics card (i.e., capable of run 1024x768 screen resolution in 15/16 bit color). One gigabyte of free disk space is necessary.

If you are using scrap hardware, an adequate machine for the **X** Window System should not have less than an Intel 486 100 MHz processor and 8 megabytes of RAM. Network servers can run on a 386 with 4 megabytes of RAM and a 200-megabyte hard drive. Note that scrap hardware can be *very* time consuming to configure.

Note that recently some distributions are coming out with Pentium-only compilations. This means that your old 386 will no longer work. You will then have to compile your own kernel for the processor you are using and possibly recompile packages.

What hardware is supported? Will my sound/graphics/network card work?

About 90% of all hardware available for the PC is supported under LINUX. In general, well-established brand names will always work, but will tend to cost more. New graphics/network cards are always being released onto the market. If you buy one of these, you might have to wait many months before support becomes available (if ever).

To check on hardware support, see the *Hardware-HOWTO* http://users.bart.nl/˜patrickr/-hardware-howto/Hardware-HOWTO.html

This may not be up-to-date, so it's best to go to the various references listed in this document and get the latest information.

Can I view my Windows, OS/2, and MS-DOS files under LINUX?

LINUX has read and write support for all these file systems. Hence, your other partitions will be readable from LINUX. In addition, LINUX supports a wide range of other file systems like those of OS/2, Amiga, and other UNIX systems.

Can I run DOS programs under LINUX?

LINUX contains a highly advanced DOS emulator. It will run almost any 16-bit or 32-bit DOS application. It runs a great number of 32-bit DOS games as well.

The DOS emulator package for LINUX is called `dosemu`. It typically runs applications much faster than does normal DOS because of LINUX's faster file system access and system calls.

It can run in an **X** window just like a DOS window under Windows.

Can I recompile Windows programs under LINUX?

Yes. WineLib is a part of the Wine package (see below) and allows Windows **C** applications to be recompiled to work under LINUX. Apparently this works extremely well, with virtually no changes to the source code being necessary.

Can I run Windows programs under LINUX?

Yes and no.

There are commercial emulators that will run a virtual 386 machine under LINUX. This enables mostly flawless running of Windows under LINUX if you really have to and at a large performance penalty. You still have to buy Windows though. There are also some Free versions of these.

There is also a project called Wine (WINdows Emulator) which aims to provide a free alternative to Windows by allowing LINUX to run Windows 16 or 32 bit binaries with little to no performance penalty. It has been in development for many years now, and has reached the point where many simple programs work quite flawlessly under LINUX.

Get a grip on what this means: you can run Minesweep under LINUX and it will come up on your X Window screen next to your other LINUX applications and look exactly like what it does under Windows—and you don't have to buy Windows. You will be able to cut and paste between Windows and LINUX application.

However, many applications (especially large and complex ones) do not display correctly under LINUX or crash during operation. This has been steadily improving to the point where Microsoft Office 2000 is said to be actually usable.

Many Windows games do, however, work quite well under LINUX, including those with accelerated 3D graphics.

See the *Wine Headquarters* http://www.winehq.com/faq.html for more information.

I have heard that LINUX does not suffer from virus attacks. Is it true that there is no threat of viruses with UNIX systems?

A virus is a program that replicates itself by modifying the system on which it runs. It may do other damage. Viruses are small programs that exploit social engineering, logistics, and the inherent flexibility of a computer system to do undesirable things.

Because a UNIX system does not allow this kind of flexibility in the first place, there is categorically no such thing as a virus for it. For example, UNIX inherently restricts access to files outside the user's privilege space, so a virus would have nothing to infect.

However, although LINUX cannot itself execute a virus, it may be able to pass on a virus meant for a Windows machine should a LINUX machine act as a mail or file server. To avoid this problem, numerous virus detection programs for LINUX are now becoming available. It's what is meant by virus-software-for-LINUX.

On the other hand, conditions sometimes allow an intelligent hacker to target a machine and eventually gain access. The hacker may also mechanically try to attack a large number of machines by using custom programs. The hacker may go one step further to cause those machines that are compromised to begin executing those same programs. At some point, this crosses the definition of what is called a "worm." A worm is a thwarting of security that exploits the same security hole recursively through a network. See the question on security below.

At some point in the future, a large number of users may be using the same proprietary desktop application that has some security vulnerability in it. If this were to support a virus, it would only be able to damage the user's restricted space, but then it would be the application that is insecure, not LINUX per se.

Remember also that with LINUX, a sufficient understanding of the system makes it possible to easily detect and repair the corruption, without have to do anything drastic, like reinstalling or buying expensive virus detection software.

Is LINUX as secure as other servers?

LINUX is as secure as or more secure than typical UNIX systems.

Various issues make it more and less secure.

Because GNU software is open source, any hacker can easily research the internal workings of critical system services.

On one hand, they may find a flaw in these internals that can be indirectly exploited to compromise the security of a server. In this way, LINUX is *less* secure because security holes can be discovered by arbitrary individuals.

On the other hand, individuals may find a flaw in these internals that they can report to the authors of that package, who will quickly (sometimes within hours) correct the insecurity and release a new version on the Internet. This makes LINUX more secure because security holes are discovered and reported by a wide network of programers.

It is therefore questionable whether free software is more secure or not. I personally prefer to have access to the source code so that I know what my software is doing.

Another issue is that LINUX servers are often installed by lazy people who do not take the time to follow the simplest of security guidelines, even though these guidelines are widely available and easy to follow. Such systems are sitting ducks and are often attacked. (See the previous question.)

A further issue is that when a security hole is discovered, system administrators fail to heed the warnings announced to the LINUX community. By not upgrading that service, they leave open a window to opportunistic hackers.

You can make a LINUX system completely airtight by following a few simple guidelines, like being careful about what system services you expose, not allowing passwords to be compromised, and installing utilities that close possible vulnerabilities.

Because of the community nature of LINUX users, there is openness and honesty with regard to security issues. It is not found, for instance, that security holes are covered up by maintainers for commercial reasons. In this way, you can trust LINUX far more than commercial institutions that think they have a lot to lose by disclosing flaws in their software.

Appendix E

The GNU General Public License Version 2

Most of the important components of a Free UNIX system (like LINUX🐧) were developed by the *Free Software Foundation* http://www.gnu.org/ (FSF). Further, most of a typical LINUX🐧 distribution comes under the FSF's copyright, called the GNU General Public License. It is therefore important to study this license in full to understand the ethos of Free ⟍Meaning the freedom to be modified and redistributed.⟍ development, and the culture under which LINUX🐧 continues to evolve.

Preamble

The licenses for most software are designed to take away your freedom to share and change it. By contrast, the GNU General Public License is intended to guarantee your freedom to share and change free software–to make sure the software is free for all its users. This General Public License applies to most of the Free Software Foundation's software and to any other program whose authors commit to using it. (Some other Free

573

Software Foundation software is covered by the GNU Library General Public License instead.) You can apply it to your programs, too.

When we speak of free software, we are referring to freedom, not price. Our General Public Licenses are designed to make sure that you have the freedom to distribute copies of free software (and charge for this service if you wish), that you receive source code or can get it if you want it, that you can change the software or use pieces of it in new free programs; and that you know you can do these things.

To protect your rights, we need to make restrictions that forbid anyone to deny you these rights or to ask you to surrender the rights. These restrictions translate to certain responsibilities for you if you distribute copies of the software, or if you modify it.

For example, if you distribute copies of such a program, whether gratis or for a fee, you must give the recipients all the rights that you have. You must make sure that they, too, receive or can get the source code. And you must show them these terms so they know their rights.

We protect your rights with two steps: (1) copyright the software, and (2) offer you this license which gives you legal permission to copy, distribute and/or modify the software.

Also, for each author's protection and ours, we want to make certain that everyone understands that there is no warranty for this free software. If the software is modified by someone else and passed on, we want its recipients to know that what they have is not the original, so that any problems introduced by others will not reflect on the original authors' reputations.

Finally, any free program is threatened constantly by software patents. We wish to avoid the danger that redistributors of a free program will individually obtain patent licenses, in effect making the program proprietary. To prevent this, we have made it clear that any patent must be licensed for everyone's free use or not licensed at all.

The precise terms and conditions for copying, distribution and modification follow.

GNU GENERAL PUBLIC LICENSE
TERMS AND CONDITIONS FOR COPYING, DISTRIBUTION AND MODIFICATION

0. This License applies to any program or other work which contains a notice placed by the copyright holder saying it may be distributed under the terms of this General Public License. The "Program", below, refers to any such program or work, and a "work based on the Program" means either the Program or any derivative work under copyright law: that is to say, a work containing the Program or a portion of it, either verbatim or with modifications and/or translated into another language. (Hereinafter, translation is included without limitation in the term "modification".) Each licensee is addressed as "you".

Activities other than copying, distribution and modification are not covered by this License; they are outside its scope. The act of running the Program is not restricted, and the output from the Program is covered only if its contents constitute a work based on the Program (independent of having been made by running the Program). Whether that is true depends on what the Program does.

1. You may copy and distribute verbatim copies of the Program's source code as you receive it, in any medium, provided that you conspicuously and appropriately publish on each copy an appropriate copyright notice and disclaimer of warranty; keep intact all the notices that refer to this License and to the absence of any warranty; and give any other recipients of the Program a copy of this License along with the Program.

   You may charge a fee for the physical act of transferring a copy, and you may at your option offer warranty protection in exchange for a fee.

2. You may modify your copy or copies of the Program or any portion of it, thus forming a work based on the Program, and copy and distribute such modifications or work under the terms of Section 1 above, provided that you also meet all of these conditions:

   a) You must cause the modified files to carry prominent notices stating that you changed the files and the date of any change.

   b) You must cause any work that you distribute or publish, that in whole or in part contains or is derived from the Program or any part thereof, to be licensed as a whole at no charge to all third parties under the terms of this License.

   c) If the modified program normally reads commands interactively when run, you must cause it, when started running for such interactive use in the most ordinary way, to print or display an announcement including an appropriate copyright notice and a notice that there is no warranty (or else, saying that you provide a warranty) and that users may redistribute the program under these conditions, and telling the user how to view a copy of this License. (Exception: if the Program itself is interactive but does not normally print such an announcement, your work based on the Program is not required to print an announcement.)

   These requirements apply to the modified work as a whole. If identifiable sections of that work are not derived from the Program, and can be reasonably considered independent and separate works in themselves, then this License, and its terms, do not apply to those sections when you distribute them as separate works. But when you distribute the same sections as part of a whole which is a work based on the Program, the distribution of the whole must be on the terms of this License, whose permissions for other licensees extend to the entire whole, and thus to each and every part regardless of who wrote it.

Thus, it is not the intent of this section to claim rights or contest your rights to work written entirely by you; rather, the intent is to exercise the right to control the distribution of derivative or collective works based on the Program.

In addition, mere aggregation of another work not based on the Program with the Program (or with a work based on the Program) on a volume of a storage or distribution medium does not bring the other work under the scope of this License.

3. You may copy and distribute the Program (or a work based on it, under Section 2) in object code or executable form under the terms of Sections 1 and 2 above provided that you also do one of the following:

   a) Accompany it with the complete corresponding machine-readable source code, which must be distributed under the terms of Sections 1 and 2 above on a medium customarily used for software interchange; or,

   b) Accompany it with a written offer, valid for at least three years, to give any third party, for a charge no more than your cost of physically performing source distribution, a complete machine-readable copy of the corresponding source code, to be distributed under the terms of Sections 1 and 2 above on a medium customarily used for software interchange; or,

   c) Accompany it with the information you received as to the offer to distribute corresponding source code. (This alternative is allowed only for noncommercial distribution and only if you received the program in object code or executable form with such an offer, in accord with Subsection b above.)

The source code for a work means the preferred form of the work for making modifications to it. For an executable work, complete source code means all the source code for all modules it contains, plus any associated interface definition files, plus the scripts used to control compilation and installation of the executable. However, as a special exception, the source code distributed need not include anything that is normally distributed (in either source or binary form) with the major components (compiler, kernel, and so on) of the operating system on which the executable runs, unless that component itself accompanies the executable.

If distribution of executable or object code is made by offering access to copy from a designated place, then offering equivalent access to copy the source code from the same place counts as distribution of the source code, even though third parties are not compelled to copy the source along with the object code.

4. You may not copy, modify, sublicense, or distribute the Program except as expressly provided under this License. Any attempt otherwise to copy, modify, sublicense or distribute the Program is void, and will automatically terminate your rights under this License. However, parties who have received copies, or rights, from you under this License will not have their licenses terminated so long as such parties remain in full compliance.

5. You are not required to accept this License, since you have not signed it. However, nothing else grants you permission to modify or distribute the Program or its derivative works. These actions are prohibited by law if you do not accept this License. Therefore, by modifying or distributing the Program (or any work based on the Program), you indicate your acceptance of this License to do so, and all its terms and conditions for copying, distributing or modifying the Program or works based on it.

6. Each time you redistribute the Program (or any work based on the Program), the recipient automatically receives a license from the original licensor to copy, distribute or modify the Program subject to these terms and conditions. You may not impose any further restrictions on the recipients' exercise of the rights granted herein. You are not responsible for enforcing compliance by third parties to this License.

7. If, as a consequence of a court judgment or allegation of patent infringement or for any other reason (not limited to patent issues), conditions are imposed on you (whether by court order, agreement or otherwise) that contradict the conditions of this License, they do not excuse you from the conditions of this License. If you cannot distribute so as to satisfy simultaneously your obligations under this License and any other pertinent obligations, then as a consequence you may not distribute the Program at all. For example, if a patent license would not permit royalty-free redistribution of the Program by all those who receive copies directly or indirectly through you, then the only way you could satisfy both it and this License would be to refrain entirely from distribution of the Program.

   If any portion of this section is held invalid or unenforceable under any particular circumstance, the balance of the section is intended to apply and the section as a whole is intended to apply in other circumstances.

   It is not the purpose of this section to induce you to infringe any patents or other property right claims or to contest validity of any such claims; this section has the sole purpose of protecting the integrity of the free software distribution system, which is implemented by public license practices. Many people have made generous contributions to the wide range of software distributed through that system in reliance on consistent application of that system; it is up to the author/donor to decide if he or she is willing to distribute software through any other system and a licensee cannot impose that choice.

   This section is intended to make thoroughly clear what is believed to be a consequence of the rest of this License.

8. If the distribution and/or use of the Program is restricted in certain countries either by patents or by copyrighted interfaces, the original copyright holder who places the Program under this License may add an explicit geographical distribution limitation excluding those countries, so that distribution is permitted only in or among countries not thus excluded. In such case, this License incorporates the limitation as if written in the body of this License.

9. The Free Software Foundation may publish revised and/or new versions of the General Public License from time to time. Such new versions will be similar in spirit to the present version, but may differ in detail to address new problems or concerns.

   Each version is given a distinguishing version number. If the Program specifies a version number of this License which applies to it and "any later version", you have the option of following the terms and conditions either of that version or of any later version published by the Free Software Foundation. If the Program does not specify a version number of this License, you may choose any version ever published by the Free Software Foundation.

10. If you wish to incorporate parts of the Program into other free programs whose distribution conditions are different, write to the author to ask for permission. For software which is copyrighted by the Free Software Foundation, write to the Free Software Foundation; we sometimes make exceptions for this. Our decision will be guided by the two goals of preserving the free status of all derivatives of our free software and of promoting the sharing and reuse of software generally.

NO WARRANTY

11. BECAUSE THE PROGRAM IS LICENSED FREE OF CHARGE, THERE IS NO WARRANTY FOR THE PROGRAM, TO THE EXTENT PERMITTED BY APPLICABLE LAW. EXCEPT WHEN OTHERWISE STATED IN WRITING THE COPYRIGHT HOLDERS AND/OR OTHER PARTIES PROVIDE THE PROGRAM "AS IS" WITHOUT WARRANTY OF ANY KIND, EITHER EXPRESSED OR IMPLIED, INCLUDING, BUT NOT LIMITED TO, THE IMPLIED WARRANTIES OF MERCHANTABILITY AND FITNESS FOR A PARTICULAR PURPOSE. THE ENTIRE RISK AS TO THE QUALITY AND PERFORMANCE OF THE PROGRAM IS WITH YOU. SHOULD THE PROGRAM PROVE DEFECTIVE, YOU ASSUME THE COST OF ALL NECESSARY SERVICING, REPAIR OR CORRECTION.

12. IN NO EVENT UNLESS REQUIRED BY APPLICABLE LAW OR AGREED TO IN WRITING WILL ANY COPYRIGHT HOLDER, OR ANY OTHER PARTY WHO MAY MODIFY AND/OR REDISTRIBUTE THE PROGRAM AS PERMITTED ABOVE, BE LIABLE TO YOU FOR DAMAGES, INCLUDING ANY GENERAL, SPECIAL, INCIDENTAL OR CONSEQUENTIAL DAMAGES ARISING

OUT OF THE USE OR INABILITY TO USE THE PROGRAM (INCLUDING BUT NOT LIMITED TO LOSS OF DATA OR DATA BEING RENDERED INACCURATE OR LOSSES SUSTAINED BY YOU OR THIRD PARTIES OR A FAILURE OF THE PROGRAM TO OPERATE WITH ANY OTHER PROGRAMS), EVEN IF SUCH HOLDER OR OTHER PARTY HAS BEEN ADVISED OF THE POSSIBILITY OF SUCH DAMAGES.

END OF TERMS AND CONDITIONS

How to Apply These Terms to Your New Programs

If you develop a new program, and you want it to be of the greatest possible use to the public, the best way to achieve this is to make it free software which everyone can redistribute and change under these terms.

To do so, attach the following notices to the program. It is safest to attach them to the start of each source file to most effectively convey the exclusion of warranty; and each file should have at least the "copyright" line and a pointer to where the full notice is found.

```
<one line to give the program's name and a brief idea of what it does.>
Copyright (C) 19yy  <name of author>

This program is free software; you can redistribute it and/or modify
it under the terms of the GNU General Public License as published by
the Free Software Foundation; either version 2 of the License, or
(at your option) any later version.

This program is distributed in the hope that it will be useful,
but WITHOUT ANY WARRANTY; without even the implied warranty of
MERCHANTABILITY or FITNESS FOR A PARTICULAR PURPOSE.  See the
GNU General Public License for more details.

You should have received a copy of the GNU General Public License
along with this program; if not, write to the Free Software
Foundation, Inc., 59 Temple Place, Suite 330, Boston, MA  02111-1307  USA
```

Also add information on how to contact you by electronic and paper mail.

If the program is interactive, make it output a short notice like this when it starts in an interactive mode:

```
Gnomovision version 69, Copyright (C) 19yy name of author
Gnomovision comes with ABSOLUTELY NO WARRANTY; for details type 'show w'.
This is free software, and you are welcome to redistribute it
under certain conditions; type 'show c' for details.
```

The hypothetical commands 'show w' and 'show c' should show the appropriate parts of the General Public License. Of course, the commands you use may be called something other than 'show w' and 'show c'; they could even be mouse-clicks or menu items–whatever suits your program.

You should also get your employer (if you work as a programmer) or your school, if any, to sign a "copyright disclaimer" for the program, if necessary. Here is a sample; alter the names:

Yoyodyne, Inc., hereby disclaims all copyright interest in the program 'Gnomovision' (which makes passes at compilers) written by James Hacker.

<signature of Ty Coon>, 1 April 1989 Ty Coon, President of Vise

This General Public License does not permit incorporating your program into proprietary programs. If your program is a subroutine library, you may consider it more useful to permit linking proprietary applications with the library. If this is what you want to do, use the GNU Library General Public License instead of this License.

Index

H

P

X

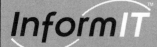

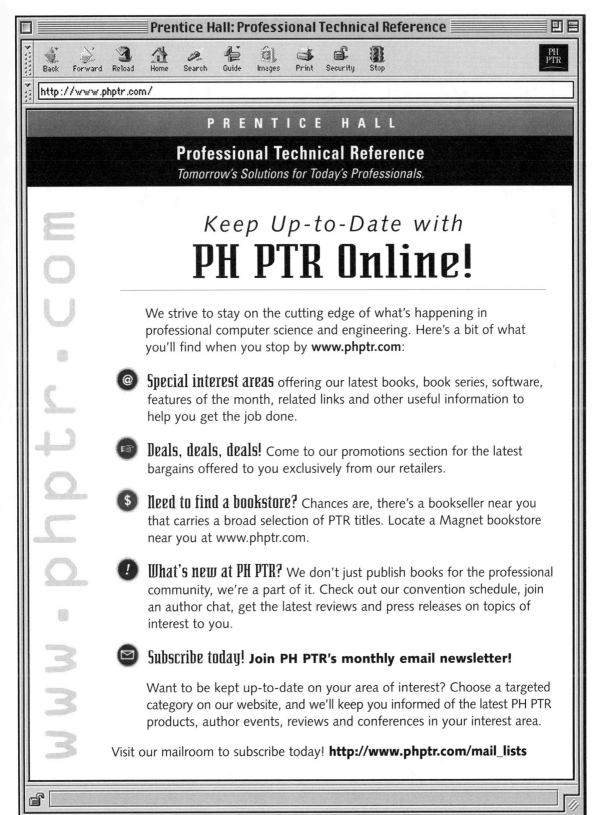

LICENSE AGREEMENT AND LIMITED WARRANTY

READ THE FOLLOWING TERMS AND CONDITIONS CAREFULLY BEFORE OPENING THIS SOFTWARE MEDIA PACKAGE. THIS LEGAL DOCUMENT IS AN AGREEMENT BETWEEN YOU AND PRENTICE-HALL, INC. (THE "COMPANY"). BY OPENING THIS SEALED SOFTWARE MEDIA PACKAGE, YOU ARE AGREEING TO BE BOUND BY THESE TERMS AND CONDITIONS. IF YOU DO NOT AGREE WITH THESE TERMS AND CONDITIONS, DO NOT OPEN THE SOFTWARE MEDIA PACKAGE. PROMPTLY RETURN THE UNOPENED SOFTWARE MEDIA PACKAGE AND ALL ACCOMPANYING ITEMS TO THE PLACE YOU OBTAINED THEM FOR A FULL REFUND OF ANY SUMS YOU HAVE PAID.

1.   **GRANT OF LICENSE:** In consideration of your payment of the license fee, which is part of the price you paid for this product, and your agreement to abide by the terms and conditions of this Agreement, the Company grants to you a nonexclusive right to use and display the copy of the enclosed software program (hereinafter the "SOFTWARE") on a single computer (i.e., with a single CPU) at a single location so long as you comply with the terms of this Agreement. The Company reserves all rights not expressly granted to you under this Agreement.

2.   **OWNERSHIP OF SOFTWARE:** You own only the magnetic or physical media (the enclosed software media) on which the SOFTWARE is recorded or fixed, but the Company retains all the rights, title, and ownership to the SOFTWARE recorded on the original software media copy(ies) and all subsequent copies of the SOFTWARE, regardless of the form or media on which the original or other copies may exist. This license is not a sale of the original SOFTWARE or any copy to you.

3.   **COPY RESTRICTIONS:** This SOFTWARE and the accompanying printed materials and user manual (the "Documentation") are the subject of copyright. You may not copy the Documentation or the SOFTWARE, except that you may make a single copy of the SOFTWARE for backup or archival purposes only. You may be held legally responsible for any copying or copyright infringement which is caused or encouraged by your failure to abide by the terms of this restriction.

4.   **USE RESTRICTIONS:** You may not network the SOFTWARE or otherwise use it on more than one computer or computer terminal at the same time. You may physically transfer the SOFTWARE from one computer to another provided that the SOFTWARE is used on only one computer at a time. You may not distribute copies of the SOFTWARE or Documentation to others. You may not reverse engineer, disassemble, decompile, modify, adapt, translate, or create derivative works based on the SOFTWARE or the Documentation without the prior written consent of the Company.

5.   **TRANSFER RESTRICTIONS:** The enclosed SOFTWARE is licensed only to you and may not be transferred to any one else without the prior written consent of the Company. Any unauthorized transfer of the SOFTWARE shall result in the immediate termination of this Agreement.

6.   **TERMINATION:** This license is effective until terminated. This license will terminate automatically without notice from the Company and become null and void if you fail to comply with any provisions or limitations of this license. Upon termination, you shall destroy the Documentation and all copies of the SOFTWARE. All provisions of this Agreement as to warranties, limitation of liability, remedies or damages, and our ownership rights shall survive termination.

7.   **MISCELLANEOUS:** This Agreement shall be construed in accordance with the laws of the United States of America and the State of New York and shall benefit the Company, its affiliates, and assignees.

8.   **LIMITED WARRANTY AND DISCLAIMER OF WARRANTY:** The Company warrants that the SOFTWARE, when properly used in accordance with the Documentation, will operate in substantial conformity with the description of the SOFTWARE set forth in the Documentation. The Company does not warrant that the SOFTWARE will meet your requirements or that the operation of the SOFTWARE will be uninterrupted or error-free. The Company warrants that the media on which the SOFTWARE is delivered shall be free from defects in materials and workmanship under normal use for a period of thirty (30) days from the date of your purchase. Your only remedy and the Company's only obligation under these limited warranties is, at the Company's option, return of the warranted item for a refund of any amounts paid by you or replacement of the item. Any replacement of SOFTWARE or media under the warranties shall not extend the original warranty period. The limited warranty set forth above shall not apply to any SOFTWARE which the Company determines in good faith has been subject to misuse, neglect, improper installation, repair, alteration, or damage by you. EXCEPT FOR THE EXPRESSED WARRANTIES SET FORTH ABOVE, THE COMPANY

DISCLAIMS ALL WARRANTIES, EXPRESS OR IMPLIED, INCLUDING WITHOUT LIMITATION, THE IMPLIED WARRANTIES OF MERCHANTABILITY AND FITNESS FOR A PARTICULAR PURPOSE. EXCEPT FOR THE EXPRESS WARRANTY SET FORTH ABOVE, THE COMPANY DOES NOT WARRANT, GUARANTEE, OR MAKE ANY REPRESENTATION REGARDING THE USE OR THE RESULTS OF THE USE OF THE SOFTWARE IN TERMS OF ITS CORRECTNESS, ACCURACY, RELIABILITY, CURRENTNESS, OR OTHERWISE.

IN NO EVENT, SHALL THE COMPANY OR ITS EMPLOYEES, AGENTS, SUPPLIERS, OR CONTRACTORS BE LIABLE FOR ANY INCIDENTAL, INDIRECT, SPECIAL, OR CONSEQUENTIAL DAMAGES ARISING OUT OF OR IN CONNECTION WITH THE LICENSE GRANTED UNDER THIS AGREEMENT, OR FOR LOSS OF USE, LOSS OF DATA, LOSS OF INCOME OR PROFIT, OR OTHER LOSSES, SUSTAINED AS A RESULT OF INJURY TO ANY PERSON, OR LOSS OF OR DAMAGE TO PROPERTY, OR CLAIMS OF THIRD PARTIES, EVEN IF THE COMPANY OR AN AUTHORIZED REPRESENTATIVE OF THE COMPANY HAS BEEN ADVISED OF THE POSSIBILITY OF SUCH DAMAGES. IN NO EVENT SHALL LIABILITY OF THE COMPANY FOR DAMAGES WITH RESPECT TO THE SOFTWARE EXCEED THE AMOUNTS ACTUALLY PAID BY YOU, IF ANY, FOR THE SOFTWARE.

SOME JURISDICTIONS DO NOT ALLOW THE LIMITATION OF IMPLIED WARRANTIES OR LIABILITY FOR INCIDENTAL, INDIRECT, SPECIAL, OR CONSEQUENTIAL DAMAGES, SO THE ABOVE LIMITATIONS MAY NOT ALWAYS APPLY. THE WARRANTIES IN THIS AGREEMENT GIVE YOU SPECIFIC LEGAL RIGHTS AND YOU MAY ALSO HAVE OTHER RIGHTS WHICH VARY IN ACCORDANCE WITH LOCAL LAW.

ACKNOWLEDGMENT

YOU ACKNOWLEDGE THAT YOU HAVE READ THIS AGREEMENT, UNDERSTAND IT, AND AGREE TO BE BOUND BY ITS TERMS AND CONDITIONS. YOU ALSO AGREE THAT THIS AGREEMENT IS THE COMPLETE AND EXCLUSIVE STATEMENT OF THE AGREEMENT BETWEEN YOU AND THE COMPANY AND SUPERSEDES ALL PROPOSALS OR PRIOR AGREEMENTS, ORAL, OR WRITTEN, AND ANY OTHER COMMUNICATIONS BETWEEN YOU AND THE COMPANY OR ANY REPRESENTATIVE OF THE COMPANY RELATING TO THE SUBJECT MATTER OF THIS AGREEMENT.

Should you have any questions concerning this Agreement or if you wish to contact the Company for any reason, please contact in writing at the address below.

Robin Short
Prentice Hall PTR
One Lake Street
Upper Saddle River, New Jersey 07458

About the CD

The CD included with this book contains a formatted HTML version of the complete text. The CD is readable from Windows and from most platforms that support a web browser. All the example scripts and commands shown in this book are presented in a blue font. These examples can conveniently be pasted from your web browser for your own use. Errata on the CD will be posted at http://www.icon.co.za/~psheer/rute-errata.html.

Technical Support

Prentice Hall does not offer technical support for this software. However, if there is a problem with the media, you may obtain a replacement copy by emailing us with your problem at:

```
disc_exchange@prenhall.com
```

Colophon

This book was typeset in TeX by Paul Sheer using the LaTeX 2_ε book class and the `palatino` style. It was converted to PDF using `dvipdfm`, and to HTML with LaTeX2HTML. Illustrations were produced with Xfig 3.2, GIMP 1.1, and lots of help from the `autotrace` package.